Environmental Law in Norway

Environmental Law in Norway

Fifth Edition

Hans Christian Bugge

This book was originally published as a monograph in the International Encyclopaedia of Laws/Environmental Law.

Founding Editor: Roger Blanpain
General Editor: Frank Hendrickx
Volume Editor: Kurt Deketelaere

Wolters Kluwer

Published by:
Kluwer Law International B.V.
PO Box 316
2400 AH Alphen aan den Rijn
The Netherlands
E-mail: lrs-sales@wolterskluwer.com
Website: www.wolterskluwer.com/en/solutions/kluwerlawinternational

Sold and distributed by:
Wolters Kluwer Legal & Regulatory U.S.
920 Links Avenue
Landisville, PA 17538
United States of America
E-mail: customer.service@wolterskluwer.com

ISBN 978-94-035-4657-5

e-Book: ISBN 978-94-035-4677-3
web-PDF: ISBN 978-94-035-4667-4

This title is available on www.kluwerlawonline.com

The Author

Hans Christian Bugge (born 1942) is Professor Emeritus of Environmental Law at the Department of Public and International Law, University of Oslo. He holds a Doctorate in Regional Planning from the University of Paris II (Doctorat de spécialité) (1972) and is Dr juris from the University of Oslo on a thesis on responsibility for pollution in Norwegian law (1998).

He teaches and does research in Norwegian, European and International Environmental Law, including Climate Law.

Before he became an academic lawyer in 1991, he held various senior positions in Norway's Ministry of the Environment from 1972 to 1982, *inter alia*, Director of the State Pollution Control Authority, and Director General of the Department for Urban and Regional Planning. He also served as Deputy Director in the Planning Department of the Ministry of Finance (1976–1977).

Furthermore, he has worked extensively with development and third-world issues, as Secretary General of the Norwegian voluntary development organization Redd Barna (Save the Children Norway) (1982–1991), and as State Secretary for Development Cooperation from 1986 to 1987. He served also as personal advisor to Norway's Prime Minister, Mrs Gro Harlem Brundtland, in her work as chair of the UN World Commission on Environment and Development.

He has been vice-chairman of the Board of the National Research Council of Norway and has chaired several research committees in the field of environment and development.

From 1998 to 2003, he chaired a governmental commission to review Norway's legislation in the field of regional and land-use planning.

From 1999 to 2009, he served as chairman of the board of the Centre for Development and the Environment at the University of Oslo.

From 2001 to 2003, he held the position of Vice Dean for Research at the Faculty of Law, University of Oslo. From 2005 to 2012, he chaired the faculty's Research Group in Natural Resources Law.

From 2015 to 2021, he was vice chair of the Council on Ethics of the Norwegian Government Pension Fund Global ('The Petroleum Fund').

He has lectured widely in Norway and abroad and has been advisor to the Ministry of Environment and Tourism in Namibia. He has authored and edited several books and a number of articles in the field of Norwegian and international environmental law and sustainable development.

The Author

Table of Contents

List of Abbreviations

ASMA	Antarctic Specially Managed Areas
ASPA	Antarctic Specially Protected Areas
BAT	Best Available Techniques
CBD	Convention on Biological Diversity
CCS	Carbon Capture and Storage
CFC	Chlorofluorocarbons
CITES	Convention on International Trade in Endangered Species of Wild Flora and Fauna
CPA	Norwegian Climate and Pollution Agency (until 1 July 2013)
EC	European Community
ECHA	European Chemicals Agency
EE Products	Electrical and Electronic Products
EEA	European Economic Area
EEA Treaty	Treaty/Agreement on the European Economic Area
EEC	European Economic Community
EEZ	Exclusive Economic Zone
EFTA	European Free Trade Association
EIA	Environmental Impact Assessment
EMAS	Eco-management and Audit Scheme
ESA	EFTA Surveillance Authority
EU	European Union
EU-ETS	EU Emission Trading System
FCCC	Framework Convention on Climate Change
GDP	Gross Domestic Product
GHGs	Greenhouse Gases
GMO	Genetically Modified Organisms
IMO	International Maritime Organization
IPPC Directive	Consolidated Directive 2008/1/EC on Integrated Pollution Prevention and Control, Replaced by Directive 2010/75/EC on Industrial Emissions

List of Abbreviations

IUCN	International Union for the Conservation of Nature
LRTAP	Convention on Long-Range Transboundary Air Pollution
MARPOL	International Convention for the Prevention of Pollution from Ships
MCE	Ministry of Climate and Environment
MPE	Ministry of Petroleum and Energy
NDA	Nature Diversity Act
NEA	Norwegian Environment Agency
OECD	Organisation for Economic Co-operation and Development
OSPAR	Convention for the Protection of the Marine Environment of the North-East Atlantic
Ot.prp. or Prop. L	Formal Proposal for a New Act, Presented by the King in Council (the Government) to Stortinget (the Parliament)
PBA	Planning and Building Act
PCA	Pollution Control Act
PCB	Polychlorinated biphenyl
PDO	Plan for Development and Operation
PEFC	Programme for the Endorsement of Forest Certification
PIC	Prior Informed Consent
POP	Persistent Organic Pollutant
PPP	Polluter Pays Principle
RBD	River Basin Districts
REACH	Registration, Evaluation, Authorisation and Restriction of Chemicals
SDR	Special Drawing Right
SPCA	State Pollution Control Authority
St. meld. or Meld. St.	'*Stortingsmelding*', White Paper Presented by the King in Council (the Government) to Stortinget (the Parliament)
St.prp. or Prop. S	'*Stortingsproposisjon*', Formal Proposal for a Budgetary or Other Decision (Not New Legislation), Presented by the King in Council (the Government) to Be Taken by Stortinget (the Parliament)
TCM	Technology Centre Mongstad
UN	United Nations
UN/ECE	United Nations Economic Commission for Europe
VOC	Volatile Organic Compounds
WFD	EU Water Framework Directive (Directive 2000/60/EC)

General Introduction

Chapter 1. General Information

§1. Geography and Population

I. Geography

1. Norway is situated in the Northern Europe. Together with Sweden, it forms the Scandinavian Peninsula. In the south, west and north, it is surrounded by the sea: Skagerak, the North Sea, the Norwegian Sea and the Barents Sea. To the south, across the Skagerak, is Denmark. To the east, it borders Sweden, Finland and Russia.

2. Mainland Norway has a surface of 324,000 km^2. It stretches some 2,000 km from its southernmost point to the northeastern border with Russia. Nearly half of the country is situated to the north of the Polar Circle, and it boasts Europe's northernmost point Kinnarodden, which is close to the North Cape, as well as the world's northernmost city, Hammerfest. Its long coastline consists of some 240,000 registered islands and numerous fjords.[1] To a very large extent, Norway and its people are turned towards the sea. Off its coasts, Norway has a very important continental shelf,[2] and a 200 nautical miles Exclusive Economic Zone (EEZ).[3] The continental shelf and the EEZ cover large parts of the North Sea, the Norwegian Sea and the Barents Sea. Together, the sea area under Norwegian jurisdiction is six times bigger than the land area.

3. Svalbard – internationally better known as the Spitzbergen[4] – is an archipelago situated about 400 miles north of mainland Norway. The group covers some 61,000 km^2. It belongs to Norway, but has a special status under international law.[5] The island of Jan Mayen between Iceland and Greenland also belongs to Norway.

1. Altogether the coastline of Norway, including islands, constitutes 101,000 km.
2. Act of 21 Jun. 1963 No. 12.
3. Act of 17 Dec. 1976 No. 91.
4. Spitzbergen is the name of the largest single island of the archipelago.
5. This is defined in the so-called Svalbard Treaty of 9 Feb. 1920 ('Treaty between Norway, United States of America, Denmark, France, Italy, Japan, the Netherlands, Great Britain, and Sweden concerning the Spitzbergen'). The treaty came into force in 1925. Nearly thirty countries have joined the treaty later. A legal analysis of the treaty is found in G. Ulfstein, *The Svalbard Treaty* (Scandinavian University Press 1995).

In addition, two islands in the South Atlantic Ocean, Bouvet Island and Peter I Island, and Queen Maud's Land in Antarctica, are under Norwegian jurisdiction as dependencies.[6]

4. Norway is a mountainous country. On the mainland, some 55% of the land area is situated above the limit of coniferous forest, and a large part of this is mountains, mountain plateaus and glaciers. Its highest mountain is Galdhøpiggen of 2,469 m, situated in the Jotunheimen mountain range in the southern part of the country. Around 23% of the land area is productive forest, 10% unproductive forest and marshland, 6% freshwater lakes and watercourses, 3% cultivated land, and only some 2% urban and other built-up areas.

5. Norway's main natural resources have traditionally been the fisheries off its coasts, the forests and various minerals including iron and copper. Svalbard is rich in coal. The fisheries and the forests are still important for the country's economy.

Norway is extremely rich in rivers and waterfalls, and hydropower is a main energy source. From the beginning of the twentieth century, this has been the basis for an important ferro, ferroalloy, aluminium and chemical industry. Even today, some 99% of the country's electricity comes from hydropower. Norway neither burns coal nor uses nuclear power plants to produce energy.

Since the beginning of the 1970s, the resources of oil and natural gas on the Norwegian continental shelf in the North Sea, the Norwegian Sea, and – more recently – the Barents Sea have become the country's most important natural resource. The activity and economic importance have increased steadily. Norway is the third largest exporter of gas in the world, and also an important oil exporter. There are sufficient petroleum resources for several decades of production at the present level. Important parts of the continental shelf, in particular in the Barents Sea, are still unexplored.

II. Population

6. With its population of 5.5 million (2023), Norway is one of the most thinly populated countries in Europe with fifteen persons per km^2. The annual population growth rate has been close to 1% on average over the last couple of decades, mainly due to immigration. Average life expectancy at birth in 2018 was 81 years for men and 84.5 years for women.

The great majority are ethnic Norwegians. In addition, the indigenous people of the Samis number some 40,000.[7] Traditionally, the majority of the Samis live in the northern part of the country and other areas where reindeer herding has played an important role as a lifestyle and economic base. Today, however, Samis live throughout the country. In the north, there is traditionally also a small Finnish minority.

---

6. Act of 27 Feb. 1930 No. 3.
7. In addition, there are some 30,000–40,000 in total in Sweden, Finland, and Russia. Within the Sami population, there are several groups, with considerable cultural and language differences, etc.

During the recent decades, Norway – similar to other Western European countries – has witnessed significant immigration from Asian, African and Latin American countries, the Balkan states, and, most recently, from Ukraine. Altogether, some 20% of the population was classified as 'immigrants' (first-generation immigrants and persons with both parents born in a foreign country) in 2023.

Three-quarters of the population live in cities and urban settlements, and the number is rising steadily. The vast majority lives in the southern part of the country. In 2023, the capital, Oslo, has some 720,000 inhabitants, with another 300,000 living in the larger Oslo area. The most densely populated area of the country is around the Oslo fjord. Important regional centres are the cities of Kristiansand (67,000), Stavanger (146,000), Bergen (286,000), Trondheim (215,000), Bodø (55,000), and Tromsø (80,000).

§2. Legal and Political Structure

I. General

7. Norway is a constitutional monarchy.[8] Its written constitution – henceforth referred to as '*Grunnloven*'[9] – was adopted by a specially summoned constitutional assembly on 17 May 1814.[10] It is the oldest written constitution still in force in Europe. However, a number of constitutional amendments have been adopted over the years, and some of them have in fact changed the constitution considerably.[11] In addition, several important constitutional changes have taken place since 1814 without formal changes in Grunnloven – even in contradiction to the basic ideas of the original version of Grunnloven. To some extent, they have been accepted as customary constitutional law. In particular, the 1814 Constitution was based on a clear division of power between the King as the executive, the Parliament – henceforth referred to as '*Stortinget*' – as the legislature, and the judiciary. Gradually, following the resolution of a dramatic confrontation between the King and Stortinget in 1884 by a Court of Impeachment procedure, a parliamentary system was introduced. Since then, with the exception of the Second World War years, the parliamentary system has never been challenged. The government must have the support of Stortinget. The core of this is the legal obligation for the government to resign if the majority of Stortinget give a vote of no-confidence. This is now laid down in Gunnloven section 15.

8. Norway has been a kingdom since the Viking age. From the end of the fourteenth century until 1814, Norway was under Danish rule. The kings in Copenhagen were kings of Denmark and Norway. Between 1814 and 1905, Norway was in a personal union with Sweden, the Swedish King being also the King of Norway. In 1905, Norway decided unilaterally to break up the personal union with Sweden and elected its own king. The Danish Prince Carl was elected as king and became King Haakon VII, grandfather of the present king, King Harald V.
9. 'Grunnloven' means 'the Constitution' – it is a word in the definite form.
10. The day 17 May is Norway's National day.
11. Amendments to Grunnloven require a two-third majority in Stortinget, and a general election must take place between the formal presentation of the proposal, and its adoption (Grunnloven Art. 121).

8. In connection with its 200 years anniversary in 2014, *Grunnloven was subject to considerable modifications and amendments*. Most significantly, a number of the most important human rights were explicitly included in a new chapter on Human Rights. Here, a general section (section 92) states that the authorities of the State shall respect and ensure human rights as they are laid down in Grunnloven and in binding international human rights treaties. Among the human rights now laid down in Grunnloven are the right to life and prohibition of death penalty and torture (section 93), right to freedom (section 94) and freedom of movement within the country (section 106), right to be treated by an independent judiciary under a just and public procedure (section 95), prohibition of retroactive legislation (section 97), the principle of equality under the law (section 98), freedom of speech (section 100) and organization (section 101), right to respect for privacy and home (section 102), and the right of the child to be treated with dignity, and the best interest of the child to be the primary consideration (section 104).

The former section 110b on the right to a good and healthy environment was somewhat strengthened and became section 112 (*see infra*).

At the same time, the language of Grunnloven was modernized, and an official text in Norway's second language, New Norwegian, was adopted.

9. An election for the 169 members of Stortinget is held every four years. Stortinget has only one chamber and acts as a single body. Most decisions are taken by a simple majority. However, there are special rules for legislative matters. A proposal for an act has to be adopted twice by a simple majority, with a minimum of three days between the two decisions.[12] According to Grunnloven, the King has suspensive veto in legislative matters, but this has lost its practical significance.

10. According to Grunnloven, *The King* is vested with the executive power. However, the expression 'The King' in Grunnloven has at least three different meanings: the King in person (at present His Majesty King Harald V), the King and the Cabinet sitting together ('the King in Council'), and the executive power, or the government, in general. Important decisions taken by the government, including most regulations and all matters to be presented to Stortinget, are taken by the King in Council, which constitutes the highest level of the executive power. At the annual opening session of Stortinget, the King presents the government's political programme to Stortinget. However, the King in person enjoys full immunity, and is not responsible in relation to Stortinget. A vote of no-confidence pursuant to section 15 only applies to the Prime Minister and the members of the Cabinet. At the same time, the political power of the King in person has become very limited. Although the King is active and important as a symbol of national values and national unity, his formal role is mainly ceremonial. He/she may, however, play an active role in choosing a new Prime Minister when parliamentary elections or a vote of no-confidence requires changes of government, and the political situation is unclear. Formally, the candidate for the post of Prime Minister is summoned by the King and asked by him to form a new government.

12. Grunnloven Art. 76.

11. The government has the obligation to provide Stortinget with all information necessary for its proper work, and to carry out its decisions. The institution of impeachment is established by Grunnloven[13] and regulated by a special Act.[14] However, the procedure of impeachment has not been used since the 1920s, and it is today generally regarded as obsolete. But regardless of legal obligations, a majority of Stortinget may at any time adopt a vote of no-confidence of a minister or the government as a whole on the basis of political disagreement.

12. General election is held every four years. At present (2023), nine political parties are represented in Stortinget. Since 1961, no single party has had absolute majority in Stortinget. During this period, various governments – several of them coalition governments – have been in office, several of them with only a minority support in Stortinget. There is no dissolution mechanism in the Norwegian constitutional system. Neither does referendum form part of the system, but consultative referenda may be decided on a case-by-case basis by Act.[15]

13. The Sami people have their own elected assembly, *Sametinget*, with mainly budgetary and executive functions.[16] Sametinget discusses and decides on matters of common concern to the Sami population and provides funds for Sami activities and measures of interest to the Samis.[17] On the basis of special Acts, Sametinget may be given decisive power in certain matters and formal status as body entitled to comment. One example is certain matters related to Sami cultural heritage objects pursuant to the Cultural Heritage Act.[18] Article 108 of Grunnloven states: 'It is the responsibility of the authorities of the State to create conditions enabling the Sami people to preserve and develop their language, culture and way of life.'

The role of Sametinget and some legal issues related to Sami language and culture are defined in the Sami Act.[19] Questions of rights of the Sami people to land and other natural resources in their traditional areas of living and herding are important political and legal issues. By an Act of 2005,[20] the ownership of a major part of the county of Finnmark, with a significant Sami population, was transferred from the Norwegian State to a new institution called 'Finnmarkseiendommen' (the 'Finnmark Property'). The Sami population, through Sametinget and its representatives in the board, has an important role in the management of the Finnmark Property and thus on the management of the land and natural resources where they have exercised – and some still exercise – their traditional semi-nomadic lifestyle and activities linked to reindeer herding.

---

13. Articles 86–87.
14. Act of 5 Feb. 1932 No. 2.
15. Since 1905, there have been only six referenda at national level in Norway. The most recent examples are the two referenda on Norwegian entry into the EU, in 1972 and 1994. In both cases, the Norwegian population voted no to membership, by a narrow majority.
16. Established by Act of 12 Jun. 1987 No. 48 (The Sami Act).
17. Based on the State budget voted by Stortinget.
18. Act of 9 Jun. 1978 No. 50.
19. Act related to the Sami Parliament and other Sami legal issues (The Sami Act) of 12 Jun. 1987 No. 56.
20. Act related to law and management of land and natural resources in Finnmark (The Finnmark Act) of 17 Jun. 2005 No. 85.

14. At the *county level,* public tasks are shared between the county authorities and the State authorities at the county level under the leadership of the county governor (*statsforvalteren*). Each of the fifteen[21] counties has its own assembly (*fylkestinget*) elected through a direct vote every four years.[22]

The 356 *municipalities*[23] also have councils elected through a direct vote every four years. During the last decades, the general trend in Norway has been to give increasing authority and new tasks to the county level and to the municipalities.

15. The *single judiciary* has three levels: the local courts (*tingrett*), the regional courts of appeal (*lagmannsrett*) and the Supreme Court (*Høyesterett*). In most cases, lay judges serve together with legally trained judges at the local courts and Courts of Appeal. In criminal cases, the Court of Appeal consists of two professional judges and five lay judges.

The courts are independent from the government as well as from Stortinget in the sense that their decisions are final and may not be overruled by either.[24] However, they have been administered by the government, and the judges are appointed by the King in Council. Through a recent reform, the courts are now administratively more independent from the government. The central administration of the ordinary courts falls under the National Court Administration (NCA). NCA has several important functions and works to make conditions favourable for the courts in order to ensure reasonable and efficient operation. The board of NCA is appointed jointly by the King in Council and the Stortinget.

16. The Norwegian courts have general competence. Norway has neither a general administrative court system nor a special constitutional court. In some areas, such as labour and social security cases, special courts of first instance have been established. However, appeals are as the rule heard in the ordinary court system.

The Norwegian courts have the right and duty to try constitutional questions in cases that are brought before them, such as the constitutionality of Acts and of decisions by State or municipal authorities, to be applied in individual cases. This is since 2015 explicitly stated in Grunnloven Article 89. Their competence to review decisions by the public administration is normally limited to the legality of the decision. This includes the question of interpretation of the rule, and whether the rule applies to the case in question. They also control that the decision is based on correct facts and procedure and that it is not arbitrary or clearly unreasonable, or in other respects represents a *détournement de pouvoir.*

17. The ombudsman – 'Sivilombudet' – is an important element in Norway's public administrative and legal structure.[25] Sivilombudet is appointed by Stortinget and has a 'watchdog function' on behalf of Stortinget. His/her task is to control the

21. Until 1 Jan. 2024 the number is eleven.
22. The capital, Oslo, has in some respects a double status as both county and municipality, and has a special institutional system.
23. In 2017.
24. This follows from Grunnloven Art. 88.
25. Originally Act of 22 Jun. 1962 No. 8, revised in 2021 by Act of 18 Jun. 2021 No. 121. Until recently the title was 'Sivilombudsmannen' – The Parliamentary Ombudsman. In order to a make the title

practice of public administration – at State, regional and municipal levels – with the purpose of ensuring the correct and reasonable application of Acts and regulations. Any citizen may present his/her case to Sivilombudet. He/she has no power to make binding decisions, but gives his/her opinion on the legality and reasonableness of the case. In most cases, but not all, the administration follows his/her opinion, and changes its decision accordingly. He/she may also give general comments on the legislation and how it is applied, and may suggest changes and amendments (for more information, *see infra* Part V, Chapter 1 §3).

II. Decision-Making Power and Competencies

18. At the State level, the decision-making power, other than that of the courts, is divided between Stortinget and the King in Council as the executive power. The main lines of this division of power are spelt out in Grunnloven. It should be understood, however, in the light of the more recent parliamentary system.

19. Norway is not a member of the European Union (EU) but is a member of the European Economic Area (EEA), based on the Treaty/Agreement on the European Economic Area (EEA Treaty) with its Protocols and Annexes.[26] This means that most of the rules adopted by the EU in relation to the European Internal market – 'the four freedoms' – are to be applied in, and are in fact adopted by, Norway. The EEA Treaty differs in principle from the EU treaties in the sense that it does not provide supranational authority.

20. Stortinget is the *main legislative body*. All Acts have to be adopted by Stortinget, while regulations pursuant to the Acts normally are adopted by the government. Stortinget also adopts *the annual State budget*. Furthermore, Stortinget may instruct the government in all fields of State policy. This is mainly done through general political guidelines, based on the deliberations of white papers presented to Stortinget by the government. It is legally accepted that Stortinget may also instruct the government in individual administrative cases. However, this is often politically controversial, and it is rarely done. By way of formal delegation, the Stortinget delegates much of the power of law and policy implementation to the government. Norway has a tradition of framework legislation in the field of public law. This is why many issues are governed by regulations of the government or ministries.

'sexually neutral' (as part of a general trend in Norwegian public administration), its full title in English is now 'The Parliamentary Ombud for Scrutiny of the Public Administration', in Norwegian simply 'Sivilombudet'.

26. Agreement on the European Economic Area between the European Community, its individual Member States, and the EFTA member countries Austria, Finland, Iceland, Lichtenstein, Sweden and Norway of 2 May 1992 with later amendments of 17 Mar. 1993, and Agreement between the EFTA member countries Iceland, Lichtenstein and Norway on the establishment of the ESA and the EFTA Court of 2 May 1992 with later amendments (Austria, Finland and Sweden having become members of the EU before the final negotiations). The agreements were implemented in Norwegian law by Act of 27 Nov. 1992 No. 109.

21. In many policy areas, the State administration is organized at *three levels.* The ministries develop government policy, prepare the government's proposals to the Stortinget and issue regulations. Specialized directorates or agencies, subordinate to the ministries, prepare policy documents for the ministries and decide individual permit cases. In many policy areas, the State also has an administration at a regional level, or at the county level under the leadership of the county governor, for planning issues and decisions of regional or local importance. The county governor also carries out formal control of the activities of and decisions by the municipalities in general, and is instance of appeal for many decisions made by the municipalities.

22. The national policy during the last decades has been to transfer power and competence from the State to the county level and even further to the municipalities.[27] The main tasks and competencies of the *counties* are in the fields of regional development policies, higher education, public transport and regional roads. They are also responsible for regional planning at the county level on the basis of the Planning and Building Act (PBA).[28]

23. The *municipalities* are responsible for many public services such as nursery schools and primary education, primary health service and social service, local roads and public transport, recreational areas, sewage, and waste disposal. The municipalities also have important competencies in the field of spatial planning, and they issue building permits.[29] Increasingly, they are given authority in other fields of environmental policies, such as management of protected areas.

§3. Economic Characteristics

24. At the beginning of the twentieth century, Norway was among the poorest countries in Europe. Most of the population made their living from small farms, and from both farms and fishery along the coast. A considerable part of the population immigrated in particular to the USA during the last decades of the nineteenth century and the first decades of the twentieth century due to poverty and lack of opportunities in Norway. But the living conditions improved gradually during the twentieth century.

During the last decades, Norway has been in *a privileged economic situation,* mainly due to its rich energy resources: hydroelectric power for metal production and other heavy industries and very considerable offshore petroleum resources. The country has also rich fisheries and a significant aquaculture industry, and a major fleet of international merchant ships. The country's Gross Domestic Product (GDP) was some Norwegian kroner (NOK) 5,500 billion in 2023. This corresponds to around USD 100,000 per capita (depending on the exchange rate between NOK and

27. An important exception is the hospitals. In 2001, responsibility for regional hospitals was transferred from the counties to the State. The hospital sector is organized in regional health trusts.
28. Act of 27 Jun. 2008 No. 71. *See infra* Part III.
29. *See infra* Part III.

USD) which is the second highest in Europe after Luxembourg. Over the last few decades, the average annual growth in GDP has been in the order of 2%–3%, except in 2020 when the GDP fell, mainly due to the Covid-19 pandemic. According to official previsions, the positive trend will continue for at least another decade. The inflation rate has traditionally been low, not exceeding 3% on average over the last ten years, but has risen sharply since 2022 and was around 6% from 2022 to 2023. The State has a considerable budget surplus when the income from the petroleum sector is included. Most of the State income from the petroleum sector is put into the Government Pension Fund Global (formerly known as the State Petroleum Fund), which invests in stocks and bonds on the international markets and is kept outside the ordinary State budget.

Compared to most other industrial states, the unemployment rate has been quite low for many years: around 3%. However, it rose temporarily during the Covid-19 pandemic, but is down to some 2% in June 2023.

In 2023, the public sector represented around 65% of the GDP when the offshore petroleum sector is excluded. This is the highest level among the Organisation for Economic Co-operation and Development (OECD) countries. The State has an important share of ownership in the most important industries such as petroleum.

A major source of income for Norway is its offshore petroleum production. In 2023, the oil and gas industry constituted some 25% of Norway's GDP and 65% of its export revenues. These figures are particularly high in 2023 mainly due to the extraordinary high price on natural gas. Metal industry, traditional fisheries and aquaculture, and shipping are also very important. Due to its important export of oil and gas, Norway has a considerable export surplus.

25. For decades, Norway pursued an active *policy of regional development.* Its industry is, to a large extent, based on the exploitation of natural resources. Petroleum, traditional fisheries and aquaculture, forests, and hydropower are all rather widely spread geographically. This – combined with important incentives for regional development and support – has made possible a rather balanced regional development. In addition, high priority has been given to the protection of the agricultural sector. Norwegian agriculture is based on relatively small family farms in the valleys and along the fjords, and remains strictly regulated.[30]

Nevertheless, during the last decade, there has been a clear population movement from rural to urban areas, and from the northern towards the southern part of the country, in particular, towards the Oslo area. The population is declining in many small municipalities along the coast, and in the inner part of the country.

§4. Social and Cultural Characteristics

26. The welfare system in Norway – although not without weaknesses – is relatively well developed. Health service and education, including higher education, are for the most part free. Every citizen is secured a minimum State pension from the age of 67.

30. Agriculture is not covered by the EEA Agreement.

Until recently, the Norwegian society was more egalitarian than most other Western societies, with relatively small economic differences between social groups. Over the last couple of decades, however, the economic gap between the well-to-do and the less well-off has been widening. A considerable number of relatively poor people have emerged, at the same time as the number of what may be called 'super rich' has increased. This has become an important and much-debated political issue, where a distinction between the 'left' and the 'right' political parties is increasingly becoming clear.

27. Culturally, Norway stayed for many years rather homogeneous, although with certain regional differences as to lifestyle, dialects and so on. There are two official Norwegian languages, standard Norwegian and 'New Norwegian' which is a formal blend of dialects spoken mainly in certain valleys and along the Western coast. The dominant religion is Lutheran protestant. More than 80% of the population, and some 90% of 'ethnic Norwegians', belong to the Lutheran church.

However, over the last few decades, Norway has rapidly become *a multicultural society.* Lifestyle and culture have become more manifold, mainly due to immigration from all parts of the world. A significant part is refugees from conflict areas in Asia and Africa. The number of immigrants and persons born in Norway with immigrant parents was 1.1 million in 2023, which corresponds to 20% of the population. Nearly half of these (48%) come from European countries, mainly Poland, Lithuania, Sweden, and more recently from Ukraine. There are also important immigrant groups from Somalia, Pakistan, Iraq, and the Philippines, to mention just a few. The immigrants tend to settle down in the major cities. In the capital Oslo, 34% of the population are immigrants or children of immigrants. At present, there are some 180,000 Muslims in the country.

28. Until 2012, the Evangelical-Lutheran religion was the official religion of the State of Norway. This was laid down in Grunnloven Article 2. The Lutheran church was a State institution. By an amendment of Grunnloven in 2012, the State and the Lutheran church split; the church has now become independent of the State. The Lutheran protestant church is no longer a State religion. Article 2 now reads: 'Our values will remain our Christian and humanist heritage. This Constitution shall ensure democracy, a state based on the rule of law and human rights.' However, the Evangelical-Lutheran church 'will remain the Established Church of Norway' and will as such be supported by the State. This is laid down in Grunnloven Article 16. And the King shall at all times profess the Evangelical-Lutheran religion (Grunnloven Article 4).

29. The ethnic origin and language of the indigenous *Sami* people are, as mentioned, very different from Norwegian. The Sami language belongs to the Finno-Ugric linguistic group and consists of several quite different dialects. Traditionally, the Sami culture and semi-nomadic lifestyle were closely linked to reindeer herding, fishing and hunting. Today, only a small minority of the Samis have reindeer herding as their living, and Samis live all over the country although there is a concentration of Sami people in the northernmost county, Finnmark.

30. Outdoor recreation, such as skiing, hiking and hunting in the forests and mountains, and boating along the coast, is an important part of the Norwegian lifestyle. According to a recent poll, 90% of the population enjoy hiking, skiing and/or other outdoor recreation activities, twice or three times a week on average. An important legal basis for this is the public's right of free access to private as well as public land, which includes bathing, camping, and so on. These rights have a long tradition, and may be seen as customary law. However, they are formally established in the Outdoor Recreation Act.[31] In addition, it is quite common for Norwegian families to have, or have access to, at least one small holiday house or cabin for recreation along the coast or in the mountains.

§5. Main Environmental Problems

31. Norway is thinly populated and has vast areas of forests, mountains and coastal areas where nature is abundant and pollution and other environmental problems are seemingly small.[32] However, the country is situated far north, and nature is in many ways marginal. Many animal and plant species have their northern limitation in Norway. This makes the nature vulnerable to even small changes in environmental conditions. Svalbard is special in this sense since it is covered by snow and ice more than half the year, and the flora and fauna live under extreme conditions.

32. Norway is very dependent on its natural resources for its economy. Pollution and overexploitation may seriously damage the fisheries and the forestry. Since less than 4% of the land is arable, it is very important to manage agricultural land in a sustainable manner. Also, the Norwegians' love of nature and preference for outdoor activities are important premises for environmental policy.

33. With a Ministry of the Environment[33] and an *active environmental policy* since 1972, Norway has managed to considerably reduce some of the environmental problems. This is particularly true for industrial pollution from major stationary sources, reduction of the discharge of chemicals and urban wastewater into fjords and watercourses and reduction of eutrophication due to agriculture in some lakes and rivers. The pollution situation in several important lakes and fjords has improved over the last few decades due to cleanup projects, but many fjords, including the Oslo fjord, are still in a rather bad environmental situation. In the same period, many natural areas have been formally protected. National parks, protected landscapes and nature reserves now cover 17.6% of the mainland land area, and

31. Act of 28 Jun. 1957 No. 16. *See infra* Part 2, Ch. 9, §3.
32. The information in this paragraph is taken mainly from the website Miljøstatus.no (in English version: environment.no) which is the official website, with environmental data from public authorities, and with the NEA as the main responsible authority.
33. MCE from 2014.

65% of the area of Svalbard. But some types of landscapes are still badly represented here. And problems are on the rise due to increase in such factors as car traffic, recreational activities including the building of recreational houses, waste production and consumption in general.

To a considerable extent, causes of Norway's environmental problems are also found outside Norway, such as long-range transport of air pollution, and pollution of the sea and coastal waters, from sources in other European countries.

There has been a general improvement in *local air quality* in Norway since the 1990s. But there are still considerable problems in several cities. Norway has national targets for concentrations of particulate matter and NO_2. The limit values for NO_2 are from time to time exceeded in the largest cities. In addition, there are legally binding limit values laid down by the Pollution Regulations. Although there is a downward trend in levels of particular matter, the limit values are exceeded from time to time.

34. The main environmental problems may be summarized as follows:

- acidification of lakes and forests in southern Norway, mainly due to long-range transport of air pollution (although the conditions have much improved);[34]
- pollution of inland lakes and rivers, and narrow fjords, mainly due to runoff from agriculture and urban wastewater;
- pollution of some fjords, such as the Oslo fjord, mainly due to lack of treatment of nitrogen in sewage and runoff from agricultural land;
- pollution in some fjords by deposit of industrial chemical waste;
- marine pollution, in particular pollution of the North Sea, partly due to discharge from offshore petroleum production;
- high air pollution levels in some of the major cities, in particular, NOx pollution in winter;
- noise from traffic in urban areas; nearly 40% of the population experience a noise level of at least 55 dBA outside their homes.
- increasing levels of some toxic chemicals in the environment, while others are declining; one special area of concern is the increasing concentration of persistent chemicals, such as Polychlorinated biphenyls (PCBs), in polar bears and other organisms in the Arctic;
- steadily increasing amount of waste, and at the same time reduction in recycling and reuse, in spite of political objectives to the contrary; Norway is on top in Europe in waste production per capita;
- the disposal of hazardous as well as household waste is not always good enough;
- the fragmentation and diminishing of wilderness areas due to infrastructure development, forestry, etc., threatening the biodiversity;
- diminishing numbers of many threatened species, in particular bird species along the coast (although some species are on the increase due to special protection measures);

34. In recent years, the area touched by acidification has been slowly decreasing. This is due to the successful cooperation in Europe since the 1970s to reduce emissions of SO_2 and NO_x, under the 1979 Convention on Long-Range Transboundary Air Pollutants with its subsequent protocols.

- 4,957 species were defined as threatened in the 2021 Norwegian Red List, corresponding to 21% of all assessed species;
- reduced stock of some important fish species, such as cod, in some sea areas surrounding Norway, in particular the North Sea, and in some fjords such as the Oslo fjord, and a threat of further reductions if strict quotas are not agreed upon by the relevant parties, and respected;
- reduction of agricultural land in the valleys and around cities in spite of an agreed political objective to protect the country's sparse agricultural land;
- increasing stress on fauna and landscape in certain coastal areas, due to more recreational houses and activities;
- motorized traffic in wilderness areas, which encroaches upon the land and disturbs the fauna. Svalbard is faced with particular problems in this respect, with a very vulnerable tundra nature, and a rapidly expanding tourist industry;
- destruction of valuable cultural heritage due to neglect or lack of knowledge.[35]

A general problem is the difficulties connected to an effective *implementation* of the legislation.

More detailed information will be given in connection with the various chapters.

35. Norway has a high level of *energy consumption and production,* and the highest consumption of electricity per capita in the world, based on hydropower. This is partly due to the high consumption of electricity in parts of Norway's major industries such as production of aluminium and ferroalloys. But since the price of electricity is generally low, private consumption is also very high. As a consequence, many rivers and lakes in Norway have been developed for power production, and their environmental value has been seriously reduced. The further development of major hydropower projects is now close to its limits, and further increase in electricity demand has to be covered mainly by other sources. Norway has been slow in developing alternative energy sources. However, the country has very good natural conditions for wind energy. Over the last ten years, the development of wind power has been a political objective and subsidized by the State. Several major wind farms have been established, mainly along the coast. However, there is now (2021) a strong and rising opposition against the further development wind major wind farms onshore due to the often massive destruction of nature by the farm itself and the required infrastructure of roads and power lines. Development of wind farms at sea is being prepared. Also, there is a rapid development of small-scale hydropower plants in the many smaller rivers in the country. This is also controversial from a nature conservation point of view. Nuclear power has been banned in Norway since the early 1970s and is still ruled out as unacceptable and not the solutions to the climate problem. Two gas-fired power plants were constructed in the early 2000s, but following several years of unprofitable operations they were closed in 2017.

35. It is estimated that 1% of valuable objects of cultural heritage disappears annually.

Chapter 2. Basic Principles of Environmental Law

§1. Constitutional Provisions

36. Norway's written constitution, 'Grunnloven', is *lex superior* to ordinary legislation. Judicial review of legislation is an important element in the Norwegian constitutional system. Since 2015, this principle is explicitly laid down in Grunnloven Article 89. The ordinary courts have a right and a duty to set aside an Act in individual cases if it finds it in contradiction with a constitutional rule, or interpret the Act in such a way that its application in a given case does not violate the constitution.

I. The Articles on Retroactivity and Compensation for Taking

37. Two general articles in Grunnloven are worth mentioning as relevant in the field of environmental protection: *Article 97 on retroactivity* and *Article 105 on compensation for taking.* In addition, Grunnloven has a special Article 112 about the right to a healthy environment.

38. *Article 97* states that *no law may be given retroactive effect.* Over the years, this article has been subject to much legal discussion.[36] There are numerous Supreme Court cases, many in the court's plenary, in which the question has been whether or not an Act, or the application of an Act, has retroactive effect in violation of Article 97. The question is how the rule should be interpreted in various situations. Its legal core is clear: A person may not be punished for an action which was lawful when it was carried out, by way of the introduction of retroactive legislation. However, outside this area, the rule is subject to interpretation. Through the many decisions by the Supreme Court, it is now usually interpreted as applicable only to retroactivity which is 'clearly unreasonable or unfair'. However, whether an Act violates Article 97 or not may be a very difficult question. Often the issue of retroactivity may itself be doubtful. And when deciding whether it is violating Article 97 as it has been interpreted, the court must make a broad assessment of the effect of the rule on the case in question. The outcome depends on several factors, such as the actual field of law, the type of right affected, the purpose of the Act in question, the need to give it a certain retroactive effect, and the gravity of the infringement. Even if Stortinget itself has expressed views on the retroactivity and has accepted a certain retroactive effect as compatible with Article 97, the courts may overrule this judgment, although they will be reluctant to do so.

39. Article 97 does not prevent the legislator from introducing *stricter general rules for ongoing activities,* as long as it applies to the future. Thus, existing polluting industry may be faced with a new Act that prohibits pollution and requires a

36. The most recent major work on the issue is the doctoral thesis by Professor Benedikte Moltumur Høgberg, 'Forbud mot tilbakevirkende lover' ('The Prohibition of Retroactive Legislation') (Oslo 2010). However, there are several later decisions by the Supreme Court.

permit.[37] This is clearly not in violation of Article 97. An Act may also allow the authorities to lay down stricter terms in permits already issued if the environmental problems so require. Furthermore, it is also quite clear that a polluter may be asked to clean up and remove polluted soil, even if the discharge or burying of the waste was perfectly legal when it took place (whether the present landowner may be ordered to clean up the soil even if he/she has not caused the pollution is a separate question to which we shall return in Part I, Chapter 5).

When it comes to *compensation for damage*, the main rule in Norwegian law is that the compensation rules in force at the time of the damaging act apply. However, this is not an absolute rule. In certain fields of law, the time of the *effect* of the damage has been accepted as decisive for liability instead of the time of the act which *caused* the damage. This is an interesting question in the field of pollution damage. Often, some time may pass between the moment a polluting activity takes place and the moment the damage is done and identified. The rules on liability for pollution damage introduced in 1989 explicitly apply to 'an existing state of pollution', for example, a polluted soil, even if it was caused by an earlier act.

40. According to Grunnloven Article 105, *a citizen is entitled to 'full compensation' if his property is taken for a public purpose.* It applies directly to expropriation. It raises several important and difficult questions which have been much discussed in Norwegian legal theory and are subject to many well-known court cases, in particular the following:

(a) What is meant by 'full compensation'?
(b) May restrictions on the use of land give the landowner the right to 'full compensation' for his/her economic loss?

These questions, and the case law related to them, raise a number of complicated issues. Only the main lines shall be presented here.

Both issues are highly relevant from the perspective of environmental law. Many types of regulation of land-use, for example, due to land-use plans pursuant to the PBA,[38] may have an environmental purpose. Whether compensation must be paid or not may, of course, be very important for society's possibility to lay down such regulations and thus to protect valuable nature.

41. Ad a): What is meant by 'full compensation'? The starting point is that the citizen shall have compensation for all his/her economic loss caused by the expropriation. He/she shall be put in the same economic situation 'as if the expropriation had not taken place'. As far as compensation for expropriated land is concerned, further precisions of this rule have been laid down in the Act on Compensation for

37. Legislation to this effect was introduced for water pollution and air pollution in 1970 and 1972, respectively.
38. Act of 27 Jun. 2008 No. 71.

Expropriation of Real Property.[39] The main rule is expressed in its Article 4: The landowner has the right to be compensated for the 'market value' of the property, but its 'use value' to the landowner if this is higher than the market value. By 'market value' is meant the likely price for the property if it would have been subject to 'an ordinary buyer' sale in the open market (Article 5). This should be based on the most likely future use of the property, having regard, *inter alia*, to approved land-use plans for the area.[40] If the value increases due to the expropriation itself, or because of public investments in connection with the expropriation or other relevant public investments during the last ten years, such value increase should not be compensated (Article 5, paragraphs 3 and 4). Compensation for 'use value' shall be based on the normal yield from the use from the property, based on the type of future use which is most probable for the property in question (Article 6). The owner of an expropriated forest will be compensated for the loss of his/her income from normal and likely logging activity – logging which corresponds to the natural growth of the forest, thus being sustainable in the long term. Expropriation of the property right to a waterfall for the purpose of hydropower development raises some special questions that will be discussed in Part II, Chapter 8, §2.

42. Ad b): The question of *compensation for restrictions on land-use* is another important issue in Norwegian environmental law. Strict regulation of land-use through land-use plans, special protection of natural areas and so on may be essential in order to protect environmental values. If the landowner is entitled to compensation for the economic loss resulting from such regulations, environmental protection may become very expensive, if not impossible, in many cases. It is clear that Article 105 does not apply directly to this situation, as its text covers expropriation only. However, the question is whether the principle of 'full compensation' in Article 105 should be applied to regulations by analogy, and the possible criteria for such an application.

43. The main principles were defined in an important decision by the Supreme Court in 1970:[41] In 1965, an Act introduced a general prohibition to build within 100 m from the shoreline along the coast. The owner of a small island was thus prevented from building a house on his island, and claimed compensation for the reduced value of the island. The Supreme Court, sitting in plenary, unanimously rejected the claim. It stated that, as the main rule, a landowner is not entitled to compensation for economic loss due to general regulations on land-use for the purpose of environmental protection. The question of compensation is solved on the basis of 'general legal principles' and should be based on a broad, case-by-case assessment.

39. Act of 6 Apr. 1984 No. 17. This Act replaced an earlier Act on the issue of 26 Jan. 1973. This was found partly unconstitutional for not always giving 'full compensation', by the Supreme Court (by a narrow majority) in the famous *Kløfta* case (Norsk Retstidende 1976, 1).

40. The effects of land-use plans for the compensation is a very complicated and rather controversial issue in itself. It has been the subject of several important decisions by the Supreme Court during the last couple of decades. The main rule is that compensation is based on the value of the property when it is used in accordance with the plan.

41. Norsk Retstidende 1970, 67.

Since 1970, the question of compensation for regulations has come before the Supreme Court in numerous cases. The restrictive line of the 1970 decision has consistently been upheld. Compensation according to 'general legal principles' may only be given in 'particularly exceptional' cases. Compensation will only be given if the restrictions, and the resulting economic loss, are very significant, and appear as 'extremely unfair' to a limited number of landowners compared to others. Compensation for the loss of the option to build on or in other ways exploit one's property in the future is generally not given; there is no generally protected 'right to build' in Norwegian law.

44. The right to compensation for economic loss due to regulation may be established by ordinary legislation. Such legislation may provide for compensation which is not strictly required according to Grunnloven. The Nature Diversity Act (NDA)[42] Article 50 establishes that a landowner is entitled to compensation for the economic loss incurred when his/her land is protected pursuant to the Act to the extent the protection *makes current use of the property more difficult.* This rule was introduced in 2009. It replaced rules in the former Nature Protection Act[43] which had different compensation rules for different categories of protected areas. Compensation may also be given if a local development plan pursuant to the PBA[44] renders a property virtually useless (PBA, Article 15-3). We shall return to these issues in more detail in the respective chapters.

II. The Article on Environmental Protection

45. In May 1992, Stortinget unanimously adopted an article on environmental protection in Grunnloven – Article 110b. In connection with the 200-year anniversary of Grunnloven in 2014, this article was slightly strengthened and became Article 112. It is included in its new Part E Human Rights, and its purpose is to protect both the natural environment as such and the human right to a good environment. Hence, it explicitly links human rights and environmental protection. The text of the article now reads as follows:

> Every person has the right to an environment that is conducive to health and to a natural environment whose productivity and diversity are maintained. Natural resources shall be managed on the basis of comprehensive long-term considerations which will safeguard this right for future generations as well.
>
> In order to safeguard their right in accordance with the foregoing paragraph, citizens are entitled to information on the state of the natural environment and on the effects of any encroachment on nature that is planned or carried out.
>
> The authorities of the state shall take measures for the implementation of these principles.

42. Act of 19 Jun. 2009 No. 100 Relating to the management of nature diversity (Nature Diversity Act – henceforth NDA). We shall revert to this issue under Part II, Ch. 2, §1.
43. Act of 19 Jun. 1970 No. 63.
44. Act of 27 Jun. 2008 No. 71.

The adoption of Article 110b in May 1992 coincided with the opening of the United Nations (UN) Conference on Environment and Development in Rio de Janeiro. However, such a constitutional amendment was first proposed already in 1972 at the time of the UN Conference on the Human Environment in Stockholm.

Article 112 is an important political symbol and guideline. But it is more than a symbol; it has *legal implications* as well. It introduces both substantial and procedural environmental rights at the constitutional level.[45]

46. Paragraph 1 describes *substantial rights* for the citizens related to the environment. The right includes, but goes beyond, the health aspect. The article also recognizes citizens' right to a natural environment whose productivity and diversity are preserved. Through the second sentence, the objectives and values of sustainable development are implicit. It seeks to give the fundamental ethical idea of intergenerational equity a legal expression and legal status, although in a general form. The precautionary principle may be regarded as implicit as well, in the principle of comprehensive and long-term considerations. The wording of right for the individual indicates an anthropocentric perspective. However, it is clearly meant to protect the environment generally as a public good, as well as the inherent value of nature.

47. Paragraph 2 expresses *procedural rights* for the citizens to information in relation to the environment, with the objective of making the substantial rights expressed in paragraph 1 effective. First, the citizens have a right to information about the state of the natural environment. They should have access to all relevant information about the status and trends in environmental quality: pollution levels, biodiversity, and other important environmental criteria. Important aspects of this are the health risks inherent in various types and levels of pollution, and hazardous substances used in production or in products. The preparatory document of Stortinget on the article expresses the view that this general right to environmental information only applies to information which already exists. It does not in itself imply an obligation – neither for public authorities nor for private industry – to carry out research or studies in order to develop new knowledge and make it known. However, this interpretation seems unnecessarily strict, and it is disputed. This point is partly covered by the last part of the paragraph, which gives the principle of Environmental Impact Assessment (EIA) constitutional status. In 2003, Stortinget adopted a new Act on the Right to Environmental Information, with more detailed provisions to ensure this right.[46] As far as 'effects of any encroachments on nature that are planned or commenced' are concerned, Norway has, since 1992, a comprehensive system of EIA laid down in the PBA.[47]

---

45. A thorough analysis of Art. 110b is found in Ole Kristian Fauchald, *Forfatning og miljøvern – en analyse av Grunnloven §110b* (Constitution and Environmental Protection – an Analysis of Grunnloven §110b) in *Tidsskrift for Rettsvitenskap* 1–2, 1–84 (2007). The modified Art. 112 has been discussed in the book edited by Ole Kristian Fauchald & Eivind Smith (eds), *Mellom jus og politikk. Grunnloven §112 (Between Law and Politics, Grunnloven §112)* (Fagbokforlaget 2019). It contains a number of chapters on Art. 112, with different views on its meaning and legal importance.
46. Act of 9 May 2003 No. 31. For details, *see infra* Ch. 2, §2.
47. Act of 27 Jun. 2009 No. 71 Chs. 4 and 14, *see infra* Ch. 2, §4.

48. The third paragraph of Article 112 states that the authorities of *the State shall take action* to have the above-mentioned principles implemented. This is a somewhat stricter formulation than in the former Article 110b, putting a clearer obligation of action on the authorities. The 'authorities' are both the legislative and executive authorities. Both Stortinget as legislator and the government have obligations pursuant to Article 112. It should be underlined that the obligations thus placed on the State institutions are relevant as a fundamental guideline for all segments in society and sector authorities, thus underpinning the principle of integration. To the extent decision-making in relevant fields of law has been delegated from the State to regional or municipal authorities, the State must take the necessary measures to ensure that the rights inherent in Article 112 are properly respected and applied by these bodies through necessary instructions and/or control mechanisms.

49. What, then, is *the legal role and significance of Article 112* within Norway's legal system? Clearly, Article 112 implies a general obligation for the institutions of the State to take measures to fulfil the rights described in the article: issue necessary legislation and regulations, ensure the proper implementation of the legislation, develop plans and economic instruments, take other actions, and provide the necessary financial means. But is this obligation only political, or is it also a legal obligation in the strict sense: Can the fulfilment of – or failure to fulfil – the duties laid down in Article 112 be subject to any sort of legal control or review by the judicial system? Can the courts play a role in preventing violations of Article 112 or failure to fulfil the rights it lays down? This has for many years been a matter for discussion between Norway's legal scholars, with different views.

Norway's *system of judicial review of legislation* and other public decisions in light of the constitution is laid down in Grunnloven Article 89.

50. The question of the legal meaning of Article 112 came before the Supreme Court for the first time in 2020, in the so-called *Arctic oil case*.

In 2016, a coalition of environmental groups (Greenpeace Nordic Association and Nature and Youth together with the Grandparents Climate Campaign as intervener) initiated proceedings at the Oslo District Court against the Government of Norway through the Norwegian Ministry of Petroleum and Energy (MPE). Stortinget had decided to open new parts of the Barents Sea north of Norway for petroleum activities, and on this basis the government had offered forty exploration licences to thirteen oil companies in the area. Some of these are very close to the limit of the Arctic winter ice. The organizations claimed that this decision was in violation of Article 112 first *paragraph*, mainly because of the emission of CO_2 that might follow from the production itself and even more from the burning of the exploited petroleum, be it in Norway or – more likely – outside Norway, and also the threat of this activity to the Arctic biodiversity. They also claimed that it violates Article 112 second *paragraph* on the basis of unsatisfactory and outdated assessments of climate effects and other environmental effects of this activity.

The government strongly rejected these arguments. Its principal standpoint was that Article 112 only lays down a duty to take active measures and cannot be interpreted as a barrier to a political decision such as this made by Stortinget and the government. In any case, the environmental effects of the decision are not serious enough to violate the article, and the procedure followed included a fully satisfactory EIA.

The organizations lost the case in the district court as well as in the Court of Appeal. They appealed further to the Supreme Court which considered the case in plenary in November 2020.

51. In its decision of 22 December 2020, the Supreme Court by eleven votes to four upheld the lower courts' ruling. Four judges deemed the licences invalid because of lack of assessment of the impacts of emissions from the burning of the exploited petroleum outside Norway. However, the court unanimously reasoned that although Article 112 of the Norwegian Constitution protects citizens from environmental and climate harms, it only allows for judicial review in very limited conditions. These were not met in the case.

On the basis mainly of a backward-looking analysis of the preparatory works to the article, the court stated that the article is clearly relevant to the climate problem and that it has legal meaning and importance in several ways: providing guidance to the lawmaker and also to the executive when exercising discretion in administrative decision-making, and as a principle of interpretation of legal texts. It may be applied directly in cases where there is a lack of adequate legislation on a given environmental problem.

In the court's view, Article 112, third paragraph, clearly establishes the legal duty of the State to adopt adequate environmental measures in order to fulfil the rights expressed in its first and second paragraphs. The court also recognizes that the State has a corresponding duty to avoid actions that are violating these rights; thus, Article 112 also serves as a barrier to the legislative and executive authorities. But the court did not agree with the organizations that the article provides the citizens with individual rights.

The issue of judicial review of the State's fulfilment of its duty to either take or avoid certain actions according to the third paragraph thus becomes a key question. In the view of the court, judicial review is possible only in situations where the duty is *grossly neglected* by Stortinget. Hence, the court established a very high threshold for setting aside legislative and other decisions that the Parliament has taken or has consented to. It defines Article 112 as a 'safety valve'. The court did not provide any reasoning for why it set the threshold so high and where it derived it from. It did not elaborate on the elements that are relevant for deciding whether the condition of 'gross neglect' is fulfilled. It did not, either, elaborate on the content of the rights expressed in paragraphs 1 and 2, which the State has to both fulfil and avoid violating. At the same time, it argues that judicial review may be less limited in relation to the procedural requirements in Article 112, second paragraph.

52. In light of this, the court was then quick to find that this high threshold was not passed in the case before it. To justify this conclusion, it referred mainly to a number of general and specific measures the Norwegian State has taken to reduce emissions from petroleum production and more generally, such as a CO_2 tax, a renewable energy initiative, support to carbon capture and storage (CCS) technology, and not least participation in the European emission trading system (EU-ETS) which covers the petroleum activity on the Norwegian continental shelf. The court found that emissions from the burning of petroleum outside Norway were relevant, but only to the extent it could harm conditions and interests in Norway, thus limiting the geographical scope of the rights laid down in Article 112. It did not mention that neither the Stortinget nor the government had adopted any measures to address emissions from exported petroleum. The precautionary principle was not discussed. Even more surprising, the rights of future generations which is at the core of the climate problem and explicitly laid down in the first paragraph of Article 112, was not mentioned. Neither did the court consider the development in the understanding and the severity of the climate problem, and the developments in national and international environmental and climate law more generally, since the article was adopted in 1992.

Not surprisingly, the court was criticised for being backward-looking and not quite up to the challenge. The decision now defines the content and legal status of Article 112, but it leaves many questions open for further discussion and development.[48]

The Supreme Court decision has been appealed to the European Court of Human Rights. The result is expected in 2024.

53. Article 112 may play its most important legal role as *a factor of interpretation of legislation,* including of Grunnloven itself. Norway's Supreme Court has already, in a few cases, referred to the former Article 110b as an argument for interpreting the law in favour of environmental considerations.

In one case,[49] a permit to start a stone-crushing plant close to a residential area was refused by the Ministry of the Environment according to the Pollution Control Act (PCA). The main reason was the noise and other inconveniences from the traffic of heavy trucks to and from the plant. Formally, the permit system of the PCA does not apply to transport. This being the case, the crusher plant company argued that the permit could not be refused because of the problems related to the transport. However, the Supreme Court found the Ministry's refusal legally valid. It used Article 110b as an argument for interpreting the PCA in such a way that – although it did not apply directly to transport – environmental problems related to the transport of stone crush could nevertheless form the main basis for refusing a stone-crushing plant close to a residential area.

In another case, a property had been leased to a company with an activity which led to considerable soil pollution. The activity closed down, and so did the company. The State pollution authority found it necessary to clean the site and remove the polluted soil, and required that a part of the costs should be paid by the owner of the land. The legal question was whether the landowner could be held responsible for the pollution caused by the former leaseholder. This was a question of interpretation of the expression 'the responsible for pollution' in Article 7 of the

48. There are a number of comments to the Supreme Court decision, including in particular three articles In the Norwegian law journal Lov og Rett No. 03/21.
49. Norsk Retstidende 1993, 528.

PCA. The Supreme Court used Article 110b as an argument for a wide interpretation of the expression. As a consequence, the landowner – having leased the land to the polluting activity – was found to be 'responsible' under Article 7.[50]

Article 112 may influence the interpretation of other articles in Grunnloven and constitutional principles not expressed in Grunnloven itself. For example, it could influence the interpretation of the above-mentioned Article 97 on retroactivity and of Article 105 which ensures a citizen 'full compensation' in case of expropriation, including the question of compensation for 'regulatory taking', in a way which is beneficial for the environment.[51]

III. The Articles on Protection of Life and Privacy/Homes

54. In 2014, in connection with its two hundred-year anniversary, important new Articles were included in Grunnloven, in particular a number of key human rights. To a large extent, these were meant to reflect the corresponding rights laid down in international conventions, mainly the 1950 European Convention on Human Rights (ECHR). The convention has no explicit article on something like a right to environmental quality. However, in particular, two of the articles in ECHR have been applied by the European Court of Human Rights to environmental problems, thus linking environmental protection and human rights: Article 2 on the Right to Life and Article 8 on the Right to Respect for Private and Family Life. Consequently, the corresponding articles in Grunnloven are equally relevant also in relation to environmental issues. However, they may be somewhat less important because of the specific article on the right to a healthy environment in Grunnloven Article 112 which to some extent 'absorbs' the articles on right to life and right to private and family life as interpreted by the European Court of Human Rights.

55. The *right to life* is laid down in ECHR Article 2. Its first sentence reads: 'Everyone's right to life shall be protected by law'. The corresponding first sentence of Article 93 in Grunnloven states: 'Every human being has the right to life. No one may be sentenced to death.' In several cases, the European Court of Human Rights has found that Article 2 has been violated in cases where accidents due to bad environmental conditions neglected by the State have resulted in deaths.[52] A similar interpretation of Grunnloven Article 93 is possible, although such a case may as well be covered by Article 112.

The *right to private and family life* is expressed in Article 8. Its first paragraph states: 'Everyone has the right to respect for his private and family life, his home and his correspondence.' The corresponding Article 102 first sentence in Grunnloven reads: 'Everyone has the right to the respect of their privacy and family life, their home and their communication.' In numerous cases, the European Court of Human Rights has found that bad environmental conditions – mainly local pollution and noise, or a threat of such conditions, are a violation of the right to a home

50. Norsk Retstidende 2012, 944. This question will be discussed further *infra* in Part I, Ch. 1, §2, III.
51. An example is a case before the Supreme Court in 1993, *see* Norsk Retstidende 1993, 321.
52. *See* as examples the cases *Öneryildiz v. Turkey* (2004) and *Budayeva and others v. Russia* (2008).

in Article 8.[53] In the *travaux préparatoires* of Article 102, there is no mentioning of this important interpretation and aspect of Article 8. It is possible that such cases are fully covered by Article 112, but the issue remains open. In the above-mentioned Supreme Court case *Arctic oil*, the court found that Articles 93 and 102 did not provide an independent, additional basis to support the claim besides Article 112.

§2. Basic Objectives, Principles and Notions as Expressed in Legislation

56. The most fundamental objective and principle in Norwegian environmental law is the objective of *sustainable development.* As mentioned, this is indirectly and to some extent expressed in Grunnloven Article 112.[54] It is also laid down explicitly in several Acts such as the Genetically Modified Organisms Act (GMO Act) (1993)[55] and the Planning and Building Act (PBA) (2008).[56] In addition, the concept of sustainable use/sustainable resource management is expressed in different ways in several Acts either explicitly or implicitly. Examples of this are the Agricultural Land Act (1995),[57] the Aquaculture Act (2005),[58] the Marine Resources Act (2008)[59] and the Nature Diversity Act (NDA) (2009).[60] We will come back to each of these Acts in later chapters.

57. There is *no legal definition of sustainable development* in Norwegian legislation. In *travaux préparatoires* and policy documents, reference is usually made to the report from the World Commission on Environment and Development ('Brundtland Commission'),[61] which brought the concept to its present status. The report defines sustainable development as 'a development that meets the needs of the present, without compromising the possibility of future generations to meet their own needs'. This is a broad definition, including as well economic development and poverty alleviation in poor countries, a social goal of more equal distribution of wealth between rich and poor globally, protection and sustainable use of the natural resource base and the environment, and intergenerational justice. However, a close analysis of the use of 'sustainable development', 'sustainable use' and similar wording in Norwegian legislation reveals that the meaning of the expression varies considerably, and that the objective is more related to a sustainable management of the resource for the benefit of the respective industry and the Norwegian society than

53. *See* https://www.echr.coe.int/documents/fs_environment_ENG.pdf.
54. *See* the former section.
55. Act of 2 Apr. 1993 No. 38 Art. 1.
56. Act of 27 Jun. 2008 No. 71 Art. 1-1.
57. Act of 12 May 1995 No. 23 Art. 1.
58. Act of 17 Jun. 2005 No. 74 Art. 1.
59. Act of 8 Jun. 2008 No. 37 Art. 1.
60. Act of 19 Jun. 2009 No. 100 Art. 1.
61. The Commission was chaired by the then Prime Minister of Norway, Mrs Gro Harlem Brundtland. The author served as an advisor to Mrs Brundtland in this work.

the broad meaning of the concept as defined by the Brundtland Commission.[62] It thus remains somewhat unclear what its real legal meaning and importance is in Norwegian law.

58. With the adoption in 2015 by the UN General Assembly of the seventeen Sustainable Development Goals, the principle – or concept – of sustainable development has become extremely wide, covering a number of different social, economic and environmental objectives. In light of this, one may ask what the legal content and role of the principle really are in 2021. Nevertheless, *in the perspective of environmental law,* it has a fairly clear meaning: the core is protection of the natural environment as it is, for the benefit of future generations as well as for its value in itself.

In spite of lack of clarity, and although it is not expressed explicitly in Grunnloven, it is fair to say that the principle of sustainable development – *in this core meaning* – is a general principle of Norwegian law. This means that the long-term consequences of activities on the environment and the natural resource base must be assessed and given the necessary weight in order to avoid its destruction, when decisions are taken, in all sectors of society.

59. The *principle of integration* is closely related to the principle of sustainable development and may in fact be seen as an essential element of it. It means that environmental objectives and considerations must be integrated into all sectors of society. This was an important point in the sustainable development strategy of the Brundtland Commission. Each industry and public sector should be responsible for the environmental effects of its activity. They should all take necessary measures to prevent and control harmful effects and ensure sustainable development. The principle is expressed in the Treaty of the Functioning of the EU (Article 11), and also in the Agreement on the European Economic Area (EEA Agreement), Article 73, to which Norway is a part.

The principle is to a large extent implemented in Norwegian policy and law. In some sector Acts, it is clearly stated that the protection of the environment is a part of its objective. In addition to the above-mentioned Acts that express the objective of sustainable development or sustainable use, one may mention the Petroleum Act[63] and the Forestry Act[64] in this respect. And even if it is not said explicitly, it is a general view that every authority has the legal duty to assess the possible environmental effects of a decision or an action and take them into consideration in decision-making. Norway's system of EIA implements the relevant EU directives in the field and applies broadly.[65] In addition, principles laid down in the NDA[66] shall ensure that decisions by a public authority are based on scientific knowledge with regard to, *inter alia*, effects on the nature diversity. However, the legislation

62. *See* Markus Jerkø, 'Det norske formålet "bærekraftig utvikling"' (The Norwegian Objective of 'Sustainable Development') in *Tidsskrift for Rettsvitenskap* 3,354–388 (2009)
63. Act of 29 Nov. 1996 No. 69.
64. Act of 27 May 2005 No. 31 Art. 1.
65. This issue will be treated in detail *infra* in §4.
66. Act of 19 Jun. 2009 No. 100 Relating to the Management of Natural Diversity, hereinafter 'Nature Diversity Act' or 'NDA'. The Act will be treated thoroughly in Part II *infra*.

usually leaves it to the sector authority to decide how to balance the environmental considerations against the primary objective of the Act in question, and other relevant considerations.

60. Another objective and principle in environmental legislation, which at the same time may be seen as a main element of sustainable development, is the *principle of protection of nature and its capacity for long-term production and renewal,* and thus protection of biodiversity. Several expressions of this are found in Norwegian Acts, in addition to the wording in Grunnloven Article 112. For example, the introductory article of the NDA states that:

> The purpose of this Act is to protect biological, geological and landscape diversity and ecological processes through conservation and sustainable use, and in such a way that the environment provides a basis for human activity, culture, health and well-being, now and in the future, including a basis for Sami culture.

Rules to the same effect are also found in other Acts, such as the Pollution Control Act (PCA) (1981),[67] the Wildlife Act (1981),[68] and the Salmonids and Freshwater Fish Act (1992).[69] We shall revert to these Acts.

61. Several pieces of legislation lay down *a general prohibition to harm nature or the environment,* and/or require special regulations or an individual public permit to do so. This principle is in reality a key aspect of the environmental dimension of sustainable development and is expressed in Norwegian law, *inter alia,* in the PCA which states (Article 7 first paragraph):

> No person may possess, do or initiate anything which may entail risk of pollution unless this is permitted by law pursuant to §§8 or 9, or permitted in accordance with decisions (permits) pursuant to §11.

The principle is similarly found in several other pieces of legislation. The Agricultural Land Act (Article 9 paragraph 1) requires a public permit to take agricultural land for any other use than agriculture. The NDA (Article 15) states, *inter alia,* that harvesting and other removals of animals that occur naturally in the wild are generally prohibited and must be authorized by statute or a decision pursuant to statute. Unnecessary harm and suffering caused to animals occurring in the wild and their nests, lairs and burrows shall be avoided. The GMO Act requires a permit to introduce such organisms into the natural environment. The general Penal Code[70]

67. Act of 13 Mar. 1981 No 6. Concerning Protection Against Pollution and Concerning Waste hereinafter 'Pollution Control Act' or 'PCA'.
68. Act of 22 May 1981 No. 25 Art. 1.
69. Act of 15 May 1992 No. 47 Art. 1.
70. Act of 20 May 2005 No. 28. *See infra* Part IV, Ch. 2, §2.

lays down a general prohibition of serious harm to the environment through pollution, waste disposal, damage to protected species, areas and cultural heritage (Article 240).

62. The principle of ecosystem approach and cumulative environmental effects is rather newly established in Norway's environmental law, at least in the explicit sense. It is laid down in Article 10 of the NDA in the following way:

> Any pressure on an ecosystem shall be assessed on the basis of the cumulative environmental effects on the ecosystem now or in the future.[71]

One may say that this follows from the other principles that have already been mentioned. However, to assess the cumulative effects of several activities, partly existing, partly planned, may be difficult in practice. The principle of ecosystem approach in water management is gradually made operational through Norway's implementation of the *EU Water Framework Directive* (WFD)[72] which has been included in the EEA Agreement. This requires, *inter alia*, that the authorities establish water quality objectives for all freshwater sources and coastal water. For further details, *see infra* Part I, Chapter 3.

The ecosystem approach and cumulative environmental effects are also laid down as explicit principles of the management of Norway's vast marine resources in its territorial waters and the 200 nautical miles EEZ, and on its continental shelf, which as mentioned cover large parts of the North Sea, the Norwegian Sea, the North Atlantic and the Barents Sea. This is stated in *management plans for these sea areas* adopted by Stortinget on the basis of comprehensive white papers from the last years. These management plans are the result of an ongoing and thorough interministerial work, which involves a number of ministries, public agencies and research institutions. The plans are adopted by Stortinget. They thoroughly describe all aspects of the marine environment and the various activities in the areas. On the basis of the environmental analyses, they lay down principles, guidelines and precise directives for these activities in the various parts of the sea area. They are not legally binding, but they serve as the basis for decisions pursuant to the respective sector legislation in such policy areas as offshore petroleum activity, fisheries, marine transport, and protection of marine biodiversity. They can best be characterized as a 'soft' form of marine spatial planning.

The last white paper, covering all sea areas under Norwegian jurisdiction, was presented to Stortinget and adopted in 2020.[73] In its introduction, it states:

---

71. A similar rule is laid down in the Svalbard Environment Act (Act of 15 Jun. 2001 No. 79) Art. 8, *see infra* Part II, Ch. 9, §4.
72. Directive 2000/60/EC.
73. Meld. St. 20 (2019–2020) 'Helhetlige forvaltningsplaner for de norske havområdene – Barentshavet og havområdene utenfor Lofoten, Norskehavet, og Nordsjøen og Skagerrak', and Innst. S. 382 (2019–2020). English version: Meld. St. 20 (2019–2020) Report to the Storting (white paper) 'Norway's Integrated Ocean Management Plans – the Barents Sea-Lofoten area; the Norwegian Sea; and the North Sea and Skagerrak'.

> In this white paper, the Government describes how it intends to continue and consolidate Norway's integrated, ecosystem-based ocean management plan system. ... The purpose of the management plans is to provide a framework for value creation through the sustainable use of marine natural resources and ecosystem services and at the same time maintain the structure, functioning, productivity and diversity of the ecosystems. The management plans are thus a tool both for facilitating value creation and food security, and for maintaining the high environmental value of Norway's marine areas.[74]

Further, it states, *inter alia*:

> The management plans implement an integrated, ecosystem-based management regime by evaluating the cumulative effects of all human activities on the marine environment and by managing the use of the oceans in a way that maintains the natural functions of ecosystems and ecosystem services. Ecosystem services are a vital basis for long-term value creation. Norway's ocean management plans are also integrated in the sense that they bring together all relevant parts of the public administration.[75]

63. The *precautionary principle* may, in its broadest sense, be seen as part of the principle of sustainable development. It addresses the issue of risk and uncertainty, and prescribes generally a safety margin in environmental matters. The popular version is that the environment and future generations shall have 'the benefit of the doubt'. *'in dubio pro natura'*. It has two different but closely related aspects: On the one hand, lack of full scientific certainty about possible serious environmental effects of a product or an activity should not be used as an argument for not taking measures to prevent such effects. Here, the principle is proactive, it requires action, and hence works as a 'sword'. On the other hand, if a planned activity may entail serious environmental effects but these effects are uncertain but may be serious, the activity should not take place. Here, the principle works as a 'shield' against harmful activities.

General prohibitions and control systems, like the one established by the PCA, may be seen as (implicit) expressions of the precautionary principle in a broad sense. Furthermore, this Act also prohibits actions that only create a *risk* of pollution (*see* Article 7 paragraph 1), thus establishing a safety margin. The GMO Act explicitly states that permits can only be given if the introduction of organisms into nature does not represent any risk of harm to health or the environment.

For a long time, the precautionary principle in its more precise meaning was not explicitly expressed in Norwegian legislation,[76] and its status as a general principle

74. *Supra* p. 7.
75. *Supra* p. 15.
76. With the exception of the Svalbard Environment Act Art. 7, which explicitly states that 'the precautionary principle shall be applied when a decision has to be taken without full knowledge of possible environmental effect. In this case, the authority shall be exercised in a manner designed to avoid possible damage to the environment'. The precautionary principle is also mentioned in the preamble

of Norwegian environmental law was somewhat uncertain. In the 2009 NDA, however, it has explicitly been laid down as a general principle to be applied as a guideline across Norway's legislation, as far as the protection of nature diversity is concerned. Its Article 9 expresses it as follows:

> When a decision is made in the absence of adequate information on the impacts it may have on the natural environment, the aim shall be to avoid possible significant damage to biological, geological or landscape diversity. If there is a risk of serious or irreversible damage to biological, geological or landscape diversity, lack of knowledge shall not be used as a reason for postponing or not introducing management measures.[77]

This definition of the principle is also laid down as a general principle for Norway as 'a sustainable society', in the State budget for 2021. Nevertheless, it is evident that many aspects of Norwegian economy and lifestyle are far from reflecting the principle of precaution in this sense. Therefore, uncertainty as to the exact meaning and scope of the principle, as a general principle in Norwegian law, remains.

64. The *principle of prevention* is closely related to the precautionary principle. Again, general control and permit systems in such Acts as the PCA, the Agricultural Land Act and the GMO Act show the extent to which this principle dominates Norwegian environmental law. Another example is the Product Control Act.[78] This Act orders anybody who produces, imports, markets, processes, uses or in any other way handles products that may cause harmful effects to health or the environment, to take reasonable measures to prevent or limit such effects (Article 3 paragraph 1). It also provides the environmental authorities with a wide authority to take measures of control and issue necessary regulations (Article 4) in order to prevent environmental harm from products.

Another important application of this principle is the general rule in Norwegian law that environmental problems should be solved also through regional and local spatial planning. This is clearly stated, *inter alia*, in the PCA (Article 11 paragraph 4). The PBA[79] establishes a system of comprehensive planning at State, county and municipal levels. Approved land-use plans are legally binding for the landowner, and serve as legal framework or guidelines for the implementation of sector legislation. For example, a discharge permit according to the PCA has to be in accordance with or approved by the municipal planning authority. However, the relationship between the planning system and the sector legislation varies considerably, *see infra* Part III.

65. The *Polluter Pays Principle* (PPP) is also fundamental. The principle is complex and has several meanings. It is both a principle of economic efficiency and

---

to the 1992 EEA Agreement. For further reading: Hans Christian Bugge, *Norway*, in Nicolas de Sadeleer, *Implementing the Precautionary Principle. Approaches from the Nordic countries, EU and USA*, London 2007.

77. *See also infra* Part II, Ch. 1, §2.
78. Act of 11 Jun. 1976 No. 79. For further details, *see infra* Part I, Ch. 1, §3.
79. Act of 27 Jun. 2008 No. 71.

a principle of fair distribution of burdens connected to pollution.[80] Although not explicitly expressed in Norwegian pollution law, it is implicit in many aspects of the relevant legislation. It follows from the above-mentioned principle of a general prohibition of pollution that nobody has an *a priori* right to carry out a polluting activity. This also means that a polluter must accept regulations to limit pollution without any economic compensation, and has to cover the costs of the necessary measures to prevent pollution or repair damage. This is stated in the PCA (Article 2 paragraph 5). As a main rule, a polluter is strictly liable for damage caused by the pollution.[81] Public subsidies for cleanup measures are only given in exceptional cases, within the framework of the EU/EEA Guidelines on Environmental State aid, in particular for the remediation of contaminated sites.

The PPP in a wide sense means that a polluter shall be charged the externalities of the pollution – that is, the social and environmental costs of the remaining pollution. Environmental taxes and charges are an instrument to this effect. The Norwegian authorities support this broad understanding of the PPP, and have introduced various types of 'green taxes'.[82]

Recently, the PPP has been extended beyond the field of pollution in Norwegian environmental law. It is laid down as a general principle in relation to the protection of nature diversity in the NDA Article 11 which states:

> The costs associated with preventing or limiting any damage caused by a project to biological, geological and landscape diversity shall be borne by the project owner, unless this is unreasonable in the light of the nature of the project and of the damage.[83]

66. The *principle of Best Available Techniques* (BAT) was for some time a matter of dispute in Norway. Economists criticized it from the perspective of economic efficiency. It was deliberately not included in a clear form in the PCA of 1981. Instead, the relevant guideline in the Act (Article 2 paragraph 3) states that:

> the prevention and abatement of pollution and waste shall be based on the technology which, on the basis of a total appraisal of present and future use of the environment and of economic consideration, gives the best results.

However, in practice, the pollution control authorities have to a large extent applied the BAT principle in a stricter sense when issuing pollution permits. With the formal adoption in Norwegian law of the EU Integrated Pollution Prevention

80. *See* Hans Christian Bugge, *The Principles of Polluter Pays in Economics and Law*, in *Law and Economics of the Environment*, E. Eide & R. van den Bergh (eds) (Juridisk forlag 1996) and Hans Christian Bugge, *The Polluter Pays Principle: Dilemmas of Justice in National and International Contexts*, in *Environmental Law and Justice in Context*, Jonas Ebbesson & Phoebe Okowa (eds) (Cambridge University Press 2009).
81. Pollution Control Act, Ch. 8. For details *see infra* Part IV, Ch. 1, §3.
82. For details, *see infra*.
83. A similar rule is laid down in the Svalbard Environmental Act Art. 9.

and Control (IPPC) Directive,[84] the principle clearly applies to all installations covered by that principle. From April 2002, the principle is explicitly laid down more generally in the rules on the application procedure for pollution permits pursuant to the PCA.[85] An annex to the regulation gives a definition of the principle which is in accordance with that of the EU directive.

Since 2009, this principle is also explicitly laid down in the NDA – although in a similarly 'soft' version as in the PCA – and so it also applies to the work to protect nature and biological diversity. Its Article 12 reads:

> In order to prevent or limit damage to biological, geological or landscape diversity, use shall be made of such methods and such techniques and siting of industrial and other activities as, based on an overall assessment of past, present and future use of such diversity and economic factors, produce the best results for society at large.

67. As a basis for the regulation of hazardous substances, *the principle of substitution* has been formally adopted. It is explicitly stated in the Product Control Act[86] (Article 3a). Any activity using a product that contains a chemical which may be hazardous to health or the environment shall consider the use of less risky alternatives. Such an alternative shall be applied if the costs or inconvenience are not unreasonable.[87]

68. The *principles of recycling and of life-cycle assessment* of products should also be mentioned. PCA Article 2, no. 4 states that waste is to be recycled or reused unless this is not justified when all environmental, resource and economic considerations are taken into account.[88] Increasingly, regulations are introduced, which require that the public authorities – and private citizens – take into consideration the total environmental effects of products when decisions are made. This includes the effects of the production, including the use of raw materials, the effects of the use of the product and the effect of the product as waste.

The Product Control Act[89] gives the legal basis for this approach, as it provides the authorities with a wide discretionary power to make regulations and decisions about such aspects as the production, import, labelling, content, handling and use of a product, and disposal of the product as waste (*see infra* Part I, Chapter 1, §3).

The Public Procurement Act[90] requires that State, county and local authorities, and institutions under their control, shall take into account life-cycle costs and environmental effects when they are planning a procurement (Article 6).[91]

---

84. Initially Directive 96/61/EEC, consolidated as Directive 2008/1/EC and further developed into Directive 2010/75/EC of 24 Nov. 2010 on industrial emissions (integrated pollution prevention and control).
85. Regulation of 1 Jun. 2004 No. 931 on Pollution Control Ch. 36.
86. Act of 11 Jun. 1976 No. 21. *See infra* Part I, Ch. 1, §3.
87. *See* for details *infra* Part I, Ch. 1 §3.
88. *See* for details *infra* Part I Ch. 4.
89. Act of 11 Jun. 1976 No. 79.
90. Act of 16 Jul. 1999 No. 69.
91. Introduced into the Act by Act No. 80 of 2001.

69. Mention should also be made of the *principle of non-discrimination* in the meaning of giving equal treatment and weight to environmental effects inside and outside Norway. If activities in Norway have environmental effects outside Norwegian territory, such effects shall be regarded as equal to effects within Norway. This principle is stated in the PCA (Article 2 paragraph 6). The Nordic Environmental Convention of 1974 between Denmark, Finland, Norway and Sweden establishes this principle, and also gives citizens of the four countries equal rights within the other countries' administrative and judicial system in environmental matters. The Convention is incorporated into Norwegian law through a special Act.[92]

70. Finally, *the principle of a knowledge-based management of the environment* should be mentioned. This is laid down in NDA Article 8 related to the management of nature diversity. Its first paragraph states:

> Official decisions that affect biological, geological and landscape diversity shall, as far as is reasonable, be based on scientific knowledge of the population status of species, the range and ecological status of habitat types, and the impacts of environmental pressures. The knowledge required shall be in reasonable proportion to the nature of the case and the risk of damage to biological, geological and landscape diversity.

In the second paragraph, it adds:

> Furthermore, the authorities shall attach importance to knowledge that is based on many generations of experience acquired through the use of and interaction with the natural environment, including traditional Sami use, and that can promote the conservation and sustainable use of biological, geological and landscape diversity.[93]

§3. The Right to Environmental Information

I. Introduction

71. The *principle of participation and access to information* concerning the environment follows from general principles of Norway's public administrative law, and is also expressed in environmental laws and regulations. Public decision-making in Norway is generally quite open and transparent. The various interests and parties in a given case have the right to be informed individually or through public procedures, and to express their opinion, usually at several stages of the case before a final decision is made. The procedures for land-use planning, pollution permits and other permits for important projects, and the establishment of protected areas, all include provisions for information, public hearings and/or other mechanisms for

92. Act of 9 Apr. 1976 No. 21.
93. Unofficial translation.

public participation. The right to environmental information and to EIA is explicitly laid down in Grunnloven Article 112 second paragraph.

72. The general *Act on Access to Public Documents*[94] provides the public with a widely defined right of access to public documents. However, this Act is not entirely clear and adequate in all aspects related to information about environmental matters. In order to comply fully with the EU directive on environmental information[95] and the 1998 United Nations Economic Commission for Europe (UN/ECE) Convention on Access to Information, Public Participation in Decision-making and Access to Justice in Environmental Matters (the 'Aarhus Convention'), a special *Act on the Right to Environmental Information and Participation in Decision-making in Environmental Matters* (hereinafter 'Environmental Information Act') was adopted in 2003.[96] In addition to implementing the mentioned international rules, this Act clarifies the various rights and duties that follow from the general principle of right to environmental information laid down in Grunnloven Article 112.

II. Act on Environmental Information

73. *The purpose* of the Environmental Information Act is to ensure public access to environmental information and thereby make it easier for individuals to contribute to the protection of the environment, to protect themselves against health and environmental damage, and to influence public and private decision-makers in environmental matters (Article 1). The Act shall also promote public participation in decision-making processes of relevance to the environment. It is meant to implement the rules in the Aarhus Convention in Norwegian law.

The Act entails new obligations for *public authorities* to have knowledge and hold information about the environmental aspects and effects of their activities and to provide information to the citizens about environmental conditions and environmental consequences of their activities and decisions. It similarly also requires that *private enterprises* have knowledge and hold information about the environmental aspects and effects of their activities and provide such information to citizens upon request. The Act is supplemented by the Act on Access to Public Documents as well as many sector acts and regulations with specific rules on the public's right to information and participation in decision-making procedures in connection with spatial and land-use planning, development projects and protection measures.

74. In the Act, 'environment' is broadly defined. It means 'the external environment including cultural heritage and cultural environments' (Article 2(2)). Consequently, also archaeological sites and architectural monuments are covered.

94. Act of 19 May 2006 No. 16.
95. The present Directive 2003/4/EC.
96. Act of 9 May 2003 No. 31. The Act was based on Norwegian Public Reports NOU: 2001: 2.

'Environmental information' is also a broad concept, in accordance with the definition in the Aarhus Convention Article 2 no. 3, as defined in the Act Article 2(1) as follows:

> Environmental information means factual information about and assessment of:
>
> (a) the environment;
> (b) factors that are being planned or have been implemented in the environment, the properties or content of products, factors related to the operation of undertakings and activities, and administrative decisions and measures, including individual decisions, agreements, legislation, plans, policies and programmes, as well as related analyses, calculations and other assumptions used in environmental decision-making;
> (c) human health and safety and conditions of human life to the extent that they are affected or may be affected by the state of the environment or such factors as are mentioned in subparagraph b.

The Act applies to Norwegian public authorities and to undertakings that are established in Norway (Article 4).

75. The right to environmental information is linked to a duty for both public agencies and private enterprises to hold information – that is *a duty to have knowledge* – about environmental aspects of their activities. All 'public agencies' – a concept which is defined broadly in Article 5 – shall *hold environmental information* of a general ('superior') nature which is relevant and pertains to their responsibilities or activity, and they have a duty to make such information public (Article 8). To take a simple example, the Ministry for Transport and Communication must have adequate knowledge about the pollution and other environmental effects of car traffic in the country.

Furthermore, all public agencies and private undertakings must have knowledge about such environmental aspects of their activities that may have an 'appreciable' ('not insignificant' in the Norwegian language) effect on the environment (Article 9). For example, a chemical factory must have precise knowledge of the environmental risks of both its production and its products, and a farmer must know the properties and possible effects of the pesticides she uses.

76. The right to environmental information corresponds broadly to the duty to have knowledge. Everybody – 'any person' – has a right to get such information from a public authority as the authority is required to hold on the basis of the duty of knowledge.

The right applies to State, county and municipal bodies. The broad definition of environmental information means that people are entitled to know, *inter alia*, whether public authorities follow up their own goals concerning environmentally friendly operation, and about the environmental consequences of public plans, programmes and decisions. The public body shall make the information easily accessible to the public.

77. According to Article 11 of the Environmental Information Act, information from a public body may be refused if it may be exempted from publication pursuant to the Access to Public Documents Act.[97] Hence, these two Acts are linked. The Access to Public Documents Act, together with the general Public Administration Act,[98] contains a number of exceptions from the general principle of public access to information. The most important is the exception for information which is subject to *confidentiality*, including information about technical devices and solutions, procedures, operational matters and business relations, etc., which is important for *competition reasons* to keep confidential in the interest of the person whom the information concerns.[99] Environmental Information Act Article 14 lays down special procedural rules for the identification and possible disclosure of what the enterprise in question may consider to be confidential commercial or industrial information. A decision to disclose such information may be appealed by the enterprise.

However, it is important to underline that information may only be refused pursuant to the Environmental Information Act if there is *a real and relevant reason* to do so in a specific case. When considering whether there is a real and relevant reason, the environmental and public interests in favour of disclosure shall be weighed against the interests in favour of refusal. If the environmental and public interests outweigh the latter, the information shall be disclosed (Article 11 paragraphs (1) and (2)).

78. A request for environmental information from a public authority may also be refused 'if it is formulated in too general a manner or does not provide an adequate basis for identifying what the request actually means' (Article 10(3)).

79. Notwithstanding the exception rules, the public shall *always have access* to information about:

(1) pollution that is harmful to health or which may cause serious environmental damage;
(2) measures to prevent or reduce such damage; and
(3) illegal encroachment on or illegal damage to the environment.

This is explicitly laid down in Article 12 of the Act.

80. The Act lays down detailed *rules of administrative procedure* when a member of the public requests information from a public body. Refusal of a request for environmental information may be appealed to the immediately superior public authority.

81. The right to environmental information pursuant to Environmental Information Act does not only relate to information from public authorities. Everyone is

97. Act of 19 May 2006 No. 16.
98. Act of 10 Feb. 1967.
99. Act of 19 May 2006 No. 16 Art. 13 and Act of 10 Feb. 1967 Art. 13.

entitled to *environmental information also from 'public and private undertakings,* including trade and industry, and other organized activities' (Article 16 and Article 5(2)). It applies to such information as the enterprise must have knowledge about pursuant to Article 9, that is 'factors related to the undertaking, including factor inputs and products, which may have an appreciable effect on the environment' (Article 16(1)).[100] By this, the Act goes an important step further than both the Aarhus Convention and the EU directive on environmental information which both limit the right to information from public bodies.

The right to information from enterprises also applies to information about effects on the environment from production or distribution of a product taking place outside Norway, to the extent such information is available. The enterprise shall request such information from the previous sales link if this is necessary to enable it to answer the information requested. For example, a dealer in wooden furniture may be required to know and disclose whether imported furniture has been made of wood from a threatened tropical forest (Article 16(2)).

The same *exception rules* as for information from public authorities apply *mutatis mutandis* to information from undertakings and other organized activities. Particularly important – and difficult – in this respect is the exception rule for technical devices and solutions, procedures, operational matters and business relations, etc., which is important for *competition reasons* to keep confidential in the interest of the person whom the information concerns. This issue is quite complex. The general understanding, however, is that this exception is to be applied in a restricted way, and that the interest of the enterprise of secrecy always must be weighed against the interest of the public concerned to have access to the information.

82. The Act lays down detailed *procedural rules* for the disclosure of environmental information from enterprises and other organized activities (Article 18).

The enterprise may provide the information in the form it finds appropriate. However, the information shall be comprehensive and comprehensible in terms of the information need expressed by the applicant. If the request for information can be answered adequately through available public registers, reports, etc., the applicant may be referred to making use of such sources of information. Several enterprises may choose to fulfil their information obligation jointly.

When a request for environmental information has been received, the recipient shall make a resolution and make the information available as soon as possible and – as the main rule – not later than one month after the request has been received. If a request is refused, the enterprise or activity shall refer to the provision which is the basis for the rejection, and inform about the possibility to ask for a more detailed explanation, as well as about the right to appeal.

Refusal of a request for environmental information from an enterprise or an activity may be *appealed* to a special institution established by the Act, named the *Appeals Board for Environmental Information.* The board has eight members, three of which shall have private enterprise background, and three others shall represent

---

100. In a case from 2010, the Supreme Court found that the owner of a major forest area in Oslo must make public detailed maps about the parts of the forest with old, and thus pristine trees presumed to be important for the protection of biodiversity (Norsk Retstidende 2010, 385).

non-governmental environmental or consumer organizations or the media. The deadline for appeals is three weeks from the time the applicant has received information about the refusal for the enterprise or activity.

83. The Environmental Information Act also has a special chapter on *public participation in decision-making processes* related to development of legislation, plans and programmes which are relevant to the environment (Chapter 5, Article 20). This general rule was new in Norwegian law, but the principles have – to some extent – been followed in practice. It implements the articles on participation in the UN/ECE Convention on Access to Information, Public Participation in Decision-Making and Access to Justice in Environmental Matters (Aarhus Convention).

In connection with the development of such legislation, plans and programmes, public authorities shall provide opportunities for the public to present comments. This shall be done at such stages in the process and within time frames that provide opportunities to influence the outcome.

When the public authorities prepare legislation, plans and programmes which may have a significant effect upon the environment, a *public hearing* shall be held in due time before a final decision is taken. For the purposes of the hearing, an account of the environmental impact of the proposal shall be available. A public hearing is, however, not mandatory if other forms of participatory measures are considered to be more relevant, and if a hearing would be impossible to carry out for practical reasons, or is considered manifestly unnecessary. Drafts of parliamentary reports (white papers) and bills may be exempted from public hearing.

III. Other Relevant Legislations

84. The Act on Control of Products and Consumer Services (Product Control Act)[101] has important rules about information about products that may be harmful to health or the environment. In this field, the Act was considerably amended in 2003, as part of the reform on the right to environmental information and was thus linked to the adoption of the new Environmental Information Act. The Act gives the public the right to information about products from public authorities (Article 9), as well as from the producer, importer, seller or user of products (Article 10). Generally speaking, the rules are based on the same principles as the rules in the Environmental Information Act as concerns the general right to information, exceptions to the right, and procedures. Further details on this Act will be presented *infra* in Part I, Chapter 1, §3, and Part I, Chapter 8, §1.

85. The Accounting Act[102] lays down rules on the proper accounting and annual reporting for institutions such as joint-stock companies and various other types of corporations, societies and associations, as well as State companies.

Article 3-3a paragraph 10 of the Act states that the annual report of a company or society must give information on those aspects of the activity, including its use of

101. Act of 11 Jun. 1976 No. 79.
102. Act of 17 Jul. 1998 No. 56.

raw material and its products, which may have an appreciable – 'not insignificant' – effect on the environment. This corresponds to the knowledge requirement pursuant to the Environmental Information Act. Detailed information must be given regarding the possible effects of the various activities, and the measures taken or planned to prevent or reduce adverse environmental effects.

In 2019, a new important Article 3-3c was included in the Act. Companies of a certain size must provide information about their *'social responsibility'*: the integration in their business strategies, day-to-day running of the company and in relations with clients, considerations related to human rights, workers' rights, non-discrimination, social conditions, the environment, and prevention of corruption. This information should cover guidelines, principles, procedures and standards used by the company and how these are applied, an assessment of results and expectations with regard to further work. If the company does not have such guidelines, principles, procedures and standards, this should be stated explicitly.

The information should be included in the company's annual report or another public document.

In 2021, Norway adopted a new Act on public *'sustainability disclosure'* in the financial sector and a framework for sustainable investments.[103] It incorporates the two key EU regulations in this field[104] into Norwegian law.

86. The Labelling of Consumer Goods Act[105] provides the government with the necessary authority to issue regulations on the marking and labelling of consumer products (Articles 3 and 4). Such regulations may include information on energy and resource use of the product, and its environmental effects (Article 3(1)(c)). Pursuant to this, regulations have been laid down, *inter alia*, on label information concerning both the energy use and noise level of electrical household equipment in accordance with EU rules in this field.[106] Article 8 gives the government the authority to issue regulations requiring that consumer products should give the consumer necessary information about the product's use of energy and other resources, as well as its environmental effects when a product is marketed, advertised and exhibited. The amendment made it possible to implement EEA rules in this field, such as the EU directive on the availability of consumer information on fuel economy and CO_2 emissions in connection with the marketing of new motor vehicles.[107] The Act (Article 9) also provides for the introduction in Norway of the system for awarding the *EU environmental label* as laid down in the Parliament and Council Regulation (EC) No. 66/2010 on the EU Ecolabel,[108] which is presented as an attachment to the Labelling of Consumer Goods Act.

103. Act of 22 Dec. 2021 No. 161.
104. Regulation (EU) 2019/2088 of the European Parliament and of the Council of 27 Nov. 2019 on sustainability-related disclosures in the financial sector and Regulation (EU) 2020/852 of the European Parliament and of the Council of 18 Jun. 2020 on the establishment of a framework to facilitate sustainable investment, and amending Regulation (EU) 2019/2088.
105. Act of 18 Dec. 1981 No. 90.
106. Regulation 10 Jan. 1996 No. 16. For details *see* Part I, Ch. 8, §2.
107. EU Parliament and Council Directive 1999/94/EEC.
108. The directive is supplemented by Commission Regulations (EU) 782/2013 and 1941/2017.

87. Hence, the EU environmental label is applied in Norway. However, it plays a less important role than the well-established *Nordic ecolabelling system*, named the 'Nordic Swan'. The Nordic Swan Ecolabel is common to the five Nordic countries Denmark, Finland, Iceland, Norway and Sweden and was introduced by the Nordic Council of Ministers. It is a semipublic institution. It is formally independent of the government, and is not based on legislation or regulations. In Norway, it is mainly financed by the producers who obtain the licence to use the label. A small part of the budget comes from the government, and the government appoints the board chairman. To have the right ('licence') to use the label, a product or service has to meet a number of criteria which have been established for each product or service type. The work is based on the standard for ecolabelling in ISO 14024. So far, criteria have been established for 250 product groups for which it is felt that ecolabelling is needed and will be beneficial. Everything from washing-up liquid to furniture and hotels can carry the Swan label. More than 1,000 licences covering 3,500 products have been assigned. The label is usually valid for three years, after which the criteria are revised and the company must reapply for a licence. In this way, we ensure that products better suited to the environment are constantly being developed.

There is a close cooperation between the Nordic Swan and the EU Ecolabels. They have a common secretariat, and there is a mutual discussion and exchange of information between the systems. To a large extent, the criteria are similar.

88. For some years, a *State of the Environment report* was presented as a government white paper to Stortinget with regular intervals. In addition to special issues, these reports gave the Stortinget an opportunity to discuss broadly environmental policy. However, this information has in recent years instead been included mainly in the annual budget proposal for the Ministry of Climate and Environment (MCE).

§4. The General System of EIA

89. The *principle of EIA* is expressed in the environmental article of the Constitution, Article 112 paragraph 2 (*see supra* Chapter 2, §1). The general framework in Norwegian legislation is laid down in the PBA, Chapters 4 and 14 and the detailed substantive rules in a comprehensive regulation.[109] These rules implement the two EU directives on EIA, the project directive[110] and the directive on environmental assessment of plans and programmes ('SEA Directive').[111] They apply to virtually all types of projects and land-use plans that may have a significant impact on the environment, the society and the local community.

---

109. Regulation on environmental impact assessment of 21 Jun. 2017 No. 854, hereinafter 'the Regulation'.
110. Directive 85/337/EEC with later amendments and replacements, the latest Directive 2014/52/EU.
111. Directive 2001/42/EC.

90. The purpose of the rules on EIA is to elucidate the effects of projects that may have a significant impact on the environment or the society and community in general. EIA shall ensure that such effects are properly assessed and taken into account in a land-use plan and/or when a decision is taken as to whether, and on what conditions, a project with environmental and social impacts may be carried out.

For projects, the duty to carry out an EIA lies with the developer of the project. For land-use plans, the duty lies with either the relevant planning authority (most often the municipality) or – in the case of a 'private plan'[112] – with the developer, which also as a rule must cover the costs.

The Regulation defines the types of projects and situations which require an EIA. Generally, this system is in accordance with the EU directive. In particular, it makes the same distinction between two groups of projects (and plans for such projects): projects that due to their type and size always require an EIA ('Annex I projects') and projects that require an EIA if they may have significant environmental or societal effects ('Annex II projects').

91. In order to understand the system, it is important to be aware of the links between the land-use planning system and important industrial and infrastructure projects in Norwegian law. Land-use plans at the various levels, pursuant to the PBA, are as the main rule, decisive for the development and localization of infrastructure and major industrial and other projects. Most infrastructure projects are planned and approved through this system, and important industrial and other projects require a local development plan in addition to a permit from the sector authority in question. Thus, in Norway, the EIA system is primarily included in the spatial and land-use planning system.

92. For some types of land-use plans and projects, the EIA is – as mentioned – *mandatory*. As far as *land-use plans* are concerned, an EIA is required for regional plans and municipal plans that provide guidelines and framework for projects listed in Annexes I and II, including all municipal master plans and local development plans of the type called 'area regulation'. It is also required for *projects* that may have significant environmental and societal effects and for local development plans that include such a project. These are listed in Appendix I to the Regulation which *grosso modo* corresponds to – and fulfils – Annex I in the EU EIA Directive. They include major industrial projects – such as oil refineries, major hydropower and wind power plants, thermal power stations, and chemical, metal, and pulp and paper factories, as well as industrial farms, big shopping centres, and golf courses. They also include major infrastructure projects – such as motorways, other major roads, railways, major waste disposal and wastewater treatment plants, and military training fields. For each category, the Regulation defines minimum criteria for the rules to apply. The rules also apply to changes or extensions of existing projects if the change or extension itself satisfies these criteria.

112. The land-use planning system will be presented in detail in Part III *infra*.

93. For other types of projects and land-use plans, an EIA is required if it is found to have possible significant effects, based on a case-by-case assessment. In order to ensure predictability and simplify the administrative work, *the Regulation defines certain relevant criteria* for this group as well. The system is based on a double set of criteria spelt out in Regulation Article 10. One set of criteria relates to *the type and size* of the project. The other set relates to possible *environmental effects.* An EIA is, generally speaking, required also for middle-sized projects if they will entail or be in conflict with:

(a) areas protected pursuant to the NDA[113] or the 'Marka Act',[114] 'selected habitat types', 'priority species',[115] protected watercourses,[116] national salmon rivers or salmon fjords, objects sites and areas protected pursuant to the Cultural Heritage Act;[117]
(b) threatened or endangered species and their habitats, valuable landscapes, valuable cultural heritage sites, important mineral resources, Sami economic activities in the open land in general, and in reindeer herding needs and interests in particular; areas of and recreational interests;
(c) national policy guidelines and decisions pursuant to the PBA;[118]
(d) important changes in the use of land which is formally designated as 'areas for agriculture, nature, outdoor recreation or reindeer herding' in a municipal master plan or as 'agricultural land' in a local development plan and is important to agriculture;
(e) increased pollution in areas where adopted environmental quality standards are exceeded;
(f) negative impact on people's health, for example, due to water or air pollution;
(g) significant pollution or emissions of Greenhouse Gases (GHGs);
(h) risk of serious accidents as a consequence of natural risks such as landslides, avalanches or floods.

An EIA is required if at least one of these criteria is met on the basis of an individual case-by-case assessment.

94. The *EIA procedure* is laid down in detail in the Regulation. It has several stages. It is to a large extent integrated into the ordinary procedure for land-use planning and applications for permits and licences pursuant to sector legislation. Hence, in Norwegian law, the EIA is not an independent procedure but integrated into and a part of the ordinary decision-making process. It is also noteworthy that Norway has implemented the two EU directives – the project EIA directive and the SEA Directive – into the legislation as one common system which includes both.

113. Act of 19 Jun. 2009 No. 100.
114. Act of 5 Jun. 2009 No. 35.
115. For an explanation of these concepts, *see infra* Part II.
116. Pursuant to the Water Resources Act of 24 Nov. 2000 No. 82.
117. Act of 9 Jun. 1976 No. 50.
118. *See infra* Part III.

The procedure varies according to the type of plan or project. It is generally simpler for projects listed in Annex II than for projects in Annex I.

First, the developer must send a notification of the planned project to the relevant authority, with a presentation of the project and its possible impacts on the environment, natural resources and the community (Article 9). The notification must be sent as early as possible during the preparation of the project, at the latest in connection with the application in question.

If an EIA is mandatory for the project in question (Regulation, Appendix I), the notification must also include a proposal for a 'study programme' – a programme for what issues are to be treated in the EIA and how the EIA is to be carried out. In the case of a public land-use plan, the planning authority must always present a programme for the planning process (called 'plan programme'). This must include a study programme for the EIA.

If the project and the corresponding plan are of an Appendix II type, the authority first has to decide whether an EIA is required on the basis of the criteria laid down in the Regulation Article 10. If an EIA is required, the developer has to carry it out.

The study programme or plan programme shall give information about the plan or project in question, the issues and possible problems it raises and which are important for the environment and the society, the issues to be studied and assessed and the methods used to this effect, relevant and realistic alternatives and how these are to be assessed, and the procedure to be followed, including participation by vulnerable groups (Article 14).

The proposed study programme or plan programme is made public, and forwarded to all interested parties, including relevant authorities and organizations (Article 15). All interested parties may have influence on the issues to be assessed. On the basis of the proposal and comments received, the competent authority finally prescribes the study programme or plan programme (Article 16). This is then carried out either by the developer or – for regional and municipal land-use plans – by the regional or municipal planning authority as part of the planning process.

95. As far as *administrative responsibility* is concerned, the Norwegian EIA system is based on the *principle of integration,* in the sense that each sector authority is 'competent authority' for its type of activity and also for the EIA. The road authorities are competent authorities for EIAs for roads, the energy authorities for EIAs for energy projects and so on. These competences are spelt out in the annexes to the regulation for each type of project. For land-use plans pursuant to the PBA and also a number of activities which require a local development plan, the municipality as planning authority is the competent authority. Hence, there is, in the Norwegian system, no 'independent' authority that lays down the rules for the EIAs, assesses draft EIAs and approves or rejects EIAs.

The regulation (Article 5) states explicitly that the responsible authority must act 'objectively' and have the necessary competence. It may happen that the competent authority also is the developer of a plan and a project. This double role is of course very problematic. The regulation states that in such a case, the two roles must be kept administratively separate as far as possible. This is in accordance with a similar rule in the EU EIA Directive.

The general responsibility for the EIA system is shared between the Ministry of Local Government and Regional Development and the MCE. But the environmental authorities are not in general the 'competent authority' for each EIA and the requirements related to various types of projects. Their opinion on a plan- or study programme or EIA is important, but the final decisions on the programme, the content of an EIA and whether an EIA is satisfactory are taken by the relevant 'competent authority' which is the municipality or sector authority that takes the final decision. Some may claim that this system is in fact to let the fox mind the henhouse. It is fair to criticize this system from an environmental point of view. A recent study has shown that many EIAs, although accepted by the relevant authority, are not sufficiently thorough and precise, and not satisfactory with regard to methodology.[119]

96. The possible impacts of the plan or project are assessed through the study programme. The findings shall be included in the final proposal of a land-use plan and/or in the application for a permit or licence pursuant to the relevant sector legislation. The proposal or application must give an account of the plan or project, its objective, design and various environmental and societal impacts, and its vulnerability to climate change and natural disasters. It shall also account for the 'relevant and realistic' alternatives to the proposal that have been considered and the reasons for the final choice among several possible alternatives (Article 19). Furthermore, based on already existing information, it shall describe the present environmental condition and how this will develop if the proposed plan or project is not carried out (the 'zero-alternative') (Article 20).

97. Further details on *the content and form of the EIA* are given in the Regulation (Article 21) which to a large extent corresponds to Annex IV of the EU EIA Directive. As to possible effects, the assessment must include possible effects on nature diversity, ecosystem services, cultural heritage, recreation, landscape, pollution, including emissions of GHGs, water resources, land (soil) and mineral resources, the Sami cultural and natural basis, transport needs, energy solutions, public health, the effects of climate change, including risk of accidents and sea-level rise, avalanches and floods, and the environment for children and youth. It is explicitly stated that the assessment must include positive, negative, direct, indirect, temporary and permanent, short-term and long-term effects, and also possible trans-boundary effects.

The assessment shall describe the methods used in the assessments (Article 22) as well as planned measures to avoid, limit, mitigate and if possible compensate significant damage, including monitoring arrangements (Article 23).

98. When the competent authority has received the proposal or application with the EIA, it shall make it public and circulate it to relevant authorities and organizations, and make it available to the public, for comments. If, on the basis of the

119. *Evaluering av konsekvensutredninger etter kapittel 5 i forskrift om konsekvensutredninger*, Rapport, Multiconsult, Oslo (2021) (Evaluation of environmental impact assessments pursuant to Article 5 in the regulation on environmental impact assessment).

comments, the responsible authority finds that the EIA is not fully satisfactory, it may require additional studies carried out, as the basis for the final decision (Article 27).

99. The EIA, as included in the plan proposal or project application, shall be taken *'properly into account'* when the final decision on the plan or project is made (Article 29).

The decision and the grounds for it shall indicate how the EIA and the comments received have been evaluated and taken into consideration. In particular, it shall explain the reasons for the preferred choice between several possible alternatives.

100. If a project is likely to have significant adverse effects *across the national borders* into another State, a procedure of information to and consultation with the authorities of this State is required, pursuant to Article 14-4 of the Act and further rules laid down in the Regulation (Articles 33–35). These rules are meant to implement the international rules on EIA in a transboundary context, notably the 1991 UN/ECE Convention on EIA in a Transboundary Context (Espoo Convention) and the corresponding rules inherent in the EU directives on EIA.

101. Finally, the regulation lays down rules on *sanctions for violations* of the rules (Articles 36 and 37). This is in accordance with and satisfies the requirements pursuant to the EU EIA Directive. Violations may, for example, be not to follow the procedural rules of the regulation, not to comply with demands from the authorities and orders to correct wrongs under threats of a coercive fine, not to give correct information about a plan or project and so on. In ordinary cases, such violations will be met by an 'infringement fine' laid down administratively pursuant to PBA Article 32-8a and Regulation Article 36. A maximum fine, according to Article 36, is NOK 400,000 (corresponding to around USD 50,000). A violation by intent or gross negligence is subject to ordinary fines or even a prison sentence of up to two years in the most serious cases (PBA Article 32-9).

102. The EIA rules in the PBA do not apply to *offshore activities*. For such activities, there are special EIA rules in a regulation pursuant to the *Petroleum Act,*[120] based on the same principles as the general EIA rules. This regulation requires that an EIA be carried out at *two different stages* of petroleum activity: First, when a decision is to be made whether to open a new area on the continental shelf for exploration and possible subsequent exploitation. In this case, *the petroleum authorities* are themselves responsible for the EIA. Whether or not to open an area is ultimately decided by Stortinget. Second, when a developer has got licence to exploit a new field, an EIA shall be included in the subsequent proposal for the Plan for Development and Operation (PDO) of the field (more about this in Part II Chapter 7, §4 *infra*). Here, *the developer* – the company that holds the right to the resource – is responsible. However, the same principles and main procedures apply in both situations.

In both situations, the procedure starts with a draft 'study programme', which describes the planned development and possible impacts on the environment and

120. Act of 29 Nov. 1996 No. 72 and Regulation of 27 Jun. 1997 No. 653 on Petroleum activity.

other activities. After a hearing among authorities and important interest groups with a minimum deadline of six weeks, the study programme is decided by the MPE. On the basis of the approved study programme, the EIA shall describe the impacts of the activity on economic and environmental conditions, including measures to prevent and repair negative effects. It shall, *inter alia*, describe possible alternatives to the proposed development plan, describe the affected environment, assess possible environmental impacts, the need and system for environmental monitoring and so on. The EIA is to be presented to the Ministry. It is made public and sent to relevant authorities and organizations for comments. On the basis of the hearing, the Ministry decides whether the EIA is satisfactory or if further studies are needed before approval. Provided that no significant environmental effects are envisaged, the Ministry may exempt a project from the EIA duty if its daily production will be less than 4,000 barrels of oil or 500,000 m^3 of natural gas, and even bigger projects if they are not expected to have transboundary environmental effects. If significant transboundary effects are possible, the principles and rules of mutual information and consultation of the Espoo Convention apply.

Chapter 3. Historical Background

103. The historic development of Norwegian environmental law may be described in four phases: Before 1887, between 1887 and 1970, between 1970 and 1992, and after 1992. The main lines have been the development within five areas of law: harbour law, water pollution law, neighbour and air pollution law, urban and land-use planning law, and nature conservation law.

Norway's environmental law has developed mainly through new legislation, in response to new types of problems and needs, and increasing conflicts of interests over environmental issues. During the last decades, important parts of new environmental legislation are the result of rules established at the international level through international conventions, or through the EU directives and regulations, most of which apply to the EEA area and thus to Norway through the EEA Agreement, since 1992.

Norwegian courts, however, have – generally speaking – played only a modest role in the development of environmental law in Norway.

§1. Early Roots: Environmental Law Before 1887

104. Until the mid-1800s, there were few sources and rules on environmental protection in Norwegian law. In fact, the harbours were the first 'protected environment' in Norway. Some local regulations from as early as the 13th century prohibited the throwing of waste into the harbour, in order to prevent it from being filled in. A national rule to this effect was adopted already in 1735. In some cities, there were early local regulations on privies and stinking waste, as those adopted by Oslo (then Christiania) in 1595, and on water pollution from tanneries. But general rules on water and air pollution, neighbour nuisance, and so on, did not appear until the nineteenth century.

105. The first piece of *pollution legislation* came in 1848, prohibiting sawmills from discharging sawdust into rivers in the vicinity of harbours. This was during the first period of industrialization in Norway, which is clearly reflected in the legal development. New acts on urban planning for the major cities required that certain polluting and inflammable activities be established in the outskirts of the cities. The first general Act on health and sanitation came in 1860. This act gave municipal health councils the competence to regulate and even prohibit activities harmful to people's health.

106. This period also saw the first *court cases about neighbour nuisance*. These raised fundamental questions of a landowner's rights and duties in relation to his/her neighbours, in particular with regard to pollution and similar nuisance and damage. In a famous case from 1874 on the possible compensation for neighbour nuisance from a gasworks,[121] the seven judges of the Supreme Court split into three

121. Norsk Retstidende 1874, 409.

fractions on the compensation issue. The issue appeared as both sensitive and controversial. It was decided to establish certain principles through legislation, and a legal commission to this effect was appointed in the late 1870s, chaired by the most prominent legal scholar at the time, Professor Torkel Aschehoug.

§2. 1887–1970

107. In 1887, the *Neighbour Act* was adopted, based on the Commission's recommendations. It laid down the general principle of Norwegian neighbour law: If an activity causes 'unusual or unforeseen' harm to the neighbours, the neighbour should be compensated for his/her loss, on the basis of strict liability. This was further developed into the principle in the present Neighbour Act of 1961[122] of compensation for 'unreasonable' damage or nuisance.

This Act of private law did not apply adequately to widely spread emissions of air pollutants from modern, large-scale industries. In fact, it encouraged the 'high stacks' solution to pollution problems. In the new Act of 1961, a licence system for important sources of air pollution was included. This preceded the present system of the PCA.

108. That same year, 1887, Norway also got its first comprehensive *Act concerning the Use of Watercourses.*[123] It confirmed the legal tradition of private ownership of watercourses and riverbeds in Norway. At the same time, it recognized the many conflicts of interests inherent in the exploitation of water resources, and the need for a trade-off between these interests. Certain activities that could be 'harmful to other interests' were not allowed without special permission. The Act introduced the first general rules on freshwater pollution. For industrial activities, it was generally forbidden without a permit to discharge any type of waste into the river if this could damage other interests. This principle was maintained in the new Watercourse Act of 1940. In 1970, a special *Act on Water Pollution* was adopted. This Act covered all main sources of pollution of groundwater, watercourses and the sea, and established a general permit system for polluting activities.

Also, in 1970, an *Act on oil spill contingency* was adopted.

109. The first *Nature Protection Act* was adopted in 1910. It provided the first legal basis for nature protection. However, it had a very limited field of application as it only concerned the protection of animal and plant species in defined areas and geological sites. A new Nature Protection Act of 1954 provided the authorities with the legal basis for protecting natural sites and larger areas. The first national park in Norway, the Rondane National Park,[124] was established in 1962. The next step was the *Nature Conservation Act* of 1970.[125] It introduced three types of protected areas:

---

122. Act of 16 Jun. 1961 No. 15.
123. Lov om Vasdragenes Benyttelse m.v. of 1 Jul. 1887.
124. Rondane is a mountain area in the southern part of Norway, popular for hiking and skiing.
125. Act of 19 Jun. 1970 No. 63.

national parks, protected landscapes and nature reserves with different legal conditions and effects. On the basis of this act, the number of national parks, protected landscapes and nature reserves increased rapidly. In 2009, it was replaced by the NDA.

110. In the field of *urban and land-use planning*, the first legislation – which only applied to the major cities – appeared in the mid-1800s. A general Act on urban planning and building regulation was adopted in 1924. This applied only to buildings in urban areas. In 1965, this Act was superseded by a very comprehensive Building Act. This established a nationwide system of comprehensive planning – including land-use plans, at regional, municipal and local levels – and it tied the traditional system of building permit to the land-use plans. This Act gave the municipalities the legal basis for controlling land-use within their territory, and not only in the urban areas. It was replaced in 1985 by a comprehensive PBA, which again was replaced in 2008/2010 by the present PBA.

111. In the 1960s, environmental issues appeared for the first time on the national political agenda. It reflected the increasing awareness of the environmental crisis in many parts of the world, not least in USA with the publishing of Rachel Carson's famous book 'Silent Spring' in 1962. In Norway, the main issue during the 1960s was the controversies over some major *hydropower development projects*. These threatened to destroy some of the most beautiful and spectacular rivers and river valleys in the country. Furthermore, the public became sensitive to the serious pollution of watercourses, lakes and fjords, and the air pollution from heavy industries, as well as the need to protect the shoreline in the central parts of the country from too intense development that became evident.

As a result, the government started a work to meet the challenges. An Act adopted in 1965 introduced a general prohibition on building within 100 m of the sea. And as mentioned, new legislation on nature conservation and water pollution was adopted in 1970, the European Nature Conservation Year.

§3. 1970–1992

112. Since 1970, Norway has had a comprehensive and generally ambitious environmental policy, which includes important administrative and legal developments. As mentioned, a new Act on Nature Conservation and a Water Pollution Act were adopted in 1970. The Ministry of the Environment was established in 1972, immediately before the UN Conference on the Human Environment in Stockholm. In the following years, the State Pollution Control Authority (SPCA)[126] was established, and the existing Directorate for Wildlife and Freshwater Fish was developed into a Directorate for Nature Management. Norway's institutions for land and sea mapping were also attached to the Ministry, thus strengthening the system for the analysis and management of natural resources. Also, responsibility for the protection of cultural heritage was transferred to the new ministry.

126. Later gradually developed into what is now the NEA.

113. During the 1970s and 1980s, important *new legislation* was adopted. A new Act on the control of hazardous chemicals and other products – the Product Control Act[127] – was adopted in 1976. Other pieces of pollution legislation (air pollution, water pollution, oil spills, waste, etc.) were brought together into one comprehensive PCA in 1981.[128] In 1989, a special chapter on liability for pollution damage was introduced into this Act. An act to regulate and limit motorized transport in nature and watercourse was adopted in 1977[129] and a new Cultural Heritage Act in 1978.[130] The Building Act was, as mentioned, further developed into a new PBA of 1985.[131] The general system of EIA[132] was introduced into this Act in 1989. We also adopted new Acts on the protection and management of wildlife (1981)[133] and salmonid and freshwater fish (1992).[134]

§4. Developments Since 1992

114. Developments in Norwegian environmental law since 1992 have been much influenced by two factors: The development of international environmental law and the EU law through the EEA Agreement.

115. In 1992, inspired by the UN Conference on Environment and Development in Rio de Janeiro, Stortinget adopted the environmental article in Grunnloven, Article 110b (to become a slightly modified Article 112 in 2014). At the same time, the concept or principle of *sustainable development* was explicitly introduced into Norwegian legislation for the first time (1992 Municipality Act).[135] Since 1992, environmental principles, such as the precautionary principle, the principle of integration, and so on, have appeared more clearly in the discussion of environmental policy and law. The Rio conference also led to increased public attention and policy developments in such fields as climate change and protection of biodiversity. The principle of cost-effectiveness has also come much to the forefront, in particular in relation to the climate policy.

116. Norway joined the EEA in 1992, making Norway party to the internal market of the EC. As a consequence, the European environmental legislation, as developed through European Community (EC) and later EU regulations and directives, has played an increasingly important role in the development of Norway's environmental law. Although most of Norway's environmental acts themselves have not

127. Act of 11 Jun. 1976 No. 79. Its field of application was later extended to certain hazardous consumer services.
128. Act relating to the Protection against Pollution, and to Waste (Pollution Control Act or PCA) of 13 Mar. 1981 No. 6.
129. Act of 10 Jun. 1977 No. 82.
130. Act of 9 Jun. 1978 No. 50.
131. Act of 14 Jun. 1985 No. 77.
132. *See supra* §2, IV.
133. Act of 29 May 1981 No. 38.
134. Act of 15 May 1992 No. 47.
135. Act of 25 Sep. 1992 No. 107.

been much changed due to EEA rules, these rules have influenced important parts of environmental policy and the *implementation* of the relevant acts, to a large extent through new regulations pursuant to the acts. The influence of EU legislation has been particularly important in the fields of air and water pollution, hazardous chemicals and waste. Furthermore, the EC directives on environmental information and EIA have led to important changes in Norway's rules in these fields. Also, the general EEA rules to limit trade restrictions and promote free competition within the EEA influence the development of Norway's environmental law. We shall revert to these issues in later chapters.

117. This period has also been marked by the development and progress in other parts of *international environmental law*. The most important examples are the 1992 UN Framework Convention on Climate Change (FCCC) and the 1992 UN Convention on Biological Diversity (CBD). They both influence Norway's environmental and climate change policy to a large extent and have made new legislation necessary. Norway ratified the Kyoto Protocol in 2002, and much attention was paid to the development and application of the flexible mechanisms pursuant to the protocol.

118. The same is the case with the UN/ECE Convention on Access to Information, Public Participation in Decision-Making and Access to Justice in Environmental Matters (Aarhus Convention), which, as mentioned, together with the EU directive on environmental information resulted in the 2003 Environmental Information Act.[136] Other important examples are the amendments to the Montreal Protocol under the Vienna Convention on the Protection of the Ozone Layer,[137] the new protocols under the UN/ECE Convention on Long-Range Transboundary Air Pollution (LRTAP),[138] and the UN Convention on Persistent Organic Pollutants (POPs) (Stockholm Convention).

119. Also, in the field of *marine pollution*, there has been important international progress over the last decades, with effects on national environmental policies. One example is the establishment of the 1992 Convention for the Protection of the Marine Environment of the North-East Atlantic (OSPAR), and the obligations to reduce discharges of a number of hazardous substances to the sea, in particular from land-based sources. Another example is the important revisions of the international rules on oil pollution from ships, with the adoption of the 1992 Convention on Civil Liability for Oil Pollution Damage (London Convention). This convention introduces new rules in this field compared to the earlier 1969 Convention on the

136. Act of 9 May 2003 No. 31. *See supra* Ch. 2, §3.
137. Amendments adopted in Copenhagen 1992, Vienna in 1995, Montreal in 1997, and Beijing in 1999. In 2016 was adopted the very important Kigali Amendment which aims to limit the production and consumption of the hydrofluorocarbons (HFC) which are potent GHG.
138. The 1991 Geneva Protocol concerning the Control of Emissions of Volatile Organic Compounds (VOC) or their Transboundary Fluxes, the 1998 Aarhus Protocol on Heavy Metals, the 1998 Aarhus Protocol on POPs, and the 1999 Gothenburg Protocol to Abate Acidification, Eutrophication and Ground-level Ozone.

issue. These changes also required new legislation which was incorporated into a new Maritime Act in 1994[139] and, to a lesser extent, a new Ship Safety and Security Act.[140]

120. The 1981 PCA, the 1976 Product Control Act and the 1978 Cultural Heritage Act have remained basically unchanged since they were adopted. Some important amendments have been adopted, though, and the application of the Acts has in several respects becomes stricter and more precise, which is partly due to new international rules, not least the implementation of EU regulations and directives.

Several important new Acts have been adopted since 1992. In 1993, Norway got its first comprehensive Act on GMO.[141] It establishes sustainable development as a main objective of the Act, and the precautionary principle as the basic principle for its application. In 1996, a special Act on supervision and control of environmental conditions was adopted. This established a special State service – much similar to the general police – for the protection of nature and control of violations of relevant legislation, in particular related to wildlife and protected areas.[142] An important new element is the rules in the already-mentioned 1998 Accounting Act[143] which requires accounting information about activities that may have a 'not insignificant' effect on the environment. The 2003 Environmental Information Act has also been mentioned. In 2000, a new comprehensive Water Resources Act[144] replaced the outdated 1940 Watercourse Act. The comprehensive Svalbard Environmental was adopted in 2001.[145] A new Act on Allowances and Trade in Emissions of GHG was adopted in 2004[146] which implemented the EU Directive on the EU Emission Trading System (EU-ETS)[147] and Norway's obligations under the Kyoto Protocol. This was amended in 2012 in order to comply with the revised EU-ETS Directive for the period of 2013–2020 and 'Kyoto 2'.[148] The most important new legislations are two major new Acts: a new PBA (2008) and the NDA (2009). These will be presented in detail *infra* in Part III and Part II.

139. Act of 24 Jun. 1994 No. 39.
140. Act of 16 Feb. 2007 No. 9.
141. Act of 2 Apr. 1993 No. 38.
142. Act of 21 Jun. 1996 No. 38.
143. Act of 17 Jul. 1998 No. 56.
144. Act of 24 Nov. 2000 No. 82.
145. Act of 15 Jun. 2001 No. 79.
146. Act of 17 Dec. 2004 No. 99.
147. Directive 2003/87/EC.
148. Directive 2003/87/EC as amended by Directive 2009/29/EC and further amended and consolidated in Directive (EU) 2018/410 for the 4th period of EU-ETS 2021–2030.

Chapter 4. The Role of Government Institutions in the Shaping and Administration of Environmental Law and Policy

121. Norway has *a parliamentary system of government*, which means that the government must have support in the Parliament, 'Stortinget'. Norway's environmental policy and law have developed through a close, mutual relationship between Stortinget and the Government. Although environmental policy is not the most controversial area of politics, there may be clear distinctions between the various political parties on certain topics.[149] For nearly fifty years until 2005, Norway had mostly minority governments. They have sought support for their environmental policy through regular white papers on environmental issues. In a period from 1999 to 2007, the government presented biannually a Report on the Government's Environmental Policy and the State of the Environment as a white paper to Stortinget. However, since 2007, this report has been included in the annual State budget for the Ministry of the Environment in a shortened version. In addition, environmental information and policy proposals are found in white papers on more specific issues.

122. A basic principle in the Norwegian legal system is the so-called *principle of legality* – the basic 'rule of law' principle in Norwegian law. It is customary law but also laid down in Article 113 in Grunnloven which states: 'Infringement of the authorities against the individual must be founded on the law.' Broadly speaking, this principle means that any burden – financial or other – put on the citizen by public authorities must be decided as a formal Act in accordance with the rules of procedure for new legislation in Grunnloven,[150] or in regulations pursuant to an Act.[151] Taxes and charges can only be decided for one year at a time, usually as part of the annual State budget. So, Stortinget has full control and the last word of both the legislation and the taxation in the environmental field.

123. Most of the legislation, taxes and charges adopted by Stortinget have been presented to Stortinget by the government, formally by 'The King in Council'. Proposals for new Acts, as well as budget proposals, are presented by the government to Stortinget in the form of a 'Stortingsproposisjon' (shortened 'Prop L' for legislation and 'Prop S' for financial and budget matters), which literally means a proposal to Stortinget. A white paper – a document presented by the government to Stortinget for discussion only – is called 'Stortingsmelding' (shortened Meld. St.).

Stortinget is of course free to change the government's proposals. Also, any member of Stortinget has the right to initiate new legislation, and to forward other proposals for decision by Stortinget on any subject.

149. At the general election in September 2013 'The Environmental Party the Green' won a seat in Stortinget for the first time. In 2023, the party has three seats in Stortinget.
150. Articles 76–79.
151. Of course, this does not apply to relations governed by private law, such as ordinary payment for public service, private law contracts between a citizen and a public authority, work on the basis of an employment agreement, etc.

124. The *Acts adopted by Stortinget may be rather general* in their content and broadly formulated. Often, they establish important substantive and procedural principles, but they leave it to the government (or the counties or municipalities) to issue necessary regulations and decide individual cases, often within a rather wide legal framework which leaves much discretion to the executive authority. This type of 'flexible' legislation is predominant in the field of environmental law. The most important Acts, such as the PCA, the Product Control Act, the Cultural Heritage Act, the Wildlife Act and the NDA, contain important principles and rules, not least rules of procedure. But generally speaking, they leave considerable discretionary power to the government to implement these through regulations and individual permits.

125. Within the government, there is a *'vertical' distribution of competence* between ministries, directorates and the State administration at regional and county level. The ministries develop government policy, prepare the government's proposals to Stortinget and issue most of the regulations. Directorates or agencies usually have the necessary specialist and technical knowledge in the relevant field, and have been given legal competence to decide individual permit cases and issue regulations of a purely technical character. In the field of environment, for more than forty years, the Norwegian Directorate for Nature Management and the Norwegian Climate and Pollution Agency (CPA) have played a key role in preserving nature, reducing pollution, and shaping Norwegian environmental policy. From 1 July 2013, they merged into a single agency for environmental matters, the Norwegian Environment Agency (NEA), under the Ministry of the Environment which from 2014 is MCE. Under this Ministry is also the Directorate for Cultural Heritage. In some environmental policy areas, the State also has an administration at the county level, most often under the leadership of the State county governor, with formal authority for certain planning issues and decisions within pollution control and nature protection of regional or local importance only.

126. The 'horizontal' distribution of power between the various ministries is a particularly important and difficult issue in the field of environmental management. The institutional structure tends to be complex, because of the many interrelationships in the field of environment and economic development. Most sectors in society comprise activities which affect the environment. As a consequence, measures to protect the environment, while ensuring the natural base in the long term, will inevitably mean short-term restrictions on some type of activities and sectors. National and international environmental considerations may go against strictly local preferences and priorities. The choice of institutional framework for solving such conflicts of interest is very important. This is partly a 'technical' question of coordination and division of functions, but, more importantly, it is a question of distribution of power between various interests, sectors and institutional levels.

A key question is whether each sector should take responsibility for, and have regulating authority over, 'their' environmental effects, or whether the environmental authorities in the strict sense should have general competence to ensure proper environmental management in all sectors.

127. As mentioned, Norway favours *the principle of integration.* This implies that each sector has the primary responsibility for the environmental effects of its activity. In many acts, which have as their main purpose to develop and regulate certain economic activities, and exploit a natural resource, there are also articles and clauses which aim at the protection of the environment. At the same time, the environmental legislation in the strict sense rests with the MCE and the directorates under its responsibility. MCE also has the general responsibility to monitor and assess the environmental situation in the country and identify necessary measures. It is a further task of the Ministry to develop general environmental policies, and propose policy measures that cross sectors. In the field of international cooperation, MCE has a central position in close cooperation with the Ministry of Foreign Affairs and other relevant ministries. All proposals related to ratification of international agreements and implementation of relevant EU directives and regulations in the field of environment are formally presented to Stortinget by the Ministry of Foreign Affairs.

128. The Ministry for Local Government and Regional Development is responsible for *regional and spatial planning* on the basis of the PBA, and in that capacity shares the responsibility for the EIA system with the MCE. However, as already mentioned,[152] sector ministries and agencies, and the municipalities, have the authority to initiate and regulate individual EIAs within their respective fields of responsibility.

In the field of *pollution control,* MCE is responsible for issues under the PCA, which covers most of the pollution from stationary sources, including CO_2 emissions and other GHGs, the GHG Emission Trading Act, and environmental issues under the Product Control Act. Much authority in this field has been given to the NEA,[153] such as the issuing of individual pollution permits. Here, the Ministry serves as the appeal body. Some types of cases have been further delegated to the county governor. When it comes to pollution from *transport*, the role of the Ministry is mixed. As to pollution from road transport, the main legislation lies with the Ministry of Transport and Communication and the Norwegian Public Roads Administration. Pollution from ships is regulated by the Maritime Act and the Ship Safety and Security Act which, in general, comes under the responsibility of the Ministry of Trade, Industry and Fisheries and the Norwegian Maritime Authority. In the field of pollution from ships, however, MCE is responsible, and the Norwegian Maritime Authority[154] is subordinate to this Ministry in this important field.

129. The MCE is further responsible for *nature conservation measures, and management of biological diversity, including protected areas,* on the basis of the 2009 NDA together with the 1981 Wildlife Act and the 1992 Act on Salmonid and Freshwater Fish. In these policy areas as well, the Ministry is assisted by the NEA. MCE is also responsible for the implementation of important parts of the 1993

152. *See supra* Ch. 2, §4.
153. At http://www.miljodirektoratet.no/. Until 1 Jul. 2013 the Norwegian Climate and Pollution Agency.
154. At http://www.sjofartsdir.no.

GMO Act. Also, measures to promote and protect the interests of *outdoor recreation* – an essential part of the Norwegian lifestyle – come under the responsibility of this Ministry.

Furthermore, MCE and the subordinate Directorate for Cultural Heritage are responsible for the protection of cultural heritage, on the basis of the 1978 Cultural Heritage Act. National museums, however, are the responsibility of the Ministry of Culture.

130. Some important parts of environmental policy are not under the responsibility of the MCE.

The general *management of water resources* lies mainly with the MPE[155] and the Norwegian Water Resources and Energy Directorate under that Ministry. The main legal basis is the Water Resources Act of 2000. It is also responsible for the 1917 Water Resources Development Act[156] which concerns the development of watercourses for hydroelectric power, and for the 1990 Energy Act.[157] The close link between water management and energy production in Norway is historical. For nearly a century, the most important economic use of the watercourses was the development of hydroelectric power, and thus water management was to a large extent an issue of energy policy. As a consequence, the development of national plans for the protection of watercourses has also been the formal responsibility of the MPE, with the participation of the (former) Ministry of the Environment. The main responsibility for energy policy in general, including the development of renewable energies, also lies with the MPE.[158] It is also the responsible ministry for the petroleum activities on the Norwegian continental shelf pursuant to the 1996 Petroleum Act.[159]

Forest management and environmental issues related to agriculture come mainly under the Ministry of Agriculture and Food. The main acts are the Agricultural Land Act[160] and the Forestry Act.[161]

The management of *sea fisheries* is the responsibility of the Ministry of Trade, Industry and Fisheries, pursuant to the 2008 Marine Resources Act[162] and the 1999 Act on the right to participate in fisheries and catch (Participation Act).[163] This includes all living resources in the sea except wild salmon,[164] but including also sea mammals such as whales and seals. This is due to the fact that whaling and sealing traditionally have been important industries in Norway, and they have been regulated by legislation similar to that of the fisheries. So, whales and seals are not covered by the Wildlife Act, but subject to special legislation (*see infra* Part II, Chapter 3). The

155. From 2024 the name is Ministry of Energy.
156. Act of 14 Dec. 1917 No. 17.
157. Act of 28 Jun. 1990 No. 50, *see* details in Ch. 8, §2 *infra*.
158. However, the central State agency for financial support for renewable energy and energy-efficiency projects, Enova, lies under the MCE.
159. Act of 29 Nov. 1996 No. 72.
160. Act of 12 May 1995 No, 23.
161. Act of 27 May 2005 No. 31.
162. Act of 6 Jun. 2008 No. 37.
163. Act of 26 Mar. 1999 No. 15.
164. The management of wild salmon comes under the Act of 15 May 1992 No. 47 on Salmonid and Freshwater Fish Act, with the MCE as the responsible ministry.

Marine Resources Act also covers shellfish and corals. Furthermore, the Ministry of Trade, Industry and Fisheries is the responsible authority for regulation of aquaculture under the 2005 Aquaculture Act[165] – an industry of considerable economic importance to Norway. The Ministry of Transport and Communication, supported by the Norwegian Coastal Administration, is responsible for contingency planning to prevent pollution accidents along the coast, and for taking the necessary actions when an accident such as an oil spill from a ship occurs. The main rules on contingency and organization of actions in such cases are laid down in PCA Chapter 6.

165. Act of 17 Jun. 2005 No. 79.

Chapter 5. Sources of Environmental Law

§1. International Law as a Source of National Environmental Law

131. Generally speaking, international law has played and plays an important role in the development of Norway's environmental law. Norway is party to virtually all the most important global and regional environmental treaties, including climate agreements.

In Norwegian law, the *dualist principle* applies to the relationship between international law and national law. International conventions and agreements have to be formally internalized into national law through internal legislation adopted by the competent national authority. However, international law is always a source of interpretation of national law. The *principle of presumption* is important in this regard. It says that Norwegian law is 'presumed' to comply with international law. If there appear to be contradictions between a rule in Norwegian law and the international rule, the national rule should as far as possible be interpreted in accordance with the international rule.

132. In some legal fields, international law has become national Norwegian law by *special acts*. The most important example is the field of human rights. In 1999, the main human rights conventions were made Norwegian law through a special Act:[166] the European Convention for the Protection of Human Rights and Fundamental Freedoms with protocols, the International Covenant on Economic, Social and Cultural Rights and the International Covenant on Civil and Political Rights with the optional protocols of 1966 and 1989. Later, the UN Convention on the Rights of the Child and the Convention on the Elimination of All Forms of Discrimination against Women and some of the protocols under these conventions have been added to this list. None of these conventions have articles which relate explicitly to environmental issues. However, some articles are applicable – and have been applied – also to environmental conditions, *see supra* Chapter 2, §1, III.

133. Norway is not a member of the EU, but is as mentioned member of the *EEA*. The EEA comprises the Member States of the EU and three members of the European Free Trade Association (EFTA): Iceland, Lichtenstein and Norway, and is based on a special agreement between these parties.[167] In essence, the EEA Agreement means that all secondary legislation regarding EU's internal market – 'the four freedoms' – adopted by EU also apply to these three EFTA countries. Thus, in reality, Norway has *grosso modo* the same rights and obligations as the member countries of the EU in all issues which are relevant for the internal market. This applies to general principles on the functioning of the internal market, as well as regulations and directives adopted by the EU. It is a clearly stated objective in the EEA Agreement to develop and apply uniform rules within the whole of EEA, and also to interpret the rules similarly.[168] As environmental matters in the EU to a large

166. Act of 21 May 1999 No. 30.
167. Agreement on the EEA, as amended by protocol of 17 Mar. 1993.
168. Several articles in the EEA Agreement, *see* in particular Arts 1, 6 and 105.

extent are related to the internal market, the environmental legislation in the EU is important also for the development of environmental law in Norway. This includes EU legislation related to climate.

134. The *EEA rules reflect the EU rules.* The EU secondary legislation that existed in 1992 was included in the EEA Agreement when it was adopted in 1992. Since then, new EU regulations and directives that relate to the internal market and are defined to be 'EEA relevant' have subsequently been formally adopted as part of the EEA Agreement by the EEA. However, the EEA is not a supranational institution similar to the EU. The EEA Agreement is an 'ordinary' international treaty. Decisions by the EEA Council do not create internal Norwegian law directly. In accordance with the dualistic principle, the competent Norwegian authorities have to make the necessary decision to implement it, in order to make it national law. However, the national Act on the EEA Agreement[169] states clearly that in case of conflict between an Act or a regulation which is meant to implement EEA rules and another national Act or regulation, the EEA regulation prevails.[170]

135. In the *climate* field, Norway and EU have entered into a special agreement which ties Norway's climate policy to the main elements of EU climate policy and law. Formally, this agreement is independent of and not included in or part of the EEA Agreement. We shall revert to it, and to the link between Norway and EU in the field of climate law in general, *infra* in Part 1, Chapter 2, §2.

136. The *EFTA Surveillance Authority (ESA)* follows and controls the implementation of the EEA rules by the three EFTA States, quite similarly to the authority and function of the European Commission in relation to the EU members.[171] The ESA may bring the EFTA States before the *EFTA Court* for breaches of the treaty, including failure to implement secondary legislation properly. The EFTA Court consists of members from the EFTA countries. It is independent, but it is stated in the EEA Agreement that it shall take due account of the decisions of the European Court of Justice. The EFTA Court treats similar cases as the ECJ and applies the same rules as they are reflected in the EEA Agreement. In reality, there is a high degree of conformity between the decisions of the European Court of Justice and the EFTA Court. The decisions of the court are a legal source in Norwegian law. So far, there have been few cases in the environmental field. In 2015, the court found that Norway violated the EU air quality directive as the level of some air pollutants in several cities exceeded the levels laid down in the directive.[172]

169. Act of 27 Nov. 1992 No. 109.
170. Act of 27 Nov. 1992 No. 109 Art. 2.
171. A special agreement between the three EFTA States establishes the EFTA Surveillance Authority and the EFTA Court. This is linked to the EEA Agreement, but the EU Member States are not parties to this agreement. These institutions are 'internal' to EFTA although they apply the EEA rules.
172. Directive 2008/50/EC. EFTA Court case E-07/15.

§2. National Environmental Law Sources

137. The main sources of Norwegian environmental law are the *acts and regulations*. The main part is within public law, providing the rules and principles, and the necessary legal basis, for regulations and individual permits or conservation measures. Within private law, there are special acts, *inter alia*, on neighbour nuisance responsibility,[173] on liability for pollution damage[174] and on the public's right of access to and passage through private land, bathing, picnicking and camping on private land and so on.[175] We shall revert to all of these.

The Act on the public's right of access to and passage through private land is based on old *customary* Norwegian law. Apart from this, there are few issues regulated by customary law in the environmental field.

138. *Court practice* is a relevant legal source in Norwegian jurisprudence. Decisions by the Supreme Court create precedents, and should be followed in similar later cases. So far, however, there are surprisingly few court cases on environmental law issues in Norway. The reason for this may, at least in part, be the dominant use of flexible rules in Norwegian environmental law which leaves much discretion to the administration. In the Norwegian legal system, a discretionary decision by the administration cannot be overruled by the courts on its content provided that it is legal: That the proper procedure has been followed and the content of the decision is within the legal framework of the act and rule in question. The courts' review is thus generally limited to whether the administration has interpreted the rule correctly, whether the rule applies to the case in question, and whether the proper procedural rules have been followed.

Many environmental court cases concern the question of economic compensation to landowners for their economic loss in cases of nature protection, and the question of compensation for nuisance in traditional neighbour cases, on the basis of the Neighbour Act. Compared to many other European countries and the US, Norway has had very few court cases about liability for pollution damage or responsibility for cleaning up polluted soil, except for two Supreme Court cases.[176] It is possible that settlements in such cases rather take place outside the court system.

139. *Decisions and legal interpretations by public authorities,* in particular the ministries, are accepted as a legal source in the Norwegian legal theory. The legal weight of this source is, however, disputed, and it is anyway regarded as rather weak. Also, decisions and considerations by the *Parliamentary Ombudsman* are a legal source, but with only limited weight. So far, most environmental cases before the Parliamentary Ombudsman have been in the field of planning and building law.

140. *Legal theory* is of importance as a legal source in Norway. Increasingly, environmental law is the subject of legal research and textbooks. There are

173. The Neighbour Act of 16 Jun. 1961 No. 15.
174. The Pollution Control Act of 13 Mar. 1981 No. 6, Ch. 8.
175. The Outdoor Recreation Act of 28 Jun. 1957 No. 16.
176. *See infra* Part I, Ch. 5.

comprehensive monographs about the protection of nature in Norwegian law,[177] pollution and nuisance responsibility,[178] the PBA[179] and the Cultural Heritage Act.[180] A recent book covers international, European and Norwegian climate law.[181] There are also several books and articles giving an introduction to and an overview of Norwegian environmental law and its development, and of the relationship between international environmental law, EU law and Norwegian law.[182] In the course of the last few years, the question of the legal content and status of Grunnloven Article 112 on environmental rights has been a much-debated topic. Over the last decades, numerous master theses have been published on specific legal issues such as the international regulation of climate change, protection of biodiversity, GMO, the right to environmental information, the use of voluntary agreements in environmental law, issues of compensation for environmental damage, and so on.

177. I.L. Backer, *Naturvern og naturinngrep* (Oslo: Universitetsforlaget, 1986). However, since the adoption in 2009 of the Nature Diversity Act, this is no longer up-to-date. *See* now the commentary to the Nature Diversity Act by I.L. Backer, *Naturmangfoldloven med kommentarer*, (Oslo: Universitetsforlaget, 2010).
178. H.C. Bugge, *Forurensningsansvaret* (Oslo: Tano, 1999); E. Stavang, *Naborettens forurensningsansvar* (Oslo 1999).
179. T.J. Pedersen et al., *Plan- og bygningsrett,* 3rd ed. (Oslo: Universitetsforlaget, 2018) and F.A. Innjord & L. Zimmermann (eds), *Plan- og bygningsloven med kommentarer* (Oslo: Gyldendal, 2020).
180. J. Holme, *Kulturminnevern. Rett. Forvaltning Håndhevelse* (Oslo: Økokrim, 2001).
181. H. C. Bugge (ed.), *Klimarett* (Oslo: Universitetsforlaget, 2021).
182. *See* Selected Bibliography *infra.*

Part I. Pollution Control

Chapter 1. General Legal Framework

§1. Overview

141. Pollution and waste is a political and legal field which is strongly influenced by international agreements. This clearly marks Norway's work in the field. Norway is party to virtually all major regional and global conventions concerning air pollution and climate change, marine and water pollution, control of chemicals, and waste disposal and trade in waste.

Furthermore, as a member of the EEA since 1993, Norway has adopted and implemented – or is preparing the implementation of – nearly all secondary legislation of the European Communities/E U in the fields of pollution control, control of hazardous substances and products, waste disposal, and so on. This has been a very important factor in the development of Norwegian policy and law in this field.

Since much of Norway's legislation is quite broadly formulated and often has a 'framework' character, it leaves much discretion to the authorities. Therefore, the international conventions and EU legislation mainly influence the *application* of the laws through regulations and individual decisions. The main acts have, to a considerable extent, remained unchanged for close to four decades. However, the *substance* of the pollution and waste policy and the more detailed legal rules in this field have changed considerably and generally become stricter. An important trend has been the introduction of more precise obligations and rights both for various private actors and for public environmental authorities.

142. The problem of pollution and waste is subject to several pieces of legislation in Norwegian law, although this legislation is probably less dispersed than in many other countries. Since 1981, the country has a general act, the *PCA*,[183] that covers all types of *pollution from stationary sources,* as well as *waste management.* The Act also deals with contingency and response for accidental pollution, and *liability for pollution damage*. The Act establishes an integrated system to prevent and control various types of pollution from most types of stationary sources. Since the rules apply similarly to air, water and soil pollution, as well as noise, the main

183. Act relating to the Protection against Pollution, and to Waste (Pollution Control Act or PCA) of 13 Mar. 1981 No. 6.

presentation will come in this general chapter, while more detailed and special rules and regulations concerning the various types of pollution will be specially treated in Chapters 2–8 *infra.*[184]

However, some sector problems of pollution emissions are regulated by other Acts. They shall be mentioned briefly in the following paragraphs, and treated in more detail in later chapters.

143. Pollution from mobile sources, in particular from *means of transport,* is regulated mainly through sector Acts and regulations: Emissions from cars by the *Road Traffic Act,*[185] from aeroplanes by the *Aviation Act,*[186] and from trains by the *Railway Act.*[187] Pollution from vessels is regulated by two different Acts. Technical measures to prevent regular discharge of pollutants and waste, and safety measures to prevent pollution through accidents, as well as rules on control and enforcement, are laid down on the basis of the *Ship Safety and Security Act.*[188] The rules on liability for oil pollution damage are included in the *Maritime Act.*[189]

144. For regulation of local pollution, the *PBA*[190] is relevant. Through *land-use planning and zoning,* local pollution problems such as noise pollution may be prevented or reduced. It is important to note that the construction of roads and railways has to be based on plans pursuant to the PBA. In detailed land-use plans, some regulations on pollution and noise may be laid down, although they should not interfere with general regulations or individual permits pursuant to the PCA. Furthermore, the PBA requires that all new construction have a proper solution for sewage treatment, preferably linked to a public sewage system. It also requires that land for construction be satisfactory from an environmental point of view, thus addressing the problem of soil pollution from the perspective of construction safety. These issues will be dealt with in more detail in Part III *infra.*

145. Local pollution affecting health may be dealt with under the *Public Health Act.*[191] An important chapter on 'environmental health' provides the State and local health authorities with competence to adopt regulations and take decisions to prevent activities which present hazards to human health, and if necessary to issue injunctions. This will be presented in detail *infra* in section 4. In the field of private law, the *Neighbour Act*[192] still plays an important role as regards local nuisance. It

184. From 1 Jul. 2004, most of the special regulations pursuant to the Act have been put together as chapters in two major regulations: Regulation No. 930 of 1 Jun. 2004 on recovery and treatment of waste ('The Waste Regulation'), and Regulation No. 931 of 1 Jun. 2004 on Pollution control ('The Pollution Regulation').
185. Act of 18 Jun. 1965 No. 68.
186. Act of 11 Jun. 1993 No. 101.
187. Act of 11 Jun. 1993 No. 100.
188. Act of 16 Feb. 2007 No. 9.
189. Act of 24 Jun. 1994 No. 39.
190. Act of 27 Jun. 2008 No. 71.
191. Act of 24 Jun. 2011 No. 29.
192. Act of 16 Jun. 1961 No. 15.

is mainly an Act on compensation, laying down a right to compensation for unreasonable and unforeseeable neighbour nuisance. This issue will be dealt with *infra* in section 5, as well as in Part IV.

146. Another important Act in this field is the Act Relating to the Control of Products and Consumer Services (*Product Control Act*).[193] It lays down a general principle of caution for anyone who trades in, or uses, *products that may be hazardous to health or the environment.* It provides the environmental authorities with an important tool for regulating and controlling the production, import, transport, use and disposal as waste of hazardous products, as well as the content of hazardous substances in products, labelling, and so on. This Act will be described in further detail in Chapter 8 *infra.*

147. Norway also has certain environmental *taxes and charges.* These are mainly based on the general legislation on special taxes, but there is one special Act on tax on carbon dioxide emissions ('CO_2 tax') from offshore petroleum activities.[194] The various taxes will be mentioned in later chapters in connection with the pollution problem in question. There are also several important *agreements* between the MCE and various groups of companies with the objective of reducing emissions and waste problems. We shall revert to these later.

148. Administratively, pollution control policy and legislation fall mainly under the authority of the *MCE.* The Ministry defines the main lines of policy, prepares matters for the government ('The King') and Stortinget and issues general regulations. The Ministry also decides important cases of appeal on decisions taken by subordinate bodies, such as pollution permits issued by the NEA pursuant to the PCA.

NEA is the main subordinate body to the Ministry in this field.[195] This agency has the necessary expertise to monitor the national environment and to propose new policy measures and regulations. It decides applications for pollution permits according to the PCA, and environmental cases under the Product Control Act, and has important functions related to climate change and the Greenhouse Gas Emission Trading Act (GGETA).[196]

The *State county governor* has the authority to decide certain cases of local and regional importance only, and oversees the activities of the municipalities. One example is the approval of certain facilities for hazardous waste.

The *municipalities* are responsible for solving certain local problems, and have legal authority in these fields. One area of responsibility is wastewater treatment, and permission for individual treatment solutions. Another task is local waste collection and disposal. The municipalities should also develop an emergency response system in order to deal with local pollution accidents.

---

193. Act of 11 Jun. 1976 No. 79.
194. Act of 21 Dec. 1990 No. 72.
195. Until 1 Jul. 2013, it was the CPA (before 2010 named Norway's Pollution Control Authority). On 1 Jul. 2013, CPA merged with the Directorate of Nature Management into one consolidated environmental agency under the Ministry with the aim of strengthening the environmental policy and make it more coherent.
196. Act of 17 Dec. 2004 No. 99.

In the following section, the expression 'the pollution control authority' will be used generally to cover the authority at all levels.

§2. The Pollution Control Act

I. General Principles of the PCA

149. The 1981 Act relating to Protection against Pollution and to Waste – the PCA – is *the central piece* of Norwegian pollution legislation. This Act brought together several earlier separate Acts on water and marine pollution, air pollution, and oil spill prevention. It also introduced the first adequate legal basis for waste disposal and waste management in Norwegian law.

As mentioned above, it addresses all types of emissions into the air, water (including the sea) and soil. It addresses prevention of pollution, restoration, and liability and compensation for pollution damage. It gives environmental authorities competence to issue regulations as well as individual permits for polluting activities. It establishes a comprehensive set of rules, and it facilitates an integrated approach to pollution prevention and control.

150. The *purpose* of the Act is:

> to protect the outdoor environment against pollution and to reduce existing pollution, to reduce the quantity of waste and to promote better waste management. The Act shall ensure that the quality of the environment is satisfactory, so that pollution and waste do not harm human health or adversely affect welfare, or damage the productivity of the natural environment and its reproductive capacity (Article 1).

Thus, the Act is based on the *principle of prevention*. However, the purpose is not to reduce or remove pollution 'for its own sake', as it were, but in order to bring it to, and keep it at, a level which is satisfactory from the point of view of health, welfare and the natural environment. This means that a certain level of pollution may be accepted, provided that it does not exceed hazardous levels and is kept within the assimilative capacity of nature.

151. 'Pollution' is *broadly defined* in the Act (Article 6) as:

(1) the introduction of solids, liquids or gases to air, water or soil;
(2) noise and vibrations;
(3) light and other radiations to the extent decided by the pollution control authority;[197]
(4) effects on temperature,

197. In 2010, a new regulation, the Pollution Control Act applicable to radioactive substances and waste, *see infra* Ch. 7. Radiation, including radioactive radiation, is generally covered by a special Act, the Act on Radiation Protection of 12 May 2000 No. 36, *see infra* Ch. 7.

> which cause or may cause damage or nuisance to the environment (Article 6 paragraph 1).

It is not required that each emission individually may cause damage or nuisance to the environment. Even an emission which in itself has an insignificant effect is covered by the definition if it consists of a substance or substances of a nature which – in a certain quantity – may cause environmental damage or nuisance. This is the case, for example, with CO_2 emissions from numerous small combustion sources. It is also clear that the emission of substances which are abundant in nature itself – such as salt, phosphorous, nitrogen and lead – also comes under the definition, provided that the increased quantity of the substance due to human discharge may cause damage or nuisance. Certainty as to the possible harmful effects is not required; the wording 'may cause' means that a certain possibility suffices.

The threshold of the relevant damage or nuisance is very low. The Supreme Court has decided that even minor damage to the microflora in the soil on the polluter's own property was pollution according to the definition.[198]

The concept includes the introduction into the environment of microorganisms, such as bacteria and probably algae, that may be harmful.[199] But it does not cover the introduction into the environment of GMOs, which is regulated by the GMO Act.[200] Neither does it include natural phenomena, such as a landslide into a river, or the sudden blooming of an algae species along the coast.

Article 6 paragraph 2 states that the term 'pollution':

> also means anything that may aggravate the damage or nuisance caused by earlier pollution, or that together with environmental impacts such as are mentioned in items 1–4 (in para. 1, see above) causes or may cause damage or nuisance to the environment.

An example of this is a river dam for production of hydroelectric power, which reduces the quantity of water in the river, thus aggravating the existing pollution in the river.

152. In accordance with the principle of prevention, the Act lays down *a general prohibition against pollution,* and even the risk of pollution (Article 7). This prohibition is combined with a duty to take necessary measures to prevent pollution and to limit the damage if pollution has occurred.

It follows that whoever wants to carry out a polluting activity will need a legal basis that makes it allowed to do so. Some types of pollution are legal according to the rules

198. Norsk Retstidende 1998, 2011.
199. The introduction of organisms which are alien to the natural environment may have serious effects. An increasing problem is the discharge from ships of ballast water from other parts of the world; the water often contains microorganisms that are not found in the receiving water environment and that may disrupt the local biota. The problem is now regulated at the international level through the 2004 Convention for the Control of Ships' Ballast Water and Sediments, The Convention is implemented in Norwegian law through Regulation 8 Sep. 2017 No. 1368 on the Treatment of Ballast Water on Ships and Movable Installations, pursuant to the Ship Safety and Security Act.
200. Act of 2 Apr. 1993 No. 38, *see infra* Part II, Ch. 9.

of the Act itself (Article 8) or are subject to specific regulations (pursuant to Article 9). Otherwise, a special pollution permit is needed (pursuant to Articles 11–16).

Any pollution which does not comply with the rules of the Act itself, regulations or an individual permit is thus illegal and may be punished (Article 78). Similarly, it is a criminal offence not to act with proper care to prevent or limit pollution.

153. The Act applies not only to new polluting activities but also to any polluting activity that had started before the Act entered into force. The authorities may order an activity that existed before 1981 to reduce or eliminate its pollution. This is not regarded as a violation of the above-mentioned constitutional prohibition of retroactive legislation (Grunnloven Article 97).

Activities that had obtained a pollution permit pursuant to the earlier legislation and activities which did not require a permit before could nevertheless continue without applying for a permit according to the new Act. However, the pollution control authority could at any time issue regulations to further restrict and limit pollution from these activities. They could also decide that such activity needed a permit in order to be lawful after a specified time limit. This is clearly stated in the Act itself (Article 86).

In particular, during the 1970s and 1980s, Norway carried out important cleanup programmes in various branches of industry. These were based partly on the earlier legislation, partly on the PCA. The legal basis for these programmes was not disputed.

Although mostly uncontroversial, the retroactivity issue has nevertheless raised doubts in relation to some problems which are not explicitly solved by the Act itself. One example is the duty to clean up polluted soil when the pollution took place before the Act was adopted and was regarded legal at the time. This question will be discussed in more detail *infra* in Chapter 5.

154. The Act contains *several important principles,* some of which are spelt out as guidelines in Article 2. A general guideline is that the Act:

> shall be used to achieve a level of environmental quality that is satisfactory on the basis of an overall evaluation of human health and welfare, the natural environment, the costs of the measures implemented, and general economic considerations (Article 2 No. 1).

155. This underlines what is implicit in Article 1 on the purpose of the Act. The main objective is, of course, to prevent pollution and protect the environment. But *it shall be implemented with due regard to other interests,* economic interests in particular. It thus requires that a trade-off is made between environmental considerations and other social needs and objectives. This makes the Act a very flexible tool for the development and implementation of environmental policy. But this type of legislation may be criticized for being too lax and leaving the task of environmental protection to the political priorities at any given time.

156. This is elaborated further in Article 2 No. 3 which states that efforts to prevent and limit pollution and waste problems:

> shall be based on the technology that will give the best results in the light of an overall evaluation of current and future use of the environment and economic considerations.

This cautious – and conscious – wording means that the Act does not itself require a strict application of the principle of BAT. But in practice, *the BAT principle* has been generally accepted and implemented in Norwegian pollution policy.[201] And since 2004, this line of policy has been further strengthened through Norway's implementation of the EU directive on integrated pollution prevention and control – 'IPPC Directive'.[202] The directive is implemented in the 2004 Pollution Regulation,[203] Chapter 36. Its Annex II defines BAT in full accordance with the corresponding annex of the directive. Thus, the Regulation lays down stricter general conditions for pollution permits than what is required by the Act itself.

157. A second principle is that the pollution authorities shall coordinate their work with that of the regional and land-use planning authorities according to the PBA.[204] *The land-use planning system* should work together with the PCA to prevent and limit pollution (Article 2 No. 2). As mentioned, proper land-use planning is essential, in particular in order to avoid some types of local pollution problems. Pollution problems should as much as possible be solved for larger areas on the basis of regional and local plans (Article 11 paragraph 4). Furthermore, regional and municipal plans should serve as guidelines for the implementation of the PCA. If a polluting activity will conflict with such a plan, the pollution control authority shall grant a permit only with the consent of the planning authorities (Article 11 paragraph 4).

158. The *principle of polluter's responsibility* is expressed in Article 2 No. 5, which states:

> The costs of preventing or limiting pollution and waste problems shall be met by the person responsible for the pollution or waste.

The meaning of this wording is to state *the PPP* as a general guideline. The costs of abatement measures have to be fully covered by the polluter and not, for example, by the State through financial support or subsidies. The formulation also gives support to the principle of strict liability for pollution damage,[205] as well as for pollution taxes and charges aiming at internalizing the social and environmental costs of pollution.

However, this general guideline does not answer the difficult question of who 'the person responsible' is when there are several relevant factors and actors contributing to pollution. We shall return to this issue later.

---

201. At least in the version referred to as BATNEEC: BAT Not Entailing Excessive Costs.
202. Originally Council Directive 96/61/EC, consolidated as Directive 2008/1/EC and further developed into Directive 2010/75/EC of 24 Nov. 2010 on industrial emissions (integrated pollution prevention and control).
203. Regulation of 1 Jun. 2004 No. 931.
204. *See infra* Part III.
205. *See infra* Part IV.

159. The fourth principle expressed in Article 2 No. 4 concerns waste disposal:

> Waste shall be managed in such a way as to minimize damage and nuisance. Waste shall be recycled preferably by preparing it for re-use or recycling of the material, unless recycling is not justified on the basis of an evaluation of environmental and natural resource considerations and economic factors.

In waste policy, significant effort is made to reduce waste and to collect and recycle waste products. We shall return to this issue in further detail in Chapter 4.

160. Article 2 No. 6 lays down 'the *principle of non-discrimination*' as follows:

> Pollution and waste problems resulting from activity in Norwegian territory shall be counteracted to the same extent irrespective of whether the damage or nuisance takes place within or outside Norway.

For example, when the pollution authority considers an application for a pollution permit, the possible effects of the pollution on the territory of other States – or areas outside national jurisdiction such as the high seas – are as relevant as the effects within Norway. As regards possible effects on the other Nordic countries – Denmark, Finland, Iceland and Sweden – the principle of non-discrimination also flows from the Nordic Environment Convention of 1974, which was implemented as Norwegian law through the Act of 9 April 1976 No. 21.

161. Several other principles flow directly or indirectly from the text of the Act. It is fair to say that the Act is based on *the principle of prevention, the principle of attacking the pollution at the source,* as well as *the precautionary principle.* There are no explicit references in the Act to these principles. However, they are implied in the system of the Act, with its general prohibition of pollution, and public control of all polluting activities. The precautionary approach can be said to be implicit in the system by the definition of 'pollution' ('... which cause or may cause damage ...') and by the fact that it is considered illegal not only to actually pollute but also to create *a risk* of pollution (Article 7). An activity may thus be prohibited pursuant to the Act because it creates a risk of pollution.

Furthermore, the *principle of EIA* is compulsory as part of the procedure for a pollution permit application.

II. The Field of Application of the PCA

162. *Geographically,* the PCA applies generally to sources of pollution, as well as waste and sources of waste, within Norway's realm, and to any threat of pollution within the realm. It also applies to sources of pollution or any threat of pollution within the EEZ of Norway if the source of pollution is a Norwegian vessel or installation, or otherwise to the extent decided by the King (Article 3). Regulations have been issued concerning the right of Norwegian authorities to investigate violations of rules to prevent pollution from vessels, and intervene in case of a pollution or risk of pollution from an accident at sea. These questions will be discussed further in Chapter 3, §3 *infra.*

163. Subject to limitations, the PCA applies to *the offshore petroleum industry* on the Norwegian continental shelf. In general, this industry is regulated by the Petroleum Act and several comprehensive regulations pursuant to that act. However, a pollution permit, pursuant to the PCA, is required for those aspects of the petroleum activity that regularly result in pollution, such as CO_2 emissions from the combustion of gas, and the discharge of wastewater, waste chemicals, drill cuttings and so on. The pollution control authority may also issue regulations concerning treatment of waste from petroleum activity on the basis of the PCA (Article 4).

164. Safety measures to prevent pollution *accidents in the petroleum industry*, such as oil spills, and to curb an actual spill, are regulated through the Petroleum Act[206] and regulations pursuant to that Act. If in case of a pollution accident, public cleanup activities are required, the general rules on the handling of accidental pollution in PCA Chapter 6 apply in combination with special regulations on safety measures and contingency in the offshore petroleum industry.[207]

165. The PCA applies mainly to emissions from stationary sources. In the field of *transport*, the Act applies to pollution from roads, railways, harbours and airports only to the extent decided by the pollution control authorities (Article 5 paragraph 1). A special Regulation states that the Act applies to pollution from polluted sediments in ports.[208] No other such decision has been made, which means that the Act does not generally apply to pollution typical to these transport facilities. However, the legal situation is unclear. Certain types of pollution which are not specific to transport facilities are covered, such as wastewater and sewage, emission from combustion and so on. It is also clear that the Act applies, for example, to the use of chemicals for deicing and other purposes at airports.

166. As regards *harbours,* the field of application is somewhat unclear. The idea behind the exception was that pollution in and from harbours should be covered by the Harbour and Navigable Waters Act.[209] However, this Act does not cover pollution. It is thus commonly understood that most types of discharge from buildings and installations in a harbour are covered by the PCA. The Pollution Regulation Chapter 20 has rules on the treatment of waste from ships, etc., in harbours.[210] And

206. Act of 29 Nov. 1996 No. 72.
207. In particular, a general Regulation of 27 Jun. 1997 No. 653 on the petroleum activity with later amendments, and Regulation of 12 Feb. 2010 No. 158 on Health, the environment and safety in the petroleum industry and some onshore installations, with later amendments.
208. Regulation 1 Jun. 2004 No. 931 Ch. 3.
209. Act of 21 Jun. 2019 No. 70.
210. These rules implement the relevant EU directives in the field: Directive 2000/59/EC as amended by Directive 2002/84/EC, Directive 2007/71/EC, Directive 2010/65/EU and directive (EU) 2015/2087.

the recent operations of removal and cleanup of sludge with toxic substances in Norwegian harbours are based on this Act.

167. As mentioned earlier, regulation of pollution from individual means of transport – *cars, trains, ships and aircraft* – is not covered by the PCA but by sector legislation and the Product Control Act. However, in case of a pollution accident from such means of transport, such as an oil spill from a vessel, or a spill of chemicals from an accident on the road, the duty pursuant to the Act to take measures to limit the damage (Article 7), and the rules on cleanup actions and so on (Chapter 6) apply fully. Also, the rules on *liability and compensation* (Chapter 8) apply fully to pollution damage from transport facilities and infrastructures, and transport means, unless other, more specific rules apply (such as the rules in the Maritime Act on liability for oil pollution from ships). For details, *see infra* Part IV, Chapter 1.

III. The General Duty to Avoid Pollution

168. Article 7 paragraph 1 of the Act states the fundamental principle of Norwegian pollution law:

> No person may possess, do, or initiate anything that may entail a risk of pollution unless this is lawful pursuant to the Act itself (Article 8), regulations pursuant to the act (Article 9) or an individual permit (pursuant to Article 11).

Violation of this rule by intent or negligence is subject to penalty according to Article 78 of the Act. The wording is meant to cover all types of actions and other causes of pollution or risk of pollution (except those sources to which the Act does not apply).

The creation of a *risk* of pollution is illegal in itself. However, the risk must be of a certain probability; theoretical possibility alone is not enough. Also, there must be a fairly direct cause-effect relationship between the action and the pollution risk.

It follows from the wording that possession of something that may create a risk of pollution is in itself a violation of the general prohibition. This is important for the issue of responsibility for polluted soil. Although the law is not entirely clear in its wording, it is the prevailing view that the owner of a polluted site is responsible for the effects of the pollution, and has a duty to carry out necessary cleanup and restoration measures. We shall return to the issue of responsibility for polluted soil in Chapter 5 *infra.*

169. The general prohibition in Article 7 paragraph 1 implicitly means *a duty to take every necessary action to prevent pollution or a pollution risk.* In paragraph 2 of Article 7, this duty is described in more detail as follows:

> If there is a danger of pollution contrary to this Act or decisions pursuant thereto, the person responsible for the pollution shall ensure that measures are taken to prevent such pollution from occurring. If pollution has already occurred, the said person shall ensure that measures are taken to stop or remove the pollution or

limit its effects. The person responsible also has a duty to take steps to mitigate any damage or nuisance resulting from the pollution or from measures to counteract it. The duty laid down in this paragraph applies to measures that are in reasonable proportion to the damage and nuisance to be avoided.

170. Unquestionably, the rule states a *strict responsibility* for action. It is the objective fact of pollution or a risk of pollution that entails a duty to act, regardless of any kind of negligence.

As the general rule, the duty to take action according to this rule also implies the duty to cover the costs of the actions taken. This follows from the principle expressed in Article 2 No. 5 (*see supra* section I). However, there may be situations where a person has a duty to act or initiate actions, for example, to limit an accidental pollution, but the costs must be covered by others, for example, the company running the polluting activity.

171. As can be seen, the wording is not very clear as to *who has the duty to take action.* Who is 'the person responsible for the pollution'? In most situations, this is quite clear and does not create any uncertainty or problem. The pollution is, for example, caused by an industrial activity, and it is clear that the owner of the factory is the responsible party. But there are also situations where several physical and/or legal persons may be seen as 'the person responsible'. There may be a chain of causes and events leading to the pollution, and thus several actors who contribute to the violation of the law. There may also be a complex system of ownership and management relationships behind the polluting activity. For example, waste from a chemical factory A may be stored by a storage firm B on a site owned by C, which is the subsidiary company of D. If a leakage occurs, is A, B, C or D 'the person responsible' according to Article 7 paragraph 2? Or are they all 'the person responsible', and if so, how are the legal obligations to be executed and divided between the parties? Even more complex situations may easily be envisaged.

The wording itself does not give a clear answer. The *travaux préparatoires* say that the responsible person must be defined in each case, depending on the circumstances. The main guideline is that the person who is 'nearest' to carry out the necessary action is the responsible one. It has to be a person in an adequate formal position, and with practical possibilities to act. Most often, this will be either the owner or the operator of the activity, or both. But as the example shows, under certain circumstances, several parties may be described as 'owner' or 'operator' of the polluting activity.

The rule on responsibility in Article 7 is meant to be broad and flexible. It is clear that *several persons* – physical as well as legal persons – may be defined as 'the responsible person' in a given situation.

172. Article 7 paragraph 2 is somewhat unclear also as regards *the extent of the duty* to take action. The last sentence indicates that the duty is limited by cost considerations. The duty does not extend to actions which are unreasonably costly compared to the environmental effect. But this only serves as a limit in rather extreme cases. Most often, all actions necessary to prevent and mitigate pollution damage – for example, to clean up and restore contaminated soil – will be within the limits of the legal obligation.

In order to properly implement the EU directive on environmental liability,[211] Norway in 2013 adopted some rules related to the application of Article 7. These are laid down in regulations, which in reality simply repeat or make more precise the general rules in Article 7 and other Articles in the PCA.[212] If there is an imminent risk of environmental damage through pollution, the responsible party shall notify the relevant authority and take the necessary action. The authority may order the responsible party to take specific actions or carry out the necessary action itself.

Anyone may request the pollution control authorities to order measures pursuant to Article 7 or take necessary action itself. This is explicitly stated in Article 84 of the Act. This article was included in the Act as part of Norway's implementation of the EU directive on environmental liability.[213] The authority is obliged to consider such a request if it is put forward by a physical or legal person who is affected or may be affected by a significant environmental damage or otherwise has a special interest in the case. The request must be based on adequate information. If the authority chooses not to take any action, this is formally regarded as a 'single decision' pursuant to the Public Administration Act, and as such it may be appealed. This is one of the very few rules to this effect in Norwegian law; the general rule is that there is no right to appeal if a public body chooses not to use its authority.

173. The pollution control authority may order the person responsible to take the necessary measures to fulfil his/her duty pursuant to Article 7 (Article 7 paragraph 4). This possibility may seem unnecessary since the duty to act to prevent or limit pollution flows directly from Article 7. However, since the wording of Article 7 is general and not clear in all respects, a public order may be necessary to remove any confusion and create a clear legal basis for further public action. The authority has a wide margin of discretion when issuing such orders.

174. If the responsible person does not implement a public order based on Article 7 paragraph 4, the pollution control authority *may itself arrange for the measures to be carried out.* The authorities may do this also in a situation of urgency, or if it is uncertain who is responsible for taking the necessary measures (Article 74, first paragraph). The same rule applies in the case where a person has been ordered to remove waste.[214]

In such a case, the costs, damage or losses incurred by the public authorities may be claimed from the person responsible for the pollution or waste problem.

If the person responsible cannot pay, or if he/she is unknown, the costs may also be claimed from the injured party or the person whose interests were served by the

211. Directive 2004/35/EC.
212. Regulation of 1 Jun. 2004 No. 931, The Pollution Regulation Ch. 40, adopted by Regulation of 3 Jul. 2013 No. 856.
213. Directive 2004/35/EC.
214. In case of pollution or risk of pollution on the high seas or the outer part of Norwegian territorial waters, special regulations apply, based on international rules on intervention on the high seas. These issues will be dealt with in connection with marine pollution in Ch. 3 *infra.*

measures. This particular 'victim pays' rule is one of the few exceptions to the general rule of 'polluter pays', which applies generally in Norwegian pollution law.

The authority may also decide to waive the claim if the claim will otherwise impede the claims of other injured parties, or it would be unreasonable to make the claim (Article 76 paragraph 3).

175. In such a case of intervention by the pollution control authorities, the authorities may decide that *the use of, or damage to, another person's property is permissible* provided that the benefit obtained 'is substantially greater than the damage or nuisance caused'. When a property is used or damaged in such a way, the owner is entitled to adequate remuneration. The authority is responsible for such remuneration, with the State as guarantor (Article 75).

In many cases of accidental pollution, such as oil spills, municipalities will have costs resulting from prevention and cleanup activities. Such costs may – subject to further regulations – be fully or partly covered by the State.[215]

These special compensation rules in fact overlap with the general rules on liability and compensation for pollution damage, which will be discussed in detail in Part IV *infra.*

176. If the responsible person fails to fulfil his/her duties according to Article 7 within a reasonable time limit, or in case of urgency, also *private parties may take the necessary measures* on his/her behalf, and have their costs covered by the responsible person. The condition is that the measures were taken in order to protect his/her property or prevent damage to it, and were implemented with due care. This follows generally from the principle of *negotiorum gestio,* which is a principle of customary Norwegian law. It is also explicitly stated in the PCA, Article 76 paragraph 2.

IV. Polluting Activities Which Are Not Generally Prohibited

177. The Act itself defines certain *polluting activities which are not prohibited* by the Act itself. They are prohibited only to the extent specific regulations have been issued to this effect (Article 8). Gradually, the most important of these activities have become subject to regulations limiting discharges and emissions. The discharge of sanitary wastewater is never allowed without a permit, unless it is in accordance with the relevant regulations (Article 8 paragraph 1).

Nevertheless, there are still some important activities that are exempted from the general prohibition of pollution.

178. 'Ordinary pollution' from *fisheries, agriculture and forestry* is legal (Article 8 paragraph 1 No. 1), unless subject to special regulations. The meaning of 'ordinary pollution' may vary with time and place. Generally speaking, the pollution is legal if the way the activity is carried out, as well as the type of pollution that it entails, complies with common practice in the area.

215. The general issue of contingency and actions against accidental pollution will be dealt with in §2, VI *infra.*

It is clear, however, that this exception only applies to pollution from traditional and small-scale fishery, agriculture and forestry activities. Pollution from large-scale 'industrial' activities in the agriculture sectors is not legal without a permit. Discharge from large-scale animal production[216] needs a pollution permit. Neither is pollution from the fish industry and fish farming legal without a permit.[217]

There are a few important regulations in the agricultural sector to which we shall return in Chapter 3, §2, III *infra.*

179. Likewise, 'ordinary pollution' from *housing, recreational houses, offices, schools,* hotels, warehouses and so on – except the discharge of sanitary wastewater – is exempted from the general prohibition, as far as it is not restricted by regulations. This includes emissions from combustion for heating, ordinary noise and so on. Also, pollution from temporary construction works is legal according to the Act, even if noise, dust and so on may create serious nuisance in the vicinity. These exceptions are explicitly stated in Article 8 paragraph 1 Nos 2 and 3.

It should be noted, however, that the health authorities may lay down restrictions on these activities on health grounds, pursuant to the Public Health Act.[218] Also, the neighbours may claim compensation for unreasonable nuisance according to the Neighbour Act.[219]

180. Also, pollution from the activities of the *armed forces* is exempted from the general prohibition. However, the Act applies in full to pollution from permanent defence installations which are not primarily used for combat purposes, such as teaching and training centres, offices, permanent training fields for artillery, and naval yards (Article 8 paragraph 2).

181. A final general exception is found in paragraph 3 of Article 8, which states that *pollution that entails only insignificant*[220] *damage* does not need a pollution permit, and thus the general prohibition in the Act does not apply.

This rule has created some confusion. The point is that small emissions from 'daily life', even if they are not covered by the exceptions of 'ordinary pollution', are legal according to the Act itself, and do not need any individual or regulatory permit. An example is the burning of dry leaves and branches in private gardens in residential areas, which is common in the countryside in springtime. It is, however, understood that the authorities may issue regulations relative to such sources (here again, the local health authorities may interfere on the basis of the Public Health Act, and the Neighbour Act may be used for injunction and compensation claims).

216. Industrial animal production is not very common in Norway, where most of the agriculture is small scale, and takes the form of family farms in the valleys and along the coast.
217. On regulation of fishing and fish farming (aquaculture) *see infra* Part II, Ch. 6.
218. Act of 24 Jun. 2011 No. 29.
219. Act of 16 Jun. 1961 No. 15. There have been several court cases related to nuisance from construction works. In a Supreme Court case, a restaurant was compensated for its economic loss due to heavy noise from the construction of a nearby highway (Norsk Retstidende 1969, 757).
220. The literal wording is 'not worth mentioning'.

However, this exception is not meant to cover those types of numerous small pollution sources which, taken together and cumulatively, add up to significant effects. Typical examples of this are CO_2 emissions from the burning of oil for heating in ordinary homes (which, however, in fact was generally prohibited from 2020), or the emission of ozone-depleting substances from numerous small sources. The Act may be fully used to control these emissions.

182. In addition to these general exceptions laid down in the Act itself, the authorities may issue *regulations* which make some polluting activities legal, or which establish general control or licensing systems for certain pollution sources.[221]

Article 9 of the Act offers the pollution control authority *a wide legal framework for regulations.* Regulations may contain:

- emission standards for various types of pollution or polluting activities;
- environmental quality standards and enforcement measures if the standards are exceeded;
- standards for polluting installations and production;
- standards for pollution control equipment and approval systems for such equipment;
- qualification requirements for personnel.

A number of regulations have been issued on the basis of Article 9. We shall return to some of the more important ones under the relevant chapters.

The legal basis for regulations is, however, not limited to Article 9. Many other Articles in the PCA authorize the issuing of regulations on specific issues. Some of these will be mentioned in the following paragraphs.

183. Environmental quality standards may be adopted through regulations pursuant to Article 9. So far, Norway has adopted quality standards for some air pollutants with local effect,[222] and for noise.[223] These implement the EU directives in these fields. Their general objective is to further people's health and well-being, and to protect vegetation and ecosystems. These regulations will be treated in the following chapters on air pollution and noise.

To date, no environmental quality standards have been adopted in the water sector, except for drinking water. However, *the Water Framework Directive*[224] *applies to Norway through the EEA Agreement,* and its implementation[225] will have major implications for the regulation of water pollution based on water quality criteria and standards. This will be treated more thoroughly *infra* in Chapter 3, §2.

---

221. This is stated explicitly in Art. 11 para. 2.
222. Regulation of 1 Jun. 2004 No. 931 Ch. 7.
223. Regulation of 1 Jun. 2004 No. 931 Ch. 5.
224. Directive 2000/60/EC.
225. Regulation of 15 Dec. 2006 No. 146 on the framework for water management.

V. The Licence System for Polluting Activities

184. The PCA establishes a general licensing system for polluting activities. Such a system existed also before 1981. However, earlier legislation treated air pollution and water pollution separately, and did not adequately cover the generation and treatment of waste. With the 1981 Act, Norway got a system of integrated pollution control, based on the same principles as were later introduced at the European level through the IPPC Directive.[226]

All polluting activities which are covered by the PCA, and which are not explicitly exempted from the Act itself (Article 8) or exempted through regulations pursuant to Article 9 need a licence according to the rules in Chapter 3 of the Act. This is explicitly provided in Article 7 paragraph 1. In practice, the system of individual licences mainly applies to industrial installations and activities of some size.

The key articles on this issue are Articles 11 and 16. The main principle is laid down in Article 11. The pollution control authority may, on application, issue a licence or permit for any activity that may lead to pollution.[227] The licence may cover all types of pollution: air, water and soil pollution, as well as noise and waste problems. It lays down necessary conditions for a permit, such as limitations on these types of pollution. It may also lay down conditions related to energy efficiency. So, in this way, it is possible to consider all aspects of pollution from an installation or activity together in an integrated way.

185. The Act provides the authorities with *a wide margin of appreciation* when deciding an application and laying down conditions. This flows from paragraph 5 of Article 11, which says:

> When the pollution control authority decides whether a permit should be granted and lays down conditions pursuant to Article 16, it shall pay particular attention to the nuisance arising from the pollution of the project, as compared with any other advantages and disadvantages of the project.

This wording must be interpreted in the light of the purpose of the Act and the above-mentioned guidelines in Article 2 of the Act. No doubt, the prevention of pollution is the main objective and concern when applications for pollution licences are decided. Other environmental concerns, such as the protection of flora and fauna and a natural site, are also highly relevant. However, social and economic aspects, including the costs of the pollution abatement measures, should be taken into account as well. This means that the Act itself prescribes a flexible approach, and the final outcome of an application may be decided on the basis of political priorities.

186. Most often, the question is not whether the activity should be permitted or not, but *what conditions are needed* to keep the pollution at an acceptable level.

---

226. Council Directive 96/61 EC, now consolidated and further developed into Directive 2010/75/EC of 24 Nov. 2010 on industrial emissions (integrated pollution prevention and control).

227. In special cases, the authorities may also issue such a permit without an application in advance (Art. 11 para. 1).

Article 16 paragraph 1 defines a broad framework for possible conditions in a permit. Any condition which works to prevent damage or nuisance from pollution, and to promote efficient use of energy, is accepted. Conditions relating to protection and cleanup measures, and recycling are explicitly mentioned. Although the Act itself does not state it clearly,[228] it is common practice to require the BAT to be applied. As mentioned, this principle has been explicitly laid down in the regulation on the procedure of pollution permit applications[229] when applied to installations covered by the EU directive on industrial emissions (integrated pollution prevention and control (IPPC)). If the present technology is not satisfactory to meet the environmental needs, the activity may nevertheless be permitted, but on condition that improved technology is developed and applied at a later stage. A permit may be given for a limited time. In addition, it is common to lay down specific conditions related to monitoring, inspection by the pollution control authorities, reporting and so on.

187. Articles 11 and 16 also apply to industrial installations that are covered by the *CO_2 emission trading system* pursuant to the special Act on emission trading which is linked to the EU-ETS.[230] These installations still need a formal permit pursuant to PCA. However, for these installations, the permit may not lay down a fixed emission limit of GHG. The installations may emit as much of GHG annually as is covered by emission allowances ('quotas' in Norwegian terminology) which are rendered to the relevant authority by the end of the year. We shall revert to this issue in Chapter 2, §4, II.

188. Article 16 also permits *other important conditions.* If pollution from the applicant's activity will permanently preclude or impede the use of the environment for a particular purpose, such as recreational activities along a river, it can be required that measures are taken elsewhere for the benefit of that activity, or that financial support be provided to promote such measures (Article 16 paragraph 2).

A condition may also be that the polluter, by agreement or expropriation, acquires areas that become heavily polluted, or reserve them for special purposes (Article 16 paragraph 2). In extreme cases, if the pollution will make a neighbouring property 'unsuitable for the purpose for which it is used', the owner or other rightholders of the neighbouring property may require the polluter to acquire his/her property on the basis of the principle of 'full compensation', as applied in expropriation cases.[231] However, this provision has only been applied in very few cases.

It is also said explicitly in the Act (Article 63) that a pollution permit may include the condition that security shall be provided in respect of possible liability to pay compensation pursuant to Chapter 8 of the Act, which concerns liability and compensation for pollution damage.

---

228. *See* discussion in Ch. 1, §2, I.
229. Regulation of 1 Jun. 2004 No. 931 Arts 36–38. The regulation implements the IPPC Directive as consolidated and developed into Directive 2010/75/EU of 24 Nov. 2010 on industrial emissions (integrated pollution prevention and control).
230. Act of 17 Dec. 2004 No. 99 and Regulation 23 Dec. 2004 No. 1851 with later amendments.
231. The principle of 'full compensation' in expropriation cases is laid down in Art. 105 of Grunnloven, *see supra* General Introduction, Ch. 2, §1, I. It is further defined in the Act on Compensation for Expropriation of Real Property of 6 Apr. 1984 No. 17.

189. In a pollution licence to two gas-fired power plants on Norway's West coast, strict limitations on the emissions of nitrogen oxides (NOx) were necessary to prevent further acidification in the area. The possible measures in the power plants were not sufficient. In addition, a condition was that certain ferries in the area installed gas-fired motors, in order to reduce their – quite substantial – NOx emissions. This was accepted on the basis of Article 16, provided that this *third-party solution* was clearly defined, under the full legal responsibility of the permit holders (the power plants), and subject to the ordinary control and enforcement mechanisms of the PCA. It was also seen as necessary in order to comply with the IPPC Directive that the gas-fired power plants themselves apply the BAT and that the third-party solution is only acceptable as a supplementary measure to BAT.

190. The procedure of permit applications is laid down partly in the Act itself (Articles 12–15), partly in a regulation.[232] Most of the applications for a pollution permit are to be addressed to the State NEA,[233] under the MCE or the county governor. The application must contain all information necessary to decide on whether a permit should be given, and on what conditions. This includes sufficient information on the activity itself including the use of raw material and energy, as well as technical solutions to prevent pollution and limit waste generation, how it relates to existing land-use plans, the present conditions in the surrounding environment and the possible environmental effects, the various interests affected by the activity, and costs and benefits of the project in general (Regulation Article 36-2).

The authority shall inform in writing other relevant authorities, as well as all interested parties, of the content of the application,[234] and invite comments within a certain time period of not less than four weeks. Usually, the application with all relevant information is made public, and anybody may present his/her views. A public hearing may also be part of the procedure.

For projects that may have significant environmental or social effects, the general rules on EIA apply. These are laid down in the PBA, Chapters 4 and 14 and the Regulation pursuant to these articles[235] which implements the two EU directives in the field, the EIA directive and the SEA Directive. The application must include a

232. Regulation of 1 Jun. 2004 No. 931 Ch. 36.
233. As already mentioned, this agency was established 1 Jul. 2013 by uniting Norwegian Climate and Pollution Agency and the Directorate for Natural Management.
234. It is not quite clear from the Act or the regulation to what extent interested parties have a right to written information. The general principle of Norwegian administrative law is that those persons whose rights or obligations are directly affected have procedural rights as a 'party' to an administrative decision (Administrative Procedure Act of 10 Feb. 1967 Art. 16). Whether this includes people who will be seriously affected by a polluting activity is a matter of some doubt. Landowners and other rights holders in the nearest vicinity of the new installation will be accepted as parties. However, this is not decisive, since the application – and in case the EIA – will be made public and anybody may present views on the matter, and these have to be taken into account.
235. Regulation of 21 Jun. 2017 No. 854. *See* the presentation of these rules *supra* in the General Introduction, Ch. 2, §4. The Pollution Control Act also has rules on EIA in Arts 13–15. Although formally still in force, these rules have in practice been superseded by the general EIA system pursuant to the PBA.

summary of the EIA, including a presentation of the various alternatives that have been considered for the project. The EIA has to be taken into account by the authority deciding the application.

As the main rule, the permit must be given in writing. It must *give the reasons for the decision.* Also, all parties and relevant authorities shall be informed of the decision in writing. There is a general rule of appeal in Norway's administrative law,[236] which applies to permit decisions. Both the applicant and any interested party, including environmental organizations, may *appeal* a decision within three weeks. If the decision is made by the NEA, the appeal goes to the Ministry of Climate and the Environment.

191. For activities and installations covered by the IPPC Directive, the regulation lays down certain substantial guidelines as well, in accordance with the Directive. *A number of principles apply* when deciding an application (Regulation Article 36-8):

- The BAT should be applied.
- Significant pollution harm may not be accepted.
- Emissions of hazardous chemicals of priority should be reduced or eliminated, as far as technically and economically feasible.
- Production of waste should be avoided as far as possible. Produced waste shall be recycled or – if recycling is not technically and economically possible – it must be disposed of in such a way that environmental harm is avoided.
- Energy should be used in an efficient way.
- Measures should be taken to prevent accidents and limit their consequences.
- Safeguards must be taken in order to avoid future pollution in case the activity comes to an end.
- Information about the emissions from the activity shall be available to the public.

192. As mentioned, a pollution permit may be given for a limited period of time. It may also be *modified, and even revoked*, under certain conditions. These conditions are defined in PCA Article 18.

According to general principles of administrative law, the alteration or reversal of an administrative decision is accepted only under specific circumstances. It is particularly difficult to have a decision altered negatively if the decision is to the benefit of a citizen such as a permit.[237] In such a case, a reversal of the decision must be deemed necessary due to significant public interests and the threshold is high.

Article 18 of the PCA defines *the legal framework for changes and reversal of a pollution permit* much wider, and at the same time in more precise terms. New conditions may be laid down which may be more or less stringent than in the original licence, depending on the circumstances.

A licence may be altered or even withdrawn if:

236. Administrative Procedure Act of 10 Feb. 1967 Art. 28.
237. Detailed conditions are spelt out in Administrative Procedure Act Art. 35.

(1) the damage or nuisance caused by the pollution proves to be significantly greater than or different from what was anticipated when the licence was issued;
(2) the damage or nuisance can be reduced without unreasonable costs to the polluter;
(3) new technology makes substantial reduction of the pollution possible;
(4) the conditions laid down in a permit are not necessary to prevent the pollution; or
(5) the advantages to the polluter or others of relaxing or rescinding the conditions laid down in a permit will be significantly greater than the damage or nuisance to the environment that will result.

In addition, the above-mentioned general principle of alteration of administrative decisions may be applicable. Regardless of these conditions, a permit may be withdrawn or altered if more than ten years have passed since it was issued, and there are environmental reasons for the withdrawal.[238]

When decisions are taken pursuant to Article 18, the costs involved for the licensee in an alteration or reversal, and any other advantages and disadvantages that result, shall always be taken into account by the authorities (Article 18 paragraph 3).

193. The issue of possible changes in a licence may arise on various bases. The initiative may come from the authorities. They monitor the environmental situation and follow the technical development in different industrial branches. Changes in these conditions may lead to one of the situations covered by Article 18, which justify modifications of the licence. Also, the licensee may demand that the conditions of the licence are made less strict if the conditions have changed in a way that justifies such a change. A special rule applies to companies under the CO_2 Emission Trading Act.

In addition, Article 19 demands that *a licensee notifies the authorities* if he/she plans a major renewal of equipment, which makes it possible to prevent or reduce pollution significantly better than the licence presupposes. This may result in stricter conditions in the licence.

As a final 'safety valve', Article 7 paragraph 3 makes it illegal to continue to pollute in accordance with a licence if the situation has changed in a way that is in accordance with the conditions in Article 18 No. 1 or 2 (*see* above). In such a case, the licensee has the duty to raise the issue of changes with the authorities if the damage from the pollution becomes significantly greater than anticipated in the licence, or the damage may be reduced without unreasonable cost to the licensee.

194. The closing down of an industrial activity or installation raises special problems. There may be a danger of future pollution from the installation, from waste left behind, or from contaminated soil. These problems may, of course, seriously aggravate if the closing down is due to bankruptcy or liquidation of the responsible company. Article 20 provides that the owner or user shall take the necessary action to prevent pollution if a facility is closed or operations stopped. If pollution continues after the activity has stopped, the pollution control authority shall

238. This rule has been applied in a few cases, one of which was disputed and came before the courts, but was upheld, *see* Norsk Retstidende 1995, 738.

be notified, and may require the necessary measures to be taken to prevent pollution. The authority may also order the owner or user to provide a guarantee for the payment of future expenses and any liability for damages that may arise.[239]

A person who wishes to start up a licensed enterprise after it has been closed for more than two years must notify the authority, which decides whether a new application for a permit is needed (Article 20 paragraph 3).

VI. Pollution Accidents

195. Chapter 6 of The PCA regulates obligations and rights in case of *pollution accidents*. The legislator had in mind in particular oil spills from ships,[240] but the rules apply generally to all types of accidents resulting in 'acute'[241] or uncontrolled pollution.

The Act defines the tasks and responsibilities of private operators as well as municipal and State authorities in the field. Close cooperation between many actors is often necessary to cope with an accident. Chapter 6 lays down the basic rules for this.

196. The starting point here is *a general obligation* on the part of any person or company responsible for an activity that may entail a risk of a pollution accident. They have a duty to establish 'the necessary *emergency response system* to prevent, detect, stop, remove and limit the impact of the pollution' (Article 40 paragraph 1). The emergency response system shall be 'in reasonable proportion' to the probability of an accident, and to the extent of the damage and nuisance that may arise. This obligation is within the framework of the general duty, pursuant to Article 7 of the Act, to prevent pollution, limit its effects and mitigate damage. This duty is further clarified by the rules of Chapter 6.

197. The authorities may, by regulations or individual decision, define more precisely the obligation of private parties to establish an adequate emergency response system (Article 40 paragraph 2). In this connection, they may require that *contingency plans* be submitted for approval (Article 41). It may also order private actors to cooperate, and to develop joint contingency plans (Article 42). Altogether, some seventy land-based industry companies have been explicitly required to establish contingency plans. Private companies have a general duty to support and assist municipalities and the State when accidents occur.

198. The offshore petroleum industry is subject to special requirements, pursuant to regulations, as regards accident prevention and contingency. According to the

239. This is, of course, a rather theoretical solution in case of bankruptcy or liquidation. The issue of responsibility in such a case will be discussed further in particular in relation to soil pollution, *see infra* Ch. 5.

240. Chapter 6 is partly based on a former Act on Oil Spill Contingency of 1970, which was adopted much as a result of the 'Torrey Canyon' accident off the southern coast of England in 1967.

241. 'Acute pollution' is the exact expression used in the Norwegian Act. We prefer to use the expression 'pollution accident'.

general Regulation on petroleum activity,[242] a number of general principles apply, the purpose of which is to reduce risks of accidents. Rightholders and operators in the petroleum industry have a general duty to prevent or limit damage or risk of damage to persons, the environment and material goods in accordance with the relevant legislation, and in all stages of the activity, and even to further reduce risks 'as far as possible'. In this, they should apply the technology and organization which gives 'the best results' when possible risks and present and future uses are considered, and the costs are not clearly disproportionate compared to the risk reduction which is achieved. In case of uncertainties in these regards, 'solutions that reduce the uncertainty' shall be applied (Regulation, Article 11).

A special chapter (Chapter IV) in the regulation deals with contingency (*beredskap*). The 'operator' of an oil or gas field shall ensure that the contingency is well coordinated in case of simultaneous use of several installations and vessels, and also coordinated with public contingency plans. The operator is responsible for taking the necessary measures in case of an accident or a risk of an accident (Article 20). Furthermore, the operator shall cooperate with operators of other oil/gas fields to ensure the necessary contingency (Article 21), and the system shall be properly coordinated with the public contingency system (Article 22). All the companies that are operators on the Norwegian continental shelf have together established an important joint contingency organization[243] with available equipment and personnel offshore, and along the coast. The aim is to 'ensure that oil recovery preparedness is always dimensioned in keeping with the needs and contingency plans of the operating companies'. A number of organizational, operational and technical requirements with the objective of reducing accident risks in the petroleum industry – partly general and partly more detailed – are laid down in three other major regulations pursuant to several different Acts, including the PCA Chapter 6.[244] We shall revert to some of these issues in the section on petroleum in Part II, Chapter 7, §4.

199. For activities using *hazardous chemicals,* a comprehensive regulation lays down more detailed rules on preventive measures and so on.[245] This regulation implements the 'Seveso III Directive' of the EU[246] and covers many different industrial activities. 'The responsible' for such activities must take all necessary

---

242. Regulation of 12 Feb. 2010 No. 158 on health, environment and safety in the petroleum industry and some land-based installations (called *Rammeforskriften* – 'The Framework Regulation').
243. Norsk Oljevernforening for Operatørselskap (Norwegian Oil Contingency Association for Offshore Operators), NOFO. This association has now twenty-one members – all the companies operating petroleum activities on the Norwegian continental shelf. It has oil spill equipment at five main stations onshore and runs information and education courses and carries out exercises.
244. Regulation of 29 Apr. 2010 No. 611 on management and duty of information in the petroleum industry and some land-based installations (*Styringsforskriften* – 'The management regulation'), Regulation of 29 Apr. 2010 No. 613 on operation of activities in the petroleum industry (*Aktivitetsforskriften* – 'The activity regulation'), and Regulation of 29 Apr. 2010 No. 634 on design and equipment of installations in the petroleum industry (*Innretningsforskriften* – 'The installation regulation').
245. Regulation of 3 Jun. 2016 No. 569 on Measures to prevent and limit the effects of major accidents in activities with dangerous chemicals, pursuant to the Pollution Control Act, the Product Control Act and several other Acts in the field of health and safety, with later amendments.
246. Council Directive 96/82/EEC (Seveso) as amended by Directive 2003/105/EC (Seveso II) and Directive 2012/18/EU (Seveso III).

measures through systematic work to prevent major accidents and limit the effects of such an accident on humans, the environment and material values. It must at any time be able to document that the necessary measures have been taken to this effect.

The regulation requires that notification on the activity, the type and amount of chemicals used, planned activities, the characteristics of the surrounding environment and so on be given to the relevant authority, the Directorate for Civil Protection and Emergency Planning. They must develop a document which describes the strategy to prevent and limit accidents, as well as a contingency plan for measures to be taken if an accident occurs, and issue 'safety reports'. If an accident occurs, they must provide all affected citizens with complete information about the situation and the measures to be taken. After the accident, a full report has to be made to the authorities.

200. Municipalities shall establish the necessary emergency response system to deal with minor pollution incidents that may take place in the municipality as a result of the ongoing activities there, or result in damage within the municipality, and which is not adequately covered by private contingency and necessary actions by the polluter (PCA Article 43). The pollution control authorities may require municipal contingency plans to be presented and approved. They may also order several municipalities to cooperate and develop joint contingency plans (Article 44). On the basis of this, thirty-two 'contingency regions' have been established, based on cooperation between municipalities. These regions cover all the municipalities in the country.

201. The State shall establish an adequate contingency system to deal with *major pollution accidents* which cannot be controlled effectively by the private and/or the municipal contingency systems (Article 43 paragraph 2). The State coordinates State, municipal and private contingency planning, as well as actions in case of major accidents. In particular, State plans and State participation are necessary to cope with major oil pollution from ship accidents along the Norwegian coast, which happen regularly. If the polluter is not able to cope with such an accident, the State takes over the responsibility for necessary actions. The Norwegian Coastal Administration under the Ministry of Transport is responsible for this task. There is close cooperation with other State agencies, such as the Norwegian Maritime Authority, the Petroleum Directorate, the NEA, the Directorate for Civil Protection and Emergency Planning, the National Defence including the Coast Guard and the Civil Defence.

202. In order to promote cooperation and the efficient use of resources, the authority sees to it that the emergency systems of private parties are adapted to the municipal and State emergency response system (Article 40 paragraph 2), and that private, municipal and State emergency systems are coordinated.

203. When an accident, or risk of an accident, occurs, the person responsible, as well as any member of the public, must notify the nearest police immediately

(Article 39 paragraph 1).[247] The responsible person shall *initiate all necessary measures to prevent or limit the damage* (Article 46 paragraph 1). If this is not done, or the measures are not adequate, the municipality shall take steps to deal with the accident and at the same time notify the State authorities (Article 46 paragraph 2). The State authorities shall provide the necessary assistance, as shall other municipalities, as much as possible (Article 47 paragraph 1). If a major accident has occurred, or could occur, the State authorities may wholly or partly assume full command of the necessary actions (Article 46 paragraph 3).

204. In case of municipal or State emergency actions, private parties who have a duty to establish an emergency response system (*see* Article 40) may be *ordered* to place the equipment and personnel included in their contingency plan at the disposal of the municipality or the State authority in charge. Similarly, municipal resources may be ordered to be included in a State action. If necessary, any public authority has a duty to provide equipment and personnel to combat the pollution. In particular, fire brigades, the Civil Defence and even armed forces may be mobilized in such situations.

Also, if there is a risk of very serious pollution damage, any person may be ordered to provide assistance in the form of equipment or personnel (Article 47 paragraph 2).

205. These rules and obligations also apply to *operations outside the national borders*. In such cases, the State authorities may decide that equipment and personnel shall be placed at the disposal of the authorities of another State (Article 47 paragraph 3). This is in line with Norway's commitment through international agreements between Norway and neighbouring countries about cooperation to prevent and combat oil spills and other major pollution accidents: the Copenhagen Agreement between the Nordic countries and the Bonn Agreement. The 1969 Bonn Agreement is the mechanism by which the North Sea States, and the EU, work together to help each other in combating pollution in the North Sea Area from maritime disasters and chronic pollution from ships and offshore installations; and to carry out surveillance as an aid to detecting and combating pollution at sea. The North Sea States are Belgium, Denmark, France, Germany, Ireland, the Netherlands, Norway, Sweden, and the United Kingdom of Great Britain and Northern Ireland.

There is also cooperation between Norway and Russia in this field.

206. The costs of operations to prevent, limit or mitigate damage from a pollution accident may be considerable. In particular, the cleanup actions after major oil spills along the coast often become extremely costly.

'The person responsible' has the primary responsibility to carry out the necessary actions, and at his/her own costs. This will normally be the owner and/or the operator of the activity or installation that has caused the accident. For oil spills from

247. Regulation of 9 Jul. 1992 No. 1269 on Warning of a pollution accident or risk of a pollution accident, as amended by regulation of 31 Aug. 2001 and 27 Jun. 2007. For offshore petroleum activities, special rules are laid down in Regulation of 29 Apr. 2010 No. 634.

ships covered by the special rules on liability for oil spills from ships in the Maritime Act,[248] the owner of the ship is – as the main rule – strictly liable for damage, including costs of cleanup actions. However, considerable assistance is often needed from other private parties, and from the municipal and State contingency organization. All the costs involved in these efforts are also to be covered by the party responsible. This follows from the general rules on responsibility in cases of public action on behalf of the person responsible in Articles 74–76 of the PCA, *see supra* III. To make this clear, Article 47 paragraph 5 explicitly states that any person that has provided assistance in emergency situations covered by Chapter 6 is entitled to remuneration in accordance with Article 75.

In addition, the rules on liability for pollution damage apply (*see infra* Part IV).

The costs of cleanup measures to be paid to the public authorities pursuant to the rules in the PCA to cover their costs are not limited by the limitation on liability for oil pollution pursuant to the international rules for liability for oil spills from ships and the corresponding rules in the Maritime Act. This was recently made clear in a decision by Norway's Supreme Court.[249]

VII. General Rules on Monitoring, Inspection and Enforcement

207. The PCA lays down a number of general rules, including penal provisions, concerning *monitoring, inspection and enforcement.* In addition, more detailed rules may be defined in regulations and in individual licences.

The main principle is that the pollution control authority has the right and the duty to monitor the general pollution situation, as well as the pollution and waste from individual sources. It shall seek to counteract pollution and waste problems primarily by means of advice, guidance and information. And it shall ensure compliance with the provisions of the Act and of decisions made pursuant to the Act (Article 48).

The State, through the county governor, may control the legality of municipalities' implementation of their obligations that follow from a number of articles in the PCA (Article 48a).

The pollution control authority demands *payment of a fee* for the handling of an application for a pollution permit, and for inspections and controls. The level of the fees is fixed in a regulation,[250] and varies according to the size and type of the activity in question.

208. The pollution control authority may order any person who possesses, does or initiates anything that may generate pollution or result in waste problems *to provide the relevant authorities with information* necessary to enable them to carry out

248. Act of 24 Jun. 1994 No. 39, Ch. 10. These rules implement the international conventions on liability for oil spill: International Convention on Civil Liability for Oil Pollution Damage of 1992, and International Convention on Civil Liability for Bunker Oil Pollution Damage of 2001. These rules will be treated in detail *infra* in Part IV, Ch. 1, §4, II.

249. Case HR-2017-331-A.

250. Regulation of 1 Jun. 2004 No. 931 Ch. 39, pursuant to Art. 52a of the Pollution Control Act.

their tasks pursuant to the Act. Information from other public authorities may also be required. This may be done by regulation or individual decision (Article 49).

If special reasons so indicate, the pollution control authority may require that information be provided also by any person who works for the person who has the duty to provide information (PCA Article 49 paragraph 1).

These obligations are not limited by any duty of secrecy. If there are conditions and facts that may lead to a criminal case, the general rules in Norwegian and European penal procedure law apply, whereby the accused may choose to abstain from presentations or explanations to enlighten the case from a certain stage in the investigation. However, the fine line between the duty to inform pursuant to the PCA and the right not to give information that may be harmful to the informant in a criminal case ('self-incrimination') may not always be entirely clear.

209. The enforcement of the Act is based on *a general right to inspection* for the pollution control authority. According to Article 50, the authority shall be given free access to property, where pollution or a waste problem may occur or has occurred or which is or may be exposed to pollution or waste problems, provided that this is necessary in order to exercise its duties. It may require documents and other materials to be submitted for inspection.

As a rule, the authority shall contact management representatives before an inspection takes place (Article 50 paragraph 3).

210. An important point is that the pollution control authority may order private actors to carry out *examinations and investigations,* with the purpose of determining the possible pollution from an activity, effects of the pollution and how the pollution should be prevented or controlled. Such an order may be addressed to any person who possesses, does or initiates anything that results in, or there is reason to believe may result in, pollution (Article 51). This rule applies correspondingly to any activity that results in or may result in waste problems.

The broad and somewhat vague definition of the person that can be made responsible for the investigation may create uncertainty. For example, Norway's Supreme Court has found that a mother company could be ordered to carry out investigations of polluted soil on a property that had been owned and used by a fully owned daughter company.[251]

211. It is a fact that some investigations of this kind may be quite costly. For example, it may be a complicated task to investigate a case of soil pollution in order to define the cause and extent of the problem, and the appropriate measures to solve it. The Act simply states that the authorities may order such investigations as *may reasonably be required* (Article 51 paragraph 1) to clarify these issues. Hence, the extent of the duty to investigate depends on many factors, such as the presumed seriousness of the case, the costs involved, the economic situation of the responsible party, and also whether the problem is due to negligence or not.

251. Norsk Retstidende 2010, 306. *See* further *infra* Ch. 5, §2.

The pollution authority may decide how investigations and analyses should be carried out, including that they must be carried out by a person approved by the authority (Article 52).

If there is pollution on a property or in the soil of a property, the authority may register this in *the public cadastre* pursuant to the rules in the Cadastre Act[252] (PCA Article 51a). They may also register legal obligations related to pollution on the property.

212. An increasingly important tool to monitor compliance with the Act, regulations and licences is the compulsory *internal control systems.* This system is defined through a regulation (Article 52b).[253] The regulation applies to all private and public enterprises and organizations with employees, and which are covered by the PCA and have employees, the Product Control Act and other Acts related to the protection of the work environment, health and public safety.

All the activities to which the regulation applies must have an adequate system of internal control related to the environment, health and safety. The obligation to ensure that such a system is in place rests with the one responsible for the activity, which means the owner and/or the leader of the activity. Cooperation with the employees is required (Regulation Article 4).

Through this system, the authorities may direct its control and inspection activities towards the firm's internal control system itself, instead of detailed inspections of emission limits, equipment and so on.

The lack of an adequate internal control system is subject to penalties in the same way as other violations of the PCA.

213. To properly apply these rules in the field of pollution control, the firm must, *inter alia:*

- ensure that relevant Acts, regulations and licences are accessible, and that they are known and familiar to key personnel;
- establish objectives for the work to prevent and limit pollution;
- identify pollution problems and risks, and make plans for the effective reduction and emergency actions;
- develop an adequate organization for the work on pollution issues, with clear lines of responsibility;
- develop routines for reporting and correcting possible violations of rules and regulations in the field of pollution applicable to the activity.

Most of these tasks must be documented in writing, and as necessary be expressed in plans, programmes, instructions and so on.

252. Act of 17 Jun. 2005 No. 101.
253. Regulation of 6 Dec. 1996 No. 1127 on Systematic Work on Health, Environment and Safety (usually called the 'Regulation on Internal Control'), with later amendments, pursuant to Art. 52b of the Pollution Control Act and several other Acts in the field of environmental protection, health and safety. For offshore petroleum activities special rules are laid down in Regulation of 29 Apr. 2010 No. 611.

214. A proper application of the regulation on internal control will, to a large extent, satisfy the requirements of the *voluntary international schemes and standards* in this field, such as the ISO 14,000 scheme, and the EU Regulation on Voluntary Participation by companies in the industrial sector in an Eco-management and Audit Scheme (EMAS).[254] However, these standards are more detailed and specific than the national regulation. The EMAS regulation has been adopted in Norwegian law through Article 52c in the PCA, and by incorporation in a regulation pursuant to the Act.[255]

215. Norway has also incorporated[256] the EU regulation concerning the common European *Pollutant Release and Transfer Register* (E-PRTR)[257] whereby Norway through NEA reports on polluting emissions to air, water and soil and transport of hazardous waste and substances in Norway in accordance with the detailed rules in the regulation and its annexes.

216. An important sanction in case of violation of a regulation or licence is the *coercive fine*[258] described in Article 73. The pollution control authority may impose such a fine when a contravention is discovered. The authority often chose, as a first step, to set a deadline for the responsible person or company to correct and remedy the matter. If the person or company responsible fails to meet the deadline, the fine becomes effective. A coercive fine may also be imposed in advance and then become effective from the date when the contravention starts.

It may be decided that the fine shall continue to be effective for as long as the unlawful situation persists, or that it is payable each time a contravention takes place.

The Act does not set any maximum level for the fine. This is left to the discretion of the pollution control authority. The fines may in fact be quite high, in order to make it unprofitable for the polluter to continue the contravention.

The use of a coercive fine is not formally defined as a penalty in Norwegian law, and thus may be decided by the administration. It does not exclude penal measures for the same contravention. In a case in 2015, the Supreme Court stated that a coercive fine pursuant to PCA Article 73 is not a penalty in the sense of Article 4 No. 1 in Protocol No. 7 to the (European) Convention for the Protection of Human Rights and Fundamental Freedoms. So, it does not violate the right pursuant to this article not to be tried or punished twice.[259]

217. The PCA has a chapter on *penalty and penal measures* (Chapter 10). This makes a reference to and is meant to implement the EU directive on the protection of the environment through criminal law.[260] Its main article (Article 78) has recently

254. Regulation (EC) 1221/2009 of 25 Nov. 2009 as amended by Regulation (EU) 2017/1505 and Regulation (EU) 2018/2026.
255. Regulation of 1 Jun. 2004 No. 931 Ch. 38, as amended by Regulation of 13 Jul. 2012 No. 756.
256. In Regulation of 1 Jun. 2004 No. 931 Ch. 38B.
257. Regulation (EC) No. 2006/166 of 18 Jan. 2006.
258. Earlier this was named 'pollution fine' in the Act.
259. Norsk Retstidende 2015, 392.
260. Directive 2008/99/EC of the European Parliament and of the Council of 19 Nov. 2008.

been considerably sharpened with regard to the possible sanctions.[261] This reflects the fact that illegal pollution appears to be rather common. The present government presented in 2020 a white paper on environmental crime[262] which describes the problems of identifying and punishing violation of environmental law in general, not least pollution law including pollution accidents and waste law.

218. PCA Article 78 makes it a criminal act, with intent or by negligence, to contravene an obligation (emanating/originating) from the Act, or from regulations or an individual licence pursuant to the Act. The examples listed explicitly in Article 78 are:

- to possess, do or initiate anything that may cause pollution contrary to the Act or regulations;
- to fail to take necessary measures according to the general duty rule in Article 7, or the rule on emergency planning in Article 40, or contravene conditions laid down in a pollution licence according to Articles 11 and 16, and Article 41 on emergency plans;
- to fail to provide notification and information to the pollution control authority in situations where this is required by the Act;[263] and
- to fail to comply with orders issued by the pollution control authorities to take measures pursuant to Articles 49–51 of the Act.

A contravention may generally be punished with fines, a maximum of one-year imprisonment or both (Article 78 paragraph 1). However, if the contravention has resulted in a risk of great damage or serious nuisance, or there are otherwise especially aggravating circumstances, imprisonment for a term not exceeding three years may be imposed. If the contravention resulted in a risk of serious or irreversible damage to biological diversity, or danger to human life or health, a term of maximum five years may apply (Article 78 paragraph 2).

Article 79 lays down similar penalties for *unlawful waste management*. This topic will be treated below in Chapter 4.

Until now, there have been very few cases of imprisonment due to pollution crimes in Norway.[264] However, heavy fines are imposed more and more often. The maximum fine until now has been NOK 4 million (corresponding to some USD 500,000), for the negligent discharge of 4 kg of mercury into a Norwegian fjord.

219. As part of the reforms of the penalty rules in 2019, a new type of reaction was introduced for violation of pollution legislation, in PCA Article 80, called

261. The government's proposals to Stortinget are laid down in Prop. 77 L (2018–2019) of 5 Apr. 2019, *see also* Innst. 322 L (2018–2019).
262. Meld. St. 19 (2019–2020) Miljøkriminalitet.
263. Similar rules apply to contraventions of the rules and regulations related to waste and waste disposal as set out in Art. 79 (*see infra* Ch. 4).
264. However, in a recent case before the Supreme Court the owner of a site for chemical waste, including storage tanks was sentenced to two years in prison for intent and gross negligence in the treatment of used petrol. The result was a major explosion with emissions creating serious health effects in the local community (Norsk Retstidende 2012 p. 65).

'administrative (infringement) fine' ('overtredelsesgebyr'). Such a fine may be laid down by the administration, thus providing the pollution control authorities with a more flexible and simpler sanction than through an ordinary criminal and penalty case before the courts. Such a fine is, nevertheless, regarded as a penalty or punishment in the meaning of this concept in the European Convention on Human Rights. Consequently, the authority has to choose between an administrative fine and an ordinary penalty pursuant to Article 78 in a case of contravention.[265]

Article 80 provides the pollution control authorities with the possibility to, by regulation, introduce this type of sanction in case of violation of a number of rules in the Act or in regulations pursuant to the Act. These include, for example, the general obligation to prevent pollution, lack of necessary actions to limit a pollution, violation of conditions laid down in a pollution permit, or violations of emergency obligations in case of a pollution accident.

Physical individuals may only be subject to a contravention fee if the contravention has been wilful or due to negligence (Article 80 paragraph 3). The possibility to lay down such a fee is limited in time to two years after the contravention ended (Article 80 paragraph 4).

220. In addition to the penalty rules in the PCA, the general Penal Code[266] has a *general article on serious environmental crime, Article 240.* According to this article, imprisonment for a maximum of fifteen years may be imposed on whoever wilfully or by gross negligence pollutes the air, water or soil in such a way that the living environment is significantly harmed, or creates the risk of significant harm, and on whoever stores, leaves or discharges waste or other substances which creates an obvious risk of such effects.

221. According to a general rule in the Penal Code, Articles 27 and 28, *an enterprise may be fined* if an act made on behalf of the enterprise is punishable. The enterprise may also be sentenced to lose its right to operate, or to operate in certain forms. By 'enterprise' is meant any type of company, cooperative society, association, organization, foundation, estate or public institution or body.

This rule applies even if no single person meets the culpability or the accountability requirement, for example, if the contravention is due to organizational weaknesses, lack of proper internal control systems and so on. This is very relevant in cases of contraventions of rules and regulations in the field of pollution control, and it has been used on several occasions.

The courts decide on the use of penalty for institutions in each case. To a large extent, the question is left to the discretion of the court. When considering the issue, the court must take into account several factors listed explicitly in Article 28:

(a) the preventive effect of the penalty;
(b) the severity of the offence, and whether a person acting on behalf of the enterprise has acted culpably;

265. *See* Protocol No. 7 to the Convention for the Protection of Human Rights and Fundamental Freedoms, Art. 4 Right not to be tried or punished twice.
266. Act of 20 May 2005 No. 28.

(c) whether the enterprise could have prevented the offence by use of guidelines, instruction, training, checks or other measures;
(d) whether the offence has been committed in order to promote the interests of the enterprise;
(e) whether the enterprise has had or could have obtained any advantage by the offence;
(f) the financial capacity of the enterprise;
(g) whether other sanctions arising from the offence are imposed on the enterprise or a person who has acted on its behalf, including whether a penalty is imposed on any individual person; and
(h) whether agreements with foreign states prescribe the use of enterprise penalties.

§3. The Product Control Act

222. Besides the PCA, the *Product Control Act*[267] is the main general legal instrument in the field of pollution prevention and control. Increasingly, pollution problems are due less to stationary point sources, and more to numerous 'diffuse sources', such as the use and the disposal as waste of products that may contain hazardous substances or otherwise have harmful effects. To regulate the content, use and final disposal of products has for several decades been a very important part of Norway's environmental policy and law.

The 1976 Product Control Act aims to meet this challenge. Its purpose is to prevent products from causing damage to health, or environmental hazards – such as disturbances of ecosystems, pollution (including noise), waste problems or the like (Article 1). Over the years, the Act has been amended, extended and strengthened several times in order to adequately meet new problems and challenges. Since 1993, the purpose of the Act is also to prevent consumer services (such as organized river rafting, sport diving, etc.) from causing damage to health. Since 1999, the Act also aims at promoting energy efficiency of products.[268]

The Act is a typical *framework Act*. It gives the government wide possibility and discretion to adopt regulations and decisions regarding products and their use. Its key objective and function is clearly to *prevent* damage to health and the environment through the regulation of products and the use of products. It does not contain rules on responsibility and liability for damage from products. Such rules are laid down in a different Act, namely the Act relating to Product Liability.[269]

267. Act of 11 Jun. 1976 No. 79 Relating to the Control of Products and Consumer Services (The Product Control Act).
268. The authority is divided accordingly between the MCE (and the NEA), the Ministry of Justice and Public Security (and the Norwegian Directorate for Civil Protection), which has the overall responsibility for the Act, and the Ministry of Oil and Energy. Authority in some limited areas is also given to the Ministry of Health and Care Services, the Ministry of Trade, Industry and Fisheries (and the Maritime Directorate), the Ministry of Agriculture and Food, and the Ministry of Transport. As regards environmental including climate issues, the NEA is the key authority. The special rules on energy efficiency of products will be presented *infra* in Ch. 8 §2. The rules on consumer services will not be further dealt with in this monograph.
269. Act of 23 Dec. 1988 No. 104.

More than fifty hazardous substances, products and group of products are regulated pursuant to the Act (*see* below).

223. The Act has *a wide field of application,* defined in its Article 2. It applies to the production, including testing, and to the import, placing on the market, use and other handling of products, including transport and final disposal as waste.

By the term 'product' is meant raw materials, auxiliary materials, intermediate products and finished goods of any kind (Article 2a). The product control authorities may decide by regulations or individual decisions that a product be exempted in whole or in part from the scope of the Act (Article 2 paragraph 2), but no such decision has been taken until now (2021). So, the Act applies to *all* products.

224. The Act lays down *a general duty to take due care* (Article 3). This is supplemented by rules on penalty for violation of the duty by negligence or intent (Article 12)[270] or administrative fine (Article 12a).

225. Article 3 paragraph 1 states:

> Any person who produces, imports, markets, processes, uses or in any other way handles products that may present hazards to health or the environment, shall act with due care and take reasonable measures to prevent or limit such effects.

This general duty applies to professionals as well as to private individuals – 'the man in the street'. What 'due care' means, in practice, has to be answered on a case-by-case basis; the preparatory work does not give much guidance. The requirements are, necessarily, less strict for ordinary people than those for professional actors. Professional actors have to take the necessary active measures in order to prevent health or environmental damages from the products and the handling of products. For many types of hazardous products, there are precise regulations, for example, with regard to labelling of the product with the necessary warnings, rules on the handling of the product and on its disposal as waste. In that case, the general duty of care in Article 3 will normally be fulfilled if these rules are followed.

Professionals also have a special obligation to be properly informed about the characteristics of the products: Any person who produces or imports products has the *duty to obtain such knowledge* as is necessary to evaluate whether they can cause hazardous effects (Article 3 paragraph 2). However, the extent of this duty has to be proportionate, taking into account, on the one hand, the possibility and the costs of getting such information and, on the other hand, the potential harms and hazards the product may cause.

226. Producers and importers also have a *duty to provide users of 'consumer products'* and recipients of consumer services *with adequate and relevant information*, and also in a suitable form, so that they may be able to assess the safety of the products or services and if necessary avoid any inherent risk (Article 3 paragraph 5). The term 'consumer product' means any product intended for consumers or that

---

270. *See infra.* However, there have been very few criminal cases on the basis of this article, if any.

can reasonably be expected to be used by consumers (Article 2a paragraph 3). The information shall be clear, easily available and adapted to the needs of users and recipients. The provision of such information does not exempt any person from compliance with the other requirements of the Act. The extent of these obligations of knowledge and information to the public is, however, not entirely clear, for example, the obligation of an importer with regard to the imported product. They have to be adequate and at the same time proportionate on the basis of an assessment in each case.

A violation of these duties by intent or gross negligence is subject to penalty (Article 12).

These duties of care do not apply to the issue of the energy efficiency of products.

227. Another important principle of the Act is *the principle of substitution* provided in Article 3a. This rule was adopted in 1999. This principle applies to professional actors only, but this generally includes any type of organizations, companies and other institutions, including public institutions and authorities. An enterprise using a product that contains a chemical substance which may have hazardous effects on health or the environment has a duty to consider alternatives that present less risk. This duty is independent of other obligations that follow from the Act and relevant regulations. The principle applies to every product which contains chemicals that may have negative effects on health or the environment. The product may either be a chemical in itself, for example, used as raw material in an industrial process, or it may contain hazardous chemical components. If an alternative exists which is less risky to health and the environment, this alternative must be chosen. The condition is that this does not involve 'unreasonable costs or inconvenience'. This will partly depend on how serious the risks are. The responsible actor is not obliged to research the possible effects of the chemical in question, but he/she must seek information about what is already known about this.

228. As mentioned, the Act gives the State product control authorities *a wide legal basis for more detailed rules and decisions* concerning specific products or types of products. A general condition is that such rules or decisions are necessary – 'required' – to prevent hazardous effects on health or the environment (Article 4).

Such rules or decisions shall, in principle, be in the form of *regulations* related to certain types of products.

Regulations may be made applicable for the entire country or for limited geographical areas. For example, differences in environmental conditions, such as eutrophication in certain lakes, may require stricter rules on the use or content of certain products in some parts of the country than in others.

229. Article 4 paragraph 1 lists *the possible content of rules and regulations* that may be adopted. The product control authorities may make decisions concerning:

(1) the production, import, placing on the market, labelling, use and other handling of products;
(2) return and deposit schemes, recovery and waste management systems, etc., in relation to products;

(3) the way in which products shall be designed or composed, and maximum limits for noise and releases of polluting substances from products;
(4) whether or not products may be produced, imported or placed on the market without prior approval by a public authority; and
(5) prohibition of the production, import, placing on the market or use of products.

In 2021, more than fifty hazardous substances, products and group of products (some of them large) are explicitly regulated pursuant to Article 4, with regard to the content, composition, labelling, use and/or disposal as waste. Most of these are included in the general Regulation related to restrictions in the use of chemicals and other products that may be hazardous to health and the environment,[271] but also in other regulations. Not least, Article 4 is the main legal basis for the Regulation on Registration, Evaluation, Authorisation and Restriction of Chemicals (REACH)[272] which implements the EU REACH Regulation 1907/2006. Another important regulation is Regulation on notification on export of certain dangerous chemicals.[273] We shall return to some of these in the following chapters.

230. If it transpires that *a product that is already on the market* in fact represents an unacceptable risk to health or the environment, the authority may lay down regulations and injunctions in order to prevent or reduce the risk of such effects (Article 6a). Such decisions or injunctions may be addressed to anyone who produces, imports, processes, markets or in any other way handles a product. They may include:

(1) publishing a warning to distributors or users;
(2) recalling the product from users or distributors;
(3) rendering the product harmless.

It may then also be prohibited to export products that entail an unacceptable risk to health or the environment.

231. An essential element in the Act is *the duty to provide information to the relevant authorities* (Article 5). Everybody is obliged, when required by the relevant authority, to provide the information which is necessary for the implementation of the Act and rules pursuant to the Act. Public authorities are obliged to provide information regardless of the duty of secrecy.

The authority may require that any person who produces, imports products or put projects on the market shall submit a representative sample of the product or initiate

---

271. Regulation of 1 Jun. 2004 No. 922 on restrictions in use of chemicals and other products hazardous to health and the environment hereinafter 'the Product Regulation' with later amendments, the most recent by Regulation of 4 Feb. 2017 No. 130.
272. Regulation of 30 May 2008 No. 516, hereinafter 'the REACH Regulation' with later amendments.
273. Regulation of 4 Nov. 2020 No. 2293. It implements obligations pursuant to the Rotterdam Convention on the PIC Procedure for Certain Hazardous Chemicals and Pesticides in International Trade.

such investigations as may be necessary in order to assess the properties and effects of a product and cover the costs of such investigations (Article 5 paragraph 2). The authority may decide that the costs shall be shared between several relevant actors or be borne in whole or in part by the public authorities (Article 5 paragraph 3).

Article 5 is the legal foundation for the whole system of information and approval required for marketing hazardous substances and products, which will be further described in Chapter 8, section 1. Detailed rules on information obligations towards the public are found in Articles 9 and 10, *see infra.*

232. When special circumstances so indicate, the authorities may impose a *temporary prohibition* on the production, import, marketing, use or other handling of products, until sufficient information has been submitted. The same applies if there is good reason to doubt whether the given information is correct (Article 6 first paragraph).

When necessary in order to evaluate the characteristics of a product and to lay down further provisions pursuant to Article 4, a prohibition may be imposed for a period not exceeding six months calculated from the time when adequate information is available. When special reasons so indicate, such a prohibition may be extended for a further six months (Article 6 paragraph 29).

233. Furthermore, the Act itself obliges a producer, importer or distributor who receives information indicating that a product which has been put on the market by him/her constitutes a substantial risk to health or the environment must *immediately notify* the product control authorities of such effect (Article 6b). When notification of unsafe consumer products is made, the information to the authorities shall include specification of the steps that have been taken to prevent the products from presenting an unacceptable risk to consumers. The State government may lay down further provisions on this duty.

234. By an amendment in 2003, the Act was given new rules on *the public's right to information about hazardous products.* This is an important part of the 2003 reform on rights to environmental information, and thus linked to the 2003 Environmental Information Act (*see supra* General Introduction, Chapter 2, §3). This right applies to information from public bodies (Article 9) as well as information from the producer, importer, seller and user (Article 10).

235. Article 9 states that *everybody is entitled to obtain information from a public body about products* that have or may have negative effects on health or the environment if that body has the information that is asked for, and the information is not explicitly exempted from the right to information. 'Public body' is defined broadly, with reference to the definition of this notion in the Environmental Information Act.[274] It does not only include public institutions but also other actors, including private companies, that exercise public functions or offer services to the public, and is formally controlled by a public body.

274. *See* General Introduction Ch. 2, §3, I.

The exceptions to the information obligation also correspond to the exceptions listed in the Environmental Information Act. A demand for information may be denied if it is formulated in too broad or vague terms. It may also be denied if there is a genuine and objective need to do so, and the information sought may be withheld from public disclosure pursuant to the Freedom of Information Act.[275] When considering whether there is a genuine and objective need to withhold the information, the environmental and public interest served by disclosure shall be weighed against the interests served by the refusal. If the environmental and public interests outweigh the latter, the information shall be disclosed.

236. A request for information that is subject to a statutory *duty of secrecy,* in particular for competition reasons, may be refused. However, information on health and environmental effects of products, the reasons for such effects, and measures to prevent or mitigate such effects may never be denied (Article 11 paragraph 2, *see infra*).

Refusal of a request for information may be appealed to the superior public authority.

237. Article 10 concerns the right to *information from the producer, importer, seller or user* of a hazardous product. Everyone is entitled to information from these actors about the following:

(a) whether the product contains components or properties that may affect health or the environment;
(b) what the names or characteristics of these components and properties are;
(c) how the product must be handled to prevent effects as specified in section 1;
(d) possible significant injury to health or environmental disturbance caused by production and distribution of the product; and
(e) who the producer or importer of the product is (Article 10 first paragraph).

238. The right mentioned in (d) also applies to information about effects on the environment from production or distribution of a product *outside Norwegian borders,* to the extent that such information is available. The enterprise shall request such information from the previous sales link if this is necessary to enable it to answer the information request (Article 10 paragraph 2).

239. A request for information *may be refused* if it is 'manifestly unreasonable', and if the information requested concerns technical devices and procedures, as well as operational or business matters, 'which for competition reasons it is important to keep secret in the interests of the person whom the information concerns' (Article 10 paragraph 3).

275. Act of 19 May 2006 No. 16.

Refusal of a request for information may be appealed to *the Appeals Board for Environmental Information.*[276] Generally speaking, the provisions of the Environmental Information Act concerning payment, administrative procedures and appeals, apply.

The producer, importer, processor, and distributor of a product shall transmit information to which these rules apply to the next link in the supply chain.

240. In this field, *the issue of confidentiality* due to business interests poses particular problems. It is generally not in the interest of a producer to make known individual qualities and properties of the products, such as the content of various chemical substances in the product. However, the Product Control Act requires that full information about products and their properties is given to the authorities. Therefore, the Act contains a special Article on confidentiality (Article 11).

The general rule is that everybody must observe confidentiality concerning any information he/she may acquire when carrying out his/her duties under the Act. Such information may, *inter alia,* relate to a product's composition or properties, production methods, research findings, commercial analyses and other trade secrets that other enterprises may be able to exploit to the detriment of the enterprise that has provided the information. Nor may the information be used in connection with the person's own activities. A violation is subject to punishment by fines or even a maximum of six months imprisonment (Article 12 paragraph 2).

However, the duty of secrecy shall not prevent the provision of information on *the product's effects on health and the environment,* an explanation of the causes of such effects to the extent necessary. The same applies to information about relevant precautionary measures to prevent or reduce negative effects of products (Article 11 paragraph 2). A public body may require that the actor in question identify those parts of the requisite information which must be kept secret for competition reasons.

Before information that is subject to a statutory duty of confidentiality is disclosed, the person whom the information concerns shall be given the opportunity to express an opinion within an appropriate time limit. If the public authority wishes to disclose information that is subject to a statutory duty of confidentiality, the person whom the information concerns shall be notified. The decision to disclose the information may be appealed under the provisions of section 15 of the Environmental Information Act, which apply correspondingly. An appeal has a suspensive effect (Article 11, paragraphs 6 and 7).

241. The Product Control Act also contains such rules as are necessary for the *effective control, supervision and enforcement* by the authorities.

With regard to *supervision,* the King will decide which instance shall be responsible for ensuring the implementation of this Act and any decisions made under the Act.

The supervisory authority shall be given free access to buildings, means of transport, storage facilities, installations, areas, and the like where products that may

276. *See supra* General Introduction Ch. 2, § 3, II about the Environment Information Act and the Appeals Board for Environmental Information.

have negative environmental effects are present. The authority may also undertake the necessary sampling and control of such products. Unless important considerations indicate otherwise, the supervisory authority shall draw up written reports on the results of such controls. The King may make regulations relating to internal control and internal control systems to ensure compliance with requirements laid down in or under this Act (Article 8). The general rules under Norwegian law on internal control systems apply in the same way as related to the PCA (*see supra* §2, VII).

242. The King may make regulations relating to *fees for dealing with applications* for permits or the like under the provisions of this Act or regulations issued under the Act, and for control measures carried out to ensure compliance with the provisions of the Act or decisions under it. The amount of the fees shall be such that the total fees do not exceed the costs incurred by the product control authorities in connection with the administrative process or the control system. Fees are enforceable by execution proceedings (Article 8a).

243. The system of *sanctions and penalty* in case of contraventions and violations of the Act, or of regulations and decisions pursuant to the Act, has been considerably sharpened recently, as part of a general reform in the field of environmental crime.[277]

A contravention of the Act or of any regulation or decision pursuant to the Act, by intent or negligence, may be *penalized* by fines, imprisonment for a term not exceeding one year, or both (unless a stricter penalty provision applies). Has a contravention caused danger to a person's health or well-being or significant environmental damage or nuisance, a maximum of three years imprisonment may be applied. A breach of the general duty to take due care may be punished only if the contravention is wilful or caused by gross negligence. Aiding and abetting are penalized in the same way (Article 12).

Pursuant to special regulation, an *administrative 'violation fine'* may be ordered by the relevant authority in case of contravention of a number of rules and obligations pursuant to the Act, including breach of the general duty of care and information obligations in Article 3, the principle of substitution in Article 3a and, generally, duties and obligations laid down in regulations (Article 12a).

In addition, in the event of a contravention, the authorities may require the responsible party to correct the situation within a specified time limit, and impose a *coercive fine* which takes effect if the corrections have not been done within the time limit (Article 13).

§4. The Public Health Act

244. The Public Health Act[278] can be applied to prevent or reduce local pollution. The purpose of the Act is to improve the general health situation of the population, promote its well-being, good social and environmental conditions, and

277. Act of 21 Jun. 2019 No. 54 amending the Product Control Act.
278. Act of 24 Jun. 2011 No. 29.

contribute to the prevention of mental and somatic illnesses, disorders or injuries. It shall ensure that adequate and long-term measures to this effect are carried out by municipalities, counties and the State and a good coordination between these actors (Article 1). The Act provides the necessary legal foundation for the public health work in the country, including health service, and decisions and actions to prevent any hazard or risk to public health. In particular, it defines in detail the division of responsibility and tasks within the health service sector between the municipalities (Chapter 2), the counties (Chapter 4) and the State (Chapter 5), as well as rules on cooperation between the various authorities, health competence in the municipalities, health contingency and State control of the public health work in municipalities and counties (Chapter 6).

245. The Act has a special chapter on *Environmentally Related Health Protection* (Chapter 3). Pursuant to this chapter, the State and municipal health authorities[279] have important environmental tools at their disposal. To some extent, the competences overlap with those of other authorities, such as the pollution control authority pursuant to the PCA. This may create some confusion. In practice, however, a certain division of responsibility has developed.

The notion of 'environmentally-related health protection' is meant to cover all those factors in the environment that may directly or indirectly affect people's health. They include biological, chemical and physical, as well as social environmental factors (Article 8 paragraph 1).

246. The central health authorities – the Ministry of Health and Care Services – may issue *regulations on environmentally related health protection*. This includes regulation of air quality, water and water supply, noise, environmental hygiene, and prevention of accidents and injuries (Article 8 paragraph 2).

247. A general regulation pursuant to the Act applies to all activities that may affect health conditions, directly or indirectly.[280] It defines the general responsibilities of the municipality in the field of public health related to environmental conditions, to take health effects into account in spatial planning pursuant to the PBA, to monitor factors that may influence health conditions, and so on. It also lays down general obligations for activities and development of properties. It generally states that activities shall be planned and run in such a way that noise and vibrations are kept to a minimum, that emissions of pollutants do not present a risk to health, and so on. In addition, there are several special regulations, such as a regulation on the sources and quality of drinking water[281] and environmentally related health protection such as hygienic conditions in various buildings and institutions.[282]

---

279. Formally this is the municipal council, but it may delegate certain authorities to the chief doctor.
280. Regulation of 25 Apr. 2003 No. 486 on environmentally related health protection, with later amendments, the most recent by Regulation of 11 May 2021 No. 1471.
281. Regulation of 22 Dec. 2016 No. 1868 on water supply and drinking water, pursuant to the Act of 19 Dec. 2003 No. 124 on Food Production and Food Safety.
282. One example of this is Regulation of 13 Jun. 1996 No. 592 on bathing installations, public swimming pools and saunas, with later amendments. Another example is Regulation of 1 Dec. 1995 No. 928 on environmentally related health protection in nursery schools and schools, with later amendments.

The Act mentions in particular the possibility of regulations which order a person, who plans to carry on certain types of activities that may affect health, to inform the municipality. Through regulations, such enterprises may be subject to approval by the municipal health authorities, pursuant to the necessary conditions (Article 10).

248. Notwithstanding such State regulations, the municipal authorities may order a person who plans, or who carries out, a type of activity that may affect health, to *provide the municipality with such information as is necessary* for proper implementation of the Act. Such information may also be required from an employee of the enterprise, and notwithstanding confidentiality rules. The responsible party may also be ordered to provide the public, clients, and others any information on aspects of a property or enterprise, which may affect health (Article 12 paragraph 3). Anyway, the responsible party has a duty to provide information regardless of such an order if possible health effects are obvious (Article 12 paragraph 2).

249. The municipal authorities may also order the person responsible for a property or an activity to perform *an assessment of possible health impacts* of the property or activity. Such an order may, however, be issued only if the disadvantages connected with the assessment, including the costs, are proportionate compared to the possible health problems in question (Article 11).

The municipal authorities may order an *investigation* of a property or an enterprise if this is necessary for the implementation of its work according to the Act. Those performing such an investigation shall have unlimited access to the property or enterprise, relevant documents and other materials, and so on. The costs are to be covered by the person responsible for the property or enterprise (Article 13).

250. Probably the most powerful tool for the municipal health authority in the field of environmental protection is the competence to issue *injunctions* – order that a property or activity be rectified – if the situation has a direct or indirect negative impact on health or is in violation of the provisions prescribed pursuant to the Act (Article 14). Rectification may only be demanded if the rectification is reasonable in proportion to the health considerations that justify the rectification. The person responsible for the property or activity may be ordered to change or correct it within a fixed time limit, at his/her own expense. The municipality may lay down a coercive fine which runs from the date it should have been changed or corrected in order to have the measures carried out (Article 15).

If there is an imminent risk of damage to health, the municipality shall suspend all or portions of the entity or activities until the situation has been rectified or there is no longer a hazard. If necessary, the suspension may be carried out with assistance from the police (Article 16).

251. These rules authorize the health authorities to *order changes to or even the termination* of an activity or a property. Obviously, this may have serious economic and other consequences for the person concerned. The wording of the rules is broad. The question is, however, in what types of situations and under what conditions it may be used.

The expression 'direct or indirect negative impact on health' is far-reaching. It includes environmental quality in a broad sense: all types of pollution, radiation and waste problems are in the core of its field of application. It applies to pollution from activities as well as installations as such.

Although it is not explicitly stated, the rules must be understood as implying a lower 'tolerance limit'. Some nuisance must be accepted in daily life in modern society. However, it is unclear where this limit is under various circumstances. It is not clear either whether this limit varies according to the persons who are affected. To some extent, the health authorities may order an activity to avoid certain disturbing activities if there is a particularly sensitive person in its vicinity. However, the measures may not be unreasonable or disproportionate to the health risk involved.

These are some of the legal questions which the Act itself leaves open, and to which there are, at present, few clear answers.

252. The responsible person is subject to *punishment* if a contravention of the Act or a regulation has been made by intent or negligence. The penalties are fines and/or a maximum three-month imprisonment (Article 18). The above-mentioned general penalty clause of Article 240 of the Penal Code may also be applied in such case, as may Articles 27 and 28 concerning penalties for companies and other institutions.

253. Furthermore, the relevant authority may lay down *administrative 'violation fines'* on anyone who wilfully or through negligence has violated provisions in Articles 10 to 14 and Article 16 of the Act. The same applies to the violation of regulations pursuant to the Act when it has been stipulated in the regulations that violation will entail such a sanction (Article 17).

254. Finally, if the deadline for fulfilment of an order to rectify a situation is not met, then the municipality may impose *coercive fines* on the addressee of the order in the form of a one-time or daily fine. The coercive fines must be stipulated at the same time as the order or in connection with the stipulation of a new deadline for fulfilment of the order. The size of the coercive fine will be determined based on how important it is that the order be fulfilled and what costs it is assumed to entail. The coercive fines fall to the public purse. Coercive fines may be recovered by execution proceedings (Article 15).

§5. The Neighbour Act

255. The Neighbour Act[283] is part of Norwegian private law. It has for more than 100 years been very important in relation to *local environmental issues,* and in particular pollution, including noise pollution. Since the 1981 PCA at the outset does

283. Act concerning the Legal Relations between Neighbours of 16 Jun. 1961 No. 15.

not cover 'ordinary pollution' from housing, recreational homes, offices, hotels and primary industries, nuisance problems emanating from such activities are mainly regulated by private law through the Neighbour Act. However, the Act is not an adequate instrument for the regulation and control of pollution in general.

The most important aspect of the Act is the rule on *strict liability for 'unreasonable or unnecessary' damage or nuisance* to neighbours. As we shall *see infra* in Part IV, this principle applies generally to damage from pollution, also pollution which is not violating the PCA. The chapter on liability in the PCA, Chapter 8, is connected to the Neighbour Act through its Article 56. The principle also applies as a basis for compensation in case of expropriation for public purposes, such as roads. This will be further discussed in Part IV.

256. The present Neighbour Act finds its roots in the first Norwegian Neighbour Act which was adopted in 1887. The main principle of Norwegian neighbour law has been somewhat modified but has not been fundamentally changed since then and is now expressed in Article 2, first paragraph of the present Act:

> No person may have, do or initiate anything which unreasonably or unnecessarily leads to damage or nuisance to a neighbouring property. Included in the term nuisance is anything that may be considered dangerous.

The following paragraphs in Article 2 further define elements and conditions that have to be taken into consideration when deciding whether a damage or nuisance is unreasonable or undue:

> When deciding whether an act is unreasonable or unnecessary, importance should be attached to what is technically or economically feasible to prevent or limit the damage or nuisance. Also, local nature diversity considerations shall be taken into account.
>
> Furthermore, when deciding whether something is unreasonable, importance should be attached to what may be expected, having regard to the local conditions, and to whether it differs from the usual ways activities are carried out locally.
>
> Even if something may be expected, or is usual according to the paragraph 3, it may be regarded as unreasonable if it results in a considerable worsening of the user conditions of a limited group of people.[284]

This legal standard, as interpreted, is called the general 'tolerance limit' in Norwegian neighbour law. How to interpret it in different circumstances has been – and still is – an important and difficult issue in Norwegian law, in particular in relation to noise from new roads and airports. We shall return to this question *infra* in Part IV, Chapter 1, §2. By an amendment in 2009, consideration shall also be given to the local biodiversity.

284. Unofficial translation by the author.

257. The Act lays down rules on some specific issues which are of minor, but practical importance in neighbour relations: Unless it is important for the owner or for the local biodiversity, a tree should not be higher than three times its distance from the next-door neighbour's property, if it could cause harm or nuisance to the neighbour (Article 3). In many residential areas in cities, this rule is decisive when trees take away sun or a fine view from the neighbouring properties. A hedge may be up to 2 m regardless of this rule. Whoever initiates building activities, digging, blasting or similar activities must take the necessary precautions to prevent landslide, stone bursting and so on which may harm the neighbour (Article 5).

258. When a landowner plans to build, plant, dig, or start industrial or other activities on his/her property, he/she must inform the neighbours in advance (Article 6). A neighbour may require a special assessment procedure ('neighbour assessment') to decide how the activity may be carried out in order to avoid unreasonable or undue damage or nuisance (Article 7).

In case of violation of the Act, the neighbour may – in addition to or as alternative to compensation – require an injunction in order to have the harmful activity changed or halted (Articles 10–12). Today, these rules play a limited role along with public law regulations, in particular the PCA and the PBA. Article 10 of the PCA states explicitly that they do not apply to activities covered by the pollution permit system pursuant to that Act. Formally, however, a building may be moved or changed, and the neighbour may have the right to compensation, on the basis of the Neighbour Act even if it has got a building permit according to the rules of the PBA.[285] Hence, the Neighbour Act works independently of public regulation.

§6. The Development of New Instruments for Pollution Control and Waste Management

259. In addition to, and combined with, these main legal systems, a number of new and alternative instruments have been developed to control pollution.

Environmental taxes have been introduced, most notably as regards CO_2 emissions from offshore petroleum installations and cars. These will be presented in Chapter 2, § 4 II *infra*. In waste policy, a number of *deposit/return systems* have been established, *see* Chapter 4 *infra*.

Voluntary agreements are also applied, particularly in the waste sector (*see* Chapter 4). In the field of air pollution, three agreements have been concluded between the industry branches and the MCE, for the reduction of SO_2 and NO_x emissions. These agreements are linked to the permit system in the PCA. Their legal status is not always entirely clear. They combine elements from private law and public law, which may lead to uncertainties on important legal issues. For this reason, they have been somewhat controversial.

There is a tendency towards more 'flexible' approaches to the regulation of pollution. In particular, in the field of emission of GHGs, Norway applied the flexible mechanisms laid down in the Kyoto Protocol. It remains to be seen whether it will

285. *See infra* Part IV, Ch. 1, §2.

apply the mechanism which has finally been established under the Paris Agreement Article 6. Anyway, since 2008 Norway is party to the EU-ETS, and nearly 50% of the Norwegian CO_2 emissions are included in this system which will continue to be a major factor in Norway's climate policy towards 2030 and beyond.

We will return to these issues in detail in the following.

Chapter 2. Air Pollution and Climate Change

§1. Introduction and Overview

260. Although Norway is thinly populated, with vast, partly uninhabited forests and mountain areas, *air pollution is a serious challenge* for national environmental policy and law. In some sectors, important improvements have been achieved over the last four decades, while other problems have increased.

261. At the *local* level, many Norwegian cities experience high levels of pollutants in the air during certain periods, particularly in winter. The most significant pollutants are particulate matter (dust), nitrogen dioxide, sulphur dioxide and ground-level ozone. Road traffic and the use of fuel wood and petroleum for heating account for most of the emissions. Also, carbon monoxide (CO), PAHs and benzene contribute to bad local air quality. Around certain types of factories, in particular cement and certain ferroalloy factories, emissions of dust may be a problem for the local neighbourhood.

262. The main *regional* air pollution problem is emissions of *sulphur dioxide (SO_2), nitrogen oxides (NO_x) and ammonia (NH_2),* an important part of which is due to transfrontier and long-range transport of air pollution. A deficiency of lime in the bedrock and soil makes parts of Norwegian nature particularly vulnerable to these pollutants. During most part of the last century, *acid rain* made numerous lakes in the southern part of the country too acidic even for ordinary freshwater fish to live, and it also was presumed to affect the forests. The deposit of airborne nitrogen also contributes to eutrophication.

263. The conditions have improved during the last decades, not least due to international agreements. In Europe, there has been more than 60% reduction in emissions of SO_2 and 20% reduction in emission of NOx since 1990, and the quantities reaching Norway have accordingly been reduced considerably. However, acidification is still one of the most serious threats to the country's biodiversity. The tolerance limit for sulphur in freshwater has for several years been exceeded in about 10% of the country's surface water. In large areas in southern Norway, the freshwater fauna is seriously damaged. In important parts of the country, the pollution level in the lakes has now been reduced to an acceptable level and fish and other living organisms are back. This is the good news. However, many lakes are still without fish.

A problem of a similar nature is increased levels of ozone in the lower part of the atmosphere (the troposphere). It is regarded as a carcinogen at the local level, and it has adverse effects on health, vegetation and materials, and is particularly a significant cause of forest damage. Such *ground-level ozone* is formed by chemical reactions between oxygen, nitrogen oxides (NOx) and Volatile Organic Compounds (VOCs) in the presence of sunlight. Norway's emissions of VOCs increased steadily until 2001, due to increased production and transport of petroleum.[286] Emissions have been somewhat reduced since then, but they are still too high.

264. These problems have been the focus of much of Norway's national and international efforts in the field of air pollution. The main international instrument in this field is the 1979 UN/ECE LRTAP. The Convention, with subsequent protocols, has required considerable reductions of emissions of sulphur,[287] NOx[288] and VOCs,[289] although the critical loads are still exceeded in parts of the country. These international obligations are the basis for the application of the national legislation in this field. Norway has an obligation to reduce emissions of SO_2 with 10%, NOx with 23%, VOC with 40%, ammonia with 8%, and particulate matter (PM2 and PM5) with 30% compared to the levels in 2005. Particles of *heavy metals and persistent chemicals* also spread over long distances through the air. These problems are therefore also treated in the context of regional problems. Emissions of heavy metals like lead and cadmium have been very much reduced, mainly due to the fact that the use of leaded petrol has phased out.

265. Emissions of *global* importance are mainly of CO_2 and other GHGs, and of ozone-depleting substances. Norway's emissions of GHGs have been more or less steady over the last twenty years. The Kyoto Protocol required a significant reduction of emissions by Norway.[290] We fulfilled our Kyoto obligations – and even exceeded our obligations – mainly through the use of the flexible mechanisms in the Kyoto Protocol, and in particular through the participation in the EU-ETS.

In the field of ozone-depleting substances, such as Chlorofluorocarbons (CFCs), however, a significant reduction of import and consumption has taken place since Norway ratified the Montreal Protocol to the Vienna Convention, while emissions still take place due to the use and disposal as waste of existing equipment containing these gases.

The work to prevent and reduce air pollution is based on several pieces of legislation. Several types of legal and economic instruments are used.

266. Air pollution is regulated by several Acts and several types of instruments. The PCA covers emissions from stationary sources, and is particularly important for preventing and reducing air pollution from industry, including petroleum installations on the continental shelf, incineration of waste and combustion for heating.

286. An important part of the emissions is leakage during the loading of oil into tankers, and it took time to find technical solutions to this problem.
287. Sulphur protocols of 1985 (Helsinki), 1994 (Oslo), and 1999 (Gothenburg, revised in 2012), all ratified by Norway.
288. Nitrogen protocols of 1988 (Sofia) and 1999 (Gothenburg, revised in 2012), both ratified by Norway.
289. VOC protocols of 1991 (Geneva) and 1999 (Gothenburg, revised in 2012), both ratified by Norway.
290. According to the 1997 Kyoto Protocol, Norway could increase its emission by 1% as annual average during 2008–2012 compared with the 1990 level. However, since the emissions at that time had increased considerable since 1990, a net reduction was required in the order of 10% compared to the 1990 level to meet this obligation. We shall go into more detail on this topic *infra* §4 II.

Rules in the Act itself, as well as regulations and individual permits, apply (*see* the presentation of the main lines of the Act *supra* Chapter 1).

Regulation of emissions from mobile sources, in particular cars, aircraft and ships, is based on *sectoral legislation for road traffic, air traffic and shipping*, respectively.

Emissions related to the use or transport of other products, as well as disposal of waste, are mainly controlled through the use of regulations on the basis of the *Product Control Act.*

Furthermore, local air pollution may be the subject of local regulations or decisions by the local health authorities pursuant to the *Public Health Act.* Within the framework of private law, the *Neighbour Act* may serve as the basis for injunctions and compensation.

267. For the sake of method, this chapter treats the legal issues of local, regional and global air pollution separately. One must bear in mind, however, that many types of air pollution and hazardous substances may have detrimental effect at local, regional and even global levels, due to the long-range transport of pollution and the accumulation in the environment of many persistent chemical substances. The sequence of the chapter will be as follows:

– local air pollution (§2);
– regional air pollution (§3);
– global air pollution and climate change (§4).

§2. Local Air Pollution

I. Rules and Regulations Pursuant to the PCA

268. The general rules of *the* PCA *apply fully to local air pollution.* Pollution permits, which are issued according to Article 11, are regularly subject to conditions to prevent emissions into the air, even if their effects are only local. For example, the cement industry has been ordered to remove most of its dust emissions.

Local emissions from ordinary activities within the primary industries, housing, offices, hotels and so on fall within the general exception from the duty to avoid pollution, according to Article 8 of the Act. For some activities, emission regulations have been issued.

269. Pursuant to the Act, a *regulation on local air quality* has been issued.[291] It applies to the content in the air of sulphur dioxide (SO_2), nitrogen dioxide (NO_2) and nitrogen oxides (NOx), dust (particulate matter – PM2.5 og and PM10), lead, benzene, carbon monoxide (CO), arsenic (As), cadmium (Cd), nickel (Ni), benzo(a)pyrene (B(a)P) and mercury (Hg). It lays down a rather complex system of

291. Regulation of 1 Jun. 2004 No. 931 Ch. 7. The regulation implements EU Directives 2000/69/EC, 1999/30/EC, 96/62/EC, 2002/3/EC, and 2004/107/EC.

maximum acceptable levels, objectives, and thresholds, and which require certain actions. The levels are partly hourly, partly for twenty-four hours, and – for all substances – a maximum annual middle level combined with maximal numbers of exceedings which can be accepted per year (Regulation Article 7-6).

In case such a level is exceeded in a region or in a greater urban area, a plan has to be developed with measures necessary to correct the situation (Article 7-9).

In addition, the regulation defines certain '*alarm levels*' for SO_2 and NOx in an area of a certain size, and in particular in a greater urban area, and which last more than three hours. Alarm levels are levels of concentration of a substance in the air which has health effect for the population even under short exposure. If an alarm level is exceeded, the municipality must inform the public about this and its cause, what is expected with regard to future development (changes in concentration and its causes, geographical extension, duration) and what measures particularly vulnerable people should take to prevent possible health effects (Article 7-10).

270. An *owner of an installation* which 'significantly' contributes to a risk of exceeding the various maximum levels and thresholds must take necessary abatement measures to ensure that the levels and thresholds are not exceeded and cover the costs (Article 7-3). Measures taken in one area must not result in increased levels in other areas. If certain alarm levels are exceeded, the owner of the contributing installation may be required to inform the public and cover the costs of providing such information. The NEA can order several owners of relevant installations to cooperate in taking the necessary measures. The owner is not exempted from the obligation to take necessary measures pursuant to these rules even if the emissions in question have been permitted through the permit system in PCA (Article 7-3 paragraph 5). For installations with a permit in accordance with BAT, the permitting authority may demand supplementary and further measures in order to achieve the threshold (Article 7-3 paragraph 2).

When assessing whether a source contributes 'significantly', only local sources shall be taken into account. The installation owners must also contribute to necessary measuring and monitoring.

271. *The municipality* is the main authority responsible for the implementation of the regulation. The municipality shall establish monitoring stations and carry out monitoring, according to specific requirements in the regulation (Article 7-4).[292] The municipality may also order a survey and report with proposals for necessary measures to be taken by the owners of the relevant installations to ensure that the limits are not exceeded. It may require the necessary investigations and information to be provided and order that the necessary measures are carried out. An annex to the regulation defines in detail the content of an assessment of measures to be carried out. In special circumstances, the municipality may also order that measures are taken by other operators than the owner of the installation that contributes 'significantly' to the problem.

---

292. However, the State is responsible for monitoring stations for ground-level ozone outside urban areas in some parts of the country.

The regulation provides the municipality with the authority to regulate emission from small-scale combustion installations, such as oil combustion installations in ordinary homes, which otherwise is legal according to Article 8 of the PCA.

The NEA may decide how costs of necessary measures are to be distributed between the relevant installation owners. The municipality may decide that the costs of reports, and of monitoring activities, are to be covered by the installation owner(s) (Article 7-5).

272. It is recognized that some of the ambient air quality standards are exceeded in Norway today, in particular when meteorological conditions are unfavourable, mainly during winter time. That also means that Norway fails to fulfil its obligations according to the EU Directive 2008/50/EC on ambient air quality and cleaner air for Europe, which has been included in the EEA Agreement. Based on a complaint from the Norwegian Association of Asthma and Allergies, the ESA brought Norway before the EFTA Court in 2015. In its decision, the EFTA Court found that Norway during the years from 2009 to 2012 had failed to fulfil its obligations under this directive since the thresholds had been exceeded in some Norwegian cities.[293]

273. It has for some time been clear that measures to reduce the present air pollution levels are necessary. In many urban areas, a policy of reducing car traffic through toll stations, parking restrictions and improved public transport has been carried out for many years, and stricter measures are now being taken.

The regulation on local air quality may have a preventive effect, in particular, through better land-use planning in connection with new roads and factories, and the localization of housing areas, schools and hospitals. However, its rules are rather technical and complex, and appear to be difficult to apply in situations of existing pollution with numerous sources of emission.

274. Another regulation of practical importance is the regulation on *maximum sulphur content in petroleum products.*[294] In most of Norway, the maximum sulphur content in heavy fuels being burned is 1% (weight) and 0.1% in light fuels. In the cities of Oslo (the capital) and Drammen, the burning of heavy fuels is prohibited altogether without a special permit from the pollution control authorities. Regardless of these limits, large fuel combustion installations (with a burning capacity of more than 500 kg of fuel per hour) or with a maximum emission of more than 10 kg SO_2 per hour must always apply for a pollution permit pursuant to Article 11 of the PCA. The owner of the incineration installation is responsible for the implementation of these rules.

275. Certain *emission regulations* have been laid down pursuant to the PCA. The rather comprehensive and detailed regulation on the *burning of waste*[295] requires

293. Judgment of 2 Oct. 2015 in Case E-7/15.

294. Regulation of 1 Jun. 2004 No. 931 Ch. 8 as amended by Regulation of 10 Aug. 2006 No. 964, which implements EC Directive 75/716 as amended by Directive 87/219, and EC Directive 93/12 as amended by Directive 1999/32.

295. Regulation of 1 Jun. 2004 No. 930 Ch. 10, which implements EC Directive 2000/76.

that new as well as existing installations for the burning of all types of waste obtain a general waste treatment permit according to Article 29 of the Act and a pollution permit according to its Article 11. The permit may not exceed certain emission limit values laid down in the annexes to the regulation. Furthermore, it must, *inter alia*, include a list of the types of waste that are treated, and state the capacity of the installation and the various methods for measuring and analysing emissions. If the installation shall treat dangerous or infectious waste, the permission must lay down maximum hourly quantity limits for the waste burned and maximum quantities of the dangerous substances, such as PCB, PCP, chlorine and heavy metals.

A special regulation on emission from *crematoriums* was adopted in 2004.[296] It lays down maximum emission thresholds for dust, mercury, and carbon monoxide (CO) and certain technical rules related to burning. The chimney must be at least 10 m and at least 3 m above the roof level.

One of the objectives of the Regulation on *manure of organic origin*[297] is to avoid local pollution, in particular stench, from the storage and spreading of *animal manure.*

II. Regulations Concerning Mobile Sources, in Particular from Road Transport

276. The above-mentioned ambient air quality limits may indirectly influence the environmental problems connected with land transport. However, direct regulations in the form of technical requirements, emission standards of vehicles and limitations of hazardous substances in fuel, as well as regulation of the use of vehicles, have so far been the most important instruments.

277. The Road Traffic Act[298] is the most important piece of legislation in relation to air pollution from cars. It gives the road authorities a wide margin of authority to lay down the necessary regulations on the use of vehicles, such as traffic rules, as well as technical requirements for various types of vehicles.[299] After amendments, it gives the necessary basis for various types of regulations aiming at the prevention and control of air pollution from motor vehicles.[300]

278. One type of regulation is to *direct various types of traffic to certain roads* or areas. For example, it has been a policy in many Norwegian cities to direct the

296. Regulation of 1 Jun. 2004 No. 931 Ch. 10.
297. Regulation of 4 Jul. 2003 No. 951 with later amendments, *see infra* Ch. 3, §2, III.
298. Act of 18 Jun. 1965 No. 4.
299. Most of the regulations are issued by the Road Directorate, under the Ministry of Transport.
300. The most important rules to this effect are found in four main regulations pursuant to the Act: Two Regulations on technical requirements and approval of vehicles, parts and equipment: Regulation of 25 Jan. 1990 No. 91 and Regulation of 4 Oct. 1994 No. 918 with subsequent amendments, which implements the numerous EU directives in this field; Regulation of 25 Jan. 1990 No. 92 on the use of vehicles with subsequent amendments; Regulation; and Regulation of 21 Mar. 1986 No. 747 on traffic (the 'Traffic Rules') with subsequent amendments.

traffic to certain main streets and ring roads, in order to protect the city centres and important housing areas from traffic pollution and other nuisances. This may be done through the use of traffic signs on the basis of Article 5 of the Road Traffic Act and also through the introduction of tolls pursuant to Article 27 of the Road Act (*see* below).

Furthermore, the Road Traffic Act is used to lay down *speed limits* (Article 6), which may have an effect on emissions of pollution, and noise in particular. This includes the possibility of a temporary reduction of local speed limits, for example, during winter or on days when the air pollution level is expected to be higher than normal. In Norway, particulate matter from cars, in particular cars with studded tires, creates serious local pollution of particulate matter in some cities during winter. The general speed limits in Norway are 50 km/h in towns, 80 km/h on ordinary roads outside towns, and 90, 100 or 110 km/h on the highways.

The Act also gives the authorities the possibility to lay down *regulations on parking* in urban areas (Article 8). Strict parking regulations, and paying for parking, may contribute to limiting the urban traffic. The authority to decide on parking issues is left to the municipalities.

The Traffic Rules laid down in Regulation of 21 March 1986 No. 747 include *a general prohibition on idle running* of a vehicle, or any other use of a vehicle which entails 'unnecessary' noise or emission of air pollution, within or in the vicinity of buildings (Article 16 paragraph 1). The term 'unnecessary' makes this rule somewhat vague.

279. On the basis of Article 27 in the Road Act,[301] the government with the consent of Stortinget may designate public roads as *toll roads*. The main purpose is to obtain necessary funding for the construction or improvements of roads. Most of the major road constructions in Norway are partly financed by tolls.

280. In urban areas, income from toll may also be used for the construction of public transport systems like railways and urban underground lines. Road toll is also used as *an instrument to limit car traffic* in urban areas. A reform of the Road Act Article 27 in 2018[302] has made it possible to develop a flexible toll system which contributes to environmental improvements and climate change mitigation. The toll may vary according to the type and weight of the vehicle, the environmental characteristics of the vehicle, at what time of the day the driving takes place, etc. The capital Oslo and several other major cities in Norway have accordingly developed flexible toll systems with the objectives of reducing air pollution in the city centre and mitigate emissions of GHG.

281. The Regulation on technical requirements of vehicles[303] is the legal basis for *exhaust emission limits*. It lays down the general requirement that a vehicle

301. Act of 21 Jun. 1963 No. 23 Art. 27.
302. By Act of 15 Jun. 2018 No. 38.
303. Section 25 in Regulation of 4 Oct. 1994 No. 918 on technical requirements for vehicles, pursuant to the Road Traffic Act, with subsequent amendments.

should be equipped and maintained in such a way as not to emit harmful gases or smoke. Through proper maintenance the emissions should not change significantly compared to the emission level of the new car.[304] The technical rules contain detailed regulations on maximum emission of the most important air pollutants from cars: hydrocarbons (HC), carbon monoxide (CO), nitrogen dioxide (NO_2), and particles. The rules implement the EU regulations and directives regarding emission standards for vehicles.[305]

Since 1994, emissions from all petrol-driven cars have been controlled as part of the periodical EEA roadworthiness tests. The control of emission levels of air pollutants is an important part of this control.

The *quality and chemical content of fuel* is also very important for the actual pollution from cars. The rules on this are not given pursuant to the Road Traffic Act, but in a particular chapter in the Product Regulation pursuant to the Product Control Act.[306] There are detailed quality requirements for petrol and diesel as well as biofuels. In 1985, Norway adopted strict rules to limit *the content of lead* in petrol for cars. There is virtually no lead in petrol today,[307] and lead pollution in air in Norway is now well below the level believed to cause injury to human health. There is also a strict regulation of sulphur in petrol.[308]

Another type of policy effort is the encouragement of the use of cars with energy sources other than petrol, in particular electricity, by easing the tax on electric cars. *See* further *infra* §4 II.

The Labelling of Consumer Goods Act,[309] Articles 8[310] and 9 give the government the authority to issue regulations requiring that consumer products give the consumer the necessary information about the product's use of energy and other resources, as well as its environmental effects and a regulation to this effect has been laid down.[311] The main objective of this amendment is the implementation in Norway of the EU directive on the availability of consumer information on fuel economy and CO_2 emissions in the marketing of new motor vehicles.[312]

282. Extensive use of *studded tyres* during winter is a significant source of pollution by particulate matter (dust) in Norwegian cities. A 1999 regulation pursuant to the Road Traffic Act[313] gives the municipalities the authority to introduce a charge for the use of studded tyres in order to reduce the use. This instrument is applied by some of the larger cities, including Oslo.

---

304. Regulation of 4 Oct. 1994 No. 918 Art. 25-2 No. 1.
305. The most recent being Regulation (EU) 2019/631.
306. Regulation of 1 Jun. 2004 No. 922 pursuant to the Product Control Act Art. 4, Art. 2-20 and Annex IV.
307. The maximum level of lead in petrol is 0.005 g/l.
308. The maximum level of sulphur in petrol is 10 mg/kg.
309. Act of 18 Dec. 1981 No. 90.
310. Introduced into the Act by Act of 15 Jun. 2001 No. 89.
311. Regulation of 11 Jul. 2001 No. 829 on labelling of motor vehicles with later amendments.
312. EC Directive 1999/94 as amended by Directive 2003/73/EC.
313. Regulation of 7 May 1999 No. 437 with later amendments.

III. Injunctions to Prevent or Reduce Local Pollution

283. If pollution of a local nature creates a health risk, harm or nuisance in the neighbourhood, any person affected may initiate an injunction to have it changed or terminated. This may be done either on the basis of private law, namely the rules in the *Neighbour Act*[314] (*see supra* Chapter 1, §5), or through the public law mechanism pursuant to the *Public Health Act*[315] (*see supra* Chapter 1, §4).

§3. Regional Air Pollution

284. As mentioned, the reduction of regional air pollution is an important field of *regional cooperation*, mainly within the framework of the UN/ECE Convention on the LRTAP. The subsequent protocols under this convention lay down the reduction obligations for Norway as regards emission of sulphur dioxide (SO_2), nitrogen oxides (NOx), ammonia (NH_3) and VOC. The Norwegian emissions have been reduced steadily during the last couple of decades and seem to be within the limits of its international obligations, with the possible exception of emission of NOx which has remained at a rather high level.

To fulfil Norway's international obligations in this field, the PCA, the Product Control Act and the legislation in the transport sector are all actively applied.

The pollution permit system (*see* Chapter 1) has been the main instrument to reduce air emissions of SO_2, NOx, heavy metals and persistent chemicals from industry. In addition, several regulations have been issued, and some special taxes and charges have been introduced. The regulation on maximum sulphur content in petroleum products has already been mentioned (*see supra* §2 I). In recent years, voluntary agreements with industry have been introduced as a supplementary instrument to reduce emissions of SO_2 and NOx (*see infra*).

The mentioned limitations on emissions of exhaust gases from cars on the basis of regulations pursuant to the Road Traffic Act also contribute to the reduction of these problems.

285. The PCA applies to the main sources of *emissions of VOC*, which are the offshore loading and storing of oil on the continental shelf. The pollution permit system is relevant in this respect.

In addition, a regulation has been issued pursuant to the Act with the purpose of reducing emissions of VOC.[316] The regulation lays down maximum limits for emissions of VOC through the use of organic solvents, as further defined in an annex to the regulation. The operators have a general duty to apply all adequate measures to limit the emissions as much as possible. Certain types of particularly dangerous

314. Act of 16 Jun. 1961 No. 15.
315. Act of 24 Jun. 2011 No. 29.
316. Regulation of 1 Jun. 2004 No. 931 Ch. 9, pursuant to the Pollution Control Act and the Product Control Act. It implements EU Directive 1999/13/EC.

VOCs, which come under strict rules concerning dangerous chemicals (*see infra* Chapter 8 section A), shall be replaced by less dangerous alternatives as soon as possible (Regulation Article 9-7).

286. Reduction of *emissions of* SO_2 has been an important objective in Norwegian environmental policy since the 1970s, and has for several decades been an obligation pursuant to the Gothenburg Protocol under the LRTAP Convention. The PCA is the main instrument, but it is combined with other instruments and legislations.

Earlier, some important industries paid a SO_2 tax on the burning of coal and coke. In 2001, an agreement of intention on SO_2 emission reduction was made between the Ministry of the Environment and the main companies in such important industrial branches as aluminium, ferroalloys and refineries. The tax was removed. Instead, the companies pay a corresponding fee to a fund managed by the industries themselves, called *Prosessindustriens miljøfond* ('The process industry's environment fund'). Some forty factories participate in the fund. Its purpose is to finance measures to reduce emissions of SO_2 from the industry, including development of new technology and construction of cleansing mechanisms. During the first period, up to 2010, the objective was to reduce total annual emissions of SO_2 with 5,000 tons within 2010. This was achieved. During the period 2011–2014, the total annual emission of SO_2 from these industries did not exceed 11,000 tons, and this target is to be kept also through the present agreement period 2018–2022, in order to meet the revised Gothenburg Protocol (2012) target of 10% reduction compared to 2005.[317]

287. The PCA is also the main instrument for the reduction of *emissions of NOx* from land-based industry, but it has not yet been used to limit emissions from the petroleum installations. In 2007, the government introduced a NOx tax. However, simultaneously, a *voluntary agreement* was made between the Ministry of the Environment and the organizations of industrial and transport activities with significant NOx emissions, much like the mentioned agreement on reduction of SO_2. Members of these organizations are exempted from the tax if they instead pay a (smaller) fee[318] to a special fund which has been established – the 'NOx Fund' – and take voluntary measures to reduce emissions in accordance with the agreement. Altogether fifteen major organizations within industry and sea transport are party to this agreement, among these are the Confederation of Norwegian Enterprise (NHO) with its subsidiary Federation of Norwegian Industries, the Norwegian Oil Industry Association (OLF), as well as several organizations within the fisheries industry and internal national and local sea transport which are significant sources of NOx emissions along the coast of Norway. Nearly 900 companies are associated with the fund, which means that about 60% of NOx emissions in Norway are included. The

317. In a longer term also the limits laid down in EU Directive (EU) 2016/2284 on the reduction of national emissions of certain atmospheric pollutants will be relevant. The directive is now in the process of being included in the EEA Agreement for implementation in Norway.

318. The fee has increased steadily over the years. In 2021 the fee is NOK 10,50 (1 EUR) per kg NOx for emission from shipping, fishery, land-based industry, aviation, railway and movable rigs for petroleum exploration, and NOK 16,5 (nearly EUR 1,6) for emissions from oil and gas production. In comparison, the tax is NOK 23,50 (nearly EUR 2.3).

organizations first committed themselves to reduce their total annual emissions with 18,000 tons during the years 2008–2010. In 2010, this agreement was prolonged for the period 2011–2017. During this period, emissions of NOx from the installations covered by the agreement was reduced with 16,000 tons. In 2017, it was prolonged again for the period 2018–2025 with the objective of a further reduction of 30,000 tons on a yearly average in 2025. Again, EU Directive 2016/2284 will be relevant here.

288. As a result, Norway fulfils its reduction obligation under the Gothenburg Protocol. A side effect of these measures is a not negligible reduction also of CO_2 emissions from the same activities.

*NOx emissions from ship*s are significant sources. Rules established by the International Maritime Organization (IMO) imply restrictions on NOx emissions from ships constructed after 2000, while emissions from older ships are mainly unregulated.

§4. Global Problems: The Ozone Layer and Global Warming

I. Measures to Protect the Ozone Layer

289. The reduction of the emissions of substances that deplete the stratospheric ozone layer has been an important area in Norwegian environmental policy over the last two decades. The significant depletion of the ozone layer over Arctic areas brings the problem close to Norway. Norway has been active in international cooperation in this field from the beginning. We are party to the Vienna Convention on the Protection of the Ozone Layer, and the Montreal Protocol with its latest amendments.[319] Also, through the EEA Agreement, Norway has implemented the latest EU regulation in this field.[320] These are incorporated in Chapter 6 of the Product Regulation.[321]

290. The national objective has been to reduce and gradually end all use of substances that contribute to the depletion of the ozone layer. The consumption of hydrochlorofluorocarbons (HCFC) was eliminated in 2015. Regulations to the Product Control Act are the main legal instruments with this purpose. The application of this Act has been based on a close cooperation with the relevant industries, voluntary measures, information, and research to find alternatives. Today, all substances included in the Montreal Protocol are covered by regulations. Norway does not itself produce any of the substances in question.

319. Gradually, stricter rules as adopted by amendments to the protocol in London 1990, Copenhagen 1992, Vienna 1995, Montreal 1997 and Beijing 1999.
320. Regulation (EC) No. 1005/2009 which replaced Regulation No. 2037/2000, and with later amendments for certain substances laid down in Regulations No. 744/2010, No. 291/2011 and No. 1087/2013.
321. Regulation of 1 Jun. 2004 No. 922 Ch. 6, pursuant to the Product Control Act and the Ship Safety and Security Act.

The first regulations were issued in 1991 aiming at phasing out and terminating the manufacture, import, export and use of CFC and halons, or products containing such substances. Strict regulations to terminate the import and use of several other substances have later been issued. Since then, the import and consumption of ozone-depleting substances have dropped sharply, and is now virtually terminated in accordance with the policy objective. In accordance with the latest amendment to the Montreal Protocol, a system of licensing for import and export of ozone-depleting substances has been established. In addition to incorporating the EU legislation on the issue,[322] it generally lays down a prohibition to import or export ozone-depleting substances and products and equipment which contain or are dependent on such substances without a permit from the NEA. NEA can only give permit in accordance with the international/EU rules.[323]

291. However, there is still a problem with *refrigerators* and so on that were produced earlier, which for the most part contain such substances. The 'Waste Regulation'[324] Chapter 1 lays down rules to control the disposal of waste of such products. The CFCs must be removed and destroyed before final disposal. The municipality must provide, free of charge, reception facilities for this type of household appliance. Also, dealers and distributors must accept – when selling a new refrigerator – to take back the used one, without charge to the customer, and transport it to the municipal reception facility. The final disposal as waste of these appliances must be in accordance with the best-known technology and prevent any emission of CFCs into the air.

292. For some uses, the CFCs have been replaced by *hydrofluorocarbons (HFC) and perfluorocarbons (PFC)*, which do not attack the ozone layer to the same extent, but however have effect as GHG and thus contribute to climate change. In 1997, regulations were laid down with the objective of reducing the use and gradually phasing it out. Since 2003, import of products containing these substances has been subject to a special tax. In 2004, a system was introduced whereby the tax will be reimbursed if products with HFC and PFC are delivered to a site/installation authorized for destruction of these substances. This applies regardless of whether the substances come in bulk or as part of a product, or is mixed with other substances.[325]

293. On 15 October 2016, 197 countries adopted an amendment to phase down HFCs under the Montreal Protocol in Kigali, Rwanda, known as *the Kigali Amendment*. Under the amendment, countries committed to cut the production and consumption of HFCs by more than 80% over the next thirty years. The ambitious phase-down schedule will avoid more than 80 billion metric tons of carbon dioxide equivalent emissions by 2050 – avoiding up to 0.5° Celsius warming by the end of

322. Regulation (EC) 1005/2009 with later amendments, the most recent by Regulation (EU) 2017/605.
323. Product Regulation para. 6-2.
324. Regulation of 1 Jun. 2004 No. 930 on recycling and treatment of waste (Waste Regulation), *see* in particular about CFC Arts 1–22 para. 4 m).
325. Rules on the right to reimbursement and procedural rules are laid down in the Waste Regulation Ch. 8.

the century – while continuing to protect the ozone layer. Under the amendment, developed countries will reduce HFC consumption beginning in 2019. Most developing countries will freeze consumption in 2024, with a small number of developing countries with unique circumstances freezing consumption in 2028. Norway is rapidly scaling down the consumption of HFK, even more rapidly than required by the Kigali Amendment. The rules are laid down in the Product Regulation.[326]

II. Climate Change: Overview of Norway's Climate Policy and Law[327]

294. Climate change has been *an important – and partly controversial – political issue* in Norway ever since the 1987 report of the World Commission on Environment and Development ('Brundtland Commission') described the possible effects of increased concentration of CO_2 in the atmosphere. Nearly all political parties, as well as the Norwegian Parliament – Stortinget – on many occasions, have defined climate change as a major environmental threat, and policy objectives and measures have been developed by and large with broad political and public support.

Norway's annual emission of GHG was in 2022 in the order of 49 million tons of CO_2 equivalents, of which 83% CO_2. The emission has been reduced by only 2.4 million tons, or 4.7%, since 1990. With 5.5 million inhabitants, the average emission of a Norwegian person amounts to close to 10 tons CO_2 equivalents which is close to the OECD average: Offshore petroleum production counted for 28%, other industries 27%, road transport 21%, other transports, fisheries, etc. 18%, agriculture, and heating, waste disposal and other various sources together some 6%. Since the reduction of emission of GHGs has been an important and agreed political objective in Norway since the early 1990s, it is remarkable that only a very little emission reduction actually has been achieved over these thirty years.

295. Several governmental reports to Stortinget (*white papers*) and proposals on the issue have been presented by the government to the Stortinget over these thirty years.[328] The earlier debates mainly focused on the merits of various legal and economic instruments, and the choice between instruments, in order to fulfil the obligations of the Kyoto Protocol in the most cost-efficient way. An important issue has also been to what extent Norway should aim at reducing its own emissions 'at home' versus through the use of the flexible mechanisms in the Kyoto Protocol (or

326. Regulation of 1 Jun. 2004 No. 930 Ch. 6a.

327. Norwegian climate law is presented broadly in Hans Christian Bugge (ed.). *Klimarett. Internasjonal, europeisk og norsk klimarett mot 2030* (Climate Law. International, European and Norwegian climate law towards 2030) (Oslo: Universitetsforlaget 2021).

328. St. meld. (white paper) No. 29 (1997–1998) on the implementation of the Kyoto Protocol, St. meld. No. 54 (1997–1998) on green taxes, St. meld. No. 29 (1998–1999) on energy policy, and St. meld. No. 54 (2000–2001) on Norway's climate policy, with addition presented by the new government in St. meld. No. 15 (2001–2002), St. prp. (proposal to Stortinget) No. 49 (2001–2002) on the ratification of the Kyoto Protocol, St. meld. No. 34 (2006–2007) on Norway's climate policy and Meld. St. 21 (2011–2012) on Norway's climate policy from April 2012, Meld. St. 13 (2014–2015) on new emission reduction commitment for 2030 – a common solution with EU, Meld. St. 13 (2020–2021) Klimaplan for 2021–2030 (Climate plan for 2021–2030), and Meld. St. 26 (2022-2023) on policy on adaptation to climate change.

possible pursuant to the Paris Agreement in the future) as applied mainly through the EU Emission Trade system (ETS) to which Norway is a part through the EEA Agreement. In 2021, about 50% of the emissions are covered by the EU-ETS.

296. In 2020, Norway presented a national target of 50–55% reduction of emission in 2030 compared to 1990, as a National Determined Contribution (NDC) under the Paris Agreement, up from the initially presented 40%. This coincides with the EU 'Green Deal' target of 55% reduction in 2030 adopted by EU in 2020.

The latest (by 2023) governmental report to Stortinget on Norway's policy to reduce GHG emissions was presented in January 2021 and discussed in Stortinget in April 2021.[329] It presents a number of different activities aiming at emission reduction. At the base is the close relationship between Norway's climate policy and that of the EU. Norway shall fulfil its international obligations towards 2030 of 50–55% reduction in close cooperation with EU. Through a special agreement between EU and Norway from 2020, Norway is fully included in the EU climate system from January 2021. Both the 'Effort sharing regulation'[330] and the LULUCF regulation[331] apply to Norway in addition to the EU-ETS. This will provide Norway with important flexibility given the fact that these regulations open a certain, although limited, possibility of trading emission allowances.

Norway will implement the recent amendments in the EU-ETS system, such as the inclusion of shipping into the system, from January 2024.[332]

297. Norway is, in some respects, *in a rather special situation* when it comes to reduction of GHG emissions. Norway is among the largest net exporters of oil and gas in the world. This industry has achieved important technological improvements to reduce CO_2 emission, not least as the result of a considerable tax on CO_2 emissions that was introduced as early as 1991 (*see infra*). It has been an important incentive for the industry to reduce its emissions. However, the petroleum industry has been growing steadily and is very energy-demanding. It is the source of more than a quarter of Norway's CO_2 emissions, and the amount has been steadily increasing. The better part of the produced oil and gas is exported, and mostly to European countries. Countries that are heavily dependent on coal for their power production may find alternative and increased use of natural gas as an important element in their own policy to curb their CO_2 emissions. Therefore, at least in theory, increased production and export of Norwegian gas may contribute to a reduction of CO_2 emissions in some European countries which now receive natural gas from Norway. At the same time, however, it inevitably leads to increased emissions in Norway.

298. While the production of petroleum is an important source of the country's CO_2 emissions, fossil fuels do not play the same important role as an energy source within Norway itself as in many other countries. Some 60% of Norway's total

329. Meld. St. 13 (2020–2021) Klimaplan for 2021–2030 (Climate plan for 2021–2030).
330. Regulation (EU) 2018/842.
331. Regulation (EU) 2018/841.
332. Directive (EU) 2023/959 and Regulation (EU) 2023/957.

energy consumption, including domestic heating, is already covered by *renewable energy*, mostly from hydropower. Close to 100% of the electricity consumption in Norway comes from hydropower produced in the country.[333] This makes it difficult to reduce national GHG emissions considerably.

299. Norway's climate policy and climate-related law has become increasingly complex both legally and technically, similar to the international climate change legislation. Here, it is only possible to describe the most important policy objectives and measures in various fields, and the main legal issues.

At the international level, Norway contributed very actively to the successful adoption of the Paris Agreement and will continue to work towards its successful implementation. Norway's International Climate and Forest Initiative is an important element here. Through this, Norway contributes up to NOK 3 billion (EUR 300 million) a year to forest protection in developing countries, based on real results. This is closely linked to the development of the REDD+ mechanism and initiatives under the UN Framework Convention on Climate Change UNFCCC and the Paris Agreement.

The most recent *national policy objectives* towards 2030 and beyond are as follows:

- Norway shall be a 'low-emission society' in 2050, and reduce GHG emissions by 90%–95% compared to 1990.
- Norway shall be 'climate neutral' in 2030.
- Norway shall reduce GHG emissions by 50%–55% in 2030 compared to 1990. This will be achieved in cooperation with the EU.
- Norway will reduce emissions of GHG from deforestation and forest degradation in developing countries, in accordance with sustainable development. It is Norway's intention to continue this programme at least until 2030.
- The Norwegian society shall prepare for and adapt to climate change.

III. The Climate Act

300. In June 2017, Stortinget adopted an Act relating to Norway's Climate Targets ('Climate Change Act').[334]

The Act is inspired by the United Kingdom's 2008 Climate Change Act, but is modelled more after the (less ambitious) climate change acts adopted later in Denmark, Finland, and Sweden. The purpose of the Act (Article 1) is to promote the proper implementation of the climate targets in order to develop Norway into a 'low-emission society' by 2050. Furthermore, the Act shall encourage transparency and public debate about the status, direction and progress of this work. The targets may be reached 'in common with the EU'. This is followed up through the above-mentioned EU-Norway Climate agreement.

333. The per capita consumption of electricity in Norway is the highest in the world.
334. Act of 16 Jun. 2017 No. 60.

The target for 2030 is a reduction of GHG emissions of 50–55% compared to the 1990 level (Article 3).[335] It will most likely be changed to 'as a minimum 55%' in the course of the fall 2023.[336] The objective for 2050 is that Norway is a 'low-emission society' (Article 4). This is defined as a society where GHG emissions have been reduced to the level where it is in accordance with the main objective of a maximum of +2 degrees in the Paris Agreement. The more precise objective is a reduction of 90%–95%.[337] However, this reduction is not meant necessarily to be achieved for sources within Norway; as mentioned, it may be at least partly achieved through the use of flexible mechanisms in the EU system.

In its Articles 5 and 6, the Act lays down reporting obligations and other obligations for the government towards Stortinget: such as an assessment of the objectives every five year, aiming at a gradual and step-by-step progress in accordance with the principle to this effect in the Paris Agreement. In its annual State budget, the government must present its plan to reach the objectives, and also assess the climate effect of the budget itself. Furthermore, it shall annually inform Stortinget about:

- the development in emissions, prognoses and how the objectives may be reached;
- how Norway prepares for the probable climate change;
- how the various economic sectors outside ETS plan to reduce their emissions;
- status for Norway's 'carbon budget'.

A 'technical assessment commission' has the mandate to assess and verify the information which is to be included in these documents. The Commission discusses and develops, *inter alia*, methods to assess the effect and cost-efficiency of various policy instruments, identifies needs for methodological improvements and presents its findings in annual reports.

301. The Climate Act does not include any new instruments to attack the problem. It is the general view that *the present legislation is sufficient* to reduce emissions and stimulate a development towards a low-carbon society, and that this is mainly a matter of effective application of legal means which are at the disposal. The PCA is a starting point in this respect. It applies to GHG emissions. However, for a long time, CO_2 emissions were 'not seen as a problem', and hence not included when pollution permits were issued. Today, this is not contested. For example, all installations with GHG emissions which are included in the system of emission trading (*see infra*) must first have a permit pursuant to the PCA.

However, other instruments play a more important role in Norway's climate policy.

---

335. This was changed from 40% by an amendment to the Act adopted in June 2021, *see* proposition to Stortinget, Prop. 182 L (2020–2021), adopted by Stortinget 7 Jun. 2021.
336. Prop. 107 L (2022–2023).
337. This was changed from 80–95% by the mentioned Act.

IV. GHG Taxes

302. Since 1990, Norway has been introducing several *CO_2 taxes*. At present (2021), Norway has the following CO_2 taxes:

- A 'CO_2-part' of the general consumer tax on ordinary car petrol.
- A 'CO_2-part' of the tax on fuel oil/domestic oil. This varies with the type of oil and does not apply generally; some industrial branches pay a reduced tax, while industry included in the emission trading system and international air and sea transport and fishery are exempted.
- A CO_2 tax on national use of gas. Various industries and activities have either a reduced rate or are exempted.
- A CO_2 tax on emissions from the burning of oil and gas in the offshore petroleum industry.
- In 2003, a tax was also put on the heavy-duty GHGs, HFK, and PFK (*see supra*).

The tax on CO_2 *emission from offshore petroleum* industry has been particularly important. It was introduced already in 1991 through a special Act.[338] There is no doubt that this tax has been a very important and effective incentive to reduce emissions from petroleum installations. From 2008 the petroleum industry was included in the CO_2 emission trading system (*see infra*), and the industry had to buy their allowances in the market. The CO_2 tax was kept, but reduced from the former level to the effect that the sum of the carbon price and the tax roughly corresponded to the earlier tax level. An explicit purpose is to create an incentive for the industry to continue to reduce emissions.

In order to reduce GHG emissions nationally, it has been decided to gradually introduce *electricity from onshore sources* – mainly hydropower – as the energy needed to run the offshore petroleum installations instead of from the burning of fossil fuels from the fields. However, this measure is controversial as it will not necessarily reduce the total global emissions since the saved fuels instead will be exported and burned elsewhere. At the same time, increased electricity production onshore will have harmful effects on nature and biodiversity.

Altogether, CO_2 taxes now apply to a considerable part of the national GHG emissions. However, the tax system is not satisfactory from a strict economic point of view of efficiency. The tax levels per ton vary considerably, and significant sources are subject to only a reduced tax, or not subject to tax at all. Since the introduction of an emission trading system in Norway, some taxes have been removed or changed. In principle, activities included in the emission trading system should be exempted from CO_2 tax. However, as mentioned, this does not apply to offshore petroleum production.

In April 2021, Stortinget decided to considerably increase the general CO_2 tax gradually to reach a level of NOK 2,000 – corresponding to EUR 200 – per ton CO_2 in 2030, up from NOK 600 in 2021.

338. Act of 21 Dec. 1990 No. 72 on CO_2 Tax in the Petroleum Industry.

V. The GHG Emissions Trading System

303. EU-ETS[339] is included in the EEA Agreement, which means that Norway and Norwegian industry participate fully in this system. As a matter of fact, Norway's emission trading system has since 2005 been linked to EU-ETS, and it will continue to do so towards 2030. The legal basis is the Greenhouse Gas Emission Trading Act – hereinafter 'GGETA of 2004'.[340] The Act is supplemented by a comprehensive technical Regulation (hereinafter 'the GGETA Regulation')[341] which to a large extent incorporates the relevant EU rules.[342] This also means that Norway and Norwegian industry will be subject to the planned reduction of the EU-ETS emission 'cap' of 2.2% per year between 2021 and 2030. This will be a very important element in Norway's climate policy towards 2030.

The system now covers some 50% of Norway's emissions of CO_2 and applies to emissions from most industrial activities,[343] including in particular:

- burning of fuel with a total thermal effect exceeding 20 MW, except from combustion of hazardous and municipal waste;
- refining of mineral oil;
- coke production;
- production and processing of iron and steel, including roasting and sintering of iron ore; production of non-ferrous metals;
- production of aluminium (emissions of CO_2 and PFC), ferroalloys (CO_2), petrochemical and numerous chemical industries, including fertilizer (N_2O) (from 2013);
- production of cement, lime, glass, glass fibre and ceramic products;
- production of pulp and paper of more than 20 tons in twenty-four hours;
- production of various chemicals;
- production of oil and gas on the continental shelf is also included. From 2011, this also includes emission from mobile petroleum exploration rigs;
- CCS of GHG.

In accordance with the EU-ETS Directive, the Act also applies to *air flights* between Norway and the other countries in the EEA (with some exceptions such as military flights and flights in connection with rescue operations, humanitarian work, and scientific research in accordance with the EU-ETS Rules).[344]

As mentioned, from January 2024 the Act also applies to *shipping* in accordance with the amendments in the EU-ETS which include shipping in the system.

---

339. Directive 2003/87/EC with later amendments, the most recent being Directive (EU) 2018/410.
340. Act No. 99 of 17 Dec. 2004.
341. Regulation No. 1851 of 23 Dec. 2004 on the obligation to have allowances for GHG emissions and trade in allowances, with later amendments, the most recent of 28 May 2021.
342. Regulation (EU) 2019/331, Commission decision (EU) 2019/708, and Regulation (EU) 2019/1842.
343. GGETA Regulation Art. 1-1.
344. GGETA Regulation Arts 1-2, 1-2a, 1-2b, and 1-3.

304. Units of production/activities to which the GGETA applies must at the outset have *a permit pursuant to the PCA*[345] for the carbon dioxide emissions (in addition to a permit for any other polluting emissions). This permit is of a formal character. It is to be given if the unit is found to have a satisfactory system for monitoring and reporting of emissions. The permit may not set any emission limits. In this sense, the Norwegian system is in accordance with the EU-ETS system and the EC Directive on industrial emissions (the former IPPC Directive, *see supra*). However, it is explicitly stated in the Act that the authorities may lay down conditions for the permit, and it is generally understood that this also includes particular technical solutions.

305. The link to the PCA is important. It makes it clear that carbon dioxide emissions from the factories in question are still subject to that Act. Thus, the implementation of the GGETA is closely linked to the general work on pollution issues. The MCE and NEA are the responsible authorities.

306. The production units covered by the GGETA *must dispose of allowances* corresponding to their actual emissions each year. They acquire allowances through the initial allocation from the State, and by buying allowances in the market to the extent necessary. Before 1 May each year, the units must surrender allowances to the Norwegian Allowance Trading Registry (NATR) corresponding to the amount of emissions during the preceding year. This Registry is organized under NEA.

Any physical or legal person can trade in carbon dioxide allowances, by opening an account in the NATR. An account-holder is entitled to transfer his/her allowances to other account-holders. However, only those companies that have a permit pursuant to the PCA may *emit* CO_2 and have the duty to transfer the necessary allowances to the account. Therefore, the right to hold an allowance does not in itself imply a right to pollute.

307. As mentioned, the Norwegian rules in the GGETA and the Regulation pursuant to the Act *implement the EU-ETS Rules*. These rules, and the corresponding Norwegian rules, are complex and rather technical. It is not possible to go into any detail here.

308. An important point is the division between those industries/activities that have to pay for their emission allowances and those that are allocated freely all or parts of their allowances. This issue, and the rules about free allocation of allowances for the period 2021–2030, is regulated through EU rules, mainly the EU Regulation 2019/331, known as the 'Free Allocation Regulation'. This regulation was included in the EEA Agreement in 2020 and forms the basis for the Norwegian rules laid down in GGETA Regulation Chapter 4. The main principle is that the question of free allocation of allowances is decided by the degree of risk for 'carbon leakage' of the industry in question. Industries are divided into three main categories:

345. PCA Art. 11 para. 2. This does not apply to aviation which is not covered by the PCA.

- Industries with no risk of carbon leakage. They do not get any free allocation.
- Industries with only very limited risk of carbon leakage. From 2021 to 2025, these get 30% free allocations, with gradually further reductions from 2026 to zero in 2030.
- Industries with considerable or great risk of carbon leakage. These get 100% free allocations.

The allocation of free allowances is organized and decided by NEA pursuant to GGETA Regulation Chapter 4 based on the EU rules. NEA has allocated *free allowances to existing industries* for the period 2021–2025 and 2026–2030 on the basis of applications. They are based on benchmarks – 'emission standards' – for the various types of 'installations' within each production unit in accordance with EU rules. Historic activity level and emissions are important elements for the decision ('grand-fathering').

Aviation has been allocated free allowances by the NEA in accordance with the EU rules, pursuant to GGETA Regulation Chapter 6.

In accordance with the EU-ETS Directive, the following activities are not entitled to free allowances: electricity production and CCS (capture, pipeline transport and storage of CO_2). These activities have to buy all their allowances in the market. The main system is *the auctioning system* laid down in the EU regulation on matter.[346] Norway has incorporated this regulation into the GGETA Regulation Article 8-1.

Since the electricity power production sector has to pay for their allowances, the price of electricity increases. This increased electricity cost may be significant for such industry sectors as production of aluminium, ferroalloys, pulp and paper, and types of chemical industries with high consumption of electricity. These increased costs make them more vulnerable to 'carbon leakage'. However, the EU-ETS Directive (Article 10a No. 6) permits Member States to adopt 'financial measures .... In order to compensate for those costs and where such financial measures are in accordance with state aid rules applicable and to be adopted in this area', and based on 'ex ante benchmarks'. Norway has established such *a CO_2 compensation system* for fifteen industrial sectors, in accordance with the EU rules.

Furthermore, Norway has incorporated the detailed EU rules on *monitoring and reporting of emissions*[347] and all other technical rules related to the EU-ETS.

309. In its Chapter 5, the GGETA has rules on *sanctions and penalty in case of violation* of the obligations to report and to deliver the necessary allowance.

If by 1 April an operator has not reported its emissions the year before, the authorities shall suspend the right to transfer allowances within the registry until a satisfactory report on emissions has been provided. If the operator fails to report, the authorities may impose a *coercive fine*, which becomes effective if the operator fails to meet the deadline for remedying the matter. Deliberate omission to report at all is punishable with fines or up to three months' imprisonment. If an operator has not complied with its duty to surrender the necessary allowances – if it does not have enough allowances to cover its actual emissions – the authorities shall impose

346. Commission Regulation (EU) No. 1031/2010.
347. *See* Commission Implementing Regulation (EU) 2018/2067.

an excess emissions fine for the allowances that are lacking. The fine is settled in the Act itself at EUR 100 for each ton of carbon dioxide – the same as in the EU.

Also in line with the EU directive, the names of the operators who are subject to such a fine, and the missing volumes, shall be open to the public. In addition, failure to surrender the necessary allowances makes the uncovered emissions illegal in relation to the PCA, and punishable pursuant to that Act.

VI. Carbon Capture and Storage

310. CCS is another important element in Norway's long-term climate policy. This has to do with the petroleum activity on the continental shelf. The subsoil of the Norwegian continental shelf has the potential for large-scale storage of carbon dioxide, both in existing and abandoned oil fields and in natural aquifers. The technique of storing carbon dioxide has already been applied at two gas fields.[348] The content of CO_2 in the gas from these fields is too high. CO_2 has been removed from the gas and has been injected back into the field.

Hence, for some time, the plan has been to capture carbon dioxide from installations onshore, transport it out to the shelf, inject it and store it in the deep seabed. On a very large scale, major infrastructures for this could be developed to take carbon dioxide from other parts of Europe and store it on Norway's continental shelf. In theory, this might become an important part of the 'solution' to the problem of GHG emissions in Europe.

Norway wants to be in the forefront in developing CCS technology, and have for that purpose invested large sums in developing an advanced development and test centre for CCS technology at Mongstad (Technology Centre Mongstad – TCM).

In 2020, a major political decision was taken by Stortinget: In cooperation with important private actors, the State will invest in a full-scale CCS project, in which CO_2 will be captured from Norway's major cement plant in southern Norway, transported by ship to a terminal in western Norway, and from there transported by pipeline to the continental shelf and stored in a major aquifer.[349]

311. CCS raises a number of legal issues, many of which have been clarified through the EU directive on CCS.[350] This directive regulates the identification and exploitation of geological storage facilities, including monitoring, liability for leakages, long-term transfer of responsibility to the authority, etc. The directive is defined as 'EEA relevant' and has been included in the EEA Agreement and implemented in Norway[351] through two comprehensive regulations.[352] Several of the

348. The Sleipner and Snøhvit gas fields.

349. *See* Report to Stortinget ('white paper') Meld. St. 33 (2019–2020) Langskip – fangst og lagring av CO_2 ('Langskip' is the official name of the project. 'Langskip' means literally Long ship.) Discussed and supported by Stortinget in Innst. S. 143 (2020–2021).

350. Directive 2009/31/EC.

351. This was unclear for some time, due to the fact that Norway's official view is that the EEA Agreement applies only to Norway's territory, and not on the continental shelf.

352. Regulation 22 Oct. 2014 No. 1338 pursuant to the Pollution Control Act, inserted into the general Pollution Regulation as Ch. 35. This regulation comes under the MCE. Regulation 5 Dec. 2014 No.

rules are common for the two regulations. It is clear that the State has ownership of the seabed geological storage facilities and the exclusive right to exploit and manage these facilities. This means that a permit from the State is needed for all activities linked to CCS on the Norwegian continental shelf. The State may itself participate in transport and exploitation activities for storage of CO_2.

312. First, CCS is regulated pursuant to the Act of 21 June 1963 No. 12 on scientific research on and exploration of, and exploitation of, other natural resources in the seabed than petroleum. This Act is under the responsibility of the Ministry of Industry, Trade and Fisheries. However, the regulation in question is the responsibility of the MPE as this activity is closely related to and has many similarities with exploration and exploitation of petroleum resources on the continental shelf. CCS may also be directly a part of petroleum exploitation activity. If injection and storage are used in petroleum production with the purpose of purifying natural gas or increasing the pressure and thus enhancing oil recovery from the field, the petroleum legislation applies, namely the Petroleum Act[353] under the Ministry of Oil and Energy.

The regulation reflects to a large extent the principles and rules in the EU directive. It regulates prospecting, exploration of suitable reservoirs for storage of CO_2 under Norwegian jurisdiction, and the exploitation of, transport to and storage in such reservoirs, and the closing down and the long-term responsibility for them. It also opens the possibility of applying the regulation on transport of CO_2 from sources outside Norwegian jurisdiction. By this, it is clearly shown that Norway is ready to receive CO_2 from other countries for storage on the Norwegian continental shelf (Article 1-3).

A permit to a CCS activity (prospecting, exploration, exploitation, transport and storage) is given to a defined 'operator' designated or approved by the authorities. There may be only one operator for each facility (Article 1-8).

313. A CCS activity starts with *prospecting* of possible storage sites. A permit from the Ministry is necessary in order to start prospecting. This permit is, however, not an exclusive right to explore the area covered by the permit, and it does not give a priority right to get a permit for the subsequent exploitation (Article 2-1). The regulation gives detailed rules on the application, including the information needed, etc. When a possible storage site has been identified, a new permit is needed for a more detailed study of the site, called *Exploration permit* (Article 3-1). This is given by the King in Council and is an exclusive right, which also will include various obligations with regard to how the exploration should be carried out. The exploration permit may be given for a maximum of ten years.

314. If the reservoir is found suitable as a storage site, the next step is the *exploitation permit* for CO_2 injection and storage (Article 4-1). This is given by the King

---

1517 pursuant to the Act of 21 Jun. 1963 No. 12 on scientific research on and exploration of, and exploitation of, other natural resources in the seabed than petroleum. This regulation is the responsibility of the MPE.

353. Act of 29 Nov. 1996 No. 72.

in Council on the basis of detailed information from the applicant. The duration is decided in the permit. It has to be accompanied by a detailed plan for the development and management of the site (Article 4-5). This has to describe the economic, technical, security, industrial and environmental aspects of the activities, and all relevant factors related to the management such as geological conditions, pressure, injection and transport solutions and so on. An important procedural element is the *impact assessment* of the storage. This shall cover all the economic/industrial and environmental impacts of the activity and has to be carried out as part of the preparation for the application, and be included in the application. The regulation gives comprehensive and detailed rules on the assessment (Article 4-7–4-10). Furthermore, there are a number of conditions for a permit laid down in the regulation, related to economic conditions, insurance against pollution damage, and so on.

315. When the permit for storage activity runs out or for some other reason is terminated, the operator must see to it that the site is fully stable and secured against leakage. In that case, and after a minimum of twenty years from the start of the storage, the site may be transferred to the State (Ministry of Oil and Energy) (Article 5-8). This is an important principle. The operator, however, has to provide a financial security for possible future liability for leakage and cover the costs of monitoring of the site for a minimum of thirty years (Article 5-10).

Storage sites on the Norwegian continental shelf may be made accessible for other actors than the holder of the right to develop and manage the site – such as other producers of CO_2. This is subject to a decision by the Ministry, and has to be provided on objective and non-discriminatory conditions. In that case, the operator has to receive CO_2 from other sources. This also opens up for delivery of CO_2 from other countries around the North Sea.

316. Second, CCS is also regulated *pursuant to the PCA*. The rules are included as Chapter 35 in the general Pollution Regulation.[354] Both capture and storage will require a permit pursuant to the PCA. The *capture* (which normally takes place at an industrial installation) is regulated by the general concession system in the PCA (*see supra* Chapter 1, §2, V), while storage is regulated by the mentioned regulation pursuant to the PCA. The main rule is that injection and storage of CO_2 in geological formations require a permit from the NEA based on an application (Article 35-4). A permit may be given if a number of conditions laid down in the regulation are met. Basic preconditions are that the geological formation is suited for storage of CO_2, that the operator in question is financially solid and has the necessary competence, and that the storage does not represent any serious environmental and other risks. The operator has to provide the necessary financial security for any future costs, liabilities, etc., from the activity. The regulation lays down procedural rules for the application. Only virtually 'clean' streams of CO_2 may be stored. Waste and other substances may not be added to the CO_2, and only very low levels of other substances may be accepted. The operator shall monitor the injection and storage activity continuously according to an established plan and report to the NEA annually and if an extraordinary event occurs.

354. Regulation of 1 Jun. 2004 No. 931.

An important point also in this regulation is the system for the *closing of the storage*. It is foreseen that various events may result in the finishing of the injection and storage activity. The storage may be closed in accordance with the conditions in the permit, on the basis of an application from the operator, or pursuant to a decision by the NEA. When closure has been carried out according to the rules, and after a minimum of twenty years from the start of the storage activity, the operator may require that all commitments and possible future liabilities are transferred to the State.

VII. Emission from Road Transport

317. Some 32% of Norway's CO_2 emissions come from *the transport sector*, including road, rail, sea and air transport within Norway. This share has increased steadily over the last decades, mainly due to increased car traffic. Besides road transport, emission from sea transport along the coast and to the petroleum installations on the continental shelf is a significant part. The agreed political aim is to reduce CO_2 emissions from transport by 50% within 2030.

One important policy measure in the transport sector is to curb the increase in car traffic by developing and strengthening *public transport* as a viable and effective transport medium. In the comprehensive ten-year National Transport Plan 2022–2033 which was approved by Stortinget in June 2021,[355] one of five key objectives is to contribute to the fulfilment of Norway's climate and environment goals. It is also an agreed objective to move transport of goods from road transport to rail and sea transport. With regard to car traffic, the objective is to stimulate, through economic incentives, the purchase of electrical zero-emission or 'hybrid' low-emission cars and buses. The intention is that by 2025 all new private cars, including light vans, sold in Norway shall be zero-emission cars. Also, all new public buses used in the cities shall have zero emission or run on biogas by 2025. Within 2030 also all new vans, 75% of new long-distance buses and 50% of new lorries shall have zero emissions. Within 2030, the emissions from distribution of goods in the major city centres should be close to zero.[356]

There are *toll roads* around the city centre of Oslo and other major cities with the double objective of reducing traffic and raising funds for new and improved transport infrastructure. This may also include infrastructure for public transport (metro, etc.) in the urban area and even to cover running costs of the public transport systems. This may be decided by the State in Stortinget on the basis of proposals from the municipality in question. Increasingly, the State and the municipalities negotiate agreements in this field – called 'Urban growth agreement' – about new important infrastructure projects and the financial participation in such projects by the State.

As mentioned, most of the transport sector is subject to various CO_2 taxes through *fuel taxes*, and some of these have increased in recent years. In addition,

355. Meld. St. 20 (2020–2021) National Transport Plan 2022–2033, Innst. 653 S. (2020–2021).
356. Meld. St. 13 (2020–2021) Klimaplan for 2021–2030, p. 65.

the *taxes on new cars* vary according to – *inter alia* – the emission of CO_2. For electric vehicles, a complete tax relief has been established. This has been effective in stimulating the sales of electric cars, but is now up for debate and possible changes within a few years.[357]

The average CO_2 emissions from new cars have decreased steadily. It was 177 g/km in 2006. The aim was to reach 85 g/km in 2020, but this objective was reached already in 2017 (in the EU, the objective is 147 g/km within 2020). Also, other types of advantages are given to vehicles with low or no CO_2 emission, such as exemption from toll in toll roads and right to drive in the public transport field on motorways.

318. Introduction of *biofuel* as a part of the total fuel consumption is another element in the policy of reducing GHG emissions from transport. In this area, Norway follows the development within the EU. This part of climate policy and law is becoming increasingly ambitious but at the same time quite complex and controversial.

In Norway, a mandatory requirement of 2.5% biofuel in car fuel was introduced in 2009 and has steadily increased since then. From 1 January, the requirement is 24.5% of which a minimum of 9% shall be so-called advanced biofuel. 'Advanced biofuel' is biofuel which is not produced from food articles but instead from waste or cellulose substances (which count double in the calculation). Norway has also laid down sustainability criteria for biofuels production which are in accordance with the *sustainability criteria* laid down in EU legislation through the renewable energy directive[358] and the directive on fuel quality.[359] These rules are laid down in the Product Regulation[360] Chapter 3. The Government will promote further the development of the value chain for advanced biofuel. This is also in line with the EU directive on 'indirect land-use changes, ILUC' from 2015[361] which further amends Directive 2009/28/EC and is now being considered for implementation by Norway.

VIII. Promotion of Renewable Energy

319. Also, the *national energy policy* is an important part of the overall climate policy. It is an agreed political objective *to increase the amount of all types of renewable energy.* Renewable energy, and energy efficiency, is promoted across the various sectors and supported by State aids and other instruments.

Hydropower has for more than 100 years been the major source of energy in Norway. Most of the watercourses with the highest potential for hydropower have now been developed, or have been formally protected by parliamentary decisions (*see infra* Part II Chapter 8). To meet the increasing domestic demand, new forms of

357. Meld. St. 13 (2020–2021) Klimaplan for 2021–2030, p. 65.
358. Directive 2009/28/EC (Arts 17–19).
359. Directive 98/70/EC as amended by Directive 2009/30/EC.
360. Regulation 1 Jun. 2004 No. 922 §2-21.
361. Directive EU 2015/1513.

energy sources are being developed. Small-scale hydro projects and onshore and offshore wind power are the most important. Norway has no nuclear power plants, and there are no plans for nuclear projects.

The *EU Renewable Energy Directive*[362] with later amendments has been included in the EEA Agreement and is implemented by Norway. The EU directive requires that all countries increase their share of renewable energy considerably. Norway's energy sector was already as high as 60% based on renewables, due to our very important hydropower sector. This is by far the highest in Europe. After negotiations between Norway and the EU on the Norwegian implementation of the directive, it was agreed that our share should be increased to 67.5%, and this goal was reached after a few years. The share is now (2023) 73%.

320. An adequate legislation and institutions for *further developments of renewable energy* are in place. Legislation for hydropower development dates back to 1917.[363] Small-scale hydropower is regulated by the 2000 Water Resources Act.[364] The general Energy Act of 1990[365] and the PBA[366] provide the necessary legal framework for the development of wind power onshore. The development of offshore wind farms is regulated by Act on Renewable Energy at Sea.[367] Important steps are being taken to develop wind farms on the continental shelf. These Acts require a public permit – 'concession' – for installations for the production of hydropower and wind power. Permits are also required for the transport of electricity through power lines. The objective of these Acts is a rational or efficient production of energy, and they are all administered by the MPE.

Norway has numerous *financial support instruments* to promote the production and consumption of renewable energy and energy efficiency. The most important mechanism to this end is a State fund – *The Climate and Energy Fund.* The fund is financed mainly from the State budget. The fund is administered by a special State company, *Enova.* It was established in 2001 and is owned by the MCE. The purpose of Enova is to contribute to developing Norway into a 'low emission society', mainly through reduction of SO_2 emissions and increased energy efficiency. It has at its disposal several financial instruments and incentives to stimulate market actors and mechanisms to achieve national energy policy goals. This includes various types of support to industry and municipalities as well as to ordinary households and information programmes.

Financial support from Enova has been provided to investments in renewable energy production or consumption units, in accordance with the EU/EEA Guidelines for State aid for environmental protection/renewable energy. The Climate and Energy Fund and Enova have been important in supporting the development of wind power farms.

---

362. Directive 2009/28/EC with later amendments, and recast in Directive (EU) 2018/2001 of 11 Dec. 2018.
363. Acts of 14 Dec. 1917 Nos 16 and 17.
364. Act of 24 Nov. 2000 No. 82.
365. Act of 29 Jun. 1990 No. 50.
366. Act of 27 Jun. 2008 No. 71.
367. Act of 4 Jun. 2010 No. 21.

321. Since January 2012, the most important economic instrument to promote production of renewable energy is the *common Norwegian-Swedish market for tradeable renewable energy certificates*, called 'green certificates' or 'el-certificates'.[368] A green certificates market is an artificially created market whereby all actors providing electricity to the final consumer have to have a certain share of renewable energy formalized through a certificate. Certificates are issued by the authorities to the producers of renewable energy. The producers then sell certificates to the companies that deliver electricity to the consumer.

The Norwegian/Swedish green certificates market is regulated by a precise and rather complex set of rules, laid down in a special Act on el-certificates and regulations pursuant to the Act.[369] Certificates are issued to companies that built renewable energy production installations between September 2007 and 2020, namely installations for small-scale hydropower, and wind-, sun-, ocean-, geothermal- and bio-energy. The companies have to apply to the energy authorities to become party to the system and get certificates. If approved, they are allocated certificates for fifteen years. The power suppliers, on their side, have to have a certain part of their production ('quota') covered by certificates each year.

This system has had an important effect on the development of renewables in Norway. It was for several years a considerable incentive to develop new wind and small-scale hydropower projects, but its importance has diminished over the last years. It raises a number of legal issues at national and EU level.[370] As a hidden subsidy system, it has been increasingly criticized for creating an inefficient electricity market. It will be phased out over the next decade.

322. The el-certificate system has been particularly important for the development of *onshore wind power* in Norway. It has worked as a subsidy which has made wind power profitable, what it – at least in the first years – would not have been without the income from the el-certificates. Therefore, considerable investments have been made in a number of major new wind parks, mainly along the coast. Among the investors are many foreign companies and investment funds. At the same time, the cost of establishing wind farms has steadily decreased over the last decade.

However, increasingly, the development of wind farms has become controversial, mainly due to the negative effects on nature and local communities. During the last couple of years, there have been strong protests and civil disobedience against some of them from the local population. The local communities feel that they to some extent have been fooled. Several years may have passed since the original licence for the project was given. In the meantime, the windmills have become much larger which make them more dominant in the neighbourhood and entail more massive encroachments in the nature for the necessary roads and powerlines than what was presented and foreseen at the outset.

---

368. Sweden has had a green certificate market as a national market since 2003.
369. Act of 24 Jun. 2011 No. 39, and Regulation of 16 Dec. 2011 No. 1398.
370. An important first contribution in Norway is the Ph.d. thesis by Catherine Banet at the Faculty of Law, University of Oslo, 'Tradeable Green Certificates Schemes under EU Law. The influence of EU law on national support schemes for renewable electricity generation', defended in Oslo in August 2012.

A particular case in point is the development of two major wind farm projects on the peninsula of Fosen in Troendelag in Mid-Norway. The wind farm area is an important grazing and herding area for reindeer and thus an essential land area for the local Sami population, and the wind farm is a considerable encroachment on this grazing area, putting the future Sami reindeer activity and culture at a risk. In 2021, the Supreme Court unanimously[371] found that the development of these two wind farms represents a violation of the International Covenant on Civil and Political Rights, Article 27, which states:

> In those States in which ethnic, religious or linguistic minorities exist, persons belonging to such minorities shall not be denied the right, in community with the other members of their group, to enjoy their own culture, to profess and practise their own religion, or to use their own language.

However, at the time of the Supreme Court decision, known as the 'Fosen case', the wind farms had already been built and were up and running, producing a considerable amount of electrical power. The practical consequences of the decision have thus been controversial and subject to a heated political debate, as well as a debate among lawyers on the various legal issues involved. These issues have not been solved at the time of this writing, September 2023. The case also illustrates possible conflicts between climate considerations and human rights.

323. In this connection, the procedure for the development of wind farms has been much criticized and has now (2023) been subject to reform. Earlier, a licence for a Wind farm was given by the State energy authority pursuant to the Energy Act with only a weak formal link to the land-use planning system pursuant to the PBA, and thus the ordinary municipal political planning procedures and decisions. This often created conflict with the local community. With the 2023 reform, this has been changed. A main point has been to link the procedure more closely to the regional and municipal planning system and give the municipality a strong vote on the licence issue. Now, a licence for a wind power farm pursuant to the Energy Act cannot be given until the project has been included in – and is in accordance with – a municipal land-use plan for the area, pursuant to the PBA (*see infra*).[372] There are in addition special rules in the PBA related to the establishment of wind farms to ensure a proper procedure.

The EIA of wind farms is rather rough as it relates only to the total production of the farm (in installed effect) and the area that will be included. This does not give a proper picture of the effects on the natural environment, the neighbourhood and the local community. A 'Detail plan' for the development of the project is to be presented later. This shall describe the number of windmills, the height and placement of each windmill, the roads, power lines, etc. A full new EIA is not required in this connection, but the developer has to present an 'Environment, transport and works plan'[373] which must show how environmental and other concerns are taken into

371. Case HR-2021-1975-S *Fosen* of 11 Oct. 2021.
372. Energy Act s. 2-2.
373. In Norwegian 'Miljø-, transport og anleggsplan – MTA'.

when the project is carried out. The real effect of the wind farm therefore only appears at this stage and often comes as a (bad) surprise to the neighbours and the local community. But at this stage, protests are too late.

324. Offshore wind energy is a priority area for research and development in Norway's energy and climate policy. In the longer term, it may become a very important activity and energy source in Norway. Work has started to develop offshore energy production. So far, the costs of this production are high, and considerable State subsidies are necessary. The legal base for this development is the 'Act on production of renewable energy off shore' ('Havenergilova' or 'Offshore Energy Act').[374] The purpose of the Act is to promote the proper exploitation of renewable energy resources – wind, tide and waves – at sea, taking into consideration the need for energy, environmental protection, security, and other interests (section 1-1). The Act applies to Norway's territorial sea outside the baselines and to the continental shelf, but individual provisions can also be made applicable to internal waters.

The Norwegian State has the right to utilize offshore energy resources. A licence is required for electricity generation, conversion and transmission in areas covered by the Act.

The decision-making system for offshore energy production has many similarities with the system for offshore petroleum production (*see infra* Part II, Chapter 7 § 3). As a general rule, licences can only be obtained after the central government authorities have carried out a strategic environmental assessment and decided to open specific areas for licence applications. However, the authorities may exempt pilot projects and similar projects with a limited time frame from these requirements.

When an area has been opened for licences, licences are assigned to companies on the basis of competition, based on objective and non-discriminating criteria. These may be combined with an auction (section 2-3). The next step is a particular licence for the production and/or transmission activity in question. An application for licence is considered on the basis of a detailed technical plan for the development and management of the project. Furthermore, a full EIA must have been carried out and approved by the authorities (the Act, Chapters 3 and 4). Further details on the procedure and the EIA are laid down in a special regulation.[375]

The Act, Chapter 9, has rules on compensation to fishermen for possible loss and damage caused by the production or transmission of offshore energy, such as occupation of fishing areas, pollution, waste and other types of damage (section 9-1). Loss caused by occupation by wind farms of fishing areas, which makes fishing impossible or considerably more difficult, is compensated by the State (section 9-2). The licensee is strictly liable for damage caused by pollution and waste. This also covers pollution and waste from ships connected to the production/installations, and from transport and construction activities (section 9-3).

In 2023, two important areas were opened for offshore wind farms licences in the Norwegian part of the North Sea continental shelf: 'Utsira Nord' and 'Sørlige Nordsjø II'.

374. Act of 4 Jun. 2010 No. 21, as amended by Act of 16 Dec. 2022 No. 96.
375. Regulation of 12 Jun. 2020 No. 1192 on offshore energy.

325. As regards *products,* the Labelling of Consumer Goods Act,[376] Article 6a[377] and 6b gives the government the authority to issue regulations requiring that consumer products give the consumer necessary information about the product's use of energy and other resources, as well as its effects on the environment. This makes it possible to implement such EEA rules in this field as the EU directive on the availability of *consumer information on fuel economy and* CO_2 *and NOx emissions* in marketing new motor vehicles.[378] These rules are laid down in a special regulation.[379] It requires that an energy label has to be always presented close to the price information when a car is exhibited for sale or leasing (Regulation Article 2). The information to be provided is described in Article 3 and is in accordance with the EU rules.

376. Act of 18 Dec. 1981 No. 90.
377. Introduced into the Act by Act of 15 Jun. 2001 No. 89.
378. European Parliament and Council Directive 1999/94/EEC as amended by Directive 2003/73/EC and recommended in Recommendation (EU) 2017/948.
379. Regulation of 11 Jul. 2001 No. 829 on energy-labelling of new vehicles.

Chapter 3. Water and Marine Pollution

§1. Overview

326. Water is abundant in Norway. The country has numerous rivers, lakes, glaciers, and deep fjords, and a long coastline facing the Skagerak, the North Sea, the Norwegian Sea, and the Barents Sea. Furthermore, most of the country is sparsely populated. Therefore, there are fewer problems of water supply and water quality in Norway than in most other countries. A national survey from 2013 indicates that more than half of Norway's freshwater sources are in very good (14%) or good (43%) ecological condition. However, the survey also showed that the ecological condition was moderate (29%), bad (11%) or very bad (3%) in a considerable part of the water sources. In some parts of the country, there are significant pollution problems. These are partly not only due to long-range transport of air pollution but also due to the discharge of wastewater from urban centres and runoff from agriculture. In many local communities, the quality of the drinking water, which is usually taken from surface water sources, is not satisfactory. Industrial emissions result in the levels of heavy metals and other toxic substances in many fjords and watercourses being too high.

Marine pollution is also caused by discharge from vessels and petroleum activities on the continental shelf. The sea and the coast are also polluted by solid waste and refuse, often dumped from ships. Marine pollution is also transported to Norway's coast from other sea areas. The periodic algal blooming in coastal waters is most likely an effect of this.

So, for a long time, Norway has been faced with a number of water pollution problems. This has been a priority for environmental policy and law.

327. The work in this field in Norway is partly based on international agreements and obligations. The country puts a great deal of effort into implementing the international rules to reduce emissions according to the agreed timetables.

The States bordering the North Sea have, over several decades, developed a close cooperation with the objective of reducing the emissions of toxic substances and nutrients (phosphorus and nitrogen) into the sea. This necessitates reduction of pollution of the sea from land-based sources, and thus freshwater pollution in general. Common objectives were established early through biannual negotiations (the North Sea Agreements). More specifically, binding restrictions on emissions of toxic substances have been codified in particular within the framework of the *OSPAR Convention on the prevention of pollution of the North-East Atlantic*. This has had an important impact on the work to reduce water pollution in Norway.

The EU directives in the field of water management and pollution apply to Norway. It is evident that the *EC Framework Water Directive* for community action in the field of water policy (EU WFD) is a decisive element in future water resource policy and management in general, and pollution control in particular.[380] We shall

380. Directive 2000/60/EC.

come back to this at the end of this section, after having presented the main legislation on water pollution as it stands in 2021.

328. The national strategic objective in this field is to ensure water quality in freshwater resources and in the sea which contributes to maintaining species and ecosystems, and ensuring people's health and well-being.

Since 2005, the main focus has been on Norway's implementation of the EU WFD. The national objective today is that discharges of phosphorous, nitrogen and particles into freshwater sources and the sea, and other types of pollution, shall be reduced to a level that ensures *a good ecological condition*, in accordance with the directive. No water resource shall be declassified according to the requirements of the directive. The risk of environmental damage due to accidental pollution should be at an 'acceptable' level.

329. The *PCA* is the main instrument for the prevention and reduction of water pollution, including marine pollution. It applies equally to pollution of freshwater, groundwater, coastal waters and the sea from stationary sources, including petroleum installations on the continental shelf. Regular pollution from mobile sources is regulated pursuant to sector legislation.

The *Water Resources Act*[381] supplements the PCA. It lays down general rules and principles for the management of freshwater resources, although not directly treating pollution issues. It lays down a general rule of care for everybody in order to avoid damage or inconvenience to public and private interests in the watercourse (Article 8). It establishes a concession system for activities that may have such an effect (Chapter 3). We shall return to this Act *infra* in Part II, Chapter 8.

Of particular importance for the *marine pollution* problem are regular discharges and accidental spills from ships.[382] The rules and regulations concerning the *prevention* of pollution from ships are based on the shipping legislation, mainly the *Ship Safety and Security Act*[383] and regulations pursuant to that Act. Liability for pollution damage due to accidents at sea is regulated in the general *Maritime Act*.[384] When a pollution accident occurs, the general rules on rights, obligations, and liability in the PCA also apply.

Also, the *Product Control Act* is of importance as a tool to limit diffuse pollution through the use and waste disposal of products containing substances that are hazardous to the aquatic and marine environment. We shall return to this Act in relation to hazardous substances in more detail in Chapter 8 *infra.*

330. Spatial planning pursuant to the *PBA*[385] is an important tool for integrated land-use and water resource planning. Approved plans lay down guidelines for the application of the PCA and other sectoral Acts. The implementation of the WFD is

381. Act of 24 Nov. 2000 No. 82.
382. For example, it is estimated that spills from ships cause nearly 40% of the oil pollution of the seas.
383. Act of 16 Feb. 2007 No. 9.
384. Act of 24 Jun. 1994 No. 39.
385. Act of 27 Jun. 2008 No. 71, *see infra* §2, I and Part III.

linked to the system of planning and plans pursuant to this Act. In addition, some sectoral legislation applies to specific issues.

331. The protection of drinking water sources is based on relevant legislation for the protection of health. The general Regulation on Water Supply and Drinking Water[386] has been issued pursuant to the Act on Food Production and Food Safety (The Food Act)[387] and the Act on Municipal Health and Care Services (Public Health Act)[388] (*see supra* Chapter 1, §4). The regulation implements the EU rules in the field.[389] It lays down a licensing system for drinking water supply. This is mainly a municipal task. Protection against pollution is essential. In fact, the municipality may prohibit any activity that may present a risk of pollution of the water in a water supply system.

§2. Water Pollution from Land-Based, Stationary Sources

I. The General System of Control of Water Pollution

332. This section covers *water pollution from stationary sources*. It includes pollution of surface freshwater in rivers and lakes, of groundwater, and of coastal water. The main legal instruments are the same for the pollution of these various recipients, while the more detailed rules and regulations, such as conditions in pollution permits, may vary.

333. The management and use of water resources fall under the general planning system pursuant to the *PBA*. Through comprehensive regional and municipal planning, general objectives and guidelines may be drawn up for the use of lakes and other parts of a watercourse, and of the land bordering them. These plans may define the types of building and other activities which may be carried out in and alongside a watercourse, and lay down legally binding restrictions. Based on the wording, they may also to some extent lay down rules and regulations concerning the discharge of pollutants and water quality objectives. In practice, mainly the pollution legislation with regulations is applied. Many types of installations and activities that may influence water flow or water quality are also regulated by the *Water Resources Act*.[390] We shall return to these issues in more detail in Part II, Chapter 8 and Part III *infra*.

334. The PCA is the main piece of legislation as regards water pollution from stationary sources. Pursuant to the Act, ambient *water quality standards* may be established for various types of recipients through regulations. Until recently, no

386. Regulation of 22 Dec. 2016 No. 1868.
387. Act of 19 Dec. 2003 No. 124.
388. Act of 24 Jun. 2011 No. 29.
389. Directive 98/83/EEC as amended by Directive (EU) 2015/1787.
390. Act of 24 Nov. 2000 No. 82.

such regulations had been issued, but this is now rapidly changing with the implementation of the WFD, *see* §2, V *infra*.

335. For pollution from industrial activities, individual *pollution permits* issued pursuant to the PCA are the main instrument. Also, several regulations have been issued, for example, regulations related to discharge of wastewater with oil content from petrol stations, bus terminals and so on,[391] pollution from the cleaning and impregnating of fish farming nets,[392] discharges from factories for fish food[393] and water pollution from agricultural activities (*see infra* III).

336. As far as discharge into water of particularly *harmful substances* is concerned, a series of EU directives on emission limits and water quality levels provide an important set of norms. These have been fully incorporated into Norwegian law through a regulation pursuant to the PCA.[394]

II. The Discharge and Treatment of Wastewater and Sewage

337. The general prohibition to pollute in the PCA applies fully to the discharge of wastewater and sewage. Thus, the law requires that ordinary wastewater and sewage from households, offices, farms, industry, and so on are treated in accordance with general rules and local regulations.

338. The Act has a special chapter, Chapter 4, on wastewater and sewage treatment from households and so on. This is mainly the responsibility of the municipality, under the supervision of the State pollution control authorities. In addition, there are rules on this matter in the *PBA*, in a special *Act on Municipal Water and Sewage Charges,*[395] and in various national and local regulations pursuant to these acts.

In this field, the main tasks are left to the municipality serving as pollution control authority. The issuing of permits is often closely related to land-use plans and the system of building permits pursuant to the PBA, which is applied mainly by the municipal planning and building authorities.

339. According to the *PBA* (Article 27-2), no building is permitted unless there is *a proper solution to the discharge of wastewater*, pursuant to the pollution legislation. There is as the main rule a duty to connect to an existing sewer if it is in the vicinity of the building, but the municipality may accept another solution if

391. Regulation of 1 Jun. 2004 No. 931 Ch. 15, pursuant to both the Pollution Control Act and the Product Control Act.
392. Regulation of 1 Jun. 2004 No. 931 Ch. 25.
393. Regulation of 1 Jun. 2004 No. 931 Ch. 26.
394. Regulation of 1 Jun. 2004 No. 931 Ch. 17. The regulation incorporates the following EU directives into Norwegian law: (1) Council Directives on discharge into water: 76/464/EEC, 82/176/EEC, 84/156/EEC, 84/491/EEC, 86/280/EEC, with amendments by Directives 88/347/EEC and 90/415/EEC; (2) Council Directives on groundwater: 80/68/EEC, with amendments by Directive 91/692/EEC.
395. Act of 16 Mar. 2012 No. 12, *see infra*.

the costs are disproportionate or in case of special circumstances. An individual permit is then needed in accordance with national regulations related to the discharge from small sewage installations.[396] This regulation gives the municipalities the authority to issue individual permits for this purpose on the basis of applications. The rules related to the pollution permit system of the PCA apply. If local pollution conditions make it necessary, the municipality may issue local discharge regulations (Pollution Regulation Article 12-6).

340. Chapter 4 of the PCA lays down *several special rules* related to the discharge and treatment of wastewater, and sewers. They cover both sanitary and industrial wastewater, and rainwater runoff (Article 21). These are supplemented by general and detailed rules applying to wastewater and sewage treatment laid down in the Pollution Regulation.[397]

The pollution control authority may lay down special requirements for sewers, by regulations or in individual permits. They may decide whether all wastewater shall be transported in a common sewer or whether separate sewers shall be required for different types of wastewater (Article 22 paragraph 1). In urban and other built-up areas, connection to a municipal sewer is most often required.

It may be decided in a pollution permit for a wastewater treatment plant that it shall be constructed in such a way that it can receive wastewater from another municipality or another property. The Act contains rules on the division of costs in such a case (Article 22 paragraph 3).

As far as such emissions from industrial production are concerned, it is up to the pollution control authority to decide whether they may be discharged into the general municipal sewer and treatment plants, with or without a pretreatment, or whether they must be treated entirely separately and/or by the industry itself. This depends mainly on the type of pollutants in question, and its location.

The pollution control authority may decide that wastewater may be conducted through a wastewater treatment facility belonging to another person (Article 23 paragraph 1).

341. The discharge of wastewater and sewage is subject to a pollution permit according to the rules of the PCA. In general, wastewater and sewage must be treated, in order to remove the most serious pollutants such as phosphorus and nitrogen. Based on the North Sea Agreements the requirements vary somewhat according to the conditions in and other uses of the recipient water. There is a general distinction in the Pollution Regulation between 'sensitive areas', 'normal areas', and 'less sensitive areas'. 'Sensitive areas' are mainly the southeastern part of the Norwegian coast with corresponding river basins. Here the regulation is stricter than elsewhere. The rest of the freshwater resources are 'normal areas', and most of the coast is 'less sensitive areas'.[398]

---

396. Regulation of 1 Jun. 2004 No. 931 Ch. 12 pursuant to the Pollution Control Act. These rules apply to discharge from up to fifty 'person units'. A 'person unit' corresponds to the definition of BOF5 in the EU Directive 91/271/EEC on urban wastewater treatment.
397. Regulation of 1 Jun. 2004 No. 931 Chs. 11–16.
398. Regulation of 1 Jun. 2004 No. 931 Ch. 11, in particular Annex 1 to Art. 11-6.

The more detailed rules are laid down in the Pollution Regulation. The rules distinguish between sanitary wastewater from 'smaller' and 'bigger' urban areas.[399] With 'smaller urban areas' is meant areas with up to 2,000 persons-equivalents (p.e.) for discharge to freshwater sources and estuaries, and 10,000 for discharge into the sea. Bigger urban areas are areas that exceed these limits. For these the rules of the EU directive on the subject (Directive 91/271/EEC as amended by Directive 98/15/EC) apply.

The general rules on conditions, procedure, and so on in Chapter 3 of the PCA apply. For the building of a wastewater treatment plant for population equivalents greater than 150,000 an EIA is required pursuant to the PBA and the corresponding regulation[400] (*see* General Introduction, Chapter 2, §4).

342. The *costs* of construction, operation and maintenance of wastewater treatment installations operated by the municipality shall be borne by the municipality (PCA Article 25 paragraph 1).

In this case, the municipality may require its costs to be met in full or in part by collecting *charges* pursuant to the rules in the *Act on Municipal Water and Sewage Charges.*[401]

This Act lays down the principle that all new main water and sewage installations shall be owned by the municipality. Existing installations may be sold only to the municipality (Article 1). On certain conditions, however, and based on individual concession, the municipality may permit the establishment of a private water and sewage system or a joint of several private installations (Article 2). The Act authorizes the municipalities to charge for the connection of municipal water supply and sewer. When a property is connected to the municipal system it has to pay the municipal water and sewage charges (Article 3).

The Act also prescribes an annual user charge. The municipality decides the level of the two types of charges, within a framework which is defined in the State Pollution Regulation.[402] The basic principle is that the charges may not exceed the real costs of the municipality for water supply and sanitation respectively (Regulation Article 16-1). The owner of the property is responsible for the payment of charges, even if the property is wholly or partly hired out (Regulation Article 16-2). The charges may vary according to the real costs connected to different types of properties or buildings, or different facilities. They may also vary if the wastewater contains other types of pollution than are normally found in wastewater from ordinary households (Regulation Article 16-5).

343. The municipality is responsible for the *operation and maintenance of wastewater treatment facilities* that are wholly or partly owned by it. In the case of private facilities, the owner of the property for which the facility was originally built is responsible for operation and maintenance. The pollution control authority may, however, decide otherwise. The authority may also lay down specific regulations on

399. Regulation of 1 Jun. 2004 No. 931 Chs. 13 and 14, respectively.
400. Regulation of 21 Jun. 2017 No. 854 Annex I No. 14.
401. Act of 16 Mar. 2012 No. 12, *see supra*.
402. Regulation of 1 Jun. 2004 No. 931 Ch. 16.

the construction, operation and maintenance of such installations, including on the necessary qualifications of personnel (PCA Article 24).

The municipality is also responsible for the *emptying of small wastewater treatment plants* such as sludge separators and sedimentation tanks for removal of sludge for sanitary wastewater and rainwater runoff, as well as for collection tanks for untreated sanitary waste. The municipality may collect the necessary fees to cover the costs (PCA Article 26).

Sludge from wastewater treatment plants, sludge separators and so on may under certain conditions be used in agriculture through spreading on agricultural land. The possible uses and conditions are defined in a regulation on manure of organic origin.[403] The regulation (Articles 25–27) lays down strict maximum limits of heavy metals in the sludge, requirements of area size, classification of the quality of the sludge and allowed use areas for the different qualities, so on. The main purpose of the restrictions is to avoid pollution of the soil from hazardous substances in the sludge, and most importantly of soil on areas used for food production (*see infra* III).

III. Water Pollution from Agriculture

344. Agriculture is a major source of water pollution in some parts of Norway. Serious eutrophication of several lakes and rivers is mainly due to runoff from agricultural land, and the discharge from grass silos.

As mentioned, 'ordinary pollution' from agriculture is not in itself prohibited according to the PCA. However, the Act (Article 8) states explicitly that the pollution control authorities may issue regulations pursuant to Article 9 of the Act with specific restrictions and if necessary prohibitions to prevent and reduce pollution from any agricultural activity.

In addition to some regulations pursuant to the PCA, the agricultural authorities have issued several regulations pursuant to the *Agricultural Land Act*[404] to reduce the negative environmental effects of agriculture. The State has established several economic incentives for investments and activities to this effect.

345. The above-mentioned comprehensive Regulation on manure of organic origin[405] lays down rules and restrictions on the *production, storage and spreading of manure, and on placing manure on the market.* One of its objectives is to prevent pollution of freshwater and the sea, as well as air pollution and stench; it also aims to manage the soil wisely and protect biodiversity through the optimal use of manure as a resource in agriculture (Regulation Article 1). The phosphorous content is the most critical factor in relation to water pollution from spreading manure.

The regulation covers all sorts of manure of organic origin, such as manure from farm animals, outflow of grass silos, sewage sludge, and compost products. It lays down a general duty of internal control for all activities covered by the regulation

403. Regulation of 4 Jul. 2003 No. 951 with later amendments, pursuant to the Agricultural Land Act, the Pollution Control Act, and the Food Act. The regulation implements Directive 86/278/EEC.
404. Act of 12 May 1995 No. 23.
405. Regulation of 4 Jul. 2003 No. 951.

(Articles 5–8). It also lays down rules on the production of manure for use, such as quality requirements. There are maximum limits for heavy metals in the manure. Production and import of organic manure shall be registered and reported to the Norwegian Food Safety Authority. Articles 18–21 lay down general and more specific rules on the storage and Articles 22–27 on the use of manure. The storage must be done in such a way that pollution is avoided.

The general rule is that spreading of manure from one 'manure unity' requires 1 acre (4 daa) of fully cultivated land. One 'manure unity' is defined in an annex to the regulation, in relation to various farm animals. For example, it corresponds to one cow, two horses, seven sheep or goats, eighty hens, or three hundred ducks. In areas with serious pollution, the municipality may require a bigger area per unit (Article 24 No. 1 paragraph 5). The municipality may also approve smaller areas, on the basis of individual applications (Article 24 No. 1 paragraph 2).

The spreading of manure should preferably take place in the spring, and not later than 1 September as the general rule (Article 23 paragraph 2). Manure which is spread on an open field must be mixed into the soil as soon as possible and at least within eighteen hours.

IV. Regulations Concerning Detergents

346. In order to reduce water pollution by *phosphates in detergents,* a regulation[406] lays down strict maximum levels of phosphate in detergents which are produced in Norway or imported for sale or use in Norway. For example, it is prohibited to produce, import or place on the market detergents for washing clothes or general cleaning with a higher content of phosphorus (in weight) than 0.2%. For detergents for washing-up machines, the level is 3.8%. Also, the regulation requires producers and importers of detergents to label detergent packaging, showing not only the name of the product and the trademark of the company but also whether it contains phosphate or not. The regulation incorporates the relevant EU rules.[407]

V. Implementation of the EU Water Framework Directive

347. The EU WFD[408] is 'EEA relevant', has been included in the EEA Agreement and applies fully to Norway. The stated purpose of the directive is to 'establish a framework for the protection of inland surface waters, transitional waters, coastal waters and groundwater'. This includes the protection and prevention of deterioration of aquatic ecosystems, promotion of sustainable water use,

406. Regulation of 1 Jun. 2004 No. 922 Art. 2-12 and 2-14. *See also infra* Ch. 8, §1, III, B.
407. Regulation (EC) 648/2004 on detergents with amendments in Regulation (EC) 907/2006, Regulation (EC) 1336/2008, Regulation (EC) 551/2009, and Regulation (EC) 259/2012.
408. Directive 2000/60/EC of the European Parliament and of the Council of 23 Oct. 2000 establishing a framework for community action in the field of water policy, with later amendments.

reduction of emissions and discharges, reduction of groundwater pollution and mitigating the effects of floods and droughts.[409]

348. The WFD implies *an ecosystem approach* to the management of the rivers, lakes and coastal waters. It requires that:

> Member States shall identify the individual river basins lying within their national territory and, for the purposes of this Directive, shall assign them to individual River Basin Districts (RBD).[410]

Thus, a RBD means the area of land and sea, made up of one or more neighbouring river basins together with their associated groundwaters and coastal waters, which is identified as the main unit for management of river basins.

The directive seeks to achieve a more consistent approach to water management by framing the decisions related to the environment by sectors and planning authorities at all levels through *binding water quality objectives.* The aim is to reach 'good ecological status' and 'good chemical status' in all water bodies. 'Good ecological status' refers to the status of plants, animals and other living organisms in the water. 'Good chemical status' is about the quantity and concentration of hazardous substances in the water.

For water resources that have good environmental status today, the aim is to keep this status, and if possible improve it. For watercourses that today are 'heavily modified' the objective is an improvement to 'good ecological potential'. The Directive lays down detailed provisions for assessment and monitoring of a number of chemical and ecological parameters in the water environment, with objectives at the outset to be reached within a fifteen-year deadline.

The directive requires that each Member State shall ensure the establishment for each RBD, or for the part of an international RBD within its territory, of *a Programme of measures*, in order to achieve the established objectives.[411] For each RBD, a *River basin management plan* shall be elaborated and adopted.[412] This forms the basis for the programme of measures.

349. The situation in Norway at the outset is that some 70% of the water has very good or good status. In 25% the quality is not good enough.[413] So, also Norway has a job to do. The implementation of the directive is clearly *a challenge to Norway's legal and administrative system* in the field of water management and environmental management in general. This system has neither been based on natural geographical and hydrological units nor on binding quality objectives. Instead, it focuses on regulating activities related to water, including pollution sources, within

409. Directive Art. 1.
410. Directive Art. 3.
411. Directive Art. 11.
412. Directive Art. 13.
413. For 5% of the water the quality situation is not entirely clear.

the different sectors and sector legislation, mainly through widely formulated, discretionary rules, rather than the quality of the watercourse itself. The implementation of the directive has raised the question of how environmental objectives in the WFD may limit various sector authorities' policy formulation as well as the exercise of discretion in individual cases. To reach the water quality objectives a much closer cooperation and coordination between the various sectors and a better integration of water issues into spatial and land-use planning have been necessary.

350. The implementation of the WFD in Norway is mainly based on three Acts: the PCA, the Water Resources Act, and the PBA provide the necessary legal foundation for the implementation. In addition, necessary rules may also be laid down pursuant to the NDA.[414] Pursuant to these Acts, the Regulation on the framework for water management ('the Framework regulation'),[415] adopted in December 2006, describes the system in detail. It is supplemented by rules on water pollution in the general Pollution Regulation.[416] In addition, the Aquaculture Act also applies, as the regulation also covers coastal waters out to one nautical mile from the baseline. The aim is to provide a framework for establishing water quality objectives that ensure holistic protection and sustainable use of the water resources and ensure that approved regional management plans and related programmes of measures are assessed and updated every six years (Regulation Article 1). The MCE and MPE have together the overall responsibility for the implementation at the central level, but several other ministries and their subordinate authorities participate in the work and are responsible for the implementation of management plans and programmes of measures. The NEA has an important initiating and coordinating function.

351. Norway is divided into fourteen *RBDs*, of which ten run to the Norwegian coast and four to Sweden; these are joined to Swedish watercourses and thus form international RBDs.

The RBDs coincide to a large extent with the ordinary administrative system of ten counties, with some minor border adjustments. One RBD covers two counties. The county municipality within each RBD is made the competent authority according to the WFD.

The RBD Authority shall define, assess and update the environmental objectives for the various watercourses within the river basin. It is responsible for the coordination of the work with management plans and programmes of measures and other activities required by the regulation within the RBD. This is to be done in close cooperation with a RBD Committee. This committee consists of relevant authorities at the regional and local level such as the county governor departments of environment and agriculture, the regional offices of the Norwegian Water Resources and Energy Directorate and other relevant State agencies, the chief

414. Pursuant to a new explicit Art. 26a adopted in 2018.
415. Regulation of 15 Dec. 2006 No. 1446 with later amendments. It preceded with more than two years the formal inclusion of the WFD into the EEA Agreement by the Norwegian Parliament on 12 Feb. 2009.
416. Regulation of 1 Jun. 2004 No. 931, in particular its Ch. 16.

county medical officer, and municipal and county authorities. Furthermore, a consultative body with representatives of private and public interests in the watercourses is attached to the work.

352. According to Article 29 in the WFD Regulation the *regional management plans* for each RBD shall be prepared and adopted as *regional plans pursuant to the PBA*.[417] This implies a broad and transparent process involving all relevant authorities and interests. The plans are approved by the County Councils (the elected body at county level in Norway), and finally approved by the MCE in cooperation with the MPE. They formed the basis for further analysis and the implementation programmes – the *programmes of measures* – which are to be elaborated for each subdistrict within the RBD. The implementation programme is cross-sectoral. It defines precise measures and decisions to be taken by the various responsible authorities in order to reach the environmental objectives in the management plan.

353. The first country-wide *planning* in accordance with the Framework regulation (and the EU WFD) took place in Norway from 2010 to 2015. During this period, the management plans from the twenty-nine pilot districts were elaborated.

354. The first ordinary and country-wide *implementation* phase of Regional water management plans and Regional programmes of measures were approved by the Government in July 2016 for all the water regions, and this was reported to the ESA. They go from 2016 to the end of 2021

The second country-wide *planning* phase and updating and revision of already adopted plans has taken place from 2016 to 2021 and shall be fulfilled by the end of 2021, with implementation between 2022 and 2027, and the third planning phase from 2022 to 2028 with implementation from 2028 to 2033, and measures operational from 2028. Hence, this water planning system is a long-term commitment.

355. The WFD Regulation has an important legal effect. It necessitates a new type of cross-sectoral planning within the general framework of regional, spatial and land-use planning in Norway. The approved management plans and programmes of measures may not automatically and in themselves be legally binding in the strict sense, on the various authorities in their planning and decision-making. Their legal nature in this respect may become an issue for further discussion. But they will certainly form a very important framework and basis for sector policy and numerous decisions. The system affects the implementation of a number of Acts, such as land-use plans pursuant to the PBA, permits pursuant to the PCA, the Water Resources Act, and the Aquaculture Act, and the application of the NDA, just to mention the most important.

The main rule is that the quality of the water resources may not be reduced or deteriorate. This forms the basis and frame for any decision that may affect the water quality and means that strict limits and conditions have to be laid down, for example, in pollution permits pursuant to the PCA or the PBA. However, this rule is not without exceptions. In accordance with the WFD Article 4(7), the Norwegian

417. *See infra* Part III.

water regulation Article 12 states that new activities or new encroachments may be accepted even if they may reduce the water quality or make it more difficult to reach the targets. The conditions are that:

- this is due to changes in the physical characteristics of a surface water source or a change of water level in a groundwater source;
- or due to new sustainable human development activities that reduce the water quality from 'very good' to 'good' (and not to even lower quality).

In addition, the following conditions must be fulfilled:

- all practicable steps are taken to mitigate the adverse impact on the status of the body of water;
- the benefits to society outweigh the loss of reduced water quality; and

356. – the beneficial objectives served by the modifications or alterations of the water body cannot for reasons of technical feasibility or disproportionate cost be achieved by other means, which are a significantly better environmental option.A particular issue in the implementation of the WFD in Norway is *the consequences for the production of hydropower*. Many important rivers have been strictly regulated, and water has been diverted from the natural river course with the objective of producing maximum electric power. As a consequence, considerable parts of many Norwegian rivers have too little water under normal circumstances to uphold a good ecological status. In order to fulfil the requirements of the Water Regulation (and the WFD), changes have to be made to a number of existing concessions for hydropower production. More water has to go into the natural river, resulting most likely in less production of electric power. Until 2021, several existing concessions have been revised along these lines, and more are to come. In general, the legal basis for this is found in the possibilities offered in the concession itself which makes changes possible under certain conditions.

§3. Pollution of the Sea from Ships and Dumping

I. Rules Concerning Regular Discharge from Vessels

357. Shipping is an important industry with a long tradition in Norway. The majority of the population lives along its long coast, and the country has one of the world's major merchant fleets. So, the problem of pollution from ships is an important field in Norwegian environmental law and policy.

The discharge of pollutants from ships is a significant source of marine pollution. First and foremost, major oil spills due to accidents may seriously damage life in the sea, as well as bird life and property along the shoreline.[418] Similarly, accidents

418. There have in fact been several serious shipwrecks along the Norwegian coast during the last decades, resulting in major oil spills.

with ships transporting hazardous substances may result in ecological disasters. But also smaller spills and discharges from the day-to-day running of ships contribute to marine pollution.

The national and international rules concerning liability for damage from pollution accidents are important in this connection. These issues will be further discussed in Part IV *infra.*

In this section, we shall look at the rules related to the control of *pollution from ordinary shipping activities,* and various *rules to prevent accidents* and limit the damage when an accident risk occurs. To a large extent, the national legislations in these areas reflect international rules.

358. The PCA does not apply to *regular* pollution from individual means of transport, such as vessels. Instead, these issues are regulated by the *Ship Safety Act.*[419] This Act applies to Norwegian vessels of more than 24 m in length wherever they are geographically. Within the limitations of international law, it also applies to foreign vessels in Norwegian territorial waters, and in the EEZ, and on Norway's continental shelf (Article 3).

359. The Act lays down important principles and provides a framework for more detailed regulation of pollution from ships. The Act has a special chapter on 'Environmental safety' (Chapter 5). It covers discharges into the sea of all types of substances, including deliberate dumping of waste, as well as emissions into the air. It does not apply to activities related to exploration, extraction and exploitation of petroleum and other natural resources on the continental shelf. There are several comprehensive regulations on pollution pursuant to this Act, and in particular its Chapter 5.[420]

360. The Ship Safety Act itself lays down *general principles and rules with regard to the prevention of pollution* and other environmental effects from ships. As the main rule, pollution by discharge or dumping or by burning of hazardous substances is prohibited, unless in accordance with other rules in the Act or regulations pursuant to the Act. Exceptions are if pollution is necessary for the ship's safety, health reasons, to save lives, or if it is caused by damage to the ship and all reasonable measures have been taken to prevent it (Article 31).

A ship shall be designed, built and equipped in such a way that no pollution in violation of Article 31 is caused (Article 32). It shall be run and managed in such a way that pollution is avoided (Article 33). It shall be properly equipped and have a contingency plan to prevent and if necessary limit and abate any pollution that may be caused (Article 34). If there is a risk of pollution, it has to immediately inform the relevant authority and report on planned measures to limit the effects. After the incident a report must be presented to the authority.

---

419. Act of 16 Feb. 2007 No. 9.

420. There are a great number of important regulations with the objective of preventing accidents. Many of these were revised through a new set of regulations of 4 Jun. 2002 and 30 Jun. 2003. These regulations will not be treated further here.

Furthermore, a ship shall deliver hazardous substances to special reception facilities onshore if these substances cannot be treated properly on board the ship (Article 35).

A ship that is permanently taken out of operation shall be disposed of in such a way that there is no health or environmental risk (Article 36).

The ship's captain is responsible for the implementation of the rules regarding the management of the ship in order to prevent pollution and corresponding regulations (Article 37). Other members of the ship's crew have a duty to contribute to the prevention of pollution in their respective positions and functions (Article 38).

With regard to all these issues, the authorities may lay down detailed regulations. In Norway, the responsibility in this field is shared between the Ministry of Trade, Industry and Fisheries and the MCE. The MCE is the primary responsible ministry for the regulation of pollution from ships, working in close cooperation with the Norwegian Maritime Authority and other relevant agencies.

361. The main regulation pursuant to the chapter on environmental safety is the general *Regulation on the Environmental Safety for Ships and Movable Installations.*[421] This regulation, and in particular its many annexes, contains a comprehensive and rather complex set of rules of mainly technical character. It covers all types of pollution and waste from ships. It builds on, and implements, the International Convention for the Prevention of Pollution from Ships (MARPOL) of 1973 with amendments of 1978 and consolidated version of 2017 and the various technical regulations pursuant to this convention, to which Norway is a party. The Regulation mainly refers to these rules and incorporates them in annexes to the Regulation. It also incorporates the many EU directives and regulations in this field.[422]

As the Act itself, the regulation applies to Norwegian ships, including recreational boats, and moveable (petroleum) installations. Within the framework of international law it also applies to foreign ships and installations within Norway's territorial waters, EEZ and continental shelf. In accordance with the MARPOL rules, foreign ships that voluntarily go to a Norwegian port are also subject to the rules on prevention of oil spill accidents and pollution accidents by hazardous liquid substances transported in bulk.

362. The rules cover such issues as:

- documentation of the content of the goods;
- prevention of oil pollution from ships and movable installations (MARPOL Annex I) (Article 4);
- prevention of pollution from hazardous liquid substances transported in bulk (MARPOL Annex II) (Article 7);

421. Regulation of 30 May 2012 No. 488, with later amendments, the most recent in Regulation of 17 Dec. 2020 No. 2985.
422. Directive 98/34/EC, Directive 93/12/EC with later amendments, Directive 96/98/EC, Directive 2000/59/EC with later amendments, Regulation (EU) No. 53/2012, Regulation (EC) No. 782/2003 amended by Regulation (EC) No. 536/2008, Directive 2005/35 EC amended by Directive 2009/123/EC, Directive 2016/802/EU, and Directive 2001/81/EC.

- prevention of pollution from sewage from ships and movable installations (MARPOL Annex IV) (Article 9);
- prohibition of discharge of sewage and wastewater in Norwegian waters;
- prevention of pollution from waste (MARPOL Annex V);
- prevention of air pollution from ships and movable installations (MARPOL Annex VI) (Article 12);
- international certificates (Article 18).

For example, the MARPOL Annex II on pollution of hazardous liquids transported in bulk lays down detailed rules on the construction of ships transporting various types of hazardous substances, handling of substances during loading and unloading, equipment, measures and routines to control and monitor possible pollution, registration and certificates, inspection by maritime authorities and so on.

Use of *organic tin components in ship paint* was prohibited in 1993. The rules were amended in 2003 and are incorporated into the Regulation (Article 17).[423]

363. One set of rules deals with the prevention of pollution from *waste disposal*. A ship (the captain) has the duty to deliver waste to reception facilities onshore (Article 16). As laid down in MARPOL Annex IV, it is generally prohibited to discharge plastics in any form into the sea. In special, closed sea areas such as the Mediterranean, the North Sea, and the Baltic Sea, it is also prohibited to discharge all other types of waste from the running of the ship, except food refuse which may be discharged outside 12 nautical miles from the nearest shore. Outside these special areas, other types of waste than plastics may be discharged outside 25 nautical miles from the nearest shore (12 nautical miles for food refuse).

364. The municipalities and port authorities may be ordered to establish adequate *facilities to receive and treat waste from ships*. A special chapter in the Pollution Regulation[424] with detailed annexes lays down more specific rules, which implement international (MARPOL) and EU rules in the field.[425]

An adequate system for the reception of waste – including waste oil – and load remains from ships is to be established in every port. This is the responsibility of the owner of the port, the port authority or the municipality, depending on the ownership of the port (the 'port responsible'). The responsibility includes receiving the waste and remains and disposing of it in accordance with a suitable plan. Such a plan is to be developed in cooperation with interested parties and be in accordance with technical rules laid down in an annex to the regulation. Regional plans may be developed.

The ship captain is responsible for informing the port of expected delivery of waste in due course before arrival, and for actually delivering waste and load remains to the reception facilities in the port.

423. Regulation (EC) 782/2003.

424. Regulation of 1 Jun. 2004 No. 931 Ch. 20 on delivery and reception of waste and load remains from ships, pursuant to both the Ship Safety Act, the Pollution Control Act and the Act of 26 Jun. 1998 No. 47 on recreational and small boats.

425. Directive 2000/59/EC as amended by Directive 2002/84/EC, Directive 2007/71/EC, Directive 2010/65/EU and Directive (EU) 2015/2087.

The costs of running the reception facilities and receiving the waste shall be covered by fees paid by the ships. The regulation gives detailed rules on how to calculate the fees. Intentional or negligent violation of the rules may be punished with fines or a maximum of a four-month term of imprisonment.

365. The rules on *discharge of sewage and wastewater in Norwegian (territorial) waters* are found in the Regulation on the Environmental Safety for Ships and Movable Installations Article 10. Increasingly, such discharge is polluting fjords and coastal waters in Norway. The rules generally prohibit the discharge of wastewater and sewage from ships in watercourses and in coastal waters closer than 300 m from the nearest shore, including islands. This prohibition applies to all types of ships, including recreational boats, as well as movable rigs, unless they have a cleaning equipment in accordance with the MARPOL rule IV/9.1 requirements. If not, the ships must instal necessary tanks on board in order to comply with this rule. Ships to which the MARPOL rule IV/2 applies may discharge sewage at a certain distance from the shore in the sea area between Norway and Denmark.

The Norwegian Maritime Authority may nevertheless in special situations give exceptions from these rules for ships which do not fall under MARPOL rule IV/2, for example, for ships that are particularly valuable and protected as cultural heritage, and these requirements will be in conflict with the ship's protection value (Article 10, paragraph 4).

If necessary, a municipality may lay down stricter rules for ships not certified for international navigation and of either more than 400 gross tons or certified to transport more than fifteen persons. This follows from Chapter 23 of the general Pollution Regulation.[426] In this, they shall take into account the access to onshore reception facilities. The municipality may also lay down less strict rules, provided that the environmental effects have been properly assessed. Cooperation between several municipalities is encouraged in these matters.

Wilful or negligent violations of this rule are punished by fines or a maximum of a four-month term of imprisonment.

366. Since 2019, Regulation Article 10a lays down special rules for the discharge of sewage and wastewater in the Norwegian fjords which are included in the UNESCO World Heritage site *West Norwegian Fjords Heritage*.[427] Discharge of sewage is prohibited for ships certified for more than fifteen persons, and discharge of wastewater for vessels over 2,500 tons or certified for more than 100 persons. Until 2024, the authorities may allow exceptions for local vessels. These measures are part of a comprehensive set of rules to prevent pollution in the World Heritage Fjords, to least related to air pollution (Article 14a–14e). Exceptions from the rules may be given to vessels protected as cultural heritage (Article 14f).

---

426. Regulation of 1 Jun. 2004 No. 931.

427. These are the Geirangerfjorden/Synnulvsfjorden area, and the Nærøyfjorden/Aurlandsfjorden area. *See* https://www.riksantikvaren.no /en/world-heritage/west-norwegian-fjords.

367. On the issue of *double hull for oil tankers*, Norway follows the EU rules laid down in the 2002 EU regulation.[428] This regulation has forced the phasing out of tankers with single hull and the construction of tankers with double hull faster than according to IMO rules through the key rule in its Article 4 that no oil tanker shall be allowed to operate under the flag of a Member State, nor shall any oil tanker, irrespective of its flag, be allowed to enter into ports or offshore terminals under the jurisdiction of a Member State after the anniversary of the date of delivery of the ship in the year specified in the article, normally thirty years after its construction. The final deadline was 2015, after which date a double hull is generally required as a condition for entering a port in a Member State of EU and Norway.

368. In 2009, Norway adopted a regulation on the prevention of spreading of alien organisms through *ballast water and sediments from ships*. This regulation was amended in 2017.[429] This regulation implements the International Convention for the Control and Management of Ships' Ballast Water and Sediments, adopted by IMO in February 2004 and ratified by Norway in 2006. The Regulation applies to Norwegian ships and movable installation. Within the framework of international law, it also applies to foreign vessels and movable installations in Norway's territorial waters and EEZ and on Norway's continental shelf. It does not apply to ships that are certified to stay within these sea areas, ships not constructed for transport of ballast water, or ships that have permanent ballast water in closed tanks. Furthermore, it does not apply to ships less than 50 m with a maximum of 8 m^3 ballast water capacity or used solely for recreation, competition or rescue operations (Article 1).

The main principle is that ballast water which has been taken on board the ship outside the Region of the Norwegian Sea/the Barents Sea/the North Sea as defined by Annex 1 must be exchanged at a certain distance from land before being unloaded in Norwegian ports. A minimum of 95% of the water must be exchanged. Alternatively, the ballast water must be cleaned before discharge or delivered to a reception facility onshore. As the main rule, unclean ballast water may only be discharged into sea areas of more than 200 m depth and 200 nautical miles from the nearest coast or – if this is not physically possible – at least 50 nautical miles from the nearest coast. The regulation lays down some further exception rules. They do not apply if the captain finds that the replacement may represent a risk to the stability of the ship and thus a danger to the crew or the passengers, due to bad weather or problems with the ship or its equipment. However, the maritime authorities may lay down stricter rules if this is required by extraordinary environmental conditions such as algae blooming.

As an alternative, the ballast water may be cleaned and then discharged, and Regulation Article 2 lays down rules for this. The cleaning must be in accordance with technology accepted by IMO guidelines before it is discharged and contain only a very limited number of organisms capable of living as specified in the article.

---

428. Consolidated Regulation (EC) 417/2002, amended by Commission Regulation (EC) 1163/2009.
429. Regulation of 8 Sep. 2017 No. 1368 on treatment of ballast water on ships and movable installations, pursuant to the Ship Safety Act.

Ships are required to have a *plan* for the management of the ballast water and sediments (Article 7) and to keep a *Ballast Water Record Book* which may be surveyed and inspected in Norwegian ports.

369. For vessels and movable installations, a special system of *environmental declaration* has been established by regulations.[430] This is a voluntary system of reporting on environmental measures taken by the vessel, in order to comply with the existing national and international norms related to discharge of pollution into the sea (and into the air as well). The environmental declaration must be in accordance with specific rules and is addressed to the Norwegian Maritime Authority. The Directorate confirms the reception of the declaration. The ship owner is responsible for the reporting and its correctness.

This system is connected to the tax system for shipping companies. A part of the tax on shipping companies is the 'tonnage tax', pursuant to Articles 8–16 of the general Tax Act.[431] According to the rules, this tax may be reduced for vessels and movable installations which satisfy environmental rules and regulations as laid down by the Norwegian Maritime Authority. The Environmental declaration forms the basis for such a tax reduction.

370. Dumping of waste into the sea is prohibited by Norwegian law. 'Dumping' is defined as the deliberate discharge of waste other than the waste generated by the running of vessels or ordinary fishing activities. This means that it is strictly forbidden to take waste created onshore out into the sea to get rid of it. This has been prohibited in Norway since 1972. The present regulation on the issue dates from 1997.[432] It is based on the general prohibition on dumping pursuant to the OSPAR Convention.[433] The *burning of waste at sea* is also prohibited.[434]

The prohibition also applies to the placement of any material in the sea or watercourse which does not correspond to its initial purpose.

In special cases, however, dumping of some types of substances and material may be permitted, namely mud and stone, waste from the fishing industry, and other types of waste which may create unacceptable risk or damage if they are disposed of on land. Dumping may also be legal due to situations of force majeure, such as bad weather, or a threat to human life or a ship's safety.

Dredging is prohibited without a pollution permit in accordance with the PCA.

371. In the field of maritime law, *the rules on jurisdiction* are particularly important, and complex. It is clear that Norwegian authorities have the jurisdiction necessary to enforce the rules and regulations in relation to Norwegian vessels, that is,

430. Regulation of 28 Nov. 2000 No. 1194 on Environmental Declaration related to Environmental Differentiation for Vessels and Movable Installations as later amended.
431. Act of 26 Mar. 1999 No. 14.
432. Regulation of 1 Jun. 2004 No. 931 Ch. 22 pursuant to both the Ship Safety Act, the Act of 26 Jun. 1998 No. 47 on recreation boats, and the Pollution Control Act.
433. Norway is also party to the international Convention on the Prevention of Marine Pollution by Dumping of Wastes and Other Matter of 1972 ('London Convention').
434. Regulation of 1 Jun. 2004 No. 931 Ch. 21.

vessels sailing under the Norwegian flag. The difficult question is, however, what steps may be taken towards vessels of other nationalities. This is an important question of the international law of the sea.

The rules as presented below are in accordance with the international regime of the law of the sea. Some regulations have been issued pursuant to the PCA, thus partly extending the geographical scope of that Act, pursuant to its Article 3 (*see supra* Chapter 1, §2, II).

372. The Ship Safety and Security Act, Chapters 7 and 8, lay down the necessary legal basis for the authorities' *control, investigation and enforcement* if a ship has violated the rules on prevention of pollution, and there is good reason to believe that it represents an unacceptable risk of damage to the marine environment. They may hold the ship back, or order it to seek harbour, to follow a special sea route, or to unload. Such decisions may be taken regardless of the nationality of the ship.

Within the framework of the international law of the sea, Article 53 of the Act authorizes the authority to stop and board any ship suspected of breach of international or national rules to prevent pollution.

The general framework rules in the Act are supplemented and specified through two regulations: the Regulation on the control of foreign ships and movable installations in Norwegian ports[435] which implements EU law on port State enforcement, etc.,[436] and the special Regulation on investigation, stopping and boarding of foreign ships suspected of violation of environmental rules.[437]

373. Most of the same rules that apply to ships apply to *movable installations for petroleum activity,* such as movable drilling rigs, on the continental shelf. As mentioned, and as follows from the Regulation on Environmental Safety for Ships and Movable Installations, most of the technical rules to prevent pollution from ships also apply to movable installations.

II. Rules Concerning Pollution Accidents at Sea

374. In case of a *pollution accident or a risk of an accident at sea,* such as an oil spill, several important legal questions arise. The question of liability and compensation for damage will be discussed *infra* in Part IV. Here we shall look into the responsibilities for necessary actions, and the jurisdiction of the authorities in this respect.

Contrary to the situation for regular pollution from ships, which is regulated pursuant to the Ship Safety Act, the general rules in the *PCA* apply in cases of accidental pollution from ships, or of a risk of such pollution. According to PCA Article 46, which refers to the general rule in Article 7 of the Act, the responsible person shall take

---

435. Regulation of 24 Nov. 2014 No. 1458 on Port state control, pursuant to the Ship Safety Act.
436. Directive 2009/16/EC as amended by Directive 2013/38/EU, Regulation (EU) 428/2010, Regulation (EC) 802/2010 and Regulation (EC) 801/2010 with later amendments.
437. Regulation of 2 Jul. 2007 No. 850 pursuant to the Ship Safety Act, with later amendments.

reasonable measures to prevent and limit pollution, mitigate the damage and if possible restore the environment. The pollution authorities may order the responsible person to take the necessary actions in this regard (Article 7 paragraph 4).

375. There is no absolute rule in Norwegian law concerning the types of measures to be taken in different accident situations. This is left to the discretion of the responsible party and the authorities. In case of an *oil spill* at sea, the use of booms to collect and contain the oil and of sucking equipment is generally preferred to the use of a chemical dispersant.

A regulation lays down rules for the use and composition of chemical oil spill dispersants and shore cleaning agents.[438] It implements EU rules on the issue.[439] All dispersants and cleaning agents for oil spills must be tested for toxicity and must satisfy strict requirements laid down in Annex 1 to the regulation. Usually, the use of certain dispersants is approved as part of the contingency plan which is required and approved pursuant to Articles 40 and 43 of the PCA (*see supra* Chapter I, §2, VI). The use of dispersants must be authorized in each case if it is not included in the plan (Regulation Article 19-4, paragraph 2). Dispersants shall be used when this method, everything considered, results in the least environmental damage compared to other methods (Regulation Article 19-6). The assessment in this regard must be documented.

376. If the responsible party does not carry out the necessary actions, the authorities, or private parties, may do it *on his/her behalf and at his/her expense*, according to the rules in Articles 74–76 of the PCA. Depending on the magnitude of the accident, the municipality and/or the State pollution control authorities shall take the necessary actions to prevent and limit the damage, and provide adequate cleanup, on the basis of the existing emergency response system and contingency plans pursuant to the rules in the PCA Chapter 6.

377. In order to clarify the types and extent of possible measures that may be taken in such a situation *outside Norwegian territorial waters,* a special regulation has been issued. It defines the competence of the pollution control authorities to take action on the high seas and in Norway's Extended Economic Zone in case of pollution or risk of pollution of the sea by oil or other substances due to an accident at sea.[440] Experience from several shipwrecks along the Norwegian coast during the last decade illustrates clearly the need for these rules.

The regulation gives the authorities the right to take all necessary measures to prevent or limit serious and imminent risk of damage to the coastline or interests attached to it (Regulation Article 3). Such measures may be to take the vessel away

438. Regulation of 1 Jun. 2004 No. 931 Ch. 19 pursuant to the Pollution Control Act and the Act of 15 Jun. 2001 No. 79 Act on the Svalbard Environment.

439. Directive 98/34/EC.

440. Regulation of 19 Sep. 1997 No. 1061 on interventions on the high seas and in Norway's Extended Economic Zone in case of pollution or risk of pollution of the sea by oil or other substances due to an accident at sea, pursuant to the Pollution Control Act. It is based on the 1969 International Convention on Intervention on the High Seas in case of Pollution or the Risk of Pollution (the 'Brussels Convention') and its Protocol of 2 Nov. 1973.

or sink or destroy the vessel or its load. The necessary personnel and equipment may be ordered to take part in such an action.

When considering such a measure, the authority shall consider possible harm to sea life, birds and animals, and their living environment, and whether protected species, protected areas, cultural heritage, beaches of public interest and so on are affected. In any case, the measures have to be proportionate and reasonable compared to the risk in question (Regulation Article 3 No. 3). The measures must be proportional to the damage or risk of damage, must not go further than what is reasonable and necessary in the case, and cease when the purpose is achieved (Article 3 No. 4).

Furthermore, the authorities have a duty – if time permits – to consult with other affected States, in particular the ship's flag State, other interested parties, and independent experts appointed by the IMO before a final decision on such a measure is taken (Regulation Article 4).

378. According to PCA Article 76, the *responsible party has the duty to cover the costs* of the actions taken by public authorities and private parties to prevent and limit pollution damage, including cleanup. This applies regardless of whether or not the accident is due to negligence on the part of the responsible party.

These rules have no limitations as to the extent of the liability. However, as far as oil spill from ship accidents is concerned, there are special rules on liability in the Maritime Act.[441] These rules are based on the international conventions on liability for oil spills.[442] According to these rules, the shipowner has strict liability for oil spill damage, as the main rule, but the liability is limited.

441. Act of 24 Jun. 1994 No. 39.

442. 1969 International Convention on Civil Liability for Oil Pollution Damage with later developments. *See infra* Part IV, Ch. 1, §3.

Chapter 4. Waste

§1. Overview

379. The disposal of waste has become an increasingly important and complex field within environmental law. In some areas of waste policy, Norway had already a well-developed system in 1992 when the country became a member of the EEA through the EEA Agreement. In some respects, Norway was quite advanced in this field. Since 1992, the waste sector has increasingly been influenced by the development of *EC waste legislation*. The Waste Framework Directive[443] applies to and is being implemented in Norway.[444]

In this area, the general rules in the PCA serve as the legal basis and framework; this is clear from the full title of the Act: Act on Protection against Pollution and on Waste. *A number of regulations have been issued pursuant to both the PCA and the Product Control Act.* So, the detailed rules are to be found in the regulations, not in the Act itself. Since 1 June 2004, all regulations concerning waste and waste disposal have been put together into a single comprehensive *Regulation on recovery and treatment of waste* (the Waste Regulation).[445] To a large extent, the regulations implement the comprehensive and complex rules on waste treatment and trade in waste laid down in EU regulations and directives. It must also be seen and interpreted in light of the numerous cases on waste before the European Court of Justice. In addition, other types of instruments are applicable. Charges, as well as various types of voluntary arrangements, including formal agreements between the authorities and key actors, have turned out to be particularly useful in this field of environmental policy. The MCE and the NEA are the responsible authorities at the central level. The municipalities have authority and play an important role with regard to local waste management and in particular household waste.

380. The inclusion of waste management in the *PCA facilitates an integrated approach to pollution and waste problems.* The line between pollution and waste may be difficult to draw. Often, waste from industrial production may either be discharged into water and create water pollution, be burned and thus create air pollution, or be turned into solid waste and deposited. A general objective of recycling and reuse of waste is a key to avoiding and combating water, air and soil pollution. A common legal system facilitates an optimal solution to these problems. However, the Act implies certain legal differences between pollution and waste. Since the distinction between waste and pollution is difficult in many situations, this may create some problems. Also, an object may be 'waste' from one point of view and for one actor, but a valuable resource from another point of view and for another actor. This raises several questions about the definition of 'waste'.

443. Directive 2008/98/EC as amended by Directive (EU) 218/851 of 30 M.

444. A thorough presentation of Norwegian and European waste law is provided in Einar Bratteng, *Avfallsrett* (Waste Law), Universitetsforlaget, Oslo, 2020.

445. Regulation of 1 Jun. 2004 No. 930, pursuant to the Pollution Control Act and the Product Control Act with many later amendments, the most recent of Regulation of 4 May 2021 No. 1397.

381. The waste treatment of products may also be regulated pursuant to *the Product Control Act.* This gives the environmental authorities the possibility of considering all aspects of a product, in a 'life cycle' – or 'cradle to grave'/'cradle to cradle' – perspective. The material, design, content of various substances, labelling and so on may all have a bearing on the possible and optimal treatment of a product as waste. In this sense, too, the Norwegian legislation facilitates an integrated approach.

§2. The General Rules on Waste in the PCA

382. The PCA *applies equally to pollution and waste problems.* The purpose of the Act is to protect the environment against pollution, and to 'reduce the quantity of waste and to promote better waste management' (Article 1 paragraph 1). The Act 'shall ensure that the quality of the environment is satisfactory, so that pollution and waste do not result in damage to human health or adversely affect welfare, or damage the productivity of the natural environment and its capacity for self-renewal' (Article 1 paragraph 2). The general principles of the Act are common to the two problem areas. In addition, the Act has a special chapter on waste (Chapter 5).

The *general guidelines* for the implementation of the Act also apply to waste problems. It is stated explicitly in Article 2 No. 4 that:

> Waste shall be managed in such a way as to minimize damage and nuisance. Waste shall be recycled preferably by preparing it for re-use or recycling of the material, unless recycling is not justified on the basis of an evaluation of environmental and natural resource considerations and economic factors.

As with pollution, the costs of preventing or limiting waste problems shall be covered by the person responsible for the waste (Article 2 No. 5).

383. The term 'waste' is defined in Article 27 of the Act. For the purpose of the Act:

> 'waste' means 'movables and chattels or substances that someone has discarded, intends to discard or is under an obligation to discard. It does not include wastewater and emissions of gases into the air'.

It is clear that solid waste products from industrial production, including sludge and dust, are considered waste. Also, buildings and other installations become waste when they are demolished or removed and can no longer be used. Wrecked cars are 'waste'. Pursuant to a recent amendment, shipwrecks are also defined as waste.

The definition and delimitation of 'waste' as a legal concept is important but raises a number of difficult questions in light of the policy objectives of increased reuse, recycling and other recovery of resources. As the EU Waste Framework Directive applies to Norway, the definition of waste in Norwegian legislation is meant to be in conformity with the definition of waste in the directive and as interpreted by case law by the European Court. It also follows the definition in the directive of what is a 'by-product' and consequently not 'waste'.

384. Article 27 second paragraph states that objects and substances are *not* 'waste' but *'by-products'* if they:

- are produced as an integrated part of a production process which primarily aims at producing a different product;
- can be used directly without any further processing other than normal industrial practice;
- can be used in a way which is lawful;
- will not lead to considerably higher hazards to health and the environment than what would follow from corresponding other objects and substances; and
- further use of the object or substance is certain.[446]

This rule implements the definition in WFD Article 5.

385. Article 27 third paragraph states that objects and substances that have been classified as waste *shall cease to be waste* when they, as a minimum:

- have undergone recycling;
- are commonly used for specific purposes;
- there exists a market or a demand for it;
- fulfil the technical requirements for the specific purposes and meet applicable requirements and standards for the product;
- will not lead to considerably higher hazards to health and the environment than what would follow from corresponding other objects and substances.

These rules are meant to implement WFD Article 6.

The pollution control authorities may lay down regulations in order to define more precisely what is to be 'waste' according to the act, but this has not yet (September 2023) been done.

386. Since, as we shall see, the rules and in particular the responsibility for the collection and disposal of the waste depend on the type of waste in question, the Act distinguishes between *three main types of waste* which are defined in Article 27a:

(1) household waste;
(2) industrial waste;
(3) special waste.

---

446. *See* for comparison Directive 2008/28/EC Art. 5.

'Household waste' ('husholdningsavfall') means waste from private households, including large objects such as furniture, and so on.

'Industrial waste' ('næringsavfall') means waste from public and private enterprises, and institutions.

'Special waste' ('spesialavfall') means waste that cannot appropriately be treated together with household waste or industrial waste because of its size, or because it may cause serious pollution or risk of injury to people or animals.

Also 'recycling' is defined in Article 27a as 'any measure the main result of which is that waste comes to use by replacing material that would otherwise have been used, or that waste has been prepared for this'.

387. The general principles and rules on waste and waste problems are similar to those related to pollution. At the outset, PCA lays down a *general prohibition against littering* (Article 28). It is prohibited to empty, leave, store or transport waste in such a way that it is unsightly or may cause damage or nuisance to the environment. If a person has contravened this rule, he/she shall provide for the necessary cleanup measures. The municipality may order any person who has discarded, emptied or stored waste in contravention of this rule to remove it, tidy it up within a specified time limit, or cover reasonable costs incurred by others in removing or tidying up the waste (Article 37 paragraph 1).

If the responsible person does not carry out the terms of such an order, the municipality itself may arrange for the measures to be implemented, at the cost of the responsible person. In this situation, the general rules on actions by public authorities or third parties in Articles 74–77 of the PCA apply (*see supra* Chapter 1, §2, III).

The question of who is the responsible person may be raised in these cases. Several persons may be regarded as responsible, and subject to the order by the authority: the owner of the waste, the one who possesses it, or any other person who is in a position which makes it reasonable to hold him/her responsible for the proper disposal of the waste.

388. Although not stated explicitly, it is clear that the rules also apply to such large objects as *shipwrecks, wrecked aircraft, cars and so on.*[447] In such cases, Article 37 paragraph 2 states explicitly that an order to remove or tidy up the object may be addressed to the person who was the owner of the object when it was left behind in violation of Article 28, and to the owner at the time the order is issued.

This rule is an important clarification, in particular in cases of shipwrecks. Norway has seen many shipwrecks along its coasts that have simply been left behind by the owner, or sold as scrap iron, and then left behind by the scrap dealer. It is important that the owner of the ship at the time of the accident may be held fully responsible for the final removal of the wreck.[448]

447. Until 2017 this was said in Art. 28, but the formulation could be misunderstood, and it was deleted.

448. Altogether, some 2,600 shipwrecks have been identified along the Norwegian coast. Some of them represent a potential pollution problem, mainly due to the danger of leakages from oil tanks.

389. When a person finds illegal waste a nuisance, he/she may require the municipality to make an *order to remove the waste* or cleanup. The decision of the municipality whether or not to act is considered to be a formal decision even if no order is issued (Article 37 paragraph 3). A decision not to order the removal of waste may be subject to administrative appeal by the interested party, according to the general appeal rules in the Public Administration Act.[449]

390. It follows from this that *a public licence is needed for the collection and treatment of waste* which may create pollution or nuisance (Article 29 first paragraph). A licence is given by the relevant authority in accordance with the rules on pollution permits as provided in Chapter 3 of the Act, in particular Articles 11 and 16 (*see supra* Chapter 1, §2 V).

Usually, a licence for a waste disposal facility is given on certain conditions. These may, for example, relate to the transport and storage of the waste, and to the way it shall be treated, such as the modes and extent of recycling, use of the waste as a source of energy and so on. The authority responsible varies according to the type of waste in question.

391. *Household waste* is the responsibility of the *municipality*. The municipality shall have waste storage sites or waste treatment and disposal plants for household waste and sewage sludge, and has a duty to receive such waste and sludge. The NEA may, however, determine in regulations or in individual cases that a municipality shall also have facilities for special waste and industrial waste, and a duty to receive such waste (Article 29 paragraph 3).

The municipality shall also make necessary arrangements for the *collection* of household waste. The modes and methods for the collection are decided by the municipality, but the pollution control authority may order the municipality to introduce schemes for sorting the waste, by regulation or in individual cases, taking into account the costs compared to the positive environmental effect of such a measure (Article 30 paragraph 1).

The municipality may issue the regulations necessary to ensure appropriate and hygienic storage, collection and transport of household waste. No person may collect household waste without the consent of the municipality (Article 30 paragraph 3). It may also issue regulations requiring that municipal waste collection shall apply only in built-up areas, and that certain types of household waste, and certain properties, shall be excluded from the collection (Article 30, paragraph 2).

392. *Industrial waste* may be disposed of in two ways (Article 32). It may be delivered to *an authorized waste treatment and disposal plant*. Alternatively, it may be *recycled* in such a way that it seizes to be waste or in other ways becomes useful by replacing materials that would have otherwise been used. The responsibility for its proper disposal rests with the enterprise or institution that creates or produces the waste. However, ordinary waste from fisheries, agriculture, forestry, etc., may

449. Act of 10 Feb. 1967 Ch. VI.

be disposed of differently provided that this is to be regarded as 'ordinary pollution' from these activities in the sense of Article 8 paragraph 1 of the Act.[450]

The Act gives the municipality neither a duty nor a right to collect and treat this type of waste. However, the pollution control authority may, by regulation or in individual cases, accept exceptions from these rules (Article 32 paragraph 2). They may also order the enterprise to deliver the waste to a municipal waste treatment facility (Article 32 paragraph 3).

Often, the activity in question needs a pollution permit according to Article 11 of the Act. In such cases, the proper disposal of the waste will be defined in the pollution permit on the basis of a general evaluation of the best solution to the pollution and waste problems which it generates.

393. Special waste, including hazardous waste, raises a number of problems, legal as well as technical.

The main principle in the PCA is that the pollution control authorities may take the necessary decisions concerning the disposal of special waste in order to prevent pollution or other types of harm, injuries or nuisance to people or the environment. The authorities may order the municipality to collect special waste, and order the waste producer to deliver the waste to the municipal system or other authorized waste collectors (Article 31 paragraph 1).

Most often, an enterprise that generates such waste needs a pollution permit. The permit may lay down conditions related to the disposal of the waste. The authorities may also issue such regulations as are necessary for the appropriate and proper storage, collection, transport and treatment of such waste (Article 31 paragraph 2). We shall return to some of the relevant regulations.

Any facility for collection and treatment of special waste needs a public licence according to PCA Article 11 (Article 29).

394. The PCA prescribes *recycling and other reuse of waste* as the preferable way of waste disposal. This is expressed in Article 2 No. 4 as a general guideline of the Act. Since the Act was adopted in 1981, the principle of recycling has gained strong support as a main approach to the waste problems of modern society.

Article 33 lays down further rules to this effect. It states that the pollution control authorities may, by regulations or individual decisions, require that waste shall be recycled or treated in another way. Such decisions may, for example, concern (Article 33 paragraph 2):

- preparation for reuse;
- recovery and recycling of materials;
- use of the waste as an energy resource;
- collection, keeping, sorting and destruction;
- binding objectives for recycling, including objectives for preparation to reuse and recycling of material.

---

450. *See supra* Ch. IV.

Several of the regulations concerning industrial waste and special waste require the recycling or reuse of products or substances.

When making such decisions, due consideration shall be given to whether the overall environmental benefits are in reasonable proportion to the costs incurred and to the costs of other methods of dealing with the waste (Article 33 paragraph 3).

Such decisions may apply to any person that manufactures, imports, markets or uses products that generate waste, and to any person that collects or possesses waste (Article 33 paragraph 4).

Increasingly, the principle of *extended producer responsibility* is applied. This usually implies an obligation to take the product back when it has become waste.

395. If no voluntary agreement is reached between the parties, a decision pursuant to Article 33 paragraph 4 may also apply to *any person that can use or treat waste from others.* A condition is that this is necessary to ensure a satisfactory treatment of waste that may be hazardous to health or the environment, or it is necessary in order to achieve a satisfactory system for the collection and treatment of waste (Article 33 paragraph 4). This rule is necessary in order to ensure sufficient use – and thus sufficient income – for proper collection and disposal installations for hazardous waste. It is combined with a rule saying that whoever delivers his/her waste to a waste disposal plant shall cover the costs involved. If, however, the possible income from the waste exceeds the costs involved in the treatment, the recipient shall pay a reasonable sum for the waste. The parties may have the compensation issue decided by arbitration (Article 33 paragraph 5).

396. The Act also requires that the costs of the municipal waste disposal, including transport and final treatment, shall be covered by *a municipal waste fee* (Article 34). The fee shall cover the full costs, including both capital and operating costs. However, the income from the fee may not exceed the actual costs incurred by the municipality for waste collection and treatment. Nevertheless, waste management fees vary widely from one municipality to another.

The Act states explicitly that the municipality should create different fees in cases where this may contribute to waste reduction and promote recycling (Article 34 paragraph 2).

The fee is normally to be paid by the owner of the property to which a waste collection scheme applies, or by a lessee if he/she has a lease of thirty years or more.

397. It is up to each municipality to organize the collection of household waste. The PCA provides the legal basis, but the local regulation and organization are decided by municipal decrees. Many municipalities have adopted plans for waste reduction and management. The tasks in this connection are often organized in intermunicipal organizations and companies.

398. A national organization – Norwegian Waste Management and Recycling Association, shortened to 'Avfall Norge' ('Waste Management Norway') – assembles approximately 100 municipal and inter-municipal solid waste organizations, corresponding to about 95% of Norway's municipalities, and an equal number of private companies in the waste sector. In all, the members take care of the waste from 95% of Norway's population.

Avfall Norge works to assist the municipalities and private enterprises in their work with solid waste problems including – not least – measures to increase recycling and reuse. It is a nationwide resource for public services and private companies alike. In order to facilitate recycling and reuse, sorting of waste has become an important issue in waste policy. Most municipalities have established waste collection systems which require or facilitate the *sorting of waste at source,* that is, at each household. As a result of this, together with the deposit/return system for beverage packaging (*see infra*), some 83% of household waste was recycled in 2012, including used as energy.

399. For certain types of consumer waste and *litter*, the Act has special provisions. Any person who runs a general store, petrol station, kiosk or similar sales outlet, or runs a campsite or other types of tourist facility, shall ensure that waste receptacles are provided, as well as ensure that these are emptied, and the necessary cleanup is carried out. At other excursion spots and heavily visited areas, the municipality is responsible for this (Article 35).

Along *public roads,* the public roads authorities shall provide waste receptacles, and arrange for them to be emptied. They are also responsible for the clearing up of the roads and the areas along the roads within the road boundaries. The pollution control authorities may order the owner of the road to provide public toilets along the road, to the extent necessary (Article 36).

§3. Regulations Concerning Hazardous Waste

400. As mentioned, since 1 June 2004, all regulations concerning waste and waste disposal have been put together into a single comprehensive *Regulation on recovery and treatment of waste* (Waste Regulation).[451] The general rules on the disposal of hazardous waste are included in its Chapter 11. They are based on the general rules of the PCA, and implement the various EU directives on waste disposal.[452]

I. General Regulation Concerning Hazardous Waste

401. This regulation covers *keeping, transport and management/disposal* of all the waste types included in the European Waste List (Annex 1 to the regulation), as well as other wastes where the content of dangerous substances exceeds certain maximum limits laid down in Annex 2 to the regulation. Waste which is covered by

451. Regulation of 1 Jun. 2004 No. 930, pursuant to the Pollution Control Act and the Product Control Act with later amendments.
452. Directive 91/689/EEC as amended by Directive 94/31/EEC, supplemented by Decisions 2000/532/EC, 2001/118/EC, 2001/119/EC, and 2001/573/EC.

the regulation may nevertheless be exempted from it if it is not regarded as dangerous or does not exceed the limits in question (Waste Regulation Article 11-2 paragraph 4).

It is up to the possessor of the waste to find out whether the regulation applies to his/her waste (Article 11-2 paragraph 5). He/she also has to prove that the conditions for exemption apply.

402. The main rules of the regulation fully accord with the rules in the PCA: Whoever keeps, transports or handles hazardous waste must take necessary measures to prevent risk of pollution or injury to people or animals.

Hazardous waste shall not be mixed with other wastes. Nor shall different types of hazardous waste be mixed together if this may create risk of pollution, or other problems in connection with the disposal of the waste (Regulation Article 11-5).

403. Whoever handles hazardous waste needs *a permit from the pollution control authority* pursuant to the PCA Article 11 (Regulation Article 11-6). Hence, this is treated similarly to a polluting activity. However, there are quite a few exceptions to this as defined in the regulation (Article 11-7). For example, a factory that handles its own waste in accordance with a pollution permit does not need a special waste disposal permit. Neither do municipal waste reception facilities, provided that they are run in accordance with technical requirements laid down in Annex 3 to the regulation.

A permit is not needed, either, if the dealer of a hazardous product takes back the product, or similar products, as waste. Take-back arrangements are getting more and more common. Increasingly, regulations provide that the producer or dealer must treat the products as waste.

404. Any enterprise or activity that generates hazardous waste has a *duty to deliver the waste* to a person or a firm who is authorized to handle special waste according to a pollution permit, or to an enterprise outside Norway in accordance with the rules on transfrontier transport of waste.[453] The waste must be delivered at least once a year if the quantity exceeds 1 kg. If an enterprise is closed down for more than three months, the waste must be delivered immediately (Regulation Article 11-8). The person who has a duty to deliver shall have a documentation in writing showing where the waste has been delivered.

405. This duty to deliver does not apply to enterprises which have a permit from the pollution control authority to treat their waste itself, pursuant to Article 11 of the PCA. When an enterprise delivers waste to the receiving facility, it must *give information* about the type of waste in question, its origin, content and characteristics, in order to ensure safe handling. It must fill in a *declaration sheet,* which must accompany the waste during subsequent transports. The packaging must be clearly marked with the number of the declaration sheet (Regulation Article 11-12). As much as possible, households must also give the necessary information if they deliver hazardous waste (Regulation Article 11-11).

---

453. Rules on this are laid down in the same regulation Ch. 13.

The person or company who handles and treats hazardous waste must ensure that the waste is properly declared and that the declaration sheet is present during further transport and handling. The receiver of such hazardous waste must, before the fifteenth of the following month, send a copy of the declaration sheet to the pollution control authorities (Article 11-13).

It is not allowed for enterprises to transport hazardous waste without a valid declaration sheet in accordance with Article 11-12. The sheet shall then immediately be handed over to the person who takes over the waste for further disposal. This rule does not apply, however, if the transport is done by the producer of the waste himself (Article 11-14).

The pollution control authorities have established *a system of fees for the declaration of hazardous waste.*[454] Enterprises that receive, in the first instance, waste, which must be declared according to the regulation, must pay a fee to the NEA. The fee is to cover the costs of the declaration system. At present, the fee amounts to NOK 15 per ton of waste up to 1,000 tons (Regulation Article 12-2). No fee shall be paid for waste beyond 1,000 tons.

The regulation has general rules on monitoring, control, coercive fines and penalties for violations, etc., in its Chapter 19.

406. Each *municipality* shall arrange for *necessary facilities to receive hazardous waste* from ordinary households, and from enterprises with small amounts of special waste, such as farms, etc. This obligation is limited to 1,000 kg per waste possessor per year (Regulation Article 11-10). The municipality is not obliged to establish and run such a facility itself. It may be left to a private waste company. But the municipality must *see* to it that it fulfils the necessary requirements. An annex to the regulation describes the standard requirements to a municipal reception facility. The municipality cannot charge ordinary households when they deliver hazardous waste to such a facility. The municipality must cover the costs through the general municipal waste fee pursuant to PCA Article 34.

II. Regulation Concerning Transfrontier Transport of Waste

407. Included as *Chapter 13* in the general Regulation on recovery and treatment of waste, this regulation *incorporates* into Norwegian law the *EU regulation on monitoring and control of waste transport* within, into and out of the EU, as laid down in the 2006 Regulation on shipment of waste with later amendments and supplements.[455] It also complies with the international Convention on the Control of Transboundary Movements of Hazardous Wastes (the 'Basel Convention'), which also is a basis for the EU regulation. Furthermore, the regulation is founded on the decision by the OECD on control of transfrontier transport of waste for

454. Regulation of 1 Jun. 2004 No. 930 Ch. 12.

455. Regulations (EC) 1013/2006 with numerous later amendments, the latest by Commission Regulation (EU) 2020/2174 of 19 Oct 202. For transport of waste to states that do not apply the OECD decision, the regulation (EC) 1418/2007 with later amendments apply. These regulations build on earlier EC legislation on transfrontier transport of waste, namely Directive 84/631/EEC and regulation (EEC) Nr. 259/93.

recycling.[456] The Norwegian national regulation itself is short, as it in the main simply refers to, and incorporates the EU regulations.

The EU regulations are very comprehensive, detailed and technical, but the main principles are quite simple and shall be presented in the following.

408. The EU regulations regulate *the right of the Member States of the EEA to prohibit or permit export and import of waste* and lays down rules of procedure for waste transport. It applies to all types of waste, but distinguishes between three main categories of waste, listed in annexes to the regulation – the 'green', 'orange', and 'red' lists. The regulation with the annexes lays down very detailed and special rules for transport of different types of waste between EEA States (Part II), within EEA States (Part III), export from and import into the EEA area from third countries (Parts IV and V), and transit through the EEA area (Part VI). In Norway, the NEA is 'competent authority' and correspondent responsible for informing or advising persons or undertakings making enquiries.[457]

409. As general rule, shipment of waste shall be *subject to prior information* to the authorities in the receiving country through a written document or a special contract, and written *prior consent* from the receiving State before it can take place. The document must give sufficient information about the type of waste, its movements and plan for final disposal or recycling in order for the authorities to be able to decide on the case and take necessary measures to protect people's health and the environment. Priority should be given to recycling and solving the problem at the source and in accordance with the subsidiarity principle. The regulation, Annex II, lists restrictions and conditions for the shipments of different types of waste to various countries.

The receiving country may lay down *objections* to shipments of waste according to some procedural rules and under certain conditions defined in some detail in the regulation, which are somewhat different for waste destined for *disposal* (Regulation Article 11) and waste destined for *recovery* (Article 12).

410. With regard in particular to *exports of waste from the EEA area to third countries*, the regulation again distinguishes between exports of waste for disposal and exports of waste for recovery. Export of waste for *disposal* is generally prohibited (Article 34).[458] For exports of waste for *recovery*, the rules are somewhat more complex. Exports of waste for recovery to countries which come under the OECD decision – that is 'developed', OECD countries – are by and large permitted under the general rules on Prior Informed Consent (PIC) (Article 38). On the other hand, exports of certain types of wastes destined for recovery to developing countries[459] are prohibited (Article 36). This includes household waste and various types of

456. OECD Council Decision of 30 Mar. 1992 as amended in 2001 (C(2001)107). Appendixes to this was further modified in 2020 and was effective in 2021..

457. Regulation (EC) 1013/2006 Arts 53 and 54 and Norway's Waste Regulation Art. 13-2.

458. Regulation Art. 34(1). Under some conditions and limitations defined in the article, the prohibition does not apply to export of waste for disposal from EU to an EFTA country which is also party to the Basel Convention.

459. Formally Countries to which the OECD decision does not apply.

hazardous waste. However, non-hazardous waste may under certain conditions be exported also to developing countries for recovery, and the regulation provides special procedural rules for this in Article 37.

III. Regulations to Prevent Environmental Harm from Final Disposal of Waste

411. In 2002, a general *regulation on landfills of waste* was adopted. It is now included in the general Regulation on recovery and disposal of waste,[460] Chapter 9. It implements the EU rules on the landfill of waste.[461] Its objective is to ensure that landfill of waste is done in a safe and controlled manner in order to prevent and reduce harm to the environment and people's health (Regulation Article 9-1). It applies to all types of waste landfills, with a few exceptions, and to areas for storage of waste (Regulation Article 9-3). It prohibits a number of waste types in landfills, such as biologically degradable waste other than polluted soil and waste/sludge from sewage treatment, liquid waste, explosive and inflammable waste, infectious waste from hospitals, and so on, car tyres and milled car tyres, and other types of waste not allowed by the authorities for waste reception. The regulation also lists waste which cannot be disposed of in subterranean deposits (Article 9-4).

Landfills must be classified according to the following three categories: landfills for hazardous waste, 'ordinary' (non-hazardous) waste, and inert waste (Regulation Article 9-5). Only waste that has been subject to treatment may be disposed of in landfills (Regulation Article 9-6). Treatment is defined as physical, thermal, chemical or biological processes, including sorting, which changes the character of the waste, reduces the risks involved and makes it easier to handle or recycle (Regulation Article 9-3i). The regulation defines what types of waste may be deposited in the three different categories.

A landfill must have a pollution permit pursuant to the PCA Article 11. To get a permit, the landfill must be in accordance with numerous technical requirements laid down in the annexes to the regulation (Regulation Article 9-7). The regulation defines the information required for an application (Regulation Article 9-8). Every landfill must have a satisfactory financial guarantee for the obligations inherent in the permit. The costs of the landfill shall be covered by a fee paid by those who deliver waste to the landfill (Regulation Article 9-10).

412. A general *Regulation on the incineration of waste* came into force in 2003, and is included in the general Waste Regulation[462] Chapter 10. Its purpose is to ensure a proper and controlled burning of waste, in order to prevent and reduce hazards to health and the environment to the extent possible (Article 10-1). It lays down general rules and requirements for waste incineration, and implements the EU directive on the matter.[463] It applies to both 'pure' waste incineration installations

460. Regulation of 1 Jun. 2004 No. 930.
461. Directive 1999/31/EC as amended by decision 2003/33/EC.
462. Regulation of 1 Jun. 2004 No. 930.
463. Directive 2000/76/EC.

and incineration installations where waste is burned together with other materials for the production of energy or goods ('combined incineration installations'). It does not apply to certain other types of waste incineration, mainly wood and other vegetable materials from agriculture and forestry, which is not classified as hazardous, and radioactive and explosive waste (Regulation Article 10-2).

The regulation reflects the general principles in the PCA. A pollution permit is needed for the incineration of waste (PCA Article 29 and Regulation Article 10-4). An application must provide the necessary information on the type and characteristics of the waste and so on. The conditions for a permit must satisfy a number of general requirements in the regulation itself (Regulation Article 10-7–10-19) as well as more detailed and comprehensive technical requirements laid down in the annexes to the regulation. These define, *inter alia*, maximum emission limits for various substances emitted into the air from waste installations and combined installations, temperature, and so on. They also lay down requirements for monitoring and measuring (Regulation Article 10-20 to 10-28).

The regulation requires certain registration procedures when waste is received for incineration. Furthermore, it lays down rules for the running of the installation.

The energy from ordinary waste incineration installations should be exploited as far as possible (Regulation Article 10-10).

§4. Rules, Regulations, and Voluntary Agreements Concerning the Disposal of Particular Types of Waste

413. The general principles and rules on waste disposal in the PCA and the general regulations on special waste and the treatment of different types of waste are necessary, but they are not sufficient to ensure the reduction and gradual elimination of various types of waste. In this field, a combination of regulations, financial incentives, voluntary agreements, and information is often useful. To some extent, it is necessary to consider each type of waste separately, and 'tailor' the choice of instruments to the type in question. Often, cooperation is needed between the authorities, the producers and dealers of a product, the users, and the relevant waste collector in order to achieve a workable solution. This method has been used with some success in Norwegian waste policy. In the following paragraphs, we shall present some of the most important schemes in this respect.

414. A return system for *end-of-life vehicles* has been in place since the 1970s. It encourages car owners to deliver their scrapped vehicles to a proper collection site, and promotes the recycling of the materials. The rules governing this are found in the general Waste Regulation[464] Chapter 4. They implement the EU rules in this field.[465]

The regulation establishes *extended producer responsibility* in this important area. 'Producer' includes importers of vehicles. Producers are responsible for

464. Regulation of 1 Jun. 2004 No. 930 Ch. 4.
465. Directive 2000/53/EC ('ELV Directive') with numerous later amendments through Commission Decisions and Directives, the most recent (2021) Commission Delegated Directive (EU) 2020/363.

receiving and handling end-of-life vehicles as waste. The obligation for each producer corresponds to his/her share of the car market in Norway in the actual year. Before 1 January 2006, the producers had to ensure that 85% (by weight) of their share are recycled, of which 80% are recycled as material and the rest is used as energy. By 2015, 95% of the share must be recycled, of which 85% must be recycled as material and the rest used as energy (Regulation Article 4-4). The obligation shall be fulfilled by participation in an approved return system. The producers shall ensure the public is provided with satisfactory information about the system.

The pollution control authorities shall approve return systems for end-of-life vehicles. Whoever runs a treatment facility for such vehicles, needs a pollution permit from the pollution control authorities (Regulation Article 4-5). The treatment facility must satisfy a number of technical requirements to avoid hazards to the environment. Parts that contain certain dangerous chemicals must be removed before the ordinary treatment. Since 1 July 2003, it has been prohibited to produce or import vehicles containing lead, mercury, cadmium and chromium, except for certain specific uses.

When an end-of-life care is delivered to an authorized treatment facility, the owner receives an amount of money presently (March 2017) NOK 3,000 (corresponding to EUR 300) for a passenger car and NOK 5,000 (EUR 500) for trucks. The regulation gives detailed rules on the registration, payment and so on.[466]

415. Electrical waste and electronic products (EE-products) such as computers, TV-sets, fridges, electric cookers and washing machines, vacuum cleaners, cell phones and numerous other products is one of the fastest growing waste streams in EU, as well as in Norway. They are subject to special and quite comprehensive rules in Norway's general Waste Regulation[467] which governs the reception, collection, recycling and other proper treatment of these products. The purpose is to reduce the environmental problems caused by such products, through recycling of material and proper disposal of the hazardous substances they may contain. The regulation is based on the principle of responsibility for producers, including importers, and dealers. It implements the EU directives in this field[468] but goes somewhat further. It is supplemented by regulations[469] on limitation of the use of certain hazardous substances in such products, and substitution of such substances by safer alternatives. In particular, this applies to heavy metals such as lead, mercury, cadmium, flame retardants such as polybrominated biphenyls (PBB) and polybrominated diphenyl ethers (PBDE). Here again, Norway implements the EU rules in the field.[470]

416. The main lines in the regulation regarding waste disposal of EE products are as follows:

466. Regulation of 1 Jun. 2004 No. 930 Art. 4-8 to 4-13.
467. Regulation of 1 Jun. 2004 No. 930 Ch. 1 with later amendments.
468. Directive 2012/19/EU which replaced Directive 2002/96/EC with later amendments. It became effective in February 2014.
469. Regulation of 1 Jun. 2004 No. 922 Ch. 2a.
470. Directive 2002/95/EC ('RoHS 1' Directive) repealed by Directive 2011/65/EU ('RoHS 2').

> The *retailer* of EE products has the duty to accept free of charge scrap EE products which are consumer waste. He/she also has to accept free of charge EE products which are waste from production against new purchase of an equivalent quantity of new products. This applies to similar types of products as the one he/she sells, regardless of brand and manufacture. He/she has then the obligation to sort, keep and transport it safely, so that it is suitable for further handling. He/she shall ensure that it is transported to a special collection point established by the producer. If no such collection point exists, the retailer must keep the product until it is collected by a return company. The product may also be delivered to an authorized treatment installation (Regulation Articles 1-4 to 1-6).

The *municipalities* are obliged to ensure adequate facilities for the reception of waste EE products, the sorting and storing of these products, and transport to a collection point. They have a duty to receive EE waste and to inform the public about the need to separate EE waste from other types of household waste (Regulation Article 1-7 to 1-9).

Producers including importers of EE products are to be registered in a national register, called the 'EE Register' (Regulation Article 1-25). Producers must cover the cost of collecting, sorting, reuse, recycling, disposal and other treatments of EE waste by way of *membership in a return company* approved by the NEA. The membership shall cover the types of EE product that the producer produces in or imports into Norway. The duty to be member of a return company applies to producers of final products as well as components to EE products (Regulation Article 1-10). Producer shall inform their customers about the need to separate EE waste from other wastes and about the system for return of EE waste (Regulation Article 1-12).

417. The regulation lays down a comprehensive and detailed set of rules about the approval, functioning and reporting obligations of *the return companies* (Regulation Chapter V). Return companies shall be registered[471] and must be approved by the NEA (Article 1-13).To be approved, a company must be able to carry out the activities which the regulations require of these companies. A return company has the obligation to go and get EE waste from retailers and municipalities independent of the product's manufacture free of charge (Article 1-14 a). This is a key principle. The content of this obligation is further regulated in Annex 1 to the Regulation. Furthermore, they shall ensure that the waste is collected, transported and managed properly and with due care and in accordance with existing rules and regulations treated properly which means reuse and recycling of the materials as far as possible. It includes ensuring that the various actors involved have the necessary licences (Article 1-18).

The Regulation (Article 1-18a) lays down obligations for the return companies to achieve a high level of recycling. It decides the *rate of recycling that shall be achieved* for different types of product groups, varying between 75% and 85%, further specified with regard to the share of reuse or material recycling within these figures.

471. Detailed rules on registration of return companies are laid down in Annex 2 to the Regulation.

Also, the return companies must ensure that the special rules on *export and import of waste* are followed. There are some particular rules on export and import of EE waste in the EE Regulation Part VII. It lays down detailed rules on testing of each EE (waste) product, documentation of relevant information about the products and. The waste products must be protected from damage during transport, loading and unloading, etc. (Article 1-24). In addition, the comprehensive set of general rules on export of waste applies (*see supra*).[472]

418. The EE regulation also lays down rules concerning the obligations for *waste managers* (Regulation Chapter VI). A general obligation is to manage the waste properly with the use of the BAT. The EE waste has to be registered when brought into or taken out of the treatment facility. It shall be recycled, preferably by being prepared for reuse or recycling of the material unless considerations of the environmental or economic conditions do not justify this (Article 1-22). Article 22 lists a number of hazardous substances that, together with liquids, as the main rule must be removed at the start of a recycling process.

419. Batteries which are harmful to the environment are regulated[473] in accordance with the EU rules in this field.[474] The system is similar to the one for EE waste. It establishes a system for return and safe disposal of batteries and lays down responsibilities for retailers, producers and for return companies.

Retailers have the duty to receive free of charge scrapped batteries of the same categories as the retailer sells, and without a duty for the customer to buy new batteries (Regulation Article 3-4). He/she has the duty to separate batteries from other wastes and to keep them in a safe place.

Producers, including importers, are obliged to be members of a return company (Regulation Article 3-7), and they have a right to become member of such a company on equal conditions (Article 3-9).

Return companies for batteries have the duty to establish a collection system in the geographic area of their members, to actually collect the batteries, and to dispose of the batteries in accordance with rules laid down in the Regulation. They shall collect 95% of the members total production and import of lead batteries and industrial batteries, and 30% of portable batteries, calculated in weight and per year (Regulation Article 3-11). Furthermore, they have to ensure that the material of the major part of the collected batteries are recycled.[475] Return companies also have a duty to inform the public about the health and environmental effects of batteries and about the collection system (Regulation Article 3-14). They need an approval by the NEA. Their obligation may be limited to certain types of batteries. A reporting and documentation system is also prescribed (Regulation Article 3-13).

---

472. *See supra* and Ch. 13 of the Waste Regulation of 1 Jun. 2004 No. 930.

473. Regulation of 1 Jun. 2004 No. 930 Ch. 3, as amended by Regulation of 24 Oct. 2012 No. 989. There are also rules on batteries in Regulation of 1 Jun. 2004 No. 922 (the Product Regulation).

474. Directive 2006/66/EC as amended by Directive/2008/103/EC and Decisions 2008/763/EC and 2009/603/EC.

475. Rules on rates of recycling and their calculation and reporting are laid down in EU rules, namely Regulation (EU) 493/2012 which is incorporated into the Battery Regulation Article 3-18.

The final stage is a proper *final treatment*. The return company is responsible for the safe disposal and treatment of batteries. They must be treated as hazardous waste, and has to be delivered to waste disposal units which are properly equipped and have the necessary permissions to treat hazardous waste (*see supra*).

Generally, batteries must be properly labelled.[476] Certain types of batteries are *prohibited to produce, import, export or sell altogether*: batteries with a mercury content and portable batteries with cadmium content above certain levels.[477]

420. Similarly, the disposal, collection and recycling of *discarded tyres* from motor vehicles and trailers is strictly regulated, in the Waste Regulation of 1 June 2004 No. 930 Chapter 5.[478] The disposal of tyres in refuse tips or landfills is prohibited (Regulation Article 5-4).

Distributors of tyres are obliged to accept discarded tyres free of charge, limited to a reasonable amount of the category of tyres sold by the *retailer* (Regulation Article 5-5). The *manufacturer/importer* is obliged to collect discarded tyres free of charge from distributors in the geographical area where the producer's tyres have been sold, limited to a reasonable amount of the category of tyres sold. This obligation can be fulfilled by a third party (Regulation Article 5-5). The manufacturer/importer is obliged to ensure that the tyres are recycled (Regulation Article 5-6). There are also obligations related to reporting (Regulation Article 5-7).

421. Waste oil is regarded as hazardous waste. The general rules on hazardous waste in the Waste Regulation Chapter 11 apply also to waste oil. The general public may deliver waste oil freely to collection sites in accordance with municipal waste collection systems. For industry, there is normally a fee for delivery of larger amount of waste oil to the proper treatment facilities. However, in order to stimulate the collection and proper treatment of *waste oil,* a charge and refund system for waste oil, such as lubricating oil, was introduced in 1994. A charge is paid for import or production of oil, but this is (partly) refunded (to the collector) when waste oil is delivered to an authorized treatment facility. The refund makes it cheaper to deliver the oil, and it may even make it free of charge. The collector has to apply for refund to the NEA. Also waste oil from ships sailing in Norwegian waters is included in this system. At present, some 85%–90% of waste oil is collected in Norway.

422. There are special rules in Chapter 14 of the Waste Regulation on the handling of *isolation glass with PCB* as waste. The *municipalities* are obliged to receive a maximum of 500 kg of such glass per year per unit of waste holder for households and small enterprises, and free of charge if it is classified as household waste (Regulation Article 14-3). The *producers, including importers,* must ensure that waste-holders can deliver such glass for proper treatment at a reasonable price,

476. Regulation of 1 Jun. 2004 No. 922 (the Product Regulation) Art. 2-18.
477. At present (June 2017) 5 pm for mercury and 20 pm for cadmium. Regulation of 1 Jun. 2004 No. 922 (the Product Regulation) Art. 2-17.
478. Pursuant to the Product Control Act of 11 Jun. 1976 No. 79, *see supra* Ch. 1, §3.

corresponding to their market share of this type of glass. They must participate in a return system which is approved by the NEA. They must also provide sufficient information about types of glass with PCB, and about the waste disposal system and where to deliver PCB glass (Regulation Article 14-4). Anyone who buys more than 200 isolation glass pane must ask and be able to document that the seller participates in an approved return system (Regulation Article 14-5).

The approved return companies must report annually to CPA (Regulation Article 14-6).

423. To reduce the waste from *packaging,* Norway for a long time applied several instruments, and agreements with the respective branches played an important role. There were agreements about plastic and metal packaging, carton packaging for beverages, and brown paper. The results of these agreements have been very positive.

However, in 2017 these agreements were replaced by a general *Regulation on Packaging waste.*[479] It implements the EU directive on packaging and packaging waste[480] which applies to Norway through the EEA Agreement. It applies to all packaging marketed and used in Norway (Article 7-2) except packaging for beverage. Its objective is to reduce the environmental problems from the use and final disposal of packaging, and increase recycling and reuse of packaging. It aims to reduce the amount of packaging through increased reuse and collection of used packaging and packaging waste (Article 7-1). The regulation covers all types of packaging (except for beverage) used for wrapping, protection, handling or delivery from producer to consumer and presentation of goods, and regardless of material (Article 7-3). Components of the packaging is included in the concept to the extent it is integrated into the packaging.

Packaging that is marketed in Norway has to comply with some general requirements laid down in an annex to the regulation. The essential points are that the packaging must not be heavier or more voluminous than necessary, and that it should be designed and marketed in a way which maximizes the possibilities for reuse or recycling. 'Recycling' may include material recycling, utilization of the packaging for energy production or in composts, or biodegradable packaging.

424. All producers and importers of packaging and packaged products have a duty to prevent waste from packaging (Article 7-6). Producers who contribute at least 1000 tons of a certain type of packaging annually have a duty to finance collection, sorting and proper treatment of used packaging and waste through membership in a *'return company'* approved by NEA (Article 7-5). Approval is based on applications from interested companies. The application must document the ability of the company and the necessary plans to fulfil the obligations laid down in the regulation (Article 7-14). Every producer of a certain type of packaging has the right to participate in the return company (Article 7-11).

---

479. Regulation of 23 Aug. 2017 No. 1289 on packaging waste, included as Ch. 7 in the general Waste Regulation (Regulation of 1 Jun. 2004 No. 930).
480. Directive 94/62/EEC as amended by Directives 2004/12/EC, 2005/20/EC, and 2013/2/EU.

Article 7-9 lays down that the return company shall:

(a) collect packaging waste from industry and municipalities;
(b) receive packaging waste from collectors;
(c) collect and receive a reasonable amount of the type of packaging its members have introduced into the market, and for which the return company has been approved;
(d) ensure material recycling of at least 30% plastic packaging, except expanded polystyrene (isolation material), 50% expanded polystyrene, 60% cardboard, 65% brown paper, 60% metal, 60% glass and 15% wood packaging;
(e) ensure that packaging for hazardous waste shall be collected and recycled safely so that there is no risk of hazards to humans, animals or the environment;
(f) have enough financial reserves for a minimum of six months of operations.

Furthermore, the return company has an obligation to provide proper information to consumers and professional operators about the system for disposal of packaging waste, including an annual national information campaign (Article 7-10). The company must report annually to NEA about the activities, including the amount of packaging waste generated during the year, the amount collected, recycle rates, etc. (Article 7-12).

425. As far as *beverage packaging* is concerned, a deposit/return system applies, based on general rules in the Waste Regulation,[481] whereby the consumer may deliver free of charge empty beverage bottles and cans for recycling in the shops they are bought. The system is organized by the producers and importers of beverage in cooperation with the distributors/retailers and is subject to approval by the NEA.

This system stimulates the reuse and recycling of beverage packaging. In 2013, nearly all bottles in glass and plastic were returned, recycled and/or reused. The general return rate is in the order of 80–95 for the different categories.

As for *paper in general,* no national regulation applies. However, recycling is promoted through the system for waste sorting in each municipality.[482]

481. Regulation of 1 Jun. 2004 No. 930 Ch. 6.
482. The rate of recycled paper rose rapidly during the 1980s, but has been fairly steady since the beginning of the 1990s.

Chapter 5. Soil Pollution

§1. Introduction

426. Soil pollution and land contamination are problems in Norway as in most other industrial countries. But, the problems are limited compared to the situation in many other countries.

The main challenge, in Norway as elsewhere, is the pollution or risk of pollution from activities such as the discharge or burying of hazardous substances into the ground or on the sea bottom in harbours and fjords, from former industrial activities, or effluents from old waste dumps. Some of the main problems are related to waste from mines which have been closed down.

427. The PCA applies the *general rules to pollution of the soil*. The definition of 'pollution' in the Act covers 'the introduction of solids, liquids or gases to air, water or ground'. By 'ground' is meant the soil and the bedrock.

Thus, from a legal point of view, pollution of the soil is treated in the same way as pollution of air and water. Soil pollution is generally prohibited, unless it is legal according to the rules in the Act itself, regulations or a pollution permit (Article 7, *see* the full presentation of the main rules of the Act in Chapter 1 *supra*).

In relation to soil pollution, the legal borderline between pollution and waste may often seem artificial. In particular, waste disposal in the form of storage of waste on a waste site, or waste deposit in landfills, often involves a risk of leakage and effluents. In case of such a risk, the rules on pollution and on waste both apply.

428. For several years, the cleanup and restoration of waste dumps and contaminated sites has been an important issue on Norway's environmental agenda.

A *State programme* of identifying contaminated sites and dumps was carried out between 2000 and 2005. This is the basis for a major cleanup programme which is still (2017) ongoing. A special plan for the cleaning of the sea bottom in ports and fjords was adopted in 2006 and forms the basis for an ongoing cleanup programme for this.

The authorities work together with the relevant landowners to find practical solutions to the problems. The work is based on the PPP: the starting point is that the landowner or owner of the watercourse or port is responsible for carrying out the measures and cover the costs (PCA Article 7 paragraph 2). If measures are not taken by the responsible party, he/she may be ordered by the pollution control authority to take the necessary measures pursuant to PCA Article 7 paragraph 4 (*see* §2 *infra*).

There are considerable State funds available to finance cleanup actions wholly or partly in cases where:

- the State itself is the party responsible;
- it is difficult or impossible to find a person responsible who has the necessary financial means;
- an immediate action is needed; or
- when the situation is such that it is unreasonable that the 'responsible party' must cover all the costs.

The programme also applies to removal or emptying of shipwrecks. A regulation from 2015 defines the procedural rules for applications and basic criteria for assignments of the financial support.[483]

Financial contributions by the State may – at least partly – explain why very few cases concerning the question of responsibility have come before the Norwegian courts, in spite of the fact that the legal rules on the responsibility for cleanup measures are not entirely clear.

§2. Responsibility for Cleaning up Contaminated Sites

429. Contrary to the situation in many other countries, Norway has *no special legislation* or regulations concerning the cleanup and restoration of polluted soil and contaminated sites. Thus, the general rules of the PCA apply to this problem. There are few keys to the solution of these issues in the *travaux préparatoires.*

However, it is clear that the issue of cleanup and restoration of contaminated soil primarily is governed by the general public law on pollution and waste control.

430. The starting point here is the general prohibition in Article 7 paragraph 1 'to possess, do, or initiate anything that may entail a risk of pollution unless it is lawful … '. If there is a danger of pollution contrary to the Act or a decision pursuant to the Act, 'the person responsible for the pollution' shall ensure that measures are taken to prevent such pollution from occurring. If pollution has already occurred, the responsible person 'shall ensure that measures are taken to stop or remove the pollution or limit its effects'. He/she also has a duty to 'take steps to mitigate any damage or nuisance resulting from the pollution … ' (Article 7 paragraph 2). These duties are limited to 'measures that are reasonably proportionate to the damage and nuisance to be avoided'.

Hence, the responsible person has a broadly defined duty to prevent soil pollution, to remove existing soil pollution and to limit the possible effects of soil pollution. A reasonable interpretation is that the Act lays down a direct obligation to clean up already contaminated sites, to a reasonable extent. However, the wording of the rules is quite general, and in many situations, it may seem to be somewhat unclear what the responsible person is required to do, if anything at all.

431. In practice, the obligations are often clarified and cleanup measures initiated by the pollution control authorities. According to Article 7 paragraph 4, *the authorities may order* the person responsible to carry out clearly defined measures to fulfil his/her obligations according to paragraph 2. A similar rule applies to clearing up illegal waste according to Article 37 of the Act.

If the person responsible does not carry out such an order, the pollution control authority may arrange for the measures to be implemented itself. At the outset, the responsible person must cover the costs of such an action. This situation is governed by the general rules in Articles 74–77 of the PCA.

483. Regulation of 26 Jun. 2015 No. 808 on state grant for actions to clean up contaminated sites and contaminated bottom of the sea and of lakes.

432. Often, it is necessary to perform *a survey or examination* of the actual pollution situation on a site which is presumed to be contaminated. Such an examination may in itself be quite expensive. The question is whether the authorities may order the person responsible to carry out such an examination.

Article 51 of the PCA provides the necessary legal basis to this effect. The authority may order any person responsible, according to Article 7, to arrange or pay for examinations and similar measures that may reasonably be required, in order to, *inter alia,* ascertain the cause of or impact of pollution that has occurred, and 'ascertain how the pollution is to be combated'. In a Supreme Court case from 2010, a foreign chemical company was found to be responsible for carrying out an examination of possible polluted soil pursuant to Article 51 on a site owned by a daughter company. The daughter company had produced paints on the site, but most of the soil pollution had been caused by earlier owners of the site which also produced paint.[484]

433. The question has been raised whether these rules may be applied *retroactively:* Does the duty to clean up a contaminated site or waste dump apply also to sites that were polluted before the general obligations inherent in the PCA came into force? This issue has been somewhat controversial.

Article 97 of Norway's written constitution – Grunnloven – states that: 'No law may be given retroactive effect.' This rule has been the subject of extensive discussion among legal scholars, and has come before the Supreme Court in numerous cases. It is interpreted as restricting only retroactive legislation which is clearly unreasonable or unjust. The considerations differ from one area of the law to the other. Whether or not Stortinget as the legislator has accepted – explicitly or implicitly – a certain retroactivity or not is relevant here but not decisive.[485]

The PCA applies explicitly to already existing enterprises and activities, and to existing waste dumps (Article 86). Contaminated sites are not explicitly mentioned in this respect. However, in a 1979 decision, the Supreme Court held that a new Act might oblige the owner of a waste dump to remove it, even if it had been legally set up.[486] As a rule, the legislator may always introduce new legislation in order to correct a situation which society now finds unacceptable.

434. On the basis of these principles of interpretation of the rule in Article 97 of the Grunnloven, a reasonable conclusion is that 'the person responsible' may now be ordered to examine a contaminated site, and to clean it up to a reasonable extent, even if the contamination is due to activities that were legal at the time they were carried out.

In fact, most of the existing soil pollution is probably due to discharges and burying of hazardous substances which were illegal when they were carried out, although the earlier legal regime may have been somewhat unclear. In that case, there is no problem of retroactivity at all.

---

484. Norsk Retstidende 2010, 306.
485. *See* further discussion of Art. 97 Grunnloven *supra* in General Introduction, Ch. 2, §1, I.
486. Norsk Retstidende 1979, 1279.

435. But another difficult question remains: Who is to be regarded as 'the person responsible'?

If the property in question is owned by the same person who undertook the pollution, the answer is simple and clear: He/she is the person responsible and he/she can undoubtedly be ordered to clean up. Often, however, the situation is different. The contaminated land may have changed ownership, even several times, since the actual pollution took place. The crucial question is whether only the initial polluter can be regarded as 'the person responsible', or whether also the subsequent owners of the site, and the present owner in particular, can be ordered to clean up the site and cover the costs.

436. In this author's view, pursuant to a reasonable interpretation of Article 7 of the PCA, *the present owner may be ordered to clean up*, even if the contamination has been caused by earlier owners of the site. This was confirmed by the Supreme Court in a 2012 case – the first Supreme Court case on the matter.[487] In that case, the landowner was found to be 'responsible' for the cleanup and had to pay a part of the costs that roughly corresponded to the increased value of the property as a result of the cleanup (the State covered a greater part of the costs). This solution is important from an environmental point of view, and thus in accordance with the purpose of the Act. It is also often a quite reasonable solution, as the present owner normally also gets the economic benefit through the increased value of the cleaned up site. This is underpinned by the rule of Article 28-1 in the PBA (*see infra* Part III) which in essence prohibits new constructions on a contaminated site. The owner's responsibility is also important in order to get the buyer of a site to examine it properly before the purchase, in accordance with the principles of *due diligence*. This in turn will clearly work to prevent landowners from polluting their soil, as this normally will reduce its market value considerably.

However, as an absolute rule, it may have unreasonable consequences for the present landowner in certain cases. Therefore, some exceptions to the rule may be justified. In the mentioned case the Supreme Court stated that there might be exceptions to the main rule of landowner responsibility in very special cases where this would be manifestly unreasonable.

437. It could be argued that the present owner should be responsible only if he/she was aware of the contamination when he/she purchased the land, or if there was reason to believe that it could be contaminated. However, such a rule would place a very heavy burden of proof on the pollution control authority, and in fact introduce an element of private law into a public law issue. In an earlier case concerning responsibility for the removal of waste from a site, the Court of Appeal held that the underlying rights and obligations between different parties must be sorted out between the parties. This was also the view of the Supreme Court in the above-mentioned case. It is an impossible task for the authorities to clarify such relationships as a prerequisite for stating responsibility.

487. Norsk Retstidende 2012, 944. In this case, the pollution had not been caused by the landowner, but by the industrial activity of an earlier lessee of the site.

438. According to Article 28-1 of the *PBA*,[488] it is prohibited to build on a site which is not environmentally safe. In practice, this means that a person who wants to build on a contaminated site must clean it up properly before he/she can obtain a building permit. This rule applies regardless of whether the present owner is responsible for the pollution, or whether he/she knew about it when he/she purchased the land.

A special regulation, pursuant to the PCA,[489] specifies the obligations of the developer during *construction or digging on contaminated soil*. The developer must always examine the soil before he/she starts the works. If there is reason to believe that the soil is polluted above certain concentration levels (specified in the annex to the regulation), a full investigation must be made. The developer must take the necessary measures to reduce the concentration to acceptable levels, and to prevent any dispersion of the pollution and risk to health and the environment. He/she has to present a plan for such measures to the local authorities, in connection with the application of the building permit required by the PBA. The plan has to be approved by the local authorities. When the works have been carried out, the developer must present a report on the matter to the authorities. If soil pollution is discovered after works have started on a piece of land, the developer has to stop the works, make the necessary examinations, and present a plan of measures to the authorities.

439. The question is also whether *other actors* than the person who actually polluted the soil and the present owner of the site may be found responsible and ordered to clean up and/or cover the costs. The PCA itself does not give a clear answer to such questions, and case law is limited.

In relation to waste dumps, the question has been raised about a possible responsibility for the person(s) who has (have) delivered or transported the waste to the waste dump. Such a responsibility cannot be excluded, although the law is unclear on this point.

440. Furthermore, the question has been raised whether, in the case of *bankruptcy* of the owner of the contaminated site, a mortgagee, or the bankruptcy estate may be held responsible for covering the full costs of the cleanup. Again, the key question is how the wording 'the person responsible' in Article 7 should be interpreted in relation to the various possible situations.

Most probably, they will be responsible if they take over the site and continue the activity. But according to Norwegian bankruptcy law,[490] the bankruptcy estate may as a rule abandon properties of the debtor that have no value. It is possible that the estate may legally abandon the site if it is ordered by the authorities to clean it up, but the criteria for this are not at all clear. Nevertheless, the estate is fully responsible and liable for damage if its own activities on the site lead to contamination and damage.

---

488. Act of 27 Jun. 2008 No. 71. *See infra* Part III.
489. Regulation of 1 Jun. 2004 No. 931 Ch. 2.
490. Act of 8 Jun. 1984 No. 58.

The phase between environmental law and bankruptcy law raises many questions to which Norwegian law at present does not have clear answers. The solution will to some extent depend on the circumstances of each case.

§3. Special Regulations

441. There are special rules to prevent the risk of pollution from *buried oil tanks.*[491]

The problem relates mainly to steel tanks in petrol stations and other enterprises. It also relates to tanks for domestic fuel oil, many of which are buried in private gardens and so on. Corrosion and other technical failures may easily cause leakages. The regulation applies to tanks with a capacity of more than 3,200 l, in urban areas and in other areas where a leakage may pollute groundwater or in other ways damage valuable natural, cultural, recreational or agricultural areas (Regulation Article 2). The municipality may decide that it should apply to smaller tanks as well.

The main rule is that the person responsible must inspect the tank regularly to ensure that the tank is in proper order. If a tank is not in proper order, it must either be repaired or be removed from use (Regulation Article 5). Tanks which are not in use must be emptied (Regulation Article 8). New tanks must satisfy certain technical criteria (Regulation Article 4).

The rules that are laid down in the Regulation on *manure of organic origin*[492] are important in order to prevent soil pollution from the spreading of manure, in particular sewage sludge, on agricultural land. The regulation lays down strict rules on such spreading, with maximum limits for content of heavy metals, area requirements, and so on (*see also supra* Chapter 3, §2, III).

491. Regulation of 1 Jun. 2004 No. 931 ('Pollution Regulation') Ch. 1.
492. Regulation of 4 Jul. 2003 No. 951.

Chapter 6. Noise Pollution

§1. Introduction

442. Noise pollution is *one of the most serious environmental problems* in Norway – if not *the* most serious – when it comes to effects on human health and well-being. According to the latest national survey, some 2.1 million Norwegians (of a total population of 5.3 million) are affected by noise above 55 dBA, of whom 1.9 million – 90% – from road traffic. These figures have increased steadily over the last couple of decades. For more than 500,000 persons, noise is a serious problem, and 200,000 have their night sleep disturbed.

443. In 2007 new national *noise policy objectives* were laid down: The general nuisance caused by noise should be reduced by 10% within 2020 compared to 1999. In addition, the number of persons most exposed (with indoor noise over 38 dB) should be reduced by 30% within 2020 compared to 2005. However, by 2021 no significant improvements are registered; apparently more people – not less – are affected, mostly due to increased road traffic and increased population in urban areas. The MCE stated in its annual budget document for 2021 that the 2020 targets are not being met.[493]

444. *Several types of public instruments are needed*, and are actually applied, for the prevention and abatement of noise. Land-use planning and building control, pursuant to the PBA, is an important tool to prevent many noise problems. In this connection, environmental quality standards in the form of maximum acceptable noise levels play an important role. But this is not sufficient. In addition, the problem has to be reduced at the source.

445. Noise is explicitly included in the definition of pollution in the PCA. This means that the general rules of the Act apply to the prevention and reduction of noise, in the same way as to other types of pollution. Emission of noise is prevented and reduced through regulations and decisions pursuant to both the PCA (noise from stationary sources) and the Product Control Act (noise from products). The legislation regulating the various types of transport provides the basis for rules on noise from sources such as road and air traffic, railways, and motorized traffic in connection with recreation. Local health authorities may intervene if noise is a threat to people's health, pursuant to the Public Health Act.[494]

An important regulation relating to the abatement of noise is the Pollution Regulation[495] Chapter 5 pursuant to the PCA which implements EU Directive 2002/49/EC as amended by Directive (EU) 2015/996 (*see* §2).[496] It is supplemented by State

493. Prop. 1 S. (2020–2021) Ministry of Climate and Environment, p. 23.
494. Act of 24 Jun. 2011 No. 29.
495. Regulation of 1 Jun. 2004 No. 931.
496. Directive 2002/49/EC of the European Parliament and of the Council of 25 Jun. 2002 relating to the assessment and management of environmental noise.

guidelines for noise in land-use planning (*see* §3). Regulation of noise from products are laid down pursuant to the Product Control Act and relevant sector legislation (*see* §4).

In this field, *private law* also plays a role through the general obligations and the compensation rules in the Neighbour Act. These have been particularly important in relation to noise from roads and airports. These issues will mainly be discussed *infra* in Part IV.

§2. Noise from Stationary Sources: Assessment and Action Plans

446. The Pollution Regulation Chapter 5 *on noise assessment, action plans and maximum limits for ongoing activities*[497] pursuant to the PCA is a central piece of legislation regarding noise abatement. It has several objectives. One is to establish minimum noise levels for indoor noise and ensure that these are applied. Another is to prevent and reduce harmful effects of noise exposure through assessment of noise, public information about noise problems, and action plans and measures to reduce noise (Regulation Article 5-1). It applies to airborne, external noise caused by human activities, except from households. As mentioned, this regulation implements the EU directive relating to the assessment and management of environmental noise. This set of rules are important for the planning of new infrastructure and for the placing of various noise-sensitive activities.

447. Part II of the Regulation establishes maximum *acceptable levels of indoor noise* in residential houses, nursery schools, educational institutions and health institutions. This applies to noise from public roads, railways, civil and military airports, harbours, other types of transport terminals, and industry (Regulation Article 5-4 to 5-10).

If the noise level exceeds 42 dB(A)[498] on a twenty-four-hour basis, measures must be taken by the owner of the installation that causes the noise in order to reduce the noise to that level (Article 5-4). The owner of an infrastructure or an installation which creates noise has a duty to assess the indoor noise situation and update the assessment every five year (Article 5-5). The pollution control authority may order assessment measures to be taken, and that several actors cooperate. The assessment methods are laid down by the pollution control authority. To get clear results, assessment of the noise level may be supplemented by actual measuring (Article 5-7).

If there is a risk that the 42 dB(A) level is exceeded, the owner of the infrastructure or installation causing this noise shall consider measures to prevent it (Article 5-8), and he or she shall take the necessary measures to avoid that the level is significantly exceeded (Article 5-9). If necessary measures are not taken, the authorities may order relevant measures, including ordering several actors to cooperate in

497. Regulation of 1 Jun. 2004 No. 931 Ch. 5.
498. 42 dB $L_{pAeq,24h}$.

carrying out these measures. The owner of the infrastructure or installation is responsible for the running and maintenance of the measure taken on the property, typically and including noise baffles.

448. Furthermore, the Regulation Part III (Article 5-11 to 5-14) lays down rules and requirements with regard to *mapping, assessment and measures to control outdoor noise*, called 'strategic noise mapping'. Before June 2012, noise maps for the preceding year were to be established for noise exposure from the major highways (more than 3 million vehicles a year), railways (more than 30,000 trains per year), airports (more than 50,000 flights per year), and urban areas of more than 100,000 inhabitants. The assessment covered noise levels over 55 Lden and 50 Lnight. These maps are to be updated every five years. In urban areas the assessment shall cover noise from public roads, railways, aviation, harbours, other types of transport terminals, and industrial installations covered by the EU 'IPPC-directive' (Article 5-11).[499] The owner of the infrastructure or installation is responsible for the assessment. In urban areas the municipalities have a coordinating role (Article 5-12).

The assessments shall be based on methods laid down in EU Directive 2002/49/EC as amended by Directive (EU) 2015/996. It shall be the basis for *action plans* made by the responsible owners with the aim to reduce the noise problem, with due information to the public and participation by interested parties. Detailed rules are laid down in annexes to the regulation, in accordance with the EU directive (Article 5-14).

The fact that the noise problems continue to increase in Norway indicates that the application of this regulation is far from satisfactory and that stronger and more active measures must be taken to turn the negative trend.

§3. Noise in Land-Use Planning

449. The general system of regional and municipal spatial planning pursuant to the PBA is highly relevant for the prevention and reduction of noise problems.[500] Through good planning, noise problems can be avoided by careful location of different activities which, on the one hand, create noise such as a highway, and, on the other hand, are particularly vulnerable to noise such as a residential area, a school or a hospital.

The MCE has issued comprehensive *Guidelines for the treatment of noise in land-use planning*.[501] They provide rules and recommendations for the treatment and limitation of noise in land-use planning and in decisions of building permits pursuant to PBA, and generally when establishing a noisy activity or installation. The guidelines apply to noise from most sources, including roads, aviation, ports, industrial installations, rifle ranges, motorsport arenas, and wind turbines. They apply in particular to the planning of new residential areas and areas for activities

499. Now Directive 2010/75/EU.
500. This system will be thoroughly presented in Part III.
501. The guideline has been regularly updated, the most recent version is State Guideline T-1442/2021, in force from 11 Jun. 2021.

vulnerable to noise in the proximity of an existing noisy source, and for the planning of new noisy activities such as a new road or the extension of an existing road.

The guidelines aim at achieving a satisfactory indoor noise level, a satisfactory noise level in outdoor areas related to residential houses, schools, etc., and a 'quiet side' in such areas. They provide a system of mapping of noise level and identifying different 'noise zones'[502] to be used in land-use planning and decisions with detailed recommended maximum noise limits from various noise sources, at various hours (day/night) and for different environments such as residential houses and other vulnerable institutions. There are special recommended noise limits for such areas as urban parks, churchyards, and recreational areas within or close to urban areas. These recommendations also apply to recreational homes. Furthermore, noise should be kept at a minimum in protected nature areas. They also give advice about measures to mitigate the noise problems from various sources.

450. The guidelines provide detailed recommendations on the treatment of noise in the various types of land-use plans. The responsibility lies with the municipality as the main planning authority (*see infra* Part III). The county governor is the State authority in the field, and may intervene if noise problems are not taken properly into account in the municipal planning.

In *municipal master plans*, the noise level in different parts of the plan area must be assessed through a noise map. This map serves to clarify what types of buildings and activities may be located in different zones. The plan may lay down precise rules for the treatment of noise in subsequent *local development plans* and when issuing building permits.

In both master plans and local development plans, the municipality may lay down noise limits in certain areas, define 'silent areas' (e.g., in recreational areas) and designate a 'restriction zone' with regard to new construction due to noise problems, for example, in connection with an airport (PBA Article 11-9 and 11-8, paragraph 3, a.). In addition, a local development plan may lay down specific and binding provisions concerning the buildings and activities covered by the plan, with the purpose of limiting local noise problems which the plan would otherwise entail.

When planning a noise-sensitive building/installation, the actual noise situation and possible future development must be assessed at an early stage and play an important role in the placing and design of the building in question. The recommended maximum noise levels must be applied. It is explicitly stated that schools and preschools should not be placed in a 'red noise zone'. Similarly, the noise problem and possible effects must be an important issue to assess and take into consideration when planning noisy infrastructure, installations and activities. For noisy activities, the owner of the activity is responsible for providing such assessment and necessary maps.

Noise from *construction works* is often a serious problem although limited in time. The guidelines lay down special noise limits for construction works, which vary according to the length of the construction period (more or less than six months) and are somewhat stricter during the night than during the day. If it is too

502. A general distinction is between 'yellow zones' and 'red zones'.

difficult or impossible to keep the activity within the noise limits, this can be accepted for shorter periods only, and the neighbouring population must be properly informed beforehand.

The guidelines also provide a number of recommendations for preventing and abating noise.

451. According to the general rules on *environmental impact assessment*,[503] an EIA has to be carried out for a new municipal master plan, and also for a local development plan if it will cause significant noise. The assessment must include an assessment of possible noise problems and suggestions regarding possible measures to limit the noise.

452. Land-use planning instruments are not least important for the *prevention of noise from airports.* The above-mentioned guidelines for noise in land-use planning serve as guidelines mainly for the municipalities when developing land-use plans and controlling building around airports. The core principle is that the noise level must be measured and/or calculated. Two different noise zones around the airport are defined on the basis of differences in noise levels. The guidelines define the types of activity that either could be permitted or should not be permitted in the various zones. This should serve as the basis for the development of the municipal master plan and the local development plan. Only buildings which comply with adopted plans are permitted.[504]

453. The Aviation Act[505] provides the legal basis for regulations concerning *noise from air traffic.* Article 9-1 of the Act states explicitly that the Ministry[506] may issue regulations with the objective of preventing nuisance from noise. For the most important airports, restrictions have been issued on night flights. Also, compulsory flight routes for take-off and landing have been defined in order to avoid – as much as possible – the most densely populated areas.

§4. Noise from Products, Including from Cars and Aeroplanes

454. The prevention and reduction of noise is an explicit objective of the *Product Control Act* (Article 1). The general rules of the Act apply, such as the general obligation to handle and use products carefully in order to prevent risk and damage to health and the environment (Article 3), *see* the general presentation of the Act in Chapter 1, §3.

455. Pursuant to Article 4 of the Act, regulations may lay down maximum noise emission limits for various products, and specify technical requirements, measuring

503. In the PBA, Chs. 4 and 14, and Regulation of 19 Jun. 2017 No. 854 on EIA pursuant to PBA.
504. In addition, regulations pursuant to the Air Traffic Act may prohibit certain types of constructions and activities in the vicinity of the airport for reasons of safety, etc.
505. Act of 11 Jun. 1993 No. 101.
506. The Ministry of Transport.

methods, labelling rules and so on to this effect. They may also define the responsibilities of producers, importers and retailers.

Specific regulations concerning noise from such *machines* as transportable compressors, lawn mowers, dozers, excavators and loaders are since 2002 included in a general Regulation on Machines,[507] which implements the relevant EU directives.[508] Its Annex XIII lays down comprehensive rules on noise emission from machines and other equipment for outdoor use, including noise limits for various machines, labelling, etc.

456. As mentioned, *noise from vehicles* is the major noise problem in Norway. There is a comprehensive set of rules with the aim of limiting noise from vehicles. These are laid down in Regulation on technical requirements and approval of vehicles, parts and equipment.[509] The general rule is that vehicles should not be 'unnecessarily' noisy (Article 24-1). The regulation lays down precise noise limits for different types of vehicles, motorcycles, mopeds, and tractors. The rules implement the quite comprehensive EU rules.[510]

Special rules pursuant to the Product Control Act prohibit the use of *motorized recreation boats* without a proper exhaust box.[511]

457. An *aeroplane* must comply with a number of technical requirements, including noise, in order to obtain an 'environment certificate', which is compulsory for all aeroplanes flying in Norway.[512] Norwegian air authorities issue environment certificates for planes registered in Norway. Foreign planes must have a proper certificate according to the rules in its country of registration, provided that there is an agreement of mutual recognition of such certificates between Norway and the country in question (Aviation Act Article 4-4). An exemption may be accepted in individual cases (Article 4-4 paragraph 3). A contravention of the rules on 'environment certificate' is subject to a penalty of a maximum of two years' imprisonment or a fine (Article 14-5).

The requirements are defined through regulations pursuant to the Aviation Act (Article 4-1). A special regulation has been adopted concerning emissions of noise and other pollutants from civil aeroplanes.[513] The regulation implements the relevant EU directives and regulations, and international rules in this field. Ongoing work at the international level[514] aims at the tightening of noise requirements, and the phasing out of the noisiest planes.

507. Regulation of 20 May 2009 No. 544 with later amendments, pursuant to the Product Control Act and other Acts.
508. Directive 2000/14/EC relating to the Noise in the Environment by Equipment for Use Outdoors, as amended by Directive 2005/88/EC.
509. Regulation of 10 Apr. 1994 No. 918 pursuant to the Road Traffic Act with later amendments, Ch. 24.
510. Directive 96/20/EC, Directive 92/97/EC, Directive 70/157/EEC as amended by Directives 1999/101/EC and 2007/34/EC, and furthermore ECE-reg. nr. 51-01, Directive 97/24/EC Ch. 9 as amended by Directives 2006/27/EC and 2009/108/EC, Directive 97/24/EC as amended by Directives 2006/27/EC and 2009/108/EC, and Directive 2003/77/EC.
511. Regulation of 1 Jun. 2004 No. 931 Ch. 6.
512. Aviation Act Ch. IV.
513. Regulation of 19 Jul. 1993 No. 4047 as amended by Regulation of 25 Mar. 2002 No. 303.
514. In particular, through the International Civil Aviation Organisation (ICAO).

Chapter 7. Radiation and Vibration

§1. Overview

458. There are numerous sources of *radiation* of different types in modern society, including X-rays, which require special care and regulation. Norway has no nuclear power plants, and is thus faced with fewer problems in this field than do many other countries. Nevertheless, as the 1987 Chernobyl accident clearly illustrated, the problem of nuclear radiation does not know national borders. Also, various types of radiation are common for a number of uses, in Norway as in other industrial countries, not least in the field of medicine. Radiation may be necessary and beneficial, but it also may involve serious health and environmental risks. Legislation for the proper control of a wide variety of radiation is needed.

The main instrument to this effect in Norwegian law is the Radiation Act, adopted in 2000.[515] As a supplement, the PCA may be made applicable to radiation pursuant to a decision to this effect by the government.[516] In 2010, a regulation was adopted with the purpose of regulating the use and waste disposal of radioactive substances on the basis of the PCA.[517] It follows that dangerous chemicals, hazardous waste and radioactive substances will be treated equally and according to the same principles. This will strengthen the legal basis for the handling and disposal of radioactive substances and waste. Included in the regulation are limit values for radioactive waste and emissions that will require a pollution permit.

As regards *vibration,* the PCA applies fully already. Also, the Neighbour Act is relevant in this respect.

§2. The Radiation Act

459. The purpose of the Radiation Act is *to prevent harmful effects* of radiation on human health and the environment (Article 1). It applies to any type of production, import, export, transport, transfer, possession, installation, use, or waste disposal of radiation sources (Article 2 paragraph 1). It also applies to human activities that entail an increase in the natural level of ionizing radiation (Article 2 paragraph 2). It further covers contingency planning and emergency response system for radiation accidents (Article 2 paragraph 3).

Its field of application is *both ionizing and non-ionizing radiation.* Ionizing radiation means radiation from radioactive substances, X-rays, and radiation from particles. Non-ionizing radiation means optical radiation, radio-frequency radiation, electrical and magnetic fields, other radiations with similar biological effects, and ultrasound.

'Radiation sources' is a key concept in the Act. It is defined as radioactive substances, products or equipment containing radioactive substances, as well as installations, instruments or equipment that may cause radiation (Article 3).

---

515. Act of 12 May 2000 No. 36 on radiation protection, and use of radiation.
516. PCA Art. 6 para. 1.
517. Regulation 1 Nov. 2010 No. 1394.

460. The Act lays down *a general obligation for anyone who handles radiation sources, to act carefully,* in order to avoid any risk to human health or the environment. This includes human activities that entail an increased natural ionizing radiation. When considering the proper level of care, the advantages of the activity as well as the risks involved must be taken into account. Radiation doses must not exceed the prescribed limits (Article 5).

Enterprises covered by the Act shall take all necessary measures to protect the employees, other persons, and the environment from radiation. Particularly vulnerable employees, such as pregnant women, shall be afforded special protection (Article 8). Necessary instruction and training for all employees is required, as well as proper information to visitors (Article 7).

The Ministry[518] may by regulation determine maximum acceptable limits for work and stay in places where natural ionizing radiation is increased by human activities (Article 10).

461. The Act provides the authorities with a broad legal basis for issuing the necessary *regulations* for virtually all aspects and types of activities in relation to radiation sources (Article 12). Notably, they may establish systems of approval or notification for the production, import, export, transport, possession, use, waste disposal, and so on of radiation sources (Article 6).

Special regulations may be issued concerning the safe disposal of radioactive waste, including regulations on take-back obligations and other compulsory return arrangements (Article 9).

462. The Act applies to the use of *radiation for medical purposes.* It lays down general principles for such use (Article 13). It must always be carried out in accordance with the accepted medical methods for examination and treatment. The person responsible must thoroughly consider the need for radiation on the basis of a broad assessment of, on the one hand, the risks involved, and, on the other hand, the advantages for individuals and society in general, and possible alternative methods. A *substitution principle* is inherent in the rules: radiation should be avoided if the same result may be reached by other methods without considerable disadvantages. As low doses as possible for the purpose should be applied. Regular control of doses is prescribed.

463. The Ministry may order enterprises covered by the Act to develop the necessary contingency plans for *radiation accidents,* and carry out 'preparedness' exercises. They may also be ordered to inform the persons in the vicinity of the enterprise about possible risks (Article 15).

If an accident occurs, the government may order State and municipal authorities to organize evacuation, access restrictions in certain areas, and necessary securing of foodstuffs, drinking water and so on (Article 16). In such cases, exemptions may be made from established dose levels and other rules and requirements (Article 17).

518. Ministry of Health and Care Services.

464. The Act has a set of rules about *inspection, control, and injunction,* and about sanctions in case of violations of the Act. A coercive fine may be applied if a fixed time limit for correcting a contravention is not met.

Whoever wilfully or negligently violates the Act, or an order pursuant to the Act, may be punished with fines or a maximum of a three-month term of imprisonment. If the violations have, or could have, entailed a serious risk to health or the environment, the maximum term of imprisonment is two years (Article 23).

Chapter 8. Other Sectors

§1. Hazardous Substances

I. Introduction

465. The introduction of toxic chemicals, including heavy metals, into the environment is one of the most serious threats to the natural environment in Norway as well as globally. Many chemicals are toxic and at the same time persistent, decompose extremely slowly in the natural environment, may be spread widely by wind and sea currents, and accumulate in the food chain. Some substances are carcinogenic or generate allergies. Others may have a disturbing effect on genes and the reproductive capacity. The level of some of the 'old' substances like DDT and PCB shows a certain decline. On the other hand, new hazardous substances appear in Norway's nature, with increasing levels.

466. The prevention and control of the spreading of hazardous substances is one of the most significant fields of action within Norway's environmental policy. The general policy objective is to reduce the concentration of the most dangerous substances to their natural level. For man-made substances, the long-term policy objective is the virtual elimination of concentrations in nature. According to the internationally adopted 'generation objective', the emission of substances that constitute a serious threat to the environment should be eliminated within a generation, or by the year 2020.[519] More precise and stricter objectives, based on their gradual phasing out, have been established for the most dangerous substances. Norway has established a 'priority list' of hazardous substances that should be eliminated from production and use. In 2021 the list contains sixty-six substances.

To a large extent, the national efforts in this important field are based on international agreements and conventions, and internationally agreed criteria. Through the EEA Agreement, Norway is implementing the relevant EU directives and regulations in the field, the most important being the regulation on REACH.[520] The 2001 UN Convention on POP (the 'Stockholm Convention'), which Norway has ratified, also plays a role in the shaping of Norway's policy.

467. There are many sources of introduction of hazardous substances into the environment, and the prevention and control requires a broad set of instruments.

Some significant sources have been treated in earlier chapters, such as emission into air and water from stationary sources, and from transport, and the disposal of hazardous waste. The *PCA*[521] is the main legal tool to this effect. However, the *Product Control Act*[522] is even more important. This Act provides the basis for the

519. This objective has been established within the framework of the OSPAR Convention.
520. Regulation (EC) 1907/2006. The regulation has been implemented in Norway through Regulation of 30 May 2008 No. 516 on Registration, Evaluation, Authorization and Restriction of Chemicals (REACH).
521. Act of 13 Mar. 1981 No. 6.
522. Act of 11 Jun. 1976 No. 79.

general systems of assessment, control and regulation of the production, marketing, use and treatment as waste of a wide variety of hazardous substances and products. A number of important regulations in this field have been adopted pursuant to this Act.

Other Acts may also be relevant. Most hazardous substances are also controlled through *The Working Environment Act*[523] and the *Fire and Explosion Prevention Act.*[524] Pesticides and herbicides are controlled through regulations pursuant to the *Food Act.*[525]

II. General Rules of the Product Control Act and the Product Register

468. The Product Control Act is the main legal instrument for the prevention and control of pollution from hazardous substances as products. The main content of the Act is described *supra* in Chapter 1, §3. It applies to the various stages in production, including testing, import, marketing, use and other handling of products (Article 2 paragraph 1). 'Product' is defined broadly as raw materials, subsidiary materials, and semi-manufactured and finished products of all kinds (Article 2 paragraph 2). This means that the Act applies to any hazardous substance and product, regardless of whether it is only used as a raw material in the production, or is itself a finished product. The Act lays down a *general duty of care* for any person who produces, imports, markets, processes, uses or in any other way handles products that may cause hazards to health, or to the environment in the form of disturbing ecosystems, pollution, waste, noise or the like. They are to act with due care and implement reasonable measures to prevent or limit such effects (Article 3 paragraph 1).

469. Article 4 provides the authorities with a basis for taking such decisions as are necessary in order to prevent hazards to health and the environment. As a rule, such decisions shall be made in the form of regulations, and shall apply to a certain type of products. Their application may be limited to certain geographic areas.

Another important rule is *the duty of substitution.* Any enterprise using products containing a chemical that may have the said effects shall assess whether there exist alternatives which entail less risk. The enterprise must choose such an alternative if this can be done without unreasonable cost or inconvenience (Article 3a). Apparently, this rule works more as a general encouragement to industry than a strict legal requirement that is controlled by the authorities.

470. The Act has detailed rules on *the duty to provide the information necessary* for the proper implementation of the Act, when required by the authorities. Public authorities must provide such information regardless of the duty of secrecy (Article 5 paragraph 1). The authorities may require that any person who produces or imports products shall submit a representative sample of the product or initiate such investigations as may be necessary to evaluate the properties and effects of a product. The costs of such an investigation shall, as a rule, be borne by the producer or importer

523. Act of 17 Jun. 2005 No. 62.
524. Act of 14 Jun. 2002 No. 20.
525. Act of 19 Dec. 2003 No. 124.

concerned (Article 5 paragraph 2). Also, the authorities may initiate such investigations, and may require the producer or importer to bear the costs of investigation (Article 5 paragraph 3).[526] There is also a general obligation to provide information about products to the public (Articles 9–11). For details, *see* Chapter 1, §3.

471. The Product Control Act forms, together with other Acts in the field of public health, occupational health and safety, the basis for *the Product Register*. This is the central register for chemical products in Norway. The information in the register gives the government and the public a good overview of the use of hazardous substances in Norway. The information is used in connection with health, environmental and safety issues. It is managed by the NEA.

There are about 25,000 products registered in the Product Register. The number increases with about 500 products every year. Declaration of chemicals to the Product Register gives the authorities knowledge about hazardous substances and mixtures on the Norwegian market. The information from the Product Register is used by many State authorities and institutions for such purposes as:

- the government's control (inspections) of product labelling and chemical documentation;
- risk analysis of chemical substances or product types;
- general supervision of chemical substances on the Norwegian market;
- basis for advice and guidance in emergency poisoning given by the Poison Control.

472. The Product Register is based on a national Regulation on declaration to the Product Register.[527] It applies to chemicals classified according to the EU 'CLP Regulation'[528] that are produced in or imported into Norway (and not in transit only) (Article 1). The substances are covered by the national Regulation relating to *classification, labelling, and packaging of substances and chemicals*[529] which incorporates the CLP Regulation into Norwegian law.

473. The duty to declare chemicals to the Product Register is set out in the Regulation on declaration. CLP Article 45 regulating notifications to Poison Centres in Europe are also valid in Norway. The NEA is together with the Norwegian Poison Information Centre appointed body. Notifications according to CLP Article 45 have to be done in the European Chemicals Agency (ECHA) portal for Poison Notifications (PCN-portal) from 1 January 2021. Chemicals registered in the Product Register are covered by a transition period to 1 January 2025 on some conditions.

---

526. For further details on the Act, *see* the presentation in Ch. 1.
527. Regulation of 19 May 2015 No. 541 on Declaration of chemicals to the Product Register, pursuant to the Product Control Act, the Act on Inflammable Goods of 21 May 1971 No. 47, the Act on Fire and Explosion Protection of 14 Jun. 2002 No. 20, and the Occupational Health Act of 17 Jun. 2005 No. 62.
528. Regulation (EC) 1272/2008 of 16 Dec. 2008 on classification, labelling and packaging of substances and mixtures, with numerous later amendments.
529. Regulation of 16 Jun. 2012 No. 622 with later amendments.

III. Regulation on Registration, Evaluation, Authorization, Restriction, and Trade of Chemicals

A. *General Regulation*

474. From 2008, Norway has been implementing the EU Regulation on Registration, Evaluation, Authorization, and Restriction of Chemicals (REACH).[530] The EU rules are incorporated into the national REACH regulation.[531] This replaced earlier national rules in this field. The fundamental principle is that the manufacturers and importers of substances and products have *an obligation of knowledge* about the qualities of their substances and products, and *an obligation to communicate the information* to the authorities and the public through registration. These are conditions for marketing a substance within EEA.

The REACH rules and system are very complex and highly technical, with different deadlines for various activities and substances. It is not possible here to go into any details; the REACH system, including the central executing institution ECHA, is more adequately presented elsewhere. In the following, only the main lines of the system will be presented.

The NEA is the central authority in Norway for the execution, coordination and follow-up of REACH, with the MCE as the responsible ministry.

475. Registration: Manufacturers and importers within the EEA area shall register all chemical substances and mixture of substances to ECHA if the quantity exceeds 1 ton per year per manufacturer or importer (REACH Article 6). To some extent, there is a duty also to register substances of more than 1 ton in finished products (articles). The obligation applies regardless of whether the substance is to be classified or not. To simplify research, several manufacturers and/or importers of the same substance may share information and register together. A registration fee has to be paid to ECHA.

What data about the substance that must be registered depends on the amount of substance produced or imported, as described in detail in REACH annexes VII to X.

If the registration obligation in accordance with REACH is not fulfilled, it is illegal to market the substance within the EEA (Article 5).

476. Evaluation: The national chemicals authorities and ECHA shall evaluate the registration documents in order to decide whether more information about the substances is necessary. There are two main types of evaluation: evaluation of the *documents* and evaluation of the *substances.*

The purpose of the evaluation of *documents* is to assess whether the information given is in accordance with the requirements. More information may be required. It will be evaluated whether more tests are necessary to determine the possible effects of the substance in question. Tests on animals must be approved by ECHA.

530. Regulation (EC) 1907/2006 of 18 Dec. 2006, with numerous later amendments.
531. Regulation of 30 May 2008 No. 516 with later amendments, the most recent by Regulation of 4 May 2021 No. 1691.

With regard to evaluation of *substances,* the work includes developing criteria for prioritizing substances to be evaluated, taking into account the dangerous qualities of the substance, level of exposure, total amount of the substance on the market, and so on. Substances presumed to be dangerous to health or the environment shall be listed in the 'Community Rolling Action Plan' (CRAP). The evaluation work is to be divided between national authorities. They shall evaluate whether more knowledge and information are necessary and whether new rules for approval or restrictions of the marketing of the substance are needed.

477. Authorization: The system of authorization shall ensure the necessary safety, that substances which are particularly dangerous to health or the environment are properly controlled and restricted. This will result in the development of less dangerous substances in accordance with the substitution principle, or altogether alternative technologies. The authorization system applies regardless of the annual amount of the substance on the market. The REACH regulation lays down complex rules for this procedure, which requires extensive testing. This may be scientifically complicated and costly and take time.

478. Restriction: The REACH regulation makes it possible to prohibit or restrict production, import, use and marketing of dangerous substances in the entire EEA area, if the substance poses an unacceptable risk to health or the environment. The restriction is designed as a 'safety net' to manage risks that are not addressed by the other REACH processes.

Any substance on its own, in a preparation or in finished product (article), may be subject to a restriction if it is demonstrated that risks need to be addressed on a community-wide basis. A restriction dossier needs to justify that the proposed restriction is the most appropriate risk management measure to address these risks.

All prohibitions and restrictions in force are included in REACH Annex XVII. Most of these were prohibited or restricted pursuant to earlier directives, in particular Directive 76/769/EEC.

There are also several other directives with restrictions on the production, marketing and treatment as waste of products, which in Norway has been laid down in the Product Regulation (*see infra*),[532] and to some extent in the Waste Regulation[533] (see, e.g., above Chapter 4, §3).

479. Another relevant set of rules is the *Regulation on notification of export of certain dangerous chemicals.*[534] This regulation implements obligations pursuant to the Rotterdam Convention on the PIC Procedure for Certain Hazardous Chemicals and Pesticides in International Trade. It applies to chemicals covered by the procedure of explicit PIC in accordance with the convention, as well as certain chemicals which are prohibited or strictly regulated pursuant to Norwegian law[535] (Article 2

532. Regulation of 1 Jun. 2004 No. 922.
533. Regulation of 1 Jun. 2004 No. 930.
534. Regulation of 4 Nov. 2020 No. 2293.
535. Listed in Annex 1 to the regulation.

paragraph 1). It does not apply to such substances as radioactive material, waste, medicines, food, and chemicals used in food (Article 2 paragraph 2).

480. The key rule is that export to a State member of the Rotterdam Convention of chemicals covered by the regulation is prohibited if the chemical in question is subject to legal limitations in the importing country, and these have been notified according to the rules in the general 'PIC-circular' (Article 5 paragraph 1). It is also as the main rule prohibited to export chemicals to a State party that has not published rules on import, with some exceptions (Article 5 paragraph 2). In case of export of a chemical which is prohibited or strictly regulated according to Norwegian law, but not subject to export prohibition, the exporter must inform the responsible authority, the NEA, in advance. A standard form is to be used which is in accordance with the reporting form for chemicals in the REACH regulation. The authority then informs the importing State. When this has been confirmed, the export may take place (Article 6). Chemicals covered by the mentioned EU Regulation on classification, labelling and packaging must be marked accordingly.

B. Regulations Concerning Specific Substances and Groups of Substances

481. There are special regulations *on the use and so on of a number of dangerous chemicals.* Most of these are laid down in the general Product Regulation, Chapter 2.[536] They prohibit and/or lay down strict rules about the production, import, export, trade and use of the most dangerous chemicals. They implement the numerous EU Regulations, Directives and Decisions in this complex field.

482. Among the substances covered are:

- PCB (Regulation Article 2-1), lead shots (Article 2-2), mercury and mercury compounds (Article 2-3 and 2-4), octylphenol (Article 2-5), methylolacrylamide (Article 2-6), PFOS in firefoam (Article 2-9), textiles containing pentachlorophenol (Article 2-10), and wood treated with chromium (Article 2-11), heavy metal in packaging (Article 2-15), batteries (Article 2-16 to 2-18a), VOC in paint (Article 2-24 to 2-26), sulphur in fuel for ships (Article 2-27), products containing asbestos (Article 2-31).
- As mentioned *supra* in Chapter 3, § 2, IV, there are strict regulations on the content of phosphorous in detergents (Article 2-12 to 2-14).

Also for such chemicals as POPs and substances containing *fluoro-compounds*, Norway has incorporated the EU rules.[537] This is laid down in the Product Regulation Chapters 4 and 6a, respectively. There are special rules also to restrict

536. Regulation of 1 Jun. 2004 No. 922.
537. Regulation (EC) No. 850/2004 of 29 Apr. 2004 on persistent organic compounds with later amendments, Regulation (EC) No. 842/2006 of 17 May 2006 on certain fluorinated GHGs, and several others regarding substances with fluoro-compounds.

the production, trade and use of substances that may contribute to the depletion of the *ozone layer* (Product Regulation Chapter 6, *see supra* Chapter 2).

As regards *biocides*, Norway has implemented the latest EU regulations[538] through a special Regulation on biocides in 2017.[539] Generally speaking, the national regulation incorporates the comprehensive set of EU regulations and decisions in this complex field, with necessary adaptations. All permitted biocide products according to Regulation (EU) No. 528/2012 Article 3 litra c must be registered in the Product Register when imported, marketed or used on the Norwegian market. Registration is based on a declaration from the responsible subject which must provide the necessary information about the name, the type of product and the active substances in the product (Regulation Article 2-2).

483. A special category of hazardous substances is *microbiological products.* A regulation has been adopted with the purpose of preventing microorganisms in such products from damaging human health or the environment.[540] It applies to products that may involve releasing microorganisms into the outdoor environment. Microorganism is defined as 'any microbiological entity that is able to reproduce or transfer genetic material, including viruses, bacteria, single-celled plants and animals and microscopic yeast and moulds' (Regulation Article 3).

Examples of microbiological products are certain products for sanitary cleaning, deodorizing, cleansing drains and cleaning up oil spills. The regulation governs the declaration and labelling of such products that are imported to, manufactured in or marketed in Norway. Any person who manufactures or imports such products or places them on the market in Norway must declare any information necessary for the assessment of the risk the product poses to health and the environment. The label must indicate the area of application of the product and recommended precautions in connection with use.

C. Agricultural Pesticides

484. Until 2004, *pesticides*[541] were subject to a special Act.[542] The main rule of the Act was that all pesticides must be approved by the agricultural authorities, on the basis of an assessment of their properties as regards toxicity and effects. Pesticides for scientific uses only were exempted (Article 3). An approval was valid

538. Regulation (EU) 528/2012 concerning the making available on the market and use of biocidal products, with later amendments.
539. Regulation of 18 Apr. 2017 No. 480 with later amendments, the most recent by Regulation 23. Apr. 2021 No. 1393.
540. Regulation of 22 Jan. 1998 No. 93 on declaration and labelling of microbiological products that may be introduced into the natural environment, pursuant to the Product Control Act, with later amendments. It implements the EU directive in the field, Directive 83/189/EEC, with subsequent amendments.
541. This includes mainly insecticides, fungicides and herbicides, of which herbicides are the most important group.
542. Act of 5 Apr. 1963 No. 9.

for five years. Also, any person who wants to produce, import or sell pesticides must as a rule have a permit from the authorities (Article 7).

In 2004, this Act was replaced by a new, comprehensive Act on Food Production and Food Safety (the *Food Act*).[543] This Act does not explicitly repeat the rules of the Pesticides Act. It leaves a more general discretionary power to the authorities to control the use of pesticides and other products in the food production industry. The intention is, however, that the control of pesticides shall be based on the same principles as before. The rules are now laid down in a comprehensive regulation on pesticides and herbicides.[544] This regulation incorporates the very complex set of EU regulations in this field.[545]

§2. The Rational Use of Energy

485. Energy efficiency and the rational production and use of energy are important objectives of Norway's energy policy and energy law. The regulation of energy production and trade is an important legal field. Although many rules in this field clearly have indirect effects on the consumption and use of energy, it is too broad and complex to be discussed further in this monograph.[546]

As far as the more *direct regulation of energy use* is concerned, saving and rational use of energy was until recently mainly promoted through information, including labelling, and economic instruments – such as taxes on electricity and domestic fuel – and certain public subsidies for energy-saving measures through the Climate and Energy Fund and the State company Enova (*see supra* Chapter 2, §4 II).

Over the last decades, several legal rules and mechanisms have been introduced with the purpose of strengthening the legal basis for increased efficiency in energy use.

486. The first was an amendment to Article 16 in the PCA. This article defines the legal framework for conditions to be laid down in a pollution permit pursuant to Article 11 of the Act, or in regulations. According to the amendment, a pollution permit or regulations may include conditions aimed at promoting efficient use of energy which is used in, or generated by, the activity covered by the permit or regulation. This amendment was necessary in order to implement properly the EU IPPC Directive[547] which requires that energy-efficiency measures are considered as part of an integrated pollution permit.

543. Act of 19 Dec. 2003 No. 124.

544. Regulation of 26 Jul. 2004 No. 1138 with later amendments.

545. In particular, Regulation (EC) nr. 1107/2009 and Regulation (EU) nr. 540/2011 with numerous later amendments.

546. The main Acts in this field are Act of 29 Jun. 1990 No. 50 on the production, conversion, trade, distribution, and use of energy (the Energy Act) and Act of 29 Nov. 1996 No. 72 on petroleum activity. Act of 14 Dec. 1917 No. 17 on Watercourse regulation is also important. Some aspects of this Act will be discussed in Part II Ch. 8.

547. Directive 96/61/EC as consolidated in Directive 2008/1/EC and now reformed in Directive 2010/75/EC of 24 Nov. 2010 on industrial emissions (integrated pollution prevention and control).

It should be noted that energy efficiency, or energy-saving, is not explicitly mentioned among the objectives of the PCA (Article 1). Therefore, it was necessary to state clearly in the text of Article 16 that conditions to this effect can be imposed as part of a pollution permit.

487. The second amendment was the introduction of a new Article 4a in the *Product Control Act*. In order to promote energy-efficient products, the State authorities may issue decisions concerning, *inter alia:*

(1) maximum limits for the energy consumption of products, including rules on assessment methods and so on;
(2) production of, and trade in, products;
(3) labelling of products;
(4) technical documentation of the energy-efficiency characteristics of products; and
(5) declaration in writing confirming the full concurrence between the label information and the real energy consumption of the product.

As a rule, such decisions should be issued in the form of general regulations concerning certain types of products.

488. The main regulation pursuant to this article is the Regulation on environment-friendly design of energy-related products (Eco-design Regulation).[548] This incorporates the EU Eco-design Directive[549] and lays down maximum allowable consumption of a number of different electric products, including ordinary households products like limps, television, refrigerators, freezers, drying machines, air conditioners, office equipment. The products with a higher consumption cannot be marketed. The producer, and if necessary the dealer, has the duty to ensure that their products fulfil the requirements. They also must put a 'CE-label' on the machine.

489. Third, the *Labelling of Consumer Goods Act*[550] was amended in order to provide the government with the necessary authority to require information on the energy use of consumer products in the form of marking and labelling (now in Article 3). This may include information on a product's use of energy and other resources, and its environmental effects, when a product is marketed, advertised or exhibited. This has made it possible to implement EU rules in this field. The EU directive on the availability of consumer information on energy efficiency of household equipment[551] is incorporated in Norwegian law in a Regulation from 2013.[552]

---

548. Regulation of 23 Feb. 2011 No. 190. The Ministry for Oil and Energy is the ministry responsible in this field.
549. Directive 2009/125/EC establishing a framework for the setting of ecodesign requirements for energy-related products.
550. Act of 18 Dec. 1981 No. 90.
551. Council Directive 92/75/EEC of 22 Sep. 1992 on the indication by labelling and standard product information of the consumption of energy and other resources by household appliances.
552. Regulation of 27 May 2013 No. 534.

Also incorporated are the EU rules on Fuel economy and CO_2 emissions in connection with the marketing of new motor vehicles.[553]

490. In 2009, the *Energy Act* was amended to include a Chapter 8 on *energy performance of buildings.* In case of sale of an existing building or construction of a new building, the owner has the obligation to present a valid energy certificate for the buyer. The same is required in case of rent in relation to the tenant. This shall provide information about the energy qualities of the building, an energy label and a list of possible measures to improve energy efficiency. The certificate is valid for ten years. The rules implement the EU rules in this field.[554] Further rules are given in a regulation.[555]

For all professional and public buildings of more than 1,000 m^2, the owner shall provide a summary of the energy label visible for the users of the building.

553. Directive 1999/94/EC of the European Parliament and of the Council of 13 Dec. 1999 relating to the availability of consumer information on fuel economy and CO_2 emissions in respect of the marketing of new passenger cars.
554. Directive 2002/91/EC of the European Parliament and of the Council of 16 Dec. 2002 on the energy performance of buildings.
555. Regulation of 18 Dec. 2009 No. 1665 on energy-labelling of buildings and energy assessment of technical installations.

Part II. Nature Conservation and Management

Chapter 1. Introduction

§1. BACKGROUND

491. Traditionally, the concept of nature conservation has been perceived as an important part of the environmental policy in the narrow sense, based on special legislation for the conservation and protection of species and valuable nature areas. The 2009 *NDA* (DNA),[556] as the central piece of legislation to this effect, is an essential part of the environmental legislation. However, legal protection of areas and species does not in itself ensure the long-term conservation of valuable nature and biodiversity. After all, most biodiversity is found outside the protected areas, and even nature within protected areas may easily be subject to pollution and other types of environmental stress due to activities outside the area. Therefore, it is essential that the value of nature and biodiversity is assessed and taken duly into account in all sector policies and legislation, in the spatial and land-use planning at State, county and municipal levels, and in the application of the Acts that regulate industries and other economic activities which are based on natural resources and which may have an effect on nature and biodiversity.

492. Norwegian environmental policy is to a large extent based on *the principle of integration.* All sectors have a responsibility for taking environmental considerations into account when defining goals and applying the relevant legislation. Many of the most important sector Acts regarding the exploitation of natural resources have environmental protection as part of their objective, and/or state explicitly that environmental consideration shall be taken into account in its application. Further details will be presented under the various chapters.

In addition, some sector Acts institute a legal protection for certain natural resources. For example, the Marine Resources Act[557] establishes principles for the management of the living marine resources. The Water Resources Act[558] regulates

556. Act of 19 Jun. 2009 No. 100 Relating to the Management of Biological, Geological and Landscape Diversity (NDA). The Act replaced the 1970 Nature Protection Act.
557. Act of 6 Jun. 2008 No. 37 on the Management of Wild Living Marine Resources (Marine Resources Act).
558. Act of 24 Nov. 2000 No. 82 on Watercourses and Groundwater (Water Resources Act).

activities in the lakes and watercourses, and gives formal status of Protected Watercourses to those watercourses which Stortinget has explicitly exempted from hydropower development. These and other Acts will be treated thoroughly in subsequent chapters.

493. Norway's policy and law in the field of nature conservation and management is significantly influenced by *international law* in the field. The EEA Agreement does not include nature conservation in the strict sense, as this is not regarded as an issue of the EU internal market and the 'four freedoms' which are at the core of this market. As a consequence, neither the EU Birds Directive[559] nor the Habitats Directive[560] – and the follow-up work through Natura 2000 – apply to Norway. However, Norway is party to all the most important global and regional conventions in the field of nature protection, such as the 1992 CBD, the 1971 Ramsar Convention on Wetlands, the 1973 Washington Convention on International Trade in Endangered Species of Wild Fauna and Flora (CITES), and the Convention on the Conservation of European Wildlife and Natural Habitats (Bern Convention). The Bern Convention is particularly important with regard to the management of wild animals in Norway, and not least the predators.

494. As regards the management and protection of living marine resources, Norway is party to the 1946 International Convention for the Regulation of Whaling, the 1980 Convention on Future Multilateral Cooperation in North-East Atlantic Fisheries, the 1982 Convention for the Conservation of Salmon in the North Atlantic Ocean, and the 1995 Agreement Relating to the Conservation and Management of Straddling Fish Stocks and Highly Migratory Fish Stocks.

495. These conventions and agreements have been, and continue to be, important for both the development and application of Norway's legislation on conservation and management of living natural resources and biodiversity.

496. In 2021, some 17.5% of the area of mainland Norway is legally protected as national park, protected landscape or nature reserve. Some 6% of the sea area within the baseline is protected. In addition, 55% of the area of Svalbard is protected. There are more than 3,000 protected areas in the country, of which forty-seven are national parks[561] and some 200 protected landscapes. Nature reserves make up the great majority, close to 2,500. Mountain and glacier areas make up a large part of the national parks. For most other types of nature and landscapes, the level of protection is less than 10% nationally, which is the level of protection which is recommended by the International Union for the Conservation of Nature (IUCN) for each of the most important types of nature and landscapes. There are fifteen marine protected areas and more are being prepared.

559. Directive 2009/147/EC which replaced the earlier Council Directive 79/409/EEC of 2 Apr. 1979, known as the earliest piece of EU legislation on the environment.
560. Council Directive 92/43/EEC of 21 May 1992.
561. Of these are forty on the mainland and seven on the Spitzbergen islands.

§2. General Objectives and Principles of Protection and Management of Nature Diversity

497. The first legislation with the purpose of protecting valuable natural sites in Norway was adopted at the beginning of the twentieth century. Since then, a large number of sites and areas with particular natural beauty and of recreational or scientific value have been protected by a formal decision by the State. The first national park was established in 1962.[562] This work intensified after the adoption of *the Nature Protection Act* in 1970. The Act established a new basis and framework for such protection, with four types of protected areas and sites: *national parks, protected landscapes, nature reserves* and *natural monuments.* It also included provisions for the protection and preservation of species of plants and animals. This Act was replaced in 2009 by the *NDA.* In addition to national parks, protected landscapes and nature reserves, this Act introduced two new categories of protected areas: *habitat management areas* and *marine protected areas.* Furthermore, it introduced new types of instruments for the protection of particularly valuable and threatened species and types of natural habitats: 'priority species' and 'selected habitat types', respectively. We shall take a closer look at all these concepts.

498. The overall *purpose* of the NDA, as laid down in its Article 1, is:

> to protect biological, geological and landscape diversity and ecological processes through conservation and sustainable use, and in such a way that the environment provides a basis for human activity, culture, health and well-being, now and in the future, including a basis for Sami culture.

499. The expression 'conservation and sustainable use' reflects an important point: the Act is not an Act for strict conservation only. It is based on the idea that biodiversity is also a resource to be used, and that biodiversity considerations have to be balanced against other social and economic objectives. It is explicitly stated (Article 14, paragraph 1) that 'measures under this Act shall be weighed against other important public interests'. And Sami interests are treated specially: When decisions are made under the Act that directly affect Sami interests, due importance shall be attached, within the framework that applies to the individual provision, to the natural resource base for Sami culture (Article 14, paragraph 2).

500. The Act is about the protection and management of *nature.* It does not generally cover domesticated species (although a few articles also relates to domesticated species). It is meant to contribute to the protection of nature influenced by human activities, and so indirectly also protection of cultural heritage although this task is mainly taken care of through the special cultural heritage legislation.[563] It applies fully to nature on Norwegian land territory, including river systems, and in Norwegian territorial waters. Outside the territorial waters, on the continental shelf and in Norway's 200 miles EEZ, only a few of the articles of the Act apply. In these

562. Rondane National Park in the (former) counties of Oppland and Hedmark in southern Norway.
563. Act of 9 Jun. 1978 No. 50 on Cultural heritage.

areas, other Acts are more important, in particular the Marine Resources Act which also provides the government with the authority to protect living marine resources and establish protected areas (*see infra* Chapter 6). Only Chapter VII of the NDA on access to genetic material applies to Svalbard ('Spitzbergen') and the island Jan Mayen. The King may decide that other provisions shall apply to these island areas. However, nature is protected by other Acts in these areas, in particular by the comprehensive and quite strict Act of 15 June 2001 No. 79 relating to the protection of the environment in Svalbard (*see infra* Chapter 9, §4), and the Act of 27 February 1930 on Jan Mayen.

501. The NDA does not in itself protect anything. It provides the government with the *authority* – the discretionary power – to protect areas and species, as it deems necessary. The extent to which this authority actually is used, and nature is protected, is left to political considerations and decisions. The government – the King – must decide to formally protect an area, a type of nature or a species in each individual case. The Act provides *the legal framework* for the different types of protected areas: its purpose, its quality and the legal effects of the protection, as well as the procedure to follow. It provides general *objectives and guidelines* for the protection of the different types of protected areas and species, but it does not itself define the exact restrictions on the land-use and other activities neither within each type of protected area nor within each individual area. This must be decided through special regulations by the government for each area, according to the protection objective and needs.

502. The Act lays down important *'management objectives'* for habitat types,[564] ecosystems,[565] and species.[566] These shall guide and influence the implementation of the various instruments in the Act. For *habitat types and ecosystems,* the objective is:

> to maintain the diversity of habitat types within their natural range and the species diversity and ecological processes that are characteristic of each habitat type. The objective is also to maintain ecosystem structure, functioning and productivity to the extent this is considered to be reasonable (Article 4).

The last sentence should be understood as a general reference to proportionality in the implementation of the Act. For *species,* the objective is:

> to maintain species and their genetic diversity for the long-term and to ensure that species occur in viable populations in their natural ranges. To the extent

564. 'Habitat types' is defined in Art. 3 as 'a homogeneous environment, including all plant and animal life and environmental factors that operate there, or special types of natural features such as ponds, habitat islands in fields or the like, and special types of geological features'.
565. 'Ecosystem' is defined in Art. 3, as 'a relatively well-delimited, homogeneous natural system where plant, animal, fungus and microorganism communities interact with one another and with the non-living environment'.
566. 'Species' is defined in Art. 3 of the Act as 'a group of living organisms distinguished according to biological criteria'.

necessary to achieve this objective, areas with specific ecological functions for different species and other ecological conditions on which they are dependent are also to be maintained (Article 5).

This objective does not apply to alien species and *'alien organisms'*, however. An alien organism is defined as 'an organism that does not belong to a species or population that occurs naturally in an area' (Article 3). The genetic diversity of *domesticated species* shall be managed in such a way that it helps to secure the future resource base.

503. Article 6 lays down *a general duty of care.* 'Any person' shall act with care and take all reasonable steps to avoid causing damage to biological, geological and landscape diversity contrary to the management objectives set out in Articles 4 and 5. This duty of care applies to individuals in their private capacity as well as in their professional work. It also applies to companies, organizations and public bodies. The general duty of care requires that everybody have adequate knowledge of the relevant natural values, and the possible effects on nature diversity on their activities. It also requires that harmful activities are avoided as far as it is possible and reasonable for the person or institution in question. If an activity is carried out in accordance with a permit issued by an official authority, the duty of care is considered to have been fulfilled if the conditions for the permit are still satisfied. Some other articles in the Act have additional rules which define the duty of care in more detail in special relations.

504. The Act also lays down *several general principles* which apply to decision-making by public authorities which may have an influence on nature biodiversity. These principles shall serve as guidelines for the exercise of public authority regardless of the sector legislation which apply to the case. In this sense, the NDA is meant to play a very important *cross-sectoral role*. The principles also apply when an administrative agency allocates grants, and to the management of public real property. Decisions shall state how these principles have been applied in the case in question (Article 7).

505. Article 8 lays down *a general principle of knowledge* which goes further than what follows from the general duty of care in Article 6. All decisions by public authorities that affect biological, geological and landscape diversity shall, as far as is reasonable, be *based on scientific knowledge* of the population status of species, the range and ecological status of habitat types, and the impacts of environmental pressures. The criterion 'scientific' implies that the knowledge must be objective, based on proper scientific methods and possible to verify. The knowledge required shall be in reasonable proportion to the nature of the case and the risk of damage to biological, geological and landscape diversity. It is stated explicitly that the authorities shall attach importance to knowledge that is based on many generations of experience acquired through the use of and interaction with the natural environment, including traditional Sami use, and that can promote the conservation and sustainable use of biological, geological and landscape diversity. This rule supplements the general duty of knowledge of environmental conditions and effects which is laid down in Norway's Act on the Right to Environmental Information[567] (*see supra* General Introduction, Chapter 2, §3).

506. Article 9 states *the precautionary principle* as follows:

> When a decision is made in the absence of adequate information on the impacts it may have on the natural environment, the aim shall be to avoid possible significant damage to biological, geological or landscape diversity. If there is a risk of serious or irreversible damage to biological, geological or landscape diversity, lack of knowledge shall not be used as a reason for postponing or not introducing management measures.

This means that the precautionary principle is generally introduced in Norwegian environmental law. Until now, the legal content and status of the principle has been somewhat unclear. The principle applies both in its 'defensive' (first sentence) and in its 'offensive' meaning (second sentence). With 'defensive' is meant that the principle is used to limit or restrict activities that may have a harmful effect on the environment. By 'offensive' is meant that the principle is used as an argument to justify active measures to halt or change a possible harmful development, such as – for example – climate change, even if there still is some uncertainty with regard to the possible environmental threats and effects.

The legal importance of this principle as laid down in the NDA is, however, uncertain. How the principle is applied and weighed outside the application of the NDA itself is very much left to the various sector authorities to decide, when they make decisions pursuant to their own legislation – legislation with a purpose which may be very different from, and often opposite to, nature protection. There is a major challenge for the environmental authorities to influence other authorities so that the principle is applied properly and consistently across the various sectors.

507. Article 10 lays down the principle of ecosystem approach and cumulative environmental effects:

> Any pressure on an ecosystem shall be assessed on the basis of the cumulative environmental effects on the ecosystem now or in the future.

Although the 'principle of ecosystem approach' is mentioned in the title of the article, it mainly deals with the duty of assessing all possible effects on the ecosystem together. It means that the authorities, when developing plans and making decisions, have to consider the effect on biodiversity of both already existing activities and planned activities that may influence the diversity in the future, and base their decision on the total effect. This is essential in order to avoid that many 'small decisions' with seemingly insignificant effects in themselves, *in sum* lead to serious and

567. Act of 9 May 2003 No. 31.

unacceptable harm on the biodiversity. The nature and the characteristics of the eco-system in question, possible tolerance limits, and the possible effects on these factors shall be the starting point and central issue in planning and decision-making.

508. Article 11 states that:

> Costs associated with preventing or limiting any damage caused by a project to biological, geological and landscape diversity shall be borne by the project owner, unless this is unreasonable in the light of the nature of the project and of the damage.

Here, the *principle of 'polluter pays'* is extended to apply to other types of damage to nature than those caused by pollution. It follows that the costs to prevent damage to the diversity, and costs to restore damage, must be covered by the owner of the activity that has caused the harm. This rule can be applied when a permission is given to an activity which will harm the diversity pursuant to sector legislation. Then necessary measures to limit the damage may be ordered or carried out at the expense of the project owner.

Within the NDA itself, Article 11 is supplemented by a system of *environmental compensation* in case of contravention (Article 74). Any person that contravenes provisions laid down in the Act or pursuant to the Act or provisions that serve to implement objectives and principles set out in the Act shall, if so ordered by the competent authority, pay environmental compensation to the State. The decision as to whether an order shall be made and the determination of the amount of environmental compensation will take place after an overall assessment of the importance of the environmental assets concerned, the possible extent and duration of the environmental damage, sanctions imposed on the offender and any other circumstances.

509. The Act (Article 12) also lays down *the principle of environmentally sound techniques and methods of operation.* In order to prevent or limit damage to biological, geological or landscape diversity:

> use shall be made of such methods and such techniques and siting of industrial and other activities as, based on an overall assessment of past, present and future use of such diversity and economic factors, produce the best results for society at large.

The principle of 'best siting' is not the least important one here. It is often possible to avoid damage to nature by simply siting an activity, a building, an infrastructure or an installation at a different place than was originally planned. The various alternatives for important infrastructures such as major roads and airports are good examples. Many Norwegian Acts give both the State and local authorities the legal possibility to require that an activity, construction or installation is placed in such a way that environmental damage is reduced or avoided, for example, as a condition for a permit. This is a recurrent issue, for example, in the siting of polluting activities and in land-use planning. Often, a trade-off has to be made between alternatives where economic arguments may counter environmental concerns.

Article 12 does not give a clear answer as to the weight of the best siting principle and thus to how this conflict is to be solved. Again, this is left to the discretion of the authority in question. However, the Act clearly requires that the issue of best location has been properly assessed and considered, and this assessment has to be made explicit in the final decision according to the rule in Article 7.

510. A new instrument that may be applied is *quality norms for biological, geological and landscape diversity* (Article 13), for example, concerning the distribution or abundance of a species or the range or ecological status of a habitat type. Such quality norms are to be decided by the King and serve as guidelines for planning and decision-making. They supplement environmental quality objectives laid down pursuant to other Acts, such as the PCA, and the Water Resources Act. If such a quality objective is not achieved, or if there is a risk of this, the environmental authority should draw up a plan for ways of nonetheless achieving the quality objective, in consultation with other authorities concerned. Such plans may entail a need to establish further regulations under the NDA or other statutes.

The first (and so far only) quality norm for nature was laid down in 2013 for *wild stocks of Atlantic salmon* (Salmo salar).[568] In Norway's many rivers there are several hundred different wild stocks of salmon, each belonging to a specific river and with its genetic characteristics. Many of these are seriously threatened, by various causes, and many are already extinct. The purpose of the quality norm is to contribute to the maintenance and reconstruction of these wild stocks of salmon to a level which ensure diversity within this species while exploiting the possibilities for production and harvesting. It shall provide the authorities with a proper basis for the management of these stocks and decisions that may affect them. The objective is that 'good quality' for each stock is maintained, or reached as soon as possible. Nevertheless, the MCE may, together with other interested ministries, decide exceptions to this objective if important societal consideration must be given more weight than that of the wild salmon. This, of course, weakens the legal strength of the norm. An annex to the regulation defines the quality norm in detail. It consists of two subnorms: (a) spawning stock and harvesting potential and (b) genetic integrity. An annex describes the assessment methodology linked to these subnorms.

§3. Enforcement of the NDA

511. The enforcement of the NDA consists mainly of control to ensure that the provisions for each protected area are respected and implemented. Initially, this is a task for the ordinary local police. In areas owned by the State or the municipality, they have a responsibility in this respect. Private landowners cannot be ordered to carry out controls.

512. In 1996, a special State organization for surveillance and enforcement of legislation concerning the protection of natural and cultural heritage values – *State*

568. Regulation of 20 Sep. 2013 No. 1109.

Nature Inspectorate – was established.[569] Its purpose is to safeguard national environmental values and prevent environmental crime, through surveillance and inspection as well as information and guidance (Article 2). The implementation and enforcement of the NDA is an important part of its responsibility.

The Inspectorate has staff members in the various counties. They are most of the time out in the field, controlling activities in protected areas and so on. They work closely together with the local police and may be given some police functions, working under the instruction of the police.

513. The NDA itself has a number of instruments of enforcement. A person who is responsible for activities that violate the Act or decisions pursuant to the Act must take measures to stop the activity, to prevent (further) damage and if possible to restore the damaged environment, as far as the measures needed are not manifestly unreasonable when costs, environmental effects and the nature of the acts are considered. The authorities may order the person responsible for violating the Act or decisions pursuant to the Act to take the necessary action to stop such activities (Article 69). The same applies in the case where an activity which is in accordance with the Act or a decision pursuant to the Act, turns out to have serious unforeseen effects for the nature diversity (Article 70). In this case, the authority may require restitution of the earlier natural status, provided that such measures do not led to unreasonable nuisance for the responsible person. If such an order is not carried out by the responsible person, the authority may itself have the necessary measure carried out, at the cost of the responsible party (Article 71).

514. The Act has rules on administrative seizure and confiscation of objects obtained by illegal activities, such as objects covered by the prohibitions laid down in the CITES Convention and the corresponding Article 26 in the Act, and of rules in Chapter IV on alien species (Article 72a and 72b) (*see infra*). Furthermore, the authorities may lay down a *coercive fine* (Article 73) which may be used for the purpose of having the rules in the Act or regulations properly implemented. Persons who have violated rules in the Act or in regulations pursuant to the Act may also be ordered to pay a compensation to the State, in the Act (Article 74) called *'environmental compensation'*.

515. In case of a violation, several *penal provisions* may come into force. Article 75 in the NDA states that any person who wilfully or negligently contravenes a prohibition pursuant to the Act or regulations pursuant to the Act is liable to a fine or imprisonment for a term not exceeding one year. In particularly serious cases, imprisonment for up to three years may be imposed.

In addition, the general environmental provision in *Article 240 of the Penal Act* may be applied. If an area protected through the NDA is 'considerably damaged', wilfully or by gross negligence, a penalty of as much as six years of imprisonment may be imposed. The same applies if a person wilfully or by gross negligence reduces a natural stock of protected organisms that are threatened nationally or internationally. Furthermore, according to Articles 27 and 28 of the same Act, a

569. Act of 21 Jun. 1996 No. 38.

company may be punished with fines if a person has contravened the Act on behalf of the company, even if the subjective conditions for punishing that person are not present in the case.[570]

A recent example of penal cases before the Supreme Court may be mentioned as illustration: In 2020, a company producing salmon fry for the aquaculture industry took out more water from a lake protected as a nature reserve (*see infra*) than was allowed in the reserve regulation. This resulted in the drying up of part of the reserve. The company was fined NOK 250,000 (USD 25,000).[571]

570. We shall return to general issues of criminal liability in Part IV, Ch. 2 *infra.*
571. Case HR-2020-955-A.

Chapter 2. Protected Areas

§1. General Objectives and Provisions for Protected Areas

516. In addition to the general purpose of the Act in Article 1 and the management objectives of nature types, ecosystems and species in Articles 4 and 5, the Act also lays down some *general objectives for protected areas* under the Act in Article 33. Protected areas on land, in river systems and in the sea under the Act shall promote the conservation of:

(a) the full range of variation of habitats and landscape types;
(b) species and genetic diversity;
(c) endangered natural environments and areas with specific ecological functions for priority species;
(d) major intact ecosystems, also making them accessible for low-impact outdoor recreation;
(e) areas of special conservation value;
(f) natural environments that reflect human use through the ages (cultural landscapes) or that are also of historical value, and facilitation of forms of use that help to maintain biological, geological and landscape diversity;
(g) ecological and landscape coherence at national and international levels; or
(h) reference areas where environmental trends can be monitored.

When a decision is made under another Act or statute to protect the natural environment in an area, importance should be attached to these objectives. If such decisions made under another Act or statute are part of a plan that covers areas protected by a decision under the NDA, the government may prescribe provisions to ensure that the protection provided by the various statutes is coordinated in order to promote the objective of the plan.

517. Protected areas are formally established by the government – King in Council – by means of *regulations. For each protected area, a* regulation is adopted. This describes more precisely the purpose and objective of protecting the area, including the natural and cultural qualities such protection is intended to safeguard and the state that protection is intended to achieve. It also defines the limits of the protected area, affected properties and provisions regarding use of the area. The geographical extent of the protected area shall be consistent with the purpose of protection. In determining the limits of the protected area, the important factor is to safeguard ecological functions of significance for achieving the purpose of protection and the resilience of the ecosystem to external pressures. Regulations relating to marine protected areas shall state whether the purpose of protection applies to the seabed, water column, water surface or a combination of these.

518. The regulation defines *the restrictions on the various activities* which are required, and what active measures must be taken in order to protect the environmental values in the area (Article 34). The regulations may prohibit or regulate activities or access or passage which alone or when combined with other use may undermine the purpose of protection. Special rules may be prescribed for different parts of the area when this is compatible with the function of the part in achieving the purpose of protection. The regulation establishing a protected area shall not preclude the continuation of sustainable use that reinforces the purpose of such protection (Article 34).

The decision to protect an area shall give the grounds of the biological, geological and landscape diversity and other qualities that are protected in and by the protection decision, and of how the latter helps to fulfil national objectives and international obligations (Article 46). As the main rule, a draft strategic management plan shall be presented when a decision is made to protect an area. When an operational management plan is also relevant, it shall be part of the strategic management plan. The protection decision shall be made public. It shall be registered judicially and be publicly accessible in electronic format with associated maps (Article 46).

519. The Act has a special provision (Article 40) for areas that are given a special *status pursuant to international conventions.* Examples are wetlands pursuant to the Ramsar Convention and natural areas and sites on the United Nations Educational, Scientific and Cultural Organization (UNESCO) World Heritage List pursuant to the World Heritage Convention. The effect that the convention in question attributes to such status also applies as Norwegian law. This means that the prescriptions in the convention as regards the protection of the cultural and natural values in such an area automatically apply to the area in question, even if such rules have not been laid down in the regulation for the area. Mere recommendations from the organs of such conventions, however, will not have the same automatic effect, and their implementation will require a formal decision/regulation.

520. An important question is whether there may be issued *exemptions to the regulation for a protected area*, for example, if the government wants to carry out a new project which will serve a useful purpose but which is in conflict with the protection. Article 48 of the Act provides the authorities with a certain discretionary power to grant an exemption, on certain conditions. The conditions are that the exemption is not contrary to the purpose of the protection decision and that it cannot make a significant impact on the conservation value. An exception may also be accepted if safety considerations or important public interests make it necessary. When weighing other important public interests against the interests promoted by the protected area, particular emphasis shall be placed on the importance of the protected area for the overall network of protected areas. It is also of importance whether a corresponding protected area can be established or developed elsewhere. In that case, the owner of such a project may be required to bear reasonable costs arising from the safeguarding, establishment or development of such a corresponding area.

If a permit is required for a project under both the protection regulations and other legislations, the project owner may choose to submit parallel applications for permits. In such cases, a decision shall first be made under the protection regulations pursuant to the NDA, unless otherwise provided by the protection regulations or the consent of the protection authority. This is in order to avoid that a permit given to a development project by another (sector) authority may be used as an argument in favour of exception in the case pursuant to the NDA.

521. Another important issue is the question of *compensation to the landowner or user* for the restrictions laid down in a protected area. All types of protected areas may consist of private land, wholly or in part. The main rule in Norwegian law is that restrictions on land-use due to legislation, regulations or public plans or decisions do not entail compensation. Compensation may only be granted in exceptional cases (*see supra* General Introduction, Chapter 2, §1, I). Until 2009, according to the former Nature Protection Act, this principle applied to national parks and protected landscapes. When an area was protected as a nature reserve, however, the landowner could claim 'full compensation' for his/her economic loss on the basis of the same rules and principles as exist for expropriation.

The NDA (Article 50) established *new and substantially different rules*. The same rules now apply to all categories of protected areas. Thus, a landowner or a holder of rights in property that is wholly or partly protected as a national park, protected landscape, nature reserve, habitat management area or marine protected area is entitled to compensation from the State for financial losses incurred *when protection makes current use of the property more difficult.* Hence, what is compensated is the increased costs of or the reduced income from his/her activity because the protection measures have made this activity 'more difficult'. This rule differs considerably from the general principle in Norwegian law as regards compensation for restrictions on economic activities based on general legislation and public plans. Both the expression 'current use' and 'more difficult' raise difficult questions of interpretation. So far (2021), there have been only a few court cases on these issues in lower and appeal courts, but no decisive case on the issues in the Supreme Court.

522. The Ministry may make regulations regarding *the temporary protection* of specified areas in order to prevent damage to their conservation value (Article 45). The provisions of the Public Administration Act regarding individual decisions apply in respect of private landowners and rightholders, who are affected by the decision. When a specific habitat type is in danger of being permanently lost, the King may make regulations prescribing limitations and prohibiting activities and access or passage that may further jeopardize the continued existence of the habitat type. When a temporary protection decision is made, the further administrative process towards final protection shall continue without undue delay. The effect of a temporary protection decision is limited to four years from the time the decision was announced. However, the Ministry may extend the effect of the temporary protection decision by up to two years.

523. In areas that are protected the authorities may mark the boundaries of the protected area and carry out *active management measures in the area,* pursuant to Article 47. The authority shall, if possible, enter into an agreement with the landowner whereby the latter shall carry out specified maintenance measures. The authority may also enter into agreements with organizations with an interest in the matter or other persons to the effect that they shall carry out such maintenance measures. Management may include measures to maintain or achieve the necessary protection, including measures to channel access or passage, removal of vegetation or alien tree species and restorative measures. No management measures that entail the harvesting of natural resources or a significant change in the state of the natural environment as it was when the protection process began may be carried out under this section. If management measures affect private property or rights in the protected area, the owner or rightholder shall as far as possible be notified in advance. Any financial benefits arising from the implementation of management measures accrue to the landowner or the rightholder. If possible, a draft operational management plan for the protected area shall be presented at the time the protection regulations are laid down.

524. NDA Article 49 concerns *activities located outside a protected area* which may harm or cause damage within the protected area. If an activity for which a permit is required under another statute may have an impact on the conservation value of the protected area, the conservation value must be taken into consideration when deciding whether a permit should be granted, and when setting conditions.

Pursuant to the PBA (Article 11-8, paragraph 3, c) a municipal master plan may lay down restrictions on the land-use in areas bordering a national park or a protected landscape, in order to prevent significant damage to their conservation values ('buffer zones'). This may be done in connection and coordination with the adoption of the regulation for the area pursuant to the NDA.

§2. The Various Categories of Protected Areas

I. National Parks

525. The legal category of *National Park* is defined in Article 35 of the NDA. 'Large areas of natural habitat that contain distinctive or representative ecosystems or landscapes and where there is no major infrastructure development' may be protected as national parks. No activity that has a lasting impact on the natural environment or cultural heritage is permitted in a national park, unless such impact is essential to achieving the purpose of protection. The regulations shall protect the landscape and its plants, animals, geological features and cultural monuments from development, installations, pollution and other activities that may defeat the purpose of protection, and ensure that people can enjoy an undisturbed natural environment. Traditionally, most Norwegian national parks were situated in mountain areas, but gradually other types of valuable nature have been formally established as national parks. In 2013 the first two national parks covering both coastal land areas and considerable sea areas including the sea bottom were established in the Oslo fjord area.[572]

572. The Hvaler national park on the east side of the Oslo fjord, and the Færder national park on the west side of the fjord.

Norway has (in 2017) forty-seven national parks in total. There are forty national parks on the mainland, and seven on the Spitzbergen islands. The size of the parks varies considerably. For example, the smallest national park[573] has an area of only 8.5 km^2 while the largest covers 3,430 km^2.[574]

526. The restrictions on land-use and other activities in national parks are decided by the government for each individual park, depending on what is needed to protect untouched nature and other values of the park. Restrictions may apply to the landowner as well as to the public at large. Generally speaking, normal and traditional activities, with limited effect on nature, are permitted, such as grazing and hiking. Pedestrian access or passage in accordance with the provisions of the Outdoor Recreation Act[575] is permitted. Such access or passage may only be limited or prohibited in delimited areas of a national park, and only if necessary in order to protect plants or animals, cultural monuments or geological features. Hunting and fishing are regulated, but will normally be permitted at reasonable and sustainable levels. However, new constructions like roads, electricity lines, hotels and recreational houses, and activities like motorized traffic,[576] mining, intensive agriculture and forestry, will normally be prohibited.

II. Protected Landscapes

527. The second type of protected area is *'protected landscapes'*, described in Article 36 of the NDA. Natural or cultural landscapes that are important in ecological or cultural terms, as a source of enjoyment or as a basis for forming an identity may be protected as protected landscapes. Cultural monuments that contribute to the distinctive character of a landscape are considered to be part of the landscape. This type of protection is used in areas which are more developed and marked by human activities than in national parks. Often, the value of protected landscapes may be partly connected to human activities such as traditional farming, fishing villages, old roads, and other cultural heritage sites and objects. Hence, the protected landscape usually combines natural and cultural values.

At present, there are some 200 protected landscapes in Norway, with a great variety of types. Some of these are adjacent to a national park and serve as 'buffer zones' for the park. Most of the protected landscapes are completely or mainly on private land. In total, they cover some 5.5% of the country's area.

528. In a protected landscape, no projects may be initiated which may *substantially alter the nature or character of the landscape*. Current activities may be continued and developed as long as the developments do not 'substantially alter the nature or character of the landscape'. Most often, those activities that were carried

573. Ormtjernkampen national park in Innlandet county in the southern part of Norway.
574. Hardangervidda national park which covers a large part of the main mountain plateau in the southern part of Norway.
575. Act of 28 Jun. 1957 No. 16.
576. Such traffic is formally covered by the general Act on Motorized Traffic on Uncultivated Land and in Watercourses (Act of 10 Jun. 1977 No. 82), *see infra* Ch. 9, §3, III.

out when the protected landscape was established, such as traditional agriculture and forestry activities, will be accepted. However, there may be restrictions on how they are carried out. New, more intensive cultivating methods, industrial developments, and larger new areas for recreational or ordinary housing will usually be prohibited or strictly limited. The regulations may include provisions regarding what may substantially alter the nature or character of the landscape, requirements relating to adaptation to the landscape, and non-pedestrian access or passage.

It is, however, not quite clear how strictly activities may be regulated in a protected landscape. Anyway, new projects must be 'adapted to the landscape'. Importance shall be attached to the overall impact of the projects implemented in the area. With regard to the parts of the protected landscape where use is essential to achieving the purpose of protection, a draft management plan to ensure that the purpose of protection is achieved shall be presented at the latest when a decision is made to establish the protected landscape. The plan may include agreements regarding land-use, the use of landscape elements or methods of operation. The plan or agreement may also contain provisions regarding financial compensation to private individuals who contribute to management of the protected landscape.

III. Nature Reserves

529. Areas may be protected as nature reserves which:

(a) contain endangered, rare or vulnerable species, communities, habitats or landscape types;
(b) represent a specific type of habitat;
(c) are otherwise of particular importance for biological diversity;
(d) comprise a distinctive geological feature; or
(e) are of special scientific interest.

Generally speaking, nature reserve is *the type of protected area with the strictest protection.* In a nature reserve no person must do anything that reduces the conservation value of the area as described in the purpose of protection. The main reason for protecting an area as a nature reserve is to retain important habitats for fauna and flora, in order to protect the species and/or for scientific purposes. An area may be completely protected or protected for specific purposes. Some of the restrictions may be limited to certain parts of the year. This is the case with many bird reserves, which usually are closed to public access only in the nesting season. Also an area which, if allowed to develop without human intervention or actively managed through habitat restoration is likely to develop such qualities, may be protected as a nature reserve.

There are some 2,500 nature reserves in Norway. Most of them have been established since 1970, mainly on the basis of countywide plans for various types of reserves. The most important groups are seabird-nesting areas along the coast, bogs and wetlands, deciduous forests, and primeval – mainly coniferous – forests.

530. The nature of the area and the purpose of the protection decide *the content of regulations and restrictions* in each case. For example, the purpose of a bog or wetland reserve will normally be both to protect a threatened type of nature in itself, in order to prevent that bogs are drained for cultivation or used as a peat resource, and to protect its bird life. As a consequence, the flora must be preserved unchanged and cannot be destroyed or taken away, the birds and their eggs and nests cannot be disturbed or destroyed, and all types of construction, development, drainage, pollution and waste disposal, the use of fertilizers or pesticides, and other activities which may have an effect on the natural environment, the fauna or flora, are strictly prohibited. In an area like this, recreational fishing may be allowed, and skiing and horse riding may be accepted in winter when the ground is frozen. The regulations may also include such *active measures* as are necessary to achieve the aim of the protection. For example, it may be necessary to remove trees that have been planted on a bog before it was formally protected, or remove ditches in a wetland in order to restore its natural conditions. Such measures must be carried out by the authorities, and may not be imposed on the landowner. Neither may the landowner be ordered to carry out or continue a certain activity, or certain methods.

531. *Protection of primeval forests* as nature reserves has been a high priority in Norwegian environmental policy during the last decade, but is also a controversial issue. It means a virtual ban on commercial forestry in the protected area. Forestry is an important income source for many Norwegian farmers. A special plan for this has been implemented, according to which approximately 3% of the productive forest had been protected in 2015. Environmental groups have criticized the plan for being too limited, but this is to a large extent a question of public funding. Since the owner of the forest is entitled to compensation pursuant to Article 50 of the NDA, the State must pay considerable amounts of money for this plan. During the recent years protected forest areas are increasingly the result of *negotiations* between the forest owner and the State in which the issue of compensation is a central question. It is a widely held view that this type of so-called *voluntary protection* is an effective instrument, because it creates less opposition among the landowners and less legal and transaction costs in nature protection.

IV. Habitat Management Areas and Marine Protected Areas

532. The 2009 NDA introduced two new categories of protected areas: 'habitat management areas' and 'marine protected areas'. An area that has or may have special importance because it fulfils specific ecological functions for one or more specified species may be protected as a *'habitat management area'* pursuant to Article 38. A prohibition may be imposed on activity and access or passage that may affect or disturb the species or the ecological conditions necessary to its existence. This category is different from nature reserves in that it aims in particular to protect certain species. For that purpose it may be necessary to protect nesting areas, breeding areas, winter lairs and so on.

533. Marine protected areas may be established within the territorial sea pursuant to Article 39 on the grounds of their marine conservation value, but also to safeguard valuable marine areas that are ecologically necessary for terrestrial species, and if they:

(a) contain distinctive or representative ecosystems and are without major infrastructure development;
(b) contain endangered, rare or vulnerable species, communities, habitats or landscape types;
(c) represent a specific type of habitat;
(d) are otherwise of particular importance for biological diversity;
(e) comprise a distinctive geological feature;
(f) are of special scientific interest; or
(g) are of special importance as an area with specific ecological functions for one or more specified species.

By 2021 there are fifteen marine protected areas in Norway and more are being prepared. The decision to establish a marine protected area must state whether the purpose of the protection and restrictions apply to the seabed, water column, surface or a combination of these elements. In a marine protected area no person must do anything that reduces the conservation value of the area as described in the purpose of protection. A marine protected area may be protected from all activity, pollution, projects and use, subject to the limitations that follow from international law. Any restrictions imposed on activity shall be proportional to the purpose of protection. Harvesting and other utilization of wild living marine resources are regulated under the Marine Resources Act within the limits of the protection regulations. Also, marine areas where protection consists solely of specific provisions regulating fishing activities shall be established under the Marine Resources Act and not under the NDA. Also, protection of marine areas outside the territorial sea falls under the Marine Resources Act (*see* Chapter 6 *infra*).

V. Protection of 'Selected Habitat Types'

534. In addition to the protection of areas as mentioned *supra* under sections I–IV, the NDA introduces a new type of mechanism, called *'selected habitat types'*. The purpose is to improve the protection of certain types of nature which are seen as threatened, *outside the areas which are formally protected*. In order to achieve the management objective of nature types which is defined in Article 4 as 'to maintain the diversity of habitat types within their natural range and the species diversity and ecological processes that are characteristic of each habitat type'. This mechanism supplements the formal protection of areas. The rules are found in Chapter VI (Articles 52–56) of the Act.

535. Habitat (or nature) types are given the status as *'selected habitat type'* through a regulation laid down by the government (King in Council).[577] In deciding whether to designate a habitat type as selected, particular importance shall be attached to whether:

- trends for or the status of the habitat type are contrary to the objective set out in Article 4;
- the habitat type is important for one or more priority species;
- a significant proportion of the natural range of the habitat type is found in Norway; or
- international obligations apply to the habitat type.

When there is documentation that shows that the status of or trends for a habitat type based on scientific criteria are significantly contrary to the above-mentioned objective in Article 4, the competent authorities shall – of their own initiative or at the request of an organization or another person who has a legal interest in the matter – assess whether regulations should be made under the paragraph 1. So, the Act lays down an *obligation to assess the need for protection* as selected habitat type. But the result of the assessment may be that the nature type is not classified as 'selected' and is not given the protection which follows from that status. Hence, there is no legal obligation pursuant to the Act to give a habitat type the status as 'selected'.

The first regulation on 'selected habitat types' was adopted in 2011. It designated five nature types as 'selected habitat type'.[578] Traditional wild fields and marshes for haymaking, hollow oaks were among these first 'selected habitat types'. In 2015, the nature type 'coastal heathery moors' was added to the list. This applies to 388 important and 284 very important sites of heathery moors along Norway's coast, covering some 830 km^2. In 2020 another two types were added to the list.

536. The status as 'selected habitat types' has several *important legal effects,* defined in Article 53. First, it is stated that special account shall be taken in exercising the general duty of care under Article 6, so as to avoid reduction of the range of the habitat type or deterioration of the ecological status of the area. More important, special accounts shall also be taken in the exercise of official authority, including the allocation of grants by an administrative agency, and in the public bodies' management of real property that belongs to them. This means that this mechanism is meant to have effect when decisions are made by various sector authorities and not least by the planning authorities in spatial planning pursuant to the PBA. Before a decision is made to carry out works in an area of a selected habitat type, the impacts on the selected habitat type must be ascertained. And the government may make regulations regarding how such impact assessments are to be carried out and processed. However, it is up to the relevant sector or planning authority to decide to

577. The municipal authorities may make regulations providing that the provisions of Arts 53–56 shall also apply to municipal management of areas of other specified habitat types in the municipality.
578. Regulation of 13 May 2011 No. 512 with later amendments.

what extent they will take the status of 'selected habitat type' into account when making decisions. This, of course, is *an important weak point* in the system.

537. *Notice* that a permit has been granted by the relevant sector or planning authority to carry out a project in areas of a selected habitat type *shall be published* in at least one newspaper that is widely read locally or in the way prescribed by the individual statutes. In the case of selected marine habitat types, the announcement shall be made in a manner appropriate to make interested parties aware of the permit. If a permit or the rejection of a permit for a project in an area of a selected habitat type is appealed against under other provisions, the superior environmental protection authority shall be given the opportunity to express an opinion on the appeal (Article 56).

538. There are special rules in Articles 54 and 55 regarding notification and possible prohibition of forestry and agricultural projects which affect areas of selected habitat types. *A forestry project* that affects areas of selected habitat types and which does not require a permit shall be notified to the municipal authorities before work on the project is started. The project may not be carried out before a reply has been received from the municipal authorities. If the municipal authorities find that the project may result in reduction of the range of the habitat type or deterioration of its ecological status, the authorities may refuse to permit the project or make further orders as to how the project shall be implemented in accordance with the provisions of the Forestry Act.[579] A similar notification rule applies to *agricultural* projects that affect areas of selected habitat types and that does not require a permit. Here, the authorities may refuse the project or make further orders as to how the project shall be implemented pursuant to the relevant rules in the Land Act.[580]

§3. Administrative Procedure for Protection Decisions

539. As a general rule, the process of getting an area protected is *initiated* either by the central environmental authorities[581] or by the environmental authority at the county level. In the recent decades, these authorities have carried out comprehensive work to identify and map important nature areas, and habitats for endangered flora and fauna and so on. On this basis, proposals for a national plan of national parks and protected landscapes, and countywide plans for nature reserves of various types (wetlands, seabird areas, etc.) have been developed. Landowners or other private citizens, or organizations may also forward suggestions for protection to the county or national authorities.

540. When a protection process commences, the Act, Article 41, requires that steps shall be taken to ensure that administrative procedures are carried out in the

579. Act of 27 May 2005 No. 31.
580. Act of 12 May 1995 No. 23.
581. The MCE and the NEA. For national parks a comprehensive plan was adopted by Stortinget in the late 1990s.

closest possible cooperation with landowners, rightholders, representatives of the local community, and other interested parties, including Sami cultural and business interests, the municipal and county authorities, the Sami Parliament and other relevant authorities. The same applies when a landowner or rightholder himself/herself offers areas for protection. The administrative process shall ensure that the purpose of protection and the conservation value, the delimitation of the area and the consequences of protection are defined as clearly as possible. The process of protection may be coordinated with a regional or municipal planning process for the area pursuant the PBA. The King may make regulations regarding such coordination.

541. According to Article 42 the competent authority shall *publish the proposal* for protection of an area, with the main consequences it is expected to have, in at least one newspaper that is widely read locally. Proposals regarding marine protected areas shall be announced in a manner appropriate to make interested parties aware of the proposal. As far as possible, landowners and other rightholders shall be informed by letter and given a reasonable time limit for submitting comments before a proposal is drawn up.

542. At an early stage of the preparations, and well before the proposal is announced, steps shall be taken to establish cooperation with any public authorities, organizations, etc., which have a special interest in the protection measure. Regulations shall be drawn up in cooperation with the central government authorities concerned.

543. When, on the basis of comments and further assessments *a draft proposal* with a detailed regulation for protection of an area has been worked out, the authority shall publish the proposal and the main consequences it is expected to have, in at least one newspaper that is widely read locally. The proposal shall describe the purpose of protection and the conservation value of the area concerned, the delimitation of the area and any qualities other than biological, geological and landscape diversity, as well as the anticipated consequences of the proposal (Article 43). As far as possible, landowners and other rightholders shall be informed by letter and be given a reasonable time limit for submitting *comments* before a final proposal is drawn up. At an early stage of the preparations, and well before the proposal is announced, steps shall be taken to establish cooperation with the various public authorities, organizations, and other parties which have a special interest in the protected area (Article 42).

544. The initiation of a proposal for protection has legal effects in itself. Article 44 states that when an announcement has been made under Article 42, an administrative agency may automatically reject an application for a permit for a project in an area to which the protection proposal applies. A permit may only be granted if the project will have no significant impact on the purpose of the proposal. When important public interests make it necessary, the government may nonetheless grant a permit for the project. Simultaneously with or after an announcement as mentioned in section 42, the Ministry may prescribe a duty to provide notification of projects that do not require a permit under other statutes for all or parts of the proposed protected area. The duty of notification shall be announced in the same way as the protection proposal.

When an announcement has been made under Article 42, a public authority *may not provide a grant* for a project in an area to which the protection proposal applies. However, the competent authority may grant exemptions from this rule if the project will have no significant impact or will have a favourable impact on the conservation of the area. These effects are limited to four years after the proposal has been announced, but the Ministry may extend the effects by up to two years.

§4. Protection According to the PBA

545. In land-use plans pursuant to the PBA,[582] areas may be protected as part of the approved plan. The rules on this differ depending on the type of plan. We shall return to these issues in Part III. Generally, it should be stated that the municipal master plans are not a strong instrument to this effect. Local development plans may give an equally strong protection as protection pursuant to the NDA. However, this tool is rarely used, partly because the municipality may have to pay compensation to the landowner. In reality, formal protection of valuable natural areas in Norway remains primarily a task for the State.

582. Act of 27 Jun. 2008 No. 71.

Chapter 3. Protection and Management of Species

§1. Management Objectives and Principles

546. The NDA is the main legal instrument for the protection and management of wild species. It is, however, supplemented by several Acts related to harvesting of wild species. The Act on Hunting and Catching of Wild Animals (Wildlife Act)[583] gives more detailed rules in particular on hunting. Similarly, the Salmonid and Freshwater Fish Act[584] provides the legal basis for a wise management of the fish resources in Norway's numerous lakes and rivers. Harvesting and other utilization of marine organisms, including marine mammals, are regulated by the Act Relating to the Management of Wild Living Marine Resources (the Marine Resources Act).[585] Furthermore, other legislations are also important for the de facto protection of wild flora and fauna in the country. In particular, general land-use planning and the system for EIA pursuant to the PBA are important factors. In the planning of land-use at the local level, and of important projects, the effects on natural species must always be taken into account. This follows from the general principles of land-use planning. Also, the manner in which forestry is carried out is very important for preservation of key habitats. This issue will be covered in connection with the Forestry Act[586] in Chapter 5 *infra*.

547. The *main objective and principles for the protection and management of all types of species* are laid down in particular in Chapter III of the NDA, on Species management. Article 5 states *the objective* in this field, which is:

> to maintain species and their genetic diversity for the long term and to ensure that species occur in viable populations in their natural ranges. To the extent necessary to achieve this objective, areas with specific ecological functions for different species and other ecological conditions on which they are dependent are also to be maintained.

The article also says that this objective does not apply to alien organisms and that 'the genetic diversity of domesticated species shall be managed in such a way that it helps to secure the future resource base'.

548. In Norwegian law, *wild animals are res nullius.* They do not belong to anybody until they have been legally killed or captured. Wildlife protection has for many years been a controversial issue in Norway, mainly because of the national policy to sustain and even increase the number of large predators – bears, wolves, wolverines and lynx – in the mountains and forests. This policy conflicts with the interests of farmers and Sami families who use the same areas as open grazing land for sheep and reindeer. Also, the owners of large forest areas are opposed, as the

583. Act of 29 May 1981 No. 38.
584. Act of 15 May 1992 No. 47.
585. Act of 6 Jun. 2008 No. 37.
586. Act of 20 May 2005 No. 28.

animals of prey diminish the stock of such animals as moose and dear which are hunted and thus of considerable economic value. In particular, the increase in the number of wolves in certain parts of southern Norway has been met with fierce opposition, and the issue has been subject to several court cases.

549. The basic *principle for the management of species* is laid down in the NDA Article 15: Harvesting and other removal of wild *animals* shall be authorized by statute or a decision pursuant to statute. By 'harvesting' is meant 'hunting, trapping, fishing and collection of plants or parts of plants (including berries and fruit) and fungi, for recreational and commercial purposes'.[587] 'Removal' means 'any form of killing or extraction of entire or parts of organisms from the natural environment, regardless of its purpose'.[588] The essence of this is *a general principle of protection*: It is prohibited to kill wild animals unless it is explicitly permitted by an Act or by a regulation pursuant to an Act. Furthermore, unnecessary harm and suffering caused to animals occurring in the wild and their nests, lairs and burrows shall be avoided.

550. Harvesting and other removal of wild *plants and fungi* are permitted to the extent that they do not jeopardize the survival of the population concerned or are not limited by statute or by a decision pursuant to statute (Article 15 paragraph 2). This does not preclude the removal of plants and fungi to prevent injury to the health of persons or animals, damage to crops, forest or other properties, to remove alien organisms, or to safeguard important public interests. Furthermore, anybody can pick *wild nuts* when eaten on the spot, and *wild flowers, berries and mushrooms* in open forest and mountain land in Norway.[589] However, the government may decide that rare and threatened wild plant species or plant communities shall be protected and preserved throughout the country or in specific areas. At present, some fifty plant species are protected.[590] They cannot be picked or otherwise destroyed or disturbed. Often, some plant species are specifically protected within national parks, protected landscapes or nature reserves, because the general regulations for such areas normally do not prohibit the picking of wild flowers.

These provisions do not preclude lawful access and passage, agricultural activities or other activities that take place in accordance with the duty of care laid down in section 6.

551. The Act itself lays down some other important *exceptions to the general protection principle*. First, small rodents, reptiles and salmonids and freshwater fish may be killed if this is necessary to prevent injury to persons or damage to property (Article 17). Hence, mousetraps are not illegal! Also killing to spare an animal unnecessary suffering is permitted in accordance with the Animal Welfare Act.[591] The same applies to killing in order to prevent an infectious disease that may have

587. Article 3, (g).
588. Article 3, (o).
589. This was originally laid down in Art. 400 of the former Penal Act, Act of 22 May 1902 No. 10 and is now laid down in Art. 5 of the Outdoor Recreation Act of 28 Jun. 1957 No. 16.
590. Regulation of 21 Dec. 2001 No. 1525 on protection of threatened species with later amendments.
591. Act of 19 Jun. 2009 No. 97 Relating to Animal Welfare.

significant social consequences in accordance with the Food Act.[592] As the main rule it is also permitted to kill alien invertebrates and invertebrates that are a nuisance or cause damage, and to remove invertebrates provided that this does not jeopardize the population in the area. The King may make regulations or individual decisions regarding harvesting and other removal of terrestrial invertebrates (Article 20).

552. A controversial issue in Norwegian wildlife policy and law relates to *the right to kill predators* – bears, wolves, wolverines and lynxes – if they attack or threat people or livestock. During the last years, the increase in the Norwegian stock of wolves in particular has created very heated political debate. The legal picture here is complicated. There are several possible legal bases for killing individual predators or reducing stocks of predators.

First, according to the Act Article 17, paragraph 2 wild animals may be killed in circumstances 'where this is considered necessary to eliminate an immediate and significant *risk of injury to persons'*. Furthermore, the owner, or a person acting on behalf of the owner, may also *kill a wild animal 'where this is considered necessary due to an ongoing or immediate attack* on livestock, domesticated reindeer, pig, dog or poultry'. Any kill or attempt to kill under this paragraph shall immediately be reported to the police.

These rules aim to limit as far as possible the unnecessary killing of large predators in Norway, in particular wolves and bears, which are threatened but which kill a considerable number of domesticated animals, mostly sheep and reindeer, which graze freely in the forest and mountains in some parts of the country. The Supreme Court has upheld a strict attitude with regard to penalties for illegal killings – that is killings where the mentioned conditions in Article 17 have not been found to be present and the killing as a consequence has been illegal. In the most serious cases, actual penalties have been several months' prison.

According to a later amendment, the government shall introduce more liberal regulations if the management objective of the species in question (*see* Article 5 of the Act) has been reached by a solid margin and for some time. In that case a regulation may open the possibility to kill bear, lynx and wolverine (but not wolf) 'where this is considered necessary to eliminate an immediate and significant risk of injury to livestock, domesticated reindeer or pig'. This may be reversed if the situation changes (Article 17 paragraph 3). And the rule may also be made even stricter through a 'priority specie' regulation (*see infra*).

In any case, when livestock and domesticated reindeer are killed or injured by predators, the State shall provide *full compensation* for the loss and consequential costs in accordance with regulations[593] (Article 19). Most of the animals are killed by wolverines and lynxes, but in some areas wolves and bears also kill a considerable number of domesticated animals. It is a condition that the owner of the animal has been careful and taken all 'reasonable' measures to prevent the attack of the predators. Another condition is that the animals have been managed and treated in accordance with the rules in the Act on Animal Welfare.[594]

---

592. Act of 19 Dec. 2003 No. 124 Relating to Food Production and Food Safety.
593. Regulations of 30 May 2014 No. 677 (lost livestock) and 4 May 2001 No. 468 (lost reindeer).
594. Act of 19 Jun. 2009 No. 97 pursuant to the Wildlife Act and the NDA.

553. Harvesting – in particular *hunting and fishing* – may only be permitted when the best available documentation indicates that the species produces a harvestable surplus. Hunting is strictly regulated in Norway. In making decisions regarding permission to harvest and regarding harvesting methods, importance shall also be attached to the function of the species in the ecosystem and the effect the harvesting may otherwise have on the biological diversity. However, the importance of the species as food or for recreation, harvesting traditions in the area in question and the possible damage that the species causes must also be taken into account when making these decisions. These rules do not apply, however, to the harvesting of alien organisms. For details, *see infra.*

554. In addition, pursuant to NDA Article 18, the government may make regulations or individual decisions permitting the *'removal' of wildlife and salmonids and freshwater fish:*

(a) to protect naturally occurring plants, animals and ecosystems;
(b) to prevent damage to crops, livestock, domesticated reindeer, forest, fish, water or other properties;
(c) to safeguard general health and safety interests or other public interests of substantial importance;
(d) for capture for the purpose of restoring stocks;
(e) for capture for the purpose of lawful breeding and farming;
(f) for research, teaching or taxonomic purposes; or
(g) which are alien organisms.

Such decisions may only be made if the removal *does not jeopardize the survival of the stoc*k and the purpose cannot be achieved in any other satisfactory manner (Article 18 paragraph 2). The rule is meant to correspond broadly with the conditions for killing of threatened species laid down in the Bern Convention Article 9. The competent authority under the Act may on its own initiative implement removal for such purposes as are mentioned in the paragraph 1 (a)–(d) and (g). The government may make further regulations regarding such removal.

555. The authorities' application of this rule is a sensitive and very controversial political issue and has been the subject of several court cases over the last years. It is the general view of environmental organizations that the rules are interpreted too liberally and that too many permits to kill predators are given, in particular with regard to wolves. An issue in point has been whether the expression under Article 18 c) 'to safeguard general health and safety interests or other public interests of substantial importance' also includes the fear and discomfort among the inhabitants in some local communities due to the increased number of wolves in the area. In a case between WWF World Wide Fund for Nature and the Norwegian State in 2021 the Supreme Court found that the formulation of Article 18 c) is wide and leave much discretion to the authorities. It may include many different public interests, and the fact that local people may be sensitive to the presence of wolves in the neighbourhood is covered by the wording. In 2017 the Stortinget debated the issue and concluded that such local sentiments could fall under the wording in litra c) and thus make killing on that basis legal. According to Norwegian law, such a statement by Stortinget has relevance as a legal source which may influence the interpretation of a rule. As a consequence, the Supreme Court found the killings of wolves in this case to be legal.[595]

556. It also considered the case in light of the corresponding Article 9, No. 1 of the European Convention on the Conservation of European Wildlife and Natural Habitats (Bern Convention) and found that the decisions in question did not violate that Article.

The municipal authorities may grant permits for the removal of *cervids and beavers* to prevent damage under (b) above, and for the removal of a beaver lodge or dam to prevent substantial damage due to flooding. The issue of permits by the municipal authorities may be appealed to the county governor (Article 18 paragraph 5).

557. The interpretation and application of these rules must be seen in light of the Norwegian system for management of wild animals, in particular of predators, The application is to be so-called *differentiated.* This means that it will vary from one part of the country to the next depending on the various interests involved. In some areas, the protection of wild animals is given a certain priority over grazing interests. In other parts of the country, agricultural interests should be protected and are given priority. Anyway, the killing of the animals is only allowed if this is the only acceptable solution. In addition, to what extent the animal species and population is threatened is as mentioned an important criterion for these decisions.

558. A major *regulation lays down further rules on the management of the predators* lynx, bear, wolverine, wolf, and golden eagle.[596] Its purpose is to ensure 'a sustainable management' of these species. Within this framework the management shall also take into account economic and social considerations.

The regulation lays down *quantitative targets* or objectives for stocks 'in Norway' of the five predators (Article 3). These are divided between the country's eight different regions for the management of predators. In accordance with the principle of differentiation there is a fixed quantitative target for the number of animals to be reached in each (Article 4). This is primarily to be seen as a target in the sense a minimum number of animals. But it also works as a 'maximum' level of the stock in question because higher numbers may on certain conditions justify a deliberate reduction of the stock through 'removals' of animals. In each region there is a 'predator committee', appointed by the MCE. The committee shall develop and adopt a management plan for the predators in the region, in close contact with the municipalities and the interested organizations and institutions. It also has the

595. Supreme Court case HR-2021-662-A.

596. Regulation of 18 Feb. 2005 No. 242 on the management of predators with later amendments, the latest by regulation 29 Jan. 2021 No. 274.

authority to make formal decisions. The management of the stocks, including deliberate killing of individual predators pursuant to the regulation.

559. Pursuant to the Regulation Article 8, the deliberate killing may take place subject to the condition that the stock in question exceed the quantitative targets adopted for the species in the region pursuant to Articles 3 and 4.

560. If a species is in *immediate danger of extinction*, the authority shall assess whether *ex-situ conservation* measures shall be implemented, if this will promote the species' survival in the natural environment (NDA Article 27).

561. The protection as well as the exploitation of *whales and seals* is regulated by the Marine Resources Act[597] and the Act on the Right to take part in (professional) Fishing and Catching (in the sea).[598,599] This will be further discussed *infra* in Chapter 6, II.

562. Svalbard is an important habitat for the *polar bear.* The polar bear is subject to a special *Act on the Catch of Polar Bears*[600] and is also covered by the *Svalbard Environment Act.*[601] The polar bear is now a protected species, according to the international Polar Bear Agreement. It is generally prohibited to kill polar bears except in emergency situations.

563. As regards *trade in endangered species,* Norway has ratified the CITES. In order to implement this convention or other international obligations, or otherwise to conserve species naturally occurring in the wild, the NDA Article 26 provides the King with the necessary authority to make regulations regarding the import and export, transport, sale and keeping or possession of living or dead specimens or parts of such. Detailed rules are laid down in a special regulation for the implementation of the Convention.[602]

§2. 'Priority Species'

564. The concept of *'priority species'* is a special instrument in Norwegian law for the protection of endangered species. The aim is to give seriously endangered species a stronger protection than what follows from the general management principles and rules in the Act. The rules are found in Articles 23 and 24 in the Act. The government (King in Council) may designate 'priority species' in regulations

597. Act of 6 Jun. 2008 No. 37.
598. Act of 26 Mar. 1999 No. 15.
599. This also means that they come under the Ministry of Fisheries and Coastal Affairs and the fishery authorities.
600. Act of 22 Mar. 1957 No. 4.
601. Act of 5 Jun. 2001 No. 79.
602. Regulation of 15 Nov. 2002 No. 1276 on Import, Export, Possession etc. of Endangered Species of Wild Flora and Fauna ('CITES Regulation') pursuant to the NDA and the Svalbard Environmental Act (*see infra*) with later amendments, the most recent by Regulation of 23 Jun. 2021 No. 2135.

(Article 23 paragraph 1). The general criteria for the selection of priority species are that the population status or trends for the species in question are contrary to the objective set out in the Act (Article 5), that a significant proportion of the species' natural range is in Norway or it has distinctive genetic characteristics in Norway, or there are international obligations related to the species.

565. When there is documentation based on scientific criteria to show that the population status or trends for a species are substantially contrary to the objective set out in NDA Article 5, paragraph 1, the competent authorities under the Act – on their own initiative or at the request of an organization or other persons with legal interests in the matter – *has a duty to consider* whether a special regulation to protect the species should be issued (Article 23 paragraph 3). There is, however, no legal obligation for the authorities to give the species the status of 'priority species' even if it is seriously threatened. This is of course a weak point in the system from a nature protection perspective.

566. When a species has been given the status of 'priority species', the authorities may lay down *strict regulations for its protection* (Article 24). They may prohibit any form of removal of, damage to or destruction of the species or specific populations of the species, and prescribe that the general rules on removal and harvesting in the NDA (Articles 15–22, *see supra)* do not apply. They may also make provisions regarding the protection of certain types of *areas* of limited extent with specific ecological functions for the species in question (however, if such area protection renders current use of the area significantly more difficult, the area should rather be protected according to the general rules on protected areas). Finally, the authorities may require that the impacts of any works planned in areas with specific ecological functions for the species concerned, may be assessed and clarified, including the identification of alternative areas that may be used to ensure the conservation of the species. The regulations may require active management measures when this is necessary in order to ensure the conservation of the species.

As far as possible, public grant schemes shall be used in a way that promotes the conservation of priority species.

In 2011 the first regulations on priority species were adopted for eight endangered species: two birds species, two beetle species, three flower species and one butterfly species.[603] In 2015 five new species were added, five plants[604] and one particularly important mammal: the mountain fox (vulpes lagopus).[605]

The competent authority under the Act may grant exemptions from a regulation on priority species if this does not result in the deterioration of the species' population status or trend, or if significant public interests make it necessary. Furthermore, the status of 'priority species' may be withdrawn if the management objective set out in Article 5, paragraph 1, has been achieved for the species in question.

603. Regulations of 20 May 2011 Nos 517–524.
604. Regulations of 22 May 2015 No. 546 and of 29 May 2015 Nos 561, 562 and 563.
605. Regulation of 23 Jan. 2015 No. 60.

§3. Alien Organisms

567. Chapter IV (Articles 28–32) in the NDA deals with alien organisms.[606] First, a *general duty of care* is laid down in Article 28. Any person that is responsible for releasing living or viable organisms into the environment shall exercise due care, and as far as possible seek to prevent such release having adverse impacts on biological diversity. If an organism is released in accordance with a permit issued by a public authority, the duty of care is considered to be fulfilled if the conditions for the permit are still satisfied.

568. Any person that initiates an activity or project that may result in the spread or release of living or viable organisms beyond their natural range *shall take reasonable measures* to prevent this. If damage is caused to biological diversity or there is a risk of serious damage to biological diversity as a result of the release or unintentional discharge of alien organisms, the person responsible shall immediately notify the competent authority, and take measures in accordance with Articles 69 and 70 (*see supra).* The government may make regulations regarding activities or projects that may entail a risk of the spread or unintentional discharge of organisms that do not occur naturally in an area, and regarding the duty of notification.

569. Import of alien species is generally prohibited. Living or viable organisms may only be imported to Norway subject to a permit granted by the competent authority under the NDA (Article 29).[607] If an organism is imported with a view to releasing it into the environment, the application for a permit shall clarify the possible effects of such release on biological diversity. No permit may be granted if there is reason to believe that the import will have substantial adverse impacts on biological diversity.

However, unless otherwise provided by regulations, no permit is required for the import of terrestrial plants and specified livestock. Nor is a permit required for the import of biological control agents for which an import permit has been granted in or under other legislations.

The government may make regulations regarding import, including requirements for permits and conditions for permits. The government may also make regulations to the effect that specific organisms may be imported without a permit, or may prohibit the import of specific organisms if this is considered necessary in order to avoid 'substantial adverse impacts on biological diversity'.

606. However, these rules do not apply to all types of alien organisms, as some organisms are regulated by other Acts. For example, GMOs are generally regulated by Act of 2 Apr. 1993 No. 38 relating to the production and use of GMOs (the Gene Technology Act). Furthermore, assessments under this chapter shall not include considerations relating to plant, animal and human life and health that are safeguarded by the Act of 5 Aug. 1994 No. 55 relating to the control of communicable diseases (Communicable Diseases Control Act) and the Act of 19 Dec. 2003 No. 124 on food production and food safety (Food Act).

607. This is now regulated through a comprehensive regulation from 2015, *see infra*.

570. As regards *release of organisms or species into the environment* Article 30 states that no person must release – without legal authority under Article 31 – or a permit granted by the competent authority:

- organisms belonging to species or subspecies that do not occur naturally in Norway, including foreign tree species, into the environment;
- wildlife belonging to species, subspecies or populations that do not already occur naturally in the district, into the environment;
- organisms, except for those belonging to a native population, to the sea or a river system unless a permit has been granted under the Aquaculture Act;[608]
- organisms that do not already occur naturally in an area into the environment if the King has made regulations requiring a permit for this purpose.

Applications for a permit to release organisms or species shall give an account of the impacts such release may have on biological diversity. The government may lay down regulations setting out requirements for applications. A permit may not be granted if there is reason to believe that the release will have substantial adverse impacts on biological diversity.

571. Nevertheless, *some release is permitted without a permit,* pursuant to Article 31 provided the general duty of care (Article 28) is observed. This applies to:

- organisms imported subject to a permit under Article 29 with a view to release;
- plants in gardens, parks and other cultivated areas, if the plants are not likely to spread outside the area, and Norwegian tree species;
- biological control agents for which a release permit has been granted in or under other legislations; and
- specified organisms if the King has made regulations to that effect.

572. Pursuant to the Act a major *Regulation on alien organisms* was adopted in 2015.[609] It lays down more detailed rules necessary to implement the main principles and rules in Chapter 4. Its general objective is to prevent the import, release and spreading of alien species which have or may have negative consequences for nature diversity (Regulation Article 1). It regulates these activities, including trade in alien species. However, domesticated species are generally not covered by the regulation as are several other species as well, mainly because they are covered by other Acts and regulations. For example, GMOs are covered by the GMO Act. Import of plants to botanical gardens is also exempted (Article 3).

Import is prohibited of a number of species listed in Annex 1 to the regulation (Article 5). On the other hand, even more species, listed in Article 7 and Annex II, are exempted from the prohibition and may be imported freely (Article 7). For the rest, an individual permit is required (Article 6).

---

608. Act of 17 Jun. 2005 No. 79.

609. Regulation of 19 Jun. 2015 No. 716 with later amendments, the most recent by Regulation of 18 Dec. 2020 No. 3156.

Release and marketing of the species listed in Annex I is prohibited (Article 9), while a number of organisms listed in Annex IV may be released without a special permit (Article 11). For the rest, a permit is required for release of wild species, subspecies and stocks which are not found naturally in the district in question, alien organisms in the sea and in watercourses and other organisms that do not belong to any local species, subspecies or stocks (Article 10).

§4. Hunting

573. Hunting is to be carried out in accordance with the general objectives and principles of the NDA, *see supra.* However, it is regulated in more detail by the *Wildlife Act*[610] and regulations pursuant to this Act.

The general purpose of the Act is to ensure that wildlife and the environment of the wildlife in Norway are managed in accordance with the NDA to ensure the protection of nature's productivity and diversity (Article 1). Stocks of the various species have to be kept at a sustainable level in the long term and within their natural living areas. Within these frameworks, wildlife may be 'harvested' to the benefit of agriculture and recreational activities.

By 'wildlife' in the Act is meant all land mammals living in the wild, and also birds, amphibious animals and reptiles. Marine mammals are not included, as the management of these is regulated, together with marine fisheries, by the Marine Resources Act.[611] Fishing of freshwater and salmonid fish is regulated by the Act on Freshwater and Salmonid Fish.[612] *The right to hunt in Norway follows the property right of the land.* This means that it partly belongs to private landowners, partly to the parties to rural common land,[613] and partly to the State as owner of important mountain and forest areas in the country. A number of small private properties may be organized as one hunting area for the common management of the game resources (Wildlife Act Article 37).

574. Hunting is a popular activity in Norway. A policy objective has therefore been *to give the public at large the possibility* to hunt at least small game. On parts of the State land there is general opportunity for the public to shoot small game like rabbit and grouse for a small fee. Where private land is concerned, the municipalities should seek agreement with private property owners to provide hunting opportunities for the public. If agreement is not reached, the State authorities may order the landowners to give public access to hunt small game, if this is desirable to keep the stock of animals at a proper level. In such cases, the authorities may issue a limited number of hunting licences ('hunting cards'), in order to keep the shooting to proper levels.

610. Act of 29 May 1981 No. 38.
611. Act of 6 Jun. 2008 No. 37.
612. Act of 15 May 1992 No. 47.
613. Rural common land is forest and mountain areas which are owned by several farmers in common. This type of ownership is found in many parts of Norway. It usually provides the farmers with necessary area for grazing, logging for the daily needs of the household, fishing, hunting, etc.

575. If, during a hunt, an animal is wounded, the hunter has the right, for a maximum of one day, to follow the animal onto a neighbouring property in order to kill it there. He/she must inform the landowner and the municipality about the incident as soon as possible.

576. If a landowner *transfers* the general right to use his/her property, the right to hunt is included, unless otherwise agreed. A landowner may rent out the right to hunt on his/her property, but for no longer than ten years at the time (Wildlife Act Article 28). The parties must make a written agreement, and an agreement for more than five years has to be reported to the municipal authorities.

577. In practice, *all hunting of wild animals and birds is regulated* in Norway. There are detailed regulations about the management of all the most important species of wild animals. The regulations define the seasons and geographical areas for the hunting of each species. Hunting of most species usually lasts from September to February.

When making decisions on these issues, the authorities must take into account to what extent the species produces a natural surplus which is worth harvesting, and that it has value as a resource. The local hunting and trapping traditions should also be taken into account, as well as possible damage caused by the wildlife. The regulations may vary between parts of the country. They may be quite detailed, specifying the number – quota – of animals that may be hunted on each individual property. They may also, for example, be specific for male and female, young and old animals, respectively.

578. Special rules apply to *animals of prey.* The four large predators are protected species. However, as mentioned, licences to kill a limited number of animals in a certain area may be issued when the animals do damage, or threaten to do damage, to domestic animals and domesticated reindeer.

579. As mentioned above, regardless of the general protection and hunting regulations the government has a widely defined authority under the NDA Article 18 to issue regulations or individual decisions permitting the killing ('removal') of wild animals, for example, if they cause or may cause damage to biodiversity, or to crop, domesticated animals including reindeer, forest, fish, water or other properties. The general condition is that the killing of the animal(s) does not threaten the survival of the stock in question, and there is no other satisfactory solution to the problem. Also, the municipality may give special permits to kill deer species and beaver if they cause or may cause serious damage (NDA Article 18 paragraph 5).

580. The Wildlife Act and regulations pursuant to the Act[614] lay down important *general rules about hunting activities.* The minimum age for shooting of small game is 16 years, and 18 years for large game. Even 14 and 15-year-olds may participate in certain types of shooting with the consent of their parents. A person who wants

614. Notably general Regulation 22 Mar. 2002 No. 313 on hunting and catching, with later amendments.

to go shooting must pass a public shooting test, pay an annual hunting fee and, if necessary, obtain a hunting licence for the area where he/she wants to shoot. For hunting moose, deer and (wild) reindeer, the shooting test must be passed every year. A fee must also be paid for each killed animal. For many animal species, the hunter must report the result of his/her hunt to the local shooting authorities (Article 50).

581. The Wildlife Act also contains certain rules about *how hunting should be carried out.* The general rule is that the animals should not suffer unnecessarily. Nor should hunting be done in a way that creates dangers for people, domesticated animals or property (Article 19). In general, only the use of guns with a maximum of two shots is permitted, but certain traps and other methods of catch may be allowed, for example, where this is necessary in order to limit damage caused by wildlife. It is prohibited to hunt from motor vehicles and aeroplanes (Article 21). Swimming deer shall not be chased or killed unless they are being pursued because they are wounded (Article 22).

The use of dogs is permitted only for hunting certain animals and birds.

582. *Illegal killing of wild animals* is regarded as quite a serious crime in Norwegian law, and in particular of species threatened with extinction. Over the last few decades, we have seen some particularly serious cases of illegal hunting of eagles, falcons and other birds of prey, and their eggs. Any violation of the Wildlife Act, or of a regulation on the basis of the Act, may be punished with fines, with a term of imprisonment of up to one year, or with a term of imprisonment of up to two years if the circumstances are particularly serious (Article 56). In addition, Article 240 of the Penal Act states that a person may be given a term of imprisonment of up to six years of imprisonment if he/she wilfully or by gross negligence 'diminishes a natural stock of protected living organisms which are threatened with extinction either nationally or internationally'.

The implementation and enforcement of the Wildlife Act is an important part of the responsibility of the State Nature Inspectorate pursuant to the Act on State Nature Inspection.[615]

615. Act of 21 Jun. 1996 No. 38.

Chapter 4. Agriculture

§1. General Introduction

583. Only 3% of Norway's territory is *cultivated agricultural land*. Of this, only one-third is suitable for cultivation of food grain. Agricultural land is found mostly around the main cities, in narrow valleys in the southern part of the country, and along the fjords in the western and northern parts. Everywhere, agricultural land is scarce, and it is seen as important to protect it against urban sprawl and development, such as new housing and industrial zones and roads.

584. In many districts, agriculture is economically very important for the local communities. Many small communities are based mainly on agriculture, and would be seriously threatened without it. For several decades, it has been an important political objective to keep *a dispersed settlement pattern* in Norway. Small-scale agriculture is a key factor for this in many parts of the country. To uphold agriculture is important also from the point of view of Norway's self-sufficiency in food products, and protection of the cultural landscape.

585. For these reasons, *the protection of agriculture and agricultural land* has been an important political objective in Norway for many years. The Norwegian agriculture is to a great extent protected from free international trade, highly regulated and also heavily subsidized by the State.[616] This is reflected in the legislation. Here, we shall concentrate on three areas of particular interest from an environmental point of view: the protection of agricultural land on the basis of the *Agricultural Land Act*,[617] planning of the use of agricultural land through the *PBA*, and the rules regarding control of transfers of agricultural properties in *the Concession Act*.[618] Issues related to pollution from agriculture are treated *supra* in Part I, Chapter 3, §2, III.

586. Traditionally, farmers' associations have a strong position in Norwegian society, and the agricultural administration has been well developed at the State, county and municipal level. These authorities are the Ministry of Agriculture and Food, the Norwegian Agricultural Authority, the County Agricultural Board, and the municipalities. The Norwegian Agricultural Authority has the competence to ensure that all schemes and regulations in the field of agricultural policy and law are administered uniformly across the country, and throughout the value chain.

587. Over the last two decades, the environmental effects of agriculture have become an important issue in environmental policy. A number of measures have

616. For example, agriculture and agricultural products are not included in the EEA Agreement which links Norway to the internal market of the EU.
617. Act of 12 May 1995 No. 23. This Act replaced the earlier Agricultural Land Act of 1955. The main principles remain unchanged from the 1955 Act. There is a long tradition of strict regulation of the use of agricultural land in the country.
618. Act of 28 Nov. 2003 No. 98.

been taken in order to reduce pollution – in particular water pollution[619] – from agriculture, and to make agriculture generally more environmentally friendly through better practices, less use of chemical fertilizers and pesticides, protection of the agricultural and cultural landscape, and so on. There are several budgetary instruments for State support for such measures. A general regulation lays down the rules for the various types of State support, and the relevant conditions.[620]

§2. The Agricultural Land Act

588. The *purpose* of the Agricultural Land Act (or Farmland Act) of 1995[621] is broad, as spelt out in its Article 1. Generally, it is to ensure that agricultural land, including forests and mountain areas, is used in the best possible way for society as a whole, and, in particular, for those who are employed in agriculture. The main emphasis should be on agricultural needs. However, it is further stated that the needs of future generations should be taken into account, thus expressing the principle of sustainable development.

It is explicitly stated that:

> the management of the land resources shall be environmentally sound, and, inter alia, take into consideration the protection of the soil as a factor of production, and the need to take proper care of the land and the cultural landscape as a basis for life, health and well-being of humans, animals and plants (Article 1 third paragraph).

589. The Act establishes three main principles:

(1) All cultivated land should remain cultivated, insofar as it may be the basis for profitable agricultural activities (Article 8).
(2) Cultivated land cannot be taken for uses other than agriculture, and cultivable land should not be used in such a way that agriculture could become impossible in the future (Article 9), unless special permission is given by the authorities.
(3) An agricultural property may not be divided into several parts without the consent of the agricultural authorities (Article 12).

590. Article 8 provides that *all cultivated land should remain cultivated.* The landowner has a general responsibility for this, and must take the necessary measures to ensure continuous cultivation on his/her land. If the landowner personally cannot carry out the necessary work on the land, he/she must let other farmers use it. This is not uncommon in Norway; nearly half of all agricultural land is rented out and cultivated by other farmers than the landowner himself/herself. Article 8 states that the obligation to cultivate may be fulfilled though a written agreement of

619. *See supra* Part I, Ch. 3, §2, III.
620. Regulation of 19 Dec. 2014 No. 1817.
621. Act of 12 May 1995 No. 23.

lease of the land of not less than ten years. The agreement must result in 'good solution' with regard to the use of the agricultural land.

The agricultural authorities can order the landowner to take necessary measures to put his/her land into cultivation, rent it to another farmer for up to ten years or order forestation of the land.

The authorities may also give dispensation from the cultivation duty in individual cases, in light of the agricultural needs, possibilities and conditions in each case (Article 8a).

The Act provides the State with a wide authority to lay down necessary *regulations*. Pursuant to Article 11 first paragraph the Ministry of Agriculture and Food may lay down regulations on how to carry out the *agricultural activities*. The objective of such regulations may, *inter alia*, be to prevent erosion and protect special natural values. Pursuant to Article 11 second paragraph the Ministry may lay down regulations about *the development of new agricultural land for cultivation* to prevent damage to nature or the cultural landscape, and emission of GHGs, including prohibition of such new developments.[622] Finally, pursuant to Article 11 third paragraph the Ministry may adopt regulations on the planning, approval and construction of *roads for agricultural purposes*.[623]

591. Article 9 of the Act establishes that *cultivated land cannot be taken for uses other than agriculture,* and that cultivable land should not be used in such a way that agriculture could become impossible in the future. 'Agriculture' includes agricultural infrastructure such as buildings and roads for agricultural purposes. It does not, however, include agricultural industry, such as dairies and slaughterhouses. Forestation is not included either.

This is an important principle in land management in Norway. It protects both the land as a resource for food production, and the soil itself. However, as an absolute rule, it would create serious difficulties for many other sectors of society, and be clearly inefficient from an economic point of view. Therefore, the agricultural authorities may permit agricultural land being put to other uses, such as housing, trade and industry, public services and roads.

This, however, is only accepted under specific special circumstances. The main condition, as expressed in Article 9, is that the authorities, on the basis of a broad assessment of the various needs, find that the agricultural interests should yield to other interests. The Act mentions some of the factors that have to be taken into account:

- existing land-use plans according to the PBA;
- possible inconvenience to the (remaining) agriculture in the area;
- consequences for the cultural landscape;
- the advantages for society of the planned activity;
- whether the change in the use of the land is irreversible or may be reversed at a later stage (e.g., if the land is used temporarily as a golf course).

622. Regulation of 2 May 1997 No. 423.
623. Regulation of 28 May 2015 No. 550, as amended by Regulation of 21 Dec. 2020 No. 3044.

The authority may attach such special conditions to the permission as it finds necessary in order to fulfil the purposes of the Act.

On this point, there is *an important link between the Agricultural Land Act and the PBA*, which is explained below, *see* §3. In areas accepted for development in approved land-use plans pursuant to the PBA the Agricultural Land Act no longer applies, according to Article 2 of this Act. The permission which would normally have been given on the basis of its Article 9, has instead been given through the formal approval and adoption of the land-use plan according to the PBA.

Similarly, a project or an activity in the energy sector that has got permission pursuant to an Act in that sector – mainly the Energy Act, the Water Resources Act or the Watercourse Regulation Act does not need a special permission pursuant to Article 9 in the Agricultural Land Act.

592. Article 10 deals with *marshes and peat-soil*. Marches and peat-soil may be taken out to make peat or other products. When this is done, there must always be left a proper layer of peat or soil, and the land has to be restored so that it afterwards can be used in agriculture, or for nature protection reasons. The abovementioned Regulation on development of new agricultural land for cultivation has an important article on marshes and peat-soil (Article 5a). The main rule is that cultivation of marshes and peat-soil is prohibited. However, the municipality may 'in special situations' give dispensation from the prohibition, for example, when a farmer loses already cultivated land to public development such as roads, or the marsh in question is the landowner's only possibility for new cultivation. Dispensation may only be given 'when the need for the new cultivation is such that it justifies that the environmental and climate considerations are set aside'. The landowner must document that cultivating the marshland is of significant importance for his overall agricultural activity.

593. The Act Article 12 lays down *a general prohibition to divide an agricultural property* into several parts. It also applies to properties that may be used for agriculture or forestry. Norwegian farms are generally rather small in size. The purpose is to prevent the agricultural area of a farm from being reduced, and farms being split into several entities, each too small for economically viable agriculture. A further fragmentation of the agricultural areas is generally undesirable. This should be seen in connection with another important legal principle in Norwegian land law: the right for the eldest child of a farmer to take over the whole farm, and at a reasonable price.[624]

Nevertheless, the agricultural authorities may give permission to a division if it leads to an acceptable structure of the agricultural activity in the area. Here again, a broad assessment must be made. Consequences for the agricultural activity, the cultural landscape, the land-use and existing land-use plans, and possible environmental or other negative effects are factors that must be taken into account. Regardless of other effects, a division may always be accepted if it has a positive effect for

624. This principle of allodial possession is a very old legal institution in Norway. Today, it is spelt out in the Act of 28 Jun. 1974 No. 58 (*Lov om odelsretten og åsetesretten*). The rules are complicated, and the subject is not regarded as relevant in the context of this monograph.

the local population and settlement (Article 12 paragraph 4). The authorities may lay down such conditions for a permission, as they find necessary.

§3. The PBA as Applied to Agricultural Land

594. The PBA establishes a *system of comprehensive planning, including land-use planning,* at the county and municipal levels. Through this planning, the various sector interests in an area should be assessed, and possible conflicts between them should be resolved. All main sector authorities are to participate in the planning. When a municipal master plan or a more detailed local development plan[625] is adopted, it is binding for the landowners. It also serves as guideline for the application of the various sectoral legislations within the plan area.

595. This planning system is very important from an agricultural point of view. In the municipal and local land-use plans, areas for agriculture will be designated. Through a systematic assessment of alternative land-use in an area, agricultural land which appears suitable for development may be protected, and housing, industry and roads located in areas that are less valuable from an agricultural point of view.

As mentioned, the main principle in Norwegian law is that agricultural land cannot be put to other uses. However, this may be necessary from time to time, in order to meet important needs in other sectors of society. Such conflicts are usually solved through the planning system in the PBA. The agricultural authorities participate in the planning, and they may have to accept that some agricultural land is taken for other uses. When the plan is formally adopted, the agricultural authorities are bound by it. As already mentioned, in areas accepted for development of housing, industry, social service buildings, and so on pursuant to the PBA the Agricultural Land Act no longer applies, according to Article 2 of this Act. The permission which would normally have been given on the basis of its Article 9 (*see supra*), has instead been given through the adoption of the plan according to the PBA.

596. If the agricultural authorities cannot accept a change of use of agricultural land as proposed in a municipal or local plan, and a compromise solution is not found, they can appeal the municipal decision to the ministerial level, in accordance with the general procedure of the PBA. In this case, the Ministry of the Municipal Affairs and Modernisation, as the ministry for planning, has the final say, after consultations with the other ministries with an interest in the matter. Certain cases have been so important and controversial that they have been decided by the Cabinet, and even discussed in Stortinget (Parliament).

597. In the *municipal master plan,* areas for agriculture are not a separate legal category. The relevant area category is *agriculture, recreation, nature protection and reindeer herding in combination* (Article 11-7, paragraph 2 No. 5). In most Norwegian municipalities, a large part of the land is forests and mountains, and there are no serious conflicts between these various activities and interests.

---

625. For details about these types of plans, *see infra* Part III.

The municipal master plan cannot be used to regulate how agricultural activities are carried out within these areas. In this respect, the jurisdiction of the municipal council as planning authority is limited. Public regulation of agriculture and forestry is mainly under the jurisdiction of the agricultural authorities pursuant to the Agricultural Land Act (*see supra*).

Within an area designated for agriculture in a municipal master plan, the plan may, however, open certain opportunities for other activities. A plan may define areas where a limited number of scattered houses, recreational houses and buildings for trade and industry can be located.

In a *local development plan,* however, separate areas for agriculture, recreation and nature protection can be set aside in the plan (Article 12-5, paragraph 2 No. 5). As a consequence, an area may be formally designated for agricultural activities, including forestry. In such areas, the authorities may lay down more detailed regulations about how the activity shall be carried out – or not carried out (Article 12-7 No. 9). This may include, for example, certain active measures to protect the land or particular environmental values. Here, the planning system pursuant to the PBA may be used to implement and supplement other instruments and mechanisms for protection of natural values and diversity, in particular the various instruments in the NDA.

§4. The Concession Act

598. Another important piece of legislation concerning agricultural land is the Act on Concession for Acquisition of Real Property (Concession Act).[626] It establishes *a general system of public licence – 'concession' – for the acquisition of real property* in Norway. This applies generally to all properties of a certain type and size.

Although its main purpose is to protect productive agricultural land and a good property and ownership structure, the Act is meant to serve other purposes as well. Article 1 on the purpose of the Act mentions, in particular, securing land for development needs, environmental considerations, public nature and recreation interests, and local settlement. It also explicitly mentions the needs of future generations.

599. The acquisition of *certain types of property does not require a concession.*[627] According to Article 4, concession is not – as a rule – required for the acquisition of plots of undeveloped ground for residential or recreational houses of less than 2 daa and has been approved as such pursuant to the PBA and the Agricultural Land Act. The same applies to plots of undeveloped ground which are designated for development in a municipal master plan or a local development plan pursuant to the PBA. Neither does it apply to built-up properties of less than 100 daa if less than 35 daa are fully cultivated. This means that ordinary homes, as well as small farms, may be transferred freely.

626. Act of 28 Nov. 2003 No. 98. The Act replaced an earlier Act on the same issue of 31 May 1974 No. 19.

627. Here we can only give a general picture. Many details are by necessity left out.

The concession requirement *applies to all sorts of acquisitions*, including heritage. It also applies to transfer of a rent of or the right to use a property for more than ten years, and to other types of agreements that to a large extent limit the owner's right to dispose of his/her property (Article 3).

600. However, concession is not required for transfer of property between spouses, to parents and children of the owner or his/her spouse, and to siblings of the owner or his/her spouse and their children (Article 5 No. 1). Nevertheless, in case of an agricultural property of more than 500 daa of productive forest or with more than 35 daa of cultivated land, these exceptions only apply if the receiver moves to, and formally, as well as in fact[628] lives on the farm for at least five years. He/she also must work the land or rent it to another farmer as supplementary agricultural land, through a written contract, for not less than ten years.[629] The same applies to a person, who has the right to take over the property as an allodial possession (Article 5 No. 2).[630] More detailed rules on the application of the concession system are laid down in regulations.[631]

The State does not need concession for its own acquisition of land (Article 5 No. 3). The same rule applies to counties and municipalities if the property in question has been designated for purposes other than agriculture in a municipal master plan or local development plan pursuant to the PBA (Article 5 No. 4).

601. As regards the issue of whether a concession shall be given or not in a given case the Act itself leaves a rather *wide margin of discretion* to the concession authority, which is the municipal council in the first instance. Since the main purpose is protection of agriculture and agricultural land, the Act (Article 9) describes the following factors that may count in favour of concession for the acquisition of agricultural land:

- whether the purpose of the acquisition supports local settlement;
- whether the acquisition gives a good solution for the agricultural activity;
- whether the person, who wants to acquire the property, has proper qualifications for agriculture;
- whether the acquisition supports the general management of the natural resources and the cultural landscape in the area.

602. For properties of a certain size, it is in addition of importance whether the agreed price is supportive to a reasonable price development (Article 9a).

603. In some parts of the country, in particular along the very attractive southern coast, there is a great demand for *recreational houses*. Well-to-do people in the

628. Article 6 states that the property must be the owner's 'real residence', based on more detailed rules pursuant to the Act of 16 Jan. 1970 No. 1 on Public Registration.
629. This follows from Art. 8 in the 1995 Agricultural Land Act.
630. *See* Act of 28 Jun. 1974 No. 58.
631. Regulation of 8 Dec. 2003 No. 1434 with later amendments, the last by regulation of 12 Dec. 2020 No. 3044, and regulation of 8 Dec. 2003 No. 1480 with amendments of 22 Sep. 2014 No. 1223.

capital Oslo and other urban areas want to buy local people's houses as summer-houses, and at a considerably higher price than its local market price as a residential house. This development has become a threat to the future stability and even the very existence of many small communities along the coast, and also in other attractive parts of the Norwegian countryside. In order to limit it, the Concession Act gives the Ministry the authority to issue *regulations that make the concession system applicable for all or parts of the residential houses* within a municipality, when residential houses are acquired for purposes other than year-round residence (Article 7). Hence, concession is not required if the property is used for ordinary year-round residence, either by the owner or by a tenant.

Concession shall anyway be granted if it is not necessary to prevent the house in question from being used for recreation. It shall also be granted if the price of the house as residential house is significantly lower than the ordinary price level for residential houses in the area (Article 10). The authority may lay down such conditions in individual cases that are deemed necessary to ensure that the purpose of the Act is fulfilled (Article 11).

Such regulations must be proposed by the municipality itself, and must be necessary to prevent residential houses from being turned into recreational houses (Article 7 paragraph 6). Today, such rules apply wholly or in part in some 30 municipalities (out of 350), mainly along the southern coast and in certain mountain areas.

Chapter 5. Forests

§1. General Introduction

604. Forests are a rich natural resource in Norway. About 23% of the land area in Norway is covered by 'productive' forest and about 5% by 'unproductive forest'. Forestry and forest-based industry – such as sawmills, and pulp and paper factories – is the third most important industry sector in the country. The main tree species are spruce, pine and birch. Large parts of the mountain areas, and the country north of the Polar Circle, are covered mainly by birch. Over the last decades, the forests have had a net increase, partly due to a milder climate and reduced logging.

Most of the forests are privately owned. Many farmers have some forest as part of their property. Thus, there are many relatively small forest properties in Norway. In addition, in parts of the country, forests form important parts of rural common land, which are owned and used in common by many farmers in a valley. An important part of the forests belongs to companies within the forest industry. The State, as well as some counties and municipalities, also owns considerable forest areas.

The country has a long tradition of forest management and development, including research and education in close cooperation with forestry organizations.

605. The Forestry Act of 27 May 2005 No. 31 is the main piece of legislation concerning forests and forestry. Legal protection of forest areas for nature conservation purpose is based on the instruments of protection of areas in the NDA: national parks, protected landscapes and – not least – nature reserves. Also, planning pursuant to the PBA may lead to restrictions on building and other activities in the forest. However, at the outset, the Forestry Act also apply to such areas to the extent forestry is not explicitly regulated pursuant to these Acts.

The forest authorities are the Ministry of Agriculture and Food, the Norwegian Agricultural Authority, the County Agricultural Board, and the municipalities. The Ministry is responsible for the government's forestry policy, while the Norwegian Agricultural Authority and the local units work to implement the policy.

§2. The Forestry Act

606. The Forestry Act applies to all Norwegian forests and 'forest fields'[632] regardless of ownership.

The objective of the Forestry Act (Article 1) is to promote a sustainable management of the forest resources in the country with a view to local and national value creation, and to protect the biological diversity, landscape, recreation and cultural values in the forest. The wording explicitly gives equal importance and weight to

632. 'Forest fields' are defined in Art. 2 as areas which are suited for forestry production and are not already in use for other purposes.

production and protection objectives. Over recent decades, provisions for the protection of the environment have been introduced and strengthened within the forestry legislation. Environmental considerations now play an important role in the forest and forestry policy and influence the way forestry is carried out.

607. The basic principle of Norwegian forestry law is that *the forest owner has the right to decide* himself/herself how to exploit his/her forest, provided that this is done in accordance with the Act, and regulations pursuant to the Act. Article 4 of the Act explicitly states that the forest owner must know the 'environmental values' in his/her forest and take these into consideration in all activities in the forest. It also states that this may restrict the way the owner manages his/her forest. The Ministry may lay down regulations to this effect and adopted an important *regulation on sustainable forestry* in 2006[633] (*see infra*). The forest owner shall also ensure that persons working in his/her forest know and follow the rules and regulations (Article 4, paragraph 2). The authorities have a general obligation to control that rules and regulations are followed and applied properly (Article 20). They have the right to enter a forest and to investigate, in order to enforce the Act effectively (Article 20). In practice, the owner often has close contact with the local forest authority about the proper management of his/her forest.

608. Several articles in the Forestry Act itself provide *guidelines for the proper management of the forest.* An important instrument for proper forestry and management of forest is *forestry planning* pursuant to Article 5. Forestry planning consists of *forest registration* and a *forestry plan.* Forest registration shall identify and describe the forest and environmental resources in a forest. The information about environmental values in the forest shall be made public, in accordance with the Environmental Information Act.[634] The forestry plan is a plan for the management of the forest resources and the forestry activities. More detailed rules are laid down in the Regulation on State aid for forestry planning and environmental registration[635] and the Regulation on sustainable forestry (*see infra*). The local forest authority may order a forest owner to carry out forest registration and make a forestry plan.

The local forest authority may prohibit felling which violates the Act or may have significant negative effects on the environment (Article 8, paragraph 2).

After felling, *reforestation* must be carried out (Article 6). In order to protect the environment, the local forest authority may prohibit certain methods in this regard, such as the introduction of new types of trees, trenching, and the use of fertilizers and pesticides.

The local forest authority may order a forest owner to report on planned felling and reforestation activities, in order to ensure that the activities are carried out in accordance with the rules in the Act and in regulations (Article 11).

633. Regulation of 7 Jun. 2006 No. 593 on sustainable forestry with later amendments, the latest by regulation 18 Aug. 2021 No. 2528.

634. Act of 9 May 2003 No. 31, *see supra* General Information, Ch. 2, § 3, II.

635. Regulation of 4 Feb. 2004 No. 449 as amended by Regulation of 17 Aug. 2021 No. 2516.

609. The 2006 *Regulation on sustainable forestry* plays an important role in Norwegian forestry. It applies to all Norwegian forests covered by the Forestry Act. Its objective is to promote a forestry that protects the environmental values in the forest and ensures proper reforestation after felling, and a generally sound forest. The owner must have full knowledge of the environmental values in his/her forest and the relevant environmental considerations in connection with forestry activities that are planned or carried out. In all forestry activities, the forest owner shall ensure that biological diversity, landscape, and recreational and cultural values are taken properly into account. As a general rule, felling can only take place where a proper registration has been carried out, pursuant to Article 5 of the Forestry Act.

The regulation was at the outset based on discussions between forestry and environmental organizations, which led to general guidelines for sustainable forestry, called Levende skog ('Living Forest'). After years of experience and further works, Norway's forestry industry decided to join the Programme for the Endorsement of Forest Certification *(PEFC)*. PEFC is the world's leading forest certification organization. It is an international non-profit, non-governmental organization dedicated to promoting sustainable forest management. In January 2016, the Norwegian forestry standards were approved by the PEFC Council as in compliance with the PEFC standards.[636] These standards with its twenty-seven requirement points are now explicitly laid down in the Regulation on sustainable forestry. A national branch of PEFC has been established.

610. The *PEFC requirements* are presented under three main themes:

(1) *Manager responsibility and planning:* The best way to implement sustainable forestry pursuant to the requirements in the Norwegian PEFC Forest Standard is to have a well-updated forestry plan and good plan procedures. Fewer and fewer forest owners are carrying out the practical measures on properties themselves – but even so, forest owners bear responsibility for ensuring that the measures are implemented as effectively as possible, both for the forest owner himself and for the community in general. The requirements linked with manager responsibility and planning focus on responsibilities and planning applicable for long-term management of the forest property.
(2) *Felling and forestry operations:* All measures linked with felling and care of the forest require a certain awareness of implementation and consideration for other interests. The requirements linked with felling and forestry operations are linked with planning and implementation where the work has to be done.
(3) *Special environmental values:* As well as using forest management to ensure that the future forest is in good condition, it is necessary to safeguard biodiversity, cultural heritage and values linked with outdoor recreation and experiences.

Several important points are listed explicitly in the regulation itself (Article 5). Important habitats and biotopes must be protected. Waste from felling must be

636. PEFS N 02 Norwegian PEFC Forest Standard.

removed from brooks, rivers and lakes, as well as from footpaths and skiing paths. Damages from transport of timber must be repaired or restored. Felling must respect and be adapted to the landscape. Sufficient amounts of trees must be kept along riverbanks and lake shores to protect the ecosystems. Dredging of natural bogs is prohibited. Also, cultural heritage must be taken into account. Reforestation with new types of trees must be reported to the local authorities and may be prohibited. Introduction of foreign species will always require a permit from the local authority.

611. The building of new *forest roads* in connection with forestry is a controversial issue in Norway. Roads facilitate the forestry, but may be harmful to environmental values by disturbing the wildlife and destroying valuable landscape elements. Not least, roads make it possible to reach forest areas that have been unaccessible and hence protected in practice and thus contain particularly valuable old forests. Therefore, the building of new roads in forests is regulated by *a national regulation on agricultural roads*.[637] A new forestry road for vehicles and tractors requires a permit by the municipality, on the basis of a public procedure where all interested parties, including State environmental authorities, have a say. For the construction of a road of more than 5 km, an EIA may have to be carried out pursuant to the EIA rules of the PBA and the regulation pursuant to the Act.[638] The decision must be taken on the basis of both forestry and environmental considerations (biodiversity, landscape, cultural heritage, etc.). The municipality may lay down the necessary conditions in each case, with a view to safeguarding environmental values.

612. In addition, the government may issue *regulations with specific restrictions on the forestry activities* in forest areas with particular values for biological diversity, landscape, public recreation, or cultural heritage (Article 13). Such a regulation has been laid down for the forestry in the forest areas surrounding Oslo[639] with the aim of managing this forest properly and sustainably in light of the needs for protection of its particular natural and recreational values. It should be seen in connection with the special Act related to the management of these areas, *see infra* Chapter 9, §3, II.

However, such regulation may not render it impossible for the forest owner to carry out a profitable forestry activity. If so, protection according to the NDA is the proper legal mechanism, with the possibility of compensation to the owner of the forest (*see supra*).

613. In case of *damage* on forests due to fire, storm felling, landslide, illness, excessive grazing by deer, attacks of insects or fungi, the local forest authority may order the forest owner to carry out necessary measures to repair the damage and

637. Regulation of 28 May 2015 No. 550 as amended by Regulation of 21 Dec. 2020 No. 3044. The rules apply generally to roads connected to agriculture, but they mainly relate to forestry roads. There are technical State guidelines for the construction of these kinds of roads.
638. *See supra* General Introduction, Ch. 2, §4.
639. Regulation of 10 Sep. 2021 No. 2698.

restore the forest (Article 10). If the measures are not carried out by the owner, the local authority itself may carry them out, at the expense of the forest owner.

614. A special category of forest in the Forestry Act is *protective forest.* This is a forest belt which is formally designated by the forest authorities because it serves as protection for other parts of the forest, or against such natural accidents as landslide, avalanche, flood, and so on. It also applies to particularly vulnerable forests in the mountain areas and along the coastline towards the sea, where logging can be detrimental to forest reproduction. The authorities may issue regulations for the delimitation and management of protective forests. In protective forests, logging may be forbidden without the permission and participation of the forest authority (Article 12).

615. The Act has rules on the *'Forest Fund'* (Articles 14–17). The forest owner pays himself/herself a charge on the timber he/she sells or uses. The charge is paid to the fund and is to be used to promote the production and management of the forest from which the charge has been paid. The purpose is to ensure that there are means for reforestation and other necessary works to make forestry sustainable.[640]

616. The Act contains a *general penal provision* (Article 22). Whoever wilfully or by negligence 'significantly' violates the Act or a regulation, or decision made on the basis of the Act, may be fined, or imprisoned up to one year.

640. Rules on the Forest Fund are laid down in Regulation of 3 Jul. 2006 No. 881.

Chapter 6. Fish Resources

§1. Marine Fish Resources

I. Introduction and Overview

617. The geographical situation of Norway makes *marine fisheries a very important resource.* There are key spawning areas in the sea off the Norwegian coast, and the fisheries along the coast and in the North Sea have always been extremely rich. High seas fisheries are also very important, particularly in the North Atlantic and the Barents Sea.

618. Norwegian fisheries have been *extensively regulated* for many years. A sound management of the fish resources, based on the principle of sustainable yields, has become increasingly vital. The stocks of some significant fish species, such as the North Sea cod and capelin, have been generally declining since the 1970s. Several stocks are now close to what is internationally estimated as *safe biological limits* for long-term reproduction. The stock of North Sea cod is even below the minimum spawning stock level which is required for safe recovery. Since these fish stocks are migratory, *international agreements* and regulations are essential. Norway is a member of both the North-East Atlantic and the North-West Atlantic Fisheries Conventions. Norway is also party to the 1995 UN Agreement Relating to the Conservation and Management of Straddling Fish Stocks and Migratory Fish Stocks. These agreements form an important basis for Norwegian fisheries policy.

Through its EEZ of 200 nautical miles, Norway has jurisdiction over the living marine resources in vast sea areas in the North Sea, the Norwegian Sea and the Barents Sea, and around the isolated island of Jan Mayen which is situated between Iceland and Greenland. Norway also claims jurisdiction over living marine resources in a special zone around the Spitzbergen islands (Svalbard), defined as a special 'fishery zone'.

619. Initially, fishing in the sea was free for everyone in Norway. However, this principle now only applies to small-scale fishing for personal consumption or recreation. *As an industry and a profession, fishing is strictly regulated* and controlled by the State. The fishery authorities – the Ministry of Trade, Industry and Fisheries and the Directorate of Fisheries with regional offices – are well developed. They exercise regulatory and surveillance functions along the coast, within the economic zone, and on the high seas. Professional fishermen and their vessels have to be registered. A special Act, the Act on Right to take part in (professional) Fishing and Catching (Participation Act)[641] lays down a number of rules and conditions in this regard (*see infra*).

620. Norwegian fisheries may be divided into *two main categories:* First, the fisheries in coastal waters and in the fjords, which are mainly carried out by local

641. Act of 26 Mar. 1999 No. 15.

fishermen from rather small boats. The catch is most often delivered directly to the local fish trader onshore. This is the traditional pattern and still important in Northern Norway. Second, the major fisheries in the EEZ and on the high seas, mainly based on big trawlers combined with freezing facilities. Trawling is generally prohibited within twelve miles from the coast. Nevertheless, since the fish stocks are a limited and vulnerable resource, there are conflicts of interest and controversies between the various groups of fishermen.

621. Fishery is therefore a sensitive and rather complicated policy area in Norway. The major challenge and objective for *fishery policy* is to keep the catch of the various fish species at a sustainable level. Another important political objective is that the fisheries contribute to industrial activity in local communities along the coast which, traditionally, have been built on and dependent of the fishery. Much of the fisheries are now based on *a quota system* (for details *see infra*). A sustainable fishery policy is made more difficult by the fact that many of the most important species are highly migratory, and scientific forecasts are uncertain. Fishing vessels from many nations harvest the same resources, not least on the high seas. Often, the fixed quotas are not as strict as the researchers recommend. There is also the problem of controlling the quotas, and notoriously some overfishing occurs.

622. *The territorial waters* of Norway extend to twelve nautical miles from the coast.[642] 'From the coast' means outside the so-called baseline – the line drawn between the uttermost points along the coast, including islands. The sea inside the baseline ('internal waters') is included in the territorial waters.

623. In the territorial waters, only Norwegian citizens and Norwegian vessels have the right to fish, catch and other types of harvesting of wild marine natural resources, pursuant to the Marine Resources Act, Article 23a and 23b. The exclusivity for Norwegian citizens and vessels does not apply to sport and recreational fishing with simple fishing equipment as defined in the Act Articles 22 and 23 (*see infra*). In the territorial waters, it is also prohibited for foreigners to make, pack, reload, etc., fish produce (Article 23 c).

624. The King may, however, make exceptions in individual cases, within specific areas (Article 23d) and may in that connection decide that the fishing activities shall be subject to Norwegian legislation.

Outside the territorial waters, Norway has an '*adjacent zone*' in accordance with international law of the sea of a maximum of 24 nautical miles from the base line. In this zone, Norway may control the implementation of legislation concerning customs, taxation, immigration and health.[643]

642. Act of 27 Jun. 2003 No. 57 on Norway's territorial sea and adjacent zone. Before 2003 Norway had *a fishery limit* of twelve nautical miles, established in 1966 (Act No. 19 of 17 Jun. 1966).
643. Act of 27 Jun. 2003 No. 57, Art. 4.

625. In 1976, Norway established an *EEZ* of 200 nautical miles from the coast.[644] Here, Norway has jurisdiction in accordance with the international law of the sea. The main purpose of the economic zone was to extend national jurisdiction over the fish resources in the zone. Here, too, the basic principle is that only Norwegian citizens have the right to fish and make fish produce. Generally speaking, the same principles apply to fisheries here as in the territorial waters. However, foreigners have fishing rights on the basis of mutual agreements between Norway and other States and in accordance with the general rules for EEZ in the international law of the sea.[645]

In the economic zone, Norwegian authorities may – within the limits of international law – issue all necessary regulations concerning the fisheries, as well as on environmental protection, scientific research, installations, pipelines, research and engagement in other economic activities.[646]

II. The 2008 Marine Resources Act

626. The Act of 6 June 2008 No. 37 on *the Management of Wild Marine Resources (the Marine Resources Act)* provides a broad basis for the exploitation and management of living marine resources. It lays down objectives and principles for the harvesting and other exploitation of all wild living resources in the sea, including fish, marine mammals, and other marine organisms and plants in the seawater as well as on the bottom, and including their genetic material. It provides the government with the necessary authority to regulate in detail the harvesting of marine organisms, and all activities that are linked to harvesting, such as storage, transport, delivery, production and marketing of living marine resources. Anadromous salmonids are exempted from the Act. The management of these species is regulated by the 1992 Salmonid and Freshwater Fish Act (*see infra*).

627. The objective of the Act is to 'ensure a sustainable and economically profitable management of the wild living marine resources and the corresponding genetic material, and to contribute to employment and settlement in coastal communities' (Article 1). Article 2 states that the wild living marine resources belong to the 'Norwegian community',[647] which means that Norwegian authorities – and these authorities only – may regulate the exploitation of these resources.

628. Within the limits of international agreements and general international law, the Act applies to Norwegian vessels, and to Norwegian or foreign activities in

644. Act of 17 Dec. 1976 No. 91 on Norway's Economic Zone. In the parts of the Barents Sea bordering on Russian waters, the borderline between the Norwegian and Russian economic zones was for a long time an issue of controversy between Russia and Norway. Finally, in September 2010 the parties agreed after long negotiations, and the borderline was determined as a compromise between the parties' primary positions.
645. UN Convention on the Law of the Sea Part V.
646. Act of 17 Dec. 1976 No. 91 Arts. 4 and 7.
647. However, by choosing the expression 'the Norwegian Community' the legislator made it clear that these resources are not formally owned by the Norwegian State.

Norwegian land territory, territorial sea and internal waters, on the Norwegian continental shelf, and in the Norwegian EEZ. It also applies to Norwegian citizens on the high seas as far as this does not conflict with the jurisdiction of other States (Article 4). However, regulations pursuant to the Act apply to activities of foreigners and foreign companies in the EEZ only if this is stated explicitly in the regulation. On the other hand, they may apply to foreigners even on the high sea to the extent this follows from international agreements (Article 5).

629. Article 7 of the Act lays down *general principles* to be taken into account in order to ensure the sustainable management of the marine resources:

- a precautionary approach in line with international agreements and guidelines;
- an ecosystem approach that takes natural habitats and biodiversity into account;
- an effective control with harvesting and other exploitation of the resources;
- a sensible distribution of the resources in order to ensure employment and settlement in coastal communities;
- optimal exploitation of the resources in light of the market and industrial conditions;
- harvesting methods and use of equipment that minimize negative effects on living marine resources;
- the management of resources that serve to ensure the basis for Sami culture.

630. Pursuant to this Act, the fishery authorities issue a great number of regulations. A central instrument in the regulation and management of marine resources is *the system of quotas*. The legal basis is found in Chapter 3 (Articles 11–14) of the Act. Quotas may be laid down for amounts of catch of various species and for time periods. The system is based on quotas at different levels (Article 11). National quotas limit the total amount of catch of a species in a given period. Within the limits of the national quotas the authorities may lay down so-called group quotas for groups of vessels and types of gear, and quotas for research and education. They may decide that a certain amount of catch must be delivered to the processing industry in certain districts of the country ('district quota'). They may fix the maximum amount of catch for each vessel and also restrict the participation of certain types of vessels in certain harvesting activities.

Furthermore, quotas are also fixed for each vessel with regard to maximum quantity of catch and time periods, and even fix a maximum allowable catch of an individual voyage and of each fish species (Article 12). These quotas are transferable. The right to acquire quotas and the rules on the trade in quotas are regulated through the *Act on the Right to take part in Fishing and Catching* of 26 March 1999 No. 15 (*see infra*).

631. The Marine Resources Act (Article 16 and others) provides the government with a wide discretionary authority to lay down the *necessary regulations and prohibitions* to ensure a sustainable harvesting of marine resources, such as:

- regulation of time periods for different types of fishing and catch;
- regulation of the number of vessels that can take part in the fishing activities in an area at any given time;

- regulation of the use of types of gear;
- prohibition to harvest certain species, in certain areas, and/or at certain time periods;
- regulation of minimum and maximum fish size;
- further technical requirements for the vessels;
- fishing methods;
- competence of the captain, etc.

when this is necessary for the (proper) management of the resources and the activities, or for the economic outcome of the fisheries (Article 21).

Usually the regulations are given for one year at the time. Regardless of such regulations, however, fishermen from certain fishing communities in Northern Norway, including communities with fishermen of Sami ethnic origin, may always continue their traditional fishing activities in the local fjords, with fishing boats smaller than 11 m. Hence, this traditional local fishery activity in the northern part of the country is protected.

The Act also covers the issue of regulations of fisheries by Norwegian citizens and vessels outside the sea areas of Norwegian jurisdiction. It gives the Ministry the authority to lay down restrictions on the participation for Norwegian vessels in fishery activities in areas which fall under the jurisdiction of other states or outside the jurisdiction of any State (Article 20).

632. The Act also regulates *sport and recreational fishing* in the sea (Article 22). Small-scale, non-professional fishing for personal consumption, recreation, and for sport, *is free for everybody* in all Norwegian waters. This is generally legal and regarded as a public right which most Norwegians enjoy along the coast, in particular during summer. Fishing is allowed with both hand line and fishing rod, as well as fishing-nets less than 210 m and a limited amount of traps and bow nets. Stricter regulations may be laid down, for example, for certain species, in certain areas and at certain parts of the year in order to avoid overfishing. *Crabs* may also be caught freely throughout the year; while there are strict time and size limits on catching *crawfish and lobster*. Lobster is severely endangered in parts of Norwegian water.

For foreign citizens, special restrictions apply pursuant to Article 23 a-d in Norway's territorial waters *(see supra).*

633. The Marine Resources Act and the Right to take part in Fishing and Catch Act[648] (*see infra*) apply to the protection, as well as the exploitation, of *whales and seals.*[649] Whaling and sealing, in Norwegian waters and elsewhere, have a long historic tradition in Norway. For certain local communities along the coast, sealing and whaling has been an important industry. However, both whaling and sealing have been considerably reduced over the last decades. The present regulations are based on the principle of sustainable harvesting. Whaling, in particular, has been strictly

648. Act of 26 Mar. 1999 No. 15.

649. This also means that they come under the responsibility of Ministry of Trade, Industry and Fisheries and the fishery authorities.

regulated on the basis of international agreements. A general moratorium on whaling was established by the International Whaling Commission in 1982.[650] However, in 1993, Norway decided to resume a limited catch of minke whales along the Norwegian coast, based on scientific assessment of sustainable yield. The stock of minke whales in Norwegian waters is estimated at some 100 000 individuals. There are, however, controversies over the size of stocks and what 'sustainable yield' means. This has put Norway at odds with many other countries on the whaling issue.[651] The catch quota of minke whales has been quite steady in recent years. In 2016, the quota was 999 animals. For the whaling season 2023, the catch quota of minke whales was 1000 animals, 83 more than in 2022. However, the catch in 2022 was only 581 whales. In September 2017, the European Parliament adopted a resolution which urged Norway to stop all commercial whaling. Nevertheless, the whaling in Norway continues.

III. The Act on the Right to Participate in Fishing and Catch (The Participation Act)

634. The second essential piece of marine fishery legislation is the *Act of 26 March 1999 No. 15 on the Right to Participate in Fishing and Catch* (the Participation Act). This Act regulates the use of vessels, and the right to participate, in salt-water fisheries, except of salmonid fish, but including catch of seals and whales. The purpose (Article 1) is to:

- adapt the capacity of the fishing fleet to the resource base, in order to ensure a sustainable management of the marine resources;
- increase the profitability in the fishery sector; and
- ensure that harvesting marine resources works to ensure employment and communities along the coast.

The Act applies to professional fishing, catch and other forms of 'harvest' of wild living marine resources with a vessel that is formally regarded as Norwegian pursuant to the rules in the Maritime Act[652] which define what is a Norwegian vessel. It also applies to such activities from vessels of less than 15 m owned by foreigners. With professional fishing and catch is meant any harvesting of marine living resources carried out by a person who has such activity as his or her livelihood and a vessel is used (Article 3).

635. A vessel may not be used for professional fishing without an 'acquisition permit' from the fishing authorities (Article 4). This permit is given to the owner of a vessel for that particular vessel and does not give the person the right to use another vessel. The fishing activity must be carried out in full accordance with the

650. Norway made a formal reservation against the moratorium, and has not been legally bound by it.
651. The catch of seals and the catch and export of minke whale are regulated by regulations pursuant to the Marine Resources Act.
652. Act of 24 Jun. 1994 No. 39.

rules and regulations laid down pursuant to the Marine Resources Act. Acquisition permit may only be given to Norwegian citizens, and to foreigners living in Norway for vessels less than 15 m. 'Norwegian citizens' also includes companies which are owned at least by 6/10 by Norwegians and has their main office in Norway and other companies as defined in the Act (Article 5). Furthermore, a vessel can only be used for professional fishing pursuant to the Act if the captain and at least half of the crew live in a municipality along the Norwegian coast or a neighbouring municipality (Article 5a). The authorities may, however, grant exceptions to this requirement. Furthermore, to obtain an 'acquisition permit', the applicant must be actively exercising professional fishing or catch and must have been involved in professional fishing or catch for at least three of the previous five years. For companies this requirement must be fulfilled by a minimum of 50% of the owners of the company. The authorities may accept exceptions to these rule as well (Article 6).

This system of 'acquisition permits' is an important legal mechanism to control and regulate the number of fishing vessels and the ownership of such vessels, and to ensure that national and local interests are ensured in the development of this important industry. The Act lays down a number of further rules and guidelines for its implementation (Article 7). To obtain permission to participate in fishing, a vessel must be properly equipped (Article 8).[653] Furthermore, the Act lays down rules for possible withdrawal of an acquisition permit (Article 11). The general rules in the Act itself are supplemented by a comprehensive regulation which covers all the main aspects of the system.[654]

636. A 'special permission' (concession) is needed for the use of an 'ocean-going vessel' for fishing and catch (Article 12).

Further rules on this are laid down in a separate regulation.[655] A number of regulations regulate in detail how the various fisheries are to be carried out, mostly related both to the various stocks of fish and the different maritime areas where Norwegian ocean-going fishing vessels are operating. Furthermore, several regulations lay down rules for fishing activities by vessels of other states, EU in particular, in the Norwegian EEZ.[656]

The Act has a comprehensive set of instruments for control and sanctions including various administrative sanctions and penalties.

§2. Freshwater and Anadromous Fish

I. General Framework

637. In Norway, rivers and lakes are abundant, and the country has rich resources of freshwater and anadromous fish, in particular salmon and trout.

---

653. Details technical rules are laid down in a Regulation of 22 Dec. 2005 No. 1682 with later amendments.
654. Regulation of 7 Dec. 2012 No. 1144 with later amendments.
655. Regulation of 13 Oct. 2006 No. 1157 with later amendments.
656. For example, Regulation of 19 Mar. 2021 No. 823.

Anadromous fish move between seawater and freshwater. Every year, the salmon moves from the sea and up the rivers to spawn, and returns to the sea. Many of the world's best salmon rivers are found along the Norwegian coast. In all, there are over 500 salmon rivers in the country, each with a genetically unique stock. Also, numerous small rivers and lakes in the mountains give good opportunities for fishing, be it as an income for the local people, or for recreation.

638. The *Salmonid and Freshwater Fish Act* of 15 May 1992 No. 47 governs all salmonid and freshwater fishing. The purpose of the Act is to ensure sustainable management of the natural stock of the various fish species and their habitats, in order to protect the biological diversity and productivity. Within this framework, the Act shall serve to further develop the fish stocks, to the advantage of the persons holding the right as well as recreational fishing interests.

Pursuant to the Act, a number of regulations have been adopted. The implementation and enforcement of the Act is part of the responsibility of the MCE, NEA and the State Nature Inspectorate.

639. The right to fish freshwater and anadromous fish in rivers and lakes belongs – as a rule – exclusively to *the owner of the river or lake* (Articles 16 and 17). Most rivers and lakes in Norway are privately owned. They are part of the properties bordering the river or lake. Along a river, the properties on the two sides own the part of the river on their side as far out as to the deepest part of the riverbed.

The right to fish may not be separated from the property right for more than ten years at the time. If the general right to use a property is transferred, the fishing right follows unless otherwise agreed (Article 19).

In some lakes and watercourses, the fishing right may belong to the community as a common resource, or be free, according to local customary law. Some municipalities may have acquired fishing rights for the benefit of the public. Some of the bigger lakes in the country are partly owned by the State.

Along the coast, the right to fish *salmon in the sea* with nets from the shore belongs to the owner of the shore, as far out as his/her property right. The exercise of this right is, however, strictly regulated and prohibited in large parts of the coast.

640. In many rivers and lakes, sport and recreational fishing is made open to the public, by way of *local fishing permits* at a reasonable price. In the good salmon rivers, however, the right to fish may be extremely expensive, even for a short time and in a small part of the river.

The authorities work to improve the possibility of freshwater fishing for the public, primarily through cooperation and agreements with the persons who hold the rights. If the public does not have reasonable access to fishing, or the resources are not exploited by the holder of the right, the authorities may order the persons who hold the right to issue fishing permits to the public, or transfer the fishing right to another person. Such measures must be limited in time, with a maximum of ten years (Article 27).

Regardless of rights and ownership, *children under the age of 16 can fish freely* with hand lines and fishing rods in all rivers and lakes in Norway before 20 August, except in rivers or parts of rivers with anadromous salmonids (Article 18). However, this right may be restricted in specific areas by the county governor if it could significantly damage fish cultivation work or the owner's own fishing. This right for children was introduced into Norwegian law in 1992. The owner of the river is not compensated for this use. In a case of principle, the Supreme Court[657] stated that the children's right to fish in private rivers and lakes is not to be regarded as expropriation, and is not in violation of the general rule in Norway's Constitution Article 105 which states that the owner of a property is entitled to 'full compensation' when his/her property is taken for a public purpose (*see* General Introduction, Chapter 2, §1, I). The possible economic loss was regarded as very limited and the owner of the river did not get any compensation.

641. In general, there are few public restrictions on freshwater fishing. The exercise of fishing activities is mainly left to the holders of the right. Nevertheless, some methods like poison, explosives, guns and artificial light are generally prohibited (Article 37).

Anadromic salmonids are, however, threatened species and legally protected pursuant to the NDA. The same applies to other fish species in rivers with anadromic salmonids. As a consequence, fishing of these species is strictly regulated by the fishing authorities.[658] The regulations lays down detailed rules on place, time of the year, type of equipment to be used, etc.[659] In the sea, the fishing of anadromic salmonids is permitted only in certain parts along the coast and with certain types of tackle, such as fishing rod and fishing line, and certain types of net.[660] Drift-net fishing in the sea was prohibited many years ago. In lakes and watercourses, only fishing rod and fishing line are permitted in areas decided by the authorities. The minimum acceptable fish length is 35 cm.[661]

II. Protection and Development of Fish Stocks and Habitats

642. The needs and interests related to freshwater fishing, and the fish habitats, are to be included and taken into account in the county and municipal planning according to the PBA. This is explicitly stated in the Salmonid and Freshwater Fish Act (Article 7 paragraph 1).

The authorities may protect the fish stock in a watercourse or parts of it, by prohibiting or strictly regulating any activity that may harm or disturb the living conditions of the fish (Article 7 paragraph 2). However, the NDA is normally chosen as a basis for such protection of an area.

It is prohibited to import living salmonid or freshwater fish without public permit (Article 8).

657. Norsk Retstidende 2004, 1985.

658. The authorities responsible for the implementation of the Salmonid and Freshwater Fish Act are the MCE, the NEA, the county governor, and the municipalities.

659. Regulation 15 Mar. 2021 No. 798 on fishing of anadromous salmon in watercourses.

660. Regulation 1 Jun. 2021 No. 1748 on fishing of anadromous salmon in the sea.

661. Regulation of 20 Jun. 2003 No. 736.

643. As mentioned, the fishing authorities may issue *regulations* about the fishing activity in a watercourse, including limitations on time periods for fishing, allowed quantities of catch, types of gear and so on, if this is necessary in order to protect the natural fish resource (Articles 11 and 34). If an accident of pollution or other environmental hazards threaten the fish the authorities may take or order any preventive measure necessary to protect the fish (Article 12).

Cultivation activities have to be approved by the authorities, either on the basis of regulations or by permission in each case (Article 10). The authorities may also order the holders of the right to carry out cultivation and other activities, if this is regarded as necessary in order to protect or properly manage the fish stock and its habitat (Article 28).

644. Over the last few decades, *the salmon stocks have declined drastically* in many of the best salmon rivers. This is particularly serious since the salmon of each river seems to have distinctive genetic features, and valuable biodiversity may disappear. It is estimated that fifty such subspecies (river stocks) have already become extinct, and among the remaining 500, one-third is reported to be threatened. Norway has an international responsibility to protect the diversity of wild salmon species and manage this genetic resource in a sustainable way.

This development has many causes, not all of them are fully known. In many rivers, there are many types of activities and encroachments that overall may have a negative effect on the fish stock. In some rivers, the industry of salmon cultivation (fish farming) is regarded as a likely important cause. This causes the spreading of salmon louse[662] and diseases that have attacked the fish on a large scale. Other stocks have been seriously disturbed by the influx of escaped cultivated salmon species from the fish farming (*see infra*). This is now by many seen as the most serious threat to the stocks of wild salmon.

645. Protection of wild salmon has become an important task in Norway's environmental policy. As a consequence, thirty-seven vital salmon rivers have been designated as *National Salmon Rivers* by Stortinget, and twenty-two adjacent fjords have been designated as *National Salmon Fjords*. In these rivers and fjords, the stock of wild salmon are subject to special protection. The decision by the Stortinget lays down rules and guidelines for various types of activities that may affect the spawning and living conditions of the fish, such as taking of water, drainage, hydropower development, fish farming, polluting activities and constructions in the river. Most importantly, aquaculture (fish farming) activities in the fjord areas are generally prohibited. Existing fish farms were to move to other areas before 2011. A special regulation lists the rivers and fjords that are covered and lays down quite precise rules with regard to the prohibition of aquaculture activities (*see infra*).[663]

The legal basis for determining National Salmon Rivers and National Salmon Fjords is not entirely clear. Apart from the rules on aquaculture laid down in the regulation the full legal effects of the designation as National Salmon River or Fjord is not very clear either. A general rule is laid down in the Water Resources Act

662. Gyrodactylus salaris.
663. Regulation of 22 Jun. 2009 No. 961.

Article 35a. It states that in the National Salmon Rivers and Fjords the salmon stocks shall be particularly protected against harmful activities. A decision or a measure that may affect the living conditions of the salmon must be based on the protection needs behind the designation of the river or fjord as a National Salmon River or Salmon Fjord. Still, in reality, the strength of the protection is much up to the discretion of the respective authorities based on their legislation. For example, the status has not prevented new major mining activities to be established in a National Salmon Fjord with massive deposit of mining waste in the fjord.

§3. Aquaculture

646. With its deep fjords and countless sounds and islands, the Norwegian coastal waters provide excellent conditions for fish farming. Over the last decades, *aquaculture, or fish farming, has become a major industry* in the country. Its export value exceeds the value of the traditional fisheries, and is next only to the export value of petroleum. It has become a significant source of employment and income for people along the coast and for local communities. Until now, the most important species have been salmon and trout. Through further research and development, the method is extended to other species as well, including cod, halibut, shellfish and crawfish, although so far with mixed results.

647. Fish farming entails some *serious environmental threats* which makes it necessary to control it strictly. The fixed nets and other installations in the sea may be destroyed in bad weather, and large numbers of fish may escape. They mix with and may – apparently – genetically disturb the wild species. This is a very serious threat to the wild salmon stocks. Also, the fish farms may breed illnesses and parasites (salmon louse)[664] that represent serious hazards both to the aquaculture industry itself and for the vulnerable stocks of wild salmon. For many years, pollution was a problem, as was the extensive use of medicine, particularly antibiotics, which may accumulate in the environment. Through research and development, these problems have gradually been reduced but are still not eliminated.

648. The *Aquaculture Act of 17 June 2005 No. 79* is the main piece of legislation. Its goal is to 'develop a profitable and competitive aquaculture industry within the framework of a sustainable development, and contribute to value creation along the coast' (Article 1). The Act covers all production of animals and plants that live in water ('aquatic organisms'). By 'production' is meant 'any measure that influence living aquatic organisms' weight, size, numbers, characteristics, and quality' (Article 2).

The main principle is that aquaculture is prohibited without permission from the public authorities (Article 4). The Act is managed by the Ministry of Trade, Industry and Fisheries and the Fisheries Directorate. A permission is given for production of a certain species on a specific site and usually for a given time period (Article 5).

---

664. Lepeophtheirus salmonis.

The authorities may lay down conditions related to ownership or change in ownership. In the beginning, permissions were mainly given to individuals with small-scale farms. As the industry has developed, larger companies are now playing a dominant role as permission holders.

649. The Act lays down certain general conditions for a permission (Article 6). A permission may be given if:

- it is 'environmentally justifiable';
- it is not in conflict with the land-use plan for the area pursuant to the PBA, nature protection regulations pursuant to the NDA, or cultural heritage protected pursuant to the Cultural Heritage Act[665] and the respective authorities pursuant to these acts have not approved the activity;
- the various land-use interests have been properly considered.

In addition, an aquaculture farm must have the necessary permissions pursuant to the Act on Food Production and Food Safety,[666] the PCA,[667] the Act on Ports and Coastal Waters[668] and the Water Resources Act.[669] Altogether, the regulation system for aquaculture in Norway is quite complicated.

What is 'environmentally justifiable' is not meant to imply absolute limits and it is not precisely defined or explained in the Act. It is to be understood as a rather flexible concept which involves a broad assessment of possible negative environmental effects on the one hand and social and economic advantages on the other hand.

650. According to its wording, *environmental considerations* are to be given much weight in the implementation of the Act. It is explicitly stated that aquaculture activities must be established, run and eventually closed down taking environmental concerns duly into account and the authorities may issue regulations to this effect (Article 10). The authority may require an assessment and monitoring of the environmental status in the area of the aquaculture site (Article 11). In case of closing down, the owner must clean up the site and remove all organisms, installations and equipment (Article 13). The authorities may require financial security for the costs of clearing and cleaning the site. They may also lay down strict conditions with regard to aquaculture activities in order to protect sea areas which are vulnerable and particularly important for aquatic organisms (Article 14). A number of Norwegian fjords with important stocks of wild salmon have – as mentioned – been designated as 'salmon fjords'. Here aquaculture is generally prohibited pursuant to a special regulation.[670]

Nevertheless, it is clear that the Norwegian aquaculture industry represents a risk to the natural environment in several ways and in particular to the stocks of wild

665. Act of 9 Jun. 1978 No. 50.
666. Act of 19 Dec. 2003 No. 124.
667. Act of 13 Mar. 1981 No. 6.
668. Act of 17 Apr. 2009 No. 19.
669. Act of 24 Nov. 2000 No. 82.
670. Regulation of 22 Jun. 2009 No. 961.

salmon. At the end of the day one may question what weight environmental concerns are given. Economic interests clearly play a very important role in the development and running of this industry which has become a very important source of income for people and communities along Norway's rugged coast.

651. As mentioned, an aquaculture farm must be established *in accordance with the land-use plan* for the area adopted pursuant to the PBA, or with the consent of the relevant planning authority – usually the municipality. Most often, an aquaculture farm will have certain negative effects on the surroundings and entail certain restrictions for other activities in the fjord or on the shore. It is necessary to assess the different interests involved before making a final decision. The Act mentions in particular possible alternative uses of the area in question, including other types of aquaculture, and various conservation interests (Article 15). A municipal land-use plan pursuant to the PBA may designate certain areas for aquaculture, and may also lay down more specific regulations, for example, with regard to the type of aquaculture.[671] Often this question ought to be considered across municipal borders, and thus belongs to the planning at county level as well (*see* Part III, Chapter 1, §4 *infra*).

652. The *procedure* for establishing an aquaculture farm follows *several steps*. The first step is that the government decides the number of new permissions that may be allocated nationwide for a certain time period, and these are distributed to the interested counties. Each county then issues a call for applications, and the given number of permissions are allocated to the applicants who are regarded as the best qualified. Local conditions are also taken into account. Then the applicant must apply again, this time to establish the farm at a certain site. At this stage, the application is considered by the municipality concerned, in light of the existing land-use plan and other interests in the area. Subsequently, the application is considered by the various sector authorities which must approve the project pursuant to their proper legislation.

653. Since 2017 a special system has been developed with the aim of reducing and preventing negative environmental effects of aquaculture, in particular the problem of parasites (salmon louse) which causes illness and is particular harmful to the stocks of wild salmon. The system is called *'the traffic light system'*. The coast is divided into thirteen 'production areas'. Areas with a high level of parasites (more than 30% of the stock expected to die from the parasites) is defined as 'red'. Here, the industry may be ordered to reduce activity/the number of fish. Areas with a moderate level of parasites (10-30% deaths) are defined as 'yellow'. Here the activity may continue at the same level. Areas with less than 10% deaths are defined as 'green'. Here the activity/number of fish may increase.[672]

---

671. There is an explicit legal basis for this in the PBA Art. 11-11 (municipal master plan).
672. The details of this rather complicated (and controversial) system are laid down in Regulation of 16 Jan. 2017 No. 61.

Chapter 7. Minerals and Petroleum

§1. Introduction

654. Historically, Norway has had an important *mining industry*. Several of its towns and cities are based historically on mining activities, mainly of copper and iron, that started in the sixteenth and seventeenth centuries. However, most of this activity has now terminated. At present, the mining industry on the Norwegian mainland is limited to some rather small-scale mining for special types of industrial minerals and stones. Some of these have significant economic value. Ordinary stone quarries and gravel pits are found all over the country and may play an important role in the local economy. Coal mining was for many years carried out in several mines on Svalbard, but is now terminated. Altogether, there are at present some 800 companies in the mining industries and nearly 5,000 people work in the sector, most of them in the industries of crushed stone, gravel and sand. However, there is no doubt that there are important mineral resources in Norway, and a potential for a major expansion of this industry in the future, provided, of course, that the market price for the products will make it profitable.

However, it goes without saying that an expansion of the mining industry is not uncontroversial, in particular because of the environmental problems which it often entails. Two major new mining projects have created strong and wide protests due to their environmental effects, in particular from the deposit in the adjacent fjord of enormous amounts of mining waste which also contain hazardous substances. In the northernmost part of the country mining activities may also interfere with and harm the traditional reindeer herding and other activities of the Sami people.

In contrast to traditional mining, the *offshore petroleum industry* has since the beginning of the 1970s grown rapidly and has developed into the by far most important industry in Norway. This has become a major policy area, and also a very important and complex legal field in Norway.

Here, only the main lines in the relevant legislation will be presented, with emphasis on aspects which are particularly relevant in an environmental perspective.

§2. The Minerals Act

655. Mining is regulated by several pieces of legislation. The main Act is the Act of 19 June 2009 No. 101 relating to the *Acquisition and Extraction of Mineral Resources (the Minerals Act)*. This Act applies to activities with the objective of surveying mineral resources for the purposes of extraction and to any extraction of mineral deposits. The Act is supplemented by more detailed rules in a comprehensive regulation.[673] The responsible authorities are the Ministry of Trade, Industry and Fisheries, and the Directorate of Mining.

673. Regulation of 23 Dec. 2009 No. 1842. Together with the Act this Regulation implements the EU legislation in the field, namely Directive 2005/36/EC with later amendments and supplementary regulations, the most recent (by 2013) being Regulation (EC) 623/2012.

The purpose of the Act is 'to promote and ensure socially responsible administration and use of mineral resources in accordance with the principle of sustainable development' (Article 1).

According to Article 2, the Act shall ensure that the following interests are safeguarded:

- value creation and industrial and commercial development;
- the foundation of Sami culture, commercial activity and social life;
- the surroundings and nearby areas while operations are being carried out;
- the environmental consequences of extraction; and
- long-term planning relating to subsequent use or reclamation of the area.

As mentioned, some potential mineral resources are situated in areas where the Sami people have traditional rights to use land and resources. The Sami rights and interests must be taken particularly into account. It is stated explicitly in the Minerals Act (Article 6) that 'The Act shall be applied in accordance with the rules of international law relating to indigenous peoples and minorities', and there are several specific rules in the Act to this effect.

656. The Norwegian mining system is based on *a main distinction between minerals owned by the State and minerals owned by the owner of the land.* Minerals owned by the State are metals with specific weight greater than five, including iron, nickel, copper, tin, zinc, silver, gold, platinum and uranium, and in addition titanium, arsenic, and ore containing such metals, and pyrrhotite and pyrite (Article 7). Alluvial gold is exempt. Other minerals belong to the landowner. These are industry minerals, stone, crushed stone, gravel, sand, clay, bog and sea ore, and alluvial gold. Search, exploration or exploitation of these resources is primarily up to the landowner.

Furthermore, the system is based on a distinction between three stages of activities: *search* for mineral resources, *exploration* of a resource to assess its value and the possibility of exploitation, and finally the *extraction* of the minerals found.

657. As the main rule *anybody may freely search* for mineral deposits on another's private land (Article 8). A search shall not obstruct the exploration, extraction or operations of other parties pursuant to the Act. The searching party shall give notice to the landowner and the user of the land one week before a search is begun, at the latest (Article 10). The searching party may undertake such works on the surface of the land as are necessary to establish the existence of mineral deposits. Measures that may cause damage of significance may not be implemented without the consent of the landowner and the user of the land (Article 9).

658. Anyone wishing to *explore deposits of minerals owned by a private landowner* must enter into an agreement with the landowner. If no agreement is reached, an application may be made for compulsory acquisition (expropriation) (Article 11). In addition to an agreement with the landowner, pilot extraction requires a special permit from the Directorate of Mining. 'Pilot extraction' means extraction that is necessary to assess the commercial viability of a deposit. Except in special cases, a permit for pilot extraction may not be granted for the extraction of more than 2,000 m^3 of matter. The permit may be made subject to conditions (Article 12).

659. Anyone who wishes to *explore deposits of minerals owned by the State* shall apply to the Directorate of Mining for an exploration permit. In principle, all citizens have a right to explore mineral deposits owned by the State. An exploration permit may only be refused if the applicant has previously breached material provisions imposed by or pursuant to the Minerals Act.

The permit gives a priority right to undertake the exploration needed to assess whether there is a deposit of minerals of such an abundance, size and nature that the deposit may be assumed to be commercially viable, or to become commercially viable within a reasonable period of time. The exploration permit grants such access to the land (including temporary storage space) as is necessary to undertake the exploration. However, the exploration permit does not grant a right of way. Measures in the ground that may cause considerable damage may only be implemented with the consent of the landowner and the user of the land (Article 19). The claimant gets *a priority right* (licence) to exploit the mineral resource within seven years from the approval of his/her application (Article 22). If necessary, this period may be prolonged by three years (Article 23 first paragraph).

Pilot extraction (Article 20) requires a special permit from the Directorate of Mining. 'Pilot extraction' means extraction that is necessary to assess the commercial viability of the deposit. Here again, a permit for pilot extraction may not be granted for the extraction of more than 2,000 m^3 of matter, except in special cases. The permit may be made subject to conditions.

660. Any party wishing to *extract deposits of minerals owned by a private landowner* must enter into an agreement with the landowner (Article 28). If no agreement is reached, an application may be made for compulsory acquisition (expropriation). The Mining Act has special expropriation rules in its Chapter 7.[674]

For minerals owned by the State, the exploring party with best priority may apply to the Directorate of Mining for *an extraction permit.* An extraction permit shall be granted if the applicant substantiates that the exploration area contains a deposit of minerals owned by the State, that is of such an abundance, size and nature that the deposit may be assumed to be commercially viable, or to become commercially viable within a reasonable period of time. Only one extraction permit may be issued in a given area (Article 29).

The extraction of mineral deposits totalling more than 10,000 m^3 of matter, and any extraction of natural stone, requires in addition an *operating licence* from the Directorate of Mining (Article 43). An operating licence may only be granted to a party that holds an extraction permit. Licence is a discretionary decision. In the assessment of whether an operating licence should be granted, emphasis shall be given to whether the applicant is qualified to extract the deposit. The licence may be made subject to conditions. The area of operation shall be fixed in the licence. An application for an operating licence shall contain a plan of operations. A licence

674. These are supplemented by the general rules on expropriation in the Expropriation Act of 23 Oct. 1959 No. 3.

may be limited in time. It may in any event be reviewed every ten year. The Ministry may issue regulations concerning operation licences and exceptions from the requirement for an operating licence.

661. The Act lays down some *general principles* for the carrying out of mineral activities which also relate to environmental aspects. Operations on shall be carried out 'in accordance with good mining practice' (Article 41). They shall be performed with caution, so that the damage caused is not greater than necessary, and 'so that the operations do not result in unnecessary pollution or unnecessary damage to the environment' (Article 48).

The exploring party, the extracting party and the working party in respect of a mineral deposit shall ensure that the area *is properly cleaned up,* both while operations are in progress and after they have been completed. The Directorate of Mining may set a deadline for the completion of cleanup works (Article 50). The Directorate may also order a party that wishes to undertake, or has initiated, exploration (including sample extraction), or operations on mineral deposits to provide financial security for the implementation of safety measures pursuant to Article 49 and cleanup measures pursuant to Article 50 (Article 51). The Ministry may issue regulations concerning the requirement to provide security.

662. In addition to the extraction permit and operating licence, *several other permits are needed* to exploit mineral resources, pursuant to other Acts. This is stated explicitly in Article 5. Pursuant to *the PBA* a local development plan and a building permit are required. At the outset, a mining activity must be in accordance with the land-use plan for the area. If necessary, the plan must be changed in order to permit mining. In a local development plan conditions for the activity may be dictated, and an activity plan may be required. A mining activity of a certain size also requires an *EIA* pursuant to the general rules on this in the PBA with regulations.[675] A pollution permit pursuant to *the* PCA is also required. *The Cultural Heritage Act* may require special studies and excavations of the site before the activity can start.

§3. Act on Mineral Activities on the Continental Shelf

663. Norway has an extended continental shelf both in the North Sea, along the Norwegian coast, and in the Barents Sea. Until now, the dominant activity has been exploration and exploitation of oil and gas. With the increased knowledge of the many important minerals which may be found on the sea bottom of the continental shelf, the Norwegian government has for some time made preparations for mineral activities there. In 2019, a special Act was adopted to this effect: The Act on Mineral Activities on the Continental Shelf.[676] Work has started to prepare for this mining activity, but the issue is politically controversial in light of fishery interests and environmental considerations in general.

675. Regulation of 21 Jun. 2017 No. 854.
676. Act of 22 Mar. 2019 No. 7.

The Ministry of Oil and Energy is the responsible ministry for this Act, and the system of the Act is in many ways similar to that of the petroleum activity and wind energy at sea: The (possible) mineral resources on the continental shelf are owned by the Norwegian State. The State has – at the outset – exclusive right to exploit these resources (Act Article 1-4). At the same time, it is foreseen that the mining activity will be carried out by private actors as follows: The first step in the process will be a decision by the government to open a specific part of the continental shelf for mineral activity. This decision must be based on an impact assessment carried out by the government (Article 2-1 and 2-2). At present (2023), this work is underway by the government. The next step is to invite companies (legal persons) to apply for right to exploration of the possible resources within the opened area (Article 3-1). This does not, however, give the company in question an exclusive right to exploitation later (Article 3-2). The third step is to invite companies to apply for the right to exploit the identified mineral resource, on certain conditions. In this connection, the authority has to spell out the criteria for the choice between several interested parties and the conditions. The company (or companies) has to be established and registered in Norway on the basis of Norwegian law.

This will be an exclusive exploration and exploitation right. The right is given for ten years with possibility of extension (Article 4-5). The rightholder obtains property right to the minerals when taken up from the sea bottom (Article 4-10). When the activity is terminated, the rightholder must clean the area on the basis of a plan approved by the authority and carry out such activities as decided by the authority (Article 5-1 and 5-2).

§4. Exploitation of Petroleum Resources on the Continental Shelf

664. The exploitation of petroleum resources on the continental shelf has since its start in 1970 become Norway's most important industry. The legislation and legal issues related to this activity are themselves a very complex and dynamic legal field. It is not possible nor opportune to treat it in any detail within the frames of this monograph. In the following, only some basic information is provided with particular relevance in an environmental perspective.

665. These resources belong to the Norwegian State pursuant to Article 1-1 of the *Petroleum Act of 29 November 1996 No. 72*, and the activity is strictly regulated through a permit system laid down in this Act and numerous regulations.[677] According to the Act Article 1-2, the petroleum resources:

> shall be managed in a long time perspective to the benefit of the Norwegian society as a whole. It shall provide income for the country and contribute to secure welfare, employment and an improved environment, and strengthen

677. Chiefly, general Regulation of 27 Jun. 1997 No. 653 on the petroleum activity ('Petroleum regulation') with several subsequent amendments, the most recent by Regulation 15 Dec. 2020 No. 2914.

Norwegian trade and industry while at the same time take regional considerations and other activities into account.[678]

666. Only the Norwegian State may exploit the resources without the licences and approvals required by the Act (Article 1-3). The State may itself participate in the activity (Article 3-6). There are distinct rules on the various phases of the activity such as the opening of a new part of the continental shelf for petroleum activity (Article 3-1), exploitation (Chapter 2) and exploration (Chapters 3 and 4) phases, and on the termination of petroleum activity (Chapter 5). For all phases a public licence from the petroleum authorities is required, based on a plan.

667. The Act and the whole system for the petroleum activity is mainly the responsibility of the Ministry for Oil and Energy, and its subordinate bodies the Norwegian Petroleum Directorate and the Petroleum Safety Authority Norway. However, also other authorities are responsible and involved, such as the MCE and the NEA with regard to control of regular polluting discharge and emissions from the activities (*see supra* Part I, Chapter 1, §2, II).

668. The first phase is *the decision to open a new part of the continental shelf* for petroleum activity. The area is divided into 'blocks' of fifteen latitude minutes and twenty longitude minutes (Article 3-2). The decision to open is in itself an important and often very controversial political issue which is decided finally by Stortinget. On this question a clear divide appears between Norway's political parties. Over the last decade, due to strong opposition from the environmental side, some parts of the continental shelf have been excluded from exploration and exploitation, at least temporarily, namely in the sea areas off Lofoten, Vesteraalen and Senja in Northern Norway, and also areas far north in the Barents Sea, near the Svalbard islands due to the vulnerability of the Arctic nature.

An *EIA* is required before it is decided to open a part of the continental shelf for exploration (*see* details on EIA in relation to petroleum activities General Introduction, Chapter 2, §2 *supra)*. The decision is to be taken on the basis of an assessment of the economic and industrial possibilities on the one hand, and the likely environmental effects, including risk of pollution, on the other hand (Article 3-1).

669. When Stortinget has decided to open an area for petroleum activity, petroleum companies can apply for *exploration licence* (Article 2-1*)*. An exploration licence gives a company – or several companies together – the right to explore the possibility of petroleum resources within a clearly defined area of the continental shelf, through geological and geotechnical activities, etc., including drilling. An exploration licence is valid for three years. The licence does not give an exclusive right, and neither does it give a priority right to a subsequent exploitation licence. The Petroleum regulation, Chapter 2, lays down detailed rules on exploitation licence, what is required from the applicant, and the content of the licence.

678. Unofficial translation by the author.

670. At a suitable time thereafter the government invite through an announcement the companies to apply for *exploitation licence* (concession) in blocks in the opened area. The companies then have a deadline of minimum ninety days to apply for the right to exploit one or several blocks in the area, or parts of blocks. The licence can only be given to a company registered in Norway. It gives an exclusive right to exploration of, drilling for and extraction of petroleum in the block(s) in question (Article 3-3). There is often a competition between the companies for exploitation licences. The assignment of licences shall be based on fair an objective criteria, and on the requirements and conditions laid down in the announcement (Article 3-5). When a licence is given, the Ministry shall designate an operator of the licence. The licence is valid for ten years but may be prolonged to thirty years as the main rule and fifty years in special cases (Article 3-9). If the licensee does not find petroleum in the blocks, the blocks may be 'returned' to the authorities (Article 3-14).

The Act does not require a special EIA in connection with the application and approval of an exploitation licence.

671. The Act has *further rules on the exploitation activity* in Chapter 4. An important principle is that as much as possible of the petroleum in a field should be extracted and should be carried out in accordance with proper technical and economic principles (Article 4-1). Before the exploitation starts the licensee shall present for approval by the authorities a *PDO* of the oil/gas field (Article 4-2). This forms the basis and framework for the project and is hence an important document. It shall describe all the relevant aspects of the project: economic, technical, safety and environmental, and information about how the installations will be disposed of when the activity is terminated. The Ministry may, under special circumstances, require the rightholder to carry out a thorough assessment of environmental effects, including risk of pollution, and effects for other activities for a larger area.

In the Supreme Court 'Climate case' the issue was whether new exploitation licences in parts of the Barents Sea was violating the environmental Article in Gunnloven Article 112 (*see supra* General Information, Chapter 2, §1, II). The court stated that the EIA in connection with a future PDO should assess the climate effects of the future emissions both from the production and from the burning of the exploited (and mainly exported) petroleum.

Another important statement by the Supreme Court in the case was that an exploitation licence does not automatically give a right to exploit the oil or gas field(s) it covers. A final approval is needed: the approval of the PDO. This is in line with Article 4-2 paragraph 5 which states that the licensee may not, without the Ministry's consent, take on significant contractual obligations or start construction works until the PDO has been approved. This means, in practical terms, that the licensee must accept the conditions for the project laid down by the authorities and adjust the project accordingly. It is rather unrealistic to stop a project at this stage and it has apparently never happened. A company may be exempted from the PDO by ministerial decision.

Chapter 4 contains a number of rules for various situations which are not essential in an environmental perspective. Of great practical importance, however, is the question of delivery and connected transport of the exploited petroleum. This is decided by the authorities (Article 4-11). Most of the petroleum from the Norwegian continental shelf is exported to United Kingdom and continental Europe through pipelines. However, a significant part is also sent to industrial installations in Norway, such as the oil refinery at Mongstad in western Norway and the important facility for the treatment of natural gas to natural gas in liquid form (LNG) at Melkøya outside the town of Hammerfest far north.

672. Chapter 5 of the Petroleum Act deals with the termination of a project and *closing down of petroleum installations*. The responsible company shall present a plan for the termination to the authorities. This must be done at the earliest five years before expected closing date and at the latest two years before (Article 5-1). The plan must present proposals for possible further use or, more realistic, a proposal for final disposal of the installations including complete removal. The plan shall give the authorities the information and assessment necessary for the authority to take the decision on how to deal with the termination and how to dispose of the installation, pursuant to Article 5-3.

673. In addition to these central licences pursuant to the Petroleum Act and connected regulations, a petroleum project needs several other licences or permits. Pollution control is an important part of the picture. In spite of technological progress, regular and accidental marine pollution from the petroleum activity is a problem. 'Regular pollution' is governed by the PCA, and strict conditions are laid down in pollution permits pursuant to the Act. This Act is also the basis for rules and requirements concerning contingency for oil spills, pursuant to its Chapter 6 on accidental pollution.[679] All petroleum companies on the continental shelf cooperate on this through a joint organization. There are important regulations on safety measures to prevent such accidents pursuant to the Petroleum Act.[680]

The Act has special rules on *compensation for pollution damage* from petroleum (Chapter 7), and for damage suffered by Norwegian fishermen if they experience an economic loss due to the petroleum activity (Chapter 8). The rules lay down strict liability for the 'licensee', that is, the company or companies who hold the exploration or exploitation right in question. These rules will be dealt with in more detail *infra* in Part IV, Chapter 1, §4.

According to a special Act, the offshore petroleum activity must pay a special tax on its *CO_2 emissions*.[681] Since 2009, offshore petroleum activities are covered by the 2004 *Emission Trading Act* (*see* Part I, Chapter 2, §4) and hence included in the EU-ETS.

---

679. *See supra* Part I, Ch. 1, §2. Norway experienced a serious blowout on the Ekofisk field in 1977.
680. The main regulation in this field is the Regulation of 12 Feb. 2010 No. 158 on Health, environment, and safety in the petroleum activity and some onshore installations (the 'framework regulation') with later amendments. Important rules are also found in three other comprehensive regulations from 2010: Regulation of 29 Apr. 2010 on management and reporting in the petroleum industry (the 'management regulation'), Regulation of 29 Apr. 2010 No. 612 on technical and operational issues (the 'technical and operational regulation'), and Regulation of 29 Apr. 2010 No. 613 on the exercise of petroleum activities (the 'activity regulation').
681. Act of 21 Dec. 1990 No. 72.

674. It goes beyond the framework of this monograph to give a full picture of the complex regulation of offshore petroleum activities. However, it should be made clear that *the petroleum activity is a controversial issue in Norwegian politics* for several reasons. On the one hand, it provides valuable employment and a major income for the society. On the other hand, it has negative environmental effects through regular discharges into the sea and considerable carbon dioxide emissions. In spite of a generally high safety standard of the petroleum activities on the Norwegian continental shelf, there is always the risk of an accident resulting in a major oil spill with possible serious effects on fishing resources, bird life and the coastal environment.

Therefore, the petroleum activity is an area of both conflicts and compromises in the Norwegian society. In particular, the question of future petroleum activity along the northern part of the Norwegian Coast and in the Barents Sea is controversial. As mentioned, some important areas have been (temporarily) protected from petroleum activity, but other environmentally vulnerable areas have been opened for quite substantial activity, and further expansions are under preparation.

In order to identify the various interests and manage these areas sustainably, the government has developed and presented to Stortinget comprehensive and subsequent *integrated management plans* for the exploitation and protection of marine areas outside Norway: the Barents Sea and the sea off the Lofoten islands, the Norwegian Sea and the Norwegian part of the North Sea and Skagerak.[682]

These plans seek to strike a balance between the various interests. They identify, on the one hand, areas that may be opened for petroleum exploration and subsequent exploitation, and, on the other hand, areas which shall be protected from such activity for environmental and/or fishery consideration. These plans have served to create considerable cross-political consensus in this sensitive field of Norwegian politics. However, they do not solve all issues, and controversies regularly raise over issues related to the further development of the petroleum industry.

During the last years, the debate has been increasingly heated in light of the general global need of reducing emissions of CO_2. *CO_2-emissions from the petroleum industry* are the major source of GHG emissions in Norway. The emissions from burning of the oil and gas produced in Norway are many times higher. On this basis, there is a considerable support in Norway for a gradual reduction of the petroleum activity; some political parties even propose an immediate end to further exploration of new gas and oil fields. This debate is reflected in the mentioned court case between environmental organizations and the Norwegian State on the opening of new areas in the Barents Sea for petroleum. The organizations maintained that this was violating the environmental Article 112 in Grunnloven, but lost in all courts.[683] One of the arguments used by the Supreme Court against the organizations' view was the fact that the activity – as mentioned – has been subject to a particular CO_2

682. Originally, there were individual plans for each of these three areas. Now one common document has been developed which was presented to Stortinget in 2020, *see* the white paper Meld. St. 20 (2019–2020) on comprehensive management plans for the Norwegian sea areas.

683. The Supreme Court decision is Case 2020-2472-P dated 22 Dec. 2020. *See* the more detailed presentation of the case *supra* in General Information, Ch. 2, § 1, II.

tax since 1991 and is included in the EU-ETS. Hence, it was the view of the court that the State had taken adequate measures to combat the climate effects of the petroleum sector, and consequently Grunnloven Article 112 was not violated.

Chapter 8. Watercourses

§1. Introduction and Overview

675. Rivers, lakes and waterfalls form an essential and striking part of the Norwegian landscape and scenery. Due to the humid climate and the generally hard bedrock, *water is abundant.* It is often the rivers and waterfalls that form the beauty and characteristics for which Norwegian valleys and fjord areas are renowned. They are essential as habitats for fish, animals and plants.

Rivers and lakes have always played an important role in the daily life of Norwegians for transport, fishing, rafting of timber, and general recreation. Most of the drinking water is provided by surface water sources. Rivers and lakes have also served as recipients for sewage, and for polluting discharge from industry and agriculture.

676. Not least, the rivers have for more than a century been the most important source of energy in Norway. *Hydroelectric power* has been fundamental to the country's development of its heavy industry and economic and social development in general. The Norwegian aluminium, ferroalloy, and fertilizer industries – just to mention the most significant – are among the most important in the world, based entirely on hydroelectric power. The consumption of electricity per capita is the highest in the world, and virtually all electricity in Norway comes from hydropower.

With all the various interests connected to rivers and lakes, it is evident that the development of watercourses for power production has been a controversial issue for a long time, and in particular since the mid-1960s. The hydropower development issue played an important role in the growing environmental consciousness and environmental movement of the time. Two of the most important cases of civil disobedience in Norway were over hydropower projects.[684]

The two main Acts related to watercourses are the Watercourse Regulation Act of 14 December 1917 No. 16 and the Act on Watercourses and Ground Water (Water Resources Act) of 2 November 2000 No. 82. In addition, the Pollution Control and Waste Act (PCA) of 13 March 1981 No. 6 is the central Act for controlling water pollution. The PBA of 27 June 2008 No. 71 is also an important legal tool for the management of water resources.

677. In Norwegian law, *rivers and lakes are mostly private property.* 'A watercourse belongs to the owner of the land it covers.'[685] This rule has a long legal tradition. If the two sides of a river or lake have different owners, the borderline usually follows the deepest part of the river or lake, unless there is a legal basis for another solution. Some of the biggest lakes have a so-called free middle area. This is not private property, but usually regarded as State property. The Water Resources

684. The development of the Mardøla river in western Norway with Europe's highest waterfall Mardalsfossen in 1970, and the development of the Alta river in Finnmark in the northernmost part of the country – with important Sami interests involved – in 1980.
685. Water Resources Act of 2 Nov. 2000 No. 82 Art. 13 para. 1.

Act states that these areas are 'at the disposal of the State', but people may use it in accordance with the customary or written law.

At the outset, the owner of the watercourse has the exclusive right to use the water flowing on his/her part,[686] including fishing. However, any member of the public has the right to take small amounts of water from a lake or river, and to bathe and move by boat without motor according to the rules of the Outdoor Recreation Act.[687] For motorized boat traffic, there are special rules in the Act on Motorized Traffic on Uncultivated Land and in Watercourses.[688]

678. The Water Resources Act states that *groundwater* belongs to the owner of the land under which the water is found. A groundwater source that extends under several properties is co-owned by the owners of the land, in proportion to the surface area of the properties (Article 44).[689]

679. Rules and regulations concerning the use of water resources date back to medieval times. In 1887, the first comprehensive Watercourse Act was adopted, later followed by the Watercourse Act of 1940. In 1917, the special Act on hydroelectric development, the Watercourse Regulation Act, was adopted[690] and is still in force. In 2000, the new *Water Resources Act* replaced the Watercourse Act of 1940. The Watercourse Regulation Act and the Water Resources Act shall be thoroughly presented in this chapter.

However, several other Acts are of importance for the protection and management of watercourses and water resources. In this field, certain problems of coordination between the various Acts and authorities are inevitable.

680. The *PBA* provides a general system of spatial and land-use planning. This system in general shall be further discussed in Part III below. The Act applies fully to watercourses and lakes. The planning pursuant to the Act shall cover the protection, use and management of watercourses. The quality and quantity of the water depend on the activities along the watercourse or lake. Hence, it is essential to integrate land-use and water resource planning properly. The planning system of the PBA makes this possible.

Regional plans may define general objectives of water management and guidelines for the application of sectoral legislation and local planning. Municipal master plans and local development plans may provide more detailed regulations of activities and constructions along rivers and lakes, including necessary restriction to protect important sources of water supply. They may also designate parts of rivers and lakes for special purposes, including recreation and nature protection. The land-use as defined by these types of plans, including the use of watercourses and the riverbed, is

686. It is somewhat disputed whether this right is based on ownership of the water, or just an exclusive right to use it. But this question is of academic interest only.
687. Act of 28 Jun. 1957 No. 16.
688. Act of 10 Jun. 1977 No. 82.
689. Before the Watercourse Act, the question of ownership of groundwater was somewhat uncertain. The main view was that the landowner had the right to exploit the groundwater on his land to a reasonable extent, but without a formal ownership.
690. Act of 14 Dec. 1917 No. 16.

legally binding for landowners. However, there are certain limitations as to the restrictions that may be laid down through plans pursuant to the PBA, and their effect in relation to other legislations. We shall return to some of these issues in Part III.

The PBA also plays a role in Norway's implementation of the *EU WFD*. This issue is treated *supra* in Part I, Chapter 3, §2, V and *see also infra* Part III, Chapter 1, §4.

681. Besides the general instruments of protection of water resources in the PBA, the Water Resources Act, and the PCA,[691] the *protection of drinking water sources* is based on relevant legislation for the protection of health, notably the Food Act,[692] the Public Health Act,[693] and the Act on Health and Social Service Preparedness.[694] The general Regulation on Water Supply and Drinking Water[695] has been issued pursuant to these Acts. The purpose of the regulation is to protect people's health by ensuring sufficient safe drinking water without distinctive smell, taste or colour. The regulation prohibits any pollution of drinking water, from all possible activities including recreational activities. In this sense, it supplements the general prohibition of water pollution pursuant to the PCA which explicitly exempts certain 'ordinary' activities from the general prohibition. It lays down water quality standards for drinking water, as detailed in an annex to the regulation. These are in accordance with the EU rules.[696] Waterworks must be formally registered by the Food Directorate. The owner of the waterworks in question – most often the municipality – is responsible for ensuring this quality and shall identify any risk that has to be prevented or reduced to an acceptable level to ensure the distribution and delivery of sufficient and safe drinking water.

682. Furthermore, the owner of the waterworks must ensure that the works have access to the necessary competence and must carry out a regular internal control of the activity and status of the works and the distribution system to ensure necessary protection and compliance with the regulation. If the quality standards are exceeded as detailed in Annex 2, the owner must take necessary steps to improve the situation. Only chemicals approved by the food authorities may be used to treat the water. The regulation lays down further rules and requirements regarding testing of water quality, reporting, emergencies, etc.

The municipality shall have knowledge of the drinking water situation in the municipality, in accordance with its general obligations pursuant to the Public Health Act and shall take the need for drinking water supply into consideration in its spatial planning pursuant to the PBA. In Norway, most waterworks are owned by the municipality or by several municipalities together (inter-communal waterworks).

691. *See supra* Part I, Ch. 3, §2.
692. Act of 19 Dec. 2003 No. 124.
693. Act of 24 Jun. 2011 No. 29.
694. Act of 23 Jun. 2000 No. 56. This Act clarifies the responsibilities and establishes systems of contingency planning in order to ensure health and social services in case of war or other types of disasters.
695. Regulation of 22 Dec. 2016 No. 1868. The Regulation implements Directive 98/83/EC as amended by Directive (EU) 2015/1787.
696. Directive 98/83/EC as amended by Directive (EU) 2015/1787.

§2. Hydropower Development: Regulation and Protection

683. Hydropower development is regulated by the Act on Concession for Right to Waterfalls, the Watercourse Regulation Act[697] and the Water Resources Act.[698] In addition, it is generally maintained that the planning system of the PBA also applies, although this is somewhat disputed. Nevertheless, the general rules on EIA in the PBA apply to hydropower developments that meet the criteria in the EIA Regulation.[699]

In this section, we shall concentrate on the Watercourse Regulation Act which at present is the most important in this field. For a century, this Act has been very important. The construction of hydropower plants has been decisive for the development of Norway's industry and for its economy in general, in many ways a prerequisite for the welfare State as we know it. A number of important rivers and lakes have been developed for hydropower production. However, today, the general view is that 'the era of big hydropower projects is over'.[700] Most of the important hydropower resources have now been developed, and the political interest has turned towards the protection of valuable rivers. In the future, modifications and modernizations of existing plants and development of small-scale hydropower plants will be the order of the day, and not major new projects.

684. The Act on Concession for Right to Waterfalls provides in several respects the legal basis for hydropower development in Norway. The purpose of the Act is to ensure that the important energy resource inherent in the country's watercourses shall be managed to the benefit of the society at large through public ownership by the Norwegian State and municipalities (Article 1).[701] The Act requires that a State concession is required for the acquiring of waterfalls of a certain size. For the biggest waterfalls, the case must be presented to Stortinget (Article 2). The main rule is that only public bodies may own waterfalls. A company may own a waterfall, but in that case, the State or a municipality must own a minimum of 2/3 of the capital of the company and the corresponding votes at the general assembly of the company.

The concession is given for an unlimited time (Article 8) and with a number of conditions which are partly general and mentioned in the Act, and partly laid down in each concession. A general condition is that 10% of the power shall be given for use by the municipality. The conditions may be revised after thirty years. In that case, the owner of the concession may renounce the concession (Article 9).

An important element in Norway's management system for waterfalls is the *right of restitution*: By the end of the concession period, the waterfall and *all assets of the project, including dams, power stations, etc., become State property*. This system was introduced as early as 1909 and has been controversial. In 2007, it was challenged by the ESA for violation of EEA Treaty, *inter alia*, because the rules

697. Act of 14 Dec. 1917 No. 16 and Act of 14 Dec. 1917 No. 17, respectively. These Acts were in 2017 subject to a major overhaul and comprehensive editorial and some substantive changes through the Act of 21 Jun. 2017 No. 101.
698. Act of 24 Nov. 2000 No. 82.
699. *See* General Introduction, Ch. 2, §4.
700. Words used by the then Prime Minister Mr Jens Stoltenberg during his New Year speech 2001.
701. At the outset, the essential objective of the Act was to prevent foreign ownership of these resources. Later concession was required for Norwegian actors as well.

treated private and publicly owned waterfalls differently. The EFTA Court found that the system violated EEA Treaty Articles 31 and 40.[702] As a consequence of the case, the Act was changed.[703] Private ownership was abandoned and public ownership is now dominant.

685. The Watercourse Regulation Act applies to projects and installations with the purpose of regulating the watercourse of a river, notably projects for hydroelectric power production. As is well known, such projects usually include the building of dams in rivers and/or lakes. The water level will rise considerably upstream of the dam, and even create artificial lakes of considerable size. Downstream of the dam, the water flow may be drastically reduced.

686. At the outset, the owner of the watercourse has the right to exploit it for hydroelectric development. However, the basic principle in the Act is that a regulation of a watercourse for industrial purposes of a certain size can only be carried out by the State or on the basis of a *State licence ('concession')* issued by the government pursuant to the Act (Article 3).[704] The case must be presented to Stortinget if the project is to produce more than 20,000 h.p., or if there are considerable conflicts of interest in relation to the project (Article 3, third paragraph). After a decision by Stortinget, the formal licence is subsequently issued by the government. In practical terms, all important hydroelectric power plants are decided by the Stortinget.

687. Article 5 states that, as a rule, a concession for a watercourse regulation shall only be granted 'if the benefits of the project outweigh the damage and nuisance it entails for public and private interests'. Also, other positive and negative effects of the project of importance for the society shall be taken into consideration. Since environmental and social and economic values are difficult to compare, decisions are in reality taken on the basis of a broad assessment of advantages and disadvantages, and are thus quite political by nature. Politically, many of these cases have been very controversial.

688. The Act lays down numerous rules concerning the possible content of a hydropower concession, and the procedure to follow.

When a concession is issued, the work must start within five years from the issuing of the concession and must be fulfilled within five years after that, but this limit may be prolonged (Article 15). A concession may be unlimited in time, or be given with a time limit (Article 6). The concession lays down a number of conditions, such as detailed regulation of maximum water height and minimum flow of water below the dam (Article 16), and in general measures to be taken to minimize the damaging effects on public and private interests, and in particular on nature, such as restoration of fishing resources, protection of cultural heritage, measures to prevent pollution and so on (Article 20).

702. Case E-2/06.
703. *See* Ot. Prp. Nr. 61 (2007–2008).
704. For some smaller projects, a licence pursuant to the Water Resources Act is required instead.

As a rule, the licensee must pay an annual tax to the State, the county and the municipality in which the project is located (Article 14). For many small mountain municipalities, the income from this tax may be considerable.

689. The conditions laid down in a concession may in general be *revised by the authorities* after thirty years. If the owner of the concession does not accept the new conditions he may renounce the concession within three months. Earlier concession given without time limit may be revised after fifty years, and regardless of earlier limitations, all concessions may be revised after 19 June 2022 (Article 8). Furthermore, the conditions may be amended on the basis of an application from the concession owner (Article 9). The owner is not free to close down the activity; a closing down requires permission from the authorities (Article 10). In addition comes the mentioned system of *restitution of the rights* and assets to the State at the end of the concession period, *see supra.*

690. The procedure shall ensure participation by all interested parties and authorities. The general rules on EIA pursuant to the PBA apply to hydropower plants generating more than 40 GWh per year, and smaller if it may have an environmental impact as mentioned in the EIA Regulation Article 10.[705]

691. According to Article 22 of the Water Resources Act, the authorities[706] may postpone further procedure, or refuse an application, in anticipation of a comprehensive plan for hydropower development within a larger area. This refers to an important system of *comprehensive planning of hydropower development* which played an important role in this sector over several decades.

For a long time, hydropower development was very much in the hands of the power companies, including the State itself as an important power producer. They bought the right to exploit rivers and waterfalls for hydropower development from the owners of land, rivers and lakes. There was no comprehensive national plan for these developments. Stortinget considered the matters case-by-case, on the basis of applications from the power producers and the recommendations of the government. The result was that some of the most valuable rivers from an environmental point of view were developed before less valuable rivers.

692. In the early 1970s it was found necessary to develop a more comprehensive approach to the issue of hydropower development in the country, in order to protect the most valuable rivers. As a result Stortinget adopted four consecutive plans for rivers that should be exempted from hydropower development, and thus protected. These plans were in part based on several subsequent priority plans for hydropower development projects, prepared by the government and adopted by Stortinget.[707] Through this, each river in Norway was classified, on the one hand, according to the technical and economic potential for hydropower, and, on the other

705. *See supra* General Introduction Ch. 2, § 4.
706. The Ministry of Oil and Energy and the Norwegian Water Resources and Energy Directorate.
707. White papers (St. meld.) No. 63 (1984–1985), No. 53 (1986–1987) and No. 60 (1991–1992) on a comprehensive watercourse plan.

hand, the environmental and other interests going against development. On the basis of this, Stortinget has on the one hand designated a number of rivers that are to be protected, and on the other hand listed other rivers that may be developed on the basis of the licensing procedure pursuant to the Watercourse Regulation Act.

693. However, this system was terminated in 2016, as Stortinget found that it no longer served a useful purpose. Each application for new hydropower development will be treated individually on its merits independent of its earlier classification. The knowledge about the environmental conditions in the rivers has been considerably improved over these years, and the planning that has been carried out will continue to be useful as an information source when considering the various cases.

694. Since the early 1970s, and partly through this process of comprehensive planning, close to 400 rivers and watercourses have been designated *'protected watercourses'* by Stortinget. Initially, the designation by Stortinget of protected watercourses was of a strictly political nature. The rivers were not protected in any legal sense. The 'protection' only meant that they could not be developed for hydropower. It did not restrict other activities that could damage the value of the watercourse and the surrounding nature, such as road building, industry or tourist activities, recreational housing and so on. As a consequence, the values of a watercourse and its surrounding nature could be considerably reduced in spite of its status as 'protected watercourse'.

In order to restrict such activities, *'National planning guidelines for protected watercourses'* were adopted in 1994 pursuant to the PBA.[708] These are guidelines for the land-use planning of importance for the watercourses, at municipal and county level. They describe the adequate restrictions and measures to apply in order to protect the values of rivers, according to their situation and conditions.

A further step was taken in the 2000 Water Resources Act. Special rules on 'Protected watercourses' give legal status to the protection, and a basis for the various authorities to control strictly all activities in the protected watercourses that may harm their natural value (*see infra* §3, IV).

§3. The Water Resources Act

I. Objective and Field of Application

695. The general objective of the comprehensive *Act of 24 November 2000 No. 82 on Watercourses and Groundwater (Water Resources Act)* is to ensure that the country's watercourses and groundwater are socially properly used and managed (Article 1).

The Act has quite a broad field of application. It applies to all surface water sources with a flow of water which is regular every year. According to the definition provided by the Act (Article 3c) this means watercourses and lakes that do not

708. Guidelines adopted as Decree by the King in Council 10 Nov. 1994, pursuant to the earlier (1985) PBA Art. 17-1 para. 1.

dry up more often than every ten years on average. This means that it covers virtually all creeks, rivers and lakes in Norway. It also covers the bottom and the riverbank up to the highest flood level. The highest flood level is defined (Article 3d) as the highest flood level which is normally experienced during a ten-year period. Where a river runs into the sea, the Act applies to the watercourse to the extent it is at a higher level than the sea at low tide, and as far out as 'the bottom of the sea is influenced by the inflow of freshwater'.[709]

II. General Principles

696. As already mentioned, the Act states that *the owner of the land adjacent to a lake or river, also owns the river or lake,* wholly or in part, depending on the circumstances. He/she may freely exploit his/her part of the watercourse, within the limits defined by Acts and regulations (Article 13). The Water Resources Act itself lays down several important limitations, while others follow from other Acts such as the PBA, the PCA, health legislation and so on.

Notwithstanding the owner's exclusive rights, *the public* has certain common rights in a watercourse. Any member of the public may take small amounts of water from a lake or river. Every citizen may also bathe, and move by boat without motor according to the rules of the Outdoor Recreation Act (Article 16).[710] Such use must be careful, and not inconvenience the owner.

697. The Water Resources Act lays down a general duty to *act with due care* to avoid damage and nuisance to public and private interests related to the watercourse (Article 5 paragraph 1). Activities in a watercourse shall be planned and carried out in such a way as to minimize possible damage and nuisance to public and private interests, to the extent that this is possible without disproportionate costs or inconvenience (Article 5 paragraph 2). It is prohibited to prevent the natural flow of water without a permit (Article 7 paragraph 1). Water must not be taken from a river or brook to such an extent that the water flow becomes lower than its regular (natural) lowest level (Article 10).

The Act states explicitly that a *natural vegetation zone* must be maintained along the riverbanks, to prevent erosion and destruction of plant and animal habitats (Article 11). The extension of such a zone may be defined by the municipality, for example, in land-use plans pursuant to the PBA.

698. A special chapter deals with *groundwater.* The groundwater belongs to the owner of the land which is situated over the groundwater source. If the groundwater source lies under several properties, it is owned in common by the owners of these properties, proportionately to the size of these properties on the surface (Article 44). Everybody shall act carefully in order to avoid that the public or private interests in the groundwater are subject to damage or inconvenience. Groundwater measures or

709. This criterion is obviously difficult to apply (Art. 2 para. 2b). The Act (Art. 2 para. 3b) authorizes the government to draw the borderlines.
710. Act of 28 Jun. 1957 No. 16.

projects must be planned and carried out in such a way that private and public interested are negatively affected as little as possible, as far as reasonable. They must fulfil all reasonable requirements to avoid danger to people, property or the environment (Article 43a).

The owner may freely take groundwater for domestic purposes including for domestic animals. More important groundwater projects which may entail considerable damage or nuisance to public interests require a public permit (concession) (Article 45), in line with what applies to projects with surface water and watercourses (*see infra*).

Anyone who drills for groundwater shall act carefully in order to avoid damage and inconvenience. He/she shall inform the watercourse authority of the drilling as soon as possible, and within three months at the latest. In case of drilling with the purpose of examining the groundwater, the results shall be reported to the authorities (Article 46).

699. The authorities may lay down *quality objectives* for watercourses, relating to the quantity of the water flow, the (maximum) content of certain substances,[711] species of flora and fauna that should be protected in the river, and so on (Article 9). Such quality objectives shall be legally binding when exercising public authority, such as in individual concession cases. This overlaps to some extent with the possibilities of establishing environmental quality objectives on the basis of Article 9 of the PCA and Article 13 of the NDA.

700. The general rules of the *Neighbour Act* apply to relations between neighbours along a watercourse (Article 6 paragraph 1). Thus the general 'tolerance limit' in neighbour law applies. A landowner who also owns part of a river or lake, may not inflict 'unreasonable damage or nuisance'[712] on a neighbour by actions in the river or lake. A landowner may be liable for damage or nuisance on the basis of the Neighbour Act, even if his/her activity is permitted according to the Water Resources Act (Article 6 paragraph 4). However, a decision pursuant to the Neighbour Act regulating the activity on a property out of neighbour considerations may not be made for an activity that has obtained a licence or concessions pursuant to the Water Resources Act. In this sense, the concession system has priority.

III. The Licensing System

701. A licence ('concession') is required for *watercourse activities and installations that may entail considerable damage or nuisance to public interests* in the watercourse or in the sea (Article 8). The authorities may define the types of activities that require a licence (Article 18). Pursuant to an amendment in 2017, the same criterion now applies to the licence requirement for activities that may affect

711. Quality norms for polluting substances, however, are laid down pursuant to the Pollution Control Act.
712. This concept is further discussed in Part IV.

groundwater (Article 45). Projects of watercourse regulation are, as a rule, covered by the licence system of the 1917 Watercourse Regulation Act, but smaller projects fall under the Water Resources Act (Article 19).

Certain types of activities are, however, permitted by the Act itself: The owner may restore a former riverbed (Article 12) and take surface water and groundwater for domestic purposes, including for domestic animals (Articles 15 and 44).

If an activity needs a permit pursuant to other Acts, such as a pollution permit pursuant to the PCA or a local development plan pursuant to the PBA, the watercourse authority may exempt it from the licensing rules of the Water Resources Act. A coordinated procedure may also be prescribed (Article 20).

702. A licence may only be issued 'if the advantages of the activity or installation exceed the disadvantages for public and private interests in the watercourse', in a long-term perspective (Article 25). To this effect, necessary conditions may be set out in the licence, such as conditions with the purpose of protecting the river as a natural biotope (Article 26 paragraph 1). The activity or installation must not in any case reduce the flow of water below its regular (natural) lowest level (Article 10 and Article 26 paragraph 2).

The licence may be limited in time, and subject to revision after a certain time (Article 26 paragraph 4). Regardless of special review provisions in the licence, a licence may be modified by the authorities at a later stage, if so needed in special cases due to public or private interests (Article 28).

703. Comprehensive plans for the use and protection of a watercourse may be developed. Article 22 of the Water Resources Act explicitly states that such plans should preferably be developed pursuant to the planning system of the PBA (Article 22 paragraph 3). An important element in this work is now the implementation of the EU Water Framework Directive (WFD).[713]

An application for a licence may be postponed or refused if central authorities have started a planning procedure, and the activity may influence the planning (Article 22 paragraph 2). When adopted, such a plan is the basis for licence decisions. An application for an activity or installation may be refused without further reasons, if it is contrary to the plan (Article 22 paragraph 1). This refers mainly to the system of comprehensive watercourse plans described under §2 *supra,* which was abolished in 2016.

704. The licensing procedure corresponds to that of other similar licences, such as the procedure for a pollution permit according to the PCA. The application must give all necessary information. It is made public, and all interested parties and authorities are free to present their views. The general rules on EIA in the PBA apply.

---

713. Directive 2000/60/EC establishing a framework for community action in the field of water policy, *see supra* Part I Ch. 3, §2 V.

IV. Protected Watercourses

705. Chapter 5 of the Act deals with so-called protected watercourses. They are protected from future hydropower development pursuant to a decision by Stortinget. In principle, no hydropower development may take place in a protected watercourse.

In order to preserve the natural values of these watercourses, the Act lays down a number of rules and restrictions as regards activities in or along the watercourse. Article 33 states that other restrictions on activities or measures may be laid down pursuant to other Acts, such as the NDA, or in legally binding land-use plans pursuant to the PBA.

706. The following restrictions apply to activities in or along protected watercourses, pursuant to Article 35 of the Act:

- Existing installations may not be used for new activities without a licence. Even changes of activities within the framework of a licence may require a new licence if they influence the natural values of the watercourse. Extension of existing installations is only allowed if the environment is not impaired.
- A licence is required for the restoration of a former riverbed.
- The authorities may demand that all new activities or installations shall be notified to the authorities.
- The authorities may limit the amount of water which may freely be taken out for domestic purposes.
- The watercourse authorities may decide that the natural vegetation along the riverbanks shall be replanted. If this results in a pecuniary loss for the landowner (e.g., if the riverbank is cultivated), he/she shall be compensated.

707. In a protected watercourse, an application for a licence may be refused without further procedure. However, it may also be permitted. When considering the issue, the protection of the natural values of the river shall be predominant. If a licence is issued, it must describe how these values are affected, and why the licence nevertheless has been issued.

More detailed guidelines for the planning of land-use and so on in relation to protected watercourses have been given as State planning guidelines pursuant to the PBA.[714]

V. Monitoring and Enforcement

708. The Water Resources Act contains several rules with the purpose of ensuring its proper *implementation and enforcement.* The watercourse authorities are responsible for the general monitoring of the condition of rivers and lakes and how they develop, and of watercourse activities (Article 53). The authorities may inspect

714. Regulation of 10 Nov. 1994 No. 1001.

watercourse installations, and demand all relevant information from the party responsible (Article 55). They may instal necessary monitoring devices and other instruments (Article 56). They may carry out studies and investigations, and order the party responsible to do it, or to bear the costs (Article 57).

The party responsible must ensure that the internal control systems are in order so as to comply with the relevant rules and regulations (Article 54).

709. In case of *violations* of a rule, regulation or licence, any person with 'legal interest', including environmental organizations, may demand that the situation be corrected. If such a situation is brought to the knowledge of the watercourse authority, it may order the party responsible to take necessary measures to remedy the matter, and if need be to order the party to stop the activity. The same applies in any situation that may involve damage or nuisance to people, property or the environment (Article 59).

To ensure the implementation of such an order, a coercive fine may apply from a given date (Article 60). The authority may also carry out or organize the necessary measures itself, at the cost of the party responsible (Article 61).

Violations of the Act or regulations and decisions pursuant to the Act, intentional or by negligence, are punishable with fines or up to three months of imprisonment. In case of threat of significant harm to people, environment or property, or if there are aggravating circumstances, a two-year term of imprisonment may be imposed. The same applies if harm has been done to people or natural assets in a protected watercourse (Article 63). A fine laid down by an administrative decision by the water authority ('overtredelsesgebyr') may also be applied (Article 60a).

Chapter 9. Other Issues

§1. Regulation of GMOs

I. Introduction

710. The production and use of GMOs are governed by the Act of 2 April 1993 No. 38 Relating to the Production and Use of GMOs, etc. (Gene Technology Act). The Act generally corresponds to the relevant EU directives which apply to Norway,[715] with some departures. With certain special exceptions,[716] it applies to all types of GMOs, and to substances and products that contain GMOs (Article 2). GMOs are defined as 'micro-organisms, plants and animals, whose genetic composition has been modified by the use of gene or cell technology' (Article 4b). By an amendment to the Act in 2004, a special chapter with strict rules on cloning was included. However, cloning is not primarily an environmental issue and will not be treated further.

The purpose of the Act (Article 1) is:

> to ensure that production and use of GMOs and production of cloned animals is acceptable when taking ethical and social considerations into account, in accordance with the principle of sustainable development, and without adverse effects on health and the environment.

711. The Act makes a fundamental distinction between *contained use of GMO* (Chapter 2) and deliberate *release of GMO into the environment* (Chapter 3).

The Ministry of Health and Care Services and the MCE are the responsible State ministries respectively for these two parts of the Act. A national Commission on Biotechnology serves as an advisory body to the government and informs the public in this field. The Commission's statements are public.

II. Contained Use

712. *Contained use* is defined as:

> any operation where GMO are produced, cultivated stored, destroyed or used in another way, in a closed system, with physical barriers, possibly combined with other measures, in order to limit contact with people and the environment, and in order to ensure a high level of protection (Article 5).

715. Directive 90/220/EEC as amended by Directive 2001/18/EC as amended by Directive (EU) 2018/350, Directive 2004/35/EC and Directive 2009/41.
716. Mainly genetically modified cells of plants and animals if the result could have been reached through traditional methods (Art. 2 para. 2).

Contained use is mainly for research purposes, notably for medical and veterinary research.[717] It may take place in approved laboratories or installations only, subject to necessary safety measures to prevent harm to health and the environment (Article 6). There are special regulations for contained use of genetically modified animals,[718] and animals in combination with microorganisms,[719] and for contained use of genetically modified plants.[720] A special regulation deals with the contained use of GMO for certain educational purposes.[721]

Contained use shall be reported to, or approved by, State authorities. An approval in advance is always necessary for certain types of use involving modification of vertebrates or the transfer of genetic material from humans to animal, plants or microorganisms. The State authority may demand an assessment to be carried out on the possible impact of an accidental release of the GMO into the environment (Article 8).

III. Deliberate Release

713. For *deliberate release,* a formal approval by the relevant State authority is always necessary. Here, we are faced with important environmental concerns. The rules of the Act are meant to prevent any risk of harm to health and the environment from deliberate release. Here, the environmental authorities are the ones responsible.[722]

714. 'Deliberate release' is defined at Article 8 of the Act. Generally speaking, it includes all types of production and use of GMOs which cannot be regarded as contained use. The main point is that the GMO in one form or another gets in direct contact with humans or the natural environment. It is thus *a broad concept.* It covers, for example, release for research purposes (field experiments), for industrial purposes and for the purpose of cleaning up (such as an oil spill), and GMOs in greenhouses, aquaculture farms, stables and so on which have not been approved for contained use. It also covers routine discharges of GMOs from contained use, deposit of waste containing living GMOs, sale of products that contains GMOs, and import and transport of GMOs.

715. Deliberate release, as a rule, always needs an *approval by the MCE.* Article 10 defines the legal framework for these decisions. It lays down strict conditions for approval. The release may not be allowed if there is a *risk* of detrimental effects to health or the environment. In this respect, the Act is based on a precautionary principle in a strict sense. If this basic condition is fulfilled, the decision is based on a broad discretion of advantages and possible disadvantages. It is explicitly stated that

717. The Ministry of Health and Care Services is the ministry responsible for this part of the Act.
718. Regulation of 21 Dec. 2001 No. 1602.
719. Regulation of 21 Dec. 2001 No. 1600 implementing Directive 90/219/EEC and Directive 98/81/EC.
720. Regulation of 21 Dec. 2001 No. 1603.
721. Regulation of 21 Dec. 2001 No. 1601.
722. The MCE is the ministry responsible for this part of the Act with the NEA as technical agency.

much weight must be placed on whether the release provides benefits for society, and whether it promotes sustainable development (Article 10 paragraph 2). According to the preparatory work of the Act, the concept of sustainable development should be understood in accordance with the 1987 report from the World Commission on Environment and Development (the 'Brundtland report'): It should be taken in a broad sense, covering not only environmental protection but also perspectives of just distribution between rich and poor countries, and the interests of future generations.

716. Release policy is to be built on *a case-by-case basis, and step-by-step approach,* in order to gain as much experience as possible before any further commitment. A GMO product may not be approved for marketing unless it has been tested in the natural environments that may be affected (Article 10 paragraph 1).

As part of an approval, the authorities may lay down the necessary *conditions* in order to minimize the risk to health and the environment. As examples of possible conditions, the Act (Article 15) mentions in particular conditions related to the choice of technical methods, and duty to take out an adequate insurance or in other ways provide financial security in case of accident and liability, and measures to prevent and limit possible adverse effects. An approval may be limited in time.

717. An application for a release approval must contain an assessment of possible risks and impacts on health and the environment, as well as of other possible consequences (Article 11). Detailed rules on impact assessments are laid down in regulations.[723] The authorities may also decide that an application shall be subject to a public hearing well in advance of the final decision (Article 13). A public hearing is always required in cases of application for approval of release of a GMO according to the Act. The hearing process must be carried out in such a way that the public in general, and affected interest groups in particular, have access to relevant information, and have a real possibility to present their views.

718. The Norwegian policy in this field has so far been quite strict. To date (June 2017), only a handful of genetically modified products have been accepted in Norway, and no release in the form of cultivation of GMOs has been approved. A main regulation pursuant to the Act[724] prohibits explicitly the release of a thirteen various types of GMO, such as genetically modified vaccines against rabies, genetically modified maize, chicory, and oil rape, as produced by specific companies.[725] It is notable that these have all been accepted by EU through Commission decisions.

719. This is a consequence of the fact that Norwegian policy and legal practice *does not fully conform with that of the EU.* Formally, the EU directive on GMO

723. Regulation of 16 Dec. 2005 No. 1495 on Impact Assessment pursuant to the Gene Technology Act, implementing Directive 2001/18/EC as amended by Directive (EU) 2018/350.
724. Regulation of 15 Dec. 2000 No. 1268 on the prohibition of marketing certain GMOs in Norway with later amendments. It implements Directive 90/220/EEC.
725. Among these are well-known companies like Rhone Merieux (France), Novartis (Switzerland), Aventis (Belgium), Monsanto AS (USA), and Bayer CropScience AG (Germany).

release[726] applies to Norway. The GMO Act Article 10 paragraph 6 states that an approval pursuant to the Act is not necessary for the marketing of a GMO product which has already been approved for marketing in another EEA member country in accordance with the EU directive. However, Article 10 adds that the marketing may nevertheless be prohibited or restricted if it, in the view of the Norwegian authorities, entails a risk to health or the environment, 'or otherwise is contrary to the purpose of the Act'. In this connection, it should be noted that one of the purposes of the Act is to promote sustainable development. Both sustainable development and ethical considerations are important criteria for approval of a GMO release.

Nevertheless, it is the Norwegian understanding that the amendments adopted by the EU in 2001 through Directive 2001/18/EEC reduced the differences somewhat between the Norwegian rules and the EU rules. Notably, the preamble of the amended Directive makes it clear that ethical considerations may be relevant. Also, it follows from one of the annexes that the problem of resistance to antibiotics must be given special consideration.

In recent cases, altogether seven types of carnations which were genetically modified with regard to their colour,[727] and which had been formally accepted by the authorities in the Netherlands, were also accepted by the Norwegian authorities. They did not find any special risk to health or the environment of these compared to normal carnations and thus not sufficient reasons to use the special possibility in our Act to prohibit these species in spite of approval by another EEA Member State.

720. According to Article 10 paragraph 4, *export* of GMOs does not require approval, unless otherwise stated in regulations.

Transport, import and export of GMOs may be subject to general regulations instead of individual approval (Article 10 paragraph 3). The actual regulation[728] lays down a general duty of precaution: Persons responsible for labelling, transport, import, and export shall 'show due care and take reasonable measures to ensure that the handling of GMOs is carried out without adverse effects on health and the environment'. They shall ensure that the regulations are complied with (Article 4).

721. The main rule is that GMOs may be *transported and imported* without special approval if the rules regarding labelling and packaging in the regulation are complied with (Article 6). However, some GMOs cannot be transported or imported without a formal approval. Among these are all genetically modified animals except ordinary domesticated animals, and live animals and plants used as host organism to genetically modified microorganisms (Article 7).

The regulation lays down detailed rules on the contents of an application (Article 8). All transport and import of GMOs must be registered by the transporter/importer and the register must be available for the authorities (Article 9).

726. Directive 2001/18/EC as amended by Directive (EU) 2018/350.
727. In 2017 the carnation types Moonlite, Moonvelvet, Moonaqua, Moonberry, and SHD-27531-4 and in 2020 the carnation types Moonaqua og Moonvista.
728. Regulations of 2 Sep. 2005 No. 1009 relating to labelling, transport, import and export of GMOs.

722. Norway has ratified *the Cartagena Protocol* on biosafety under the CBD. This is reflected in the mentioned regulation of export of GMOs. The first time an exporter plans to export GMOs to a country outside the EEA, he/she has to obtain what in the Cartagena Protocol is called 'advance informed agreement' from the responsible authority in the importing country (Regulation Article 15). The exporter must provide the importing country with detailed and correct information about the GMO in question and its characteristics, the planned use, the risks involved in the transport and other relevant information. The required information is described in detail in the regulation (Regulation Articles 16 and 17). Export is not approved and cannot take place until the authority of the importing country has formally agreed to it in writing.

There are some exceptions to these rules, however. For example, advance informed agreement is not necessary for GMOs in transit and when the exported GMOs are meant for contained use in the importing country. It is not necessary either for export to a country that has informed the Information Mechanism under the Cartagena Protocol that advance informed agreement is not required in its case, provided that the necessary measures are taken to ensure a safe passage in accordance with the objective of the Cartagena Protocol.

IV. Rules on Implementation and Enforcement

723. The GMO Act has a comprehensive set of implementation and enforcement rules (Chapter 4). The issue of *public access to information* is a particularly important and sensitive issue in the field of GMOs. The Act explicitly states that the Public Information Act[729] applies to matters pursuant to the Act. This means that documents related to, for example, an application for approval of release are, as a rule, public. However, the Public Information Act also contains certain important limitations for, *inter alia*, secrecy reasons. Here, the GMO Act Article 12 states that certain information is public regardless of the secrecy rules in the Public Information Act, notably:

- a description of the GMO, the name and address of the user, and the place and purpose of the use;
- methods and plans for monitoring and preparedness;
- assessment of possible effects.

Also, the Act on the Right to Environmental Information[730] applies to the release of GMOs.

724. The authorities have every right to *inspect and control* sites of production and use of GMOs, investigate relevant documents and so on (GMO Act Article 18). Any person who produces or uses GMOs must, when asked, give the authorities all

729. Act of 19 May 2006 No. 16.
730. Act of 9 May 2003 No. 31.

the information which is needed for their work. Accidents and other unforeseen incidents must be reported immediately (Article 19).

The authorities may order the immediate cessation of an activity which is in violation of the Act or rules pursuant to it, or if there is a risk of harm to health or the environment (Article 20).

725. If a GMO is released into the environment in contravention of the Act, the party responsible shall take 'reasonable measures' to *prevent or limit damage* (Article 21)The same applies if an approved release turns out to entail unforeseen risks. The authorities may then order the responsible party to collect the GMO and carry out other measures to remove the organisms, and to restore the natural conditions in the area as closely as possible to the original State. If the party responsible does not carry out such an order, the authorities may carry them out at the expense of the party responsible. The rules to this effect correspond to those of the PCA (*see* Part I, §2).

726. The Act provides for *strict liability* in case an intentional or accidental release of GMO results in damage, nuisance and/or pecuniary loss. The Act explicitly refers to the rules in Chapter 8 of the PCA, which apply *mutatis mutandis* also to damage from GMO (*see infra* Part IV). Liability for damage is notwithstanding a release approval.

727. Finally, the Act provides for a system of coercive fines (Article 24), and for *criminal sanctions* in case of violations of the rules of the Act or rules pursuant to the Act. The maximum penalty is a one-year term of imprisonment, but up to four years in case of particularly aggravating circumstances (Article 25).

§2. Access to Genetic Material

728. In 2008, Norway got its first regulation on access to genetic material. This had become necessary in light of the international cooperation related to Article 15 on access to genetic resources in the Convention on Biodiversity, as well as increasing industry interest in bioprospecting in sea areas under Norway's jurisdiction. The necessary rules were introduced into both the Marine Resources Act (Chapter 2) and the Nature Diversity Act (Chapter VII). Bioprospecting on land, in the territorial water and on Svalbard is explicitly regulated by the NDA. It is also said that this Act is to be applied to bioprospecting on Norway's continental shelf and in the EEZ 'to the extent appropriate' (Article 3). The Marine Resources Act regulates bioprospecting at sea. The two Acts overlap somewhat. Since the rules in the NDA have the broadest field of application and are the most elaborate, the following presentation will mainly refer to that Act.

One should bear in mind that the general principles of the NDA, including the duty of care and the precautionary principle (*see supra* Chapter 1, §2), also apply to activities covered by Chapter VII.

729. Chapter VII in the NDA regulates *'access to genetic material and traditional knowledge linked to genetic material'*. Special rules on access to traditional knowledge were added in 2013 in order to make Norwegian legislation in full accordance with the Nagoya Protocol under the CBD which was adopted in 2010.[731]

'Genetic material' is defined in Article 3 of the Act as 'genes and other hereditary material in any biological material that can be transferred to other organisms with or without the help of technology, except for human genetic material'. Article 57 states that genetic material obtained from the natural environment is 'a common resource belonging to Norwegian society as a whole and managed by the State'. It shall be managed to the greatest possible benefit of the environment and human beings in both a national and an international context. The genetic material shall be managed in such a way that the benefits are shared appropriately and the interests of indigenous peoples and local communities are safeguarded.

730. Article 58 concerns *collection and utilization* of genetic material obtained from the natural environment. The article itself lays down merely a legal basis for further regulation. It states that the government (the King) may determine that the collection of biological material from the natural environment for the purpose of utilizing the genetic material, as well as the utilization of such material, requires a permit from the Ministry. If a collection permit has been granted, no new permit is required for subsequent utilization, but the conditions for the permit apply correspondingly to any person that acquires the material or results arising from the collection. Collection for use in public collections and for use and further breeding or cultivation in agriculture or forestry does not require a permit.

However, such a public permit does not give right to access private land. The landowner may deny access as well to the land as to the biological material from which the genetic material is to be taken.

The government may lay down the necessary regulations as regards the information the application shall contain, including information regarding use of the knowledge of indigenous peoples or local communities. The regulations may also state how the interests of landowners and indigenous peoples and local communities can be reasonably safeguarded. Conditions may be set for the further utilization of the material.

731. Article 59 regulates genetic material in *'public collections'*. A 'public collection' is a collection of genetic material that is managed by or on behalf of the State and to which any person has access on specified conditions. Public collections shall be managed in accordance with the principles set out in Article 57. The manager of a public collection has a duty to register any genetic material removed from the collection and provide public access to such information.

Any person that receives genetic material from a public collection shall refrain, in Norway and abroad, from claiming intellectual property rights or other rights to the material that would limit use of the material, such as use for food or agriculture,

731. The Nagoya Protocol on Access to Genetic Resources and the Fair and Equitable Sharing of Benefits Arising from their Utilization (ABS) to the Convention on Biological Diversity was adopted in Nagoya, Japan on the 29 Oct. 2010 and came into force on 12 Oct. 2014.

unless the material has been modified in a way that results in a substantial change. Article 59 contains various mechanisms to prevent violation of this rule. Anybody may take legal steps against a person that seeks to enforce an intellectual property right contrary to the rule. The government may lay down further regulations regarding removals from collections.[732] With regard to the removal of genetic material covered by the International Treaty on Plant Genetic Resources for Food and Agriculture of 3 November 2001 or by another international agreement, the standard conditions laid down under the agreement shall apply.

732. Article 60 regulates *genetic material from other countries.* It reflects the international discussion related to the proper implementation of Article 15 of the CBD. The import for utilization in Norway of genetic material from a State that requires consent for collection or export of such material may only take place in accordance with such consent. The person that has control of the material is bound by the conditions that have been set for consent. The State may enforce the conditions by bringing legal action on behalf of the person that set them.

When genetic material from another country is utilized in Norway for research or commercial purposes, it shall be accompanied by information regarding the country from which the genetic material has been received (provider country). If national law in the provider country requires consent for the collection of biological material, it shall be accompanied by information to the effect that such consent actually has been obtained.

If the provider country is a country other than the country of origin of the genetic material, the country of origin shall also be stated. The country of origin means the country in which the material was collected from *in situ* sources. If national law in the country of origin requires consent for the collection of genetic material, information as to whether such consent has been obtained shall be provided. If the information under this paragraph is not known, this shall be stated.

The government may make regulations prescribing that if utilization involves use of the traditional knowledge of local communities or indigenous peoples, the genetic material shall be accompanied by information to that effect.

When genetic material covered by the *International Treaty on Plant Genetic Resources for Food and Agriculture* of 3 November 2001 is utilized in Norway for research or commercial purposes, it shall be accompanied by information to the effect that the material has been acquired in accordance with the Standard Material Transfer Agreement established under the treaty (Article 61).

733. Article 61 on *access to and utilization of traditional knowledge* linked to genetic material was included in the Act in 2013. It reflects the principles and rules on these issues in the Nagoya Protocol. The interests of indigenous peoples and local communities must be ensured and respected in cases of access to and utilization of knowledge linked to genetic material which has been developed, transferred and protected by an indigenous people or a local community. The King (the government) may lay down regulations which require that access and utilization of traditional knowledge is agreed by the indigenous people or local community in

---

732. No such regulation had been laid down in June 2017.

question, and the necessary control and sanctions to this effect.[733] This can also apply to traditional knowledge which has been developed, transferred and protected in another State, provided that such consent is required pursuant to the legislation of that State.

§3. Outdoor Recreation and Motor Traffic in the Countryside

734. Large parts of Norway are covered by relatively unspoiled forests, mountains, rivers and lakes. Most of its coast is thinly populated, and ideal for boating and other recreational activities with its many fjords and islands. To Norwegians, outdoor recreation is an important part of their lifestyle, whether in the form of hiking, skiing, or boating – inland or along the coast. A prerequisite for this is the possibility to move freely in the forests and mountains, and along the shoreline, regardless of the ownership of the land. This is ensured by the Outdoor Recreation Act.[734]

At the same time, it is necessary to restrict certain types of traffic in the forests and mountain areas, in particular motor traffic. The Act Relating to Motor Traffic on Uncultivated Land and in Watercourses[735] provides the legal basis for such restrictions.

I. Outdoor Recreation Act

735. The Outdoor Recreation Act of 1957 provides the *general rules regarding the public's right of access on private land.* Although the Act was adopted in 1957, its rules express for the most part customary law with a long tradition. In Norway, it has always been possible for people to move freely in forests and mountains, on watercourses and along the coast, regardless of the ownership of the land. This customary law was developed at a time when this possibility was a social and economic necessity in a country as thinly populated as Norway, with scattered farms and villages. Gradually, access for recreational purposes played an increasingly important role, and the possibility of conflicts between the landowner and the public became evident. Hence, it became necessary to legislate on the issue with a view both to safeguarding the public's rights and to limiting it in relation to the landowner's property rights and legitimate interests. A limitation was needed also in order to protect the countryside. This is the purpose of the Outdoor Recreation Act.

736. It should be noted, however, that most of the rules of the Act are regarded as *customary law of old standing.* They have for a long time constituted important elements of public rights (*allemannsrett*) in Norwegian property law.

This fact is important for the question of the Act's application to existing situations. It is clear that the rules of the Act apply to situations which were established

733. Such regulation has not yet been adopted (September 2021).
734. Act of 28 Jun. 1957 No. 16.
735. Act of 10 Jun. 1977 No. 82.

before the Act was adopted in 1957, and in that sense have a retroactive effect. For example, facilities which violate the Act, may be removed even if they were erected long before the Act came into force. This is of particular importance as regards violations of Article 13 which prohibits a landowner from taking measures to prevent the free access and passage of the public. We shall return to this issue.

Although the Act strikes a balance between the public and private interests, its predominant objective is clearly the *protection and promotion of the public's outdoor recreation activities.* Its Article 1[736] provides that the purpose is:

> to protect the natural basis for outdoor recreation and to safeguard the public's right to and passage through the countryside and the right to spend time there, in order to maintain and promote opportunities for outdoor recreation as a leisure activity which is healthy, environmentally sound, and gives a sense of well-being.

737. An important distinction in the Act is that *between 'cultivated land' and 'uncultivated land'.* As a rule, the public has a general right of year-round access to and passage through uncultivated land, and also to some extent a right of stay. On cultivated land, however, the right of access, passage and stay is much more limited. It is thus necessary to clarify this distinction.

The Act (Article 1a paragraph 1) defines *'cultivated land'* as 'farmyards, plots around houses and cabins, tilled fields, hay meadows, cultivated pasture, young forest plantations and similar areas where public access would unduly hinder the owner or user'. Although not mentioned explicitly, it is clear that ordinary gardens are considered to be 'cultivated land'. Also, small, uncultivated plots within tilled land or hay meadows may be considered as cultivated land.

'*Uncultivated land*' is defined as 'land that is not tilled and that is not considered to be equivalent to cultivated land in accordance with paragraph 1' (Article 1a paragraph 2). In practice, the country's vast forests and mountain areas, as well as the uninhabited parts of the coast, are uncultivated land according to the definition of the Act.

These definitions are fairly clear, but there may be cases of doubt. This is notably the case along the seashore, where the line between a garden and the natural shore may be difficult to define. Here conflicts arise regularly between landowners and members of the public who want to walk along the shore, sunbathe and go swimming. Some of these conflicts end up in court, and a few have even been decided by the Supreme Court.[737] In these cases, there is a tendency that the court interprets the Act in a way that supports the public interest and right of free access.

738. As mentioned, any person is entitled to access to and passage through uncultivated land on foot and on ski at all times of the year. It must, however, be done with due *consideration and care* (Article 2). The same applies to access and passage on horseback, bicycle or the like on roads and paths across uncultivated land and in all uncultivated mountain areas (Article 2). However, the municipality,

736. This article was included in the Act in 1996 by Act of 21 Jun. 1996 No. 37.
737. *See* Norsk Retstidende 1998, 1164, 2005, 805, and 2008, 803.

with the consent of the owner or user and approval of the county governor, may prohibit such passage along specified tracks.

During the last decades several new forms of recreational activities have become popular in Norway, such as off-road bicycling, kiting, hang-gliding, intensive rock climbing and BASE-jumping. Whether these activities can be regarded as 'access to and passage through uncultivated land' is a matter for discussion. However, in practice these activities are to a large extent exercised freely and thus accepted and not regarded as violating the Act. The dominant point of view is that the right to access and passage in the Act is a flexible concept which develops in accordance with the public's interests and habits, and with activities that actually take place.

739. On *cultivated land,* any person is entitled to access to and passage on foot, when the ground is frozen or snow-covered, but not from 30 April to 14 October.[738] This right does not apply, however, to farmyards or plots around houses and cabins, fenced gardens or parks, or other areas fenced in for special purposes where public access in winter would unduly hinder the owner or user.

Notwithstanding these rules, the owner or user may prohibit passage across unfenced gardens, young forest plantations, autumn-sowed fields and newly established meadows if such passage could cause significant damage (Article 3).

Walking, horse riding, bicycling, etc., on a road or trail on cultivated land is also permitted the whole year if this is necessary in order to get access to uncultivated land, except through a courtyard. It must not hinder or be of inconvenience to the owner. The municipality may lay down prohibition of such traffic (Article 3a).

It is, as a rule, permitted to park a motor vehicle or other vehicles on uncultivated land alongside a public road. The owner of a private road may, however, prohibit access by vehicles and parking alongside the road (Article 4).

740. There are special rules on *passage on the sea and watercourses,* landing, bathing, and the like (Articles 6–8). To a great extent, the sea and watercourses may be regarded as a common. Any person is entitled to free passage on the sea by boat, and on ice-covered areas of the sea as well. On the sea along the coast there are no limitation on traffic by motorboats. However, many municipalities have introduced speed limits during summer in areas close to the shore.

On lakes and watercourses, boat traffic is generally free for everybody as well, pursuant to the rules of the Water Resources Act (Article 16). But here, there are important restrictions on the use of motorboats pursuant to the special Act governing motorized traffic on uncultivated land (*see infra* III).

741. Whether on sea or a watercourse, everybody has *the right to land a boat* on the shore in an uncultivated area for a short period of time. It is not permitted, however, to make use of a quay or jetty without the owner's or user's permission. The owner of the shore may not oppose the use by others of mooring devices (rings, bolts, etc.) in uncultivated areas, if this can take place without unduly hindering the owner or user of the land (Article 7).

738. The county governor may decide that this period shall be shorter or longer within the county or part of the county.

Any person has the right to bathe in the sea from the shore in an uncultivated area, or from a boat, at a reasonable distance from an inhabited house or cabin, provided that it does not unduly hinder or inconvenience others (Article 8). As a rule, the same applies to rivers and lakes.

742. Picnicking, sunbathing, and camping overnight is also generally allowed on uncultivated land, provided that it does not unduly hinders or is of inconvenience to others, or risk to damage young forest. Outside specially designated camping sites, camping may not take place closer than 150 m from an inhabited house. As a rule, the landowner's permission is required for a stay of more than two days, but this is not required in the mountains and other areas distant from inhabited areas (Article 9 paragraph 2).

On cultivated land, however, it is not permitted to picnic, sunbathe or stay overnight without the permission of the owner or user of the land.

Outdoor meetings, sports events such as skiing competitions, and similar events that may entail significant damage or inconvenience, may not be held without the consent of the owner or user of the land. Trails for skiing competitions, cross-country running and the like must be routed so as to avoid damage to young forest and fences (Article 10).

743. A person who passes through or spends time on another person's property, or on the sea off another person's property, shall *behave considerately and with due care* in order not to cause damage or inconvenience to the owner, users or others, or damage the natural environment. When leaving the place, he must ensure that it is in a proper state and may not create damage or inconvenience. The owner or user of the land has the right to expel persons who act inconsiderately or cause damage or inconvenience (Article 11).

744. As a rule, *the landowner may not take measures aimed at preventing the public from exercising its right of access* and passage. It is stated explicitly that 'the owner or user of land may not by means of barriers or in any other way hinder access that is permitted by this Act, unless this serves his legitimate interests and does not unduly hinder public access' (Article 13 paragraph 1). This is a very important rule. If a barrier, sign or notice contravenes this rule, its removal may be required by the municipality.

However, this rule is not clear and often creates confusion. Some types of measures are clearly prohibited, such as putting up a fence or a hedgerow, or erecting a small building with the sole purpose of barring access. Also, the Act explicitly prohibits signs saying that access and bathing are prohibited in an area where access is permitted pursuant to the Act (Article 13 paragraph 2).

It is doubtful whether the owner of a piece of uncultivated land may indirectly keep the public off by planting flowers, placing chairs and tables, building installations for bathing or a landing stage by the shore, and the like. Even if such measures may not physically hinder the public's access, it may have similar 'psychological' effect, giving the public a feeling of trespassing. The question is whether such installations 'serve a legitimate purpose', and do not hinder public access 'unduly'. This is a matter of discretion in each individual case.

745. These issues are often subject to conflicts between the public and the owners of houses and cabins, in particular – and increasingly – along the seashore. Here, free access is of particular value to the public. At the same time, privacy is very important for the landowner. In a Supreme Court decision,[739] the owner of a seashore property neighbouring a camping site had fences down to the shore on both sides of his/her property. His/her house was 60 m from the shoreline. The court found the shore to be uncultivated land and as a consequence open to access for the public. It decided that the parts of the fences closest to the shore had to be removed in order to grant such access. It did not matter that the fences had been in place since 1930 and the early 1950s. Nor did it matter that the owner had some facilities for bathing and the like close to the shore. However, the public had only the right to pass through the property along the shoreline, and not to stay there for swimming and sunbathing.

746. The rules of the Outdoor Recreation Act do not prevent the landowner from changing the use of the land on his/her property in such a way that uncultivated land becomes 'cultivated land', such as a garden. By so doing, the public's access becomes severely restricted. Nor does the Act prevent the construction of houses or cabins, which also, of course, will prevent public access to that particular area.

Constructions and installations are governed pursuant to the PBA. Although the two Acts apply side by side and independently, constructions and installations that are permitted pursuant to the PBA will most often also be acceptable pursuant to the Outdoor Recreation Act.

747. The municipality has considerable authority pursuant to the Outdoor Recreation Act. Some examples have already been given. Furthermore, with the consent of the landowner, it may lay down general rules of conduct in areas with a large number of visitors, in order to protect flora and fauna, ensure proper sanitary conditions, and so on (Article 15).

Some properties may be particularly heavily used by the public. If public access causes significant damage to the property or is a serious obstacle to the owner's own use, the municipality may decide that all or part of it shall be closed to the public (Article 16). If such a prohibition is not established by the municipality, the landowner may require that the municipality purchase his/her property (Article 18). The municipality is also authorized to make decisions in cases of conflicts and doubt, for example, as to whether a piece of land is to be considered cultivated or uncultivated, or whether a barrier is legal or not pursuant to Article 13 (Article 20). These rules are, however, scarcely applied.

The municipalities, as well as private recreation associations, may also be given the authority by State authorities to signpost and mark trails, build footbridges or carry out other measures to facilitate access to and passage through uncultivated areas (Article 35).

---

739. Norsk Retstidende 1998, 1164.

748. The public's right of free access to and passage through forests, shore areas, and mountains is regarded as an important value of the Norwegian society. However, it is now *subject to controversy and debate.*

On the one hand, increased recreational activities by the public, such as cross-country and off-piste alpine skiing, off-road bicycling, motor-boating, and motorized traffic in forests and mountains, put the country's nature areas under stress. It is rightly pointed out that the purpose of these rights, as well as their content and effects, have changed considerably over the last century. For this reason, some argue in favour of certain restrictions of the right to free access.

On the other hand, many landowners see a growing need to restrict the public's access to their land for economic or purely private reasons. Increasingly, uncultivated land becomes 'privatized' in various ways. This makes public access to recreational areas difficult, notably along the coast in certain parts of the country.

II. Protection of Nature and Recreational Interests in the Oslo Area

749. Norway's capital Oslo with its neighbouring municipalities is surrounded by vast and rather unspoiled forest areas – called 'Oslo-marka' or simply 'Marka' – and the Oslo fjord. The forests with their numerous rivers and lakes are valuable nature areas and much used by the population for skiing, hiking, camping, bathing, fishing and other recreational activities. Some parts are formally protected as nature reserves.

Altogether, the forests are situated in eighteen municipalities, with 1.2 million inhabitants in total. It has been an agreed objective for several decades to avoid developments in the forests that would significantly reduce their values. Ordinary forestry has by and large been accepted – although with some special restrictions. However, the development of infrastructure, residential areas, cabins for recreation and so on have been strictly limited. In Oslo, the 'forest limit' (*Markagrensen*) represents an absolute spatial restriction on the urban development. In other municipalities, there has been some pressure for building of cabins, forestry roads and other developments in their forests. It has thus been a challenge to manage the vast forests as a whole.

750. In 2009, Stortinget adopted a special *Act relating to the Nature Area in Oslo and Neighbouring Municipalities* (the 'Marka Act').[740] Its purpose is to promote and facilitate outdoor recreation, experience of nature, and sport in the forest area defined as 'Marka'. It shall safeguard the limitation of the area and protect its varied landscape, and natural and cultural environment and cultural heritage while also considering other sustainable uses of the area (Article 1). It is a major objective to ensure a holistic and sustainable management of the area, that is, through a stricter State control of activities and of the relevant policies of the municipalities. This is achieved partly through substantive rules in the Act and partly through the various procedural rules in the Act. The limitations of the geographical area it covers are

740. Act of 5 Jun. 2009 No. 35.

defined in detail on a map which is part of the Act. The limitations may be adjusted, and the area may be extended (Article 2).

751. The Act is closely connected to the PBA, and is also supplemented by several important sector Acts which still apply to the area. The above-mentioned Outdoor Recreation Act is the basis for the public's right to and limitation of access, while motorized traffic is more strictly regulated than in the general Act on motorized traffic on uncultivated land (*see infra*). As the main rule, forestry may be carried out in accordance with the Forestry Act. Pollution is regulated by the PCA and management of watercourses by the Water Resources Act. Land-use planning and building control in the area is generally carried out in accordance with and pursuant to the general system in the PBA, but some special rules apply. Some forest areas are protected pursuant to the NDA. For these areas, the restrictions on activities are defined in the respective regulations of protection pursuant to that Act.

752. Generally speaking, *any building, construction and other types of works and developments are prohibited* in Marka. There are, however, certain exceptions to this, such as ordinary agricultural activities including forestry and major electricity lines (Article 5). Municipal master plans and local development plans pursuant to the PBA may permit constructions for agricultural purposes, hiking paths and skiing tracks, sport facilities, necessary roads, water supply, and some other public infrastructure projects (Article 7). However, the MCE must first accept that such a plan is worked out, and the final plan must also be approved by the Ministry. Approval can only be given if the plan is not in conflict with the objective of the Act (Article 6).

The Act (Article 9) lays down strict rules for the establishment of new paths and ski tracks. A local development plan pursuant to the PBA is required for new major ski tracks. New tracks have to be accepted by the owner of the forest.

In general, new buildings and constructions may be approved only if the advantages outweigh the disadvantages for the recreation interest, the natural environment, and other public interests (Article 14).

753. *Motorized traffic* is regulated in detail in the Act (Article 10). The main rule is that motorized traffic is prohibited on 'uncultivated land' and watercourses/lakes. Motorized traffic includes transport by car, tractor, motorbike, snow-scooter, motorboats as well as taking off and landing with aircraft. 'Uncultivated land' includes roads that are not developed for ordinary car traffic and roads that are not cleared for snow during winter. It also includes small housing sites and similar plots in the area.

However, the Act lists a number of transport needs and purposes which may be carried out by some sort of a motorized vehicle, such as police, rescue and post services, transport to and from agriculture and forestry activities, military activities, maintenance of tracks and of cabins open to the public, the running and maintenance of energy systems, including power stations and power lines, and so on. Such traffic has to be carried out carefully and at such times which lead to as little damage and inconvenience for recreational activities, and as little disturbance of wildlife and other natural values as possible.

754. The Act provides a special type of protected area, namely *'recreational areas'*. Such areas are to be protected due to their natural qualities which are particularly valuable for the recreational activities (Article 11).[741] In recreational areas, no activities may be carried out which may considerably change the recreational value of the area. Hence, activities that are generally permitted pursuant to the Act itself may be prohibited in a recreational area. This is particularly relevant with regard to agriculture and forestry which may be possible pursuant to the Act itself (Article 5), but may be severely restricted and even prohibited in a recreational area. Such 'recreational areas' supplement the five types of protected nature areas that can be established pursuant to the NDA (*see supra* Part II, Chapter 2, §2). The difference between protection as a recreational area pursuant to the Marka Act and protection as a nature reserve pursuant to the NDA may in fact be very limited or non-existing. In fact, the Ministry has chosen to protect several areas in the Marka area as nature reserves pursuant to the NDA in spite of the fact that the main purpose is protection of their recreational value. Also, most of the procedural rules that apply to the establishment of a protected area pursuant to the NDA apply directly to the establishment of 'recreational areas'.

As with protected areas pursuant to the NDA, the landowner has a right to *compensation* from the State for his or her economic loss which follows from restrictions laid down in a recreational area. The condition is that the restriction *'makes current use of the property more difficult'*. Hence, what is compensated is the increased costs of – or the reduced income from – his/her activity because the protection measures have made this activity 'more difficult'. This is the same compensation rule as laid down in the NDA Article 50 for economic loss due to restrictions in protected areas.

755. Within the borders of the land area that is covered by the Marka Act, new buildings and other new activities can be carried out *only if they are permitted pursuant to a decision* by the relevant authorities. As mentioned, approval can only be given if the advantages outweigh the disadvantages for the recreation interest, the natural environment, and other public interests (Article 14).

Individual exemptions may be given by the authorities pursuant to detailed rules in Article 15. The conditions are that the objective of the Act, as laid down in its Article 1, is not considerably disregarded by the exemption. Furthermore, it is required that the advantages of the exemption clearly outweigh the disadvantages and harms for recreational activities, the natural environment or other public interests. A municipality may not grant an exemption if a State or regional authority goes against it.

756. Finally, the Act lays down the necessary *rules for its effective implementation* including sanctions. The municipality may order remedial and corrective measures when the Act or regulations pursuant to the Act have been violated. The responsible actor must take necessary actions to prevent damage or inconvenience to the environment or to repair damage that has taken place (Article 18). In order to

741. Until September 2021 five areas had been protected as 'recreational areas'.

have necessary measures carried out, the responsible actor may be subject to a coercive fine (Article 19). Violations of the Act or regulations and decisions pursuant to the Act, intentional or by gross negligence, are punishable with fines or up to one year of imprisonment. In case of threat of significant harm or if there are aggravating circumstances, a three-year term of imprisonment may be imposed (Article 20).

III. Motor Traffic on Uncultivated Land and Watercourses

757. The right of way of the public, pursuant to the Outdoor Recreation Act, only applies to access on foot, on bicycle, skis, horseback and the like – and not to motorized traffic. Motorized traffic outside ordinary streets, roads, airfields and so on is regulated, and as a rule prohibited, pursuant to the *Act Relating to Motor Traffic on Uncultivated Land and Watercourses (Motor Traffic Act).*[742] The purpose of this Act is to strictly limit such traffic with a view to protecting the natural environment and promoting public well-being (Article 1). This is an issue of considerable conflicts of interests and where State environmental authorities and the municipalities in some parts of the country tend to have different views. Generally speaking, local authorities have a more liberal attitude to motorized traffic. The Act tries to strike a balance between national and local authorities and interests. The most serious problem in this respect from an environmental point of view is the extensive use of snow-scooters in pristine, unspoilt nature in certain parts of the country. Restriction on the use of snow-scooters is, however, quite controversial in many parts of the country with vast and seemingly isolated mountain and forest areas.

The Act covers using motor vehicles (cars, motorcycles, snow-scooters, etc.), using any type of boat with a motor, and landing and taking off with motorized aircraft (Article 2 paragraph 1) on uncultivated land[743] and watercourses. Roads in uncultivated areas that are not constructed for motorcars, or which are not cleared for snow in winter, are considered to be uncultivated land.

The Act does not apply to the sea area. Hence, *motorized traffic by boats along the coast and in the fjords is free.*

758. The use of *'water-scooters'* and similar small crafts which cannot be regarded as boats is regulated pursuant to the Small Boats Act (Article 40).[744] Earlier restrictions and prohibitions on the use of water-scooters mainly due to their noise and other environmental inconveniences which they created were abolished in 2017. As a consequence, water-scooters may at the outset be used in the same ways and areas as ordinary boats. However, the State may lay down regulations to protect natural and recreational values, and may give authority to the municipalities

742. Act of 10 Jun. 1977 No. 82.
743. As defined by Art. 1a para. 2 of the Outdoor Recreation Act, *see supra* s. I.
744. Act of 26 Jun. 1998 No. 47, Art. 40. The former rules were criticized by the ESA for being too strict and thus violating EU rules on free movement of goods, and they had to be modified.

to adopt local rules. For example, in many municipalities, traffic with water-scooters can only take place at a certain distance from the shore. Anyway, drivers of water-scooters have to act with due care and the general rules for boating and navigation apply.

759. The general rule according to the Motor Traffic Act is that *motor traffic on uncultivated land (forests, mountains,* etc.*) and on watercourses is not permitted* unless otherwise determined in the Act or by decisions pursuant to the Act (Article 3). Notwithstanding this general prohibition, such traffic is permitted in some situations due to the rules of the Act itself (Article 4), rules in municipal regulations, or on the basis of individual permits accorded mainly by the municipalities pursuant to the general Regulation of the implementation of the Act.[745]

Motor traffic is generally permitted, pursuant to Article 4, for certain purposes, for example:

- police, ambulance and rescue services and the like, and public postal and telecommunications services;
- essential transport of passengers and goods to and from permanent dwellings and in connection with commercial agriculture and forestry;
- military exercises, construction and operation of public roads and the like, and scheduled and licensed transport services.

The use of motor boats is permitted on lakes with an area of 2 km^2 or more, and on stretches of river and lakes with an area of less than 2 km^2 if these form part of a navigable watercourse. The municipality may nevertheless prohibit such traffic.

It is permitted to use *electric bicycles* on uncultivated land unless prohibited by the municipality in the whole or in parts of the municipality.[746]

760. In 2015, the legislator decided to transfer much authority with regard to *traffic of snow-scooters* from the State to the municipalities, and also generally to make such traffic legal regardless of purpose. This allows for snow-scooter driving as a pleasure and 'amusement' – and as a recreational and tourist activity, even with a purely commercial objective. This may both be harmful to wildlife and other natural values and be a serious nuisance to other interests, notably other recreational interests. Politically, this was a very controversial issue. It was adopted by Stortinget by a very thin majority.

Article 4a of the Act gives the MCE the possibility to transfer to the municipalities the authority to establish special tracks for snow-scooters in uncultivated land – mainly in areas of mountains and mountain forests. However, the article lays down several restrictions and limitations with the objective of minimizing conflicts of interests and in particularly of protecting natural and recreational values. Scooter tracks may not be established in protected nature areas, proposed protected areas or

745. Regulation of 15 May 1988 No. 356 relating to the use of motor vehicles on uncultivated land and ice-covered watercourses, with later amendments, the most recent by Regulation 30 Mar. 2021 No. 1193.

746. Pursuant to Art. 2a of the general Regulation of 15 May 1988 No 356.

national areas of wild reindeer stocks. They may not be harmful or inconvenient to domesticated reindeer stocks. When planning and establishing track the municipalities shall take into consideration the possible problems of noise and other nuisances to traditional outdoor life and recreation, as well as nature diversity, residential areas, landscape, cultural heritage and safety. Before making decisions, the municipality must make an assessment of the possible impacts of the driving on nature diversity and other outdoor recreational interests in the area that will be affected by the increased scooter driving. The owner of the land must always accept a new track for snow-scooter driving.

Further details are laid down in the general Regulation relating to the use of motor vehicles on uncultivated land and ice-covered watercourses.[747]

761. Outside the special tracks for snow-scooters, where even driving for pure pleasure is permitted, the general and strict rules of the Act apply to the driving of snow-scooters. However, the general Regulation relating to the use of motor vehicles on uncultivated land and ice-covered watercourses provides the municipal council with the authority also to grant *permission to local inhabitants* to use snow-scooters for various economic purposes, such as transport to cabins situated off the roads, transport of firewood, inspection of cabins, transport of disabled persons, groups of elderly people and so on (Regulation Article 5).

In addition, the Regulation (Article 8) provides the National Environment Agency with authority – on the basis of proposals from the municipality – to permit the use of snow-scooters in some pristine areas, in order for people to reach lakes for fishing which are situated more than 5 km from open roads. In the northernmost part of the country, in the Finnmark county and the northern part of the Troms county, some special and slightly more liberal rules apply.

Pursuant to the Regulation, the municipality may also grant permission to use a motor vehicle for necessary transport of materials and equipment in connection with locally based economic activities in the uncultivated areas, such as tourist-based activities (Regulation Article 5a).

762. Furthermore, the Act provides the municipal council with the authority to issue certain *local regulation*, on the right to land and take-off with aircraft at specified locations on uncultivated land and watercourses, and on the use of motorboats on lakes with an area of less than 2 km^2 if there are special reasons for this. However, if any county authority or government agency raises objections, the county governor has the final say (Article 5). If there are 'special reasons' for it, the municipality may also grant permission for use of motor vehicles or aircraft that may not otherwise be permitted pursuant to the Act. Such permission may be given for specific purposes or specific periods of time. The municipality may impose conditions for such permission. The decision may be appealed to the county governor (Article 6).

The MCE may issue further provisions relating to the exercise of the municipality's authority pursuant to Articles 5 and 6 in order to limit the authority of the

747. Regulation of 15 May 1988 No. 356.

municipality. A special regulation prohibits permission to take ski tourists to mountaintops, glaciers and the like by helicopters for subsequent cross-country or alpine skiing.[748]

763. The *implementation and enforcement* of this Act is part of the responsibility of the State Nature Inspectorate.

Violations of the rules are not uncommon. In certain parts of the country, the population is generally opposed to the strict regulation, and violations may be difficult to discover and investigate. This is an important field for the State Nature Inspectorate and the central prosecuting authority for environmental matters (Økokrim). The rules are not always known, and not always clear either. Over the years, several penal cases have come before the Supreme Court.

The Act has the necessary rules on sanctions. These include fines for intentional or negligent violations of rules in the Act or in regulations (Article 12), and in addition a special administrative fee in case of violation of rules by the driver of a snowscooter.

§4. The Svalbard Environmental Act

I. Introduction

764. Svalbard, also known as Spitzbergen, is a group of islands in the Barents Sea far north of mainland Norway. Altogether, they cover approximately 61,000 km^2. The islands are mountainous, and for the most part covered by tundra and glaciers. They have no indigenous inhabitants, but some 1,500 Norwegians live on the biggest island of the archipelago, Spitsbergen, and some 950 Russian citizens live in the Russian mining town of Barentsburg. Svalbard is rich in coal. Apart from coal mining, tourism and scientific research are the chief activities, and these activities are presently increasing rapidly.

765. Svalbard is part of Norway, but has a *special legal status, based on the Svalbard Treaty* of 9 February 1920.[749] Norway has full sovereignty over the islands, and exercises jurisdiction over all types of activities there. The Norwegian State owns most of the land on the islands.[750] However, according to the Svalbard Treaty, all the States party to the treaty have equal rights to exploit the natural resources, such as mining, fishing and hunting, and carry out other relevant activities on the islands. This is further described in the Svalbard Treaty. It is the view of Norway that the rights of other states pursuant to the Svalbard Treaty only apply on land and within the territorial limit of 12 nautical miles at sea. This view implies

748. Regulation of 14 Mar. 1988 No. 225.

749. 'Treaty between Norway, United States of America, Denmark, France, Italy, Japan, the Netherlands, Great Britain, and Sweden concerning the Spitzbergen.' The treaty came into force in 1925. Nearly thirty countries have since joined the treaty. A legal analysis of the treaty is found in G. Ulfstein, *The Svalbard Treaty* (Scandinavian University Press 1995).

750. With the exception of some pieces of land belonging to other States as spelt out in the Svalbard Treaty and some privately owned land.

that they do not apply to the continental shelf around Svalbard. Norway has not established and EEZ around Svalbard, but instead a 'fishery protection zone'.

The Svalbard Act[751] establishes the system of authority on the islands. The highest authority is the Governor, who is appointed by the King. The Governor has a wide field of authority, which covers both police and general administrative functions. He/she may make decisions on a number of issues, as defined in special legislation. Recently, a system of an elected local council has been established for the biggest Norwegian settlement, Longyearbyen.

Norwegian private law and criminal law apply to Svalbard unless otherwise decided. In other fields of law, Norwegian law does not apply, unless explicitly stated in the relevant Act.[752]

766. The *natural environment of Svalbard is special, rich, mainly untouched and particularly vulnerable*, due to the marginal natural conditions. There are fifteen to twenty types of marine mammals, including whales, dolphins, seals, walruses, and polar bears, as well as the Arctic fox and the Svalbard reindeer. About thirty types of birds are found on Svalbard, most of which are migratory and many in great numbers. The Barents Sea is among the areas in the world with most seabirds, with about 20 million individuals during late summer.

767. With increasing tourism and interest in petroleum exploration on Svalbard, the need to take legal measures to protect its natural environment became evident several decades ago. Article 2 of the Svalbard Treaty explicitly gives Norway the responsibility for introducing and enforcing necessary measures to protect, and if necessary restore, the fauna and flora on the islands. The ordinary national environmental legislation did not apply to Svalbard. However, over the years, a number of regulations to this effect were established pursuant to the Svalbard Act. Most important, large parts of the islands were protected as national parks, protected landscapes or nature reserves in 1973. Additional nature reserves were established in 1983 and 1984, and some new parks and reserves in 2002, 2003, and 2005.

768. The maritime areas around Svalbard are important nursery and fishing grounds, notably for the North-East Arctic cod, haddock and capelin. As mentioned, in 1977, Norway established a 200-mile fishery protection zone around Svalbard, pursuant to the Act on Norway's EEZ.[753] The fishery in the zone is regulated by Norwegian authorities, but is not reserved for Norwegian fishing vessels. The main purpose is to facilitate conservation and sustainable management of the fish stocks. Further rules are laid down in a special Regulation.[754]

751. Act of 17 Jul. 1925 No. 11. This lays down the general legal framework for the status and the governing of Svalbard. It is supplemented by several other Acts, and parts of Acts, on special issues. The most important of these, for the purposes of this monograph, is the Svalbard Environmental Act of 15 Jun. 2001 No. 79.
752. Svalbard Act Art. 2.
753. Act of 17 Dec. 1976 No. 91.
754. Regulation of 3 Jun. 1977 No. 6 regarding a fishery protection zone at Svalbard, with later amendments.

769. In 2001, Stortinget adopted a comprehensive new *Act Relating to the Protection of the Environment in Svalbard (the Svalbard Environmental Act).*[755] This Act builds to a large extent on principles and rules which already apply on the basis of existing regulations. However, it also goes further in many respects. It is particularly interesting that it covers all aspects of environmental protection, including pollution control, land-use, the protection of flora and fauna, and protection of cultural heritage. It contains important environmental principles as well as rules on environmental liability. In short, the Act may be called an 'environmental code in miniature'.

II. Purpose and General Principles of the Svalbard Environmental Act

770. *The purpose* of the Act is 'to preserve a virtually untouched environment in Svalbard with respect to continuous areas of wilderness, landscape, flora, fauna and cultural heritage'. 'Within this framework, the Act allows for environmentally sound settlement, research and commercial activities' (Article 1).

Subject to the limitations imposed by international law, this Act applies to the entire land area of Svalbard and its waters out to the territorial limit (Article 2). It does not apply to the fishery protection zone around Svalbard.

771. The Act lays down *a general duty of care and duty to provide information* (Article 5). Any person who is staying in or operating an undertaking in Svalbard shall show due consideration and exercise the caution required to avoid unnecessary damage or disturbance to the natural environment or cultural heritage. A head of an undertaking shall ensure that any person who carries out work or takes part in the activities for which the undertaking is responsible is aware of the provisions set out in or pursuant to the Act.

772. The Act (Articles 6–10) provides explicitly several important *environmental principles or guidelines.* These are meant to form the basis for the exercise of authority under the Act.[756]

First, *the precautionary principle* is expressed clearly:

> When an administrative body lacks adequate information on the effects that an undertaking may have on the natural environment or cultural heritage, its authority under this Act shall be exercised in a manner designed to avoid possible damage to the environment (Article 7).

Second, *a holistic approach* to the management of Svalbard's nature is underlined. Any activity that is started in Svalbard shall be assessed on the basis of the cumulative effects on the natural environment and cultural heritage that would result (Article 8).

755. Act of 15 Jun. 2001 No. 79.
756. The same principles appeared later, similarly formulated, in the 2009 NDA (*see supra*).

Third, *the PPP* has been given a general implementation, not limited to pollution. Article 9 provides:

> the cost of preventing or limiting damage to the environment or cultural heritage shall be covered by the person that is or would be the cause of such damage. Likewise, the cost of preventing or limiting pollution and waste problems shall be covered by the person who is or would be the cause of such problems.

Also, both *the principle of* BAT and *the substitution principle* have been given a general application. Activities in Svalbard:

> shall make use of the technology that puts the least possible pressure on the environment, unless important economic considerations regarding an already existing activity indicate that a different technology should be used, and this is justifiable on the basis of an overall environmental assessment (Article 10 paragraph 1).

Chemical and biotechnological products that may cause damage or nuisance to the environment shall be replaced with products that on the basis of an overall environmental assessment pose less risk to the environment, unless otherwise indicated on the basis of important economic considerations regarding an already existing activity (Article 10 paragraph 2).

III. Protected Areas

773. A large part of Svalbard is already protected as national parks, protected landscapes or nature reserves. The Act (Article 11) lays down that there shall be protected areas in Svalbard that:

- include the full range of habitats and landscape types;
- help to maintain areas of special conservation or historical value;
- protect ecosystems on land and in the sea;
- contribute to the maintenance of wilderness and untouched nature.

Individually protected areas will be prescribed by the government (King in Council). In such areas, the government may prohibit or regulate any activity and access or passage that may harm the natural environment.

774. Four possible types of protected areas are envisaged.

Large untouched or mainly untouched areas of natural habitat may be protected as *national parks* if they may be considered valuable for research purposes or for opportunities to experience Svalbard's natural and cultural heritage. Here, no activity is permitted that has a lasting effect on the natural environment or cultural heritage. The landscape and, if applicable, the seabed with plants, animal life and geological formations shall be protected against development, construction, pollution and other activities, including access and passage, that may affect or disturb the natural environment or cultural heritage (Article 16). In 2013 there are seven national parks on Svalbard covering some 35,000 km^2.

Untouched areas or largely untouched areas may be protected as *nature reserves* if they:

- contain distinctive or vulnerable ecosystems;
- comprise a special type of habitat or special geological formations; or
- are otherwise of special importance for the flora and fauna, or of special scientific interest.

A nature reserve may be given absolute protection (Article 17). There are nineteen nature reserves at Svalbard, including one on the island of Bjørnøya (Bear island) and one on Hopen Island.

775. Areas of particular importance to the flora or fauna or that contain important or distinctive geological formations may be given protected status as *biotopes or geotopes.* In such areas, activities that may affect or disturb the flora or fauna or damage geological formations contrary to the purpose of the protection measure shall be avoided (Article §18). So far (2013) one geotope has been protected.[757]

Areas of particular value in terms of cultural history may be protected as *cultural environments* (Article 19). In cultural environments, activities that may reduce the historical value of the area shall be avoided. The cultural values in other types of protected areas may be protected through the regulations of such areas.

The government may, by regulations, grant a protected area special status under an international Convention on the protection of the natural environment or cultural heritage. The effect of this status under the Convention in question shall also apply as Norwegian law (Article 20).

776. In protected areas the Governor for Svalbard may carry out any management considered necessary for the adequate protection and make arrangements to give people access and enable them to experience the natural environment and cultural heritage within the framework of the objectives of the protection measure (Article 21).

When scientific or other special reasons so indicate, the environmental protection authorities may grant exemptions from a protection decision provided that this does not conflict with the objectives of the protection decision and will not have a significant impact on the conservation value of the area. The reasons for the decision shall include an account of how the environmental protection authorities have evaluated the impact that the exemption may have on the environment, and the weight that has been attached to this (Article 22).

757. Regulation of 26 Sep. 2003 No. 1190 on protection of the Festningen geotop area on Svalbard.

IV. Protection of Flora and Fauna

777. The provisions of the Act concerning *the protection of flora and fauna* (Chapter IV) apply to all species of flora and fauna on land and in the sea, with the exception of saltwater fish, crustaceans, and marine mammals that do not show site fidelity in Svalbard (Article 23).

The Act states, as a general principle, that the flora and fauna on land and in the sea shall be managed in such a manner that the natural productivity and diversity of species and their habitats are maintained, and Svalbard's natural wilderness is protected for future generations. Controlled and limited harvesting may take place within this framework (Article 24). The Act lays down a general protection principle: All species of flora and fauna, including their eggs, nests and lairs, are protected unless otherwise provided by the Act (Article 25).

778. The *import of live specimens* of wild flora and fauna that are established or that can become established in the wild in Svalbard may only take place in accordance with a permit issued by the Ministry or under regulations. This provision also applies to the roe and eggs of such species (Article 26). Contrary to the other rules on flora and fauna, this provision also applies to saltwater fish, crustaceans, and marine mammals that do not show site fidelity in Svalbard (Article 23(2)). The Act itself and a regulation pursuant to the Act (and several other Acts) makes it clear that the national rules which implement the CITES also apply to Svalbard.[758]

Without the permission of the environmental protection authorities, no person may introduce species of flora or fauna that do not already occur naturally in Svalbard, move indigenous species of flora or fauna, or initiate measures for the cultivation of species of flora or fauna, including releasing such flora or fauna on land or in river systems, fjords or the sea (Article 27). This provision as well applies also to saltwater fish, crustaceans, and marine mammals that do not show site fidelity in Svalbard.

779. *It is prohibited to damage or remove flora,* except as a normal result from lawful access and passage or approved activities (Article 28). The collection of fungi and seaweed for private use is permitted. The collection of flora for research or teaching purposes is permitted where this does not make significant inroads into the local populations of the flora involved (Article 29).

780. Article 30 establishes general rules regarding the protection of *Svalbard's fauna*. It is generally prohibited to hunt, capture, injure or kill fauna or damage eggs, nests or lairs unless so authorized by the provisions of the Act. Damage to or killing of single-celled animals and invertebrates as a result of lawful access or passage or approved activities, and by catches taken during lawful fishing operations, are however explicitly allowed. No person may use ships' sirens, fire shots or produce other loud noises within one nautical mile of a *seabird colony* between 1 April and 31 August.

758. Regulation of 15 Jun. 2018 No. 889 on import, export and possession of endangered species of wild fauna and flora (CITES Regulation).

The killing of *polar bears* is generally prohibited pursuant to a special Act.[759] For Svalbard the provisions of the Svalbard Environmental Act apply instead. These go further by stating that it is prohibited also to lure, pursue or otherwise seek out polar bears in such a way as to disturb them or expose either bears or humans to danger (Article 30 paragraph 4). A special Article (Article 30a) lays down a duty to be prepared to meet attacks of polar bear, including having knowledge of the danger and having means to chase an attacking bear. There have been several fatal accidents and dangerous incidents during the last years when polar bears have attacked people.

A general regulation lays down more detailed rules for the management of wildlife and freshwater fish on Svalbard, hunting, fishing, etc.[760]

781. Harvesting of fauna, including hunt, catch and fishing, and collection of eggs and down, is only permitted pursuant to further regulations. Regulations must give due consideration to ensuring that harvesting does not significantly alter the composition and development of the stocks in question (Article 31). Regulations to this effect were adopted in 2002.[761]

Article 32 draws up further rules for the harvesting. The right to harvest is in principle free. Any person over the age of 16 has the right to harvest fauna and to collect eggs and down in accordance with the regulations. However, the Ministry may, for particular species, issue regulations to the effect that they may only be harvested by permanent residents or with the permission of the Governor of Svalbard.

In the past, Svalbard was a very important area for fur trapping, especially the fur of the polar fox and the polar bear. This activity has been drastically reduced over the last few decades, but some activity still exists. The Governor may grant wildlife trappers who spend winters in trappers' cabins the exclusive right to harvest certain species within a defined area and during a defined time period. The Governor may prescribe regulations regarding the allocation of trapping areas with exclusive harvesting rights (Article 32).

782. Animals may be killed in circumstances where this is considered necessary to eliminate an immediate *risk of injury* to persons or prevent substantial material damage. The Governor may issue permits to kill animals that remain near permanent or temporary settlements, and that represent a risk of injury to people or significant material damage. Animals may only be killed in accordance with such permits if a reasonable effort has been made to use other measures to prevent injury or damage (Articles 33 and 34).

In areas that are open for general access and passage, dogs must be controlled in an appropriate manner when not on a leash.

---

759. Act of 22 Mar. 1957 No. 4.

760. Regulation of 11 Aug. 1978 No. 3765 on the management of wildlife and freshwater fish on Svalbard and Jan Mayen pursuant to the Svalbard Act, with subsequent amendments.

761. According to Regulation of 24 Jun. 2002 No. 712 on harvesting on Svalbard the special Svalbard reindeer, the mountain fox, several bird species and seal species may be hunted parts of the year.

V. Cultural Heritage

783. The Act contains rules concerning the protection of cultural heritage, which to a large extent is in accordance with the general Norwegian legislation in this field and also contains special rules due to the special historic activities and heritage on Svalbard.

784. It is stated explicitly that historical structures and sites, and movable objects, in Svalbard shall be protected and safeguarded as a part of Svalbard's cultural heritage and identity and as an element of a coherent system of environmental management (Article 38). It is generally prohibited to remove from Svalbard protected cultural heritage that is found or originated in Svalbard. In special cases, the Directorate may authorize export (Article 46).

The Act makes a distinction between fixed and movable objects, and between objects that are automatically protected pursuant to the Act, and objects which are protected by a special decision. Movable objects belong to the State, unless other ownership is documented (Article 43).

785. Structures and sites, and as a rule other elements of cultural heritage, dating from 1945 or earlier, are *automatically protected* by the Act (Article 39). For example, the simple huts that belonged to the earlier trappers of fox and polar bear are now protected. Graveyards and individual graves for humans, and pieces of skeletons on the surface, are protected regardless of time of origin. The same goes for skeleton remnants on slaughtering sites for whales and walrus. Included in an automatically protected object is a safety zone of 100 m unless otherwise decided by the Governor. Sites and objects that are automatically protected must not be harmed, unearthed, moved or removed, changed, or hidden. It is also prohibited to create a risk of such effects (Article 42). It is also prohibited to make a fire safety zone and to set up a tent when the ground is not covered by snow. Tents on frozen and snowy fields are nevertheless allowed in the safety zone.

786. Cultural heritage sites and objects with special historic value from after 1945 may be individually *protected by a decision* by the Directorate for Cultural Heritage. This may include an area around the object which is necessary to preserve the value of it in its environment. If the circumstances make it necessary, a temporary protection may be laid down in order to have the values fully clarified and the permanent protection properly assessed and prepared (Article 40).

787. When an activity or undertaking is planned, the promoter shall at his own expense examine whether it will negatively affect automatically protected cultural heritage in a manner as mentioned in Article 42 (Article 44). The Directorate shall decide as soon as possible whether, and in what manner, the project may be implemented. If it appears while project work is underway that it may have an effect on an automatically protected cultural heritage in violation of section 42, the Governor shall be notified and the work shall be suspended. In that case the Directorate decides as soon as possible if the work can continue and the conditions for it.

Finds that appear during investigations and excavations or during the operation shall be documented and preserved at the expense of the promoter. Found objects shall be delivered within one year, unless the Governor extends the deadline.

The Directorate may in exceptional cases make exceptions to decisions on conservation and conservation measures for activities or projects that do not entail significant interventions in the protected site or object.

The Act (Article 44) provides the Directorate and the Governor with the necessary general authority and possibilities to carry out investigations and documentation, and take other necessary measures to protect cultural heritage objects and sites.

VI. Land-Use Planning

788. Rules for the land-use planning system in Svalbard are laid down in *Chapter VI of the Svalbard Environment Act*. The system follows and mirrors in several ways the main pattern of land-use planning on the mainland pursuant to the PBA, which will be described in detail in the following Part III. However, land-use planning is simpler in Svalbard than on the mainland since the land generally belongs to the State. The system applies not in the entire land area of Svalbard but only in certain areas defined by the King in regulations ('planning areas') (Article 47).[762] Furthermore, while the main system on the mainland includes several types of plans (regional plan, municipal master plan, and local development plan), there is only one type of plan in the Svalbard system, simply called 'land-use plan'. The landowner, or an another actor authorized by the Ministry, is responsible for the planning in each planning area, and shall carry out a current planning for the use and protection of the land in the area (Article 48). New activities, including construction, building, demolition, digging, landfilling, and other utilization of resources, shall be in accordance with the purpose of the land-use and the supplementary provisions laid down in an approved land-use plan (Article 53). Settlements and commercial activities shall as a general rule be located in the planning areas, and in such a way that adverse environmental impact is minimized (Article 56).

789. Each planning area must have a land-use plan with supplementary provisions showing existing and future land-use for the entire planning area (Article 49). The level of detail may vary by specific need to control land-use. The plan, or parts of it, may be revised as conditions require it. At least every four years the plan authority should consider whether a revision should be undertaken.

The plan must adequately and in a precise way define and map areas for the various purposes such as development of areas for housing or economic activities, cabins, areas for cultural heritage, nature protection and recreation, areas for extraction of raw materials, research, roads and other infrastructure for communication, risk areas, areas for the management of sea areas and waterways, including special or combined areas for transport, fishing, nature and recreation areas, and nature areas protected pursuant to Chapter III of the Act (*see supra*). Within the same area multiple purposes may have permitted.

762. Regulation of 28 Jun. 2002 No. 650 on EIA and delimitation of planning areas on Svalbard.

The plan shall describe how considerations for the environment (including the natural environment, cultural heritage and aesthetics) and the local communities (including safety and children's needs) are taken care of and whether – and how – the plan may have an impact on the environment outside the planning area.

The plan may contain supplementary provisions. These may either lay down legally binding terms for the use of the area, traffic, and for the shaping of the area and of buildings in the area or they may lay down guidelines for how the plan should be carried out.

790. The Act lays down quite detailed rules for the planning procedure (Article 50). The procedure is to be open and transparent. All interested parties shall have the opportunity to be informed and take an active part. The procedure goes through various stages, and there are public information and hearings on the way. When the final hearing of the proposal has been fulfilled, the responsible actor presents the final plan proposal to the Governor for adoption. The Governor may adopt the plan when there are no major objections not been taken into account. If there still are objections, the Governor may act as mediator to find a solution. If no solution is found, the Ministry decides on the matter. The Governor or the Ministry may also lay down temporary restrictions for a maximum of one year on activities when it is necessary to revise the land-use plan for a planning area or make the existing plan more precise and detailed (Article 54). The Ministry may also carry out and adopt a land-use plan when conditions make this necessary (Article 55).

VII. Activities That Have an Environmental Impact

791. A permit (licence) is required from Svalbard's environmental protection authorities for certain undertakings listed in the Act, both outside the land-use planning areas and within land-use planning areas where there is no approved land-use plan. This applies to any physical alteration of the terrain, activities that may cause pollution, hotels, guest-houses and other places that provide overnight accommodation for the general public, changes in existing facilities or their use if it changes the nature or effects of the facility on the natural environment, and in general, all activities that may put pressure on the environment in Svalbard, pursuant to further regulations (Article 57).

792. Comprehensive and detailed rules related to all aspects of pollution control, waste management, etc., are laid down in a special regulation.[763]

793. The responsible planning authority and the Governor for Svalbard must be notified of new undertakings *within a land-use planning area with an approved plan.* The notification shall provide sufficient information to indicate whether the activity or allocation is in accordance with the plan. The activity may be started

763. Regulation of 3 Jul. 2020 No. 1517 on pollution and waste on Svalbard.

three weeks after the receipt of notification, unless the activity conflicts with the terms of the land-use plan, or the Governor has laid down a temporary prohibition.[764]

A permit from the Governor is nevertheless required before the activity is started even if it complies with an approved land-use plan, if it could have a detrimental effect on the natural environment or cultural heritage, as further described in Article 58.

If the activity is in conflict with the terms and regulations of the plan, it may not be started unless the plan is amended. The Governor may nevertheless grant permits for activities that conflict with the supplementary provisions to a plan.

794. The head of an undertaking is responsible for the carrying out of an *EIA* for activities that require permits under the Act, provided that it may have more than an insignificant effect on the natural environment outside land-use planning areas, or may have a significant and long-term effect on the environment inside a land-use planning area (Article 59). The EIA shall elucidate the effects of the enterprise on the environment in order to provide a basis for evaluating and taking a decision on the application. The Act lays down further rules regarding the impact assessment procedure, and more detailed rules are laid down in a regulation.[765]

The grounds for a decision shall indicate how the environmental impact statement and any comments received have been evaluated, and the importance attached to them in arriving at the decision (Article 61 paragraph 1).

A permit should include conditions that are designed to satisfy the purpose of the Act, such as conditions relating to the provision of security for the costs of cleanup operations in case of an accidental pollution, which is explicitly mentioned (Article 61 paragraph 2).

The head of an undertaking shall carry out regular and effective monitoring of the environment, as laid down in the licence (Article 62).

795. The Act includes provisions which give the Governor authority to *alter or withdraw a permit* or the conditions on which it was issued, if there are good reasons for this. The rules on these issues follow the same lines as the corresponding rules in the PCA Article 18 (*see* Part I, §2) (Article 63).

A permit may in any case be withdrawn if it is more than ten years since the decision was made. A permit that has not been used lapses five years after it was issued.

796. If an activity is *closed down or discontinued,* the head of the undertaking shall take the necessary steps to prevent environmental damage (Article 64). If the activity could cause environmental damage after it is closed down or discontinued, the Governor shall be given reasonable prior notice of this.

When an activity or parts thereof are discontinued, the head of the undertaking shall at his/her own expense remove from the area all surface installations, all waste and other remains that are not protected structures and sites pursuant to the rules on

764. The Governor may lay down a temporary prohibition of a maximum of one year pursuant to Art. 54, if he or she finds it necessary to change a plan or make it more detailed.

765. Regulation of 28 Jun. 2002 No. 650 on EIA and delimitation of planning areas on Svalbard.

cultural heritage. The area shall so far as possible be restored to its original condition. The Governor may prescribe what measures to be taken, including whether polluted soil should be treated. The Act provides further details on this duty.

Abandoned vehicles, vessels, aircraft, and the like must be removed by the owner.

The Governor may grant exemptions from the duty to clean up pursuant to this section.

797. A special section of the Act (Chapter VII section ii) contains *rules on pollution*. This is based on the same principles as the PCA (*see supra* Part I, Chapter 1, §2). No person may possess, do or initiate anything that may entail a risk of pollution unless this is lawful pursuant to the Act. The detailed rules on pollution control are laid down in the above-mentioned regulation on pollution and waste on Svalbard.[766] This regulation also covers collection and treatment of waste, including hazardous waste and waste from ships,

If there is a danger of illegal pollution, the person responsible for the activity shall ensure that measures are taken to prevent such pollution. The environmental protection authorities may issue orders regarding such measures. If pollution has already occurred, the person responsible shall take the necessary measures to limit the effects and restore the environment so far as possible to its natural condition (Articles 65 and 93).

798. Any release of *environmentally hazardous substances* into the environment is prohibited, except for traces of hazardous substances in ordinary discharges from household activities, and so on (Article 66). The Ministry may grant exemptions from this prohibition for existing commercial enterprises.

The Ministry may decide that certain products that contain hazardous substances may not be imported to or used in Svalbard.

It is also prohibited to release waste into the sea from a ship or other vessels. The Regulation Article 9-1 lays down an obligation for the port authorities of Longyearbyen to establish necessary reception facilities for waste from ships. However, the discharge of uncontaminated waste food from small vessels or of sanitary wastewater in the open sea is permitted (Article 67). The dumping and incineration of waste or other materials from ships or other vessels is prohibited. The Ministry may issue regulations containing exceptions from the prohibition against dumping (Article 68).

The Governor or the person so authorized by the Ministry may make an order requiring buildings inside a land-use planning area to be connected to a wastewater treatment plant. The Ministry may determine who shall have a duty to operate wastewater treatment plants and associated sewer systems (Article 69).

799. Any person engaged in an activity that could result in *accidental pollution* shall provide the necessary emergency response system to prevent, detect, stop, remove or limit the impact of such pollution. The Ministry may order the person responsible for the activity to submit contingency plans for approval. Further conditions for the approval of contingency plans may be laid down.

---

766. Regulation of Jul. 2020 No. 1517.

In the event of acute pollution or the risk of acute pollution, the person responsible shall notify the Governor without delay. Other persons also have a duty to provide notification unless this is clearly unnecessary (Article 70).

800. It is *prohibited to leave waste* outside a land-use planning area (Article 71). The Governor may in special cases grant exemptions from this prohibition. In land-use planning areas waste must be discarded or left only in places specifically designated for this purpose. Waste must be stored in such a way as to avoid it being spread. It is prohibited to import waste to Svalbard.

The regulations on waste laid down pursuant to the Act include rules and obligations with regard to collection, transport, reception, sorting and disposal of waste, that some types of waste shall be recycled or taken away for special treatment elsewhere.[767]

Regulations may also be issued relating to fees and annual charges for connection to sewerage systems and for the collection and disposal of waste. The Ministry may issue regulations relating to a waste tax to be levied on goods sold in Svalbard and to the total or partial refund of the tax on return of the packaging for such goods (Article 72).

VIII. Access and Passage, and Cabins

801. Access to and passage through Svalbard nature may in itself provide a threat to its vulnerable natural environment. These issues are sensitive, not least to the people who live permanently in Svalbard.

The Act states clearly that *the public right of access to and passage* in the natural environment, which applies on the mainland pursuant to customary law and the Outdoor Recreation Act (*see supra* §2), also applies in Svalbard. However, the Act implies certain limitations in this regard (Article 73 paragraph 1).

All access and passage in Svalbard shall take place in a way that does not harm, pollute or in any other way damage the natural environment or cultural heritage, or result in unnecessary disturbance to humans or animals (Article 73 paragraph 2).

802. The Governor may prohibit types of access and passage or modes of transport that put special pressure on the natural environment (Article 74). Outside protected areas, the Governor may prohibit or regulate access and passage in delimited areas throughout the year or at certain times of the year when this is considered necessary in order to protect the natural environment, cultural heritage, drinking water supply or scientific research (Article 75).

The Governor may also issue regulations governing camping activities. The regulations may decide that permission from the Governor is required if the period of stay exceeds a specified duration or the camp is larger than a specified size (Article 76).[768]

---

767. Regulation of 3 Jul. 2020 No. 1517 Part III, and Regulation of 11 Sep. 2009 No. 1188 on sorting and collection of waste and waste fees in Longyearbyen plan area.

768. *See* Regulation of 27 Jun. 2002 No. 731 on camping on Svalbard.

Operations of emergency and inspection activities pursuant to the Act may, if necessary, be carried out notwithstanding such limitations (Article 77).

The government may issue regulations on *fees payable by visitors* to Svalbard (Article 78).[769] The idea is that visitors should contribute to the work that needs to be done to prevent environmental damage and protect the special nature and valuable cultural heritage on Svalbard. The duty applies to visits to the land territory and internal waters. Permanent residents may not be charged such fees. The fees accrue to the Svalbard Environmental Protection Fund (*see infra*).

803. *Motor traffic,* in particular the off-road use of snow-scooters in nature areas, represents a special challenge. Here, various interests may conflict sharply. The Act states that motor traffic shall be regulated on the basis of overall considerations of the public interest and with a view to protecting Svalbard's natural environment (Article 79 paragraph 1).

Generally, motor traffic is prohibited except on roads or places constructed for this purpose unless otherwise provided for by the Act or regulations pursuant to the Act (Article 79 paragraph 2).

804. *Off-road motor* traffic on ground that is not snow-covered or on thawed ground is only permitted along special trails or for special purposes laid down by the Governor in regulations, or when there are special considerations and the Governor has issued a permit (Article 80).

Off-road motor traffic *on snow-covered and frozen ground* and on ice-covered watercourses and areas of sea may be permitted in areas and along trails prescribed by the Ministry by regulations, or for specific purposes or special reasons and the Governor has issued a permit on application. Such regulations 'shall ensure that permanent residents have more extensive rights to make use of motor traffic than visitors' (Article 81 paragraph 2).[770] Restrictions on permanent residents' motor traffic must be justified by the environmental considerations related to Svalbard or by the need to separate motor and non-motor traffic.

805. Motor traffic in *watercourses* is only lawful with the permission of the Governor (Article 82 paragraph 1). Motor traffic *at sea* may, however, take place in accordance with the general rules on access and passage at sea, unless otherwise provided in or pursuant to this Act. The Ministry may issue regulations relating to prohibition of the use of specific types of vessels, prescribe shipping lanes or areas where shipping is not permitted, speed limits and provisions regarding casting of anchor and landing. The regulations may differentiate between traffic for different purposes (Article 82 paragraph 4). The use of *water-scooters* are generally prohibited (Article 82 paragraph 3).

---

769. *See* Regulation of 22 Dec. 2006 No. 1532. The fee is (in 2021) NOK 150 per individual visit which has to be paid in connection with the travel ticket to Svalbard.

770. *See* Regulation of 24 Jun. 2002 No. 723 on use of motor vehicles and aeroplanes on Svalbard, with comments of 24 Jun. 2002.

In order to reduce air pollution from ships, ships that enter into the territorial waters around Svalbard must use types of light fuel further defined in regulation (Article 82a).

806. Motorized *air traffic* is also restricted. Aircraft may not land on ships or on the ground or water outside a landing strip that has been licensed or approved in accordance with the Air Traffic Act.[771] The Governor may on application grant exemptions from this. It is prohibited to fly an aircraft closer than 1 nautical mile from large known concentrations of mammals and birds.

The Governor may issue regulations relating to minimum flying altitudes for aircraft and to prohibitions on the use of aircraft for tourism purposes (Article 83).[772]

807. When the Governor decides whether to issue applications for permits for motor traffic, weight shall be attached to, *inter alia*, the risk of environmental damage from the traffic in question. The permit shall be limited in regard to time and place and may be restricted to apply to certain specified cases only. Conditions may be attached to the permit. The permit may be altered or withdrawn if environmental considerations so require (Article 84).

808. *Leisure cabins* may only be owned or rented by persons who are or have been permanently resident in Svalbard, or associations that have their headquarters in Svalbard and most of whose employees or members are permanent residents there. No person may own or rent more than two leisure cabins. The Governor may in special cases grant exemptions from these provisions (Article 85).

IX. Inspection and Control Measures

809. The Act (Articles 87–99) contains a number of rules concerning enforcement, inspection, control, the duty to provide information, sanctions and so on. Generally speaking, these are in accordance with similar sets of rules in the environmental legislation that applies to the mainland, in particular, the PCA. Partly, they provide the authorities with the authority to lay down further regulations or make individual decisions.

810. Article 93 states that:

> any person that has had an impact on the environment in Svalbard by contravening provisions established in or pursuant to the Act shall take the remedial action necessary to prevent further environmental impact and, if possible, to restore the environment to its original condition by appropriate action such as collection, clearing up, removal, the release of organisms, or levelling the ground.

771. Act of 11 Jun. 1993 No. 101.
772. Regulation of 24 Jun. 2002 No. 723.

However, this duty to take remedial action and to restore the environment does not apply insofar as it would be especially unreasonable in view of the cost and effect of the measures, the environmental impact of the contravention and the offender's fault and financial situation.

Within the framework of this section, the Governor may issue orders regarding the remedial and restoration measures that are to be carried out, including orders regarding the killing of living organisms to which the contravention applies or the return of living organisms or items of cultural heritage to their original location.

811. The Act (Article 98) establishes the *Svalbard Environmental Protection Fund.* The fund is financed through the special visitors tax, other duties, fines for contraventions, liability and the like as follows from various Articles of the Act. The fund shall only be used for protection measures at Svalbard, such as:

- studies and monitoring of the environmental situation, environmental effects of activities and so on;
- restitution of the environment;
- other measures to protect the natural or cultural environment;
- information and teaching activities.[773]

Items of flora and fauna that are collected, trapped or killed in contravention of this Act, or killed in accordance with section 33 paragraph 1 and section 34 become the property of the Svalbard Environmental Protection Fund. The same applies to wildlife or parts of wildlife found dead, and animals killed in the interest of animal welfare.

The Board of the Fund is appointed by the Ministry of Climate and Environment.

812. The Act includes a special section (Article 95) on tort liability, which reflects – 'in a nutshell' – the rules on liability for pollution damage in the PCA. Any person that causes environmental damage by contravening the provisions made in or pursuant to the Act is liable to pay compensation regardless of any fault on his/her part for economic loss resulting from the environmental damage, or from actions to prevent damage or restore the environment.

However, the Act goes further in the sense that it provides for compensation to be paid also for *damage to the environment as such*, regardless of economic loss. The Governor may order any person that by contravening the provisions established in or pursuant to the Act has caused appreciable environmental damage, to pay environmental compensation to the Svalbard Environmental Protection Fund. The amount of the environmental compensation to be paid is set on the basis of the value of what has been damaged, the extent and duration of the environmental damage, the fault of the offender, other sanctions imposed on the offender and general circumstances.

773. *See* for details Regulation of 30 Apr. 2007 No. 599 on grants from the Svalbard Environmental Protection Fund.

813. In order to ensure the implementation of the provisions of this Act or decisions taken pursuant to the Act, the Governor may impose *a coercive fine* payable to the Svalbard Environmental Protection Fund (Article 96).

Any person who wilfully or negligently contravenes the provisions laid down in or pursuant to the Act is subject to *penalties*: He or she faces fines or a term of imprisonment not exceeding one year. If a risk of substantial environmental damage has occurred or been caused, or if there are especially aggravating circumstances, a term of imprisonment not exceeding three years may be imposed. An accomplice is liable to the same penalties (Article 99).

814. The Governor may also order any person that wilfully or negligently contravenes the provisions of the Act to pay *a contravention charge* to the Svalbard Environmental Protection Fund. The Ministry may in regulations lay down further provisions on which contraventions may result in a contravention charge. A contravention charge may be imposed also on an enterprise if the contravention was committed by someone acting on behalf of the enterprise. This applies even if no contravention charge can be imposed on an individual person (Article 96a).

§5. ANTARCTICA

815. An important section of Antarctica, Queen Maud's Land, and two islands – Bouvet Island and Peter I Island – in the South Atlantic Ocean are Norwegian dependencies.[774] The background for this is the Norwegian expeditions to the area at the beginning of the twentieth century,[775] and the extensive whaling activities by Norwegian vessels which lasted until the 1960s. Norway thus shares the international responsibility for the protection of the environment in Antarctica.

A special and comprehensive Regulation deals with the protection of the environment and safety in Antarctica.[776] It implements the 1991 Protocol on Environmental Protection to the Antarctic Treaty,[777] which has been ratified by Norway.

The objective of the regulation is to protect the environment in Antarctica and its ecosystems, its intrinsic value including wilderness areas and aesthetic values, and to preserve the value of the area for scientific research. All activities in Antarctica shall be carried out in a safe and self-contained way (Article 1).

The regulation applies to the whole geographical area south of the latitude of 60 degrees south, and not only to the Norwegian dependencies. It applies to this area for Norwegian citizens, companies, vessels and aeroplanes, and to foreign citizens living in Norway or taking part in Norwegian expeditions to the area. However, in the Norwegian dependencies Queen Maud's Land and on Peter I Island it applies to everybody who stays there or is responsible for activities there. However, it does not apply to fishery activities and vessels on the high seas (Regulation Article 2).

774. Act of 27 Feb. 1930 No. 3.
775. The Norwegian Roald Amundsen was the first to reach the South Pole, in December 1911.
776. Regulation of 26 Apr. 2013 No. 412 on environmental protection and safety in Antarctica, pursuant to the Act of 27 Feb. 1930 No. 3.
777. The Antarctic Treaty of 1 Dec. 1959.

816. The general principle of the regulation is that all activities in Antarctica shall be planned and carried out in such a way as to minimize the effects on the Antarctic environment and the ecosystems that depend on it, so that its value for scientific research is preserved (Article 5). Activities must not have negative effect on, *inter alia,* the climate, the quality of air and water, the stocks and productivity of fauna and flora, areas of biological, scientific, historical or aesthetic importance, or the wilderness character of the area. Activities related to mineral resources are prohibited.

817. Collection of, and harmful influence on, flora or fauna, including harmful transport, is prohibited (Article 18). Import of species requires a permit from Norwegian Polar Institute. Import of dogs is prohibited (Article 19).

Waste shall be removed from Antarctica unless it can be burned properly in an environmentally satisfactory way (Article 21). It is prohibited to discharge substances or products which may harm the Antarctic environment (Article 22). Existing waste dumps and left installations must be cleaned up by the person that caused it. Norwegian Polar Institute may give exceptions to this if the possible harm by destroying it exceeds the environmental benefits (Article 24).

The Regulation also lays down clear rules for the handling of a pollution accident and for liability for damage (Chapter 7, Articles 26–32). The general rule is strict and several liability for damage. For accidents which are not linked to shipping, there is a liability limitation of 3 million Special Drawing Right (SDR) (Article 31). For spills and discharge from ships the rules in the Maritime Act[778] Chapter 9 apply (*see supra* Part I, Chapter 3, §3 II). The condition is that the owner falls under the limitation rules in the Maritime Act Article 171. For other cases, the Regulation itself lays down special liability limitation rules in Article 31.

818. Certain areas may be protected as *'Antarctic Specially Protected Areas' (ASPA)* in order to protect particularly valuable nature and wilderness areas, and areas of special scientific, historical or aesthetic value, or a combination of such values. Anybody planning a stay in Antarctica has a duty to know of such areas (Article 33).[779]

Areas with activities or planned activities may be designated as *'Antarctic Specially Managed Areas' (ASMA)*, where there may be special rules for planning and coordination of activities, cooperation between the actors, prevention of environmental effects, and so on (Article 34).[780]

Historic places and registered cultural heritage (*'Historic Sites and Monuments'*)[781] must not be hurt, destroyed or removed (Article 35). The rules in the Cultural Heritage Act[782] on export, import and return of illegally exported items apply.

778. Act of 24 Jun. 1994 No. 39.
779. In 2021 there were altogether seventy-five ASPAs in Antarctica.
780. In 2021 there were six ASMAs in Antarctica.
781. There are more than eighty registered Historic Sites and Monuments in Antarctica.
782. Act of 8 Jun. 1978 No. 50.

819. Information on any planned scientific, tourist or other activities shall be given to the relevant authority, Norwegian Polar Institute, at least one year before the activity is to take place. Anybody who plans an activity shall carry out a preliminary EIA (Article 16). If this shows that the activity will have more than insignificant or short-term effects on the environment, a full EIA must be carried out. The regulation gives detailed guidelines of what an EIA must include (Article 17). There is also a general obligation to have proper contingency plans for possible pollution accidents and accidents that may cause danger to health and life (Articles 10 and 11). The responsible has to have a proper insurance or guarantee for any economic responsibility that may arise because of accidents, rescue operations and so on. Norwegian Polar Institute decides the necessary insurance or guarantee sum (Article 12). The Institute also has the authority to decide on changes in the planned activity, and even prohibit it if this is necessary in order to avoid unacceptable environmental or other effects (Article 13). Decisions by the institute may be appealed.

The Regulation also lays down rules on duties of information, monitoring, and reporting, and on violations of the rules. A person who by intent or negligence contravenes rules in or pursuant to the Regulation may be punished to fines or a maximum of one year's imprisonment, or both (Article 40).

Part III. Spatial Planning

Chapter 1. General

§1. General Overview

820. Spatial planning is regarded as an important instrument in Norwegian environmental policy and law. The main Act in this field, *the PBA,*[783] is often referred to as 'the most important environmental act' in the country. Mainly through the land-use planning system and building control pursuant to this act, construction and other uses of land are strictly controlled in Norway. The Act was adopted in 2008.[784] It builds on earlier acts and a long tradition of urban and regional planning in the country, with roots in legislation from the first half of the nineteenth century.

821. This Act establishes a system of *comprehensive social, economic, cultural and spatial planning* in the counties and the municipalities, with the active participation of State authorities. The plans serve as guidelines for activities and decisions of municipal, county and State authorities within the plan area. Furthermore, land-use plans at the municipal level are legally binding for the landowner's future use of his/her land. They are the basis for decisions on building permits.

The regional and land-use planning pursuant to the PBA is part of the responsibilities of the Ministry of Local Government and Regional Development.[785]

822. The rules on buildings and other constructions, and on *the building permit system,* are included in this Act and regulations pursuant to the Act. Any new construction or other changes in the use of land need a municipal building permission. As the main rule, permission must be given if the building or construction is in full accordance with the land-use plan for the area, as well as with other rules in the Act or in regulations. If this is not the case, the municipality may refuse to give permission. In special cases, a permit may nevertheless be issued as an exemption, on the basis of the general exemption clause in Chapter 19 of the Act.

---

783. Act of 27 Jun. 2008 No. 71.
784. Based on a comprehensive public report: Norwegian Official Reports (NOU) 2003:14. The report was prepared by the governmental 'Planning Law Commission' which was chaired by this author.
785. Until 2014, the MCE was the responsible ministry for urban, regional and land-use planning.

823. Besides establishing the system for comprehensive regional and land-use planning, and building permission, the PBA has certain rules aiming directly at the protection of the environment.

The most important is *the general prohibition to build less than 100 m from the sea.* This is laid down in Article 1-8 of the Act. In this zone, special consideration must be given to the natural and cultural environment, outdoor recreation, landscape and other public interests. The general rule is that all types of constructions and buildings, including enclosures, are prohibited in this zone.

However, there are important exceptions to this rule. The rule is superseded by the area designation and regulation in a municipal master plan or a local development plan (*see infra*). Such plans may open the 100 m zone for development. In addition, the municipality may issue an individual exemption on the basis of the general exemption clause in Chapter 19.

824. In addition to the PBA, there are a number of *special Acts* of importance for the use of land. The most important are presented in Part II above. Some of these Acts are formally linked to the PBA. Plans which are approved according to the PBA either replace decisions according to the sectoral Act or serve as basis for such decisions. In other areas, no such link has been formally established. In that case, several Acts may apply more or less independently of each other.

§2. Purpose and General Principles of Planning According to the PBA

825. The *objective* of the PBA is expressed in its Article 1-1. The overall objective is 'to promote sustainable development for the benefit of individuals, society and future generations'. Planning according to the Act serves to coordinate the activities of the State, counties and municipalities. It shall provide a basis for decisions about the use as well as the protection of natural resources, and for development. The system of building permissions shall ensure that all constructions are in accordance with Acts and regulations. It is further explicitly stated in Article 1-1 that the Act shall ensure transparency, predictability, and participation by interested parties and authorities. It shall promote long-term solutions, and environmental and social impacts must be assessed. It shall also promote and ensure aesthetic values and the interests of children and youth. For disabled people, the principle of design for universal accessibility shall be taken into account in planning and in requirements relating to individual building projects, in particular with regard to access into houses.

826. The Act applies to *the whole mainland territory, including watercourses and the underground* (Article 1-2). It also applies to coastal waters inside of 1 nautical mile (1,852 m) from the 'baseline'. This is the line drawn between the uttermost islands and skerries along the coast which forms the basis for the 12-mile border for territorial waters and the 200-mile border of the EEZ. However, in this area, pipelines in the sea for the transport of petroleum are exempted from its field of application, as they are regulated by the Petroleum Act[786] (Article 1-3).

The Act does not apply to Svalbard. Land-use and land-use planning on Svalbard are regulated by special rules in the Svalbard Environment Act (*see supra*). However, the system for Svalbard is based on the system in PBA, although somewhat simplified.

827. Within the overall purposes of the Act, its Article 3-1 lists a number of '*functions and considerations*' for the planning pursuant to the Act. Plans shall:

(a) establish goals for the physical, environmental, economic, social and cultural development of municipalities and regions; identify social needs and functions, and state how these functions can be discharged;
(b) safeguard land resources, landscape qualities and the conservation of valuable landscapes and cultural environments;
(c) protect the natural basis for Sami culture, economic activity and social life;
(d) facilitate value creation, industrial and commercial development, and sufficient housing construction;
(e) facilitate the good design of developed surroundings, good housing environments and good childhood environments and living standards in all parts of the country;
(f) promote public health and counteract social inequalities in health, and help to prevent crime;
(g) take climate considerations by reducing emissions of greenhouse gases and adapting to expected climate change, *inter alia*, through solutions for energy, land-use and transport;
(h) promote societal safety by preventing the risk of loss of life, injury to health, and damage to the environment and important infrastructure, material assets, etc.;
(i) arrange for a holistic management of the water circulation with necessary infrastructure.

Planning shall be based on financial and other resource-related prerequisites for implementation and shall not be more exhaustive than necessary. Plans shall contribute to the implementation of international conventions and treaties within the scope of the Act. Adopted plans shall serve as a common basis for municipal, regional, central government and private-sector activity in the field of planning.

828. The PBA establishes a system of *comprehensive societal and spatial planning* – and approved plans – at regional/county and municipal levels. The plans are meant to cover all important sectors of society. Hence, the Act does not only apply to the planning of land-use. It is meant to cover broadly economic, social and cultural, as well as environmental planning.

786. Act of 29 Nov. 1996 No. 72.

One may describe the system as a *hierarchy of plans*. Regional plans shall serve as guidelines for sector and municipal plans. General municipal master plans (*kommuneplan*) draw up the main lines of the land-use and the framework for sector planning within the municipality, as well as for more detailed land-use plans called local development plans (*reguleringsplan*).

Nevertheless, the system is rather flexible. For example, the municipal planning authority may approve a local development plan even if it deviates from the general municipal plan, provided that the various State and county authorities also find the solution acceptable. Furthermore, regional plans and municipal master plans shall be reviewed, and may be modified, every fourth year.

829. The planning is the responsibility of the *highest political bodies* in the counties and the municipalities: the county council for regional planning (Article 3-4) and the local (municipal) council for municipal planning (Article 3-3). These bodies also formally adopt the plans. Thus, the planning is clearly defined as a political task and an important element in the Norwegian local democracy. The practical planning work is usually left to the administration in the counties and municipalities. However, an important aspect of the planning system is that *all public authorities* at the municipal, county and State levels, which have an interest in the planning, have both the right and the duty to participate in the planning and provide information and assistance to the planning authorities (Article 3-2).

830. The Act provides the State with various instruments to influence this planning. *State regulations and policy guidelines provide an important basis* for the regional and municipal planning. If necessary, the State may itself initiate, organize and carry out the planning, and also adopt municipal land-use plans (Article 3-5–3-7, and Chapter 6).

831. Public participation is both an important planning method and an objective in itself. Comprehensive rules on participation are laid down in Chapter 5. The planning authorities at all levels have a duty to actively inform the public about planning activities, from an early stage. Individuals and groups with interests in the planning, and the public at large, shall be duly informed about planning activities and the preparations of plans and have the opportunity to participate (Article 5-1 and 5-2). In particular, the municipality must work to ensure participation by weak groups where special efforts are needed, such as children and young people. For detailed land-use plans, the landowners and other rightholders have special rights, and must be directly informed and consulted.

There are specific rules on public information and participation for each type of plan. Planning proposals have to be made known and available for all citizens. Everybody may voice his/her opinions. When a proposal is made known, the public must be told whether there are alternatives to the proposal (Article 4-1). When a plan is adopted, it has to be made publicly known.

832. Rules on EIAs are included in the Act (Chapters 4 and 14) (for details, *see supra* General Introduction, Chapter 2, §4). The rules implement, in combination, the two EU directives on EIA and strategic environmental assessment (SEA).[787]

Chapter 4 describes the general procedure for the preparations of plans pursuant to the Act. A 'planning programme' must be prepared and laid down for each planning process. In *regional and municipal land-use plans* (master plans), which open areas for development, an SEA/EIA must always be included in the 'planning programme' and carried out as part of the planning procedure. *Local development plans* must include an SEA/EIA if the plan may have 'significant' environmental or social effects. The criterion 'significant effect' is clarified for the different types of activity in the EIA Regulation.[788]

Chapter 14 applies to projects which do not require a plan and are not included in a plan. However, the EIA Regulation applies similarly to projects as with regard to local development plans.

833. Often, there are *conflicts of interests between various public authorities.* In particular, this may be the case when it comes to future use of land, watercourses and other natural resources.

According to the Act, the municipality is the main land-use planning authority. Municipal master plans and local development plans are legally binding and thus decisive for future land-use. However, there may be important national or regional interests involved in the land-use, and State, as well as county authorities and neighbouring municipalities, must have a say. This is most relevant in relation to questions concerning natural resources and the environment. Here, local preferences and various national and regional priorities may differ.

If a municipality does not submit to views presented by a county or State authority, these *may raise formal 'objections' to the plan* on issues of national or considerable regional significance, and otherwise on issues of principle. Similarly, other municipalities may raise formal objection to a municipal plan if it is on issues of considerable significance for their inhabitants. Also, the Sami Parliament may raise objections on issues of significant importance to Sami culture or economic activities. In these cases, mediation between the parties shall take place at the county level. If no solution is found, the issue will as a last resort be decided by the Ministry of Local Government and Regional Development, if necessary, after consultation with other ministries. The Ministry may make such changes in the plan as it finds necessary. The Act lays down quite detailed rules on the application of 'objections' (Article 5-4–5-6).

If a municipal land-use plan is contrary to national interests or a regional plan, the Ministry may on its own initiative annul the plan wholly or partly or make such changes in it as are found necessary, even if there are no formal objections to the plan from other authorities.[789]

---

787. Directive 85/337/EEC with several later amendments and consolidated in Directive 2014/52/EU, and Directive 2001/42/EC.
788. Regulation of 21 Jun. 2017 No. 854. It combines the implementation of the two relevant EU directives. *See supra* General Information, Ch. 2, § 4.
789. This follows from Art. 11-16 and Art. 12-13.

834. In the following, the various plans and mechanisms of the Act will be presented and discussed, in particular, as instruments for the management and protection of the environment.

§3. Planning at the Municipal Level

I. The General Municipal Plan (Master Plan)

835. The municipality has a duty to develop and adopt a *'municipal plan'* (*kommuneplan*). This is a comprehensive plan for the future activities within the municipality. It shall, in principle, cover all sectors and activities within the municipality, and thus serve to coordinate its environmental, economic, social and cultural development. It shall define long-term objectives for the development of the municipality and for each sector, and an action programme for the coming years (Article 11-1). The action programme is usually closely linked to the economic plan of the municipality.

An important part of the municipal plan is the long-term land-use plan (master plan) (Article 11-5–11-18, *see infra*). This lays down legally binding restrictions on future construction and other forms of land-use.

As the main rule, a municipal plan should cover all activities and the whole area of the municipality. However, the municipality may also adopt plans that apply to only one or a few sectors, or cover only a part of its territory (kommunedelplan).

Several municipalities may cooperate and develop a coordinated plan across municipal borders. The Act has a special chapter on cooperation between municipalities in planning (Chapter 9).

836. A municipal plan has no clear time limit. However, the Act prescribes that each local council within its first year after an election shall adopt a *municipal planning strategy* (Chapter 10). This shall review the existing plan, assess the need for changes in the plan and identify special issues which may require attention, and new planning initiatives. This will be the basis for the municipality's further planning activities. If no changes are needed, the existing plan will serve during the full four-year election period.

837. The land-use part of the *municipal plan – the 'master plan' – is the most important legal instrument for the control of land-use.* It is meant to be a long-term plan for the spatial development in the municipality. It is based on a principle of *zoning*. In the plan, different areas of the municipality are designated for specific purposes, such as areas for future housing development, industry, public services, infrastructure, military activities and so on, as well as agricultural and nature areas that shall be protected from development (Article 11-7).

Supplementary provisions, as explicitly listed in the Act, may be adopted either for the plan area in general (Article 11-9), for each of the various area categories (Article 11-10 and 11-11), or for special zones that may cut across the different area categories (Article 11-8). However, there are formal limitations to what may be decided in a master plan. Many questions of detail have instead to be decided either through a local development plan (*see infra*) or through decisions of sector authorities based on sector legislation.

838. The intention is that the master plan draws up *the main pattern of future development* and land-use in the municipality. The main categories of zones are defined in Article 11-7 and are areas for the following objectives: construction, transport infrastructure, parks ('green structures'), defence, 'agriculture, nature, outdoor recreation and reindeer herding', and areas for use and protection of the sea and watercourses, including the adjacent shoreline. Each of these main categories may be divided and specified into more precise 'sub-categories'.

Furthermore, the rules open the possibility for the municipality in addition to specifying the designation of land-use with regard to purpose, also issue rather detailed rules and restrictions for building activities in the master plan. Thus, to a considerable extent, a master plan gives specific directives, and may even serve directly as the basis for decisions of building permits.

839. Here, we touch on a crucial issue: *the legal effects of a master plan.* Generally speaking, an adopted master plan shall serve as the basis for subsequent public planning and decision-making within the municipality (Article 11-6). As such, it is addressed to State and county, as well as municipal authorities. It also guides the private sector in its planning of future development activities.

The plan determines the possible future use of the various areas within the municipality. This is its main legal effect. It is a *legally binding* plan: any new construction, building and other new activities related to the use of land must be in accordance with the purpose of the area as defined by the plan, including supplementary regulations. In areas where no local development plan has been adopted, the master plan will serve as basis for decisions on building permits. A building permit will normally not be issued to a building or construction which is not in accordance with the plan and its supplementary regulations.

However, the plan does not in itself require any changes in *the present land-use.* A landowner may continue the actual use of his/her piece of land, even if the plan designates it with a different purpose. If the municipality wants to change the existing land-use, a local development plan is the adequate instrument because such a plan may serve as a basis for expropriation (*see infra*).

Unless it is decided otherwise, a new master plan sets aside already existing land-use plans for the area, including existing local development plans and building plans (Articles 1–5). Most often, however, such plans are maintained. It may also set aside the general prohibition to build in the 100 m zone along the sea pursuant to Article 1-8.

840. A *master plan may have a binding effect in relation to planning and decisions pursuant to some sector legislation.* It is of particular importance in this respect that the plan is decisive for the application of the Agricultural Land Act.[790] Unless explicitly decided otherwise, this Act does not apply in areas designated for

790. Act of 12 May 1995 No. 23. This follows from Art. 2 of that Act.

development in an approved master plan, or in areas where scattered homes and recreational houses are accepted. This means that the agricultural authorities cannot subsequently interfere in development projects in such areas by requiring an application pursuant to the Agricultural Land Act, which otherwise is required on agricultural land (*see* Part II, Chapter 4). Similar effects apply in relation to the Cultural Heritage Act.[791] As regards forestry, the Forestry Act applies even in areas designated for other purposes unless it has been explicitly exempted pursuant to the plan or regulations in question.[792]

841. Even if the municipal master plan restricts a landowner's future use of his/her property, and often prohibits building and other developments on the land, the landowner has *no right of appeal* of the approved plan. This is stated explicitly in the Act (Article 11-15). Neither will he/she normally have the right to compensation for his/her possible economic loss, due to lost construction opportunities. This is in accordance with the general principles of compensation for regulations in Norwegian constitutional law (*see supra* General Introduction, Chapter 2, §1).

842. The master plan is an important instrument for *the protection of the environment.* It is a tool that may prevent a piecemeal land development and degradation of valuable natural areas, and that may ensure that certain environmental values are properly taken into account and protected. This may be done through the zoning system and through restrictions included in the plan. For example, rules and restrictions can be laid down with the purpose to ensure environmental quality, aesthetics, nature, landscape and 'green areas' (Article 11-9). Furthermore, valuable nature may be protected though proper zoning. To some extent, this is possible in areas designated as 'Area for agriculture, nature, outdoor recreation and reindeer herding' which is one of the main area categories in the master plan system (Article 11-7 No. 5 and 11-11).

However, in such areas, a more precise designation – for example, into separate areas for agriculture, nature protection and recreation – is not possible. The reasoning behind this is that ordinary agriculture and outdoor recreation activities normally neither conflict nor pose a threat to nature, and therefore a 'multiple uses' approach has been accepted. It should be borne in mind that the Outdoor Recreation Act[793] provides for a general right of the public to pass over – and to some extent stay on – open, uncultivated land, such as in forests and mountains, and along watercourses. Possible conflicts between agriculture and recreation in these areas are thus regulated by the general rules in the Outdoor Recreation Act.

In areas for 'agriculture, nature, outdoor recreation and reindeer herding', ordinary agricultural activities are always seen to be in accordance with the purpose, and are allowed without a special licence. Furthermore, scattered housing, industrial activities and recreational homes may be permitted through supplementary regulations. Such regulations must define the extent and the geographic areas for such developments.

791. Act of 9 Jun. 1978 No. 50.
792. Act of 27 May 2005 No. 31 on Forestry Art. 2 para. 2.
793. Act of 28 Jun. 1957 No. 16. *See supra* Part II, Ch. 9, § 3, I.

843. The issue of construction of *secondary recreational homes* is particularly important and controversial in Norway. A considerable part of the population wants to build a recreational secondary (or even third) home, preferably along the coast and/or in the mountains. But this will often be a threat to important natural values and public recreational interests. The municipal master plan is the main tool to control the development in this sector. Increasingly, the municipalities require that the building of new recreational homes is concentrated in certain development areas, instead of being scattered. This is normally a good solution from an environmental point of view, but is nevertheless often subject to local controversies.

844. *A master plan may not be used to regulate ongoing agricultural activities.* Even in 'areas for agriculture, nature, recreation and reindeer herding', the master plan may not lay down restrictions on how agriculture and forestry activities are to be carried out. For this purpose, legal instruments other than the master plan must be applied. From an environmental point of view, this has been much criticized. For example, the master plan may not be used to protect biodiversity from agricultural or forest practices, such as logging or the building of a forestry road in an important bird nesting area, or draining a wetland in order to increase farmland. Nor may forestry practices be restricted, in order to benefit outdoor recreation, in a master plan. Restrictions may however be laid down through the adoption of a local development plan (*see infra*).

Restrictions on farming and forestry are mainly laid down pursuant to the agricultural legislation, notably the Forestry Act[794] and the Agricultural Land Act[795] (*see supra* Part II, Chapters 4 and 5) with regulations. As regards forestry, strict rules have been laid down in regulations which oblige the forest owner to identify and map environmental values in his or her forest and to manage the forest with due consideration to these values.[796]

845. The legal mechanisms and legal effects of the master plan apply also to *coastal waters, lakes and watercourses.* The application of the general categories may be extended into sea and freshwater areas.

However, the municipality may also designate specific areas as 'area for use and protection of the sea and watercourses with the adjacent shoreline' (Article 11-7 No. 6). Here, various purposes – such as traffic, ship traffic lanes, nature conservation, outdoor recreation, drinking water supplies, fishing, and aquaculture – may be specified. Supplementary regulations may be issued by the municipality in such areas as well. In addition, in order to *protect the shoreline along rivers and lakes,* the municipality may lay down special restrictions on certain types of building and construction in areas within 100 m from a watercourse or a lake with natural, cultural or recreational values (Article 1-8 paragraph 5).

846. As mentioned, there is a possibility in the Act to lay down restrictions which may go across the main zones as laid down in Article 11-7 (and described

794. Act of 27 May 2005 No. 31.
795. Act of 12 May 1995 No. 23.
796. Regulation 7 Jun. 2006 No. 593 on sustainable forestry.

above). This is also a mechanism for other authorities to have their decisions included in the plans. The purpose is to make the municipal master plan a common planning tool and land-use document for all the various sectors involved in land and resource use. This instrument is called *zones for special consideration* (Article 11-8). Such zones may, for example, lay down restriction on certain construction activities due to the noise levels, or because of risk of floods or landslides in the area, or require special considerations of biodiversity, cultural heritage values and so on. Some restrictions may be legally binding for the landowner, while others instead are meant as guidelines for the authorities in further planning and when treating individual cases.

847. The Act has detailed rules on the procedure for making a master plan (Article 11-12 to 11-16). The procedure is transparent and all interested parties – public authorities as well as organizations and individual citizens – have the possibility to comment and influence the outcome. A draft plan is presented formally to the public for comments. The municipal council itself adopts the municipal master plan. If the municipal council intends to make a decision entailing a use of land that has not been the subject of consultation during the consideration of the plan, those parts of the plan where alterations are sought must be taken up for renewed consideration.

848. The plan shall be announced and made available through electronic media. A copy of the plan shall be sent to the Ministry, county governor, regional planning authority and affected central government authorities. The municipal council's decision on the municipal master plan may not be appealed.

849. The master plan is up for consideration and discussion in the municipality at least every fourth year, and *may be altered*. The procedure for alterations is the same as for the preparation of a new plan (Article 11-17). However, the municipal council may delegate authority to adopt minor alterations to the plan.

850. Where national or important regional or municipal considerations so require, the King may decide that certain specified parts of the land-use plan shall not be subject to alteration or revocation within a specified time frame unless the Ministry has given its consent. Such decision must be made within twelve weeks of the Ministry's receipt of the plan (Article 11-18). The idea behind this rule is that some interests and objectives in the plan need a more long-term predictability than four years for planning needs, etc.

II. The Local Development Plan

851. The local development plan (reguleringsplan) is a more detailed plan for land-use than the municipal master plan. The rules are laid down in Chapter 12 of the Act. Such plans are usually made for new housing or industrial areas, a part of a city centre or a village, a road section, etc. It has a long tradition in Norwegian planning and building law. It is adopted by the local council. The local development plan is a necessary tool to decide precisely, and in detail, how various pieces of land may legally be used – and not used – in the future. Similarly, to a municipal master plan, a local development plan designates zones for various purposes, but it is somewhat more flexible than the master plan in this respect. Supplementary regulations may be issued, with more detailed rules and regulations related to the future construction and other activities in the various zones.

852. A local development plan may either be prepared by the municipality for a somewhat extended area which the municipality wants to develop or secure for certain purposes, called *'area regulation' (områderegulering)*, Article 12-2. Or it may aim at the development or protection of a small area or just one or a few constructions. In that case, it is most often prepared by a private developer or a public authority for the construction for a public purpose, called *'detail regulation' (detaljregulering)*, Article 12-3. Contrary to a municipal master plan, a local development plan is not subject to regular reviews. Normally, such a plan will be a lasting legal basis for the use of the land in question. However, it is open to modifications, and may be annulled at any time, according to the same rules of procedure as the adoption of a new plan.

853. A local development plan is often a necessary tool for implementing and carrying out a master plan. Often, the master plan itself states that, in certain zones, further development has to be based on local development plans. The Act requires that 'major building and construction works' and other activities that may have significant environmental and social effects must be based on a local development plan in order to obtain a building permit (Article 12-1). For these, a building permit may not be granted until a zoning plan exists.[797]

Thus, a local development plan is normally made in connection with real plans for construction or other developments in an area, and is thus *directed more towards the actual carrying out of projects,* than a master plan. However, a local development plan may also be used for the purpose of protection of a valuable nature or agricultural area against constructions or other developments.

A local development plan may be initiated and proposed by the municipality, any public body and also by *any citizen.* Planning based on a private initiative, for example, by a developer of a new housing area or of an industrial activity, is now quite common in Norway. In fact, most of the local development plans are 'private' in the sense that they are proposed by private actors. They are often initiated by landowners or land developers and presented to the municipality for formal adoption (*see infra*).

854. The legal effects of a local development plan are similar to those of a master plan. A local development plan is 'legally binding'. It determines the possible future use of the various zones of the area it covers. Any new construction, building

797. However, a zoning plan is not required to licensable sites for the production of energy pursuant to the Energy Act, Water Resources Act or Watercourse Regulation Act. The energy sector is partly exempted from the act.

and other new activities related to the use of land, must be in accordance with the plan, including supplementary regulations (Article 12-4).

A building permit will normally not be issued to a building or construction which is contrary to the plan and its supplementary regulations. However, a developer normally has the right to a building permit for a project which is in full accordance with the plan.

855. Similar to the municipal master plan, the local development plan does not in itself require any changes of the present land-use. A landowner may continue the present use of his/her land, unless it makes it difficult to carry out the plan at a later stage. However, contrary to the master plan, an approved local development plan provides the *legal basis for expropriation* of land (Article 12-4 paragraph 4, and Chapter 16). Thus, the plan can be used by the municipality, the county or the State, to acquire land for public purposes. So, if the municipality wants to change the existing land-use, a local development plan is the adequate instrument.

856. Like the master plan, a local development plan may have binding effect in relation to planning and decisions pursuant to some *sector legislation.* Generally speaking, the Agricultural Land Act does not apply in zones designated for other purposes than agriculture and foresting. Thus, the agricultural authorities cannot subsequently stop a project in such areas on the basis of their sector legislation. The same principle applies in relation to the Cultural Heritage Act, its Article 8. It is not necessary to apply for a permission to build on a piece of land that may contain valuable remnants of cultural heritage, if the plan designates it for such building. Possible conflicts with the relevant interests and authorities shall be solved in connection with the planning process and the adoption of the plan. As mentioned, the Forestry Act applies even in areas designated to other purposes unless it has been explicitly exempted pursuant to regulations.[798]

857. The local development plan is a very flexible legal instrument for deciding future land-use. It provides the municipality with *a wide discretionary power* in this respect. Areas may be designated for more or less any purpose. The list of possible zoning purposes mentioned in the Act (Article 12-5) corresponds to that of the municipal plan, but is more detailed. Among the purposes listed are zones for housing, cabins, industry, public and private services, extraction of natural resources, tourist activities, roads and other infrastructure, bicycle lanes, lanes for public transport, public parks, military activities, agriculture, forestry, nature protection, recreation, protection of cultural heritage, areas at sea and in watercourses for various types of activities, and protection of drinking water sources.

It is possible to combine several purposes within one zone.

858. The Act provides a *wide legal framework for supplementary provisions* in connection with the various types of zones in a local development plan. The relevant Article, Article 12-7, contains both a general legal framework for provisions and a supplementary list of possible provisions. Many types of regulations may be

798. Forestry Act Art. 2 para. 2.

issued with the purpose of protecting the environment, both in zones designated for protection purposes, and in zones for development.

For example, in zones designated as *nature protection zones,* regulations may prohibit or restrict any activity that may pose a threat to the fauna, flora and other natural values in the area, including agricultural activities. In zones designated for cultural heritage protection, regulations may lay down strict rules on the carrying out of traditional activities, modifications of existing buildings, etc.

Equally important is the possibility to lay down restrictions on the future constructions and activities in zones designated for development, with the purpose of preventing or reducing environmental harm. Examples are environmental quality norms and other measures to prevent pollution including noise, measures to protect and promote the interests of vulnerable groups including children's needs for areas for play, regulations to protect valuable nature and cultural heritage, and measures to regulate traffic and parking in the area.

859. The Act lays down *detailed rules on the procedure* (Article 12-8 to 12-13). When the work on a plan starts, the landowners in the area, neighbours and all public and private actors that may be affected by the plan shall be notified. Information about the proposal must be published in a local newspaper and through electronic media. A private developer has to present his intentions or proposal early in a formal meeting with the planning authority in the municipality. If it is favourable, the municipality may give advice and provide assistance. However, if the authority finds that the initiative should not proceed, it may put a stop to it. Such decision should be taken as early as possible in the process (Article 12-8). It may be appealed by the applicant to the municipal council.

If the project is not stopped at this stage, the private party may continue the planning procedure, which is basically the same as when the municipality itself prepares a plan. A draft plan is then to be presented to the municipal planning authorities. The authorities then decide whether the plan has enough merits to be forwarded for public hearing and other further procedures, or whether it should be rejected (Article 12-11).

For plans that may have significant social or environmental effects, a 'planning programme' must be developed pursuant to Article 4-1. This is to be made public and open to comments. It must include a formal EIA on the conditions and according to the rules laid down in the general regulation on EIA[799] (Article 12-9). When this is fulfilled, the proposed plan, including the EIA, is made public for comments. Then, the proposed plan is subject to further and possibly a final deliberation in the municipal planning authority. If it is found favourable, it is forwarded to the municipal council for the formal adoption of the plan (Article 12-10 and 12-12).

860. The general rules on 'objection' from State and county authorities and other municipalities apply to local development plans as well. Contrary to a master plan, the adoption of local development plans may be subject to appeal by the landowner, other rightholders, or other parties with 'legal interest' (*see* Part V) in the matter. Appeals may be based both on questions of law, and on the municipality's exercise

799. Regulation of 21 Jun. 2017 No. 854.

of its discretionary power when designating zones for various purposes. If the municipality maintains its decision, the appeal is forwarded to the county governor for possible mediation. If agreement is not reached it is furthered to the Ministry of Local Government and Regional Development. The Ministry may choose to uphold the plan unchanged, cancel it, or make such modifications as it finds suitable.

861. The issue of compensation may often be raised by a landowner who finds that the plan prevents him/her for exploiting his/her property, and thus entails an economic loss. There is a general article on compensation in Article 15-3. It states that the landowner has the right to compensation if a local development plan makes it impossible for him/her to build or economically exploit his/her land in any other way. The wording is complicated, and the content of the rule is uncertain. Probably, it does not go much further than the general rule on compensation for restrictions on land-use (*see supra* General Introduction, Chapter 2, §1).

862. For zones designated for *nature protection,* Article 15-3 refers to the compensation rules in the NDA Articles 50 and 51. Thus, a landowner or a holder of rights in property that is wholly or partly protected as a nature (protection) area in a local development plan is entitled to compensation from the municipality for financial losses incurred *'when protection makes current use of the property more difficult'*. Hence, what is compensated is the increased costs of or the reduced income from his/her activity because the protection measures have made this activity 'more difficult'. The fact that the municipality must pay compensation clearly works to limit the use of local development plans for nature conservation purposes. This is thus left mainly to state decisions pursuant to the NDA (*see supra Part II, Chapter 2*).

If an area is designated for public transport, a public park, and some other public purposes, the landowner may require that his/her land be *redeemed* by the authorities, and that the value of the land be compensated as if it had been expropriated.

863. A local development plan may be subject to *amendments and annulment.* In that case, the same rules of procedure apply as to the preparation of a new plan. For smaller modifications which will have limited effect on the plan as a whole, however, a somewhat simpler procedure may be followed: The decision may be taken by a subordinate body to the municipal council (Article 12-14). The same applies to annulment of a plan which is clearly in conflict with the municipal master plan.

§4. Regional Planning

864. The PBA Chapter 8 lays down the legal framework for regional planning in Norway. *Regional planning is normally carried out at the county level.* The county municipality is the responsible authority for regional planning. The plans are adopted by the county council. This is an elected political body. The regional planning shall develop common long-term objectives for the region or county and coordinate activities and decisions of the State and county authorities within the county. It shall also provide frames and guidelines for planning activities in the municipalities.

865. Regional planning shall result in the adoption by the county council of a *regional plan*. The regional plan is a comprehensive plan for the physical, environmental, economic, social and cultural development of the county (Article 3-4). It shall define long-term objectives and guidelines for the development of the county. It shall also consist of an action plan for the coming years, for the implementation of the objectives and guidelines. The action plan may if necessary be updated on an annual basis (Article 8-1).

Normally, a regional plan covers the entire county and all important sectors. However, when appropriate, a plan may be prepared for specific areas of activity, or for only parts of the county. The Act prescribes that the county council within its first year after an election shall adopt a *regional planning strategy* (Chapter 7). This shall review the existing regional plan, assess the need for changes in the plan and identify special issues which may require attention and new planning initiatives, for example, within specific sectors or in certain geographical parts of the county. This will be the basis for the county's further planning activities. If no changes are needed, the existing plan will serve during the full four-year election period.

866. A regional plan is prepared in accordance with the *general planning principles* described above in §2. State authorities at the county level as well as the municipalities have both the right and the obligation to participate. A draft 'planning programme' is developed by the county planning authority and presented to the State agencies, municipalities and other interested parties for comments before it is finally approved. The planning programme may include an SEA/EIA if the plan may lay down guidelines for future developments. Also, a draft plan shall be made public for comments by all interested parties, and public debate is to be encouraged.

The plan is adopted by the county council. If a State authority disagrees with elements in the plan, it must be submitted to the Ministry of Local Government and Regional Development for consideration. The Ministry may then make modifications in the plan (Article 8-4) and may also make modifications on its own initiative. Often consultation with other ministries, and even discussions in the Cabinet, are required. The government may decide, pursuant to a regulation, that regional plans must be formally approved by the King in Council (Article 8-1 paragraph 2).

867. The regional plan can serve as an important instrument for environmental management and policy. Many questions relating to nature and landscape protection, outdoor recreation, and so forth require solutions across the borders of any single municipality. For example, the protection of farmland in agricultural areas adjacent to urban areas depends on a conscious land policy, where the various municipalities of the city and the countryside must agree on the main lines of urban development with the purpose of minimizing negative effects on agricultural land.

Many natural areas and important biotopes and habitats cover several municipalities. Their protection requires a coordinated policy, if necessary by the State or county authorities. It is very significant that the regional plans are central in *Norway's implementation of the EU Water Framework Directive* (*see* Part I, Chapter 3, §2). The management plans for each RBD are adopted as a regional plan by each county council.

868. However, *the formal status of the regional plan* restricts its legal importance as an instrument in these respects. In practice, a regional plan is not fully equipped to serve as a land-use plan. Certainly, it shall form the basis for activity by the county municipality, and shall serve as a guideline for both State and municipal planning and activity in the county, including land-use planning. As a land-use plan, however, it is normally not legally binding neither for the municipalities nor for the landowners. Most often, its legal effect depends on its implementation by the municipalities through their municipal master plans and local development plans, and by State and county planning and decisions based on sector legislation.

However, by a special decision pursuant to a regional plan called *'regional planning decision'*, a moratorium for a maximum of ten years on certain building activities within designated areas may be laid down by the county council if this is necessary in order to protect national or regional interests (Article 8-5).

§5. State Instruments in Respect of Spatial Planning

869. According to the principles of the PBA, the local democratic (elected) bodies in the counties and the municipalities have the main responsibility for land-use and natural resource planning. However, the State also has a strong interest in the land-use and thus in the planning. Certain land-use and environmental issues are of national – and even international – importance. And many important elements in a land-use plan, such as major roads and other infrastructure projects, are to a large extent based on State financing. It is thus very important for the State to have the last say with regard to the choice of lane for such projects.

In order to ensure that State and national interests are taken properly into account, *State authorities shall participate actively in the preparation of municipal and regional planning strategies and plans.* If the municipality does not accept the views of a State authority when preparing a municipal master plan or a local development plan, the State authority may issue an 'objection' pursuant to Article 5-4 to 5-6, whereby the issue is taken to the ministerial level for decision.

In addition, the State has several instruments to ensure State and national interests in the planning.

870. The government is generally responsible and shall direct the planning activity at the national level. As the ministry responsible for the planning system, the Ministry of Local Government and Regional Development shall work to ensure that the decisions made at the national level are followed up in the county and municipal planning (Article 3-5).

To this effect, the *government (King in Council) may define general objectives and frameworks, and issue guidelines,* for the development in counties and municipalities. These shall form the basis for their planning at the local level. Every fourth year, the government shall present its 'national expectations' of the upcoming regional and municipal planning in a public document (Article 6-1). These may be made more specific in '*State planning guidelines*' (Article 6-2). Such guidelines are not in themselves legally binding for the region or the municipalities. However, if they deviate from them in the planning, the relevant State authority will often issue a formal objection to the plan.

Important examples of such guidelines are guidelines for municipal climate and energy planning and climate adaptation,[800] for management of the shoreline towards the sea,[801] for coordinated housing, land-use and transport planning,[802] for planning and decision-making concerning protected watercourses,[803] and for the strengthening of children's interest in the planning.[804]

871. By regulation, the government may prohibit for a period of ten years the initiation of specific building or construction activities within a designated geographical area (Article 6-3). The prohibition may be extended for five years at the time. Such a *State planning provision* is mainly used for intermediate protection of valuable nature areas from development, to get time to prepare a more permanent land-use plan or a protection decision according to the NDA. This mechanism was earlier used to control the construction of new major department stores.[805]

872. The State may also itself prepare and adopt a municipal master plan or a local development plan, if this is necessary to carry out important State and county development projects, or protection measures (Article 6-4).[806] It may also ex officio decide to review, and if necessary change, a municipal master plan or local development plan (Article 11-16 and Article 12-13, respectively).

§6. The 'Building Permit' System

873. Besides the planning system, the PBA also comprises the rules concerning the building permit system. According to Article 20-1 of the Act, most building and construction activities, including change of use of a building, require a permit, which is generally known as a 'building permit'. *The building permit system is*

800. Royal Decree of 28 Sep. 2018.
801. Royal Decree of 28 May 2021. The main purpose is to restrict the building of recreational homes and other types of construction along the seashore, to the detriment of recreational and natural values and interests.
802. Royal Decree of 26 Sep. 2014.
803. Regulation of 10 Nov. 1994 No. 1001. *See* about protected watercourses *supra* Part II, Ch. 8, §3, IV.
804. Regulation of 20 Sep. 1995 No. 4146.
805. Regulation of 27 Jun. 2008 No. 742 (later annulled).
806. For example, this mechanism was used in connection with the construction of a high-speed railway between Oslo city and the new main airport of Gardermoen.

directly linked to the system of land-use plans. The municipal master plans and the local development plans with supplementary provisions determine the future use of various land areas. They have a direct legal effect, in the sense that they are legally binding on the landowners and other rightholders of the land. It follows from this that an application for a building permit normally will be decided on the basis of the plan for the area.

It also follows that the applicant is entitled to get the permit if his/her building project is in accordance with the plan – and with all other relevant rules in the PBA or regulations pursuant to the Act, or with rules in other Acts (Article 21-4). However, a project which is in conflict with the plan will at the outset not be permitted. In this case, the applicant must apply for an exemption ('dispensation') from the plan pursuant to the rules and conditions in Chapter 19 of the Act.

874. The PBA contains a number of *substantial rules concerning buildings and building sites.* In addition, a number of more technical regulations have been issued pursuant to the Act. A new building or other type of construction has to comply with these rules. Without going into too much detail, some of the most important general rules, relevant for the environment, should be briefly mentioned:

All building sites must be properly provided with water, sanitation and road access (Article 27-1 to 27-5).

The site must be safe as regards environmental and natural risks, such as flood, landslide, and avalanches (Article 28-1). Every year, buildings are taken by landslides and avalanches in Norway. This raises the issue of responsibility for the authorities that have approved the plan and building in question. Based on a decision by the Supreme Court[807] the decisive factor is whether the authority in question has exercised sufficient caution and diligence when deciding the case. The rule also applies to polluted soil. No building may be accepted on a contaminated site. So, if a landowner wants to develop such a site, he/she has to clean it up before he/she can get the building permit.[808] In practice, many ordinary cases of polluted soil are solved on the basis of this rule, instead of the rules in the PCA (*see* Part I, Chapter 5). A restriction on constructions may also follow from a hazardous activity in the vicinity, such as an industrial activity. The EU directive on the control of major-accident hazards involving dangerous substances (the 'Seveso III Directive')[809] has been included in the EEA Agreement and has now become an important factor with respect to land-use planning in the areas influenced by hazardous activities in Norway.

875. A building may not be constructed *closer than 4 m from the neighbour's property* unless otherwise decided in a land-use plan or accepted by the neighbour in writing (Article 29-4).

The local authorities shall ensure that any construction covered by the Act has a 'good architectural design in accordance with its function' (Article 29-1), and that in the view of the municipality 'has good visual qualities in itself and in relation to

807. The Nissegården case, Norsk retstidende 2015 p. 257.
808. Rules to this effect is found in Regulation of 1. Jun. 2004 No. 931 (Pollution Regulation) Ch. 2.
809. Directive 2012/18/EU.

its function and its built and natural environment' (Article 29-2). It must also have 'a universal design': It must be accessible and in other respects suitable for disabled people (Article 29-3).

876. All new buildings and constructions must satisfy a number of technical rules and requirements for the sake of safety, health, energy, the environment, and the protection of lives and material values (Article 29-5), and waste treatment (Article 29-8). Many general rules to this effect are included in the Act itself (Article 29-5 to 29-9). This is supplemented by more detailed rules in regulations.[810] The Ministry may lay down further regulations with the purpose of protecting the environment, including biodiversity (Articles 28-8 and 29-10).

877. As mentioned, most building and construction activities require a permit – commonly called a *building permit* – according to Article 20-1 of the Act. This includes not only to construct a new building but also changes to an existing building, the demolition of a building, and changes in the use of a building (e.g., from housing to office purposes). It also covers various types of constructions and encroachments, such as roads, parking lots, excavations and landfills. It also includes the partition of a property.

878. The *municipality is the building authority.* An application for a building permit is to be addressed to the municipality where the property is located. Normally, the application must be formally forwarded by a professional builder, architect or entrepreneur, in the Act called *'enterprise with right of responsibility'* (Article 20-3). The Act lays down detailed rules on this responsibility. For some smaller types of projects, this is not required; the owner may himself/herself forward the application (Article 20-4). A number of small projects and activities do not require a permit at all, provided that it is in full accordance with the land-use plan for the area and the technical rules in the Act (Article 20-5). Also, a permit is not necessary if the project in question has got a licence pursuant to a different Act, such as energy projects pursuant to energy legislation (Article 20-6).

Detailed *rules of procedure* are laid down partly in the Act itself (Chapters 20 and 21), partly in a comprehensive regulation.[811] As a first step in the procedure, a preliminary meeting may be held between the applicant and the municipal authority, in order to clarify the application, present and comment on the land-use plans and other rules and regulations that apply, and generally to exchange views on the matter (Article 21-1). Also, the neighbours must be informed in advance through a written notice, and asked to give their opinion (Article 21-3).

879. If the applicant so prefers, *a permit may be issued in two stages* (Article 21-2 and 21-4). First, a 'framework permit' may be issued. This covers the main characteristics of the project, such as its outer dimensions and characteristics, and the placing. On this basis, the developer then develops the project further and eventually presents a detailed technical description and application, which is the subject

810. Regulation of 19 Jun. 2017 No. 840 on technical rules for buildings.

811. Regulation of 26 Mar. 2010 No. 488 on rules of procedure in building matters.

of the final permit, the permit to carry out the project. Construction cannot start before the full application has been received and subject to control, and approved.

The municipality also has a coordination function in relation to other authorities. It controls that the project has got the necessary permits and approvals of other relevant authorities before construction can start (Article 21-5). As the main rule, an application shall be decided by the municipality within twelve weeks (Article 21-7 paragraph 1), but within three weeks provided that the neighbours do not object, and the project is in accordance with the relevant plans and regulations. In this case, a permit is given automatically if a decision has not been made within three weeks (Article 21-7 paragraph 2).

880. As mentioned, the applicant is *entitled to a permit* if his/her project is in accordance with the relevant plan, and is not in conflict with other rules and regulations pursuant to the Act, or in the Act itself. Hence, the municipality is not free when deciding on an application; it is not provided with discretionary power in this respect.

Nevertheless, certain rules and regulations provide the building authorities with some discretionary power when deciding on a building application. For example, a building permit may be refused if the municipality considers that it does not satisfy the 'visual qualities' as expressed in Article 29-2. The precise placing of a building on a given site is also subject to some discretion by the municipality (Article 29-4). In such cases, the municipality may lay down the necessary conditions for the permit.

881. A building permit is only *valid for three years* from the issuing of the permit. If works on the project has not started within three years, or if the works have been stopped for two years, the permit is invalid (Article 21-9). These time limits may not be extended.

If the municipality wants to stop a building project which is in accordance with the existing plan for the area, it may lay down a *temporary building prohibition* (Chapter 13). This offers the municipality the opportunity to change the existing plan, or prepare a new plan for the area, and thus create a basis for refusing the application. It should be noted that such a temporary prohibition also may be laid down after the municipality has received the application. It may not last for more than four years, but the municipality may prolong it in special cases.

882. A building project which is in conflict with rules in the Act or with the relevant land-use plan and pursuant provisions will normally be refused. However, the municipality may approve it, if it finds sufficient reasons. Chapter 19 of the Act gives the municipality a general authority to make *individual exceptions* – 'dispensation' – if certain conditions are fulfilled. Dispensation may not be accorded if it will conflict considerably with the considerations and interests behind the plan or rule in question, or with national or regional interests. In addition, the advantages of a dispensation 'must be considerably greater than the disadvantages' (Article 19-2 paragraph 2).

883. As further guidelines, the Act states that special consideration shall be given to the effects of a possible dispensation on health, the environment, protection of agricultural land, safety and accessibility (Article 19-2 paragraph 3).

Nevertheless, this rule gives the municipality a considerable range of discretion to accept exemptions from plans and regulations. Many municipalities may be quite liberal in this respect. The neighbours, as well as the relevant State and county authorities, shall be notified and given the opportunity to comment before a dispensation from a plan is issued. Exceptions may only be given in individual cases, which do not imply significant changes of a plan. Significant cases must instead be treated according to the rules on amendments of plans.

Part IV. Liability Questions

Chapter 1. Civil Liability

§1. Overview

884. This part will deal with issues of liability and compensation for environmental damage and nuisance.

885. General rules on liability for *pollution damage and nuisance* are found in Chapter 8 in the PCA.[812] Also, some special sets of rules apply. Some of these apply in addition to the general rules in Chapter 8. In that case, the one who has suffered damage may base his/her claim on several Acts. Other sets of rules replace Chapter 8, wholly or partly. The relationship between the various sets of rules may be unclear and rather complicated. There is not a clear answer to all questions in this respect.

However, to a large extent, the same general principles apply regardless of the legal basis. *The main rule is strict liability for pollution damage.* If several actions and causes have worked together, the liability of the parties is *joint and several.*

The EU directive on environmental liability[813] has been included in the EEA Agreement and is implemented by Norway. Generally speaking, Norwegian law was in accordance with the rules and principles of the directive before, and only some minor amendments in the Act and the Pollution Regulation were needed to comply with it (for details *see supra* Part I, Chapter 1, §2 III).

886. The Neighbour Act[814] lays down a general principle of a right to compensation for damage or nuisance caused by activities on a neighbouring property, provided that the damage or nuisance exceeds the *'tolerance limit' in neighbour relations.* This draws the delicate line of distinction between acceptable and unacceptable neighbour damage and nuisance. This issue has been thoroughly discussed in Norwegian legal theory since the middle of the 19th century, and has been subject to numerous court decisions, including many decisions by the Supreme Court, notably in cases of noisy airports and new roads.

The principle has a broader field of application than in cases based on the Neighbour Act. It also applies to claims on the basis of the PCA, provided that the

812. Act of 13 Mar. 1981 No. 6.
813. Directive 2004/35/EC.
814. Act of 16 Jun. 1961 No. 15.

pollution that caused the damage was 'legal', for example, because it was in accordance with a pollution permit or was in some other way based on a decision by a public authority.

887. Outside the area of pollution, the rules are less certain. For damage, nuisance or economic loss caused by the introduction of GMOs into the environment, PCA Chapter 8 applies *mutatis mutandis* (GMO Act Article 23). And Article 95 of the Svalbard Environmental Act lays down similar rules as PCA Chapter 8 for all types of damage on nature and the environment at Svalbard. Several Acts lay down compensation rules for pollution damage from particular activities, such as pollution from ships (Maritime Act), petroleum activity on the continental shelf (Petroleum Act), and radiation (Nuclear Energy Act). However, with the exception of the Svalbard Environment Act there are no special Acts on liability for other types of environmental damage, such as damage to special natural values and biodiversity due to constructions or encroachments.[815] Here, the Neighbour Act may be relevant, but its field of application is quite limited. General principles of tort law will apply. Fault-based liability is the main rule in Norwegian tort law. However, strict liability applies in cases where the damage is caused by a particularly dangerous or risky type of installation or activity.

888. So, Norwegian liability law in environmental issues is not very advanced when it comes to compensation for damage on the natural environment as such. As a rule, *only economic loss may be compensated.* However, extensive measures may be required to prevent a pollution accident pursuant to the PCA Article 7 or damage to nature and biodiversity pursuant to the NDA Article 6, to limit the damage and to restore the environment. The costs of such measures must to a large extent be covered, in the last resort, by the polluter or developer who has caused the damage or risk of damage. Thus, indirectly, the liability rules also provide some protection for natural values as such.

889. In this chapter, we shall first discuss the general principle of the 'tolerance limit' of the Neighbour Act (§2) since this also partly applies to damage on the basis of the PCA. We shall then present the general rules of the PCA (§3), and rules on liability for pollution damage in some sector Acts (§4).

§2. The Neighbour Act

890. The Neighbour Act[816] has its roots in one of the first 'environmental' acts in Norwegian law, the Neighbour Act of 1887,[817] where the main principle of Norwegian neighbour law was first expressed. This principle has been slightly modified

815. Furthermore, a person violating rules in the NDA or in regulations pursuant to the Act may be required to pay a compensation to the State called 'Environmental compensation' in the Act, Art. 74, *see supra* Part II, Ch. 1, §3.
816. Act of 16 Jun. 1961 No. 15.
817. *See* about the historic roots of Norwegian environmental law in General Introduction, §3.

in the present Act, but the main idea of a trade-off between the conflicting interests by a *tolerance limit* has been maintained. The present rule is laid down in Article 2 of the Neighbour Act:

> No one may have, do, or initiate anything that may result in unreasonable or unnecessary damage or nuisance on a neighbouring property. Under the heading of nuisance also fall activities that must be regarded as dangerous.
>
> When deciding whether something is unreasonable or unnecessary, importance should be attached to what is technically or economically feasible to prevent or limit the damage or nuisance. Also, local nature diversity considerations shall be taken into account.
>
> Furthermore, when deciding whether something is unreasonable, importance should be attached to what may be expected, having regard to the local conditions, and to whether it differs from the usual ways activities are carried out locally.
>
> Even if something may be expected, or is usual according to paragraph 3, it may be regarded as unreasonable if it results in a considerable worsening of the user conditions of a limited group of people.[818]

A violation of the rule has several legal consequences. Notably, it gives the neighbour a right to compensation on the basis of strict liability (Article 9). It may also lead to an injunction (Article 10).

891. It should be noted that the wording *'neighbouring property' is given a wide interpretation.* This does not only cover properties that border on the damaging property. It also covers the neighbourhood in general, as far as it is subject to damage or nuisance. In the case of pollution, the circle may be quite wide. However, only persons who hold rights in the relevant properties may claim compensation. The Neighbour Act does not protect public interests, for example, public recreational interests on the basis of the public's right of way.[819]

The wording '… have, do, or initiate … ' implies that more or less every type of cause may be relevant. It covers activities, such as the running of an industrial activity or the construction of a building, as well as omissions.

892. The expression *'damage or nuisance' is also meant to be given a wide interpretation.* It covers first and foremost physical damage on the property, but nuisance such as noise and types of pollution, as well as aesthetical nuisance, are also clearly covered. Also, damage to personal health is covered, including psychical health problems. It covers both single incidents and long-term exposure.

The general prohibition implicit in the rule applies to damage and nuisance regardless of whether there is economic loss. However, compensation is given only if the damage or nuisance has resulted in some sort of economic loss (Article 9), either through the damage itself, the costs of repairing it, or – not least of all – in

818. The author's translation.

819. On the basis of the Outdoor Recreation Act of 28 Jun. 1957 No. 16, *see supra* Part II, Ch. 9, §3.

a reduced property value. In the following, we shall concentrate on the other conditions for compensation, namely the 'tolerance limit'.

Another important point is that a neighbour's right to compensation pursuant to paragraph 2 remains even if the activity in question has been approved by a public authority, for example, though a building permit pursuant to the PBA.

893. First, the neighbour has a right to compensation if the damage or nuisance is '*unnecessary*'. This covers situations where the activity is *intended* to cause damage or nuisance to the neighbour, where the damaging activity has no legitimate purpose, as well as situations where the activity is legitimate and useful, but is carried out in a way, or at a place, which creates unnecessary problems for the neighbours.

As it is clearly stated in Article 2, this will depend on what is 'technically or economically feasible' to prevent or limit the damage or nuisance. This criterion may refer to the placement of the activity, as well as to the way it is carried out. An activity may be found to be 'necessary' – and thus legal – if any other placement or method is significantly more difficult or costly. However, the threshold in this respect is rather high.

894. What is technically and economically feasible is an important criterion also in relation to the second condition for compensation in Article 2: '*unreasonable*'.

Here, however, importance should also be attached to 'what may be expected, having regard to the local conditions, and to whether it differs from the usual ways activities are carried out locally'. It is clear that both the type of one's activity, and the impacts, must be probable in order to avoid liability. This criterion has been subject to much discussion.

The basic idea is that some types of nuisance, and a certain level of such nuisances, are more likely to occur in certain types of neighbourhoods, and must be accepted as a more or less 'regular' activity in that kind of neighbourhood. For example, pollution and noise tend to be more easily accepted in industrial areas than in residential areas. However, even if a nuisance is possible and even likely in an area, it may still be regarded as unreasonable. The rule prescribes a rather broad assessment in this respect, where also the interests on both sides could be taken into consideration.

895. In connection with the adoption of the new NDA in 2009, the paragraph was amended to include the duty to take *local nature diversity* into consideration. This means that it, due to such considerations in addition to others, may be found unreasonable to destroy a local wood in a residential area in order to develop it for industrial purposes.

896. Traditionally, the issue of *time priority* has played an important role. The question has been whether the damaging activity was there already when the damaged neighbour bought the land or moved in. In that case, the prevailing view was that the nuisance was 'foreseeable'. This may be regarded as if the neighbour has 'accepted' the situation, and on these grounds compensation was refused. For example, this was the decisive factor in a number of Supreme Court cases during the 1960s and 1970s concerning *noise from airports*. People who had bought or inherited a house in the vicinity of the airport were denied compensation. In the court's view, even a very considerable increase in air traffic – including the introduction of jet aeroplanes – was sufficiently *probable or foreseeable* to justify that no compensation was given. In hindsight, some of these decisions may be criticized, at least with today's perspective on environmental problems.

The Supreme Court has also been reluctant to grant compensation for noise nuisance in connection with *new roads*. The prevailing view has been that noise from new roads, as well as gradually increasing noise from increases in traffic on existing roads, are 'normal' risks for people living in urban areas, and thus are not subject to compensation. A worsening of noise and other pollutions has been regarded as 'foreseeable', and, therefore, as not 'unreasonable'.

It is obvious that this understanding of the law has seriously limited the role of the Neighbour Act as an instrument for environmental protection and improvement.

897. However, a certain development is taking place in this regard. Due to a modification of the wording of Article 2 in 1989,[820] the issue of time priority is now less decisive than it was in the past. As mentioned, *a broad assessment is now required as* to whether or not damage or nuisance is 'unreasonable'. Most people are increasingly sensitive to the quality of their environment, and certain levels of noise, pollution, and so on are regarded as unacceptable by the public, as well as in environmental law.[821] If these levels are exceeded, they may be found to be unreasonable, even if they could have been expected by the neighbour. Furthermore, in many situations, it is now most probable that an *improvement* of the environmental conditions will take place, due to public regulations and the like. It follows that it may be regarded as 'unreasonable' to maintain a bad environment. In this connection, new technical possibilities for preventing nuisance are also a relevant factor, in accordance with Article 2 paragraph 2.

However, it remains to be seen how the 'tolerance limit' in neighbour law, which is mainly based on court decisions, will develop in light of these changing conditions.

One more recent Supreme Court case regarding airport noise may indicate a more flexible attitude. A medium sized airport, Gardermoen, situated in the countryside outside Oslo, was chosen as the future main national airport. The result was a major increase in flight activity and consequently in noise, pollution and other types of nuisance. The Supreme Court concluded that the shift from an ordinary medium sized airport to the main national airport was *not 'foreseeable'* for those who lived there before the final political decision was taken – even if a certain increase in noise would have been foreseeable if the airport had not been chosen to become the new national airport.[822] As a consequence, compensation was accepted.

820. This modification was made in connection with the adoption of the rules on liability for pollution damage in the Pollution Control Act Ch. 8, and was meant to improve it from an environmental point of view.
821. Formally adopted environmental quality standards are a clear example.
822. Norsk Retstidende 2006, 486.

898. What, in this connection, is *the importance of public rules and guidelines* regarding environmental quality, such as environmental quality standards? It is clear from Supreme Court decisions[823] that they are relevant for the assessment of what is unreasonable, but they are not in themselves decisive. However, their importance ought to increase – at least as the lower limit of what should be regarded as acceptable.

899. Paragraph 4 of Article 2 says that 'even if something may be expected, or is usual according to the third paragraph, it may be regarded as unreasonable if it results in a *considerable worsening* of the user conditions of *a limited group of people*'. This paragraph was introduced into the article in 1989. Its meaning is not quite clear. The legislator wanted to provide a legal remedy in situations, such as the construction of a new road, where the nuisance often hits a few of the nearest properties more significantly than the other properties in the neighbourhood. Much is left to the discretion of the court when applying this rule.[824]

900. If an activity is found to exceed the tolerance limit and thus in breach of Article 2 of the Neighbour Act, the neighbour has, as an alternative to compensation, the *right to have the situation corrected* to bring the activity within the tolerance limit (Article 10). If this is not possible, the result may be that the activity has to stop altogether. This was the decision made by the Court of Appeal with regard to a pistol range in a residential area in Oslo.[825]

There are, however, several exceptions to this main rule, as laid down in Article 10. First, *correction* cannot be required if the activity has been formally approved through a decision (permission) by the relevant public authority pursuant to the Neighbour Act itself (its Article 7), the PCA, or the Water Resources Act, or when the property has been or shall be expropriated for the purpose in question. Second, the neighbour cannot demand correction if the costs involved make it clearly unreasonable when compared with the benefits for the neighbour. Instead, the neighbour has the right to compensation which, as a minimum, must cover his/her loss (Article 10, paragraph 2).

901. If an activity continues in breach of the tolerance limit rule in Article 2, the neighbour is entitled to *compensation for his/her economic loss on the basis of strict liability.* As mentioned, the compensation rule applies even if the activity has been formally approved by a public authority – such as the municipal building authorities or the pollution control authorities.

What is to be compensated is the economic loss resulting from the breach of the tolerance limit pursuant to Article 2. The economic loss may be due to direct damage on the property, or reduced property value due to the nuisance. It may also be an indirect result, for example, if noise from construction work keeps customers

823. Norsk Retstidende 1983, 152, and 1983, 940.

824. In a case concerning noise from a new highway through a rural area, the Supreme Court found that the nuisance was significantly more serious for six out of a total of fifty neighbours. In that case Art. 2 para. 4 was found applicable (Norsk Retstidende 1996, 232).

825. Rettens Gang 1976, 84.

away from a restaurant.[826] It is the 'extra loss' due to the breach of the tolerance limit that shall be compensated. However, since the tolerance limit is based on a broad assessment of what is 'unnecessary and unreasonable', including the time priority element, the difference in economic terms may be difficult to assess clearly.

902. The rule on the 'tolerance limit' of the Neighbour Act plays its most important role in connection with the *expropriation of land* for public purposes, such as roads and airports. The key issue then is the amount of compensation to be paid to the person whose land is being expropriated. This is a complicated and partly controversial subject in Norwegian law. As a rule, the compensation shall reflect the market price of the land, based on such future use and exploitation as appears most likely.

Often, only a part of a property is expropriated. In such a case – for example, in the case of expropriation for a new road – the value of the remaining part often diminishes due to noise and other nuisances. Is this loss to be compensated as well? Article 8 in the Expropriation Compensation Act[827] states that a loss on the remaining land due to nuisance 'common in the district' may only be recovered if it exceeds the tolerance limit in the Neighbour Act (and the PCA).

Noise nuisance from a new road will normally be regarded as 'common in the district'. In such a case, the landowner will only get compensation for noise nuisance which exceeds the tolerance limit in the Neighbour Act – and this limit is high as far as noise from roads is concerned.

However, damage and nuisance on the remaining property is compensated if it is directly caused by and linked to the expropriation, and thus specific to the person whose land is being expropriated.

903. As a general rule of strict liability for damage and nuisance, Article 2 of the Neighbour Act has been an important piece of environmentally related tort law. This is illustrated by the cases concerning noise from airports and roads. However, for many decades, the courts interpreted it rather strictly, making the 'time priority rule' nearly decisive. *This has limited its importance as a tool in environmental law.* It also has other important limitations, notably that it only applies to rightholders of the neighbouring properties, and only to these persons' economic loss. Against this backdrop, it was felt necessary to develop a new set of rules on liability for pollution damage included in Chapter 8 of the PCA.

§3. Liability Pursuant to the PCA Chapter 8

I. The Field of Application of PCA Chapter 8

904. The chapter on liability for pollution damage (Chapter 8) was included in the PCA in 1989. The purpose was to clarify, unify, and to some extent strengthen

826. Norsk Retstidende 1969, 757.
827. Act of 6 Apr. 1984 No. 17.

the rules in this field for the benefit of the environment. In particular, it was felt necessary to lay down clear, general rules on strict, joint and several liability for pollution damage. 'Pollution damage' means 'damage, nuisance or loss caused by pollution' (Article 53 paragraph 2).

The chapter also applies to damage, nuisance and loss caused by waste (Article 53 paragraph 3), and by exposure to light and radiation.[828]

Furthermore, it applies fully to pollution and waste from 'permanent transport installations', such as roads and airports, and also from individual means of transport, although other parts of the Act do not apply to regular pollution from mobile transport sources (Article 53 paragraph 4). This means that Chapter 8 applies to pollution from vehicles, aircraft and – not least of all – ships, to the extent that pollution damage from these sources is not especially covered by other legislations.

905. It is explicitly stated that the chapter applies to the duty to pay compensation for pollution damage only insofar as the question of liability is not specifically regulated by *other legislation* (Article 53 paragraph 1). This means that special rules on liability for pollution from certain sources apply instead of Chapter 8. This is the case, for example, with the special rules on liability for oil pollution from ships in the Maritime Act, and pollution from petroleum activities in the Petroleum Activities Act. However, it is said in the *travaux préparatoires* that special rules in Chapter 8 may *supplement* such rules on issues which are not addressed in the special legislation.

It is also clear from the preparatory works that general rules on liability for damage during transport, including damage to third party, take precedence over Chapter 8.[829]

906. However, it is to be understood that Chapter 8 applies in cases which are also covered by *general liability rules* in other legislations – that is, rules not treating pollution damage in particular.

The question here is whether Chapter 8 replaces and in fact nullifies the general rules as far as pollution damage is concerned, or if both sets of rules apply. Although the answer to this is not quite clear, the prevailing view is that the relevant Acts all apply, side by side. In such a case, the person who has suffered a loss due to pollution damage or nuisance may invoke several Acts, such as the Neighbour Act and the Vehicle Liability Act,[830] which regulate liability for damage and loss due to car driving. However, the real importance of this is rather limited, since the rules of the PCA are generally at least as strict as, and even stricter than, the other legislations.

It is also clear that the general rules of Norwegian tort law, as laid down in the Damages Act,[831] apply insofar as the question is not explicitly regulated by the special rules in Chapter 8.

---

828. However, damage from radioactive radiation is covered by the Nuclear Energy Act. *See infra* §4.
829. There are general liability rules in the Acts concerning road transport, air transport, railway transport and transport by ship.
830. Act of 3 Feb. 1961.
831. Act of 13 Jun. 1969 No. 26.

907. Article 53 paragraph 1 states that the rules in Chapter 8 are set aside if the question of liability for pollution damage is regulated *'by contract*'. This expression can easily be misunderstood. It is meant to apply to contracts that regulate the legal relationship between the party causing the pollution and the injured party. One type of example is the standard contracts between a transport company and its customers. If transported goods are damaged by pollution caused by the transporter, the contract between the two parties is decisive for the question of compensatory damage.

In some situations, several parties may be held responsible for pollution damage. This may be the case, for example, if soil pollution due to discharges from several installations results in damage to neighbouring properties. In spite of the wording of Article 53 paragraph 1, it is clear that the polluting parties cannot make an agreement regarding the allocation of their responsibilities, which is binding for the injured parties. *Such a 'contract' cannot supersede the general rules in the Act.* In other words, a contract cannot set aside the rules of the Act in relation to third parties. Otherwise, it would be too easy to avoid responsibility, for example, by placing the obligation on a party who has not the means to cover a possible damage. But such an agreement may of course be perfectly valid between the injuring parties, regulating the final economic settlement between them.

908. As far as the *geographical scope and choice-of-law* are concerned, Chapter 8 applies to pollution damage that:

- occurs in Norway (including the territorial sea) or the EEZ of Norway;
- occurs outside these areas if the damage is caused by an incident or activity within Norwegian sea or land territory (Article 54 paragraph 1).

Damage that does not fall within this scope is nevertheless covered insofar as the Norwegian law of damages shall be applied pursuant to the relevant choice-of-law rules (Article 54 paragraph 2). In the case of measures to prevent or limit pollution damage, it is sufficient that damage *may* occur in an area as mentioned (Article 54 paragraph 3).

It is also stated that the injured party may require the issue of compensation to be decided pursuant to the provisions applicable in the State, where the pollution incident or activity took place (Article 54 paragraph 4).

909. The question of the field of application also includes its *application in time.* This touches the complex issue of *retroactivity* of new legislation. In Norwegian constitutional law, certain forms of retroactivity are accepted. The general criterion in this respect, based on the interpretation of Article 97 of Grunnloven, is whether the retroactivity leads to 'clearly unreasonable' results (*see supra* General Introduction, Chapter 2, §1, I). The judgment on this will vary according to the field of law in question. In criminal law, for example, any retroactivity will most probably be regarded as unconstitutional. As a starting point, the same strict rule applies to tort law. Here, however, some flexibility is accepted. In fact, some special Acts on tort apply to damage that was identified or occurred after the Act came into force, *even if the damaging action took place before the Act came into force*. This is 'the principle of the time of the effect', as opposed to 'the principle of the time of the cause'.

910. The retroactivity issue is relevant in cases of pollution damage, and it may raise difficult questions. A note to Chapter 8 says that it applies to 'a damaging state which exists when the chapter enters into force'. For example, in the case of polluted soil, the Act applies to damages and loss that may be the result of such pollution as existed at the time of the entry into force. This undoubtedly includes the costs of cleanup of the polluted soil. It also applies to damages caused by pollution from regular activities that were ongoing at the time of the entry into force. The note further states that the chapter applies to 'damaging incidents that occurs after the entry into force'. This clearly applies to incidents such as an accidental oil spill. The expression is less clarifying in the case, for example, of leakage from buried barrels of chemical waste. Is this a 'state' or an 'incident'?

Without going too much into the intricacies of this subject, it is safe to say that the rules of *Chapter 8 generally apply to situations where damage occurs or is identified after its entry into force* (1990), regardless of whether its cause may be found in earlier events or actions. The importance of this question should not be overestimated, however. In most cases, the earlier rules would in fact have given the same result as to liability, as the rules in Chapter 8.

II. The Basis and Subject of Liability (Articles 55–56)

911. Article 55 lays down the general rule regarding the basis and the subject of liability for pollution damage. The rule clarifies certain issues, but others are left unresolved. It establishes *strict liability as the main rule,* and defines – at least to some extent – the parties who are responsible regardless of fault. However, persons who cause pollution 'indirectly' are liable only on the basis of fault.

We shall take a closer look at the rule and some of the problems it raises.

912. Strict liability applies to the *owner* of the property, object, installation or enterprise causing the pollution damage, provided that the owner also 'operates, uses or possesses the property, and so on'. If the owner is not the operator, responsibility rests solely with *the person who actually operates, uses or possesses the property and so forth,* insofar as the damage is not due to matters for which the owner is also liable pursuant to other compensation rules.

It follows from this that the actual operator is the responsible party. If the operator is a person other than the owner, this person assumes the liability. This is the case, for example, if a farm or a factory is subject to a long-term lease. However, the owner may also be held liable pursuant to other legislations (such as the Neighbour Act).

In order to obtain legal harmony, the expression 'operates, uses or possesses' must be interpreted as being in accordance with and covering the expression in Article 7 of the Act, which makes it a duty to 'have, do, or initiate anything that may entail risk of pollution … ' (this is also the key expression in the Neighbour

Act). Generally speaking, the liability applies to pollution damage due to any type of activity, omission, condition, installation and so on.

913. The rule leaves several difficult questions unanswered. One relates to the situation where *several actors* may be regarded as the relevant owner of the property or object that causes the pollution. There is, as an example, a serious leakage of chemicals from barrels belonging to A, which are stored by B, on a site that belongs to the company C, which is owned by the corporate group D. It is possible that both A, B, C, and D may be held strictly liable on the basis of the wording and natural interpretation of Article 55.

However, if in such a case it is clear that – for example – B has taken full responsibility of the handling of the barrels, and that B also has a long-term lease of the land without any interference from C, the storage may be seen as the relevant activity in relation to Article 55. Then B must be regarded as the relevant operator and thus as solely responsible.

So far, there have not been any court cases in which these issues have been raised, and the solutions are not certain.

914. Article 55 contains an *important delimitation of the strict liability rule.* Paragraph 2 deals with the liability of parties who 'indirectly contribute to pollution damage'. Such parties are liable only if they have caused the damage 'intentionally or by negligence'. The cited examples of this are persons 'supplying goods and services, carrying out control or supervisory measures or similar means'. The list is not meant to be exhaustive, and the rule cannot be understood as in any way limiting actors that may be held liable for pollution damage on the basis of fault. Regardless of what is explicitly said in Article 58 paragraph 2, the general rule of fault-based liability in Norwegian law applies.

The question of fault depends in part on what the injured party could reasonably expect from the activity or service in question, and whether this has been disregarded.

915. To some extent, this rule may overlap with what is usually called *product liability:* the liability of a producer, importer or retailer towards the purchaser, user or consumer of a product, due to product defects. In Norwegian law, this is regulated by the Product Liability Act.[832] The purpose of this Act is primarily to protect the consumer in situations where the use of a product results in damage which would not have happened had the product not been defective. It may, however, also apply in cases where a third party is the victim of the product's weakness. This may happen, for example, in cases of pollution due to a defect tap on a tank. Not only the owner of the tank but also – probably – a third party affected by the pollution may in such case claim damage pursuant both to the Product Liability Act and to Article 55 paragraph 2 of the PCA.

916. An even more important limitation of the strict liability follows from Article 56. *For pollution that is legal,* compensation may only be claimed insofar

832. Act of 23 Dec. 1988 No. 104.

as the pollution is 'unreasonable or unnecessary' pursuant to the provisions of Article 2 of the Neighbour Act. This is the case, for example, if the pollution is in accordance with a pollution permit pursuant to the PCA Article 11, or is 'ordinary pollution' from households, agriculture, and so on according to Article 8 of the same Act.

So, if the damage is caused by a legal form of pollution, *the aforementioned 'tolerance limit' of the Neighbour Act applies*. Here, we are faced with the difficult task of applying the criteria 'technically and economically possible', and 'what may be expected, having regard to the local conditions, and to whether it differs from the usual ways activities are carried out locally' (*see supra* §2).

This rule is intricate, and raises difficult questions. The distinction between legal and illegal pollution is not always clear at the outset. For example, according to Article 8 of the PCA, certain types of 'ordinary pollution' are legal. What 'ordinary pollution' covers may in itself be a matter of dispute. Moreover, a pollution permit is not always clear enough. Even if certain conditions of a permit have been temporarily violated, it may be doubtful whether the emissions as such are illegal.

917. Applied in connection with Article 56, however, it has a somewhat wider field of application than when it is applied within the framework of the Neighbour Act itself. Therefore, some special questions arise. On the one hand, certain actors may be held liable on the basis of Article 55, even if they are not covered by the Neighbour Act. Pollution from mobile sources is a case in point.

A Supreme Court case (Norsk Retstidende 1996 p. 1122) may serve as an illustration: A reindeer herd was frightened by the noise from military planes flying at low attitude, and several animals were lost. The owner claimed compensation from the State, and he won the case. The question of 'tolerance limit' was discussed, but not clearly answered. In this case, Chapter 8 of the PCA was deemed to apply, but not the Neighbour Act (the case was ultimately decided on the basis of liability rules in the Air Traffic Act).

On the other hand, certain groups of victims are not protected by the Neighbour Act, such as the general public using the seashore for recreation. Neither are natural resources as such protected by the Neighbour Act. Such cases raise special problems of interpretation of the 'tolerance limit' rule in Article 2 of the Neighbour Act. A broad appreciation of what is 'reasonable' is necessary, taking present environmental needs, aspirations and policies into account.

The *objective* of the PCA is relevant in this connection: to prevent pollution and to limit existing pollution. This is a proactive and more dynamic objective compared to that of the Neighbour Act, which mainly serves to resolve conflicting interests between neighbours. Clearly, this must influence the interpretation of the tolerance limit when applied within the framework of Chapter 8 of the PCA.

III. The Extent of Liability (Article 57)

918. Article 57 defines the types of loss and damage covered by Chapter 8, and thus the extent of the liability for pollution damage.

A. The General Rule: 'Pecuniary Loss' Is Compensated

919. The starting point is found in Article 57, litra a): Liability pursuant to Chapter 8 'includes compensation for *pecuniary loss* resulting from pollution damage'. There is no limitation to the liability pursuant to Chapter 8.

The term 'pecuniary loss' is wide, and is subject to further interpretation. It must be understood as meaning pecuniary loss connected to a *right* in the damaged object, such as property right or a user right (in other rules, notably Article 57 litra c) and litra d); however, this is extended to economic loss in connection with the exercise of so-called public (common) rights (*see infra*)).

The loss must be the result of damage or nuisance to a property, an object or an activity based on a right in the property or object in question. Typically, if the discharge of pollution into a fjord kills the fish in a fish farm, the owner of the fish farm can claim his/her economic loss. Similarly, if the value of a property is reduced due to noise from a new airport exceeding the tolerance limit, the owner may have this loss compensated. If water pollution kills the fish in a valuable salmon river, all those who have the right to fish in the river may claim compensation for their pecuniary loss.

920. The term also clearly covers direct *personal injury,* such as health injury from air pollution requiring costly medical treatment, or resulting in subsequent economic loss.

In case of health injury, the general rules of Norwegian tort law[833] also prescribe compensation for a non-pecuniary nuisance loss – for 'lost enjoyment of living' as it were. Although such a form of loss is not covered by the expression 'pecuniary loss', there are strong reasons for accepting such claims. On this point, Chapter 8 is supplemented by general tort law.

921. However, damage and injury to nature as such is not to be compensated. Norway has not developed a system of valuing this kind of *'ecological damage'* and making it a part of tort law, unlike in certain other countries. The economic theories – and arguments – on these issues are well known in Norway, including the concepts of user value, optional value and existence value. But so far, it has not been expressed or reflected in the legal order.

However, these values are nevertheless protected indirectly by Chapter 8 because the costs of measures to protect nature as such from pollution damage may be recovered from the person responsible for the pollution according to Article 57 litra b.

922. Pollution damage will often result in various types of *consequential loss.* A typical example is an oil spill at sea which drifts on to a popular seashore. Fishermen are prevented from fishing and lose their source of income. Not only that but also hotels, shops and so on along the shore, and the various businesses which are dependent on these, may suffer economic loss.

833. The Damages Act of 13 Jun. 1969 No. 26 Art. 3-2.

In Norwegian law, damages for this type of loss may be recovered, *provided that the cause-effect relationship is sufficiently close and predictable*. This is based on a case-by-case assessment, and the dividing lines may be difficult to draw.

In some such cases, the possible effects of pollution damage may have been agreed upon by the parties, as part of a contract. If so, the contract most likely replaces the rules of Chapter 8 altogether, as stated in Article 53.

If an enterprise may claim compensation for a loss due to a temporary stop in production or the like, the employees may also claim compensation for their loss of income. This is explicitly stated in Article 57 litra e).

923. A question that has been discussed is whether compensation may be recovered for *'reduced pleasure' connected with the use of a property* or an object. For example, an oil spill makes it temporarily impossible for the owners of the recreational houses along the shore to go swimming. A new airport makes it unpleasant to stay outdoors but does not reduce the value of the property. There are strong economic arguments in favour of compensation for this type of loss. It would mean an internalization of these external environmental effects. However, the preparatory works of Chapter 8 make it clear that such loss is not included in the expression 'pecuniary loss' and cannot be recovered.[834]

Nevertheless, the costs of *measures to prevent or reduce* such nuisance may to some extent be recovered on the basis of Article 57 litra b) (*see infra*).

924. As mentioned, a polluter may be liable even if the pollution that has caused damage is perfectly *legal.* But in this case, compensation may be claimed only if the damage or nuisance in question surpasses the general tolerance limit as laid down in the Neighbour Act. This is a very important limitation of the strict liability rule for pollution damage. In such a case, only the damage which exceeds the tolerance limit may be recovered.

The tolerance limit is based on a broad assessment of what is 'unnecessary and unreasonable', including the time priority element (*see supra* §2). The difference in economic terms may therefore be very difficult, if not close to impossible, to assess clearly.

925. Pollution damage may be due to a combination of both legal and illegal sources. This is the case, for example, if fish perish in a lake due to the sum of discharges from legal and illegal sources; some of the discharges are legal, while others are not. In relation to the tolerance limit rule, this complicates matters further. What must be identified in this case is the damage caused by 'the illegal part' of the emissions, as well as that part of the 'legal part' that exceeds the tolerance limit. It goes without saying that it is difficult to make a precise assessment of such cause-effect relationships, and to estimate its economic consequences. It must be based on a rather broad, discretionary evaluation.

We shall return to the general problem of multiple pollution sources.

834. The Supreme Court had earlier denied compensation for this type of loss in a case of road noise (Norsk Retstidende 1980, 309).

B. Costs of Measures to Prevent and Limit Pollution Damage

926. The PCA Article 7 lays down *a general obligation to prevent pollution* and – if pollution has occurred – to take reasonable measures to stop or remove the pollution or to limit its effects. The person responsible also has a duty to mitigate any damage or nuisance resulting from the pollution or from measures to counteract it. This obligation implies in itself a duty to cover the costs of the necessary measures to prevent and limit pollution damage. If the person responsible does not fulfil this obligation, the rules in Articles 74–76 may come into effect. The authorities may then carry out the necessary measures to limit the pollution and mitigate the damage, at the cost of the person responsible. In other words, the authorities may claim reimbursement of their costs. Under certain conditions, private persons may have the same right to reimbursement for measures taken on the basis of Articles 74–76 (*see* Part I, Chapter 1, §2, III).

So, to some extent, such costs may be recovered on the basis of other rules than the rules on liability for pollution damage in Chapter 8 of the PCA.

927. However, the rules of Chapter 8 also apply to this type of costs. Article 57 litra b) explicitly states that liability includes 'compensation for damage, losses, nuisance or expenses incurred as a result of taking reasonable measures to prevent, limit, remove or mitigate pollution damage'. This rule raises several questions of interpretation.

Some problems connected to the overlap between the two sets of rules will be discussed below in section V.

It is clear that such costs may be recovered regardless of whether or not the pollution has threatened or damaged economic values. The costs of combating an oil spill may be recovered, even if the oil spill only threatened a wilderness area, a bird colony or other elements of nature without any economic value to rightholders. In this way, the rules indirectly imply compensation for ecological damage.

It is also undisputed that costs of measures to protect other public interests such as recreational interests are to be compensated. But here, the special rule of Article 58 applies in addition.

928. The polluter is only responsible for the costs of *'reasonable'* measures to prevent, limit, remove or mitigate pollution damage. What is regarded as reasonable in various situations depends on a discretionary case-by-case assessment. The polluter shall not cover the costs of actions which were clearly unfounded or useless.

In practice, the responsibility covers the costs of virtually all measures taken to remove the pollution, and to restore the environment to its natural status. The issue has been raised, for example, in connection with actions taken to clean up a sea shore after oil spills. It is clear that all costs necessary to remove the oil from the shore are to be covered, even if the shore is remote and of little recreational value. The same goes for costs to clean up and in other ways care for polluted birds and mammals, regardless of any economic value.

929. As the general rule, there are *no limitations* to the general liability pursuant to Chapter 8. However, Article 57 litra b) contains an important limitation as regards *damage from legal pollution.* In this case, compensation may not be claimed for expenses for measures taken to abate the pollution 'insofar as such compensation would clearly exceed the compensation that could have been claimed if the measures had not been implemented'.

To illustrate this rather vague rule, the limitation of noise from a new road may serve as example. The noise from the road reduces the value of the houses along the road. To limit the noise nuisance, the house owners want to put up a noise baffle, and to claim the costs covered by the road authorities. To the extent that the cost of the noise baffle 'clearly exceeds' the reduction in the value of the houses due to the noise, they cannot be recovered.[835] It is clear from the preparatory works that this rule shall be interpreted rather strictly.

930. This rule is clearly unfortunate when seen in the perspective of protection of ecological values. Where *the ecological damage* does not result in measureable economic loss, there is little room for recovery of the costs to take measures to prevent or restore nature. It must be underlined, however, that this limitation only applies to damage from legal pollution, that is, pollution which has been accepted by society. If the legal basis is a pollution permit according to the PCA, conditions may have been laid down in the permit in order to mitigate the negative consequences.

931. In addition to the rules already mentioned, *public (common) rights* have some special protection in Chapter 8. It is stated explicitly in Article 57c that liability covers compensation for damage, loss or nuisance when pollution 'prevents or impedes the exercise of public rights for commercial purposes'. The key example of this is loss to people exercising sea fishing for a living. This used to be a public (common) right in Norway (however, during the last decades it has been subject to detailed regulations and restriction, *see supra* Part II, Chapter 6).

932. Article 58 lays down the rule that *costs to restore the environment for the benefit of non-commercial public interests* (such as recreational interests) may be recovered from the person responsible for illegal pollution. Such claims shall be made by the municipal pollution control authority. They may also be made by private organizations working for relevant public interests, such as recreational or environmental organizations. An example here is the measures used to restore fish stocks in a watercourse for the benefit of the anglers. Even if the claim is put forward by a private organization, the compensation awarded shall accrue to the pollution control authority, which will also decide how the compensation is to be used (Article 58 paragraphs 3 and 4).

The full meaning of Article 58 is somewhat unclear when compared to the general rule in Article 57 litra b) on compensation for reasonable measures to mitigate pollution damage.

835. The rule is meant to modify slightly – to the benefit of the victim of pollution – the result of the Supreme Court decision in Norsk Retstidende 1980, 309.

IV. Causation Rules: Compensation in Cases of Multiple Causes

933. The issue of causation poses often difficult questions in the field of environmental damage. In many situations, it is difficult to identify the cause of a particular damage or other effects, due to factual and scientific uncertainty. Often, there may be *several causes or several possible causes.* Several possible sources may each have caused the damage, or the damage may be due to the cumulative effect of many sources. In some cases, only statistics will tell whether certain emissions of pollutants may cause certain types of injury, for example, when a certain illness occurs more often than average in the vicinity of a chemical factory. It is, however, impossible to identify the cases in which it has been the main cause.

There are numerous variations of possible cases in this field, and it is not possible to discuss them all in this monograph. Only the main issues and examples are treated in what follows.

934. Norwegian tort law is based on a *theory of adequacy,* which is close to the 'remoteness doctrine' and 'proximate cause doctrine' in Anglo-American Law. It is supplemented by the doctrine of 'substantial factor rule', and – in the end – by a broad, discretionary assessment of whether liability is reasonable, giving regard to the Act in question and the probability of its damaging consequences. Other factors, such as the actions and situation of the victim, may also be relevant in this connection.

935. In case of several (possible) causes, the *main rule in Norwegian tort law is that of joint and several liability.*[836] It means that each possible cause is regarded as the cause of the damage, and may be liable for the total amount of damages. This clearly applies in the situation where several actions have contributed, and together have caused the damage ('contributory causes' or 'cumulative causes'). This is the case when the damage is the result of the pollution caused by the sum of several discharges into one recipient. It also applies in situations where each one of several actions may have caused the damage, but it is impossible to find out which of the action actually caused it ('multiple sufficient causes').

In both cases, however, the substantial factor rule may exclude some of the possible tortfeasors from liability.

936. Article 59 of the PCA addresses some of these difficult questions. Its paragraph 1 states that:

> any person that causes pollution that alone or in combination with other causes of damage may have caused the pollution damage, is regarded as having caused such damage unless it is established that another cause is more likely.

836. Earlier, this was based on unwritten law, but is now stated explicitly in the general Damages Act of 13 Jun. 1969 No. 26 Art. 5-3.

This is meant to be a rule concerning *the burden of proof.* The purpose is, of course, to ease the burden of proof for the victim in those cases where it appears to be several possible causes.[837] It may, however, also play a role as a substantial rule concerning causality in these cases.

Article 59 paragraph 2 states that:

> persons that cause pollution incidents which individually or together are sufficient to cause the pollution.

937. In cases where pollution damage has been caused by *the cumulative effect of several emissions,* the importance of the different contributions may vary considerably. It may appear unfair that even a nearly insignificant contributor is fully liable and may be sued for whole damages. Article 59 paragraph 3 gives the basis for *a fair distribution of the liability* in such cases, based on a broad assessment of reasonableness. It states:

> If it can be established that other causes of damage have predominantly contributed to the pollution damage, liability for a less significant cause of damage may cease or be proportionately reduced to the extent this is reasonable. In evaluating this, the tort-feasor's contribution to the pollution damage, the type and extent of his activities, and other circumstances, shall be taken into account.[838]

938. Special problems are also raised in cases where the pollution damage has been caused by extreme circumstances such as extreme weather, a natural disaster such as earthquake, flood, or landslide, or other 'act of God', armed conflict, and so on. In contract law, such circumstances are generally defined as 'force majeure', exempting an otherwise responsible party from his/her obligations.

There is no general force majeure rule in Norwegian tort law. The law is in fact less than clear in this field. The question of liability must be based on a general assessment of causality, the application of the 'substantial factor rule', and reasonableness.

This may be seen both as a question of whether there is legal basis for liability at all, and as a question of fair distribution of the liability burden between the polluter and the victim. However, due to the general rule on burden distribution in the Damages Act and in Article 59 paragraph 3 in the PCA, it is not strictly necessary to make this formal distinction.

939. Generally speaking, a person who runs an activity that poses a risk of pollution will most probably be held liable, even if that risk is very small, and the direct cause of the pollution damage is an unforeseeable event. Most often, this result is

837. It is somewhat disputed whether this rule at all deviates from what at any rate follows from unwritten burden of proof rules in general Norwegian tort law.

838. A general rule with similar effect is laid down in the Damages Act Art. 5-2. The focus of this is, however, the fair distribution of the burden between the tortfeasor and the injured party. Art. 59 supplements this general rule by adding circumstances in connection with the various causes and contributions as a basis for a more fair distribution.

fairer than if the victim has to carry the burden of such circumstances and possible loss. The polluter should also have an incentive to take all necessary preventive and precautionary measures. Also, he/she is the one who should have adequate *insurance*.

This general rule undoubtedly applies in all types of activities which clearly involve certain risks – risks that are known and accepted, such as chemical industry, chemical waste disposals, offshore petroleum exploration and production, and transport of oil and chemicals on land or sea. For example, petroleum installations on the continental shelf are constructed to resist 'the 100-year wave'. But the risk is, of course, that one day 'the 200-year-wave' hits and destroys a platform and creates massive pollution. Liability is the natural solution when such a 'calculated risk' becomes reality.

However, when the chain of events results in consequences which are simply unforeseeable or extremely unlikely, the substantial factor rule may lead to the opposite conclusion. Also, the burden distribution rules of the Damages Act and Article 59 paragraph 3 of the PCA may be used in such cases in order to find a reasonable solution.

940. Liability for pollution damage may be lessened because of *contributory negligence* on the part of the victim. There is no special rule to this effect in the PCA. The general rule in Norwegian law, however, is that contributory negligence may lead to the reduction of the compensation, or that the liability drops altogether.[839] The solution must be based on a broad assessment of reasonableness, taking into account the actions of the parties and their respective importance, and the circumstances in general.

This is an extremely relevant issue in cases of pollution damage. The victim may have had the possibility to prevent or reduce his/her loss by taking precautionary measures, for example, by keeping away from the polluted area, or by taking active steps to prevent a spill from reaching his/her property.

However, since pollution is generally prohibited by Norwegian law, people should normally have no reason to believe that there is a pollution risk. Only if there are clear signs of a pollution risk, like a special warning or the like, will a commoner have a duty to take preventive actions.

941. The victim may have *accepted* the pollution risk. If he/she has been fully informed about the risk, and has understood and consented to it, he/she will most probably not have the right to recover compensation for his/her loss.

However, the presumption must be that he/she has not accepted a risk of being damaged or injured by pollution, even if he/she has accepted a certain activity, for example, in the vicinity of his/her property. This principle was applied in a case where a landowner had hired out a part of his/her property to a waste deposit. The nuisance from the deposit turned out to be much worse than expected. The landowner got compensation although he/she had agreed to the deposit as such.[840]

839. Damages Act Art. 5-1.
840. Rettens gang (RG) 1988, 413.

942. A difficult issue in this connection is raised when the property or the person injured by pollution is *particularly vulnerable or sensitive,* and when the damage is mainly due to this circumstance. Article 5-2 of the Damages Act generally opens the possibility for a *reduction* of the compensation on the basis of a broad assessment of reasonableness. The fact that the victim is particularly vulnerable may be a cause for a reduction.

Referring to this rule, Article 61 of the PCA states explicitly that, when making an assessment according to Article 5-2 of the Damages Act, 'the fact that the property or object is particularly vulnerable' may be taken into account. This possibility applies only to damage to 'property or object'. Most probably, this also includes possible damage to nature as such.

However, this rule does not apply to injuries to persons, such as health injuries. Here, *the general view is that a person's vulnerability to pollution is irrelevant for the liability and compensation issue.*

943. The Act has no general rule concerning *the victim's use of the damages.* For example, it is not generally required that the amount is used to mitigate the damage or restore the environment. This limits the effect of tort law as an instrument for environmental protection.

However, Article 62 is a special rule on the use of compensation awarded for housing rented out for residential purposes. The house owner cannot keep the money for himself/herself. The compensation must be used for the purpose of protection against the pollution, primarily for the benefit of the tenants. If measures against pollution are of little benefit for the tenants, the compensation may be used for other purposes that raise the standard of living or otherwise benefit the tenants. The intention of this rule is good, but it has not been applied much.

V. The Relationship Between the Rules on Damages and Those on Reimbursement When Actions Have Been Taken

944. In Part I, Chapter 1, §2, III, we have described the general duty to avoid pollution, and the duty to take all reasonable measures to prevent, stop and remove pollution, to limit its effects, and to mitigate any damage or nuisance (Article 7 paragraphs 1 and 2 of the PCA). The pollution control authority may issue an order to the person responsible for carrying out such measures. If he/she fails to do so, the authorities may themselves arrange for the measures to be implemented. In that case, *the authorities may claim reimbursement* for all their costs. In certain situations, private parties affected by the pollution may also take necessary measures to prevent and limit pollution of their property, and have an equal right to be reimbursed (Articles 74–76).

945. This situation is also covered by the wording of Article 57 litra b) concerning the type of costs and loss that may be recovered on the basis of Chapter 8 in the Act, that is the tort liability rules. Article 57 litra b) explicitly mentions the costs of 'reasonable measures to prevent, limit, remove or mitigate pollution damage'. Also, Article 58 deals with this type of measures. Typically, such measures are taken by the pollution control authorities, for example, in connection with an oil spill, or by private parties whose properties are threatened or damaged by pollution.

Thus, *a double set of rules apply in these cases:* both the rules on reimbursement according to Articles 74–76 and the rules in Chapter 8. The first is based on the polluter's obligations to public law. The second is within the framework of private tort law. In actual fact, they overlap to a large extent.

946. Some of *the basic conditions are the same.* In both cases strict liability applies, and although the responsible subject is defined differently in the two sets of rule, the solutions in this respect will be the same in most cases. The types of costs that may be recovered will also to a large extent be comparable, in spite of slightly different wording. The obligation to reimburse the costs of reasonable measures to protect the natural environment as such, regardless of economic interests and possible loss, follows from both sets of rules.

947. However, there are also *certain differences.* In most cases of accidental or otherwise illegal pollution, Articles 74–76 may provide a simpler legal basis for claims of cost recovery. However, these rules do not apply to damage due to legal pollution. They also limit the right to recovery to certain situations only, mainly when an order by the pollution control authority has not been implemented by the person responsible. Only the pollution control authority and private parties with threatened properties can claim reimbursement. The liability rules are more open in both respects, the key criterion simply being adequate causation. The special rule in Article 59 paragraph 1 on the burden of proof in case of several possible causes does not apply directly in the case of reimbursement, but the general rules on the burden of proof in such situations will probably most often lead to the same result.[841]

§4. Liability Rules in Other Acts

948. There are several special rules on liability for pollution damage in Norwegian law, besides those of the Neighbour Act and the PCA.

I. Liability Pursuant to the Petroleum Act

949. The Petroleum Act[842] regulates the *offshore petroleum activity on the Norwegian continental shelf.* This industry is the source of considerable air pollution and marine pollution as a result of its regular activity. In addition, there is always a risk of serious pollution accidents, for example, in the form of blowouts.[843] In addition, the waste problem has been serious, in particular during the first years of the

841. Also, the rules on time limitation of action and some other procedural rules may be different, but it is not necessary to go into such details.
842. Act of 29 Nov. 1996 No. 72.
843. A serious blowout took place in 1977 on the Ekofisk field in the middle of the North Sea. It was stopped one week later, and the damage to the marine environment was found to be insignificant.

activity. Numerous objects were thrown overboard from ships and installations, fell to the bottom of the sea, and created problems for trawlers and others. Exploration and exploitation of petroleum takes place in sea areas which are also rich fishing grounds and spawning areas. Therefore, the issues related to pollution prevention and damages have always been very important in petroleum policy and law in Norway.

The Petroleum Act is under the responsibility of the Ministry for Petroleum and Energy. Two chapters of the Act deal with these liability issues.

950. Its *Chapter 7 applies to damage or loss due to pollution* caused by the discharge – whether accidental or intentional – of petroleum, which covers oil and gas. It includes costs of reasonable measures to prevent and limit pollution damage, and the losses of fishermen who are prevented from fishing (Article 7-1). Geographically, its field of application corresponds to that of the PCA (Article 7-2).[844]

Pollution from types of substances other than oil and gas is not covered by the rules of Chapter 7. Here, the general rules in the PCA apply, unless the injured party is a Norwegian fisherman. Norwegian fishermen are protected through a special set of rules in Chapter 8.

951. The rules of Chapter 7 lay down *strict liability for 'the licensee'*. The licensee in the petroleum industry is a person – physical or legal – that has a licence to exploration, exploitation, production or transport of petroleum resources. Usually, there are several licensees to one oil or gas field, pipeline or the like.

Strict liability also applies to *the 'operator'* of an installation or activity, if so designated by the Ministry. If one of the rightholders is the operator (which is usually the case), claims of damages should first be directed to the operator. If the claim is not fully recovered from the operator, the other rightholders are responsible proportionate to their share in the activity (Article 7-3).

952. The rule shifts liability to the licensee/operator. It is meant to exclude other possible responsible parties from direct liability. Article 7-4 explicitly lists several *subjects that may not be liable* to the injured party, such as subcontractors and employees of the licensee, and persons who take measures to prevent or limit pollution damage when pollution has occurred.

It is explicitly stated in Article 7-5 that the responsible licensee may not claim reimbursement from such parties unless they have caused the pollution damage with intent or through gross negligence. This is an incentive for the operator and other licensees to select and supervise subcontractors and employees thoroughly, and to the greatest extent possible avoid double insurance.

953. Article 7-3 paragraph 3 includes a special rule on 'force majeure'. If the pollution damage is to a considerable extent caused by an 'inevitable natural event, war, decision by a public authority or similar force majeure' beyond the control of the responsible party, the liability may be reduced to a reasonable level. Due

---

844. *See* Part I, Ch. 1, §2, II.

account shall be taken of 'the extent of the activity, the situation of the injured party and the possibility of insurance on both sides'.

954. If petroleum activity leads to *damage or loss to Norwegian fishermen,* some special rules apply pursuant to *Chapter 8* of the Petroleum Act. These rules must be understood on the background of the conflicts of interests between the petroleum and fishing industries, and the political need to care for the fishermen. The rules have only had limited practical importance.

Chapter 8 covers damages for the fishermen's economic loss due to petroleum activity. The loss may be caused by pollution from substances other than petroleum (which is covered by Chapter 7), or waste. The loss may also be due to lost fishing opportunities in certain parts of the sea because of the oil installations and their surrounding safety zone, or result from trawls and other fishing gear hitting pipelines and other installations on the bottom (Article 8-1).

If petroleum installations make it *impossible or very difficult to fish* in an area, the State must compensate those fishermen who would normally use the area (Article 8-2). This rule has been of limited importance, partly because the relevant fish stocks migrate considerably, and the fishermen anyway take in a sufficient catch in other areas. It follows from general tort law that the fishermen have a duty to try to avoid or minimize their loss.

955. The rule on damage from pollution and waste follows the same general principles as in Chapter 8 of the PCA, and Chapter 7 of the Petroleum Act. The *licensee is strictly liable* for this type of damage, including costs of measures to prevent or reduce such damage (Article 8-3 paragraph 1).

An important rule is laid down in Article 8-3 paragraph 2. It states that the rightholder is also responsible for pollution and waste from *supply ships* and similar ships connected to the petroleum activity, even if the ships in question do not belong to the rightholder. In this case, however, the licensee may claim reimbursement from the tortfeasor or the owner of the ship.

Often in these cases, it is impossible to identify the tortfeasor. If no particular rightholder may be found liable, all rightholders in the actual installations or activity are jointly and severally liable (Article 8-4).

956. Claims pursuant to Chapter 8 of the Petroleum Act are considered by two different committees. Loss due to reduced fishing areas are covered by the State and are considered by a committee appointed by the government. Claims caused by damage from pollution and waste, notably waste objects on the seabed, are covered by the petroleum companies. The companies have formed a joint committee to look into these cases and to pay out compensation on the basis of a common responsibility.

II. Liability Pursuant to the Maritime Act

957. Shipping is an important source of marine pollution. With Norway's long coast facing important sea areas, there is considerable shipping activity within its territorial waters and in its economic zone. Regularly, Norway experiences oil spills along the coast due to shipping accidents. Norway itself also has an important merchant fleet which works internationally. Marine pollution from ships is therefore *an important part of Norwegian environmental law,* and a field of considerable public interest and awareness.

958. Chapter 8 in the PCA on liability for pollution damage applies generally, and also to pollution from ships. But in this field there are *special rules in the Maritime Act*[845] *that supersede the* PCA, pursuant to Article 53 of PCA. These rules are in accordance with the international rules in this field, notably the 1969 Convention on Civil Liability for Oil Pollution Damage ('London Convention') in the version adopted 1992, and the International Convention on the Establishment of an International Fund for Compensation for Oil Pollution of 1972 as amended in 1992 and supplemented by the 2003 protocol. These conventions apply to pollution from most – but not all – ships that transport oil in bulk.

The International Convention on Civil Liability for Bunker Oil Pollution Damage of 2001 was ratified by Norway in 2007, and the Maritime Act was amended accordingly (*see infra*).

959. The rules on liability for oil pollution from ships are found in Chapter 10 of the Maritime Act. The rules are rather complex, and we shall not go too much into details here. The main rules of the 1969/1992 Oil Pollution Convention have been incorporated into the chapter. These apply, however, only to certain types of oil, and from certain types of ships, notably tankers. Furthermore, they only apply in the territorial waters and economic zones of the States party to the convention, including Norway (except as regards costs of measures to combat the oil spill, which are covered regardless of where they are carried out).

Also, the main rules of the 2001 Bunker Oil Pollution Convention have been included in the chapter. In addition, the chapter lays down liability rules concerning oil spills in other situations as well, to some extent applying the same principles as those that are laid down in the Oil Pollution Convention. Far from all the rules of the Convention apply, however, in these situations.

In addition, the general rules of Chapter 8 in the PCA may supplement the Maritime Act.

960. The main rule is that *the owner* of a vessel, a drilling rig and other movable installations *is strictly liable* for damage or loss caused by the discharge or spill of oil from the vessel or installation. The liability also covers reasonable measures to prevent and limit pollution damage, and to restore the environment. This rule applies regardless of the type of oil, the type of vessel or movable installation, or where the pollution occurs (Articles 191, 207 and 208).

If the pollution is the result of a series of events with a common cause, the responsibility is linked to the initial event, and the respective owner. If two or more ships are involved each owner is strictly liable. They are jointly liable for damage that cannot reasonably be connected to one particular ship (Article 191, paragraph 1).

845. Act of 24 Jun. 1994 No. 39.

961. Here, too, there are special exception rules in case of 'force majeure'. Article 192 states explicitly that the owner is not liable if the pollution damage is caused by war or other armed conflicts, or a natural disaster of 'extraordinary, inevitable and irresistible' character, by an action by a third person with the intent to cause damage, or by negligence by a public authority in relation to lighthouses or other means for the navigation.

962. For ships that transport oil in bulk, the liability is thus *transferred or channelled to the owner.* The Act (Article 193) lists a number of physical and legal persons who may *not* be liable, such as the ship's crew and the owner's employees, the pilot, owners of the cargo, those who take part in the salvage of the ship in case of an accident, or in the pollution abatement work and their employees.

Recovery may, however, be claimed from such a person if he/she has caused the pollution damage by intent or gross negligence, and understood that such a damage was likely to occur. In that case, the shipowner may also claim reimbursement if he/she has covered the damages in the Court of First Instance.

963. The rules lay down *limitation of liability* for oil pollution damage from ships. The rules on this are rather complicated, and they vary slightly, depending on whether or not the situation is covered by the London Convention (as to type of ship, type of oil, and geographical area), and – for situations outside the Convention – whether or not the accident has occurred in the vicinity of a State which is party to the Convention.

Article 194 lays down the limitation rule for an oil spill from *a ship transporting oil in bulk, which is covered by the Convention.* The liability of the shipowner is limited to 4,510 million SDRs[846] for ships of less than 5,000 tons. For ships of more than 5,000 tons, the amount increases with 631 SDRs per ton, with a maximum of 89,770 million SDRs (about USD 120 million).[847] This limitation applies to all liability for pollution damage in relation to one event, and to a series of events with a common cause.

The limitation does not apply if it is proved that the pollution damage resulted from the owner's personal act or omission, or that it was committed either with the intent to cause such damage or recklessly with an awareness that such damage was likely to occur.

These rules partly overlap the rules in the PCA (Articles 7 and 74–76) on the duty to take action and reimbursements of costs of measures to prevent or reduce the effects of pollution. The PCA has no limitations on reimbursements claims. In an important court case from 2017 the Supreme Court stated that the limitation rules in

846. 'Special Drawing Rights' (SDR) is an internationally applied unity defined by the International Monetary Fund. The currency value of the SDR is determined by summing the values in US dollars, based on market exchange rates, of a basket of major currencies (the US dollar, Euro, Japanese yen, and the British pound sterling). The SDR currency value is determined weekly and the valuation basket is reviewed and adjusted every five years. At present (September 2021) one SDR corresponds roughly to USD 1.4. Source: SDR Valuation (imf.org).

847. These figures were increased in the Convention in 2000 as a result of the sinking of *Nakhoda* and *Erika*, going into effect from 1 Nov. 2003 (by an amendment to the Act of 5 Apr. 2002).

the Maritime Act do not limit reimbursement claims for the costs covered by the public authorities in connection with cleanup of a major oil spill pursuant to the PCA Articles 74–76.[848]

If the oil pollution occurs in a sea area which is not covered by the convention (in the waters of a State which is not party to the convention, or on the high seas), Article 207 applies instead of Article 194. However, the rules on limitations of liability are the same as in Article 194. With respect to ships that only transport oil as bunker, the special rules on limitation of oil pollution liability do not apply. Instead, the general rules of global limitation of shipping liability apply (Article 208 and Chapter 9).

964. Within the field of application of the international rules, the owner of a ship that transports at least 2,000 tons of oil in bulk has a *duty to be properly insured* against oil pollution liability. The insurance must cover the possible amount of the damages, as defined by the limitation rules (Article 197 paragraph 1). This obligation applies to all Norwegian ships, and to foreign ships that call at or leave a Norwegian port or installation on the Norwegian continental shelf (Article 197 paragraph 2).

The injured party may claim recovery directly from the responsible insurance company (Article 200).

965. To the extent that the damages and losses covered by the international rules exceed the limited amount pursuant to the limitation rules, compensation may be claimed from the International Fund for Compensation for Oil Pollution Damage. This Fund, based in London, is financed by a levy on oil imports.[849] From November 2003 it is limited to 203 million SDRs (about USD 280 million). The International Convention establishing the fund, as well as its 2003 Protocol establishing an International Oil Pollution Compensation Supplementary Fund, are explicitly incorporated into Norwegian law (Article 201).

The fund will also pay if the shipowner is not liable at all by virtue of one of the exceptions referred to above, or if the shipowner is financially incapable of meeting his/her obligations in full.

966. For pollution caused by discharge of *bunker oil* the rules in the International Convention on Civil Liability for Bunker Oil Pollution Damage of 2001 apply. The main rules have been included in Chapter 10, Articles 183–190 of the Maritime Act. The same basic principles apply as those already described with regard to oil pollution from oil transport in bulk: As the main rule only *the owner* of the ship is strictly liable, but other actors may be held liable if they have caused the pollution damage by intent or gross negligence, and understood that such a damage was likely to occur. The liability covers damage or loss caused by the discharge

848. Norsk Retstidende 2017.331 on liability and the duty to remove the wreck after the shipwreck of the merchant ship 'Server' on the Western coast of Norway.

849. It applies to oil companies that transport more than 150,000 tons of oil by sea per year, or purchase the same amount of oil that has been transported by sea.

or spill of oil from the vessel and reasonable measures to prevent and limit pollution damage, and to restore the environment. Furthermore, the same limitation rules apply. Also, the owner has a duty of insurance in accordance with the general international requirements (Article 186). Compensation may be claimed directly from the insurance company (Article 188).

967. If an oil spill falls under the liability rules of the *Petroleum Act,* the rules of the Petroleum Act apply. This will be the case, for example, with oil spills from a movable drilling rig. However, if the ship in question is covered by the International Liability Convention, the rules of the Convention also apply. In that case, the rules overlap; both the licensee and operator of the oil installation, and the owner of the ship, are liable. This will be the case if the spill occurs during a tanker's loading of oil from an oil installation.

968. There are no special rules in the Maritime Act regulating the liability for *other types of pollution from ships than oil.* Such cases are subject to a combination of general tort law for shipping activity (Chapters 8 and 9 in the Maritime Act), and the general rules in Chapter 8 of the PCA. It is not quite clear how these two sets of rules mutually relate. Most likely, the general rules in the PCA on strict liability for owners/operators (Article 55) and on types of damage and costs covered (Articles 57 and 58) apply. However, it is maintained that the general rules in the Maritime Act (Article 9) regarding limitation of liability must apply.

The International Convention on Liability and Compensation for Damage in Connection with the Carriage of *Hazardous and Noxious Substances by Sea* (the *'HNS-Convention'*) was adopted in 1996. In April 2010, a Protocol on the main unsolved issues to the Convention was negotiated and signed by seventy States, paving the way for ratification. Under these rules the shipowner will be strictly liable for any damage caused by HNS. Shipowners carrying HNS by sea are required to have sufficient insurance to cover their liability. The 2010 HNS Protocol will enter into force eighteen months after the date on which it is ratified by at least twelve States, including four States each with not less than 2 million units of gross tonnage, and having received during the preceding calendar year a total quantity of at least 40 million tonnes of cargo that would be contributing to the general account. As the first State Norway has ratified the protocol. However, in September 2021 only five states have ratified and the Protocol is still not in force.

III. Liability Pursuant to the Nuclear Energy Act

969. Norway has no nuclear power plants, but has several smaller installations for nuclear energy research. An *Act on Nuclear Energy*[850] was adopted as early as 1972. It establishes the necessary legal framework for the establishment and management of nuclear energy installations, including rules on liability and insurance in case of accidents resulting in damage from nuclear radiation and the like.

850. Act of 12 May 1972 No. 28 with later amendments, mainly by Act of 15 Jun. 2007 No. 37.

This comprehensive and detailed set of rules implements the international conventions and protocols in the field, to which Norway is party.[851] They implement the 2004 Protocol to the Paris and Brussels Conventions. The Act sets out strict liability for the owner of the nuclear installation. This is the physical or legal person either who has the licence to establish and run the installation, or – if a licence is not required – who operates the installation (Article 20). This rule also applies during transport of nuclear material from the installation until it has reached its destination (Article 21).

In other respects as well, the rules are generally quite similar to those regarding oil pollution from ships. Incidents of 'force majeure', like natural disasters and war, exempt the owner from liability. The liability is limited, at present, to 60 million SDRs. A lower limit may be established by the government, taking into account the size of the installation, the amount transported and so on, but never less than 5 million SDR (Article 30 No. 1). The owner of a nuclear installation has a duty to insure his/her possible liability for damages in case of nuclear accident (Article 35). In case the damages exceed the amount, full recovery may be claimed from the State (Article 40).

851. The European 1960 Paris Convention and its supplementary 1963 Brussels Convention as amended by the 1964, 1982, and 2004 Protocols, and the global 1963 Vienna Convention. The Paris and Vienna Conventions have been linked together through the 1988 Joint Protocol relating to the Application of the Vienna Convention and the Paris Convention.

Chapter 2. Criminal Liability

§1. Introduction

970. During the last decades, environmental crimes have been subject to increasing public attention in Norway. In 1989, a special central authority for the investigation and prosecution of economic and environmental crime was established ('ØKOKRIM'). Since then, the number of cases has been steadily increasing. In 2020, the government presented a white paper on environmental crime to Stortinget.[852] It describes the various types of environmental crime within the three main areas, pollution, nature conservation, and protection of cultural heritage. It draws a gloomy picture: These types of crime are widespread and the work to prevent them is often difficult. Among the types described under nature conservation are illegal hunting, fishing and other illegal killing of animals and birds, violation of the CITES Regulation on export and import of endangered species, building in violation of the PBA, violations of the Act relating to Motor Traffic on Uncultivated Land and Water Courses, and illegal import and marketing of alien species. Among the types described as crimes related to pollution are illegal pollution from petroleum activity on the continental shelf, from ships, and from industrial activity, illegal treatment of hazardous waste and export of waste, and illegal destruction of end-of-life vessels. In the cultural heritage area, the paper describes numerous violations of the Cultural Heritage Act such as the destruction of protected houses and ancient objects.

971. Each of the Acts that have been the subject of earlier parts of this monograph lays down penalties for violations of its rules and of regulations and decisions pursuant to its rules. Usually, violations are punishable if they are done intentionally or out of negligence, and they may result in fines, imprisonment, or both. These rules have been presented above, in connection with the various Acts discussed.

972. The National Authority for Investigation and Prosecution of Economic and Environmental Crime in Norway *(ØKOKRIM)* is the central State institution for the investigation and prosecution of both economic and environmental crime. ØKOKRIM is both a police specialist agency and a public prosecutor's office with national authority. ØKOKRIM's overall objective is to combat economic crime, environmental crime and laundering of proceeds of crime. Its main tasks are to uncover, investigate, prosecute and bring to trial its own cases, and to assist the national and international police and prosecuting authorities and various public agencies in the environmental field in their work to combat various types of environmental crime.

973. Another important institution for the control and enforcement of environmental law is the *State Nature Inspection* (Statens naturoppsyn), which is based on

852. Meld. St. 19 (2019–2020) Miljøkriminalitet, discussed by the committee in Stortinget in Innst. 68 S. (2020–2021).

a special Act.[853] This organization is formally placed under the Directorate for Nature Management and, thus, under the MCE. Through some sixty local offices all over the country, its task is to prevent, detect and report environmental crime, in particular violations of legislation in the fields of nature protection, wildlife management, public recreation, cultural heritage and pollution. Members of the staff spend much time outdoor, in particular in areas with important and vulnerable natural and cultural values. They work in close cooperation with the police, and may be provided with limited police authority pursuant to the Police Act.[854]

974. An important general rule in Norwegian penal law is the criminal liability for companies and other institutions – *corporate liability* – as laid down in Articles 27 and 28 of the Penal Code.[855] A company or corporation may be punished by fines if a person violates the law when acting for, or on behalf of, the company or corporation. This also covers State and municipal bodies. In one case, a municipality was punished with a fine because its waste incinerator contravened the requirements under the PCA.[856]

It is not necessary for any individual to be found guilty according to the penalty provision, and thus to be personally punishable (Article 27). The company may also be punished in situations of so-called anonymous faults. This refers to situations where a violation has occurred, but where it is difficult or impossible to identify particular persons as criminal responsible, or to bring sufficient proof in that respect. For example, the company may be punished if the general system of surveillance and oversight proves to be insufficient, or if instructions are not properly made known.[857] It is obvious that this rule is of great relevance and importance in many cases of environmental crime.

The decision to punish a company on the basis of this rule is made by the court (or the pollution control authority) in each case, on the basis of a discretionary assessment. The court shall take into account the seriousness of the Act, whether the violation could have been prevented through guidelines, instruction, training, control and the like, whether the violation has been profitable or in other ways favourable for the company, the economic situation of the company, and so on.

975. The amount of the fines for environmental crimes by companies may be quite high. In 2001, a chemical factory was fined NOK 4 million[858] for discharging 1 kg of mercury into a fjord. This has been the highest fine until now (2021).

853. Act of 21 Jun. 1996 No. 38 on the State Nature Inspection.
854. Act of 1 Oct. 1995 No. 53.
855. Act of 20 May 2005 No. 28. Articles 27 and 28 are in accordance with the corresponding Art. 48a and 48b in the former Act.
856. Norsk Retstidende 1989, 733.
857. In a case from 2007, a company was fined NOK 1.2 million (USD 150,000) pursuant to the former Art. 48a and 48b. An employee had discharged large amounts of ammonia into a river causing massive fish starvation. The company lacked instructions and proper control systems to prevent the action (Norsk retstidende 2007, 1684).
858. This corresponds to nearly USD 700,000.

However, up to now there have been only a few cases where the person responsible has been imprisoned for a violation of the pollution legislation.[859]

Imprisonment has, however, been used in several cases of fauna crimes, notably in cases of illegal hunting of protected birds of prey and other bird species for commercial purposes.[860]

The intentional killing of predators that kill or threaten to kill domestic animals is a difficult and controversial issue within the field of environmental crime. Here, the rules in the NDA and the Wildlife Act apply (*See supra* Part II, Chapter 2 §3).

§2. The General Provisions on Environmental Crime in the Penal Code

976. Articles 240, 241 and 242 of the Penal Code set forth a *general penalty provision* for environmental crime and crime related to cultural heritage. The rules were first adopted in 1993 as Article 152B of the former (1902) Penal Code, and this was included in the new (2005) Penal Code with some amendments. It covers *the most serious types of environmental crime,* and it introduced considerably stricter penalties for this type of crime than before.

977. Article 240 *paragraph 1* deals with criminal actions related to *pollution and waste disposal.* It supplements the penal provisions in the PCA. Whoever by intent or gross negligence pollutes air, water or soil, in such a way that the natural environment within an area is considerably damaged or threatened, may be punished with up to fifteen years of imprisonment. The same applies if a person causes considerable damage or poses a threat by storing, leaving or discharging waste or other substances.

978. The *paragraph 2* of Article 240 deals with intentional or grossly negligent actions which damage the *natural environment*, notably:

- to reduce a natural stock of protected living organisms which are threatened by extinction nationally or internationally;
- to cause considerable damage to an area which is protected pursuant to the 1970 Nature Conservation Act, the NDA or the Svalbard Environmental Act (as well

859. The first case is found in Norsk Retstidende 1992, 1578. The person was a captain on a foreign vessel that stranded on a reef off the Norwegian coast. The wreckage caused a very serious oil spill close to a valuable seabird reserve. Due to technical problems, the ship drifted for several days, but the captain refused assistance. The captain was found guilty of violating his duty, pursuant to the Pollution Control Act, to prevent the pollution. A similar accident took place on Norway's southern coast in 2009. The captain was sentenced to six months imprisonment for negligent violation of the Pollution Control Act and the Ship Safety Act. In a more recent case before the Supreme Court the owner of a site for chemical waste, including storage tanks was sentenced to two years in prison for intent and gross negligence in the treatment of used petrol. The result was a major explosion with emissions creating serious health effects in the local community (Norsk Retstidende 2012 p. 65).

860. In one case, the person had killed more than 200 birds of seventy-two different protected species (Rt. 1992, 1256). The result was eight months of imprisonment.

as the Acts governing the Norwegian island Jan Mayen in the North Atlantic Ocean, Bouvet Island and Peter I Island and the South Atlantic Ocean, and Queens Maud's Land in Antarctica).

Such actions may be punished with up to six years of imprisonment.

This article was applied by the Supreme Court in a case from 2016 that created much publicity and debate. A group of people in a local community which was critical to the policy on the management of wolves, made preparations together for the illegal killing of several wolves, tried to kill these wolves and actually killed one wolf. They got penalties from 1 year to 120 days in prison, and several years of prohibition of hunting.[861]

979. Article 242 deals with crimes related to *cultural heritage*. It supplements the penal provisions in the Cultural Heritage Act.[862] Whoever by intent or gross negligence causes considerable damage to objects or sites of cultural heritage which are of special national or international value, may be punished with up to six years of imprisonment. Imprisonment of up to two years applies to a person who in an armed conflict, by intent or gross negligence, uses an object or a site of cultural heritage of particular national or international value as a basis or support for military activities and by this creates a risk of damage to the object or site – unless this activity was imperative from a military point of view.

980. So far, the provisions of these articles have been applied in very few cases. This is probably mainly due to the fact that it only applies to actions with very serious consequences, be they real or only possible. The threshold is set rather high. For the prosecuting authority, it may be easier to apply the rules in the special Acts, such as the PCA or the Cultural Heritage Act. They are more precise, and violations are easier to prove. Imprisonment and quite heavy fines may be applied on the basis of these Acts as well.

One may, however, presume that the articles have a certain preventive effect.

861. Case HR-2016-09-01.
862. Act of 9 Jun. 1978 No. 50, Art. 27.

Part V. Juridical Actions by Individuals

Chapter 1. Administrative Remedies

§1. Introduction and Overview

981. Administrative remedies consist of procedures whereby persons can ask an administrative authority to revoke, annul or modify an administrative decision. In the system of Norwegian public law, the main administrative remedy is the *administrative appeal.* It is a fundamental rule in our public administrative law that any decision made in individual cases by a public authority may be subject to appeal to a superior authority,[863] unless otherwise explicitly stated. The right to appeal is, however, limited to persons who are 'parties' to the case, or who otherwise have a 'legal interest of appeal'. The authority of the appeal body is usually as wide as that of the authority in the first instance. It may control not only legal aspects but also how the discretionary power has been exercised and may thus also come to a different result as to the content of the decision. In some cases, however, the authority of the appeal body may be somewhat limited. Norway has no administrative court separated from the ordinary courts.[864]

In some Acts in the field of environment, there are special rules on the right of appeal. Normally, these replace the general rules. We shall revert to these issues below (§§2 and 3).

982. Regardless of whether a decision has been appealed or not, a citizen may always present his/her case to the Parliamentary Ombud for Scrutiny of the Public Administration. The Parliamentary Ombud is appointed by the Parliament, Stortinget. His/her role is to control, on behalf of Stortinget, the application of the legislation by the central and local administration. We shall revert to a more detailed discussion of this below (§4).

---

863. Public Administration Act of 10 Feb. 1967, Art. 28.

864. Except in certain areas of public law, notably the area of social security. A central Social Security Court replaces the local Court of the First Instance in the ordinary court system. However, the Courts of Appeal in the ordinary court system are appellate bodies for decisions by the Social Security Court. And the Supreme Court has the final word in these cases as well. A similar system applies to employment disputes, where an Employment Court, composed of representatives of the employers' and employees' unions, is first instance.

§2. General Rules on Administrative Procedure and Appeal

983. The Public Administration Act[865] lays down general rules of procedure for actions and decisions by public authorities. The Act applies to actions and decisions of a public law nature. This means the exercise of public authority as opposed to activities regulated by private law.[866] The Act covers procedural rules for both regulations and individual decisions.

These rules apply generally, to the extent that there are no other rules on the same issues in specific legislation. Quite often, other Acts make explicit reference to the general rules in the Public Administration Act, and in addition to some special rules. Even without such a reference, it is generally understood that the Public Administration Act complements rules of procedure in special legislation.

984. With regard to *individual decisions,* the procedural rights mainly apply to the *'parties'* to the case.

'Party' is defined in Article 2 of the Act. A party is 'a person to whom a decision is directed, or whom it directly concerns'. A person who applies for a pollution permit is clearly a party to the case. Also, the closest neighbours which are directly affected will be regarded as parties. Their well-being and health may be affected, or the pollution or nuisance may impair or reduce the value of their property. It is doubtful, and somewhat disputed, to what extent neighbours in a wider circle may be accepted as parties. In any case, this depends on the extent to which they may be affected by the pollution. At least, a neighbour ought to be regarded as party to the case if his/her health or the value of his/her property is at stake. An environmental organization is party to a case when the organization as such is the subject of a case or initiates it, but not just because the case is of interest to the members – even if it is important from an environmental point of view.

The party has a right to be heard after prior notification, and a right to examine the documents of the case. He/she also has the right to be informed about the decision taken, and the reason for the decision.

It should be noted that the Administrative Procedure Act only ensures these important rights for the parties. They do not apply to the general public concerned, nor to interested environmental associations. Instead, their right to be informed and participate in the decision-making are ensured through special rules of procedure to this effect in the relevant special Acts. As described, most of the Acts in the environmental field, such as the PCA, the PBA, and the NDA have themselves detailed rules on procedure for decisions pursuant to the Act, including rules on information to the public, participation, possible hearings, etc. They also may have rules on appeal.

An important rule with a general application is Article 17 of the Public Administration Act. It supplements procedural rules in the various special acts by obliging

865. Act of 10 Feb. 1967.

866. This distinction may however be difficult to draw in some cases, for example, in cases of important purchases by State or municipal authorities, and various types of public service. Increased privatization of public service, wholly or partly, gives rise to new 'grey zones' in this area.

the public authority to ensure that *all relevant information be gathered and considered 'to the extent possible'* before a decision is made. This means that the authority has a duty to actively seek useful information and opinions from all relevant actors and associations.

Furthermore, organizations as well as the general public are to have access to relevant documents in the files of administrative bodies, pursuant to the Public Information Act.[867] According to this Act, all documents related to activities and decisions by public authorities must be made available to the public on request, unless they are exempted for reasons mentioned in the Act.[868] In addition, most of the environmental Acts contain special rules of public participation, and the general rules on EIA apply.

985. Article 28 of the Public Administration Act lays down the general rule that *a decision of public administration in individual cases may be subject to appeal* to the authority superior to the authority that made the decision. The decision of the appeal body may not be appealed further.

A decision made by a subordinate State authority is to be appealed to its superior body. If the Ministry makes a decision as the first instance (which is unusual), the King in Council is the appellate authority.

A decision made by a subordinate local authority should normally be appealed to the local council or the county council (Article 28 paragraph 2). However, there are rules in the special legislation to the effect that a State authority is the appellate body in certain local decisions.

It is explicitly stated in Article 28 paragraph 3 that special appeal rules may be laid down in other legislations. However, the right to appeal cannot be removed or strictly limited to the detriment of the citizens' interest unless there are weighty reasons for it.

986. Not everybody has the right to appeal. Article 28 states that a decision may be appealed by 'a party or another person with legal interest of appeal'.

The concept 'legal interest of appeal' is rooted in Norwegian court procedure. 'Legal interest' has been the key criterion for *locus standi* in civil court cases.[869] It is generally maintained that the criterion 'legal interest of appeal' in the Public Administration Act to a large extent corresponds to the 'legal interest' concept in

867. Act of 19 May 2006 No. 16.

868. Chapter 3 of the Act. In fact, it contains a number of exceptions from the general principle of public access to information. For example, exempted here are 'internal documents', as well as external reports and so on, which an authority has ordered in connection with the preparation of a case. Also important is the general exception for *confidential information*. This includes information about technical devices and solutions, procedures, operational matters and business relations, etc., which it is important for *competition reasons* to keep confidential in the interest of the person whom the information concerns.

869. In the new Civil Procedure Act of 17 Jun. 2005 No. 90 Art. 1-3(2), this expression has been replaced by '... a real need to have the claim against the defendant settled', based on a broad assessment of the claim and the parties' connection to the case. However, the meaning is meant to be more or less unchanged.

the Civil Procedure Act,[870] though in certain aspects its field of application is somewhat wider. The argument is that it should not be more difficult, but rather somewhat easier, to appeal a decision to a higher administrative body than to put the court system to work.

In actual fact, the administrative practice is rather liberal in environmental cases. Most of the environmental legislation has rules of procedure that encourage all citizens, members of the public, to voice their opinion. By this, their interest in the case is indirectly recognized. A strict interpretation of 'legal interest of appeal' would not be in good harmony with this view.

However, a person with only an 'ideal' interest in a decision will normally be refused the right to appeal.

987. A practical question here is whether the law recognizes non-governmental *environmental associations* as having 'legal interest of appeal' in environmental cases. Based on certain cases before the Supreme Court regarding the question of *locus standi* for environmental associations, it is fair to say that they will, as a rule, have the right of administrative appeal. This right is not confined to certain associations specified in the Acts, or to solely national associations, but the association must satisfy certain (minimum) conditions related to its purpose, structure, and so on (*see* Chapter 2 *infra*). In reality, the administration has been rather liberal in this respect.

During the last decade, numerous decisions by the environmental authorities have been appealed by various environmental associations and groups in Norway. It is fair to say that environmental associations and groups carry out an important 'watchdog' function in the Norwegian society, which is generally appreciated by the public at large.

988. The general appeal procedure rules require that an *appeal be addressed to the authority that made the decision in the first instance.* The ordinary time limit is three weeks from when the decision was made known, but the limit may be prolonged by a special decision. The authority may choose to change its own decision if it finds sufficient reasons for doing so. If it upholds its decision, the case is submitted to the appellate body.

An administrative appeal of a decision does not have a suspensive effect, unless this is decided in each case (Article 42 of the Public Administration Act). Thus, the appeal does not in itself prevent or delay its implementation. A person who, for example, has obtained a pollution permit according to the PCA may normally proceed with the project even if the permit has been appealed on environmental grounds. In order to prevent irreversible actions from being taken in such a case, an action must be brought before the local court acting in a special capacity as a court of execution and enforcement (*see infra*).

870. 'Legal interest' was the explicit expression used in the former Act on court procedure in civil cases (Art. 54). In the present Civil Procedure Act of 17 Jun. 2005 No. 90, Art. 1-3, this expression has been replaced by 'a real need to have the case decided', which shall be based on an assessment of the current interest and the plaintiff's connection to the case. In reality this is meant to correspond *grosso modo* to the traditional interpretation of the former 'legal interest' criterion.

989. As mentioned, the general rule in Norwegian law is that *the appellate body has the legal competence to try all aspects of the decision:* the procedure, the legal issue, and its substantial content – the discretion exercised by the first administrative instance. It may, of course, confirm and maintain the decision. It may also revoke it, make a new decision, or return the case to the first instance to be reconsidered.

The relationship between political bodies at the local and county level and the State administration may be somewhat sensitive in Norway. The general policy is to extend the decision-making powers of the local authorities. Some decisions made by local or county authorities may, however, still be appealed to the relevant State authority, pursuant to special rules. In such cases, the State authority has a legal obligation to 'give much weight to the local self-government' when considering the discretionary part of the decision. In its decision, the authority shall make it clear how the local self-government has been weighed (Article 34 paragraph 2). This is highly relevant, for example, when a local development plan adopted by the local council, pursuant to the PBA, is appealed to the State county governor.

990. Normally, an administrative appeal relates to a formal decision made by a public authority. In environmental matters, the *inaction* of the authority faced with damage or threat to the environment may be a problem. A question is whether citizens or environmental associations may require decisions to be made to ensure the protection of environmental values, or whether they may appeal the implicit decision of passivity or inaction.

Although there are nuances here, the main rule in Norwegian administrative law is that inaction is not the same as a decision, and usually not subject to appeal or other types of enforcement mechanisms. Rules to the opposite effect must be laid down in legislation. One example of such a rule is found in Article 37 paragraph 3 of the PCA, which concerns orders to clear up waste and the like. If a person asks the municipality to issue an order to clear up illegal waste, the municipality must make a decision on the case. If no such order is issued, the inaction of the municipality is formally regarded as a decision which is subject to administrative procedure rules pursuant to the rules in the Public Administration Act Article 28, including the rules on the right to appeal.

§3. The Parliamentary Ombud[871] for Scrutiny of the Public Administration

991. In Norway, the Parliamentary Ombud (*Sivilombudet*) was established as early as 1962 by a special Act.[872] This was replaced by a new Act in 2021.[873] The Ombud is independent of the government as the 'watchdog' of Stortinget as regards

871. Until recently the title was the Parliamentary Ombudsman. In order to a make the title 'sexually neutral' (as part of a general trend in Norwegian public administration), it was changed to 'ombud'.
872. Act of 22 Jun. 1962 No. 8.
873. Act of 18 Jun. 2021 No. 121 on the Parliamentary Ombud.

the government's application of the legislation. He or she[874] is elected by Stortinget for four years and may be reelected once (Act Article 2). She reports directly to Stortinget through an annual report, which is subject to debate in Stortinget. Through this mechanism, Stortinget and its members become aware of problems in the application of the legislation, may express their views on the application of various Acts and regulations and identify areas where adjustments or reforms in the application of a law seem desirable.

The Parliamentary Ombud supervises public administration agencies. The main purpose of the Ombud is *to ensure that every citizen is treated properly and reasonably by the public administration, and that the public authorities respect and ensure the human rights.* Her function is, however, not limited to the interest of individuals; she may also look into cases where the question is whether public interest such as the environment is treated properly. She may raise issues and question rules and administrative practice ex officio. But her work is mainly based on complaints from citizens or organizations in connection with individual cases. The institution of the Ombud thus provides the citizens with an extra tool, in addition to administrative appeal and civil lawsuits. Her authority covers decisions by local and county authorities as well as State authorities at all levels.

992. However, the powers of the Ombud are different from those of an administrative authority and a court, in the sense that *the Ombud does not have the authority to make a decision in a case.* Her authority is limited in Article 12 of the Act. When she has considered a case, she expresses her opinion on the matter. If she finds that the public authority has made a mistake, has shown negligence or acted clearly contrary to good administrative practice, when treating the matter, she points it out to the relevant authority. She may state that she finds the decision illegal or clearly unreasonable. She may also express the opinion that certain facts of importance to the case seem to be questionable, or that the case may raise the issue of liability and compensation.

When an authority is criticized by the Ombud, it most often corrects the mistake and changes its decision accordingly. This is clearly the intention. In a recent case, the Ombud formally complained to Stortinget that a Ministry did not follow two recommendations. Stortinget took the opportunity to confirm the main rule that the view of the Ombud was violated, and asked the government to see to it that the authorities accept and follow up the views and recommendations expressed by the Ombud.[875] In the strict legal sense, however, the authority is not obliged to follow the Ombud's recommendation. It may find the views expressed by the Ombud simply legally wrong, unjust, or too difficult to apply, and maintain its decision.

The Ombud may itself initiate enquiries and investigations into both individual cases and more general issues. If she finds weaknesses or defects in a rule or administrative practice, she will inform the relevant authority. Serious weaknesses or mistakes will also be reported to Stortinget.

874. Presently the Ombud is Mrs Hanne Harlem, a woman, thus I chose to use 'she' in the following.
875. *See* Stortinget Dokument 4:2 (2015–2016) and Innst. 376 S. (2015–2016).

993. The formalities of the Ombud's work are quite simple. Anybody who feels that he or she has been treated unjustly by a public authority may file a complaint. Here, there is no formal requirement of 'legal interest', but the Ombud has the full discretion to refuse to consider a matter (Article 10). There are quite simple requirements as regards the form of the complaint. It must be filed within one year after the decision or action in question, and the matter must have been subject to administrative appeal and decided by the appellate body (Article 8).

The further procedure is also straightforward. There are few formal rules. The Ombud may demand access to any document or other information from the relevant authorities which she finds necessary. She will receive most of the information in writing, but she may also meet with the parties.

994. The Ombud is an important institution in Norway. However, so far, the number of cases concerning the application of environmental legislation has been limited. Often, in such cases, the petitioner is a citizen who has been denied an activity or a construction, for example, pursuant to the PBA. Only in a limited number of cases environmental interest groups have filed complaints.

Chapter 2. Judicial Remedies in Civil Cases

§1. The Court System

995. The court system functions as the ultimate legal safeguard for the citizens, in environmental cases as well as in other legal disputes. Norway has a single general court system. The ordinary courts treat all types of legal disputes and criminal cases. As mentioned, there is no general administrative court in Norway. Neither is there a constitutional court in the Norwegian court system. The ordinary courts have competence in constitutional cases as well, such as the constitutionality of legislation and decisions by public authorities.

There are *three levels* in the court system: the district courts, the higher courts (appeal courts) and the Supreme Court. In addition, civil cases have to be considered by a conciliation board before they are admitted to the district court as the Court of First Instance. Article 88 of the constitution – Grunnloven – states explicitly that the Supreme Court has the final say in legal matters. However, the Supreme Court may, on grounds of opportunity, refuse an appeal in a civil case. In criminal cases, the Supreme Court may, generally speaking, only consider legal matters, not questions of proof, or the like.

996. The rules on the court system, and the procedural rules, are laid down in three major pieces of legislation: the Court Act,[876] the Civil Proceedings Act,[877] and the Criminal Proceedings Act.[878] For the enforcement of decisions, a special Act – the Execution and Enforcement Act[879] – applies.

§2. General Issues

997. The *question of standing* is particularly important in environmental cases. As mentioned above, the key criterion for *locus standi* in civil court cases has traditionally been 'legal interest'. This expression was in the 2005 Civil Procedure Act replaced by ' … a real need to have the claim against the defendant settled'.[880] The dispute must be a live – not a moot – controversy, and the plaintiff must have a sufficiently close connection to the subject matter so as to justify the court's treatment of the dispute. Whether a person has *locus standi* is decided discretionarily in each case, and depends on individual circumstances. The core question to ask is whether the person has reasonable grounds for having the issue tried by a court. In general, the plaintiff must be directly affected by the matter, to such an extent that it justifies the use of the court system. Also, interests which are merely based on public or common rights, such as the public right of way, may be accepted if they are strong enough for the plaintiff in particular.

876. Act of 13 Aug. 1915 No. 5.
877. Act of 17 Jun. 2005 No. 90.
878. Act of 22 May 1981 No. 25.
879. Act of 26 Jun. 1992 No. 86.
880. Civil Proceedings Act Art. 1-3(2).

However, a purely 'ideal' interest in the matter is not sufficient. For example, an ordinary citizen does not have *locus standi* in a case concerning the authorities' licensing to kill wolves, based on his or her general interest in the protection of these predators.

998. Based on Supreme Court cases, non-governmental *environmental associations* generally have been accepted to have sufficient 'legal interest' in environmental cases. This principle was established by the Supreme Court in 1980, in the Alta case (*see infra*). The court accepted that the Norwegian Association for Nature Conservation could sue the government in respect of the validity of the decision to build a hydropower dam and station on the Alta river.[881]

The Supreme Court has also accepted *locus standi* for associations in a case of compensation for pollution damage. A nationwide association, with the objective of influencing lifestyle and reducing private consumption on the basis of international solidarity and environmental protection,[882] was entitled to bring an action for compensation for pollution damage to fishing and recreational areas against two chemical factories in the southern part of Norway. The local branch of the Swedish Association for Nature Conservation in the affected area was also found to have standing in the case.[883] The claim in this case was based on Article 58 of the PCA (*see supra* Part IV, Chapter 1, §3). The possible compensation would be used for fishing and recreational purposes pursuant to a decision by the municipality.

999. As these cases show, an organization may bring an action before the courts on 'ideal' environmental grounds. It is not necessary that any individual member of the organization be directly affected by the decision in question. Neither is it necessary that the organization be regarded as the one most natural to represent the interests in question.[884] Hence, this right is not confined to certain associations specified in the legislation or to truly national associations. It applies to any association, national and local, whose aim covers the matter at stake. It is generally required, however, that the association be 'serious', in the sense of having bylaws and a well-established organizational structure. It must not necessarily have general membership; a foundation may also have *locus standi*. However, it is usually maintained that an association established for the sole purpose of bringing an action to court will not be accepted as a plaintiff.

1000. In spite of the fact that environmental organizations have a relatively open access to courts, *very few environmental cases actually come before the courts* in Norway, in particular when compared with the role of the courts in environmental cases in many other industrialized countries. There may be several reasons for this. One reason may be that Norway's environmental legislation is dominated by widely formulated rules which leave much discretion to the executive bodies. As the main

881. Norsk Retstidende 1980, 569 ('Alta case I').
882. *Framtiden i våre hender* (literally: 'The Future in our Hands').
883. Norsk Retstidende 1992, 1618.
884. In the last case, neither the local fishermen nor any local association for outdoor recreational activities brought actions against the factories.

rule, the courts cannot – in the Norwegian system – try the way the administration has applied the legislation within the limits of its discretionary power (*see infra* §3, I). This clearly limits the possibility of having a decision annulled by the court. A second reason may be the relatively good opportunity for administrative appeal (*see supra* Chapter 1, §2), as well as the possible appeal to the Parliamentary Ombud (*see supra* Chapter 1, §3). A third reason may be the rules on the sharing of costs in court cases.

1001. An important element in the Norwegian system of courts and proceedings in civil cases is *the set of rules concerning the costs* of a court case. The main rule is that the winning party shall have all its costs covered by the losing party, including the costs of its own attorney. In addition, the principle of 'no cure, no pay' for legal services is rarely applied in Norway. It may thus be quite costly to lose a court case and quite risky to go to court in the first place.

It is quite likely that this risk is one of the main causes of the limited number of environmental disputes in Norwegian courts. It discourages both individuals and organizations from bringing such cases before the courts. In addition, in environmental cases, the matter is often of only limited economic importance for the plaintiff on the side of the environment, but may be of great economic importance for the defendant. The defendant may often be either the State or another public authority, or a company, with considerable resources and first-rate attorneys at its disposal. Furthermore, in cases where an environmental organization want to challenge, for example, a permit given to a development project, the project may already be underway and even finished before the case is decided by the court. An *action of temporary injunction* may prevent this (*see infra*), but the threshold is rather high in practice.

According to Article 9 (4) of the Aarhus Convention concerning access to justice, the access to court in cases covered by the convention shall be ' … fair, equitable, timely and *not prohibitively expensive*'. With regard to the court system, it may seriously be questioned whether the Norwegian system is in accordance with this requirement.

§3. Examples

I. Decisions by a Public Authority

1002. The plaintiff may demand the annulment or change of a decision made by a public authority. Such a decision may be pursuant to an environmental protection Act, such as a pollution permit pursuant to the PCA, or the protection of an area pursuant to the NDA. Or it may be a decision to develop an area, build a major road, a wind power farm, or a hydropower plant and the like, which is challenged on environmental grounds. In these cases, the defendant is the public authority that made the decision, which is to say, the State or the municipality.

The most famous environmental case of this type is the so-called *Alta case II* of 1981.[885] It concerned the decision pursuant to the 1917 Hydropower Act to construct a major dam for hydropower production on the Alta river in Finnmark in Northern Norway, a traditional Sami area. The decision was challenged on several substantial and procedural grounds, but the Supreme Court (who met in plenary) upheld the decision.

1003. What can the court decide in this type of cases? The *doctrine of judicial review* is important in Norwegian public administrative law.

1004. The starting point is that the court may review the *legality* of the decision. First, it must consider whether the legal rules in question have been interpreted correctly, whether they cover the case in point, and whether they have been properly applied to the case. If the law has not been properly interpreted or applied, the decision must be revoked.

Second, it must review the applied procedure. If there have been procedural mistakes or flaws, the consequences are left to the court to decide. If the mistake most likely did not influence the final decision, the decision must be upheld regardless of the mistake.[886] If the decision may have influenced the decision, however, the result is left to the discretion of the court, taking account of the cause and the importance of the mistake, and, in general, what a reasonable outcome would be.

1005. In Norwegian public law doctrine, the discretion of a public authority must not only comply with the wording of the authorizing rule. It must also respect certain *general principles and limitations.* In using its discretion, the public authority must assess and consider all relevant issues. The decision must not be blatantly unreasonable, or discriminate against certain parties compared to others. The court must consider whether the decision violates these principles and rules. If so, the decision will, as a rule, be revoked.

The Norwegian doctrine of public administrative law does not include a general principle of proportionality in the sense that the courts may or should review the proportionality of a decision and annul or correct a decision on that basis. But the extent of the judicial review in this respect is a matter of current discussion among legal scholars. It is maintained that a public authority has *a general duty to consider the proportionality* of its decision. If it is not clear from the decision that this has been done properly, and the court questions the reasonableness of the decision, it may be revoked. Also, by the fact that the principle of proportionality plays a real role in EU law and mark decisions by the European Court of Justice, it is foreseen that the principle will gradually move into Norwegian administrative law as a general principle as well.

1006. In order to stop a decision which permits an activity or a construction that threatens environmental resources, it is necessary to prevent its implementation

885. Norsk Retstidende 1982, 241.
886. Administrative Procedure Act Art. 41.

until the case has been finally decided. The legal mechanism which is at the plaintiff's disposal is an *action of temporary injunction* before the local court acting as a 'court of execution and enforcement'. Through a temporary injunction, the court may prohibit the execution of the decision until the matter has been conclusively decided. This function of the court is defined in the Execution and Enforcement Act, in particular in its Chapter 15.

If the plaintiff claims that a public decision, such as a pollution permit, is invalid and should be changed or revoked, a temporary injunction may be laid down by the court if it finds the claim 'probable' (Article 15-6 paragraph 1). However, this is not required in case of 'danger' if the action is not postponed (Article 15-6 paragraph 2). In any case, the court must carry out a temporary review of the matter, in order to decide whether the claim has a reasonable basis. In most cases, this actually requires a preliminary assessment of the substance of the case.[887] In a recent case, the environmental association 'Våre rovdyr' (literally 'Our predators'), which works to protect animals of prey, succeeded in stopping the execution of a decision to kill a family of wolves, by claiming a temporary injunction to this effect. The court found that the law did not authorize such a decision under the circumstances.[888]

II. Cases of Compensation

1007. There are two quite different types of cases under this heading. Claims of compensation for environmental damage may be based on special legislation such as the PCA, Chapter 8, or on unwritten tort law. The ordinary courts – from the local court to the Supreme Court – consider both the legal and the factual aspects of the claim. As already mentioned, the interpretation of 'legal interest' in such cases is wide as far as environmental associations are concerned.

Another and rather opposite type of compensation cases consists of cases of compensation required by the landowner from a public authority due to restrictions on land-use for protection purposes. This type is quite common, and most of the environmental cases before the Supreme Court concern issues on principle related to this kind of compensation. This is partly because the rules are neither entirely clear as to whether the citizen has a right to compensation or not nor entirely clear as to the size of the compensation. In these cases, the defendant is the authority that laid down the restriction.

887. One famous example is an attempt by the association Natur og Ungdom (literally 'Nature and Youth') to stop the demolition of an old farm house in connection with the construction of a new Central State Hospital in Norway. The basis for the claim was that the EIA for the hospital was insufficient. The court found that the EIA had important weaknesses, but nevertheless refused the claim on the grounds that the EIA rules at the time were unclear.

888. The Wildlife Act was later changed so as to make it possible to carry out the killing.

Selected Bibliography

Since important parts of Norway's environmental law have changed recently, not all the books in this list are updated in all their parts.

Norway's Environmental Law, General Works

Backer, I.L. 'Miljøretten' (Environmental law). In *Knophs oversikt over Norges rett,* 15th ed., edited by H. Irgens Jensen. Oslo: Universitetsforlaget, 2019.

Backer, I.L. *Innføring i naturressurs- og miljørett* (Introduction to Natural Resources Law and Environmental Law). 5th ed. Oslo: Gyldendal, 2012.

Bugge, H.C. *Lærebok i miljøforvaltningsrett* (Textbook in Public Environmental Law). 6th ed. Oslo: Universitetsforlaget, 2022.

Fleischer, C.A. *Miljø- og ressursforvaltning. Grunnleggende forutsetninger* (Managing the Environment and Natural Resources. Fundamental Conditions). 4th ed. Oslo: Universitetsforlaget, 1999.

Cross-Cutting Issues

Backer, I.L. 'The Structure of Environmental Law – A Norwegian Perspective'. In *Finnish Environmental Law Review* 1/2015, Helsinki, 2015.

Bugge, H.C. 'Norway'. In *Implementing the Precautionary Principle. Approaches from the Nordic Countries, EU and USA*, edited by N. de Sadeleer. London: Earthscan, 2007.

Bugge, H.C. 'Environmental Law's Fragmentation and Discretionary Decision-Making'. In *Law and Economics. Essays in honour of Erling Eide*, edited by E. Røsæg, H.-B. Schäfer & E. Stavang. Oslo: Cappelen Akademisk Forlag, 2010.

Bugge, H.C. 'Har vi de rettslige redskapene som trengs for en god forvaltning av våre havområder?' (Do we have the legal tools necessary for a proper management of our sea areas?). In *Forsker og formidler. Festskrift til Erik Magnus Boe.* Oslo: Universitetsforlaget, 2013.

Cabot, S.A. *Miljøinformasjonslova – overblikk og kommentarer* (The Environmental Information Act). Oslo: Kommuneforlaget, 2005.

Falkanger, T. & A.T. Falkanger. *Tingsrett* (Property Law). 9th edn. Oslo: Universitetsforlaget, 2022.

Holth, F. & N.K. Winge (eds). *Konsekvensutredninger. Rettsregler, praksis og samfunnsvirkninger* (Environmental Impact Assessment. Legal rules, Practice and Societal Effects). Oslo: Universitetsforlaget, 2014.

Jerkø, M. 'Det norske formålet "bærekraftig utvikling"' (The Norwegian Objective of Sustainable Development). *Tidsskrift for Rettsvitenskap,* 2 (2009): 354–388.

Platjouw, F.M. *Environmental Law and the Ecosystem Approach. Maintaining Ecological Integrity Through Consistency in Law*. Oxon/New York: Routledge, 2016.
Schütz, S.E. *Miljøkonsekvensutgreiing av planar og tiltak* (Environmental Impact Assessment of Plans and Projects). Bergen: Universitetet i Bergen, 2007.
Winge, N.K. *Kampen om arealene. Rettslige styringsmidler for en helhetlig utmarksforvaltning* (The Battle of the Land Areas. Legal Instruments for a Comprehensive Management of Uncultivated Land). Oslo: Universitetsforlaget, 2013.

Constitutional Law

Andenæs, J. & A. Fliflet. *Statsforfatningen i Nor*ge (The Norwegian Constitution). 11th ed. Oslo: Universitetsforlaget, 2017.
Fauchald, O. K. and E. Smith (eds). *Mellom jus og politikk. Grunnloven §112 (Between law and politics, Grunnloven §112)* (Between Law and Politics. Article 112 of Grunnloven). Bergen: Fagbokforlaget, 2019.
Høgberg, B. M. *Forbud mot tilbakevirkende lover* (The Prohibition of Legislation with Retroactive Effect). Oslo: Universitetsforlaget, 2010.

Pollution Control and Climate Law

Bratteng, E. *Avfallsrett* (Waste Law). Oslo: Universitetsforlaget, 2020.
Bugge, H.C. 'Climate Law and Policy in Norway'. In *Miljöjuridik/Finnish Environmental Law Review 3/2012*, 'Comparative Climate Law'. Vol. IIB, 2012.
Bugge, H.C. *Forurensningsansvaret* (Responsibility for Pollution in Norwegian Law). Oslo: Tano, 1999.
Bugge, H.C. (ed.). *Klimarett* (Climate Law). Oslo: Universitetsforlaget, 2021.
Stavang, E. *Naborettens forurensningsansvar* (The Neighbour Responsibility for Pollution). Oslo: Cappelen Akademisk Forlag, 1999.
Wang, Ø. *Forurensningsloven med* kommentarer (The Pollution Control Act. A Commentary), 2nd ed. Oslo: Gyldendal, 2015.

Nature Conservation Law

Backer, I.L. *Naturmangfoldloven med kommentarer* (The Nature Diversity Act. A Commentary). Oslo: Universitetsforlaget, 2010.
Backer, I.L. *Naturvern og naturinngrep* (Nature Conservation and Nature Damage). Oslo: Universitetsforlaget, 1986.

Outdoor Recreation: Legal Issues

Reusch, M. *Allemannsretten. Friluftslivets rettsgrunnlag* (The Public Right of Way. The Legal Basis for Outdoor Recreation in Norway).Oslo: Flux, 2012.

GMO and Bioprospecting Regulation

Fauchald, O.K. 'Genetically Modified Organisms and Precaution in Norwegian Law'. In *Implementing the Precautionary Principle. Approaches from the Nordic Countries, EU and USA,* edited by de N. Sadeleer. London: Earthscan, 2007.
Haugseth, E.L. *Utsetting av genmodifiserte organismer.* Oslo: Institutt for offentlig retts skriftserie, 2001.

Walløe Tvedt, M. *Norsk genressursrett* (Norwegian Law on Genetic Resources). Oslo: Cappelen Akademisk Forlag, 2010.

Water and Energy Law

Arnesen, F., et al. 'Energy Law in Norway'. In *Energy Law in Europe. National, EU and International Law and Institutions,* edited by M. Roggenkamp, C. Redgwell, A. Rønne & I. de Guayo. Oxford: Oxford University Press, 2007.

Falkanger, T. & K. Haagensen (eds). *Vassdrags- og energirett* (Water Resources and Energy Law). Oslo: Universitetsforlaget, 2002.

Petroleum Law

Hammer, U., et al. *Petroleumsloven* (The Petroleum Act. A Commentary). Oslo: Universitetsforlaget, 2009.

Planning Law

Holth, F. & N. K. Winge. *Plan- og bygningsrett. Kort forklart* (Planning and building law in short). 2nd ed. Oslo: Universitetsforlaget, 2019.

Innjord, F. & L. Zimmermann. *Plan- og bygningsloven med kommentarer* (The Planning and Building Act. A Commentary). 2nd ed. Oslo: Gyldendal, 2020.

Pedersen, T.J., et al. *Plan- og bygningsrett* (Planning and Building Law). 3rd ed. Oslo: Universitetsforlaget, 2018.

Reusch, M. *Plan- og bygningsrett i et nøtteskall* (Planning and building law in a nutshell). Oslo: Gyldendal, 2019.

Cultural Heritage Law

Holme, J. *Kulturminnevern. Rett. Forvaltning, Håndhevelse* (Norway's Cultural Heritage Law). Oslo: Økokrim, 2001.

Kahn, M.H. *Lærebok i kultuminnerett* (Textbook in cultural heritage law). Bergen, 2023.

EEA Environmental Law: Norway

Bugge, H.C. *EØS-avtalens rolle og betydning på miljøvernområdet* (The Role and Importance of the EEA Agreement in the Field of the Environment). Oslo: Europa-utredningen, 2011 (not updated).

Selected Bibliography

Index

The numbers here refer to paragraph numbers.

Index

www.ingramcontent.com/pod-product-compliance
Lightning Source LLC
Chambersburg PA
CBHW071411230926
51846CB00001B/59
9789403546575